Communist Planning versus Rationality

REVISITING COMMUNISM: COLLECTIVIST ECONOMIC AND POLITICAL THOUGHT IN HISTORICAL PERSPECTIVE

Series Editor: János Mátyás Kovács

The series will cover the evolution of economic ideas under communism in Eastern Europe (including the Soviet Union) and China. These ideas will be presented in the context of the global history of collectivist economic thought. The core of the series will include a number of country monographs, a comparative analysis and a multiple-volume anthology of studies that have not been published in English yet.

Titles in This Series

Communist Planning versus Rationality: Mathematical Economics and the Central Plan in Eastern Europe and China
Edited by János Mátyás Kovács

Populating No Man's Land: Economic Concepts of Ownership under Communism
Edited by János Mátyás Kovács

Communist Planning versus Rationality

Mathematical Economics and the Central Plan in Eastern Europe and China

Edited by János Mátyás Kovács

LEXINGTON BOOKS
Lanham • Boulder • New York • London

Published by Lexington Books
An imprint of The Rowman & Littlefield Publishing Group, Inc.
4501 Forbes Boulevard, Suite 200, Lanham, Maryland 20706
www.rowman.com

86-90 Paul Street, London EC2A 4NE

British Library Cataloguing in Publication Information Available

Library of Congress Cataloging-in-Publication Data

Names: Kovács, János Mátyás, editor.
  Title: Communist planning versus rationality : mathematical economics and
    the central plan in eastern Europe and China / edited by János Matyas
    Kovács.
  Description: Lanham : Lexington Books, [2022] | Series: Revisiting
    communism : collectivist economic and political thought in historical
    perspective | Includes bibliographical references and index. | Summary:
    "This volume examines failed attempts at modernizing the communist
    economy by means of optimal planning. It traces the rise and fall of the
    concept in Eastern Europe and China, explaining why the mission of
    optimization was doomed to fail and why it may nevertheless be
    relaunched today"-- Provided by publisher.
  Identifiers: LCCN 2022005012 (print) | LCCN 2022005013 (ebook) | ISBN
    9781793631770 (cloth) | ISBN 9781793631787 (ebook)
  Subjects: LCSH: Central planning--Communist countries. | Economics,
    Mathematical--Communist countries--History--20th century. | Mathematical
    optimization--History--20th century. | Communist countries--Economic
    policy. | Soviet Union--Economic conditions. | Europe, Eastern--Economic
    conditions--1945-1989. | China--Economic conditions--1949-
  Classification: LCC HC704 .C665 2022 (print) | LCC HC704 (ebook) | DDC
    338.947--dc23/eng/20220322
  LC record available at https://lccn.loc.gov/2022005012
  LC ebook record available at https://lccn.loc.gov/2022005013

Contents

Acknowledgments   vii

Introduction: Another "Grand Illusion"—Optimizing the Central Plan   1
    János Mátyás Kovács

Chapter 1: To Command or to Understand? Planning Concepts and
    Economic Research in Communist Bulgaria   19
    Roumen Avramov, Kaloyan Ganev, and Stefan Petranov

Chapter 2: Quantitative Economics in China: From Planned
    Economy to Socialist Market Economy   55
    Xiuli Liu, Minghui Qin, Shan Zheng, and Xin Xiang

Chapter 3: Mathematical Economics and Central Planning:
    Economic Research in Czechoslovakia under Communism   81
    Julius Horváth

Chapter 4: Theory and Political Economy of Central Planning in
    East Germany   109
    Hans-Jürgen Wagener, Udo Ludwig, and Knut Richter

Chapter 5: Mathematical Economics Outside the Neoclassical
    Paradigm?: Evolution of Planning Concepts in Hungary under
    Communism   145
    Gergely Kőhegyi and János Mátyás Kovács

Chapter 6: Between Rationality and Reality: Economics and
    Central Planning in Poland (1945–1989)   211
    Maciej Bukowski and Wojciech Maciejewski

Chapter 7: The Failure of Communist Planning: A Perspective from
    Romania   227
    Valentin Cojanu and Grigore Ioan Piroşcă

Chapter 8: Communism = Soviet Power + Planning: Planning and
  Mathematical Economics in the Soviet Union   255
  Andrei Belykh

Chapter 9: Mathematical Economics, Economic Modeling, and
  Planning in Yugoslavia   293
  Jože Mencinger

Conclusion: Rationality Found and Lost? In Search of a New
  Historical Narrative of Optimal Planning   319
  János Mátyás Kovács

Index   389

About the Editor and Contributors   411

Acknowledgments

We wish to express our gratitude to the Institute for Human Sciences (IWM), the Research Center for the History of Transformations at the University of Vienna (RECET), and the Charles Koch Foundation for generously supporting our research program. Thanks are also due to Lukas Becht for coordinating the research activities and commenting on the chapters and Ninja Bumann for working on the manuscript of the volume. Last but not least, we are very grateful to Thomas Richardson Bass for editing the volume in English. They made enormous (and successful) efforts to discover the mistakes that we, the authors, made in the text.

Introduction

Another "Grand Illusion"— Optimizing the Central Plan

János Mátyás Kovács

The main thrust of our series *Revisiting Communism. Collectivist Economic and Political Thought in Historical Perspective* has been twofold: to tell unknown stories and warn about the dangers of their repetition.

The first volume in the series (Kovács ed. 2018) discussed the evolution of the economic concepts of ownership. It focused on the utopian idea of social property and the "trap of collectivism" that prevented most economic theorists in the communist countries (and a significant minority beyond) from acknowledging even the obvious advantages of private ownership. Our contributors unveiled much of the mystery around the concept of social property in nine country studies.[1] In the real world of communism this concept worked as a party-state (*nomenklatura*) property that succeeded to populate, in the wake of sweeping nationalization and collectivization, a no man's land of ownership. Although *nomenklatura* property was complemented by various types of cooperative/communal ownership and combined with formal and informal varieties of private ownership in all countries, it stultified the imagination of economic theorists for decades to come. Regardless of the inefficiency and injustice of social or mixed (collective and private) property, they made enormous efforts to keep various blends of these on their scientific agenda.

Staying in such a trap could not be explained exclusively by a servile submission to (self-)censorship; it was also motivated by genuine scholarly and ideological convictions. Also, Eastern Bloc economists did not necessarily emulate the half-hearted attempts of their Soviet colleagues to exit the trap. Instead, their research programs resulted in a number of remarkable local solutions combining vertical and horizontal forms of collectivism with a light version of economic individualism/liberalism.[2] Usually, the emerging patterns of ownership were rather unoriginal and unsophisticated in terms of economic theory. Nevertheless, they offered posterity precious information gained from the gigantic testing ground of the Soviet empire about intermediary configurations between the principles of collectivism and individualism.

A Greek Tragedy?

In thinking about social ownership, we were cognizant of the importance of another basic concept of Marxist-Leninist political economy: central planning. The fact that today new authoritarian regimes in former communist countries show no scruples whatsoever to resort to policies of nationalization, state-led development programs, macro-regulation with targeted interventions in business life, and the like has to do, among other things, with the half-contested legacy of communist planning. Following 1989, the idea of mandatory macro-planning seemed to disappear forever, leaving virtually no intellectual history behind. The destiny of one of the "travel companions" of the doctrine of social property, namely, the theory of planned operation of that property from an imagined center of the party-state, has not been explored yet. Thus far, a small library has been filled with literature on the economic history of thousands of central plans of various lengths, which were issued in the communist world during the twentieth century. However, the books and papers dealing with the *concepts* of these plans and Soviet-style planning in general can be squeezed into a bookcase while the works (predominantly journal articles) covering the *history* of planning concepts do not occupy more than one of its shelves. Since 1989, a whole generation of scholars who have become top economic advisors and decision-makers in the ex-communist states still do not have a chance to evaluate the risks of rehabilitating even strongly interventionist ideas like central planning—a once perhaps innocent goal that proved unfeasible if not fatal to communist economies. We hope this volume will help some members of this generation think twice before they venture to make similar experiments, chasing dreams about the success of their national plans of "salvation," "reconstruction," "development," or "cooperation."[3]

Long before the Soviet era (and even before Marx tried to wrap communist thought in the scientific discourse of classical political economy), a Grand Illusion was born. As an organic ingredient of the Enlightenment-based vision of modernity, the goal of managing the economy as a whole enchanted a vast number of scholars and politicians all over the globe during the past centuries, did not die out entirely after 1989, and may return with a vengeance. With time, this goal was complemented by the illusion of planning (or "plannability"), reflecting a misguided trust in the omniscience and omnipotence of the proverbial Central Planner.[4] Famously, Marx and his early followers cherished the idea of a certain kind of decentralized and voluntary planning implemented by a horizontal network of self-managing communes (while, paradoxically, also advocating the principle of a centrally planned allocation of labor, capital, and goods in an economy organized hierarchically like a large enterprise). Furthermore, they claimed that planning the national economy in the "anarchistic" world of markets dominated by private ownership would be a *contradictio in adiecto*. However, really-existing socialism[5] taught economists to make distinctions among many kinds of ownership called "social"; and these could merge with multiple forms of planning, some of which were not even called "central." The present volume focuses on a particular type of planning concept, sometimes called "classical Stalinist planning"[6] and more acutely, on the ways of its "improvement" ("modernization") via advanced mathematical methods. In what follows, let me share some of our key working hypotheses and research questions.

Similar to the conundrum of social property, we were interested in the evolution of a widespread, lasting and—in a sense—workable invention in social engineering, namely, the concept of imperative and centralized macroeconomic planning.[7] While not ignoring the unbroken hegemony of verbal techniques of planning,[8] we have made great efforts to comprehend in an East-East comparison why and how a mathematically intensive research program, the theory of optimal planning,[9] grew out of the concept of central planning and, despite its poor performance in real life, succeeded in preserving some of its scholarly power until the last breath of communism. A rare development as it was, optimal planning models succeeded in catapulting economic thoughts and methods—invented to overcome the dire straits of Soviet-type planned economies—into standard economics in the West. Probably, this could not have happened if simultaneously similar models had not been formulated in the West[10] during the Cold War, and there had not been a growing exchange of ideas between the two blocs, epitomized by the Nobel Prize shared between Leonid Kantorovich and Tjalling Koopmans in 1975.

In this way, the Grand Illusion of central planning assisted the birth of an even grander one, the convergence of capitalism and communism. The convergence theorem anticipated not only a compromise between social and private property or between dictatorship and democracy but also a rapprochement between imperative and indicative regimes of state planning and between different designs of market institutions. This may remind the reader of hopes about the universal validity of a related hybrid project, market socialism, that, in various verbal forms, became a flagship initiative among a growing number of economists in the communist world *after* optimal planning had begun to ail in practice. In their view, there remained no other means to improve the plan than a partial rehabilitation of market institutions.[11] This—perhaps less utopian—project surfaces throughout this volume but will be discussed at great length in our third collective volume examining the evolution of market concepts in the communist era.

Talking about illusion and utopia promises no happy ending in the history of a research program that was supposed to shine light on collectivist thought by linking the economic rationality of planning to Mathematical Science (writ large) in a positivistic mood. Instead of expecting rational economic behavior from allegedly instinctive market agents or from allegedly omniscient state bureaucrats, the pioneers of optimal planning were confident about introducing rational planning procedures based on indisputable mathematical truths that were embedded in formal models. They assumed almost axiomatically that these models could be construed by the experts and conveyed to the Central Planner who would put them into practice, and the entire process of revealing, producing, mediating, and synthesizing scientific information as well as taking decisions on their basis would imply hardly any ambiguity and frictional loss. The *Gosplan*, or any national planning office in the Soviet bloc, was thought to act as a Walrasian auctioneer[12] coordinating supply and demand (rather than prices) until general equilibrium was reached. Similarly, the hierarchical institutions of the party-state, including the state-owned firms, were presumed to execute the central plan almost impeccably. Another hypothesis breeding hope for rational outcomes was that the data to be fed into the models would be both available and correct, that is, they would exist when planning begins and would not be severely distorted or concealed by any economic actor. Both the input-output tables that served as the "infrastructure" of the optimal models and the constraints and the objective functions of the latter seemed to be defined fairly unambiguously and reflect a common good. In János Kornai's (1975, 426) words, the optimal planners were fairly certain that they would not have to "throw stones in the coffee mill."

Even as expectations became much less romantic over the years, many mathematical economists[13] continued to put their faith in (a) superseding the primitively verbal methods of planning *without* abolishing central planning as such; (b) converting the Marxist-Leninist political economy of socialism into a veritable scientific discipline equipped with precise research questions and hypotheses, appropriate model-building, and procedures of accurate measurement and verification *without* joining, heart and soul, the neoclassical mainstream in the West; and (c) improving the performance of the planned economy *without* having to introduce a capitalist market economy. In the end, this *par excellence* technocratic (and, for a long time, expressly pro-communist) project failed dismally in all the three respects.

Verbal planning managed to preserve its dominance. Although official political economy lost much of its influence in some countries, the harm it had to suffer was caused by the theories of market reform confirming certain liberal tenets, that is, by theories, with which the mathematical economists did not want to flirt initially, rather than by the standards of mathematical exactitude. Finally, while input-output analysis contributed to raising the quality of central planning, optimization did not have a chance to show its strength in real life on the level of the national economy in any of the states under scrutiny.

Thus, the original mission of optimal planning proved impossible but—paradoxically—in the eyes of the "missionaries" it was not entirely unsuccessful. The neoclassical mainstream did *not* inundate economic thought in the communist world despite the fact that they opened a few of the flood gates. Moreover, no matter if cautiously liberal ideas appeared in the optimizers' research programs, they did not have to fear for decades that they or their more radical rivals, the market reformers would feel the urge to "jump" into capitalism. At the same time, as an unintended consequence, mathematical culture managed not only to slowly permeate but also uproot economic research and education in some of the communist countries. Exactly half a century after Kantorovich published his first booklet on *The Mathematical Method of Production Planning and Organization* in 1939, this culture alleviated the post-1989 breakthrough of neoclassical theory[14] in the former Soviet empire. In a sense, optimal planning accomplished an altruistic task in the long run: it provided mathematical economics with an expanding habitat, helped a small sect of scholars grow into a genuine academic community with established institutions, enabling them to survive communism and prosper in the framework of other research programs afterward.

This volume could suggest a drama in two acts: finding rationality, then losing it. However, the country chapters show that, as always, life was much more complicated. First, this two-phase sequence was characteristic of optimal planning rather than planning in general and other fields of mathematical economics. Second, the rise and the fall of somewhat rational planning concepts were sometimes difficult to take apart because—while certain (overambitious) models of optimal planning failed—others promised favorable results. The Conclusion will show what we did not really expect in the beginning, namely, that several causes of the fall of the research program were preprogrammed in its rise. Third, the concept of rationality did not fade away completely during the second act but survived under the aegis of other research programs of mathematical economics (e.g., disequilibrium analysis), and of verbal studies (e.g., market reform or even futurology). Fourth, and most importantly, the optimizers had focused not on rationality as such but on a *particular* type of it. Instead of searching, to cite Max Weber, for both value rationality and instrumental (goal) rationality, they were fascinated by the latter, more exactly, its situation-based and procedural varieties. Friedrich Hayek would call it "constructivist rationalism."

Some hoped that goal rationality would combine with value rationality, that is, the improved planning regimes would raise the well-being (including some economic freedoms) of their fellow citizens. For a long time, the loftiest value in the eyes of optimal planners was the protection of the communist system in the Cold War that not only justified the modernization efforts of the experts but also supplied them with cutting-edge techniques in analysis developed together with the military. Otherwise, their value judgements concerned the rationality of science in itself. In other words, they confined themselves to ensuring the correct application and refinement of these techniques rather than assessing the economic system they wanted to plan as inferior to capitalism in terms of both efficiency and freedom.[15]

Seeing the title of the Conclusion in the table of contents, one might expect to read into a huge intellectual and emotional tension between the phases of finding and losing rationality. Still, the destiny of optimal planning did not genuinely follow the logic of Greek tragedies: it lacked a cathartic climax before the end. The hero's rise was not interrupted by spiritual enlightenment and self-purification and it was not followed by a sudden and disastrous fall but by a protracted stagnation, frustration, fatigue, and—eventually—silent disappearance. One might even ask whether it is not blasphemy to talk about heroism in this regard, knowing that the advent of scientific planning was promoted by certain groups of the *nomenklatura*, and the program was contingent on daily collaboration between optimal planners and the party-state as well as on repeated concessions made by mathematical economists to official political economists. In the end, the optimal planners retreated from their research program in a despondent mood once central planning was abolished. Of course, both the strength and the duration of trust in making planning rational varied in the communist countries under scrutiny during those many decades. By and large, however, the 1950s and 1960s were a time of great hopes, the 1970s brought a stalemate, and the 1980s showed frustration and slow decline. In fact, rationality was not left behind by the optimal planners like a lost bag on a train but was abandoned as a hope.

The reader may have noticed that this narrative is quite pessimistic. In a twist on the title of Roy Weintraub's book (2002), prior to 1989, the official political economy of socialism "did *not* become a mathematical science" and, clearly, not a neoclassical one. Neither optimal planning and market reform nor any of their blends proved able to produce an original and robust theory of the planned economy or to force textbook political economy to become one. Intentionally or not, they delayed a profound scientific turn even on their deathbeds. Nevertheless, the main hero of our story mathematical planning did not bring its "gentle" characteristic traits that had informed a few generations of scholars in the Soviet era about "divine" standards of economic research to the grave. In this respect, our narrative does follow the pattern of Greek tragedies.[16] To put it simply, optimal planning left several concepts of neoclassical economics and advanced mathematical methods of economic analysis to posterity. Whether or not the inherited standards were "divine enough" is just one from among a whole series of questions that our research group sought in vain to answer using the relevant historical literature. The state of the art conveyed far too rosy a picture in many fields, in which huge blank spots yearned to be filled with realistic colors.

Underestimating Failure, Ignoring Success: Some Words on the State of the Art

In identifying biases and blank spots, it is far from our intentions to brag about the wisdom of hindsight. Nonetheless, much of what our research group has explored in the history of planning concepts could have been mapped without difficulty three decades ago when the Soviet empire imploded or even earlier. Although a number of prominent mathematical economists (such as Igor Birman, Aron Katsenelinboigen, János Kornai, and Tiberiu Schatteles) had started complaining publicly about some unsurmountable scientific, technical, and political obstacles to their planning initiatives in the late 1960s and early 1970s, the second act of the play with its unhappy ending has not been written until now. In the concluding chapter of this volume I will offer a detailed survey of the relevant literature.[17] What comes next is just a foretaste.

The promising overture and quick exposition of the story of optimal planning was portrayed with great erudition and compassion by authors such as Michael Ellman, Pekka Sutela, and Alfred Zauberman, three of the most profound intellectual historians in the field. During the 1960s and 1970s, no eminent economic Sovietologists and experts of Comparative Economic Systems could afford the luxury of *not* expressing their opinion about what one of them called, sarcastically, "computopia." They did not share each and every optimistic goal set by the first cohort of mathematical planners but regarded the prospects for "contaminating" textbook political economy and improving the quality of central planning as realistic. Similarly, they did not mind if market reforms would be overshadowed by streamlining the planning regimes and some of them were definitely anxious about the neoclassical leanings of their Eastern European colleagues (China was under their radar at the time). Most of the first scholarly observers stressed the market (more exactly, *khozraschet*) orientation of the new research program and benevolently underestimated the statist preferences of the optimal planners.

Typically, these observers did not reach for the arguments of Ludwig Mises and Friedrich Hayek on the impossibility of rational economic calculation in a "socialist commonwealth," which were put forward between the two wars. They instead accepted the position of Oskar Lange on fusing Marxian and Walrasian ideas. Preoccupied with the pragmatic question of which mathematical model would improve planning the most, they failed to tackle the core of the research program and ask whether any theoretically correct *and* practically feasible model could be built at all. The first analysts also were fairly uninterested in the sociological status of (and insensitive to the moral dilemmas experienced by) those local experts who decided to cooperate with the communist governments.

The Soviet story of optimal planning smothered the comparative history of the research program for too long; historians admired an unexpectedly successful scholarly advance and institutional buildup—all at the epicenter of an empire. Optimization efforts in the satellite countries were neglected, just like the delicate balance of conflict and cooperation between the mathematical planners and the market reformers, which often exerted a greater influence on the evolution of economic ideas outside the Soviet Union. Even such a conspicuous revolt against one's own research agenda like Kornai's bitter progress report about the failure of optimal planning in Hungary (1967) and his ensuing frontal attack on neoclassical economics (1971) did not prompt historians of economic thought to start writing the second act of our drama on stagnation and decline. Instead, the hype around Kantorovich's Nobel prize prolonged the victory lap of the research program while it was already well known that, despite the mushrooming of theoretical models of optimal planning, not a single communist country had ever executed a central plan even close to what mathematical planners proposed.

With time, the observers might have asked two questions:

1. Was the scientific core of the research program per se responsible for the fiasco or were the basic institutional arrangements of the planned economy operated by a communist party-state the main culprit, or both?
2. Was it worth looking for macroeconomic rationality in a centralized planning regime, in which the economic actors on each level of the hierarchy show little interest in contributing to (or are induced to work against) it when they want to attain their own (rational) goals?

Unsurprisingly, it was the heirs of the Austrian School of Economics (above all, Don Lavoie and Peter Boettke) who were among the first to ask such questions in the 1980s and 1990s. Without examining either the mathematical properties of the planning models or the political history of their reception and the sociology of the national research communities, they realized that optimal planning had entered a phase of decline. The "Austrians" contended with some satisfaction that—although the research program was on its way to what Hayek called the "competitive solution" that makes some use of the market in generating realistic information—simulation would not bring economic advantages comparable to those of genuine capitalism. At the same time, they did not shed any tears for the superficial reception of neo-classical principles by the optimal planners because they had mixed feelings about those principles themselves.

Those who, in principle, could have combined the virtues of the above-mentioned interpretations (and avoid their vices) while capitalizing on first-hand local knowledge were those few historians of economic thought who lived in the communist countries. However, except for Andrei Belykh ([1989] 2007) and some recent writings, the reader will find only a few works containing personal reminiscences or detailed ego histories (e.g., Birman 2001; Fedorenko 1999; Kantorovich 2002; Katsenelinboigen 1980; 2009; Kornai 2007; Schatteles 2007) published by insiders to this date. The latter books did shed some light on the hidden motives of authorship as well as on interpersonal relations within the academia and politics but were not always unbiased, to say the least.

Following 1989, amidst a "neoclassical revolution" in post-communist economic sciences, optimal planning once again could have found itself a hero in a totally new context. However, its unintended achievements in paving the way for a reunification of Eastern and Western economic thought were seldom recognized either by insider or outsider observers. Instead, a small but vocal group of authors (including Johanna Bockman and Gil Eyal) with numerous followers in contemporary Eastern Europe contended that the infiltration of neo*classical* ideas into economic knowledge via optimal planning set the scene for a neo*liberal* hegemony in the region and beyond—another kind of reunification, a deplorable phenomenon in their view. This—heavily ideological—narrative was moderated by including in the historical analysis important factors from the sociology and politics of science (e.g., the role of the military, East-West dialogue, expert networks and power) and case studies from Eastern Europe based on interviews and archival materials. Yet, these historians could not write the second act on the fall of optimal planning for a simple reason: they were convinced that the decay already had begun during the first act when neoclassical theory's *Homo Oeconomicus* entered the stage and unleashed the doctrine of market socialism—allegedly—under the pretext of optimizing central planning.

Fortunately, this brief overview of the state of the art does not have to end on a sad note because reservations similar to those of our research group have been expressed by a number of (younger) scholars such as Ivan Boldyrev, Till Düppe, Yakov Feygin, Olessia Kirtchik, Adam Leeds, and Eglė Rindzevičiūtė who embarked upon writing case studies on the evolution of mathematical economics in the Soviet Union in the last few years.[18] They subject the published texts to careful scrutiny and also immerse in archival and oral sources, showing a sometimes anthropological precision. These authors do not believe that the optimal planners were obsessed neoclassical theorists who "came out of the closet" as neoliberals during *perestroika*. They consider "coldwarism," that is, a special emphasis on geopolitical rivalry in general and on military demand for cybernetic development in particular, to be a key explanatory factor of the optimization of central planning. However, Eastern Europe and China hardly occur in their studies, and—with a few exceptions—the verbal reform economists and the official political economists of the USSR are only regarded as supporting actors on the stage of the evolution of economic ideas. Meanwhile, they provide an insightful typology of the mathematical planners.

The statist attitudes of the optimizers and their tight collaboration with the political elite do not prevent these historians from describing them as techno-scientists whose expertise slowly pulverized the communist regime from inside. Cybernetic utopias aside, they do not claim that the optimal planners made hopeless efforts to rationalize the communist economy. Due to a lack of "Austrian suspicion," the insistence by the Soviet planning experts on collectivist reasoning in economics goes unnoticed, suggesting that during the Brezhnev years of stagnation they insisted on the program of plan improvement for so long not because of the inertia of collectivist beliefs but of a persistent fear from repression. Finally, as regards the second act of our drama, one of the authors in this group coins the term "marcescence" but fails to link it, through a clear reference, to the impossibility of rational calculation under communism. Be as it may, the theme of optimal planning reemerged in serious historical studies; hence, the contributors to our volume did not have to start at square one.

On Methodology

Our doubts about the state of the art indicate the methodological backbone of our book. Like the previous volume on theories of ownership, we explored the evolution of planning concepts from five perspectives: chronological, thematic, qualitative, political/sociological, and methodological. In other words, the chapter authors did their best to walk the reader through the whole communist era of each selected country, map the key themes of the doctrines of central planning with a special emphasis on optimal planning, examine the scholarly quality and authenticity of discoveries[19] within this research program, check some of the political and sociocultural drivers of research, and raise a whole series of methodological issues that have been neglected by others.[20] These issues include the relationship between mathematization of planning and neoclassical economics in East-West comparison; the pattern of evolution of economic ideas from the dawn to the twilight of optimal planning; as well as the pre-communist legacies and post-communist repercussions of mathematical economics. As icing on the cake, the multiplicity of research perspectives also should provide us with a "horizontal" view of intellectual history (e.g., transfer history and *histoire croisée*) and protect us from the fallacy of methodological nationalism even if eventually we ground our comparative conclusions on country studies. Here the contributors were interested in the role played by Soviet scholars in generating and transmitting economic knowledge in the framework of the research program in other countries of the Eastern Bloc and asked whether it makes sense to look for national types of optimal planning.

In striving to offer a Big Picture with ample historical and local detail, our latest volume devotes more room to discussing the work of leading scholars since in planning studies scientific findings were more significant than in research on ownership concepts. At the same time, similar to the first volume, we insist on the "importance of small texts," to twist Quentin Skinner's phrase, as the context of a few "great texts" emerging in the communist period. Understandably, the discursive aspects of economic knowledge are given special attention also because we want to comprehend the birth of a new vernacular in a Marxist-Leninist environment, namely, mathematical language. Finally, in the background of dominant planning concepts one usually finds influential institutions and personal networks. Therefore, our volume explores how, for example, the Planning Offices "thought" in the individual countries, or in what way optimal planners drew the contours of their professional identity and situated themselves in the rivalry between textbook political economists and market reformers.

Combining internalist and externalist techniques of historical analysis, our research group remained loyal to the principle of "healthy methodological eclecticism" presented in the first volume while continuing to refrain from an "anything goes" attitude (Kovács 2018, 13–16). We needed at least a modicum of flexibility to portray two main trends, the development of optimal planning and mathematical economics, which crossed each other: the former gave rise to the latter that, in the end, "thanklessly" survived its promoter. Flexibility did not mean that the contributors abstained from making clear judgements about the scholarly merits and political implications of the works discussed. What we abstained from was passing moral verdicts with a presentist pride. In an attempt to provide a sober contextual analysis, even those of us tried to remain as impartial and permissive as possible who—as active participants or eyewitnesses of the history of planning concepts depicted in this volume—had exhibited in the communist era a strong sympathy or aversion to certain ideas described in the pages that follow. That said, experiencing the attempts at improving the planning regimes from a close vicinity had a notable advantage beyond any doubt. Those among us who took part in research and education of mathematical economics in our countries before 1989 can give a credible account of our own illiteracy in (and misreading of) then-standard neoclassical theory.[21] This fact was well known to Western observers, too, but—generously—they hid it under polite understatements.

The book the reader holds in hand is a result of the long-term research program *Between Bukharin and Balcerowicz. A Comparative History of Economic Thought under Communism* launched by the editor in 2014. In 2019, the program was transferred from the Vienna Institute for Human Sciences (IWM) to the Research Center for the History of Transformations (RECET) at the University of Vienna. The selection of countries, like many of the authors of the national chapters, remained the same as in the first volume. I am very grateful to my co-authors for their contributions to our research program. Unavoidably, both the fields and techniques of research overlap to some extent in our book series. Nevertheless, we radically deleted repetitions with a view of minimizing boredom and to encourage our future readers to browse through the volumes simultaneously.

NOTES

1. Our research program covers Bulgaria, China, Czechoslovakia, German Democratic Republic, Hungary, Poland, Romania, the Soviet Union, and Yugoslavia, that is, almost all ex-communist countries of Eastern Europe (in its Cold War sense), and China.

2. For more on the interpretation by our research group of economic collectivism under communism, see Kovács (2018, 1–22, 287–339).

3. Such designations invoke the memory of interwar development plans in Eastern Europe. As to the present, for example, the Orbán regime in Hungary calls itself the "System of National Cooperation" and launched a number of medium-term development plans during the past decade. Kaczyński's Poland introduced the "Plan for Responsible Development" in 2017 and complemented it with the program of the "New Polish Deal" in 2021. While some of the Eastern European governments are flirting with the idea of reintroducing strong state intervention under the auspices of such plans, China has not ceased to issue traditional five-year plans and longer-term development programs in the post-Mao era. In August 2021, the Chinese government accepted a five-year plan to strengthen macro-regulation. For more on the Hungarian case, see Kovács and Trencsényi (2019).

4. In this volume we use the language of the communist regimes without subscribing to the then-official meaning of the terms. In many respects, speech acts such as "mandatory central planning," the "Central Planner," the "law of planned and proportional development," and "socialist plannability" were empty shells in terms of economic reality and often referred to the opposite of their formal sense. Central planning

was neither central nor planning if one expected the term to mean a well-designed program of the organized management of the national economy from a single center, which—in contrast to capitalist spontaneity and anarchy—is based on rational principles (see notes 12 and 15) reflecting the collective wisdom of the party-state/working class/people, and so forth. It was evident that, for example, the phrase "Central Planner" denoted a layered, polycentric group of the *nomenklatura*, the "mandatory instructions" of which were shaped by a multilateral bargaining process including the addressees of these instructions. Moreover, planning was frequently culminating in administrative chaos, an extremely irrational selection of ends and means, enormous differences between the plans and the actual performance, and most surprisingly, it had an *ex post* rather than an *ex ante* nature due to its repeated revisions in the phase of implementation.

5. Besides the official jargon, the authors of the national chapters were free to apply phrases like "really-existing socialism," "Soviet-type socialism," or "state socialism" invoking illegitimate political discourse under the old regime. The widespread use of the term "communism" in the pages to come originates in the linguistic tradition of distinguishing "Western" and "Eastern" forms of socialism by calling the latter "communism" rather than in the absurd assumption that the Marxian vision of a communist society was fulfilled in any corner of the Soviet empire.

6. The term "classical system" was suggested by János Kornai (1992) in conjunction with Stalinist rule to distinguish it from the ensuing "reform system." Our previous volume and some of the national chapters of this one provide sufficient information about the deficiencies of this term. In short, these "systems" are not clearly demarcated ideal types but partly overlapping *quasi-ideal* types located between the genuine ideal types of a totally planned (centralized) in-kind economy based on party-state ownership and a totally unplanned (decentralized) market economy based on private property. The reform system does not follow the classical one but precedes it in many fields (see the NEP) while the latter was preceded by War Communism. Both are *real* types of Soviet economic history that from the end of the 1920s shows an oscillation between the two quasi-ideal types with a long-term tendency pointing toward the reform system in certain countries. Stalin's name can be linked to many phases of that oscillation in both directions: he was a cautious reformer on Nikolai Bukharin's side in the mid-1920s, a fanatic initiator of the classical system at the turn of the 1920s and 1930s, then he swung between these two roles during the 1930s and 1940s, approaching the reform system in the early 1950s again.

In the following, we will use the terms "reformer," "market reformer," "reform economist," "reform-minded economist," and "market socialist" interchangeably.

7. In the volume we will apply the conventional term of "central planning," keeping in mind that the other two adjectives (imperative and macroeconomic) are not to be ignored in a precise definition sensitive to historical change and suitable for East-West comparison. The imperative (mandatory, command-like, directive, direct) nature of central planning and the fact that it should embrace the national economy as a whole is essential in distinguishing it, on the one hand, from indicative planning under capitalism, and, on the other, from various forms of indirect macro-regulation

devoid of mandatory central instructions (targets) in certain segments of planned economies undergoing market reforms.

Taking a closer look, the adjective "central" and the noun "planning" also require clarification. To a degree, central planning always relied on decentralized procedures, and hierarchical coordination was mixed with multilateral bargaining in the entire communist epoch. In addition, planning combined economic control/regulation, extrapolation, and foresight in different proportions. Our main focus will be on macro-planning while enterprise-level planning will be examined only as far as it concerned economy-wide planning procedures. For recent broader overviews of planning theory in the East and the West, see, for example, Caldwell (2008), Döring-Manteuffel (2008), Laak (2008), Etzemüller (2009), Schulze Wessel and Brenner (2010), Matejka, Kott, and Christian (2018), Couperus, Grift, and Lagendijk (2015).

8. Both verbal and mathematical planning applied numbers and models. However, the former used formalized models rarely and these did not go beyond elementary statistics while the latter could not do without formal models and employed advanced mathematical instruments to follow (in most cases) the principle of optimization. Mathematical planners ridiculed the verbal specialists as bookkeepers with their simplistic balances. Yet, the scorn often did not pertain to the bureaucratic attitudes of the "accountants" or the roughness of their calculations but rather to the fact that this method of planning was considered to be much more exposed to arbitrary political intervention than the complex quantitative procedures.

Verbal political economy versus mathematical economics (see note 11) is also a helpful distinction to understand why and how official/textbook Marxism (more exactly, the varieties thereof) lost their monopoly. To be sure, mathematical economists did not apply their models exclusively to planning.

9. Below, the terms of "mathematical (scientific)" and "optimal" planning will be used interchangeably. The same applies to those of mathematical and optimal planner or, simply, optimizer. As it will transpire from the national chapters, the term "optimal planning" had a long and twisted prehistory until the use of mathematics in general and the concept of optimum in particular could overcome the hurdles set by communist ideologues in economic sciences. Despite its roots in Walrasian (neoclassical) theory of general equilibrium and many of its "Western" sources in the overlapping fields of input-output theory, operations research, activity analysis, and linear programming, optimal planning became an "Eastern" research program *tout court*, by and large consisting of input-output (I-O) and linear programming models that were not always fused tightly. Initially, the discipline was also called economic cybernetics, planometrics, and parametric planning. Over time, the models of optimal planning were refined considerably by including non-linear, dynamic, and stochastic methods. On the immense difficulties of making distinctions in symbolic geography between the East and the West with regard to this research program (cf. the role played by Wassily Leontief in its development), see the Conclusion.

Although there are strong arguments for using the Lakatosian term of "scientific research programme" to grasp the methodological status of optimal planning and think about its "progress" and/or "degeneration," the authors of the national chapters were not strait-jacketed: they could call it a new paradigm, theory, concept, doctrine, discipline, and so on.

10. In this volume we focus on the communist world and regard the development of the research program on the other side of the Iron Curtain, say, from Paul Samuelson to Tjalling Koopmans and George Dantzig and further, as well known.

11. In the history of communist economic thought the idea of limited marketization was as old as Lenin's New Economic Policy from 1921 or even Marx's *Critique of the Gotha Programme* from 1875. It resurfaced among political economists time and again, especially if supported by authoritative works like Stalin's *Economic Problems of Socialism in the USSR* from 1951. However, the shattering of the illusion of optimizing the central plan was a necessary prerequisite for many economic theorists to turn from modest strategies of acknowledging the "commodity-money relationships" as auxiliary tools for improving planning to increasingly radical projects of market socialism in some countries. These projects transcended Oskar Lange's models from the 1930s in two respects: they replaced his basically mathematical approach with a verbal-institutionalist one, and extended his concept of simulated markets to real ones that also include the capital market.

12. The concept of rationality (see below) was linked to the auctioneer who in the role of the Central Planner distributes and redistributes resources to those determined by the optimal model to maximize collective utility (minimize waste) in reaching equilibrium while observing certain constraints. The auctioneer may borrow certain parameters of the model from market processes (this was already the case in the first Lange models in the 1930s) but does not give up his/her dominant position in resource allocation.

13. In the beginning, mathematical economists came from "bourgeois economics" of the interwar era (the pre-revolutionary era in the Soviet case), mathematics proper, and from Marxist-Leninist political economy, or were repressed market reformers. Many of them were self-taught mathematicians until courses in mathematical economics began to be accepted at the universities. Both "mathematical" and "economics" were thorns in the flesh of censors for a long time because these terms depoliticized official political economy as well as challenged its scientific (exact) nature, not to mention the fact that the "thought police" did not understand the language the mathematical economists spoke. Symbolic emancipation was slow: the adherents of the new discipline in the communist countries had to put up with designations such as "economy and mathematical methods," "mathematics of planning," "mathematics in economic research," and "economic analysis."

14. I discussed the quality of that breakthrough in Kovács (2002; 2012). Its level was deeply affected by the ambiguities of the reception of neoclassical ideas by the optimal planners.

15. For a similar approach to the concept of rationality, see Erickson et al. (2013). For differences between their and our assessment of Cold War's impact on the evolution of economic ideas in the Eastern Bloc, see the Conclusion.

16. The author of the Soviet chapter quotes Brodsky who said in another context that "in a real tragedy it is not the hero who perishes; it is the chorus." Or both, I

would add, as demonstrated by the fate of optimal planning in many communist countries. See the Conclusion.

17. See the proper references there.

18. Some of these experts contributed to our research program in its preparatory stage.

19. Here we pay attention to the sophistication of the research program as a whole rather than to that of its mathematical constituents. Similarly, for lack of space, the authors could not delve in the methodological details of mathematical modeling (cf. Morgan 2012).

20. Cf. the Introduction of our first volume (Kovács 2018).

21. See my "Everything I Always Wanted to Know about Mathematical Economics But Was Afraid to Ask" (Kovács 2016).

BIBLIOGRAPHY

Belykh, Andrei. (1989) 2007. *Istoriia rossiiskikh ekonomiko-matematicheskikh issledovanii. Pervye sto let.* Moscow: URSS.

Birman, Igor. 2001. *Ia—ekonomist (o sebe liubimom).* Moscow: Vremia.

Caldwell, Peter. 2008. "Plan als Legitimationsmittel, Planung als Problem: Die DDR als Beispiel Staatssozialistischer Modernität." *Geschichte und Gesellschaft* 34 (3): 360–74.

Couperus, Stefan, Liesbeth van de Grift, and Vincent Lagendijk. 2015. "Experimental Spaces—Planning in High Modernity." *Journal of Modern European History* 13 (4): 475–79.

Döring-Manteuffel, Anselm. 2008. "Ordnung jenseits der politischen Systeme: Planung im 20. Jahrhundert." *Geschichte und Gesellschaft* 34 (3): 398–406.

Erickson, Paul, Judy Klein, Lorraine Daston, Rebecca Lemov, Thomas Sturm, and Michael Gordin. 2013. *How Reason Almost Lost Its Mind: The Strange Career of Cold War Rationality.* Chicago: University of Chicago Press.

Etzemüller, Thomas. 2009. "Social Engineering als Verhaltenslehre des kühlen Kopfes: Eine einleitende Skizze." In: Die Ordnung der Moderne: Social Engineering im 20. Jahrhundert, edited by Thomas Etzemüller, 11–39. Bielefeld: transcript.

Fedorenko, Nikolai. 1999. *Vspominaia proshloie, zagliadivaiu v budushcheie.* Moscow: Nauka.

Kantorovich, Leonid. (1939) 1960. "The Mathematical Method of Production Planning and Organization." *Management Science* 6 (4): 366–422.

———. 2002. "Moi put' v nauke." In *Leonid Vitalievich Kantorovich: chelovek i uchenii,* edited by Leonid Kantorovich, Vsevolod Kutateladze, and Iakov Fet. Vol. 1, 22–75. Novosibirsk: SO RAN, Geo.

Katsenelinboigen, Aron. 1980. *Soviet Economic Thought and Political Power in the U.S.S.R.* New York: Pergamon Press.

———. 2009. *Predisposition: Vospominaniia. O Vremeni, O Liudiakh, O Sebe.* https://web.archive.org/web/20120331012012/http://predisposition.us/category/ memoirs/, accessed October 30, 2021.

Kornai, János. 1967. *Mathematical Planning of Structural Decisions.* Amsterdam: North-Holland.

———. 1971. *Anti-equilibrium.* Amsterdam: North-Holland.

———. 1975. *Mathematical Planning of Structural Decisions.* Amsterdam: North-Holland.

———. 1992. *The Socialist System: The Political Economy of Communism.* Oxford: Oxford University Press.

———. 2007. *By Force of Thought: Irregular Memoirs of an Intellectual Journey.* Cambridge MA: MIT Press.

Kovács, János Mátyás. 2002. "Business as (Un)usual: Notes on the Westernization of Economic Sciences in Eastern Europe." In *Three Social Science Disciplines in Central and Eastern Europe (1989–2001)*, edited by Max Kaase, Vera Sparschuh, and Agnieszka Wenninger, 26–33. Bonn: Social Science Information Centre, Collegium Budapest.

———. 2012. "Beyond Basic Instinct? On the Reception of New Institutional Economics in Eastern Europe." In *Capitalism from Outside? Economic Cultures in Eastern Europe after 1989*, edited by János Mátyás Kovács and Violetta Zentai, 281–310. Budapest: CEU Press.

———. 2016. "Everything I Always Wanted to Know about Mathematical Economics But Was Afraid to Ask" (in Hungarian). 2000 Irodalmi és Társadalmi Havi Lap. http://ketezer.hu/2016/11/minden-amit-tudni-akartam-matematikai-kozgazdasagtanrol-de-nem-mertem-megkerdezni/, accessed October 30, 2021.

———. ed. 2018. *Populating No Man's Land. Economic Concepts of Ownership Under Communism.* Lanham: Lexington Books.

Kovács, János Mátyás, and Balázs Trencsényi, eds. 2019. *Brave New Hungary. Mapping the "System of National Cooperation."* Lanham: Lexington Books.

Laak, Dirk van. 2008. "Planung: Geschichte und Gegenwart des Vorgriffs auf die Zukunft." Geschichte und Gesellschaft 34 (3): 305–326.

Marx, Karl. (1875) 1970. *Critique of the Gotha Programme.* https://www.marxists.org/archive/marx/works/1875/gotha/, accessed October 30, 2021.

Matejka, Ondrej, Sandrine Kott, and Michel Christian. 2018. *Planning in Cold War Europe: Competition, Cooperation, Circulations* (1950s–1970s). Boston—Berlin: De Gruyter.

Schatteles, Tiberiu (Tibor). 2007. *Economie, epistemologie si previziune.* Edited by Paul Dragoş Aligică and Horia Terpe. Bucharest: Editura Tritonic.

Schulze Wessel, Martin and Christiane Brenner, eds. 2010. *Zukunftsvorstellungen und staatliche Planung im Sozialismus: Die Tschechoslowakei im ostmitteleu-ropäischen Kontext 1945–1989.* München: R. Oldenbourg

Stalin, Joseph. (1951) 1972. *Economic Problems of Socialism in the USSR*. https://
   www.marxists.org/reference/archive/stalin/works/1951/economic-problems/index.
   htm, accessed October 30, 2021.
Weintraub, Roy. 2002. *How Economics Became a Mathematical Science*. Durham
   NC—London: Duke University Press.

Chapter 1

To Command or to Understand?

Planning Concepts and Economic Research in Communist Bulgaria

Roumen Avramov, Kaloyan Ganev,
and Stefan Petranov

Economic science in Bulgaria during communism commonly is perceived as a pale, grim copy of the corresponding Soviet landscape. Although this assessment captures the broad picture, scrutiny reveals subtle trends in the history of economic ideas. Such an exercise does not discover (nonexistent) spectacular Bulgarian innovations but elaborates on the gestation of concepts shaped by an interplay of complex influences.

The chapter investigates the craft of planning from the perspective of "adjacent" economic research. Our focus is on the impact exerted on the planning paradigm by the gradual and partial mathematization of traditional economic science and by the emergence of new approaches to its conventional topics. We briefly review prewar legacies and the core canon. Then the ambiguous process of formalization is discussed. Finally, we comment in more detail on the notions of *optimal planning* and *economic growth* as well as the incipient neoclassical turn embedded in a critical revisit to the latter.

BEGINNINGS

Proto-ideas

As elsewhere, the ideas that led to the establishment of all-embracing communist planning in Bulgaria originated in the late nineteenth century propagation of Marxism and other radical reformist movements. They can be traced to the intellectual impact of the Bolshevik revolution and the eventual spread of collectivist, interventionist, or totalitarian theories. Between the two world wars planning became an acceptable idea, a tempting social experiment, and a respectable academic and political mainstream (Avramov 2018; Penchev 2018).

Typical for the periphery, economic thought in Bulgaria at the turn of the twentieth century evolved in the shadow of dominant paradigms. Political economy was understood as a blend of epigonic transfers from classical, Austrian, and historical schools; an overview of the general history of economic ideas; and a sequence of occasional glimpses on local particularities (Avramov 2007, Vol. 3; Nenovsky and Penchev 2018). Anglo-Saxon authors were of secondary importance. Ambitions for original contributions to high theory were a priori dismissed, aversion to the avant-garde was dominant, and mathematical approaches were ignored or deliberately rejected. Political economy was deemed to be a secluded domain of abstract reasoning. When shifting to the down-to-earth world of politics, university professors forgot the liberal precepts they were teaching their students.

During the interwar period, ideas related, in one way or another, to planning permeated academia. New curricula endorsed equidistant theoretical positions between totalitarian and liberal *economic systems* and promoted a synthesis of *individualistic* and socialist order. The "planned economy" was classified as an extreme but plausible model. The far-left and the far-right converged in its exaltation and in programs for modernization through nationalization and the elimination of free competition.

Attempts to institutionalize this ideology began in the early 1920s. A *Higher Economic Council* was instituted in October 1923 by a government that had emerged from a recent coup, headed by professor of Political Economy Alexander Tzankov. The council was an advisory body at the Ministry of Finance and composed of five members selected from professional associations and appointed/dismissed by the government. The naïvely rationalistic idea was to try to coordinate diverging interests ex-ante and thus avert economic policy errors. It was assumed that in this way competence prevails over political affiliation, long-term views, and stability over short-term political considerations, the public over the corporativist interest. The expected outcomes were a "general economic and financial plan" and the elaboration of draft laws and expert opinions concerning the most pressing economic issues. For over twenty years, the council functioned as a forum and maintained the ambivalence of its representative and technocratic profiles. Its existence, however, affirmed and legitimized the concept of "planned economy." Indeed, different government institutions produced elaborate sectoral blueprints like the five-year Plan for the Rationalization of

Industry (1934), the General Plan for Electrification (1941), and the detailed five-year Plan for Agricultural Economy (1941) (Penchev 2018).

A trend which pointed in the same direction was the progress of positivist economic thinking. It was fostered by a growing number of Bulgarian doctoral students abroad, but the decisive step was made in 1935 when the Statistical Institute for Economic Research (SIER) at Sofia University, directed by the Russian émigré Oskar Anderson,[1] was established with the help of the Rockefeller Foundation (Avramov 2007; 2018). Without resorting to econometrics or mathematical economics, SIER published a series of high-quality empirical studies, namely, the first estimates of Bulgarian national income and a thorough study of the business cycle. Several of the institute's members were granted fellowships at American and British universities. Together with Assen Christophoroff (SIER fellow and former LSE student), they enhanced the influence of Anglo-Saxon economic thinking and provided the foundation for targeted, selective, and informed state interventions in the economy.

Planning concepts penetrated mainstream economic thought through economic policy as well. The stabilization of the national currency in the 1920s carried out under the conditionality of the Inter-Allied Commission and the League of Nations[2] was a complex endeavor of financial planning requiring coordinated steps, consistent prospective vision, and extensive statistical data. Efforts on an even larger scale were needed to cope with the Great Depression. Some of those activities (namely, clearing policies, foreign exchange and capital controls) anticipated almost literally the functions of a future communist monobank. As early as in 1933, the League of Nations and foreign observers complained publicly that the Bulgarian government de facto follows a policy of "planned economy." By the end of the decade and during the war, the running of an even more etatized, overly regulated economy—and of an overwhelmingly state-managed banking system—involved the application of a great deal of hard planning instruments, including price setting. It was discussed whether this trajectory leads unavoidably to full-fledged planning, and where the boundaries separating it from the capitalist economy lay (Bochev 1935; Christophoroff 1943). Christophoroff delineated several stages which regrettably but logically culminate in "wartime capitalistic socialism." Although in prewar Bulgarian scholarly literature no direct reference was made to the "Socialist Calculation Debate" of the 1930s, the above-mentioned discussions implicitly touched upon the same problems.

More telling than the experts' debates was the public mood. In 1935, Stoyan Bochev[3] commented on how the First World War and the ensuing developments had molded a generalized perception that the transformation of comprehensive state interventionism from *temporary* into *permanent* order (and further into a collectivized economy) is a natural, conceivable, and even desirable trend (Bochev 1935). A few years later, Christophoroff lucidly foresaw and lamented that one of the most important consequences of the war would be the attractiveness "of the seemingly limitless possibilities of the central political authority" to shape the economy, the institutions, and the political system (Christophoroff 1943, 360). The most liberal Bulgarian politicians were convinced that the new system born from the war would confirm the compatibility of democracy with a *dirigiste*, managed economy. Hence, it is no coincidence that when the freshly installed communist-dominated regime founded the prototype of a future planning body in May 1945, the institution borrowed the name of the *Higher Economic Council*: behind the continuum in the brand stood a continuum of ideas.

The Communist Canon

In the interlude preceding the full seizure of power by the Communist Party in 1947, a couple of one-and two-year plans addressed the material and financial effects of the war. In December 1947, the industrial and financial systems were nationalized and a Planning Commission was established which took over the management of the entire economy, while the Bulgarian National Bank was transformed into a monobank. The first five-year plan was adopted for 1949–1953. In the following decade the economy achieved an impressive increase of output in key industries, which coexisted with serious mismatches and disequilibria. Both a high degree of inefficiency and many limits to resources affected virtually all production factors.

A prompt and uncompromising implementation of the Soviet model came together with the imposition of the corresponding canon. Not unlike new institutionalism today, which builds a theoretical system around the concept of *private* property, this canon considered central planning the emanation of *state* ownership and the ultimate incarnation of collective property rights. At the same time, as an instrumental field subordinated to the reigning ideology, its theoretical content was deemed of inferior status and its domain in the textbooks of political economy was of secondary importance (Avramov 2018).

The actual weight of planning, however, was higher. Since it embedded the holistic view of communism regarding the intrinsic governability of the economy according to "objective," "scientific" laws, every analytical or theoretical result of economic research reflected on the concepts of planning. Due to its key importance in economic life, it gave birth to a distinct research field, teaching departments, and careers. Planning built tangible institutional realities, social and power networks. It was the transmission belt of political goal-setting, and major decisions concerning economic structure, growth, and/or priorities were implemented with the available planning tools. The same was true of the macro/micro interface and the related motivations/ incentives of economic actors. Thus, in the post-Stalinist landscape, planning became part and parcel of the ongoing controversies among political economists on (de)centralization and "commodity-market relations" and *implicitly* entered the province of "high theory."

Notwithstanding the series of market-oriented reforms, the planning canon in Bulgaria remained fossilized. The primitive Stalinist model boiled down to a system of imperative orders: addressed to the branches (and down to the enterprises) about quantity, quality, and timing of their output; concerning labor force; and indicating the location of investments. The declared objective was to avoid "disproportions," and if they still appeared, to have contingency resources available (Lazarov 1949). This simplistic philosophy remained the backbone of the planning canon even when its original wording was abandoned and seemingly more sophisticated schemes emerged. The curricula taught at Bulgaria's leading economic university (the Karl Marx Higher Institute of Economy in Sofia—HIE)[4] did not undergo substantial change during the lifetime of the communist regime. Since the outset, the general frame was given by exogenous political objectives, translated and broken down into indicators and resources-output flows of the main branches in the "material sphere" of the economy. The key "material balances" were supposed to provide coherence for the whole, whereas the surrounding satellite plans/balances set the corresponding financial flows, prices and territorial breakdown of investment, labor, personal consumption, and services. The system was bound together by Input-Output (I-O) tables,[5] a few additional models and the planning of the national income (gross product). This 1965 version was replicated nearly verbatim until 1987–1988 (HIE 1963–1989). The related research output was published in a specialized review (*Planovo Stopanstvo*) but was of mediocre quality, the bulk of the articles being devoted to minor issues, to planning procedures, or to the management of branches and enterprises.

The conservatism in planning of economic structure and growth contrasted with chaotic regulations organizing the relations between the "center" and enterprises. Epitomized by the notion of *economic mechanism*, those rules reflected the oscillating degree of autonomy granted by the regime. Political, social, institutional, and conceptual barriers aborted the first reform experiment of 1965–1968, and only a fraction of the intended measures was implemented in an incoherent way (Petrov 1969; 2016). The subsequent reforms moved the pendulum to more centralized planning in the 1970s and back to decentralization in the late 1980s (Ivanov 2008; Marcheva 2016; Avramov 2018). A quick survey recounts five key compulsory parameters/instructions in 1966, 25 in 1975, an average of 10 in 1982–1987, and five in 1989 (Ivanov 2008, 130–32). The decrease, however, is misleading. Although at the end of its existence the regime proclaimed the implementation of a market-oriented economic system, the result was extremely inconsistent. The directive character of planning was never truly abandoned[6]; the newly established institutions (like a few "commercial banks") were not autonomous entities and plagued by contradictory regulations. In 1987 the Ministry of Finance was integrated into the mega Ministry of Economy and Planning, while the perimeter for private economic initiative and independence of state enterprises remained severely restricted. Moreover, political circumstances in the summer of 1989 strengthened compulsory planning and state intervention in the economy.[7]

Economic reforms in communist Bulgaria never were initiated by the planning establishment. On the contrary, it was a stern adherer to the canon and an obstacle to any attempt to increase the autonomy of the economy. As a rule, the proposals were instigated, digested, and filtered by party ideologues in coordination with the community of political economists. It was only after (or in parallel with) this round of purification that planning bodies were entrusted to give flesh to the decisions. An uninterrupted cycle of trial and error gave to these recurring exercises the appearance of perpetual *political* transformations. The attitudes to planning, however, were tacitly exposed to intangible intellectual influences stemming from the evolution of empirical and theoretical economic research.

A FORMALISTIC TOUCH

As a universal language of science, mathematics was the most powerful medium of novel perspectives and a natural vehicle for innovative concepts. It also had a—feared or coveted—subversive potential to undermine ideological barriers.

Always attentive to developments in Soviet economic thought, Bulgarian economists did not miss the birth of the mathematical school in the USSR at the end of the 1960s. The encounter of mathematics with conventional planning discourse, however, was not frictionless. New methods faced disdain, opposition, or hostility, and their relevance was questioned in endless scholastic debates. Mathematics and political economy remained two mutually isolated worlds; the neat separation between "mathematical" economists (mathematicians and a few economists developing/applying formal or quantitative methods) and the massive body of "verbal" economists was a fact until the very end of the regime.

Casting Mathematical Economists

During the 1950s the only potential platform for educating "mathematical" economists was offered by statistics, and statistics graduates were insufficient in number and quality. Moreover, statistics was considered mere support to more prestigious and important planning activities. Mathematics entered the economic curricula on a broader scale from 1962 onward. A general course of mathematics and courses of linear algebra and mathematical programming became obligatory for all HIE students, while tools that already had been standard in graduate economics education in the West (such as differential and difference equations, discrete and continuous dynamic optimization, and so on) were absent. In the mid-1960s the planning curriculum incorporated rudimentary mathematical methods centered on I-O models adapted to the system of national balances. A project to launch (starting in 1966) "Mathematical Economics" as a major for 20 students in the HIE was not implemented, but from the turn of the 1970s onwards cybernetics, optimization, and forecasting became tolerated (even fashionable) notions in the research agenda of the planning chair. It was only in 1980 that a curriculum of "Economic-Mathematical Methods in Forecasting and Planning of the Economy" was introduced; symptomatically, in 1989 a course on "Automated Systems for Planning Computations" was rebranded "Economic-Mathematical Models in Planning" (HIE 1963–1989).

The corresponding reading lists typically included the textbooks by Evgeni Mateev, other mainstream Bulgarian professors, and books by Soviet authors. A telling move (albeit with completely marginal impact) was the introduction of a course on "Modeling of Economic Processes" for students of political economy in 1967.[8] It briefly presented production functions, models of labor dynamics, commodities and money, distribution, "economic reproduction," and the global economy. The "bourgeois" models were taught as a separate lesson (out of a total of nine) introducing different, often inaccurately interpreted theories.[9] The references combined quarantined résumés of Soviet professional "critiques of bourgeois political economy" with a few Russian translations of Western authors. Not a single original path-breaking text was on the list. Discarding any heretic allusion to universalism in economic science, the curriculum was almost entirely dedicated to models of socialist economy. The theoretical background was fully in line with Marxist concepts and with the spirit of the Soviet economic-mathematical school. The general approach to modeling boiled down to the "cybernetic ideology" of the 1960s, including reference to Lange's *Introduction* (Lange 1965). By the mid-1980s the "socialist" and "politico-economical" orientations of the program were enhanced, the chapter on the "bourgeois models" was reduced, and further simplification of the lectures was requested.

Overall, by the early 1970s the teaching of mathematics had become routine. A technocratic blueprint for the development of the HIE (Davidov 1973) presented the economist of the future as a leader of social changes who tames the nature-like economic laws revealed by Marxism. He was supposed to be the produce of three integrated streams: economic science, management, and *mathematics/statistics*. The source of each stream was a corresponding general theory (political economy, systems and information theory, mathematics) blended into mezzo-level macro-management theories and, further down, into managerial models of branches and enterprises.

Institutions

The gradual institutionalization of mathematical methods was expected to provide decision-makers with new ideas and instruments. The emblematic move was the establishment of a specialized research unit at the Institute of Economy of the Bulgarian Academy of Sciences (IE BAS) in 1963. It was called the *Economico-Mathematical Laboratory (EML)*,[10] and its first chair was Ivan Stefanov. The same year the institute's journal *Ikonomicheska misal (Economic Thought)* opened a regular section on "Economics and Mathematics."[11] The laboratory's range of research and prestige made it a leading center in the field. Its mission was formulated as the "application of mathematical and statistical methods in economic research" because, until the 1970s, "mathematical economics" and "econometrics" were considered schools of "bourgeois" political economy. While its tasks included the "enlightening" of economists, it remained pragmatic. It was supposed that the EML would contribute to the improvement of planning, and the laboratory's agenda reflected the sinuous relations between economic science and planning concepts.

During its first years (1963–1970), the EML was focused entirely on linear programming and the I-O system, with only occasional econometric publications (estimations of sector production functions and consumer functions). Linear programming already had a well-known algorithm to solve linear optimization problems, which was considered a perfect solution for optimization on the microeconomic level. Publications analyzed optimal production plans on the micro level, optimal distribution of resources and materials, or transportation schedules. I-O models were perceived as a suitable instrument for macroeconomic planning capable of replacing traditional, simplistic methods. The research tried to clarify the possibilities of the respective models, the methods used to build them, and the precision of estimations. Opportunities for finding the optimal I-O balance were researched, but such attempts later collided with the fundamental difficulty to optimize on the macroeconomic level. Research was conducted on the relationship between centralization and decentralization, and some hopes (purely theoretical at this point) were placed on economic cybernetics.

In the next stage (1971–1976), EML's research focused on theoretical and methodological aspects of building a system for optimal planning and management of the national economy. The understanding was that it ought to be possible to create an integrated system for optimal planning and management based on uniform socioeconomic data processed through computer configurations. It was presumed that designing the necessary planning and optimization methodology was a sufficient condition to calculate optimal plans. Due to the unrealistic expectations, however, the results were unable to meet the requirements of such a super-task. Yet, the interest in these research topics was preserved and expanded further. Linear optimization was applied to a broader scope of subjects, and macro-modeling was spreading quickly as a tool to find solutions to complex tasks by using I-O models. Optimization research was extended with the help of nonlinear and dynamic programming models as well as by examining the problems of automated management systems. Micro-level research (rationalizing decision-making in production tasks, supply and warehouse planning, inventory, transportation plans, regional distribution, and so on) developed much better than macro-modeling. It turned out that building an automated planning and management system at the macro-level was not possible.

During the following years (1976–1984), EML's research was directed towards the theory and methodology of economic modeling, namely, I-O and econometric models of the national economy, and measurement of economic processes. Although this direction was much more realistic than before, the interface between economic-mathematical models and real-life planning continued to be missing. The economists-mathematicians claimed that planners were unwilling to apply their results, thus failing to utilize the options for plan improvements and optimization, whereas those who worked with traditional methods (planners included) claimed that mathematical methods were unrealistic, abstract, and impracticable. At the end of the 1970s, the adequacy of the available economic-mathematical apparatus was questioned. This was both due to the theoretical experience acquired in the meantime and to indications that the econometric models did not function properly (e.g., they proved incapable of anticipating a slowdown in growth during the second half of the 1970s). The major problem was that available tools did not account for individual behavior. Applied econometric models presupposed that economic activity develops on the grounds of one-way causality and behavior remains unchanged, while job satisfaction and other human aspects were unaccounted for. Therefore, forecasting entirely based on econometric models could deviate significantly from reality. The same applied to other classes of models using linear programming, game theory, or other optimization procedures.

Attention thus was drawn to the need to develop knowledge about individual and collective behavior which required clarifying income distribution or coordination of social interests. Other shortcomings of the developed econometric models were that they did not take into account the changes in economic structure and policy, innovation, or the impacts of external economic environment. Finally, credible data were scarce because of poorly developed statistical information and/or ideological concerns and state secrets.

As everywhere in the communist world, the idea of optimal planning and management of the economy was being compromised, EML's research turned to simulation modeling and systems analysis. A set of models for medium-and long-term economic forecasting was created which allowed for the application of a scenario approach. Among other topical fields were micro-and mezzo-level optimization, I-O models for international comparisons, identification of the key sectors of the economy, calculation of full labor and foreign currency costs, or capital intensity. Research refocused towards the Bulgarian economy; modeling was already considered an apparatus of applied research, and not as a topic in its own. In the last years of the regime the intellectual and social environment drastically changed due to the impact of the Soviet *perestroika*. The need to reform both the economy and economic science was urgent and publicly debated.

During the 1980s, the laboratory worked at its maximum capacity and had 30 employees (including 10 technical assistants). The scholarly community using mathematical methods, however, had grown beyond the EML. A number of narrowly focused units had been created at economic universities and ministries' research departments. Top-down campaigns to implement mathematical methods in the largest enterprises were organized to comply with the growing trend that became fashionable. As expected, they failed due to a lack of motivation, experience, and knowledge. Finally, a generously staffed research center at the Planning Commission dealt with models related to its activities, without challenging in any way the traditional conceptual frame of planning. As a result, the formal indicators of scientific production expanded sizably. Between 1981 and 1986, a noticeable 7.2 percent of economic research publications were in the economic-mathematical field with the same share as "Planning and Management of the National Economy" (Stoeva 1987).[12]

Among the newborn structures, most of which proved irrelevant in terms of economic theory, the only noteworthy initiative was the creation of the Research Institute for Forecasting of the socioeconomic Development of Bulgaria at the HIE in 1985. The institute was monitored by the old guard of the planning establishment (Evgeni Mateev and Ivan Iliev), and nothing in its configuration promised unconventional ideas. This unit, however, hired some of the most unorthodox young economists: it became the host institution of

Ventsislav Antonov and co-opted Ivan Kostov and Lubomir Hristov who were at the forefront in the application of quantitative and mathematical methods. Within the very conservative environment, the contributions of these scholars remained exotic. They did not influence at all the customary planning mindset and stayed secluded from the actual economic governance. The situation was in stark contrast to reformist Hungary or Poland, where many of the most prominent nonconformist economists had occupied, at some moment of their careers, leading executive positions in the planning agencies.

Personalia and Intellectual Roots

To apply quantitative methods in economic research during communism supposed a priori or ex-post departures from the profile of the standard theoretician, personified by the "verbal" political economist. Although every character in the mathematization story had his own biographical and/or intellectual motives to deviate from the mainstream, some typical features appeared throughout the years.

Ivan Stefanov (1899–1980) was an archetype of the few pre-communist economists who had enough credentials to survive in the new order. He was a diverse personality, a well-read scholar, and a political figure. In 1924 Stefanov earned a PhD in social and political studies at Humboldt University in Berlin under the supervision of Ladislaus Bortkiewicz. During the 1920s he worked in Germany and France and was a member of the Bulgarian, German, and French communist parties. After his return to Bulgaria, he was employed by the Statistical Office, cooperated with the SIER, and was a professor at the Higher School of Economics in Svishtov. As an established scholar in the aftermath of the Second World War and the seizure of power by the communists, Stefanov was appointed governor of the Bulgarian National Bank and later became minister of finance. In 1949, he was sentenced to life in a show trial against a group of prominent Party functionaries. His main "guilt" was his "wrong" position in trade negotiations with the USSR. In 1956, he was released from prison, acquitted, and permitted to continue his academic career. Stefanov took a neutral empirical approach, and in his last years he used to say in private that he followed the Austrian school and Böhm-Bawerk in particular.

The most prominent promoter of central planning based on I-O techniques was Evgeni Mateev (1920–1997). He attended a high school educating orthodox clergy and eventually graduated from the Law Department of Sofia University in 1943. A convinced Marxist, Mateev entered academia with a combative volume against the "subjective school in political economy" (1947) and was active in the closure of the venerable Bulgarian Economic Society (1895–1949). Writing on planning since the late 1940s, he had a spectacular ascension both in the university and the planning institutions, holding the positions of head of the Planning Agency (1950–1951; deputy 1959–1962) and of the Statistical Office (1953–1959). Minister without portfolio in 1963–1966 – during the climax of debates on economic reforms—he fiercely defended centralization. Mateev taught Economic Planning at the HIE and was (with short interruptions) head of the eponymous chair from 1952 to 1985. In 1968 he spent two months in the United States as a fellow of the Ford Foundation with a focus on corporate governance. By the beginning of the 1970s he occupied high-level positions in the United Nations (UN) Economic Commission for Europe and was a member of the UN Commission on Transnational Corporations. In an "Eastern version" of the convergence theory, Mateev firmly believed that corporate planning in the West was an irrefutable consecration of the planning idea. He was aware of general trends in Western economics but had a condescending, and quite dogmatic opinion about it. He treated "bourgeois" theories of value as "positivistic and formalistic." Not so far from today's illiberalism, his partial and unsystematic references to capitalist economies sought to show that "free markets" do not exist any more and that, correspondingly, "neoliberal" advocacy of free competition under socialism cannot serve as a reform model.

The reformist current of the 1960s in Bulgaria was triggered and most emphatically promoted by conventionally trained economists. The then popular adage that "in the West (under the hegemonic Keynesian paradigm) economists talk about the glories of planning, while Eastern economists talk about the virtues of the free market" was worded in the Marxist meta-language. The reformist champion Georgi Petrov (b. 1929), expressed his views on planning in the tongue and concepts of traditional political economy, and conveyed his messages by observing the lengthy demonstration patterns proper to Marxism (Petrov 1969; 2016). This language excluded any interface with mainstream economics.

From the 1960s onward, the end of the reformist effervescence coincided with the spreading of quantitative approaches that were contingent on some opening to the outside world. The EML's personnel, for instance, consisted of researchers whose qualifications were developed locally, but a significant number of them specialized in the USSR. The contacts of Bulgarian scholars in the field with their counterparts in the key Soviet academic centers (Moscow, Leningrad, and Novosibirsk) were institutionalized smoothly. On a smaller scale, relations with other communist countries also were taking shape, often in the framework of multilateral projects organized by the national academies of sciences. Practically no systematic communication was established with the West. In sharp contrast with other countries, there were no Bulgarian graduates or doctoral students at Western universities; just one scholar from the EML was sent to the United States to do research;

and limited cooperation existed with the International Institute for Applied Systems Analysis (IIASA) in Vienna.[13]

The inaccessibility of Western economic ideas, however, should be qualified. Despite the barriers for personal contacts with colleagues from behind the Iron Curtain, Bulgarian economists had access to leading scholarly journals and monographs in academic libraries (especially after the 1960s). Besides, Western titles on mathematical economics translated into Russian were numerous and easily available.[14] Although the dominant influence in the development of mathematical methods came from the Soviet Union, the impact of the West grew. Nearly one third of the sources cited by Bulgarian mathematical economists originated there, half of which had been published in Russian language. The intensity of quoting Western literature in this field was much higher than in other areas of economic studies.

The autodidactic option was thus present and tangible. Whether to choose it was a personal decision that had to be taken under stringent social constraints. The deliberate or unconscious determination to move away from the ideological domain and to dedicate oneself to genuine research implied an explicit break with the political economy of socialism, additional learning efforts, and narrowing (if not foreclosure) of the scholarly career paths. Three escapist patterns were left: (1) to adopt a coherent positivist/empiricist standpoint towards domestic economic issues; (2) to shift to a rigorous formal mathematical reasoning; and (3) to perform a neutral or quantitative research on capitalist economies. Ultimately, the true problem was the absorption of these kinds of knowledge. It could not be socialized due to ideological and political restrictions: the intimate intellectual encounter could be privatized (by those who were interested and made the corresponding effort) but barely transformed into social capital. Capitalization of this investment came only after the fall of the regime.

The entering into the scene in the early 1980s of a small informal group[15] of young economists whose most uncompromising figure was Ventsislav Antonov (1955–2014), and the changing political context in the second half of the decade altered the landscape (Avramov 2007; 2008). They overtly acknowledged the application of neoclassical instruments, without trying to twist or truncate their underlying theoretical content and assumed the policy implications of the research results. To different extent, those economists continued to use some Marxist concepts, but Marx's aura of exclusiveness was mitigated as he was put in context and in perspective.

Apprehending problems in terms of neoclassical language and using mathematical apparatus and concepts was not a superficial shift. It allowed to tackle issues that otherwise were not visible or to deal with the observable ones from uncommon perspectives. The diagnosis and the proposed therapies gained in boldness and consistency; they were far better targeted and calibrated than official views on the country's most urgent economic difficulties.

The sources of inspiration contributed to cohesion but also introduced nuances of interpretation within the group. A crucial cleavage was rooted in differences of conceptualization of the Western mainstream and of mastering of mathematical tools.[16] Antonov had a deep knowledge in mathematical economics and econometrics. He presented the overall general equilibrium setting as a theoretical continuum which starts from the "abstract theory of socialism" (Aleksandr Bogdanov; Grigorii Feldman); continues with its "brilliant defense against the Austrians by Lange in the 1930s" (a hint to the "Socialist Calculation Debate"); reappears in the optimal planning theory formulated in the wake of the reform debates from the 1960s; and still constitutes an adequate analytical frame of reference in dealing with the economic tensions of the 1980s (Antonov 1988b). Antonov's publications relied on an extensive critical reading of neoclassical works on noncompetitive equilibrium, structural disequilibrium, dynamic inefficiency, and comparative advantages. He elaborated on different types of production functions, on contemporary developments in I-O analysis, and on studies of structural change. Hristov, Kostov, and the mathematician Vassil Vesselinov, in turn, obtained important results by applying Tsukuy's turnpike theorem. The point of view adopted by Avramov highlighted implications for the socialist economies of the capitalist business cycle theories and empirics.

Economists from Eastern Europe, in their successive cohorts, offered other exciting opportunities to muse. Personal (re)discoveries of Soviet authors in the 1920s[17] were illuminating. The next Soviet component comprised the postwar mathematical school with its optimal planning wing and some more traditional growth theories. Strong interest was devoted to the findings and methods of Czech, Hungarian, and Polish economists (accessible in English or in Russian) applied to the analysis of local issues. Antonov was an attentive commentator of János Kornai's works,[18] as well as of studies made in other communist countries on investment cycles and on suppressed inflation.

Thanks to the originality of its publications, to its internal dynamics, and the impetus for self-assertion, the group gradually gained the status of an informal proponent of alternative visions of the country's most serious economic shortcomings. In that sense it inevitably became a challenger to planning's fundamentals. The claim for otherness was formulated clearly by Antonov at a November 1988 conference where he pointed out the irony:

> economists who ardently plead for the establishment of whatever markets still ignore the sad absence of 'market' for their own product and thus perpetuate the reigning monopsony in this field. If we have to be consistent, we have to

acknowledge that the creation of such a market is the first—and intellectually most important—step towards a true transformation of economic life. (1988b)

Finally, like the reformers in the 1960s, these economists did not demonstrate interest in the outside views on the Bulgarian economy. This was partly due to a sense of epistemic superiority, that is, a belief that outsiders' knowledge is inferior by default to local knowledge because it is impossible to understand the essence of a communist economy without an intimate insight in the data, the context of their production, and the background of their interpretation. Although there were good reasons for such an attitude, it also reproduced parochialism: judgments and generalizations were formulated in isolation, and they sometimes repeated conclusions reached abroad.

TOPICAL CONCEPTS

The ideas that inspired the planning canon in Bulgaria were shaped by intellectual transfers originating in both East and West. In what follows, we discuss problems of their *interiorization*. On the one hand, the reception entailed risks of tacit or open interpretational biases. On the other, the dubious rigor (related to confusion, ignorance, illiteracy, or misunderstanding) in the use of imported concepts and analytical instruments led to ambiguous readings, quid-pro-quos, incorrect statistical inferences, and inaccuracies that corrupted the implementation and/or critique of the borrowed concepts.

Optimal Planning

The most well-known case was the entangled couple of the I-O technique and the optimal planning paradigm. It is particularly complicated due to the fact that the transfer concerned a loop of ideas generated in the East which bounced back after having been processed by modern economics in the West.

Optimal planning pretended to capture the features of the economic system through analytical tools, then model those features with formal methods, and finally manage them by changing key parameters through policy action. In Bulgaria, optimal planning is usually personified by Mateev, although he accepted the Soviet forerunners only partially and often disagreed with them. He never (even implicitly) contradicted Marxism; viewed the economy as a strictly integrated vertical structure; considered state ownership the most advanced platform for streamlining information flows and implementing the best possible coordination and management of production processes. A hierarchical design was regarded as the perfect prerequisite to the establishment of centralized decision-making, where decisions at lower levels are taken in stages, in a domino-like, algorithmic way. In this respect Mateev went to extremes that bore all the signs of utopianism. In tune with some trends in the USSR, he put forward the idea that science and practical policy should aim to build a fully automated system for the management of the national economy (Mateev 1974; 1987). That presupposed the possibility to construct and implement complex algorithms that could perform any necessary actions depending on the parameters of a given economic situation. He also proposed to design algorithms that would automatize the completion of central plans, thus making human input necessary only at the programming stage. Mateev was unconcerned with evidence that such an approach never could work perfectly or maybe never work at all. Despite references to the "free and creative" impetus of the enterprises, his approach was founded firmly on the assumption of full determinism. It discounted the complexity of the economy, dismissed the randomness of the processes, and the fact that the available information was incomplete and imperfect, while optimal planning required just the opposite.

From the end of the 1970s, this paradigm found some acceptance at the party leadership level, and some of its elements were implemented superficially in practical planning. At the same time, there was no clear idea how to harness its potential and channel it to the resolution of economic bottlenecks. It required a critical mass of well-read economists and engineers whereas the number of such specialists was far below the minimum required. As a result, theoretical and practical issues were not well understood, and therefore massive amounts of "noise" were introduced in the implementation. Optimal planning was clustered around the belief that investment was the most important factor driving economic growth, and consequently increasing social welfare. Curiously, investment planning itself followed no optimality criteria. Its volume was subject to arbitrary decisions, to the erroneous conviction that there was enough knowledge on how much and where to invest, and to the omission of efficiency-based considerations. Optimal planning relied on the notion of a constant identity between labor demand and supply at a full-employment level. The role of technological progress in sparing labor resources was well known, but still that led to no conceptual changes in theory. Labor was treated broadly as an exogenous constraint with little dynamics over time, and its intrinsic heterogeneity and human capital properties went unrecognized. The developments in labor sociology and labor economy from the early 1970s on were of little help since they were not integrated in the optimal planning paradigm. Due to interdisciplinary barriers, their results were used as analytical, descriptive, or forecasting materials in sectoral planning and had a limited impact on the setting of key macroeconomic parameters.

Optimal planning applications relied on Wassily Leontief's I-O framework as their conceptual basis, on the one hand, and on linear programming as their computational tool, on the other.[19] Efficiency was not part of analysis. Instead it was assumed through the imposed values of technical coefficients. Insofar as market clearing could not be used as a criterion for price determination, "optimal"-like prices were recorded from the solution of the dual problem. Throughout the years, this approach did not experience any significant development despite some modifications.

The fact that Mateev's "anti-market" line was based entirely on the I-O paradigm was not accidental. Leontief conceived the model in physical units which suited the non-monetized Marxist mindset of socialist planners. Even with priced coefficients, the I-O table could be reduced to a simple descriptive scheme of the flows of goods that were the focal point for planning institutions. The image of an economy insensitive to the fluctuations of supply and demand and where agents are not treated as choice-making actors was tempting.

Theoretical constraints further facilitated the model's reception. In 1955, Carl Christ observed that I-O is not a truly equilibrium system because "it cannot rank . . . the function of the preference scale of those whose decisions control the economy—. . . individual consumers, and firms and government agencies" (Christ 1955, 138, 143). Circumventing the notion of equilibrium was an advantage for planners who found familiar the underlying assumption that input proportions are rigid and not affected by fluctuations of free relative prices. Western economists, in turn, agreed that Walrasian equilibrium cannot be attained by collectivist in-kind planning. John Montias noted that "the method of material balances is not inherently wasteful or theoretically unsound; it may lead to full consistency if the iteration process is carried on long enough and if the technical coefficients are accurate" (Montias 1959, 974). At the same time, he pointed out that this statement holds true under unattainable conditions. Despite possible incremental improvements, the estimation of meaningful technical coefficients is precluded by inexorable behavioral, organizational, and informational biases. More importantly, efficient allocation of resources is outside the scope of the in-kind I-O machinery and needs a consistent system of prices able to detect surplus or deficit. The conclusion was candid and irrefutable: "efficiency is not the be-all and end-all of the art of planning. The Soviet system with all its compulsion and waste is a vehicle for high rates of growth" (982). The eventual sophistication of the conceptual apparatus of Soviet optimal planning did not overcome this intrinsic dichotomy between efficiency and central planning.

The pervasive appeal of the I-O model in the communist East was rooted in the duality of Leontief's approach. Although his device was inspired by the concept of Walrasian general equilibrium, which was alien to Marxism, he deliberately accepted simplifications in order to transform the I-O system into an empirical analytical instrument (Miller and Blair 2009, 730). His pragmatic priority and concerns were comprehensible in a sociopolitical environment akin, in some respect, to the extreme conditions prevailing under central planning. Indeed, the I-O methodology and its applications were intensely developed by U.S. government agencies for the management of wartime resource allocation in an economy near full employment (731–32). The civil use of the scholarly apparatus during the Cold War was essentially for the building and checking of national accounts carried out by numerous institutions devoted to indicative planning.

Intellectual transfers are never innocent theoretically. The ideological ambiguity of I-O models was realized rapidly. By considering I-O just a matrix of products, planners ignored the neoclassical premises and implications of the model. They transformed the device and re-formatted it purposes. Its applications by planning technocrats and political officials had nothing to do with public choice and actually superseded the sovereign decisions of *free* economic agents assumed by the original model. As early as the 1950s conservative voices expressed concerns about its possible (mis)use for direct control over the economy. While acknowledging some analytical potential in the paradigm, Milton Friedman (1955, 174) was skeptical about "the grandiose dreams of predicting by I-O analysis the detailed consequences of major changes in the economic environment." Friedman declared his preference "to rely primarily on the price system, rather than the detailed physical planning for organizing the use of our resources, whether for peacetime purposes, defense mobilization, or total war." The generalized trust in the virtues of (central) planning was a facet of the global, Enlightenment-inspired, new wave of faith in rationality, fostered by the spectacular progress of mathematics, quantitative methods, and computing capacity.

The Calculation Problem

How to grasp supply and demand fluctuations in price setting and how to shape the rate of profit were core questions during the reforms in 1960s and the experiments with optimal planning. These topics led to another important case of biased intellectual transfer.

Nowhere in the Bulgarian economic literature of that period was the *Socialist Calculation Debate* mentioned, but its shadow fell in different forms. In his fervent defense of economic reforms, Petrov unconsciously espoused many of Lange's positions (or anticipated Kornai's criticism of the soft budget constraints). He pleaded for rationing through prices, arguing in Marx's spirit that value is not tangible and cannot be determined otherwise than via approximation. Petrov was skeptical about the possibilities of computer-aided price computations. His perception of the market was more "social," and in that view he was closer to Misesian (and Hayekian) non-neoclassical interpretations (Coyne, Leeson, and Boettke 2005) of the market as a lively and competitive community of economic players.

The writings of the Soviet optimal planning school, however, could not be ignored. Petrov subscribed to them intuitively, while the methodology of the quoted authors hardly was understood by him. Mateev, in turn, considered them as technically and conceptually inappropriate to serve socialist planning. He accepted possible price/wage fluctuations without identifying the process with Walrasian *tâtonnements* and without thinking in terms of equilibrium prices. Mateev focused on the I-O technical coefficients, the choice of investment projects, and the best accounting of production costs. He treated I-O as an excellent analytical frame for adequate cost calculation (i.e., price-setting), leaving the rate of profit as the only exogenous parameter. Thus, following the Marxist view, prices appeared as the sum of "objective" inputs (estimated through the I-O model) and a wisely adopted rate of return (reflecting "society's needs"). This was another departure from the theoretical fundamentals underpinning Leontief's model where real-life relative prices are supposed to reflect supply and demand, and, in line with the general equilibrium theory, the rate of profit and prices are determined simultaneously, not sequentially. Mateev opposed Kantorovich's "optimal" (in fact marginal) plan prices as supposedly static and equilibrating growth (the consumption/accumulation ratio) and efficiency only by chance. He thus rejected two basic corollaries: the "production price" model based on the average rate of profit and on marginal costs accounting for supply and demand; the idea that profit should be the key indicator of efficiency.

Twenty years later, in the late 1980s, Antonov tackled the calculation problem implicitly, in a very different form, wording, and setting.[20] He reassessed the reforms of the 1960s and questioned the very rationale of "mechanisms' games." Antonov pointed out that the appropriate incentives cannot be artificially engineered in a demonetized realm: from a neoclassical economics' perspective, they were part of a universal grid of price parameters proper to any economy. Moreover, the persistently disregarded inconsistency between the macroeconomic policy's priority (maximizing growth) and the economic mechanism was put at the forefront. Antonov underscored the need for homogeneity between the two, claiming that their inconsistency had disruptive consequences and debased the communist economy rather than reformed it. He observed that "every mechanism, differing from the traditional, needs a higher degree of freedom than provided by the central planning system" (Antonov 1988b). Only the traditional planning system was coherent and thus viable, controllable, more or less predictable, and (within its own framework) efficient. The new types of incentives corrupted the model that was not prone to reforms and every modification resulted in "abnormal" constructs.

This approach came after the disenchantment with attempts to build automatized systems for the management of the economy. Although computers had entered planning on a larger scale, their enhanced capacity was now regarded as an analytical asset, no more as a mighty proxy of the social machine. A great many economic deadlocks were still existent, and the fascination of the 1970s was over. Alongside, in Bulgaria and elsewhere in the East a gradual shift was under way in the set of applied research tools. I-O analysis attained its explanatory and descriptive limits without producing spectacular pragmatic or theoretical results. In turn, Western-inspired general equilibrium models started to gain importance. Their conceptual foundations were neoclassical, emanating an essentialist market philosophy. Thus, they served as implicit vehicles of decentralized economic options as opposed to the strong centralist bias fostered by the traditional I-O planning apparatus.

Economic Growth

Although the I-O framework was the centerpiece of theoretical and empirical research, other methodologies and topics related to planning were present in Bulgarian economic thought. Economic growth was prominent among them.

For a long time, macroeconomic production functions were the strongest contenders to Leontief's method in theoretical and empirical analysis of growth. Initially, in the second half of the 1960s, publications focused on reviewing well-established Western practices related to specification and parameter calibration. In addition, they offered some advice and warnings with regard to econometric estimation, which could be extremely valuable in applied and empirical work. Most of these were neglected: the urge to escape the caveats of oversimplification and to utilize more advanced estimation methods (such as generalized linear models), whenever data required them, was not taken to heart by most researchers. Instead, the ordinary least squares (OLS) technique became the routine, while its underlying assumptions often were downplayed or even forgotten. The technique encountered severe resistance: on the orthodox ground that it was borrowed directly from the "bourgeois" neoclassical school; and out of eagerness to defend the local mainstream gravitating to the I-O framework. The opposition eventually turned out to be futile and the production functions never lost the attention of researchers. The quasi-monopoly of the input-output method, which its followers vehemently defended, ended before they realized.

The proliferation of macroeconomic production functions was an achievement in applied research, although often at the cost of quality. In many publications time series data were used to estimate function parameters. Various functional specifications were tried (e.g., linear, parabolic, CES, and so on), though the unquestionable favorite was the Cobb-Douglas function. Besides simplicity, its good fit to the data was often put forward as an argument justifying this choice. However, as a rule, the usage of the Cobb-Douglas form lacked sufficient substantiation. The unit elasticity of substitution between factors of production was simply assumed; technological progress was just a standard mechanistic addition to the model and rarely was tackled differently than in the standard Hicks-neutral specification case; and negligence with respect to terminology was recurrent. Almost all specifications featured closed economies; the open-economy case received no tangible share of research efforts.

While authors often claimed to be using dynamic specifications of the estimated equations, in fact in most cases they included deterministic trends to an otherwise static relationship. At the same time, they ignored methodologies such as the one offered by distributed-lag models, which were already part of standard econometric work in the West. As a rule, publications were based on small samples but, once again, blind faith was put in the asymptotic properties of estimators. Those same small samples were used to derive the estimates of parameters (e.g., production elasticities), and as a result elasticities of scale often were just empirical artifacts.

The choice of different functional forms in specifying regression equations for econometric estimation seemed rather arbitrary. This left the impression that the existing knowledge on production structures was neglected, while attempts were made to infer those structures from the data. In some instances additional variables were inappropriately added to otherwise well-established theoretical constructs, which practically led to the destruction of the initial theoretical specification for the sake of getting a higher goodness-of-fit measure. Hardly ever was the issue of non-stationarity mentioned or explicitly tackled. The over-reliance on OLS was the usual (false) panacea.[21] In particular, there was full neglect of the endogeneity bias. Logically, reverse causation was rarely (if ever) studied in multiple-equation estimation frameworks. The overall conclusion is that the level of econometric knowledge among the majority of Bulgarian authors was notably unsatisfactory, far below the contemporary standards of the West, and even lower than that of most of their Eastern-bloc colleagues.

Until the early 1980s, an insignificant number of publications using the research results of Western authors produced original models that were properly constructed in terms of assumptions, specification, solution, and derivation of stability properties (cf. Milev and Assa 1977). Importantly, despite their relevance for planning, such theoretical exercises were neither meant for real-life applications nor ever found such by chance. They drew from neoclassical assumptions in model building that could not be endorsed by

Marxist theory, and their prior empirical substantiation or posterior validation was highly dubious or even infeasible. A methodological novelty in the
1980s was the interest in complete multi-equation models which contrasted
with the previous single-equation growth models (besides the ones directly
related to Leontief's framework). The main purpose was to take the model
from other (either capitalist or socialist) countries and try to reconcile it with
the available Bulgarian data. In many instances parameter calibration was
deemed acceptable, while it was clearly not, given the systematic under-or
over-fits; rudimentary system solution methods were applied; non-linearities
were avoided at all cost. Original contributions in this area were very rare.[22]

In other publications new insights touched upon partial aspects of planning. For instance, the lagged effects of investment (in a Kaleckian fashion) were investigated (Stoykov 1983); the lifespan and average age of
fixed capital were explored (Petranov 1989); and financial flows modeled
(Minassian 1989).

A specific approach developed during the 1980s was to implicitly assume
that no theory was directly applicable, and thus to rely only on what the data
said. In terms of research techniques, the corresponding publications used
cluster or principal-components factor analysis. These allowed for deriving
valuable insight in the economic phenomena from large datasets. They also
had the advantage of offering dimensionality reduction, that is, detecting
and then using only the meaningful relationships in the form of generalized
factors in the models. Such a data-driven approach was not unknown in the
West, and its epistemological flaws had already been commented in the early
1950s in the famous criticism by Tjalling Koopmans of Wesley Mitchell's
"measurement without theory" (Koopmans 1947).

NEOCLASSICAL TURN: GROWTH VERSUS EQUILIBRIUM, CYCLICITY, AND STABILIZATION

From the mid-1970s, dynamic forces in the Bulgarian economy were fad-
ing, the traditional work incentives were exhausted, and the vulnerability of
external balances increased. The scale of structural disequilibria, foreign debt
burden, and limited adjustment capacity did not bear comparison with anything before. Hard macroeconomic measures were unavoidable and a "readi-
ness for radicalism" was in the air, although its interpretation differed widely
among intellectual groups, power stakeholders, and social actors (Avramov
2008). The response of the planning establishment was trapped in the official
canon. Its explanation of the growth slowdown did not allow for identifying
Marxism-compatible endogenous causes. In turn, the a-theoretical I-O framework lacked suitable conceptual instruments. Consequently, no adequate

policy responses were proposed or implemented. At the same time, novel approaches started to appear in the scholarly community. A series of new instruments were developed, and previously ignored or "closed" research topics became researchable. In most cases, the outcomes of this research challenged the established planning practices and enforced critical rethinking of the dominant economic doctrine.

A still incoherent and marginal "neoclassical turn" began in the early 1980s with the problematization of the main mantra of central planners imbued with *growth fetishism*. This dogma reflected the subordination of optimality to the single objective function of high nominal growth rates. The problem also was sensed by the planning technocrats who started emphasizing "quality of growth"—a term that entered party documents.

Papers by Kostov, Hristov, and Antonov concluded that after the second oil shock, the acceleration of growth was not an option any more due, in particular, to the high import intensity of the economy and a corresponding sensitivity of growth to recurrent external imbalances (Kostov and Hristov 1981; Kostov 1984; Hristov 1986; Antonov 1986). Some of the results allowed for international comparison, especially within the Comecon countries. They pointed to the purposefully neglected fact that, despite being the most important growth factors, quantities, technology and investment were not the only ones. Such studies, subtly or openly, condemned the whole planning model for being founded on a "growth for the sake of growth" principle. They also were able to demonstrate (see Kostov and Veselinov 1982; Hristov 1986) that it was virtually impossible to optimize planning by means of the (dynamic) I-O model.

Academic economists applying conventional analytical methods also criticized the excessive focus on growth indicators. For instance, only one of the early growth models from the 1960s and 1970s adopted the maximization of national income as optimality criterion, while the others were oriented towards consumption-related criteria (Shapkarev 1975). In 1983, a study of the IE BAS explicitly concluded that "forcing economic growth usually generates negative unintended consequences"; that rising rates of the aggregate output do not necessarily lead to an increase in consumption; and that there is a need to replace the strategy of accelerated development with one of balanced and stable progress (*Problemi* 1983).[23] The interpretation of those statements, however, was conventional. To overcome the deceleration of growth was considered possible with the well-known measures aiming at input rationalization, technological change, restructuring, managerial and planning improvements, and reshaped incentives. The problem itself was conceived of as inertial and long-term, not requiring flexible adjustments of final demand, monetary flows, or price structure. The average annual growth forecasts until 2000 did not fall below 4 percent. A few years later, a new brainstorming in the IE BAS (encouraged by the influx of *perestroika* discourse) repeated the above-mentioned concerns but still kept the upper range of the growth rates at 5 percent (*Diskusia* 1988, 1). The dilemma between growth and equilibrium was commented cautiously by Hristo Vladov, with the opportunistic and meaningless qualification that a compromise between the two would be the solution. At the same time the party's policy goals adopted for the second half of the 1980s foresaw an annual growth rate of 5.4 percent (against the average of 3.7 percent in the previous decade), and by 1989 envisaged a totally unrealistic 6.5 percent for the next five-year plan.

The novelty of the neoclassical approach was manifold. The estimate of feasible long-term growth was reduced and the crucial role of external equilibria was stressed. Most importantly, it was argued in an iconoclastic manner that a *deliberate* economic slowdown was unavoidable. Deceleration ceased to be considered a passive, undesirable trend to become an *active* stabilization strategy. This, of course, contradicted the ideological assumption that maximization of the current growth rate is equivalent with an increase in social welfare. By taking a general equilibrium approach—and in line with Kornai's and other Eastern European economists' insights—Antonov insisted that this could be true only under extremely implausible assumptions, otherwise it leads to the exacerbation of structural disequilibria. To transpose the full employment characteristic of the initial industrialization drive in Bulgaria into the completely different conditions of the 1980s would severely harm the economy. Additional arguments in this vein referred to the experience of developed capitalist economies. Avramov emphasized that, by pursuing stabilization, they intentionally implemented deflationary and restrictive policies from the end of the 1970s (Avramov 1989; 1990). Thus, he argued, research on business cycles constitutes a natural platform for forsaking the dominant Marxist political economy and integrating "Western" and "Eastern" economic sciences. Given the exogenous shocks that hit Bulgaria's economy, a pro-cyclical adjustment via contractionary policies, was a must. In short, neoclassical equilibrium theory suggested a rearrangement in the official hierarchy of economic policy priorities by downgrading the still immovable preeminence of fast growth. In a sense, this posture was a subliminal and distant echo of the paradigmatic shift initiated by the Club of Rome's intellectual provocation *The Limits to Growth* in 1972.

The cyclical properties of the Bulgarian economy started to be systematically explored in the 1980s. Although dynamic imbalances implied instability and fluctuations of output reminiscent of capitalist business cycles, and were clearly observable from the late 1940s until the early 1980s, such a topic was an ideological taboo as the planned economy was proclaimed to be immune to instability. When uneven growth was touched upon, it was confined to technical issues and mismanagement. Interpretations refrained from any conceptual generalization and did not mention the term "cyclicity." The only tolerated notion was that of "rhythmicity" (Gatev 1976).

Most of the modeling attempts related to cyclicity followed a positivist approach, without applying dominant postwar Western paradigms. While Keynesian business cycle models required complex mathematical treatment and, more importantly, were out of fashion, the Real Business Cycle theories had—in addition to their mathematical sophistication—an unacceptable ideological (neoconservative) connotation. Spectral analysis of Bulgarian data identified recurring patterns in the behavior of macroeconomic variables (Dimitrov 1980; Antonov 1987)[24] or determined relationships among them, revealing, in particular, lagged effects. The idea of "rhythmicity" also returned to the stage (Shapkarev 1983). Moving averages were utilized to restate the obvious fact that the economy did not develop smoothly, and that the "rhythmic" recurrence of economic phenomena was in fact not that rhythmic. In direct reference to planning, those studies put forward the idea of improved efficiency as the solution. A part of the results indicated the presence of eight-year investment cycles (similar in length to the Western business cycles). In addition, five-year cyclicity of output was found and five-year planning was marked as one of the potential causes. Well-established modeling frameworks also were utilized to study the effects of external shocks on key economic variables (Kostov 1989; Avramov 1990). They shed more light on the mechanics of developments after 1975 and on the special role played by the international environment in generating cycle-like dynamics in macroeconomic aggregates.

As a rule, there was a clear-cut division between the studies of the long run (growth) and those of the short run (cycles). Combining the methodological limitations encountered by both approaches could provide a partial explanation. Another part seems to be linked to the difficulties of economic theory in general, as integrated models of growth and cycles are quite uncommon even today. Yet, in the late 1980s Antonov (1989a; 1989b; 1990) constructed such a full-fledged model of the centrally planned Bulgarian economy.[25] It was based on an original theoretical development of Michael Bruno's ideas (Bruno 1968), and managed to explain the nature of the existing structural disequilibria and the ensuing accumulation of pressures in the economy. Special attention was paid to the distinction between external and internal disequilibria, the latter being treated as much more relevant from the policy perspective. One of the most valuable contributions was the proof that disequilibria (especially the disproportionately large labor share in total income and underinvestment) imposed severe limitations on growth potential. Based on the results, the official assessment that in 1960–1985 Bulgaria's economy had exhibited equilibrium dynamics was emphatically rejected. On the contrary, real developments were characterized by constantly widening disequilibria. Expectedly, Antonov's studies remained marginalized and did not invoke qualitative shifts in the attitudes of planners and policymakers.

Antonov's approach implied the need for a consistent stabilization effort, which stemmed also from his conceptualization of inflation. The topic was completely missing from Bulgarian scholarly journals until the end of the 1980s[26] and was perceived in a primitive way by the planning authorities. Antonov legitimated the issue and unveiled the inflationary mechanisms inherent to a "reformed" Bulgarian economy with its numerous income leakages and commodity shortages. This was a system where, to a certain extent, "money mattered." His model presented a "monetized twin" of the economy and allowed to assess the inflationary potential, as well as the factors of production's equilibrium prices. It was concluded that the regeneration of shortages (i.e., suppressed inflation and structural disequilibria) is a built-in accelerator of growth and thus at the root of the traditional high growth mantra.

Those findings were in line with opinions attributed ex-post to other economists, or with conclusions reached after the opening of the communist archives (Gregory and Harrison 2005; Skidelsky 2007). But in Bulgaria in 1988 they constituted bold statements. Antonov expressed the grim future in a strict neoclassical language. Economic imbalances were unavoidable because the "disequilibrium growth" doctrine of the central planners ignored the fundamental marginalist principle of proportionality between marginal productivity and factor prices; the system is doomed because it eliminated the price of capital, maintained a negative discount rate (thus, generating a large inflationary potential), and eradicated the feedback proper to money and prices. The most important policy implication was that the fundamental cause of the system's non-viability is its *demonetization*. This reconfirmation of the impossibility of *socialist calculation* permitted Antonov to advance further and address the issues of inflation, domestic and foreign debt, and, finally, macroeconomic stabilization. He concluded that "the pressures for the monetization of the economy by the reform experiments . . . necessarily faced the resistance of the planning authorities because the 'revelation' of the real scope of shortages through prices reveals at the same time the failure of the existing organization of economic life" (Antonov 1990, 28). The incompatibility between plan and market was intuitively felt and formulated by reformers from the 1960s, but they packaged their suggestions in opaque wording and problematized only the "mechanism," not the macroeconomic objectives of the communist economy. The neoclassical approach covered both facets.

Despite their outspoken criticism, the conveyors of neoclassic ideas still were subject to subtle limitations. Even at the very end of the regime it was difficult to surmount the deeply infiltrated scent of eternity emanating from the communist institutional infrastructure. It implicitly censured the horizon, the addressee, and the scope of the proposals. The pathos reflected the urgency of a radical economic policy shift, but the absence of credible *political* alternatives and the rhetorical conventions compelled neoclassical-minded economists to direct their pleas to the existing authorities. Insofar as the core agenda imposed by the party was still dominated by the obsession of accelerating growth, the propositions took the appearance of calls for "large-scale, well-designed macroeconomic interventions." Akin to the planning mindset, economic policy still was conceived as a technocratic procedure based on *ex-ante* alternative model imitations. It was as if the regime's planning bodies could reformulate priorities as well as fine-tune and implement tools capable of reshaping and balancing the economic structure.

The move from analyzing economic growth and structure to a monetary approach brought to the fore the *problem of sequencing*. Antonov's attitude in this respect was, at first, seemingly anti-liberal. In 1988 his view was that the immediate priority is to balance the macroeconomic structure (Antonov 1988a). Decentralization was considered by him a counter-productive "democracy game" that only increases pressure on the macroeconomic variables. Accordingly, the proposed sequencing was eminently *dirigiste*: initially, let us fix (through concentrated, centralized effort) the structural imbalances, and only then start decentralizing the economy. Unleashing strongly distorted market forces only would provoke chaos.[27] This reasoning surprisingly coincided with the standpoint of economists loyal to the regime who claimed that such steps would result in stop-go policies attributed to "revisionist" Hungarian economists. The idea to temporary slow growth and reduce the standard of living in Hungary in order to facilitate structural adjustment was presented by the Bulgarian conservatives as an ideologically unacceptable failure (*Diskusia* 1988, 2). However, at a second reading and in his next publication (1988b) Antonov's attitude took a very different shape. There was no more doubt that "structural change" means imperative readjustment of relative (including factor) prices. In this context, *monetization* of the economy, that is, liberalization of prices and implementation of a comprehensive stabilization program became the immediate goals. Those policies had knocked on the door but were let in only after the fall of the regime and the closure of the Planning Commission in September 1990.[28]

At the end of the 1980s, a number of stabilization blueprints were prepared by government authorities. The most complete version was put forward by the Bulgarian National Bank (Avramov 2008). All of them stayed, however, piecemeal, hesitant, and inconsistent. Although the outlook was depicted more or less realistically and presented in an alarming tone, the proposed measures never addressed the roots of the problems. This was due to basic theoretical deficiencies, political constraints, and hierarchical or career considerations. The planning technocrats neither were equipped to design an adequate stabilization program nor able to process a reform strategy conceived in terms of equilibrium theory.

The incipient neoclassical turn was of great importance for the post-1989 transformations. Much remained to be learnt and the main ideas were further developed. But the real challenges had been tackled, and Bulgarian economic thought started to converge on mainstream economics. Expectedly, after the collapse of the regime the instigators of the turn were the most vocal promoters of shock therapy and opponents of gradualism.[29] Those economists joined the government at different levels and participated in the major reform programs of the 1990s, that is, the elaboration of the initial stabilization package, the settlement of the Bulgarian foreign debt problem after the March 1990 default, and the establishment of the Currency Board in 1997. However, the cohesion of the group reached its limits. Changing socioeconomic goals and priorities, fluid (re)configurations of the technocratic elites, and political meanders slowly dispersed the community and redefined the positions of its participants in the academic and public arena.

CONCLUSION

The evolution of the planning concepts in communist Bulgaria illustrates the intellectual and social patterns that economic ideas followed under this regime.

Planning that was supposed to embody the quintessence of the new order and entrusted to build a distinct institutional realm showed intrinsic rigidity. Its nomenklatura was, ex-officio, the administrator of the communist creed, and hence an extremely conservative community shielded from subversive influences and immune to innovative outbursts. By its very function it was a policy-taker, not a policy-setter even if sometimes it shaped the mindset of the political sovereign. Moreover, in a society where the world of ideas was arranged meticulously and hierarchically, planning matters occupied a subaltern place vis-à-vis political economy as the supreme ideological custodian.

Still, planning concepts were subject to contaminating effects. Very much like the semi-monetized grey economy undermined and coexisted with the planned façade, alien ideas besieged the canon. To make things more complicated, those ideas followed intricate trajectories across diverse conceptual, doctrinal, and (geo)political milieus. The incoming messages were corrupted, amputated, or twisted, and the result was rejection, hybridity, or incoherence. Because ideas arriving from the Western mainstream lacked a common theoretical ground with communist planning, their encounter was either dysfunctional or subversive. In turn, the winds from the East circulated more freely and were relayed according to the local sociopolitical conditions.

Planning in Bulgaria remained under double isolation. On the one hand, it proved unable to creatively digest new developments in economic research, and its major innovation (the optimality paradigm) remained more of a high-theory exercise accessible to a few scholars than a widely-adopted foundation for economic governance. Such advances seldom reached the top echelons of the party-state, and their presentation to officials was more of an art than a science. On the other hand, Bulgaria's planning technocrats stood aside from the reformist ideas. While in the Soviet Union and in other communist countries the quest for optimality (with all its ambivalence) was, to a certain extent, a driver of reformist momentum in economic science and policymaking, in Bulgaria it epitomized the status quo. Mathematization served, as a rule, the centralist positions. After all, it was perceived as a tool for *improving/enhancing*, not for *narrowing the scope* of planning.

The main positive results of planning's interactions with economic research were that they legitimized mathematical methods and experiments, contributed to the identification of some qualitative characteristics of the economy, and appreciated quantitative outlooks. It was no surprise, however, that the embryonic neoclassical turn during the late 1980s was missed by the authorities. In addressing the incapacity of communist planning to solve major economic problems, the new approach ultimately implied the superfluousness of central planning per se.

NOTES

1. An assistant of Aleksandr Chuprov, Anderson (1887–1960) arrived in Bulgaria in 1921. As a leading scholar, he was well-connected to the international research community. A member of the first body of fellows of the Econometric Society, he had contacts with Ragnar Frisch's institute in Oslo, associated SIER to the Jan Tinbergen's and Gottfried Haberler's project on business cycles at the League of Nations, and arranged a lecture (1935) of Oskar Morgenstern in Sofia.

2. The Commission was instituted by the peace treaty with Bulgaria that was signed in Neuilly, France in November 1919. The 1926 and 1928 foreign loans were contracted under the aegis of the League.

3. Stoyan Bochev (1881–1968) was a self-made financier without a university degree. During the interwar period, he served as executive director of the Sofia Stock Exchange, was a member of the board of one of the leading commercial banks, and managed the most important domestic insurance company. He was head of the Union of the Private Shareholding Companies and an active fellow (president for one mandate) of the Bulgarian Economic Society. It is mainly in this last capacity that he published numerous essays dealing with Bulgaria's economic problems.

4. Most of the time, the department of "Economic Planning" was chaired by professors who were or had been also heads of the "Planning Agency."

5. The I-O tables were confectioned by the Statistical Office since 1960. They were not published officially, but some of their versions, as well as other macroeconomic indicators not included in the public *Statistical Yearbook*, were accessible to scholars for research purposes. Until 1989 Bulgaria employed the System of Material Products. In the late 1980s tentative experimental estimates of the country's GDP were performed. They were neither adopted nor published.

6. Of course, in real life the relations between the planning bodies and the enterprises always entailed bargaining. Compromises were vital for the survival of the regime. Initially, bargaining was a completely informal process, but later on the authorities tried to partially institutionalize it. The "alternative plan" (*nasreshten plan*) was introduced as a mandatory step in the planning procedure. It was supposed to embed the "innovative energy of the collectives," to disclose "hidden reserves," and, ultimately, to upgrade the primary requirements of the center. Notwithstanding such amendments, the chaotic, and aleatory elements never disappeared and recurrently generated leakages, unaccounted flows, and monetized "market" pockets in the economy.

7. The forced mass exodus of 320,000 Bulgarian Turks from June to August 1989 was the climax of the overwhelming assimilation campaign initiated in December 1984. The economic shocks triggered by the exodus contributed considerably to the implosion of the regime. The authorities had to manage a state of emergency and, paradoxically, while the government embarked on an allegedly most radical "market-oriented" reform plan, it concurrently adopted a series of measures proper to War Communism.

8. The course was only 75 hours per year, compared to 480 hours for Political Economy (HIE 1963–1989).

9. Cournot, Gossen, Jevons, Walras, Pareto, Keynes, Kahn, Harrod, Domar, Samuelson, Hicks, Goodwin, Kalecki, Leontief, von Neumann, the Club of Rome, the Forrester-Meadows and Mesarovic-Pestel models, and Leontief's report on the future of the world economy (available in Russian) were quoted.

10. It was an unequivocal replica of the Laboratory for Mathematical Methods in the Economy established by Vasilii Nemchinov in Moscow in 1958.

11. In 1964 *Planovo stopanstvo* started an analogous but intermittent section with the same pool of authors.

12. This figure included articles discussing the construction and application of mathematical models or analyzing economic problems with the help of a more or less sophisticated mathematical apparatus. The field was positioned after "Political Economy of Socialism, Problems of Economic Science, History of Economic Thought" (18.9 percent), "Sectoral Economics" (13.3 percent), "Economics of Capitalist and Developing Countries, Critique of Bourgeois and Revisionist Theories" (11.5 percent), and "Intensification and Effectiveness of the National Economy" (7.7 percent).

13. As an exception, in 1965–1967 three EML fellows attended a high-level Master's Program organized in Yugoslavia under the leadership of Branko Horvat. Among others, George Dantzig was teaching there.

14. A far from exhaustive list of outstanding Western econometricians and mathematical economists translated into Russian includes Michael Intriligator, Kelvin Lancaster, Edmond Malinvaud, Michio Morishima, Hukukane Nikaido, Lionel Stoleru, and Gerhard Tintner.

15. Namely Ivan Kostov, Lubomir Hristov, Ventsislav Antonov, Roumen Avramov, and in a slightly different vein Ventseslav Dimitrov. The cohesion of the group was based on a distinct generational identity and a critical stance vis-à-vis the academic establishment. The community coalesced on different grounds: common university studies, teacher-student ties and institutional affiliations; cross-influences and complementarity of interests; and a continuous intense and lively theoretical and methodological debate. The intellectual closeness was reflected in mutual references and a desire to formulate a *joint* research agenda, which did not preclude differences within the group in terms of political radicalism.

16. In the late 1970s, the Sofia University's Faculty of Mathematics and Mechanics opened its doors to professionals from other areas. Ventseslav Dimitrov (researching at the time Western foreign trade theories and quantitative models), Ivan Kostov and Ventsislav Antonov seized the opportunity to earn an additional university degree in mathematics.

17. Grigorii Feldman, Viktor Novozhilov (his early writings, especially his seminal 1926 paper *Nedostatok tovarov* (Commodity Shortage), which was ignored by the reformers of the 1960s), and Nikolai Kondratiev were the most influential authors.

18. In 1987 Antonov presented Kornai's *Economics of Shortage* at the EML's seminar by sharing some disagreements with the mathematics and models in the book. This review was the first systematic comment in Bulgaria on Kornai's work, which so far had been ignored, even by reformists like Georgi Petrov.

19. It was assumed that Leontief's framework is superior to any competing methodology presented in "bourgeois" literature.

20. Although well aware of the interwar controversy and of Hayek's position, he did not discuss them in his papers. From another angle, the debate was evoked explicitly for the first time by Hristo Vladov. He took the side of Mises by questioning the monopoly of state ownership and bureaucratic management and by claiming that the aborted optimal planning experiment demonstrated the irrelevance of the Lange-Taylor proposals to mimic the market (Vladov 1989).

21. One notable exception could be found in Antonov (1985) where a two-factor CES production function was estimated by means of a nonlinear least squares procedure.

22. Rumen Dobrinsky (1990) was a notable exception in this respect, despite some methodological drawbacks that were noticed by the author himself.

23. In a symptomatic coincidence (most probably due to chance), the same issue of the review published a translation of Tamás Bauer's paper "Tensions and Cyclicality in Capital Investment." The publication was accompanied with a disclaimer that many of the author's positions were controversial.

24. The results suggested periodical movements of 3–4 years in investment and national income, as well as in manufacturing.

25. Some of the results of Antonov appeared in early 1990 due to the publication delay. They reflected, however, work done (and publicly voiced) before the end of 1989.

26. A narrative account of hidden and open inflation and the corresponding experience in some socialist countries was proposed by Belcho Ilev in (Diskusia 1988, 1).

27. In early 1989 Kostov still worried that an overwhelming financial liberalization could generate chaos. Nevertheless, he was the one who (as Minister of Finance) liberalized prices and forex trade in February 1991.

28. The issue of sequencing was raised also in the context of the reforms in the 1960s. In purely verbal and intuitive terms Petrov shared the concern that a transition to flexible prices would provoke sizable structural effects and a *temporary* slowdown of growth (Petrov 1969, 262, 290, 438).

29. As early as December 1989 Antonov published the most lucid account of the desperate macroeconomic situation and the unavoidable dramatic adjustments (Antonov 1989c).

BIBLIOGRAPHY

Antonov, Ventsislav. 1985. "Proizvodstveni funktsii s obobshteni faktori." *Ikonomicheska misal* 7: 106–118.

———. 1986. "Strukturen analiz na vanshnata targovia ot pozitsiite na natzionalnata ikonomika." *Ikonomicheska misal* 1: 44–56.

———. 1987: "Nyakoi harakteristiki na strukturnite promeni v ikonomikata: prisposobimost i tsiklichnost v promishlenostta." *Ikonomicheska misal* 5: 13–27.

———. 1988a. "Problemi na ikonomicheskia rastej v Balgaria i neposredtvenite zadachi na ikonomicheskata politika." *Annual of the Higher Institute of Economy "Karl Marx,"* Sofia, 2 (1): 44–76.

———. 1988b. *Printzipite na ikonomicheskia mehanizam: Dvadeset godini po-kasno.* Presentation at the Conference on the Problems of Public Ownership and the Economic Mechanism, Institute of Economy, Bulgarian Academy of Sciences, November 17–18, 1988 (Unpublished).

———. 1989a. "Neravnovesie i ikonomicheski rastej: vazdeistvie na strukturnite neravnovesia varhy tempa na rastej." *Ikonomicheska misal* 2: 72–85.

———. 1989b. "Neravnovesie i ikonomicheski rastej: model na tsiklichen rastej s ustoichivi strukturni neravnovesia." *Ikonomicheska misal* 5: 82–95.

———. 1989c. "Otvad magiata na slovoto ili za kogo bie kambanata." *Rabotnichesko Delo*, December 29, 1989.

———. 1990. "Teoretichni osnovi na inflatziata pri sotzializma." *Ikonomika*, June (Supplement): 16–28.

Avramov, Roumen. 1989. "Tsiklichnostta v balgarskata ikonomika: teoretichni i metodologicheski osnovi na analiza." *Ikonomicheska misal* 11: 3–16.

―――. 1990. "Tsiklichnostta v balgarskata ikonomika: vanshni shokove i vatreshni faktori." *Ikonomicheska misal* 2: 13–29.

―――. 2007. *Komunalniat kapitalizam: Iz balgarskoto stopansko minalo.* Vols. 1–3. Sofia: Fondatzia balgarska nauka i kultura, Centre for Liberal Strategies.

―――. 2008. *Pari I De/Stabilizatsia v Balgaria, 1948–1989.* Sofia: Ciela.

―――. 2018. "From Nationalization to Nowhere: Ownership in Bulgarian Economic Thought 1944–1989." In *Populating No Man's Land: Economic Concepts of Ownership under Communism*, edited by János Mátyás Kovács, 23–46. Lanham: Lexington Books.

Bochev, Stoyan 1935. "Planovo Stopanstvo." *Spisanie na Balgarskoto Ikonomichesko Drujestvo* 34: 16–28.

Bruno, Michael. 1968. "Estimation of Factor Contribution to Growth under Structural Disequilibrium." *International Economic Review* 9 (1): 49–62.

Christ, Carl. 1955. "A Review of Input-Output Analysis." In *Input-Output Analysis: An Appraisal*, 137–169. NBER Studies in Income and Wealth, vol. 18. Princeton: Princeton University Press.

Christophoroff, Assen. 1943. *Uvod v politicheskata ikonomia na voennoto stopanstvo.* Sofia: The author's publication.

Coyne, Christopher J., Peter T. Leeson, and Peter J. Boettke. 2005. "Hayek vs. the Neoclassicists: Lessons from the Socialist Calculation Debate." In *Elgar Companion to Hayekian Economics*, edited by Roger W. Garrison and Norman Barry. Cheltenham/Northhampton: Edward Elgar.

Davidov, David. 1973. *Struktura i nasoki na razvitie na Vishia ikonomicheski institute.* Sofia: HIE.

Dimitrov, Alexandar. 1980. "Za inertsionnostta v ikonomikata." *Ikonomicheska misal* 8: 41–52.

Diskusia . . . 1988. "Diskusia po problemite na kachestveno novia ikonomicheski rastej." Proceedings of the conference held at the IE BAS, June 9–10, 1987. *Ikonomicheska misal* 1: 3–42; 2: 3–30; 3: 3–39.

Dobrinsky, Rumen. 1990. "Makromodel na proizvodstvoto i parvichnoto razpredelenie na dohodite." *Ikonomicheska missal* 4: 84–96.

Friedman, Milton. 1955. "Comment on Carl Christ." In *Input-Output Analysis: An Appraisal*, 169–174. NBER Studies in Income and Wealth, vol. 18. Princeton: Princeton University Press.

Gatev, Kiril. 1976. "Otnosno sashtnostta i izmervaneto na ritmichnostta na stopanskite protsesi." 7: 42–53.

Gregory, Paul, and Mark Harrison. 2005. "Allocation under Dictatorship: Research in Stalin's Archives." *Journal of Economic Literature* XLIII (September): 721–61.

Higher Institute of Economy (HIE). 1963–1989. Fund 1643, Inventories 3, 10, 18. Chair of Economic Planning—Research Plans, Curricula, Minutes. Sofia City's and Regional Archives.

Hristov, Lubomir. 1986. "Analiz na ikonomicheskia rastej I strukturnite izmenenia v nashata ikonomika vuz osnova na magistalnia podhod." *Ikonomicheska misal* 1: 95–110.

Ivanov, Martin. 2008. *Reformatorstvo bez reformi.* Sofia: CIELA.

Koopmans, Tjalling C. 1947 "Measurement without Theory." *Review of Economics and Statistics* 29 (3): 161–72.

Kostov, Ivan. 1984. "Otnosno teoriyata i metodologiyata na kachestvoto na ikonomicheskiya rastezh." *Ikonomicheska misal* 8: 30–45.

———. 1989. "Neravnovesieto i otraslovata strategia." *Ikonomicheska misal* 3: 65–77.

Kostov, Ivan, and Lubomir Hristov. 1981. "Sravnitelno izsledvane na ikonomicheskia rastej v niakoi strani na SIV." *Ikonomicheska misal* 1: 12–25.

Kostov, Ivan, and V. Veselinov. 1982. "Prognozirane i analiz na ikonomicheskiya rastezh sas zatvoreni dinamichni modeli." *Ikonomicheska misal* 2: 115–27.

Lange, Oskar. 1965. *Wstęp do cybernetyki ekonomicznej.* Warszawa: Panstwowe Wydawnictwo Naukowe.

Lazarov, Kiril. 1949. "Planirane i Statistika." *Statistika* (2): 67–78.

Marcheva, Iliana. 2016. *Politikata za stopanska modernizatsia v Balgaria po vreme na Studenata voina.* Sofia: Letera.

Mateev, Evgeni. 1964. "Uravnenia na mejduotraslovite vruzki." *Ikonomicheska misal* 6: 73–89.

———. 1974. *Avtormatizirana sistema za upravlenie na narodnoto stopanstvo: ikonomicheski osnovi.* Sofia: BAN.

———. 1987. *Struktura i upravlenie na ikonomicheskata sistema.* Sofia: Nauka i izkustvo.

Milev, E., and I. Assa. 1977. "Analiz na dvusektoren model na ikonomichesko razvitie." *Ikonomicheska misal* 3: 83–92.

Miller, Ronald E., and Peter D. Blair. 2009. *Input–Output Analysis: Foundations and Extensions,* 2nd Edition. Cambridge: Cambridge University Press.

Minassian, Garabed. 1989. "Modelirane na finansovite vzaimodeistvia v narodnoto stopanstvo." *Ikonomicheska misal* 6: 63–73.

Montias, J. M. 1959. "Planning with Material Balances in Soviet-Type Economies." *The American Economic Review* 49 (5): 963–85.

Nenovsky, Nikolai, and Pencho Penchev. 2018. "The Austrian School in Bulgaria: A History." *Russian Journal of Economics* 4 (1): 44–64.

Penchev, Pencho. 2018. "Patiat kam sotsializma? Parviat petgodishen plan za razvitie na selskoto stopanstvo." *Nauchni Trudove na UNSS* 3: 253–80.

Petranov, Stefan. 1989. "Makroikonomicheska otsenka na vazrastovite harakteristiki na osnovnite fondove." *Ikonomicheska misal* 11: 82–95.

Petrov, Georgi. 1969. *Stokovi otnoshenia u tzenoobrazuvane pri sotzializma.* Sofia: Nauka i Izkustvo.

———. 2016. *Lajlivite reformi v Balgaria.* Sofia: The author's publication.

"Problemi na ikonomicheskia rastej v Balgaria." 1983. Report of the IE BAS presented at a conference at the Institute, June 23–24, 1983. *Ikonomicheska misal* 9: 12–47.

Shapkarev, Petar. 1975. "Problemi na narodnostopanskia optimum." *Ikonomicheska misal* 8: 73–85.

———. 1983. *Proizvodstveniyat ritam v narodnoto stopanstvo na NR Balgariya: Statistiko-ikonomicheski etyud.* Sofia: Nauka i izkustvo.

Skidelsky, Robert. 2007. "Winning a Gamble with Communism," review of *By Force of Thought: Irregular Memoirs of an Intellectual Journey*, by János Kornai. *The New York Review of Books,* 50–53. May 31, 2007.

Stoeva, L. 1987. "Naukometrichno izsledvane na spisanie Ikonomicheska misal." *Ikonomicheska misal* 6: 79–91.

Stoykov, Ivan. 1983. "Faktorat vreme pri kapitalnite vlozheniya." *Ikonomicheska misal* 3: 62–76.

Vladov, Hristo. 1989. "Diskusia po problemite na sotzialisticheskata sobstvenost, Noemvri 1988." *Ikonomicheska misal* 5: 41–44.

Chapter 2

Quantitative Economics in China

From Planned Economy to Socialist Market Economy

Xiuli Liu, Minghui Qin, Shan Zheng, and Xin Xiang

Quantitative economics was born within the planned economy of China in the late 1950s, but it was not until after reforms and opening up led by Deng Xiaoping that its development accelerated in the course of China's transition from planned economy to socialist market economy during the 1980s. The transition promoted the development of quantitative economics in China in three respects: expanding demand, stimulating supply, and accelerating internationalization. In a market economy, the uncertainty and risk of economic development are far more obvious than in a planned economy. To meet the unprecedented urgency of applying quantitative economics to economic forecasting, policy analysis, and macro-control, traditional economics[1] was gradually combined with quantitative economics in terms of both theory and application. As regards theory, mathematical economics, economic cybernetics, economic game theory were among others used to study micro-and macroeconomic issues. As for application, econometrics, input-output analysis, economic game theory, and so on were used to solve sectoral and firm-level economic problems. Thus, economics developed through an organic combination of qualitative and quantitative analysis. There were two principles to which to adhere: insistence on the guidance of Marxist theory[2] and combining it with the practice of communist economy. In the process of China's reforms, the research objectives and contents of quantitative economics constantly have been adjusted in five dimensions: they were transformed from a discipline serving the plan to one serving the market, from a supply-oriented paradigm to a demand-oriented one, from supporting the government to supporting enterprises and citizens, from contributing to centralized deci-sion-making to primarily contributing to decentralized multilevel decision-making, and from promoting direct administrative regulation to promoting indirect economic regulation. In the past forty years, quantitative economics has played an important role in revealing objective economic laws and apply-ing them to improve the level of economic management in China.

The first part of this chapter discusses the development of quantitative economics and the role it played at different stages of the contemporary economic history of China. The second part focuses on basic and applied research in input-output analysis, econometrics, economic optimization theory, and economic cybernetics. The chapter concludes with a summary and an outlook upon the future.

DEVELOPMENT OF QUANTITATIVE ECONOMICS

China began to introduce socialist public ownership at the end of 1949, and by 1952 the planned economy was basically established. To ensure scientific prediction and manage national economic plans, it was necessary to under-stand and describe the ever-changing process of social reproduction. Relying on simple traditional methods of mathematical calculation was not enough. In 1956, Sun Yefang, director of the Institute of Economics of the Chinese Academy of Sciences, proposed to carry out research on mathematical eco-nomics after visiting colleagues at the Soviet Academy of Sciences. He set up a research group, with Wu Jiapei as leader, within the national economic balance department of the institute. At the same time, another research group was established at the department of operations research in the Institute of Mathematics of the Chinese Academy of Sciences. The two groups collabo-rated in doing research on methods of mathematical economics, mathemati-cal models of socialist reproduction, and principles of intersectoral balances. Quantitative economics began to sprout in China in a way that the latter group was mainly responsible for mathematical operations to support the former group's policy analysis.

In 1962–1964, Hu Daiguang, Wu Baosan, and Sun Shizhen co-authored and published the book *Western Econometrics*. This was the first time that this subject was introduced to Chinese academic circles in a comprehensive and systematic manner. At the time, domestic scholars mainly learned from the experience of the Soviet Union and studied models for socialist repro-duction, intersectoral balance, optimization, and simulation. They focused on input-output analysis, theory of economic cycles, optimal planning, the "three theories" (information theory, systems theory, and cybernetics), and models of productivity (technological progress) and economic growth as well as employment and price theory. In building models of mathematical economics, they took the political economy of Marx and Lenin as the foundation of economic analysis. From the outbreak of the Cultural Revolution in 1966, research on quantitative economics was carried out haphazardly. Nevertheless, in 1973 Chen Xikang compiled physical input-output tables of Chinese economy for 61 products as a natural science research project with the help of Yan Shuhai, Renmin University of China, the State Planning Commission,[3] and the National Bureau of Statistics (Zhang 2010; Zhang, Wang, and Ge 2016).

Since 1979, China gradually has turned from a "planned commodity economy" to a "socialist market economy." In October 2002, the Sixteenth National Congress of the Communist Party of China (CPC) declared that the socialist market system was established in the country. It promoted quantitative economics, and academic economists continued to introduce mathematical theories and methods learned from scholars in the United States and other Western countries more freely. In 1980, with the help of Chinese Academy of Social Sciences, Lawrence R. Klein, Gregory C. Chow, Lawrence J. Lau, Xiao Zheng, Su Qingxiong, Theodore W. Anderson, Albert Ando, and others held a seven-week econometrics workshop at the Summer Palace in Beijing. As a result, traditional qualitative research began to shift to quantitative and empirical analysis. This was an important milestone in the history of quantitative economics in China. Since then, mathematical economics has been in the public eye and widely applied in various fields of economic development.

This wave of quantitative research in economics began with economic forecasting. In the early 1980s, taking the formulation of the 2000 development plan as an opportunity, some research institutions and state agencies like the National Development and Reform Commission, the Ministry of Agriculture, and the Ministry of Commerce, began to apply quantitative economic models, and the development of national and regional macroeconomic models became popular. In 1985, the Chinese Academy of Social Sciences, the State Planning Commission Computing Center (National Economic Information Center), and Fudan University began to cooperate on building a macroeconomic model for the entire Chinese economy. In December, 1985, the model was completed successfully and replaced the previous version developed by Professor Liu Zunyi in the framework of the world economic forecasting model system (Project Link directed by L. R. Klein). Based on the results of this model, the Chinese Academy of Social Sciences began to provide the Central Committee and the State Council with annual economic forecast data and published the "blue book" (*Economics of China: Analysis and Forecast*) from 1990 onwards (Wang and Wang 2010). In 1997, the National Bureau of Statistics set up a quarterly econometric model and predicted the values of consumption, investment, import and export, and GDP as a whole (Wang and Li 1999). In 1998, the Academy of Mathematics and System Science, Chinese Academy of Sciences used co-integration and wavelet transform methods to forecast quarterly money demand and monthly money multiplier (Liu and Deng 1999). Since 2005, the Center for Forecasting Science, Chinese Academy of Sciences annually published *China—Economic Forecast and Outlook*, in which—apart from the analysis of the factors affecting China's economic growth and the forecast of economic growth rate—more than ten important economic aspects such as fixed assets investment, import and export, final consumption, and CPI were predicted. With the continuous deepening of the commodity market, the economy gradually changed from supply-led to demand-led, and the forecasting model also was modified accordingly. A fixed asset utilization coefficient was added to the production function, and the variation of the coefficient explained by demand affected the change in total output, thus bringing in the feedback of demand.

Quantitative economic methods also were adopted widely in macroeconomic regulation. The Reform Office of the State Council used econometric methods to measure various schemes of control and their chain effects in designing price reform and also demonstrated the feasibility of the macro-control target in 1996 (Wang 1996). The State Planning Commission also applied mathematical models during the preparation of the Seventh Five-Year Plan in 1986. Using general equilibrium theory, the 710 Aerospace Research Institute[4] built the "national financial system control model," a dynamic model for credit and currency circulation. It determined the appropriate accumulation rate and optimized currency liquidity (National Symposium on Soft Science Research 1986).[5] The Chinese Academy of Social Sciences and other institutions used the "Avenue Model" to optimize the analysis and forecast of China's industrial structure from 1986 to 2000, providing a significant amount of basic information to the central government for the Seventh Five-Year Plan. The plan put forward principles of industrial restructuring, the so-called "first industrial policy."

The simulation of economic policy at the macro level is another important application of quantitative economics. For many years, scholars carried out a large number of research projects to provide governmental decision-making with scientific assistance. For example, Tang (1984) applied a multisectoral econometric model to evaluate and analyze population, investment, price, wages, and other domestic policies from 1963 to 1982. Based on the national agricultural input-output table, the Rural Development Research Center of the State Council developed a "rural policy analysis model" by means of systems engineering and econometric methods, to conduct a short-term agricultural prediction and a quantitative analysis of agricultural policies (National Symposium on Soft Science Research 1986). Li and Qi (1998) compared the effects of different industrial policies on economic growth. In 2000, China's economic development entered the phase of the "new normal," with a growth rate changing from high speed to medium high speed, a growth model changing from large-scale and extensive growth to quality-and efficiency-oriented intensive growth, and with driving factors changing from investment to innovation. This transition process brought many new opportunities and challenges for the development of quantitative economics. On the basis of previous studies, scholars combined the concept of sustainable development with a growing number of complex macroeconomic factors such as economic growth and inflation (Liu and Xie 2003; Liu and Xia 2010), public debt (Li, Xia, and Wang 2013), transformation performance (Jin 2005; Che and Zhang 2011), urban-rural differences (Han and Du 2012), income distribution (Liu and Xie 2003), labor supply (China's Economic Growth and Macroeconomic Stability Research Group 2007), and even private property rights.[6]

At the micro level, with the increasing prosperity of the capital market, questions like how to measure risk, how to obtain extra yield in the capital market, or how to adjust the economic growth through taxation attracted widespread attention in the field of quantitative economic research. Earlier, the compilation and application of enterprise input-output tables had been more widespread. With the improvement of research methods and the expansion of the scope of research, Chen (2007) explored tourism by asymmetric information models of game theory. Yu and Shi (2004) compared the competitiveness of Chinese and foreign banks. Zhang (2007) analyzed the impact of income and expenditure uncertainty on the current consumption of citizens from both long-term and short-term perspectives. Zhang and Song (2016) studied the effects of private property protection on the expansion of and innovation by enterprises. Jiang et al. (2017) built a theoretical model of optimal loan pricing for banks and analyzed the impact of growing competition on their information gathering behavior.

Meanwhile, catering to the development concept of innovation, coordination, greenness, openness, and sharing[7] put forward by the fifth plenary session of the Eighteenth Central Committee of CPC, scholars made use of the quantification of the relationship between resources, environment, and economic development in designing environmental regulations (Xie 2008; Zhang, Wang, and Ge 2010; Liu, Hewings, and Wang 2018), energy consumption and output efficiency (Sun et al. 2012; Liu, Muniz, and Moreno 2016) as well as the efficiency of the green economy (Zhu, Yue, and Shi 2011; Li and Su 2016; Liu et al. 2016). The main driving forces of China's transformation and industrial restructuring, and the nonlinear correlation and spillover effects between technological innovation and structural optimization also were studied.

In recent years, the development of the internet and the internet of things promoted the advent of the era of Big Data and provided new opportunities for the expansion of quantitative economic research. On the one hand, the emergence of big data changed the basis of empirical research in economics. In the past, the number of data used in quantitative economic research usually amounted only to a few hundred, resulting in problems such as a rough fit with reality and constraints on various assumptions. The ultra-large scale of data accumulated through the internet has unique advantages like timeliness, accuracy, relatively low cost, high granularity, and large sample size, which provide abundant and original information for a more comprehensive and objective investigation of the research object. Zhang et al. (2012) predicted the consumer price index by using some keywords in web search and obtained the index about one month earlier than the National Bureau of Statistics. Wang and Dong (2017) used five different forecasting methods to analyze China's quarterly unemployment rate. Heretofore, the combination of big data and quantitative economic methods has been applied to unemployment and inflation (Sun et al. 2014; Xu and Gao 2017), social consumption (Cheng and Wei 2019), real estate markets (Huo, Shang, and Xu 2013; Hong and Li 2015), and public opinion analysis (Yu 2015; Ma, Liu, and Li 2016). The development of big data methods also brought changes in the capacity of data processing and analysis and even in the research paradigm of empirical economics as a whole. Because the internet can be used for collecting economic information, it is logical to find the regression paths of economic data according to the law of large numbers, and thus enhance the reliability of quantitative economics. However, one still faces problems of data acquisition, processing of unstructured data, and data noise.

MAIN RESEARCH METHODS

Input-Output Analysis

Following the reforms, input-output theory was applied widely to the analysis and prediction of macroeconomic performance and the solution of social problems. The National Bureau of Statistics (NBS) used the input-output model to calculate the 1990 national economic plan[8] and proposed that the investment in fixed assets should be increased to the actual level of the previous year (Chen et al. 2011). Since 2007, Renmin University of China used multisectoral input-output analysis to simulate actual changes, internal economic links, and policy effects in the process of structural transformation and made concrete operational suggestions to change the mode of economic growth (Liu 2010). Applying input-output theory, the Department of National

Accounts of NBS evaluated China's industrial structure and identified the uncoordinated industrial sectors during 1978–1992, providing a basis for future industrial restructuring (Shi 2004). Liu (2018) compared the skeleton industrial structures (SIS) of China, Japan, and the United States based on input-output tables and suggested policies for structural adjustment in Chinese industries.

The input-occupancy-output technique[9] also was applied in many fields such as grain output, water conservancy, foreign trade, education, finance, and energy production. In the national grain output prediction for China (Chen, Pan, and Yang 2001; Chen, Guo, and Yang 2008) suggested a systematic integrated approach based on the input-output model of agriculture. Liu et al. (Liu and Chen 2008; Liu, Chen, and Wang 2009) combined the input-occupancy-output tables with linear programming techniques to calculate the shadow prices of productive water and industrial water in China's nine river basins. The Academy of Mathematics and Systems Science, Chinese Academy of Sciences worked out non-competitive input-output tables to analyze exports and calculated the value added of exports. It was found that if the trade surplus was calculated by the value added of exports, the Sino-US surplus would be significantly reduced (Chen et al. 2001; 2012). Therefore, then World Trade Organization Director-General Pascal Lamy suggested that trade statistics should be based on changes in the value added of each country's imports and exports. In the field of education, Chen Xikang (2004) proposed a new dynamic input-occupancy-output model that considered human capital and technology. Zhang and Chen (2008) built a dynamic model of education-economy input-occupancy-output model, and Fu and Chen (2006) constructed a multi-year-lag education-economy extended IO model with assets. Guo Jue analyzed the interaction between financial sectors and other branches based on the 1997, 2000, and 2002 financial input-output tables of China. The research results were valued highly by the Currency Gold and Silver Bureau of the People's Bank of China (Chen et al. 2011). In 2005 and 2006, Renmin University of China used input-output techniques to analyze the economic impact of the price changes of water, coal, and oil. The research results provided a reference for the Beijing Development and Reform Commission to formulate a price reform for natural resources (Liu 2010).

Econometrics

The development of econometrics in China took place in three stages:

First Stage: *1979–1991*. Entering the 1960s, mathematical economics and econometrics became the mainstream of Western economics. Influenced by this trend, Chinese economists began to introduce and assimilate econometrics after 1979. A series of translations of works by Nobel Prize winners in economics were published, including *A Textbook of Econometrics* (Klein and Hood 1983), *Quantitative Lectures* (Klein et al. 1990), *Course of Econometrics* (Klein 1991), and so on. The main textbooks or textbook translations were *Theory of Econometrics* (Koutsoyiannis 1981), *Econometrics* (Sun 1984), and *Econometrics* (Zhang and Yu 1984).

At this stage, China was in a period of transition from a highly centralized planned economy to a so-called "planned commodity economy." Theoretical research on econometrics mainly focused on the characteristics of a Chinese macroeconomic model, economic cycles, technological progress, economic growth, employment, and prices. It was guided by Marxist economic theory[10] and production-oriented. Representative monographs included: *Technological Progress and Economic Growth* (Shi 1985), *Research on China's Macroeconomic Models* (Wu and Zhang 1986), *Discussion on Macroeconomic Models* (Wang 1992), and *Cyclical Fluctuation of Chinese Economy* (Liu 2007). The application of these quantitative models solved many problems of China's economy and society at that time. First, it ensured the public's correct judgment of economic development and maintained the stability of market economy. Second, it provided a basis for the formulation of economic policies and raised their efficiency. For example, China's largest economic mathematical model (the "Avenue Model" System[11]), developed in 1986, analyzed and predicted the evolution of the industrial structure in the country until 2000 and provided a lot of important information for the central government to formulate the Seventh Five-Year Plan and the "first industrial policy" in China (Qi 1997).

Second Stage: 1992–2000. In 1992, the Fourteenth National Congress of CPC proposed that the goal of economic restructuring was to establish a socialist market economy. China's economy made a soft landing[12] in 1996–1997, and the degree of marketization was further increased. Facing changes in the economic mechanism, quantitative economics in China began to pay attention to econometric models that can be adapted to the socialist market. First, they turned from supply orientation to investment-and consumption-demand orientation. For example, Wang and Shen (2001) included a demand function in the model in order to examine the impact of consumption on the national economy. Second, the econometric models changed from serving the planned economy to serving macro-control and began to tackle policy analysis. For example, the People's Bank of China developed the quarterly macro-econometric model PBCM1[13] to describe the transmission process of China's monetary policy and predicted the implementation effect of different policy options through model simulation (Wang and Jiang 1991).

Third Stage: After 2000. In view of social problems faced by China in a new era characterized by globalization, urban and rural development disparities, insufficient energy resources, and environmental problems, the theories and methods of econometrics developed rapidly. It was extended to the research on complex models, model robustness, and semi-parameter estimation (Zhang and Fang 2011; Zhao 2012; Bai and Wang 2016), and the studies changed from classical to modern econometrics. The main models involved were factor analysis, co-integration test, VAR, ARIMA, Monte Carlo simulation, VECM, panel data model, state space model, variance decomposition, impulse response function, CVAR, and other modern econometric methods (Wu and Shen 2015).

In terms of application, the models turned from macro-to micro-analysis and from cross-section and time-series data to panel data. The main areas of research were economic growth and development (Lin and Liu 2003; Pan 2003; Long 2003; Shi and Zhao 2011), industrial structure and policy (Ling 2017; Jin, Zhao, and Lu 2006; Gan, Zheng, and Yu 2011), urban and rural development (Jiang, Deng, and Seto 2013; Wang, Tai, and Chen 2019), environmental protection and sustainable development (Zhou, Ang, and Zhou 2012; Hao and Liu 2016; Long et al. 2016; Guan et al. 2018; Liu, Hewings, and Wang 2018), income distribution and income gap (Lu and Chen 2004; Song and Xiao 2005; Chen 2007), and the capital market (Zhang and Jin 2005; Liu, Luo, and Liu 2009; Shan 2008).

To sum up, the theory and application of econometrics at this stage focused on quality and efficiency, the supply of material, cultural, institutional, and ecological products, and tried to solve the problem of unbalanced and inadequate development in China.

Optimization Theory and Game Theory

Optimization theory is also known as operations research. Modern operations research was introduced in China in the late 1950s. The "location of the wheat field" was a representative research topic to find out how to save manpower in manual harvesting at that time. In addition, the model of the "Chinese postman problem"[14] was proposed by Guan (1960). This was the first work of Chinese scholars in the field of optimization which gained international recognition before the Cultural Revolution. In the early 1970s, Yue Minyi and Han Jiye began to study sequencing theory (Yue and Han 1976; 1979) and reported their research results on the sequencing problem of a multi-machine assembly line at the Seventh International Operations Research Conference held in Japan. During the Cultural Revolution, both the popularization and promotion of optimization theory were managed by Loo-Keng Hua. For ten years after 1965, he visited more than 20 provinces and cities to explain basic optimization techniques and overall planning methods to decision-makers in rural areas and factories (Zhang and Guan 1999). Interestingly, optimization never has been seen as a method of bourgeois pseudoscience in China. In the most difficult period of studying economic theory during the Cultural Revolution, optimization was still widely promoted as a model combining theory with practice (Li 2006).

In the 1970s, the pioneers of China's optimization theory, such as Xu Guozhi and Yue Minyi, achieved a number of important results in the field of the instantaneous probabilistic problem of queuing theory, the convergence problem of nonlinear programming gradient algorithm, and the sorting problem in combinatorial optimization. In 1977, the American Mathematical Society's report on the visit of its members in China pointed out that "in terms of applied mathematics, China has rapidly reached the forefront of these fields in areas such as queuing theory" (Mathematical Planning Branch of China Operations Research Society 2014). Since the 1980s, academic exchange at home and abroad has been increasing. Under the leadership of Yue Minyi and others, domestic optimization theory has developed fast, and researchers obtained a number of theoretical and applied results of international recognition. For example, researchers divided optimization into static and dynamic methods. The former includes linear and nonlinear programming while the latter focuses on calculus of variations, optimal control, dynamic programming, and so on (Gong 2000). As for applications, researchers used optimization and decision analysis methods to study financial risk control and management as well as asset evaluation and pricing[15] (Xie 1996; Zhong and Wang 2003). Also, a stochastic dynamic programming model was applied to the calculation of optimal strategy in multiple decision-making on supply chain management (Zhang, Li, and Wang 2006). Governor of the People's Bank of China, Zhou (2019) pointed out that the main economic reason for introducing socialist market economy was the optimization of resource allocation. From the perspective of optimization theory, the link between the optimization of resource allocation and the contract responsibility system is a dual relationship[16] reflected by the Lagrange multiplier method in static optimization. Yuan Yaxiang carried out research on mathematical planning at the Institute of Computational Mathematics, Chinese Academy of Sciences, which reached a global level in the field of nonlinear programming with its applied research on the trust region method, the conjugate gradient method, and the quasi-Newton method. As regards application, in 1984, the Geographical Resources Institute proposed the "point-axis system" theory of China's organization of social and economic space and the T-shaped space structure of land development.

The Chinese Society of Optimization, Overall Planning, and Economic Mathematics was established in 1981 to do research on optimization theory. Loo-Keng Hua was the first chairman. Today, the society has more than 17,000 members and 15 provincial and municipal branches. Also, there are 20 professional branches including project management, decision-making information, and economic mathematics. Since the establishment of the society, it has actively studied and promoted the application of the "double method."[17] It played an active role in many projects, such as the formulation of economic development plans for key provinces and cities, the optimization of railway transportation, and large iron and steel enterprises, as well as the comprehensive risk analysis of several major national projects[18] (Yu 1979; He 1996; Wang and Wang 2002; Chen and Lee 2004; Tao and Xiang 2005; Liu 2006; Wang, Yu, and Li 2006; Zhang et al. 2007; Li and Luo 2008; Gao and Wang 2008; Zhou 2010; Yin 2011; Yang and Cui 2013; Li, Lim, and Xiong 2018; Zhang, Tang, and Zhou 2019; Xiao and Li 2019). China has adhered to five-year cycles of central planning since 1953, and has not interrupted them except for the period of economic adjustment between 1963 and 1965. In 2016, China started the Thirteenth Five-Year Plan. And in the same year, Nobel laureate in economics Michael Spence was invited by the Chinese government to take part in the preparation of the Twelfth Five-Year Plan. He believed that China would benefit from the five-year plan and its experiences would be worth learning in the West. [19]

In recent years, researchers have continued to combine optimization theory with major development projects. Linear programming, nonlinear programming, dynamic programming, and recursive programming are widely used in economic optimization. For example, constructing a dynamic stochastic general equilibrium model (Li, Ma, and Wang 2009; Tan and Wang 2011; Yan 2012; Zhu and Cao 2019; Shu and Hong 2019), which is used by the central bank in macroeconomic analysis and monetary policy decision-making, has become one of the most important analytical methods. In addition, experiments were made with Bayesian decision models as well as game theory. The Bayesian models, for example, are currently of great significance for the study of exiting expansionary monetary policy.

Game theory is another hot spot in the study of quantitative economics in China. Before the 1990s, game theory was discussed little in China. The earliest work published was the *Handout on Game Theory* by Wu Wenjun and others (1960) based on the lectures given by Nikolai Vorobyov[20] in Leningrad. Cui Zhiyuan published *Game Theory and Social Science* in 1988, briefly introducing game theory. Since the 1990s, the quantitative economics community has published a series of more systematic books related to game theory, such as Li Zijiang's *Game Theory and Economic Equilibrium* (1992) and Wang Guocheng and Huang Tao's *Modern Economic Game Theory*

(1996). Zhang Weiying's *Game Theory and Information Economics* (1996) was considered to be of highest quality among these books at that time. In 1998, the National Game Theory Research Institute was established and an academic seminar was held in Beijing. In 2005, the society changed its name to National Society of Game Theory and Experimental Economics, and several academic seminars have been organized since then. The application of game theory in Chinese economics has been studied more widely since the beginning of the twenty-first century. The studies include the financial game model by Pan and Wu (2013), the entrepreneur's choice of game equilibrium model by Wang (2002), the game analysis of corporate governance structure by Liu et al. (2005), the game pricing model of financial moral hazard by Wu and Zhu (2001), and game theory and economic system simulation by Li et al. (2012). In recent years, game experiments and experimental economics in general were explored in a growing number of works.[21]

Economic Cybernetics

The term "economic cybernetics" was first proposed at the World Cybernetics Conference in Paris in 1952. In the beginning, economic cybernetics only appeared as an application of cybernetics in economics. However, economics soon reconstructed itself with the help of cybernetics and tried to make the entire social and economic system and its constituent parts the object of systems analysis and control. China's renowned scientists Qian Xuesen and Song Jian (1980) said that economic cybernetics is a discipline that applies modern control theory and methods to study the evolution and optimal control of economic systems. Subsequently, this idea became a new branch of cybernetic research in China.

In the late 1970s, Wu Jiapei wrote an article on economic cybernetics discussing the prospects of its application. This might be the earliest introduction to economic cybernetics in China (Gong 1988). The earliest published work on economic cybernetics in China was Oskar Lange's *Introduction to Economic Cybernetics* translated by Yang Xiaokai and Yu Hongsheng in 1980. In the early 1980s, China began to apply economic cybernetics to the formulation of regional energy and industrial planning (Hu and Qiao 1984; Zhong 1986; Zhuang 1988; Ning 1990; Zhang 1991; Huang and Zheng 2000; Lai, Zhu, and Dong 2004; Jiang et al. 2009; Liu, Zuoren, Sun 2019). One typical case was the application of cybernetics to the study of population problems in China. Song and Yu (1985) published research results in *Population Cybernetics* that used the state space method of modern cybernetics. The observability, controllability, and stability of the population system were discussed, and optimal cybernetic methods of population policy were proposed. They ultimately designed China's population development plan (Song and Yu 1985). Later, Yu et al. (1986) built a macro-optimal cybernetic model. The model provided feedback control through the input-output equilibrium equation and determined the optimal accumulation rate as well as the optimal industrial and investment structure under the constraints of supply and demand, construction scale, and production factors.

Since the 1990s, macroeconomic regulation has become an important means of steady and rapid economic development. Many mathematical economists began to apply modern cybernetics to the economy. There are four main types of control methods in the study of China's economic system.

1. *Optimal control*—a dynamic optimization method to solve the optimal control function of the economic system, which is often used to solve optimal decision-making and planning problems in macroeconomics. In the twenty-first century, dynamic programming has been applied to economic models such as investment decision-making, multi-stage production scheduling, resource allocation, and consumer choice (Chen 2006; Huang, Fabozzi, and Fukushima 2007; Meng, Zhang, and Jia 2019).

2. *Robust control*—or how to design a fixed controller to make an uncertain economic system reach a control quality that is robust. Xiao and Lu (2002) regarded uncertainty in the macroeconomic system as disturbance signal, transformed it into a standard H∞ problem, and then applied robust control theory for system analysis and decision-making. Wu (2001) combined the macroeconomic market regulation mechanism with robust control theory. Liu and Qu (2002) aimed at a discrete dynamic model of macroeconomic system and considered the supply-demand equilibrium of the model under the condition of uncertain parameters and financial risks. By transforming it into a system that is asymptotically stable at the equilibrium point, a robust control strategy emerged.

3. *Predictive control*—adopts multi-step testing, rolling optimization, feedback correction, and other control strategies, which have good control effects. It is suitable for controlling a complicated production process, for which it is difficult to establish accurate digital models. It has great advantages in dealing with complex economic systems. At present, there are applications of predictive control in chaotic economic systems and unbalanced economic systems (Yao and Sheng 2001; Yao and Sheng 2002; Liu and Liu 2006).

4. *Fuzzy control*—to use the knowledge of fuzzy mathematics to imitate the thinking mode of the human brain, identify and assess fuzzy phenomena, give precise control quantity, and control the controlled object. Fuzzy control theory was widely used in economic forecasting (Shen, Ding, and Tan 2009), enterprise classification management (Zhang 2003), highway traffic and supply chain management (Ding and Wang 2002; Huang and Liang 2008). Additionally, grey fuzzy control[22] based on grey theory proposed first by Deng Julong in 1982 developed rapidly (Deng 1987; Jin, Li, and Zhu 2019; Zhang 2019).

Economic cybernetics emphasizes the study of economic systems from the perspective of holistic, dynamic, interconnected, and coordinated development. It is not only applicable to the macroeconomic system to strengthen the regulation of the national economy but also to the microeconomic system to strengthen the scientific management of enterprises. Economic cybernetics brought significant economic and social benefits for both the planned economy and the market economy (Wang 2008). The contribution of economic cybernetics to economic development mainly includes four aspects: (1) structural theory of economic control systems; (2) regulation of macroeconomic systems; (3) control and coordination of microeconomic systems; (4) hierarchical and decentralized control of large economic systems.

Summary and Outlook

Quantitative economics made a great progress in both theory and practical applications in China during the past 40 years. However, there are also some shortcomings due to its late start in China. Despite rapid development after the 1980s, it still ranks behind contemporary advanced economic research in the world.

Theoretical research in China was not consummate enough to define a rigorous and universally accepted paradigm, and there are still disputes about the disciplinary attributes of quantitative economics. One typical opinion is that quantitative economics is actually econometrics. According to another, quantitative economics is a discipline of regularity with a specific object of study, while others hold that quantitative economics is not a discipline but a school of thought. What is more, the main direction of the discipline's development is not clear, which will have an adverse impact on quantitative economics in China in the long run. Moreover, China is not entirely consistent with advanced Western countries on many basic issues of economics owing to its special socialist market system. There are also different approaches to understanding socialist market economy in domestic academic circles. Some scholars believe that socialism and capitalism cannot coexist, and public ownership is incompatible with the market economy. Other scholars suggest that the socialist market economy is a market economy under macro-control. Again others hold that the socialist market economy is a combination of social equity and market efficiency. Therefore, a consensus in theory will be a significant prerequisite to establishing quantitative economics applicable to China's socialist market economy.

NOTES

1. In traditional economic research, Chinese scholars usually adopted an empirical approach, made assumptions about how the economy worked, and supported the alleged rules with examples. However, because there was no generally accepted theoretical test method, the debate about the validity of theoretical assumptions never ended.

2. Marx established a theoretical system that took labor theory of value as its foundation and surplus theory of value as its core. Chinese researchers adhere to the basic principles of Marxist economic theory and apply them to institutional analysis. For example, in central planning the output and distribution indicators of social product are determined first. Then, the dynamic model of intersectoral balance table and the real value model are used to formulate the production and distribution plans.

3. The State Planning Commission established in 1952 was renamed the National Development Planning Commission in 1998, and in 2003 it was merged with some parts of the former Reform Office of the State Council and the State Economic and Trade Commission into the National Development and Reform Commission.

4. In the 1980s, Qian Xuesen founded the Chinese systems engineering school at 710 Aerospace Research Institute, and took the lead in applying space systems engineering theory to national macroeconomic and population policy decision-making. In 2003, 707 Aerospace Research Institute, 710 Aerospace Research Institute, China Aerospace Engineering Consulting Center and China Aerospace Economic Research Center were merged into China Aerospace Engineering Consulting Center. In 2011, it was renamed China Aerospace Academy of Systems Science and Engineering.

5. The National Symposium on Soft Science Research was held in Beijing on July 25, 1986.

6. In the models, instead of direct quantification, the level of private property protection was explained by using instrumental variables, such as enterprise investment and innovation.

7. "Innovation" means the promotion of new solutions in theory, system, science, technology and culture; "coordination" means that the development process should be more comprehensive, holistic, balanced and sustainable; "greenness" means saving resources and protecting the environment; "openness" means a deep integration in the world economy; and "sharing" means that the development is balanced, equitable and beneficial to all.

8. In 1987, following the advice of many scholars, the General Office of the State Council issued a notice on national input-output survey, which clearly stipulated that the survey should be conducted and input-output tables should be compiled every five years.

9. Chen Xikang was the first in the world who proposed in 1989 a static input-occupancy-output technique. It not only examines the relationship between the input and output of individual sectors, but also studies the relationship between the fixed assets, labor force and natural resources owned by each sector and their output. Later, Chinese scholars introduced dynamic and nonlinear input-occupancy-output techniques as well.

10. Marx believed that the private possession of means of production and the socialization of products would inevitably lead to periodic economic crises. The only way to solve this problem, he thought, was to introduce the planned economy.

11. This model system is composed of an avenue model, a macroeconomic optimization model, and a recursive model of the national economy. It divides China's economy into 22 sectors, and forms a system with 4,026 constraints and 4,212 variables based on scientific and technological progress, environmental protection, foreign trade, and other factors.

12. This meant that after a period of overexpansion, the national economy fell back smoothly to a moderate growth range. In 1997, the M2 year-on-year growth rate dropped to 19.3 percent and the CPI dropped to below 4 percent, while the GDP growth rate remained above 8 percent.

13. The model consists of seven modules, one of which is the money supply module. The others are macroeconomic operation modules: industrial production, incomes, retail, prices, investment, and savings deposit.

14. The model built by Guan Meigu, a famous graph theorist, was meant to help the postman choose the shortest distance while completing the task. Later, the method was widely used in other fields, too, such as the snowplow line, the sprinkler line, the police patrol line and so on.

15. For example, the Shaanxi Provincial Operations Research Association conducted a cross-impact analysis of the volatility of Shanghai and Shenzhen stock markets, an optimization analysis of development decisions in Shaanxi's fruit industry, and an evaluation of the coordinated development of Shaanxi's economy, resources, and environment.

16. From the perspective of the optimization model, the incentive mechanism of the contract responsibility system corresponds to shadow prices. To achieve optimal resource allocation, it is necessary to align actual prices with these.

17. The double method means optimization and critical path method.

18. They included economic development plans in Shandong Province and Dalian, a railway transportation plan in Lanzhou, the economic evaluation of joint venture projects, and the optimization of large enterprises such as Baosteel and Wuhan Iron and Steel (China Operations Research Institute Research Report 2012).

19. Xinhuanet. Nobel Prize economist: China's five-year plan is worth learning from the West. https://oversea.huanqiu.com/article/9CaKrnJUfvU

Accessed November 13, 2021.

20. The founder of game theory in the Soviet Union N.N. Vorobyov lectured in China in 1960 and was received by Premier Zhou Enlai.

21. According to the statistics of China journal full-text database of China knowledge resources general database, there were less than 700 academic papers dealing with game theory in China from 1965 to 1999, but more than 700 publications in 2003. By now, the number of such publications has exceeded 2,000 each year and the main topic of 70 percent of them is economics.

22. Deng Julong began to study the control problems of large-scale systems with unknown parameters in 1979. In 1982, he published a paper on the control problems of grey systems.

BIBLIOGRAPHY

Anonymous. 1986. "Progress in Soft Science in the Field of Finance." *Science of Science and Management of S.&.T.* 10: 10.

Bai, Zhonglin, and Lingling Wang. 2016. "An Approach of Estimation for Impulse Response Functions of DSGE Model." *Journal of Quantitative & Technical Economics* 33 (1): 127–41.

Center for Forecasting Science, CAS. 2021. *Economics of China: Analysis and Forecast.* Beijing: Science Press.

Che, Xiaocui, and Pingyu Zhang. 2011. "Performance Evaluation of Resource-Based Urban Economic Transformation Based on Multiple Quantitative Methods: Taking Daqing City as an Example." *Journal of Industrial Technological Economics* 2: 129–36.

Chen, Changbing. 2007. "Calculation of Various Gini Coefficients from Different Regions in China and Analysis Using the Nonparametric Model." *Journal of Quantitative & Technical Economics* 24 (1): 133–42.

Chen, Chengliang, and Wencheng Lee. 2004. "Multi-Objective Optimization of Multi-Echelon Supply Chain Networks with Uncertain Product Demands and Prices." *Computers & Chemical Engineering* 28 (6–7): 1131–44.

Chen, Jie. 2006. *Some Problems of Optimal Control and its Application in Financial Mathematics.* Shanghai: Tongji University.

Chen, Xikang, Leonard K. Cheng, Kwokchiu Fung et al. 2001. "The Estimation of Domestic Value-Added and Employment Induced by Exports: An Application to Chinese Exports to the United States." Working paper, Department of Economics, Stanford University, California.

———. 2012. "Domestic Value Added and Employment Generated by Chinese Exports: A Quantitative Estimation." *China Economic Review* 23 (4): 850–64.

———. 2008. "Yearly Grain Output Predictions in China 1980–2004." *Economic Systems Research* 20 (2): 139–50.

Chen, Xikang, Jue Guo, and Cuihong Yang. 2008. "Yearly Grain Output Predictions in China 1980–2004." *Economic Systems Research* 20 (2): 139–150.

Chen, Xikang, Xiaoming Pan, and Cuihong Yang. 2001. "On the Study of China's Grain Prediction." *International Transactions in Operations Research* 8 (4): 429–37.

Chen, Xikang, Cuihong Yang et al. 2011. *Input-Output Technique.* Beijing: Science Press.

Chen, Xikang. 2004. "Study on Input-Occupancy-Output Technique and its Non-Linearization and Dynamics." Selected Papers on Analytical Purposes of I-O Techniques in China, edited by Xianchun Xu and Qiyun Liu, Beijing: China Statistics Press, 3–16.

Chen, Yunxian. 2019. "Market Economy with Chinese Socialist Characteristics: Combination of Effective Government and Efficient Market." *Economic Research Journal* 1: 6–21.

Cheng, Tongtong, and Haiyan Wei. 2019. "Analysis and Application of Big Data in Agricultural Production and Consumption." *Shanxi Youth* 15: 12–13.

China Economic Growth and Macro-Stability Task Force. 2007. "Labor Supply Effect and China's Economic Growth Path Transition." *Economic Research Journal* 10: 4–16.

Cui, Zhiyuan. 1988. *Game Theory and Social Science.* Hangzhou: Zhejiang People's Publishing House.

Deng, Julong. 1987. *The Basic Method of Gray System.* Wuhan: Huazhong University of Science and Technology Press.

Ding, Jianmei, and Kechong Wang. 2002. "Fuzzy Control of Traffic Flow on Run-on Ramp of Expressway." *Journal of Harbin Institute of Technology* 34 (5): 671–74.

Fu, Xue, and Xikang Chen. 2006. "Chinese Education Structure for Sustainable Development: A Multiyear Lag Education-Economy Extended IO Model with Asset." *International Journal of Applied Economics and Econometrics* 14 (1): 61–78.

Gan, Chunhui, Ruogu Zheng, and Dianfan Yu. 2011. "An Empirical Study on the Effects of Industrial Structure, Economic Growth, and Fluctuations in China." *Economic Research Journal* 46 (5): 4–16, 31.

Gao, Jingmei, and Dingwei Wang. 2008. "Simulation-Based Optimization and its Application in Multi-Echelon Network Stochastic Inventory System." Paper presented at the Asia Simulation conference 2008/7th International Conference on System Simulation and Scientific Computing.

Gong, Deen. 1998. *Introduction to Economic Cybernetics.* Beijing: China Renmin University Press.

Gong, Liutang. 2000. *Optimization Method in Economics.* Beijing: Peking University Press.

Guan, Dabo, Meng Jing, David M. Reiner et al. 2018. "Structural Decline in China's CO_2 Emissions Through Transitions in Industry and Energy Systems." *Nature Geoscience* 11 (8): 551–55.

Guan, Gumei. 1960. "Graphical Method Based on an Odd-Even-Point Approach." *Acta Mathematica Sinica* 10 (3): 263–66.

Han, Liyan, and Chunyue Du. 2012. "Income Gap, Borrowing Level and Regional and Urban-Rural Differences in Household Consumption." *Economic Research Journal* 1: 15–27.

Hao, Yu, and Yiming Liu. 2016. "The Influential Factors of Urban PM2.5 Concentrations in China: A Spatial Econometric Analysis." *Journal of Cleaner Production* 112: 1443–53.

He, Shiwei. 1996. "Research on Optimization Model of Railway Marshalling Station Stage Plan." *Railway Transportation and Economy* 4: 91–94.

Hong, Tao, and Wei Li. 2015. "Analysis of Housing Price Expectations and Actual Price Fluctuations Based on Web Search Data." *Statistics and Information Forum* 11: 49–53.

Hu, Chuanji, and Qingwei Qiao. 1984. "Economic Cybernetics and Economic Forecasting." *Journal of Shanxi University of Finance and Economics* 6: 63–67.

Hu, Daiguang, Wu Baosan, and Sun Shizhen. 1964. *Western Econometrics*. Beijing: The Commercial Press.

Huang, Chongzhen, and Jingguo Liang. 2008. "Supplier Selection System Based on Rough Set and Fuzzy Control." *Statistics and Decision* 9: 161–63.

Huang, Dashan, Frank J. Fabozzi, and Masao Fukushima. 2007. "Robust Portfolio Selection with Uncertain Exit Time Using Worst-Case VaR Strategy." *Operations Research Letters* 35 (5): 627–35.

Huang, Zhongyi, and Lixin Zheng. 2000. "Economic Cybernetics and Sustainable Development of Social Economy." *Journal of Huaqiao University (Philosophy & Social Science)* 4: 25–30.

Huo, Lin, Wei Shang, and Shanying Xu. 2013. "The Construction of Real Estate Open Source Public Opinion Index and Policy Impact Research." *China Journal of Information Systems* 2: 57–66.

Jiang, Fuxiu, Zhan Jiang, Huang Jicheng, Kenneth Kim, and John Nofsinger. 2017. "Bank Competition and Leverage Adjustments." *Financial Management* 46 (4): 995–1022

Jiang, Li, Xiangzheng Deng, and Karen C. Seto. 2013. "The Impact of Urban Expansion on Agricultural Land Use Intensity in China." *Land Use Policy* 35: 33–39.

Jiang, Zhaohua, Liu Dingyi, Chen Yu et al. 2009. "Analysis on the Sustainable Development of Energy-Environment-Economic Based on Control Theory." Paper presented at the International Conference on Management Science & Engineering. IEEE. Moscow, September 14–16, 2009.

Jin, Chengwu. 2019. "The Integration of Urban and Rural Development and Theoretical Integration in China: A Critical Reference to Contemporary Development Economics Theory." *Economic Research Journal* 8: 183–97.

Jin, Jin, Zonghao Li, and Liang Zhu. 2019. "A Research on Risk Assessment of China Railways 'Go-Global' Project Construction." *Railway Transport and Economy* 41 (2): 86–91.

Jin, Yu, Chen Zhao, and Ming Lu. 2006. "Industry Agglomeration in China: Economic Geography, New Economic Geography and Policy." *Economic Research Journal* 4: 79–89.

Klein, Lawrence R. 1991. *A Course in Econometrics*. Translated by the Department of Economic Forecasting, the State Information Center. Shanghai: Fudan University Press.

Klein, Lawrence R. et al. 1990. *Econometrics Lecture*. Translated by the Chinese Association of Quantitative Economics. Beijing: Aviation Industry Press.

Klein, Lawrence R., and William C. Hood. 1983. *A Textbook of Econometrics*. Translated by Xie Jia. Beijng: Business Press.

Koutsoyiannis, Anna. 1981. *Theory of Econometrics*. Translated by Xu Kaijia and Wang Shouyong, Liaonig: Department of Economics, Liaoning Institute of Finance and Economics.

Lai, Hongsong, Guorui Zhu, and Pingjie Dong. 2004. "Population Forecast Based on Combination of Gray Forecast and Artificial Neural Networks." *Economic Geography* 24 (2): 197–201.

Li, Bin, and Yuxuan Su. 2016. "Is Industrial Restructuring Beneficial to the Development of Green Economy? An Empirical Study Based on Spatial Econometric Model." *Ecological Economy* 6: 32–37.

Li, Bingquan. 1962. "Applying Mathematical Methods in Economic Research and Planning." *Chinese Science Bulletin* 6: 16–23.

Li, Cheng, Wentao Ma, and Bing Wang. 2009. "Inflation Expectation and Macro-Economy Stability: 1995–2008. Analysis Based on Dynamic Stochastic General Equilibrium." *Nankai Economic Studies* 6: 30–53.

Li, Gang, Feng Xia, and Wei Wang. 2013. "Can Public Debt Promote Economic Growth?" *Word Economy Studies* 2: 16–21.

Li, Jingwen, and Jianguo Qi. 1998. "Characteristics of Economic Development and Pillar Industries in China's Future Stages." *Management World* 2: 89–101.

Li, Nianwei. 2008. *An Optimal Economic Model and Calculation Considering Sensitive Factors*. Guizhou University.

Li, Qingfu. 2006. "Analysis of the Social Background of Hua Loo-Keng Popularizing Overall Planning Methods and Optimum Seeking Methods." *Science of Science and Management of S.&.T.* 27 (2): 45–50.

Li, Sun, and H. Luo. 2008. "A Strategy for Multi-Objective Optimization under Uncertainty in Chemical Process Design." *Chinese Journal of Chemical Engineering* 16 (1): 39–42.

Li, Tai, Hongduo Cao, Haoke Xing et al. 2012. "Modeling and Simulation of Complex Finance Networks Based on Minority Game." *Systems Engineering—Theory & Practice* 32 (9): 1882–90.

Li, Yan, Ming K. Lim, and Weiqing Xiong. 2018. "An Optimization Model of Vehicle Routing Problem for Logistics Based on Sustainable Development Theory." In *Recent Advances in Intelligent Manufacturing*, edited by Wang Shilong et al., 179–90. Singapore: Springer.

Li, Zijiang. 1992. *Game Theory and Economic Equilibrium*. Guangzhou: South China University of Science and Technology Press.

Lin, Yifu, and Mingxing Liu. 2003. "Growth Convergence and Income Distribution in China." *World Economy* 8: 3–14, 80.

Ling, Li. 2017. "China's Manufacturing Locus in 2025: With a Comparison of 'Made-in-China 2025' and 'Industry 4.0.'" *Technological Forecasting and Social Change* 135: 66–74.

Liu, Bin, and Shuhui Deng. 1999. "Quantitative Analysis and Prediction of China's Monetary Multiplier." *Forecasting* 1: 43–45.

Liu, Bing, Sun Zuoren, and Huacheng Sun. 2019. "Path and Optimization Strategy of Energy Space Allocation under the Control of Total Consumption." *China Population Resources and Environment* 29 (1): 99–109.

Liu, Jinquan, and Weidong Xie. 2003. "The Dynamic Correlation between China's Economic Growth and Inflation." *The Journal of World Economy* 6: 48–57.

Liu, Qiyun, and Ming Xia. 2010. "The Application and Development of Input-Output Analysis in China." In *Quantitative Economics in China: A Thirty-Year Review*, edited by Zhang Shouyi and Ge Xinquan, 142–163.

Liu, Rubing. 2006. "The Optimized Model of the Medium and Long-Term Growth Rate for the National Economy Plan." *Humanities & Social Sciences Journal of Hainan University* 24 (4): 521–25.

Liu, Shucheng. 2007. *The Cyclical Fluctuation of China's Economy*. Beijing: Social Science Academic Press.

Liu, Weisong, Zhuohua Zhou, Zhang Zongyi et al. 2005. "Game Analysis of Manager's Earnings Management in Corporation Governing Structure." *Finance and Trade Research* 16 (2): 104–08.

Liu, Xiaohua, and Jing Liu. 2006. "Analysis of Disequilibrium Economic System Using Predictive Control Theory." *Control and Decision* 21 (4): 470–72.

Liu, Xiuli. 2018. "A Method to Visualize the Skeleton Industrial Structure with Input-Output Analysis and its Application in China, Japan and USA." *Journal of Systems Science and Complexity* 31 (6): 1554–70.

Liu, Xiuli, Ana Salome Garcia Muniz, and Blanca Moreno. 2016. "A Grey Neural Network and Input-Output Combined Forecasting Model: Primary Energy Consumption Forecasts in Spanish Economic Sectors." *Energy* 115: 1042–54.

Liu, Xiuli, Xikang Chen, and Shouyang Wang. 2009. "Evaluating and Predicting Shadow Prices of Water Resources in China and its Nine Major River Basins." *Water Resources Management* 23: 1467–78.

Liu, Xiuli, Geoffrey Hewings, Xikang Chen, and Shouyang Wang. 2016. "A Factor Decomposing Model of Water Use Efficiency at Sector Level and its Application in Beijing." *Journal of Systems Science and Complexity* 29 (2): 405–27.

Liu, Xiuli, Geoffrey Hewings, and Shouyang Wang. 2018. "Evaluating the Impacts of Waste Treatment Management Modes on each Sector's Price in a Macro Economic System." *Journal of Cleaner Production* 200: 188–95.

Liu, Xiuli, and Xikang Chen. 2008. "Methods for Approximating the Shadow Price of Water in China." *Economic Systems Research* 20 (2): 173–85.

Liu, Yi, Yadong Luo, and Liu Ting. 2009. "Governing Buyer-Supplier Relationships through Transactional and Relational Mechanisms: Evidence from China." *Journal of Operations Management* 27 (4): 294–309.

Liu, Yufeng, and Baida Qu. 2002. "A Control Strategy for Macroeconomic Model under Financial Risk." *Journal of Liaoning Technical University (Natural Science)* 21 (3): 376–79.

Long, Genying. 2003. "Understanding China's Recent Growth Experience: A Spatial Econometric Perspective." *The Annals of Regional Science* 37 (4): 613–28.

Long, Ruyin, Tianxiang Shao, and Hong Chen. 2016. "Spatial Econometric Analysis of China's Province-Level Industrial Carbon Productivity and its Influencing Factors." *Applied Energy* 166: 210–19.

Lu, Ming, and Zhao Chen. 2004. "Urbanization, Urban-Biased Economic Policies and Urban-Rural Inequality." *Economic Research Journal* 6: 50–58.

Ma, Mei, Dongsu Liu, and Hui Li. 2016. "Research on Network Public Opinion Analysis System Model Based on Big Data." *Information Science* 3: 25–28.

Mathematical Planning Branch of China Operations Research Society. 2014. "Overview of the Development of Chinese Mathematics Planning Discipline." *Operations Research Transactions* 18 (1): 1–8.

Meng, Qingbin, Yongji Zhang, and Junsheng Jia. 2019. "Economic Uncertainty and Optimal Corporate Assets Structure." *Systems Engineering –Theory & Practice* 2: 286–97.

Ning, Zhiping. 1990. "Application of Economic Cybernetics in Science Policy." *Science, Economy and Society* 2: 105–106.

Oskar, Lange. 1970. *Introduction to Economic Cybernetics.* Translated by Yang Xiaokai and Yu Hongsheng, Beijing: China Social Sciences Press.

Pan, Linwei, and Yaling Wu. 2013. "Establishment and Solution of Game Model of Supervision Coordination and Financial Institutions under Mixed Operation Conditions." *Statistics and Decision* 13: 52–55.

Pan, Wenqing. 2003. "The Spill-Over Effects of FDI on China's Industrial Sectors: A Panel Data Analysys." *World Economy* 6: 3–7, 80.

Qi, Jianguo. 1997. "Overview of the Development of Quantitative Economics." *Journal of Quantitative & Technical Economics* 14: 76–82.

Qian, Xuesen, and Song Jian. 1980. *Engineering Cybernetics.* Beijing: Science Press.

Shan, Haojie. 2008. "Reestimating the Capital Stock of China:1952–2006." *Journal of Quantitative & Technical Economics* 25 (10): 17–31.

Shen, Ruiling, Li Ding, and Sumei Tan. 2009. "The Application of Fuzzy Control Theory in Economic Forecasting." *Keji Jingji Shichang* 4: 3–4.

Shi, Faqi. 2004. "Coordination Analysis of Industrial Structure in China." Selected Paper on Analytical Purposes of I-O Techniques in China, edited by Xu Xianchun and Liu Qiyun, 145–54. Beijing: China Statistics Press.

Shi, Qingqi. 1985. "Technological Progress and Economic Growth." Reform 3: 43–45.

Shi, Xiusong, and Shudong Zhao. 2011. "The Regional Economic Convergence and its Mechanism in China:1978–2009." *Journal of Quantitative & Technical Economics* 28 (1): 51–62.

Shu, Changjiang, and Hong Pan. 2019. "A New Framework of Financial Vulnerability and Monetary Policy Based on Dynamic Stochastic General Equilibrium Model:

Theoretical and Numerical Simulation." *Financial Theory and Practice* 474 (1): 37–44.

Si, Ming. 2011. *The Economic Analysis of Assets Appraisal Theory.* Agricultural University of Hebei.

Song, Jian, and Jinyuan Yu. 1985. *Population Cybernetics.* Beijing: Science Press.

Song, Jian. 2010. "Excess Currency, Economic Growth, and Inflation: An Empirical Study Based on China's Macroeconomic Data from 1979 to 2007." *Financial Economics Research* 2: 16–33.

Song, Qilin. 1994. "Analysis of Urban Planning Development with Chinese Characteristics." *Modern Urban Research* 5: 8–12.

Song, Yuanliang, and Weidong Xiao. 2005. "An Analysis of Dynamic Econometric Relationship between Development of Urbanization and Income Growth of Rural Residents in China." *Journal of Quantitative & Technical Economics* 22 (9): 31–40.

Sun, Guangsheng, Tao Xiang, Wei Huang, and Xianming Yang. 2012. "Efficiency Improvement, Output Growth, and Energy Consumption—Based on a Comparative Analysis of Industrial Sectors." *China Economic Quarterly* 1: 253–68.

Sun, Shizheng. 1984. *Econometrics.* Beijing: People's Publishing House.

Sun, Yi, Lü Benfu, Hang Chen, and Tian Xue. 2014. "Inflation Expectation Measurement and Application Research from the Perspective of Big Data." *Management World* 4: 171–72.

Tan, Zhengxun, and Cong Wang. 2011. "Research on Financial Stability Effect of China's Credit Expansion and Housing Price Fluctation: A Dynamic Stochastic General Equilibrium Model Perspective." *Journal of Financial Research* 8: 57–71.

Tang, Guoxing. 1984. "China's Long-Term Multi-Sectoral Econometric Model." *The Journal of Quantitative & Technical Economics* 1 (10): 18–29.

Tao, Ran, and Jing Xiang. 2005. "Optimize the Allocation of Railway Transportation Resources and Implement Centralized Train Operation Map Compilation." *Railway Transport* 4: 52–53.

Wang, Dayong, and Wanjin Jiang. 1991. "Quarterly Macroeconomic Econometric Model PBCM1 of the People's Bank of China." *Journal of Quantitative & Technical Economics* 8: 46–53.

Wang, Di, and Dashou Wang. 2002. *Comprehensive Optimization in Engineering Decision.* Chengdu: Southwest Jiaotong University Press.

Wang, Guocheng. 2002. "Research on Entrepreneurial Choice Mechanism: Application of Game Theory Method." *China Economic Studies* 6: 22–31.

Wang, Guocheng, and Tao Huang. 1996. *Modern Economic Game Theory.* Beijing: Economic Science Press.

Wang, Jin. 2008. *Economic Cybernetics: Theory, Application, and MATLAB Simulation.* Beijing: Science Press.

Wang, Qiao, Dejin Tai, and Dezhi Chen. 2019. "The Empirical Analysis of the Impact of Financial Development on the Income Gap between Urban and Rural Residents." *Statistics & Decision* 35 (6): 165–67.

Wang, Tong. 1996. "China's Macroeconomic Regulation Model." *Forecasting* 3: 6–15.

Wang, Tongsan. 1992. *Discussions on Macroeconomic Models*. Beijing: Economic Management Publishing House.

Wang, Tongsan, and Lisheng Shen. 2001. *The Set of Economic Models of the Institute of Quantitative and Technical Economics, Chinese Academy of Social Sciences*. Beijing: Social Science Literature Press.

Wang, Tongsan, and Li Wang. 2010. "The Roadmap of Econometrics in China." *Science and Technology for Development* 5: 7–12.

Wang, Yong, and Hengxin Dong. 2017. "Prediction of China's Quarterly Unemployment Rate against the Background of Big Data—Based on the Analysis of Web Search Data." *Journal of Systems Science and Mathematical Sciences* 2: 460–72.

Wang, Yu, Xiaozhong Yu, and Jun Li. 2006. "Comprehensive Optimization Decision of Project Duration, Quality and Cost." *Statistics & Decision* 19: 42–43.

Wu, Jiapei, and Shouyi Zhang. 1986. *China's Macroeconomics Model Research*. Hefei: Anhui People's Publishing House.

Wu, Jiapei. 2008. "Yesterday, Today and Tomorrow of the Development China's Quantitative Economics." *Journal of Chongqing Technology and Business University (Western Forum)* 1: 1–4.

Wu, Meihua, and Yinggao Zhu. 2001. "An Analysis and a Model of Judging the Risk of Financial Morality." *Contemporary Economic Research* 9: 67–70.

Wu, Wenjun et al. 1960. *Handout of Game Theory*. Institute of Mathematics, Chinese Academy of Sciences, Beijing: People's Education Press.

Wu, Yong. 2001. "The Rude Stick Control Strategy of the Macroeconomic System." *Journal of Chongqing Institute of Technology* 15 (4): 22–25.

Wu, Yuanren, and Lisheng Shen. 2015. "Knowledge Mapping of Quantitative Economics in China: Bibliometric Analysis Based on CSSCI (2000–2014)." *Economic Perspectives* 8: 84–96.

Xiao, Dongrong, and Zhenyu Lu. 2002. "Analysis of the Macroeconomic System Using Robust Control Theory." *Control and Decision* 17 (5): 629–30.

Xiao, Yan, and Dengfeng Li. 2019. "The Least Square Solution Model and Method of Cooperative Games with Trapezoidal Fuzzy Numbers." *Control and Decision* 34 (4): 834–42.

Xie, Chi. 1996. 'Optimization Model in Financial Risk Management." *Forecasting* 6: 45–48.

Xie, E. 2008. "Environmental Regulation and China's Industrial Productivity Growth." *Industrial Economics Research* 1: 19–25.

Xu, Yingmei, and Yiming Gao. 2017. "Construction and Application of CPI Public Opinion Index Based on Internet Big Data: Taking Baidu Index as an Example." *The Journal of Quantitative & Technical Economics* 34 (1): 94–112.

Yan, Lili. 2012. "The Effect of Financial Intermediary Efficiency on Monetary Policy Effects: Research Based on Dynamic Stochastic General Equilibrium." *Studies of International Finance* 6: 4–11.

Yang, Xiaoyan, and Bingmou Cui. 2013. "Molten Iron Transportation Scheduling Optimization and Simulation of Iron and Steel Enterprises." *Journal of Computer Applications* 33 (10): 2977–80.

Yao, Hongxing, and Zhaohan Sheng. 2001. "Application of Prediction Feedback Control Method in Economic Chaos System." *Journal of Southeast University* 31 (5): 101–105.

———. 2002. "Improved Method for Feedback Control in Economic Chaotic Model." *Journal of Systems Engineering* 17 (6): 507–511.

Yin, Shijie. 2011. "A Brief Discussion on Optimizing Consumption Structure and Transforming Economic Development Mode." *Consumer Economy* 1: 3–9.

Yu, Guoming. 2015. "The Structural Characteristics and Analytical Findings of Current Social Lyricism—Based on the Big Data Analysis of China's Social Network Public Opinion in 2014." *Jianghuai Tribune* 5: 136–43.

Yu, Jinyuan, and Yuhe Song, Yang Zhangshu, and Minglu Wu. 1986. "National Macroeconomic Control Model and Analysis of Optimization Results." *Journal of Quantitative & Technical Economics* 3 (1): 19–24.

Yu, Li, and Jing Shi. 2004. "Comparison and Analysis of the Competitiveness of Chinese and Foreign Banks." *Modern Management Science* 10: 96–97.

Yu, Wenci. 1979. "Positive Basis and a Class of Direct Search Techniques." *Science in China, Ser. A* 1: 53–67.

Yue, Minyi, and Jiye Han. 1976. "On the Sequencing Problem of Flow Shop." Proceedings of the Seventh IFORS International Conference on Operational Research.

———. 1979. "A New Reduced Gradient Method." *Scientia Sinica* 22: 1099–113.

Zhang, Chong, Lü Benfu, Peng Wei, and Liu Ying. 2012. "Correlation between Network Search Data and CPI." *Journal of Management Sciences in China* 7: 50–59.

Zhang, Heping. 2019. "Research on Combinatory Optimization Model Based on Grey Relational Degree." *Statistics and Decision* 9: 19–23.

Zhang, Hongxia, and Xikang Chen. 2008. "An Extended Input-Output Model on Education and the Shortfall of Human Capital in China." *Economic Systems Research* 20 (2): 205–221.

Zhang, Jinfeng, and Ying Fang. 2011. "A Robust Test for Spatial Error Models." *Journal of Quantitative & Technical Economics* 28 (1): 152–160.

Zhang, Jun, and Yu Jin. 2005. "Analysis on Relationship of Deepening Financial Intermediation and Economic Growth in China." *Economic Research Journal* 11: 34–45.

Zhang, Lin. 2003. "Application of Fuzzy Control Theory in Enterprise Classification Management." *Industrial Technology & Economy* 22 (4): 85–86.

Zhang, Shou, and Qingwen Yu. 1984. *Econometrics*. Shanghai: Jiaotong University Press.

Zhang, Shouyi, Tongsan Wang, and Xinquan Ge. 2010. *30th Anniversary of Chinese Quantitative Economics*. Beijing: Social Sciences Academic Press (China).

———. 2016. *Quantitative Economics in China*. Beijing: World Scientific Publishing Company.

Zhang, Shuo, and Zengji Song. 2016. "Research on the Impact of State-Owned Equity on the Protection Level of Private Property Rights." *Chinese Journal of Management* 12: 1873–81.

Zhang, Subo, Yong Liao, Jiankang Zou et al. 2007. "Optimize the Occupation Plan of Arrival-Departure Lines in Passenger Station Based on Genetic Algorithm." *Railway Transport and Economy* 29 (11): 24–27.

Zhang, Weiying. 1996. *Game Theory and Information Economics.* Shanghai: People's Publishing House.

Zhang, Xiangsun, and Yaji Guan. 1999. "China Operations Research: Vitality for Forty Years." *Operations Research Transactions* 1: 1–5.

Zhang, Xinyu, Xiaohua Tang, and Shuai Zhou. 2019. "Study on Adjustment and Optimization of Manufacturing Industry Structure under Multiple Constraints of Environment, Economy, and Employment: Taking Northeast China as an Example." *Reform of Economic System* 3: 86–93.

Zhang, Yanmin, Yang Li, and Lihai Wang. 2006. "Research on Decision-Making Optimization of Supply Chain Management Based on Dynamic Programming." *Forest Engineering* 22 (5): 71–72.

Zhang, Yunling. 2007. "Research and Empirical Analysis of Chinese Household Consumption Measurement Model." Doctoral dissertation, Capital University of Economics and Business.

Zhang, Zhongjun. 1991. *Economic Cybernetics: The Application of Cybernetics in Economic Management.* Xi'an: Xidian University Press.

Zhao, Chunyan. 2012. "Research on the Stationarity of Smooth Transition Autoregressive Model." *Journal of Quantitative & Technical Economics* 39 (1): 152–60.

Zhong, Genyuan, and Fanghua Wang. 2003. "Anti-Dumping Tax Rate Optimization Pricing Model under a Complete Information Dynamic Game." *Journal of International Trade* 1: 1–4.

Zhong, Yueming. 1986. "Social Function of Economic Cybernetics." *Business Economy* 9: 57–58.

Zhou, Peng, Beng W. Ang, and Dequn Zhou. 2012. "Measuring Economy-Wide Energy Efficiency Performance: A Parametric Frontier Approach." *Applied Energy* 90 (1): 196–200.

Zhou, Xiaochuan. 2019. *Mathematical Planning and Economic Analysis.* Beijing: China Economic Press.

Zhou, Xiaohong. 2000. "Research on Optimization and Configuration of Railway Transportation Resources." *Railway Transport and Economy* 32 (7): 29–32.

Zhu, Chengliang, Hongzhi Yue, and Ping Shi. 2011. "Research on China's Economic Growth Efficiency under Environmental Constraints." *The Journal of Quantitative & Technical Economics* 38 (5): 3–20.

Zhu, Mengnan, and Chunyu Cao. 2019. "Sino-US Trade War and Exchange Rate Arrangement Choice: A Policy Simulation on a Dynamic Stochastic General Equilibrium Model." *Finance and Trade Research* 2: 46–63.

Zhuang, Weiming. 1988. "Economic Cybernetics and Macro Plan Management Functions." *Journal of Shanxi University of Finance and Economics* 3: 43–46.

Chapter 3

Mathematical Economics and Central Planning

Economic Research in Czechoslovakia under Communism

Julius Horváth

For devoted communists all over the world, central planning was invaluable by definition: it was seen as an antidote to the anarchy of the market, especially in the minds of those who lived through the Great Depression and were indoctrinated by Soviet political economy. Central planning, it was believed, had electrified Russia, built power stations and steel works, and organized the war economy. Initially, Czechoslovak communist leaders viewed central planning as engineering rather than as an economic activity. Slowly, the importance of economic factors increased, but planning continued to be seen as a predominantly technical issue in the eyes of planners. Their experience gained in military investment projects seemed to confirm this approach.

Views about central planning were reformed to an extent—approximately from the late 1950s and the early 1960s onward—by the rise of mathematics in economics and by the emergence of linear programming, operations research, input-output analysis, cybernetics, systems analysis, computer applications, econometrics, and similar subdisciplines. These research programs applied scientific methods to solve complex problems such as the management of large economic systems. The use of mathematics and statistics created a feeling that there was new weaponry to handle such complexities and suggested that crude planning methods, to be described below, would be replaced or at least complemented by some form of an optimal plan. Ironically, optimal planning was considered a proper scientific concept not only by many economists in the communist world but also by leading representatives of Western mainstream economics. However, this concept ignored asymmetric information and irrational incentives in the economic behavior of individuals and institutions, both of which were vital for understanding the operation of planned economies. At the time, i.e., from the 1950s to the 1980s, most neo-classical theories had similar weaknesses (Wagener 1998a, 4).

Economic theories produced in the Soviet 1920s used advanced mathematical tools, but until the mid-1950s the prevailing mode of interpretation in official political economy remained verbal. In the Stalinist spirit, the main attitude of economic theory *vis-à-vis* the regime was apologetic. Moreover, the mathematical approach to economics came to be seen as non-Marxist in both the Soviet Union and its satellite states. From the late 1950s, this situation slowly changed and in the early 1960s, mathematical economics began to be researched more intensely. As a result of de-Stalinization, the professional autonomy of researchers increased, and mathematical methods gained wider acceptance as tools of economic planning in the Soviet Union. This also helped the spread of mathematical economics in Czechoslovakia. A decisive step forward was taken in 1959 with the publication of a volume on mathematical methods in economics, edited by Vasilii Nemchinov (Barnett 2008, 5–6). Jaroslav Habr (1981) mentions that Nemchinov played an important role in persuading Czechoslovak politicians about the advantages of founding the *Ekonomicko-matematická laboratoř* (Laboratory of Economics and Mathematics) at the Institute of Economics of the Czechoslovak Academy of Sciences in Prague. Habr also speaks about the support given by prominent Czech mathematicians and statisticians such as Josef Bíly, Antonín Ter-Manuelianc, František Nožička, and Jaromír Walter to the initiative.[1]

Most likely, the new mathematical instruments made planning a bit more efficient. Nonetheless, the dire straits of the world economy in the 1970s and depleting reserves of extensive-type economic growth may have had stronger negative effects on the Czechoslovak economy than any efficiency gained from better planning by using mathematics (Kowalik 1987, 5). One might expect that mathematical methods brought a bigger increase in economic efficiency in the Soviet Union, characterized by a history of gigantic misallocations,[2] in comparison to Czechoslovakia with its more balanced and developed economy.

In this chapter we make some observations on the co-evolution of central planning and mathematical economics in Czechoslovakia. In theory, planning is a constrained maximization problem with an objective function (representing social welfare or individual utility), which is to be maximized under resource and technology constraints. Thus, in principle, it is difficult to separate planning from mathematical economics. If the economic problem is described this way, then, in principle, mathematical techniques combined with high-speed computers are likely to "solve" the problem directly and provide an efficient allocation of resources in both capitalist and socialist economies.[3] However, mathematical economists and planners differed in a number of ways, and maybe in a similar manner as market reformers differed from the official political economists of socialism. Below, we will point to some of the intricacies within the relationships among these groups of economists.

We divide the period of investigation in three stages. The first stage, preceding the communist coup in 1948, excels by its relatively high level of mathematical economics in interwar Czechoslovakia. The second stage overlaps with the first because planning started between 1945 and 1948 and continued with the introduction of central planning in the 1950s and the attempts to reform it. This stage ended during the reform years of the late 1960s. The third stage covers the so-called normalization (*normalizace, normalizácia*) period of the 1970s and 1980s. It includes the re-establishment of economic orthodoxy with the objective of making planning more sophisticated than that of the 1950s while avoiding changes that resemble the reformism (market socialism) of the mid-1960s. Geographically, we concentrate on developments in the Czech lands where most of the changes were initiated but do not disregard Slovakia.

Economic Thought in Pre-Communist Czechoslovakia

Doležalová (2018) claims that the beginning of the mathematization of economic thought in the Czech lands is associated with Georg Franz August Count Buquoy (Jiří František August Hrabě Buquoy, 1781–1851) who was one of the first scholars to use technical diagrams, mathematical formulas, and calculations in his work on the theory of national economy. Another economist with a similar thrust was Alois Lexa, knight of Aehrenthal (1777–1843). From 1863 onward, the theory of national economy as well as economic statistics were taught at the Technical University in Prague by Josef Erben (1830–1910) and Eberhard Antonín Jonák (1820–1879) (Studihrad 2018, 8). Until 1918, economics was taught also at the Law Faculty of the Czech University in Prague by professors such as Albín Bráf (1851–1912), Josef Gruber (1865–1925), and Cyril Horáček (1862–1943).[4]

The mathematical approach to economic science burgeoned in interwar Czechoslovak Republic. In this period, leading scholars in economics, statistics, insurance mathematics, and demography were well versed in their subjects and active internationally. For example, in 1934, the members of the newly founded Econometric Society included—in addition to governor of the Central Bank Karel Engliš and the founder of Slovak economic thought Imrich Karvaš—W. G. Friedrich, Jaroslav Janko, Vladimír Klonov, Dobroslav Krejčí, Peter Rastokin, Emil Schönbaum, and František Schwarz.[5]

The teaching of the above subjects reached a high level in the Czech lands,[6] while in Slovakia[7] a clear improvement was observed. In addition, several important political economists from Russia settled in Prague during the 1920s.[8]

A special status was achieved by the Austrian School of Economics in Prague and, to an extent, in Brno. Economic faculty positions at the German University in Prague, the German Institute of Technology in Prague, and the German Institute of Technology in Brno were occupied by members of that school (or of its rival, the German Historical School) continuously from 1879 to the mid-1930s.[9] Prominent Austrian economists remind us of the dissemination of their ideas in Central Europe. For example, Ludwig Mises (2013, 151) writes that "among the students of Menger, Böhm-Bawerk, and Wieser there were also non-German Austrians. Two of them have distinguished themselves by eminent contributions, the Czech[s] Franz Čuhel and Karel Engliš."

In 1882, the Austrian government reshaped Prague University as a twin—Czech and German—university. As the German University in Prague gained importance with the rise of the Austrian School in the heat of the *Methodenstreit* of the 1880s, it also helped improve the quality of teaching at the Czech University. The leading economist at the Czech University, Albín Bráf, originally was fascinated by the older generation of the German Historical School but later was influenced also by the Austrians. Nevertheless, he called for a new and distinctly Czech system of economics. František/Franz Čuhel examined the theory of needs in his 1907 book, which was published in German at the University of Innsbruck and made his fame far beyond the borders of Austria. Hudík (2007) writes that Čuhel's ordinal theory of needs, which avoids using indifference curves, and his insistence on interpersonal incomparability of utility belong to the basics of modern microeconomics. He was quoted by Fritz Machlup, Wesley Clair Mitchell, Lionel Robbins, and Eugen Slutsky. Karel Engliš fulfilled Bráf's wish to form a distinctly Czech economics. He labeled his system "teleology" and was in the process of creating a Czech school of economic thought after the war when the communists eliminated his research team (Vencovský 1997).

From Democratic through Crude Methods of Central Planning to Market Reforms: 1945–1969

In Czechoslovakia, like in other countries of the Soviet Bloc, the actual introduction of central planning was a result of the communist takeover. However, due to the economic crisis of the 1930s, the ideas of planning, and state intervention in general, were also favored by traditional democrats and not only by those close to the communist movement. In other words, the Czechoslovak state penetrated the economy after the Second World War, and the planned economy was accepted widely in economic discourse before 1948. The period of 1945–1948 was marked by large-scale nationalization in banking, industry, transport, and foreign trade.

The government program declared in Košice in April 1945 established a planning apparatus by creating the Economic Council[10] and giving it the task of constructing an overall plan of economic development and proposing measures to accomplish it. This required the agreement of all political parties in the coalition government on the state plan. A presidential decree created the State Planning Office as a technical organ of the Economic Council, which included experts delegated by all parliamentary parties. In October 1946, the Central Planning Commission submitted a draft of a two-year plan for 1947/1948 to the government and the National Assembly, which later became law. This plan was prepared in a democratic and developed country, and it was seen by the left throughout Europe as a possible model for other advanced countries[11] (Bernasek 1970, 100–103). For instance, an eminent economist of the communist era, Josef Goldmann (1947), presented the Czechoslovak postwar experience of planning as a possible road map for developed economies.

In the first two-year plan, planning meant simply setting output, resource, and employment goals for large industrial firms as part of postwar reconstruction. At the time, the Czechoslovak economy was dominated by a sizable state sector and a private capitalist sector. The concept of the "privileged purchaser" was introduced, which meant that an industrial firm did not receive state resources if it could not fulfill the demand of such a purchaser. Planning was done in an atmosphere of immense uncertainty as it was difficult to know the level of utilization in different industries and sectors. Also, planning was exposed to the growing influence of different political groups (party networks) on nationalized enterprises (Spulber 1956, 369). These characteristics of planning did not change much during the communist period.

In the Two-Year Plan and in the early years of the First Five-Year plan, planners still used financial (price, credit, and so on) indicators. Soviet-type quantitative, in-kind, material-balance planning appeared in the first years of the 1950s. Rozsypal (1981) argues that this kind of central planning was introduced only in 1953, which used to be the opinion of Josef Goldmann (1947), too. However, others claim that a large number of planning indicators were already introduced in 1949, when the Law on Planning was accepted. Markuš (1986, 112) writes that in the period between 1951 and 1953, central planning in Czechoslovakia converged on the Soviet model and the planning directives were becoming increasingly detailed. The number of in-kind directives increased in the following way: in 1949 around 100 such directives were issued, encompassing one half of total industrial production; this increased in

1950 to about 400 directives (two thirds of production) and in 1951 to 1,100 directives (80 percent of production). These directives were connected to the allocation of raw materials, energy, and also to investments (114). In such a planning system the role of prices, values, and the market in general was suppressed. At the same time, well-known weaknesses of the planned economy quickly appeared as firms began requesting resources larger than needed for efficient use. An especially large demand emerged for investment goods. In addition, the coordination of requests between different organizations under different ministries was a serious problem when drawing balances.

Already in 1952, the official opinion published in the journal *Plánované hospodářství* (Planned Economy) criticized the overcentralization of planning (Markuš 1986, 115). As a reaction, both-direction planning (*ústretové plány*)[12] was introduced. However, this method that strengthened planning from below led to an even larger demand from firms for energy and raw materials, creating additional tensions and disequilibria in various sectors of the economy and provoking the opinion that state norms also should be introduced for the consumption of materials, utilization of machines, and so on. These norms were basically disaggregated input-output ratios, and their task was to help prepare the plans. In socialist jargon, these norms were called scientific, i.e., they were to represent best engineering practice, and not necessarily economic efficiency. However, due to the enormous number of such norms and informational problems associated with them, difficulties did not ebb. Furthermore, central planners also had to take into consideration high-level bureaucratic decisions, as well as existing party and government programs. Such a complexity was difficult to coordinate manually. That is why the belief that computers could be instrumental to achieve consistency in planning emerged among a broad circle of economists.

Another "innovative" step was the introduction of a gross production indicator in 1952, with the aim to reduce the number of planning directives. The Party Conference of 1956 announced another new technique, long-term planning, which was to form the basis for annual and five-year plans. This conference also called for financial indicators to be given a larger share among the directives. These considerations led to the first "reform" in 1958, which was to contribute to the "strengthening of central management of the national economy as well as to the development of workers' initiatives based on decentralization of responsibilities." (Markuš 1986, 122). This reform did not bring any significant change, and in the early 1960s—once growth rates had slowed down significantly—further measures were taken, culminating in the so-called Šik reforms in the second half of the 1960s (see below). The reasons for the slowdown were explained by a sluggish growth in productivity and an excessive material consumption per unit of final production. Directive planning with quantitative targets or gross values was connected to managers' and workers' wages, thus motivating them to increase growth irrespective of the costs of inputs. This convinced the reformers of the need to move partially away from gross directive planning in favor of procedures favoring net production.

In the period of 1949–1953, the First Five-Year Plan was in action, followed in 1954 and 1955 by one-year plans. In 1956, the Second Five-Year Plan was introduced, and in 1961, the Third Five-Year Plan. The five-year plans offered a general framework, while the annual plans were operational projects supposed to fit well with the five-year plans, at least in principle. In reality, annual plans were often modified during the year.

A crucial part of these plans were investment and output targets for industries and sectors. The decision concerning the share of national income to be invested (accumulation rate) was determined by the objectives of rapid industrialization and of "laying the foundations of socialism." The share of gross investment in net material product was typically above 20 percent. Emphasis was put on machine tools, electricity, coal, iron, and steel. Most investment decisions were made with the intention to increase the domestic capacity of production since, especially in the early years of the regime, the country's foreign economic relations were kept at a minimum. There was not much cooperation, even with other socialist countries, despite the fact that these countries set up the Council of Mutual Economic Assistance (CMEA, Comecon) in 1949. Most of them aimed for an all-encompassing development of their own industrial sectors, even if some of these sectors were cost-prohibitive in the pre-communist period (Spulber 1956).

FROM APOLOGY TO SOPHISTICATED RESEARCH

From 1948 to the mid-1950s, the role of economists in the new regime was predominantly apologetic as the scientific atmosphere deteriorated. To create such an atmosphere, it was necessary to eliminate independent views, including those of the prewar communists with exposure to Western economic thought.[13] Of course, a similar destiny awaited important non-leftist economists as well.[14] From the second half of the 1950s, one discerns small deviations from the official doctrine. Dissatisfaction with the results of central planning led to the 1958 "reform," also known as the Rozsypal reform, named after planning expert Kurt Rozsypal.[15]

From the 1960s onward, a large amount of funds were invested in research institutes and the education of qualified personnel, and many sectors of the economy began to use mathematical methods and computer technology. Several institutions ran projects in operations research, linear programming, and long-range optimal planning. These were typically not institutes of economics but those of applied technology as, for example, the Research Institute of the Economics of Food Industry. Economists of mathematical orientation preferred to work in the industrial or sectoral research institutes of the ministries and avoid economic institutes[16] that were under tighter ideological control.

The introduction of mathematical tools in research and planning was seen by the non- or anti-socialist economists as an attempt to render additional support to the communist regime because improvements in planning were prolonging its existence.[17] However, most of those involved with mathematical economics in their research felt differently. Their research programs finally could get rid of the apologetic role of economic theory, since mathematics provided a much more subtle vocabulary in which their thoughts could be expressed[18] and whose real meaning was therefore more difficult for the authorities to capture. In addition, in the 1960s, mainstream economics in the West saw the market as a computational mechanism. It was presumed that if the market can allocate resources optimally, then planning can somehow imitate the computational iterations and achieve a similar level of optimality. However, socialist central planners were not only short of mathematical sophistication but also lacked any well-founded theoretical background. Their decisions were rather implementations of some political and developmental aims set outside the planning process.

In almost all periods, mathematical economists had to demonstrate to the political watchdogs—typically, lecturers of Marxism-Leninism or political economy, and communist party *apparatchiki*—the usefulness of mathematical methods and to prove that these were in conformity with the fundamentals of Marxist teachings. Also, the formal language of mathematical modeling was used not only because it was less likely to trigger repressive reactions from ideological supervisors but also because it helped forge contacts with Western scholars (Turnovec 2002).

The central plans were staged as optimistic targets as the authorities wanted to mobilize the population to overfulfill the plan, in particular, those directives which were recognized as priorities. However, the plans also generated shortages and disproportions. Once fear from retaliation decreased, central planning was exposed to growing criticism from both professional economists and the public as well as from some members of the *nomenklatura*. To sacrifice consumption for investment also became more difficult once the initial shock wave of communist takeover weakened.

Even if the results of mathematical economics could potentially save resources, the ministries and other decision-making bodies showed a relatively low interest in applying them. These bodies were normally less knowledgeable of mathematical methods and more aware of ideological constraints.

There was always a risk that the mathematical tools could show that plans prepared by the political hierarchy were not optimal by almost any standard.

In the 1960s, the political mood changed. Applying linear programming, operations research, cybernetics, systems theory, and so on came to be recognized as part of modern economic management as compared to old-fashioned ideological control. The latter did not die out, and was even fully rejuvenated in the normalization period during the 1970s. In the 1960s, new centers of mathematical application were opened, and a large number of research institutes were established in different sectors of the economy. One of the first mathematical applications was the so-called *meziodvětvové vztahy* (intersectoral relations) of the economy, a variant of input-output analysis. Here one should highlight the work of Habr and Korda (1960), and Bouška, Skolka, and Tlustý (1965). Habr (1959) wrote one of the first books to introduce the Czech reader to linear programming. Habr (1981) mentions that the first national accounts for Czechoslovakia were constructed in 1946. Later, national accounts based on a market approach were studied by Vladimír Nachtigal. Benáček (2010, 47) writes that, in 1962, the first input-output model was prepared at the Faculty of Mathematics and Physics at Charles University in cooperation with economists such as Jiří Bouška, Oldřich Kýn, Bohuslav Sekerka, and Jiří Skolka. According to Habr (1981), the first detailed econometric work in socialist Czechoslovakia was published in 1950 in the *Československý ústav práce* (Czech Institute of Labor) by Jan Jankovský.[19]

Gradually, the syllabi of economic courses at the universities began to contain applications of mathematical economics, and this tendency also prevailed in the 1970s and 1980s. Graduates of the University of Economics in Prague and Bratislava were taught basic calculus, intermediate statistics, linear programming, operations research, optimal planning, and some other mathematical subjects, in addition to the verbal theory of planning and political economy.

Benáček (2010, 49) reviews the institutions of mathematical economics in these decades and identifies those representing standard international scientific quality. These were centers affiliated with the *ČVUT* (Alfons Bašta, František Egermayer, A. Klvač, Milan Písek, Jiří Skolka, Antonín Ter-Manuelianc); the *VŠE* (Roman Hušek, Benedikt Korda, Jaromír Walter); the Law Faculty of Charles University (Rita Budínová, Oldřich Kýn, Bohumil Urban); and several institutes of applied research (Jiří Chlumský, J. Janiš, Vladimír Kadlec, Václav Klusoň, Miroslav Rumler, L. Smetana). Turnovec (2002) regards the main centers of mathematical economics to be the Laboratory of Mathematical Economics led by Jiří Bouška at the Institute of Economics; the Department of Econometrics headed initially by Bedřich Korda, and later by Jaromír Walter, and Miroslav Maňas at *VŠE* in Prague; and the Department of Informatics and Operations Research managed by Milan Vlach at Charles University. One should not forget about the high level of studies by Jaromír Walter in econometrics as well as Lubomír Cyhelský and Josef Kozák in economic statistics. A detailed empirical analysis of economic data was published regularly by the Statistical Office of Czechoslovakia (*ČSÚ*) and the State Bank of Czechoslovakia (*ŠBČS*).

Rychetník (1968) reviewed the state of mathematical economics at the late 1960s. From 1963 on, Bohumil Urban built the Department of Political Economy and later the Institute of Economic Sciences at the Law Faculty of Charles University where social sciences were combined with a strong background in mathematics. This institute was closed in the normalization period because it was considered by orthodox communists a "nest of revisionists and after-August emigrés."

In the first half of the 1960s, domestic reform ideas as well as reform programs from Hungary, Poland, and the Soviet Union spread gradually in the country. Likewise, Czech and Slovak economists became more knowledgeable of developments in mainstream economic theory, including different sub-fields of mathematical economics. In the 1960s, Czechoslovak economic theorists began to publish at prestigious Western publishing houses and journals. For example, the paper by Kýn, Sekerka, and Hejl (1969) was included, together with the contributions of a large number of renowned economists such as Leif Johansen, Michał Kalecki, Oskar Lange, Joan Robinson, Amartya Sen, and Robert Solow, in a book honoring Maurice Dobb. Earlier, in a volume paying tribute to Michał Kalecki, Jaroslav Habr also published together with a large number of eminent contributors (Habr 1966).[20] In this period, a variety of research programs were developed at a sophisticated level, for example, applications of the theory of production functions (Toms and Hájek 1965, 1967; Tlustý and Strnad 1968; Toms 1968, 1969). One of the most well-known contributions in this period was Goldmann and Kouba (1969) on economic growth,[21] which was translated into English and Hungarian.[22]

In the late 1960s, the economic reform movement during the Prague Spring ended with military occupation. In classifying the positions of different groups of economists concerning this movement, it seems that the protagonists of market reforms such as Vladimír Kadlec, Bohumil Komenda, Jirí Kosta, Karel Kouba, Čestmír Kožušník, Ota Šik, and Věněk Šilhán did not originate in the discipline of mathematical economics. Rather the members of this influential group in the 1950s and early 1960s were interested predominantly in studying the planned economy, and gradually distanced themselves from orthodox communist views. Some of them played a negative role in the persecution of non-Marxist economists in the early 1950s. Yet, in the second half of the 1960s, those devoted to such fields as optimal planning, statistics, and econometrics normally became supporters of the reform movement led by Ota Šik. They were involved with background studies and the preparation of some of the key documents. Nevertheless, the political work of Šik and his collaborators was relatively far from the interest and preferences of mathematical economists. Šik himself was in a peculiar situation as he had deep connections, going back to the 1940s and the early 1950s, with hardline communists, which helped him accumulate power in the early 1960s. Gradually, he lost this network and was forced to emigrate after 1968. Those who worked on reforming the planned economy and those who studied the mathematical problems of planning seemed to belong to two different camps, but they shared animosity toward official political economy.

In the 1960s, the publishing house Svoboda launched the series *Ekonomie a společnost* (Economy and Society), in which mathematical economics featured prominently. This series included, among others, *Modely socialistického hospodářství* (Models of socialist economies) by Włodzimierz Brus (1964), *Sovětští ekonomové k používaní matematiky v ekonomii* (Soviet Economists on Using Mathematics in Economics) by Vasilii Nemchinov et al. (1964), as well as translations of works by Bela Balassa, Michał Kalecki, Oskar Lange, and Lawrence Klein. The volume by Pontriagin et al. on optimal processes was translated in 1964. Benáček (2010, 49) notes that the translation of Roy Allen's books (1971, 1975) by Martin Černý helped shape the vocabulary of mathematical-economic terms in Czech language. In 1966, Rudolf Briška translated Dantzig (1966) and Kaufmann and Cruon (1969). Also, Evsey Domar's work (1957) on economic growth was translated into Slovak in the 1960s. In 1966, Vasilii Nemchinov's *Ekonomicko-matematicko metódy a modely* (Economic-Mathematical Methods and Models) was published in Slovak. Three years before, Ján Ferianc[23] had already translated Nemchinov (1964). Translations continued even during the normalization period. The publishing house *Svoboda* put out Kenneth Arrow's *Social Choice and Individual Values* in 1971, and Joan Robinson's *Exercises in Economic Analysis* in 1975. In 1974, Antonín Kotulan wrote an introduction to *Planometrie* (1974) in the Economy and Society series. Chapters in this volume were written by, among others, Abel Aganbegian, Aleksandr Granberg, Leonid Kantorovich, Anatoly Lurie, Vasilii Nemchinov, Viktor Novozhilov, and Stanislav Shatalin. They dealt with problems of optimal planning such as the optimum criteria of the national economy, optimal price structure, and economic efficiency. A volume on optimal decision-making written by Leonid Kantorovich and Alexander Gorstko was translated into Slovak in 1976. Some important translations were reserved for internal use of the Academy of Sciences, for example, those of George Stigler's *Theory of Price*, Paul Samuelson's *Economics*, and the works of János Kornai, Leif Johansen, and others.

TEACHING MATHEMATICAL ECONOMICS

In addition to shaping economic research, the communist takeover also completely changed economic education in the country. In the pre-communist era,
most economists were trained at law schools in Prague, Brno, and Bratislava.
The communists considered these institutions as centers of bourgeois
thought and removed training from them. Moreover, the Law School of Brno
University was closed. Havel, Klacek, Kosta, and Šulc (1998, 217) mention
that, because the communist party did not trust economists of the previous
regime,[24] the planned economy faced a shortage of qualified experts. The new
regime filled the positions in research and education with young candidates
prepared for work in crash courses. Interestingly enough, some of them had
matured so fast that eventually they became the backbone of the reformist
movement in the second half of the 1960s.

After having tried out different types of new socialist economic education,[25] the *Vysoká škola ekonomická, VŠE* (High school of economics) was
established in Prague in the early 1950s. It still exists today. A department of
statistics was organized there, the fresh graduates of which became renowned
statisticians such as Benedikt Korda.[26] In the academic year 1952/1953,
a Faculty of Statistics was established at the *VŠE*, mirroring the Moscow
Institute of Economic Statistics. In the next academic year, the average age
of the instructors at the Department of Statistics (that had no professors or
habilitated docents) was 29 years. This was the standard human resource policy of the new regime, in which excellent career opportunities were offered
to young academics in exchange for political loyalty (Závodský 2013a, 520).

In the early 1950s, statistics was considered a socioeconomic discipline
based on historical materialism and Marxist political economy. Initially, statistics proper was regarded as "bourgeois pseudoscience." Závodský (2013a)
describes courses offered at the *VŠPHV* in the specialization of socioeconomic statistics. These courses included political economy and historical
materialism, methods of statistics, organization of statistics, Lenin's importance in statistics, critique of bourgeois statistics, and statistics as a historical,
class, and communist science. At the same time, already in the second half
of the 1950s, serious university textbooks of statistics were published such as
Statistické metódy (Statistical Methods) co-authored by Ilja Novák, Benedikt
Korda, and Jaromír Walter in 1956, or *Obecné metody statistiky* (General
Methods of Statistics) written by Novák and Korda in 1959. The large number of co-authors served to spread political responsibility.

In 1953, the economic school in Bratislava was renamed once again
and became *Vysoká škola ekonomická, VŠE* (High School of Economics).
This name was kept until 1992. *VŠE* Bratislava as well as *VŠE* Prague

remained the foremost pedagogical institutions, with important apologetic roles for the socialist regime. However, both institutions reached a solid level of training in mathematical economics, statistics, and similar subjects. In the 1950s, at the *VŠE* Bratislava research activity was not required of the faculty from the university. However, research intensified from the 1960s (Ekonomická univerzita 2011). In 1950, the Institute of socioeconomic Statistics was founded at the predecessor of the *VŠE* Bratislava, and in 1952, it was renamed Department of Statistics and Mathematics. Among the first teachers one finds Anton Klas, Anton Kotzig, Milan Kovačka, Adam Laščiak, and Ján Svetoň.[27] In the early 1960s, the school founded its Department of Mathematical Economics with Juraj Fecanin, Adam Laščiak,[28] Jozef Sojka, and Ladislav Unčovský.[29]

NORMALIZATION OF THE ORTHODOXY: 1968–1989

Right after the Soviet invasion in August 1968, "normalization" began and tight communist party control was re-introduced at all institutions of higher learning.[30] This control remained in force basically until the collapse of the regime. Again, people were compelled to leave their jobs at the institutions of research and higher learning once they were considered disloyal.[31] In this period one also observes a large-scale emigration of leading Czech economists.[32]

In the early 1970s, the political leadership admitted some of the weaknesses of the communist model and the economic disproportions accumulated in the past. In official rhetoric the disproportions resulted from voluntarism of the 1950s and revisionist policies in the second half of the 1960s. Thus, they would not constitute inherent characteristics of the planned economy.

Following a period of relatively fast development in the early 1970s, economic growth slowed again. In the second half of the 1970s, there were external reasons for this slowdown due to the preceding oil shocks, but the re-introduction of orthodox directive planning perverted the motivations of enterprises, adversely affecting the whole economy. Economic growth was heavily dependent on increasing material inputs because productivity did not improve sufficiently. Large investments went into heavy industry again, partly because cooperation with the Soviet Union was deepened.[33] Also, a new barrier to economic growth arose as a vital resource, namely, labor, faded away.

This led the ruling elite to accelerate research on growth, productivity, efficiency, prices, planning methods, and so on. In an attempt to improve the planning mechanism, the government experimented with some new incentives on enterprise level, but also—due to ideological reasons—strengthened the mandatory character of the plan (Levčík 1986).[34] The orthodoxy of the late 1950s was brought back, however, with an interesting twist. On the one hand, pro-regime scholars maintained their apologetic approach to the planned economy in the style of the official political economy of socialism. Among them, the most influential were Jaromír Barvík, Antonín Bružek, and Zdeněk Hába. On the other, some economists—even those occupying high positions within the party-state—chose a research field, in which mathematical economics was used like in the neoclassical mainstream. For example, at the Graduate School of the Institute of Economics in Prague lectures were given in this spirit by Miroslav Hájek, Jan Klacek, Antonín Kotulán, Miroslav Toms, and others. Several research projects at the Institute of Economics also followed the logic of modern mathematical models. This applied especially to research made under the leadership of Josef Goldmann, with collaborators such as Karel Dyba, Kamil Janáček, Jan Klacek, and Václav Kupka. Works by this group of scholars belong to the finest achievements of postwar Czechoslovak economic science.

The publication outlets were usually domestic due to restrictions on publishing in the West.[35] This type of research also entailed useful inquiries into modern econometrics. For example, the Economic-Mathematical Laboratory of the institute produced the volume *Systém ekonomicko-matematických modelů* (Systems of Economic-Mathematical Models) with authors such as Jiří Bouška, Martin Černý, Karel Dyba, Dagmar Glückaufová, Miroslav Hrnčíř, and Vladimír Nachtigal, and also works like Dědek (1989), Dyba and Kupka (1983), Hrnčíř et al. (1978), and Klacek and Nešporová (1980).

Josef Goldmann published a trilogy dealing with the socialist economy. In 1975, he published *Makroekonomická analýza a prognóza* (Macroeconomic Analysis and Prognosis); in 1978, *Úvod do makroekonomické analýzy* (Introduction to Macroeconomic Analysis); and in 1985, *Strategie hospodářského růstu* (Strategy of Economic Growth). The last volume tackles the formation of goals in the planning process. He argued that planning targets should not be exogenous to the socialist economy or determined by a superior body, but they are to be discussed at multiple echelons of society. His 1978 volume that was published together with Karel Dyba, Kamil Janáček, Jan Klacek, Václav Kupka, and Růžena Vintrová reflects the state of macroeconomics in Czechoslovakia during the 1970s.[36]

Miroslav Toms was a scholar who also attempted to bring Marxist analysis closer to mainstream economic thought. Similar to Goldmann, he settled at the Institute of Economics where he remained till his premature death. In the 1970s and the 1980s, his main research focus was optimal planning and Marx's concept of the use value.[37] Toms rejected the supply dependency of the socialist economy and understood that the government's attempts at mobilizing the factors of production could not be sufficient to achieve an intensive growth of the economy without increased efficiency of these factors.

An original contribution to the analysis of socialist planning procedures was provided by Lubomír Mlčoch (see Horvath and Sommer 2018). Official socialist ideology was stressing the vertical control of society by the planning authorities. However, Mlčoch argued in a series of works that "in a closed hierarchical system, planning was an extensive cooperative game based on a deep dichotomy of actual and official rules" (Mlčoch, 2000, 11). Unfortunately, he did not test this hypothesis by a game-theoretical model. In retrospect, Mlčoch writes that planning was used as a "smoke screen for the exercise of power flowing from the monopolization of all decision-making conditions of social reproduction in the individual planning links" (11). In his view, planning was a costly social ritual to keep the social structure intact.[38] The communists did not realize that once the initial revolutionary targets were achieved, much would depend on the supply of information from the enterprises. Instead, small informal groups established indirect control over the planning process as the years passed by. Mlčoch (1990) explored how managers, together with the representatives of the *nomenklatura*, exercised property rights over the output of shortage goods, sometimes in return for favors from another group of managers. He reasoned how, during the communist period, the informal authority emerged over state-owned property. To an extent, these informal property rights were transformed into formal legal rights in the first years of the Czechoslovak transition.

In the second half of the 1980s, regular monthly seminars were organized by Václav Klaus and some of his collaborators such as Tomáš Ježek, and Miroslav Kerouš in the State Bank of Czechoslovakia (*ŠBČS*). These were held under the auspices of the *Československá vedecko-technická společnost* (Czechoslovak Scientific-Technical Society) on economic theory, mathematical economics, planning, economic policy, and similar topics. Among the participants one finds directors of the Planning Office, the State Bank, and the government, as well as those economists who were critical-minded or took anti-socialist positions. These seminars brought back the atmosphere of discussions and exchange of ideas which was interrupted in the early 1970s by the process of normalization.

In Slovak economic thought a considerable progress was achieved, especially in teaching econometrics, operations research, and mathematical foundations of economics. Related publications include a university textbook of dynamic modeling by Adam Laščiak (1985), with co-authors such as Miroslav Hysko, Josef Lauber, Miroslav Maňas, Jaroslav Samek, and Juraj Trnovský; and a textbook of optimal programming also by Laščiak (1983), with co-authors including Michal Chobot, Eduard Hozlár, Roman Hušek, Miroslav Maňas, Ján Šimkovic, Jozef Sojka, Vladimír Ulašin, and Ladislav

Unčovský. The prolific scientific work of František Turnovec also deserves special attention.[39]

CONCLUSION

In the final years of communism, quite often the task to prepare a central plan was such a monumental exercise for the planners that the "plan" for the previous year was equal to the real data published in the early part of the current year. So everything was fine on paper. The difficulty for central planners typically was caused by both exogenous events occurring in the world economy and by the fact that the annual plan was of such a low internal consistency that its implementation required constant adjustment during the year. In short, decades of experimenting with central planning did not guarantee that the plans became more accurate.

In the communist era, the level of knowledge of mathematical economics in Czechoslovakia was substantial, and some accomplishments were achieved, especially in applying the results of operations research, linear programming, and statistics. Normally, these efforts were less noticed in the international literature since there priority was given to politically-driven discussions like those on the troubled relationship between the plan and the market. The introduction of mathematical methods in planning the Czechoslovak economy did not transform central planning fundamentally. However, there were constructive mathematical applications in use in managing various sectors of the economy. Following the collapse of communism, some of those experts who specialized in such applications found good positions for themselves in academia, business, and even high-level policymaking.

NOTES

1. František Nožička (1918–2004) studied at Charles University in Prague. After the funeral of Jan Opletal on November 17, 1939, he was arrested and sent to a concentration camp. He became a professor at the newly founded Faculty of Mathematics and Physics at Charles University in 1960. He was a leading expert in linear and dynamic programming and in optimization theory (Zimmermann 1999, 103–107). Josef Bíly (1905–1970) worked as a statistician in the Ministry of Finance during the 1930s. Later, he became a famed professor at the Faculty of Mathematics and Physics at Charles University. Jaromír Walter (1923–2001) studied insurance statistics and became a professor of statistics at the High School of Economics (*VŠE*) in Prague (see Závodský 2013b, 91).

2. In the Soviet Union "the very first calculations for optimizing the structure of the country's long-range fuel-energy balance in the mid-1960s revealed shortcomings in the fuel pricing system: the price of fuel in the regions from which it was shipped was higher than the prices of the same fuel in the regions to which it was shipped, and the prices of higher quality types of fuel were lower than the prices of low-grade fuels" (Kantorovich, Albegov, and Bezrukov 1987, 8).

3. As Ludwig von Mises (2000, 28) writes, "the collection of these data, and the setting up of the corresponding equations, is a task far beyond the powers of a socialist central administration composed of mere human beings."

4. Eberhard Jonák was professor at Charles-Ferdinand University in Prague from 1860. In 1856, he published *Theorie der Statistik in Grundzügen* in Vienna, and in 1871, *Základové hospodářství* (Foundations of Economy) in Prague. After Jonák, Albín Bráf became professor of political economy at Charles-Ferdinand University. He was active in political life, too, and served as minister of agriculture in 1909. His papers were collected and published by Josef Gruber in 1922–1924. Some consider Bráf the founder of Czech economic thought.

5. Jaroslav Janko (1893–1965) was professor at the Czech Technical University from 1936, and at the Faculty of Mathematics and Physics of Charles University from 1952. For Emil Schönbaum (1882–1967), see Folta and Šišma (n.d.). Dobroslav Krejčí (1869–1936) became the first president of the Czechoslovak Statistical Office in 1919–1920. In 1935/36, he was rector of the Masaryk University.

6. After 1918, mathematical statistics and insurance theory were taught at the College of Special Sciences (*Vysoká škola speciálních nauk, VŠSN*) of the Czech Technical University. Among its graduates, one finds some of the leading postwar Czech economic statisticians such as Lubomír Cyhelský, Jaroslav Hátle, Benedikt Korda Jiří Likeš, Jaromír Walter, and others (Závodský 2013a, 87). Statistics was also taught at the Faculty of Natural Sciences of Charles University. Here, the leading professor was Emil Schönbaum. At the College of Business (*Vysoká škola obchodní, VŠO*), which from 1929 became part of the Czech Technical University (*České vysoké učení technické, ČVUT*), statistics lectures were held by František Hodáč, Jan Koloušek, Josef Mráz, and Leopold Šauer (see Závodský 2013a, 515; 2013b, 88). Benáček (2010, 48) mentions that business students at this school had to pass advanced-level exams in mathematics. At Charles University in the interwar period Vilibald Mildschuh lectured on quantitative economic subjects. He was followed by Cyril Horáček. At the German University in Prague statistics was taught by Heinrich Rauchberg (see Závodský 2013a, 516). In the academic year of 1937/1938, about 200 Slovak students joined the *VŠO* (Ekonomická univerzita 2012, 49).

7. In Slovakia economics was studied at the Law School of Comenius University where the Institute of Statistics (*Seminár Štatistiky*) began to work in 1935. In October 1940, the *Vysoká obchodná škola (VOŠ*, High School of Business) was founded in Bratislava as a private school financed by the Chamber of Trade and Industry. This was similar to the Prague *VŠO*; however, exams in higher mathematics were not required at the *VOŠ* (Ekonomická univerzita 2011, 13). In December 1944, the *VOŠ* was renamed *Slovenská vysoká škola obchodná v Bratislave (SVŠO)*. The first rector of the *VOŠ* was Jur Hronec (Georg Hronyecz), see Matematický ústav SAV n.d.)

8. One of them, Alexander M. Baykov (1899–1963) left the Soviet Union in 1920 and worked on Soviet planning issues in an economic study center in Prague under the leadership of the former liberal Menshevik Sergei Prokopovich. Baykov was part of the team publishing the journal *Russkii ekonomicheskii sbornik*. Later, Baykov moved to England and worked at University of Birmingham.

9. The list of noted Austrian economists teaching in Prague and Brno before the First World War consists of Friedrich von Wieser, Emil Sax, and Hermann von Schullern zu Schrattenhofen. In the interwar period, Robert Zuckerkandl, Hans Mayer, Franz Xaver Weiss, and Oskar Engländer followed them. Economists close to the German Historical School such as Adolf Weber and Arthur Spiethoff also worked in Prague before the First World War. In addition, Othmar Spann taught at the Institute of Technology in Brno between 1907 and 1919 (see Horváth and Krištofóry 2017).

10. The Economic Council was composed of economic ministries, the State Planning Office (later, Central Planning Commission or State Planning Commission), and the Statistical Office. The prime minister acted as the chairman of the Economic Council.

11. The preamble of the Law on the Two-Year Plan stated: "Although the Czechoslovak plan has benefited by the experiments made in other countries, the Soviet Union in particular, it has been worked out independently. We do not try to imitate these models nor to transplant them mechanically to our economic life, which has developed on different principles, and has as a result a different structure. Considering all these differences, and in keeping with our original political evolution, we are following equally original ways which suit our national character and the structure of our economic life" (George 1947, 336). Such hopes for an independent Czechoslovak road to socialism were crushed by the coup in February 1948.

12. Also called two-level planning, counter-planning, or *Gegenplanung* in the literature.

13. Ludvík Frejka (Ludwig Freund, 1904–1952) studied in Berlin and London in the 1920s. During the war, he worked in Great Britain as an economic advisor to the Czechoslovak government in exile. From 1945 to 1952, Frejka was an economic advisor to the president. In 1952, he was executed, then later rehabilitated. Another potential independent voice was Eugen Löbl (1907–1987), a Slovak economist who worked for the exile government during the war. From 1945 to 1949, he was a deputy minister of foreign trade, later sentenced to life imprisonment, and released from prison in 1960. In 1968, Löbl left for the United States. Josef Goldmann (1912–1984) also belonged to the group of independent thinkers (see below).

14. Imrich Karvaš (1903–1981) spent years in prison. The greatest Czech economist of the pre-communist era, Karel Engliš (1880–1961), was forced to move from Prague to his native village, and his followers such as Václav Chytil (1907–1980), Miloš Horna (1897–1958), Alois Král (1902–1991), and Vladimír Vybral (1902–1980) were persecuted (see Vencovský 1997).

15. Kurt Rozsypal (1916–2013) was a Czech communist economist and politician. He gave an orthodox critique of the reforms in the 1960s. He worked in high positions in the State Planning Commission until 1962, later became a professor at *VŠE,* Prague.

16. In 1953, the *Ekonomický ústav Československé akademie věd* (Institute of Economics, Czechoslovak Academy of Sciences) was created from the former *Kabinet politické ekonomie* (Cabinet for Political Economy). This institute played a fundamental role in the 1960s and the second half of the 1980s in developing reform ideas.

17. Once mathematical economics was accepted politically, it provided the planners with new arguments for the possible future improvements of the planning process. See, for example, *Státní plánovací komise* (1965).

18. Habr (1981) writes that in the early years of socialism most of the economic thinking was *"papouškováni,"* that is, a parrot-like repetition of the learned text. Compared to that, learning linear programming seemed a much more reasonable activity.

19. We were not able to find more detailed information except this quotation of Habr (1981).

20. The book was entitled *Problems of Economic Dynamics and Planning*, and was published by Pergamon Press. Contributors included Paul Baran, Fritz Behrens, Czeslaw Bobrowski, Włodzimierz Brus, Kazimierz Laski, Maurice Dobb, Ragnar Frisch, Roy Harrod, Lawrence Klein, Tadeusz Kowalik, Oskar Lange, Prasanta Mahalanobis, Vasilii Nemchinov, Joan Robinson, Richard Stone, Paul Sweezy, and Jan Tinbergen.

21. During the war, Josef Goldmann worked in the Statistics Centre of Oxford University where he joined the communist party in 1945. Later, he worked in the teams preparing the Two-Year Plan and the First Five-Year Plan. In 1952, as deputy head of the Statistical Office of Czechoslovakia, he was imprisoned for twenty years. In 1960, he left prison. Following rehabilitation, he joined the Czechoslovak Academy of Sciences in 1963 where he remained till the end of his life. Goldmann belonged to the generation who experienced the Great Depression, the break-up of Czechoslovakia, death in his family during the German occupation and considered socialism as a viable social project. He was not involved in daily reform activities; rather, he attempted to understand the actual planned economy. Karel Kouba (1927–2013) worked as director of the Institute of Economics, Czechoslovak Academy of Sciences in 1968–1969. During the period of normalization he had a low-level administrative job in Prague. Some of the Goldmann and Kouba studies written at that time could not be published in Czechoslovakia. However, one of them (Goldmann and Kouba 1984) appeared in Hungary.

22. This book analyzed the barriers of economic growth and the relationship between different factors of growth and efficiency, and discussed the application of Kalecki's model in Czechoslovakia. The authors explain the cyclical pattern of growth by the in-built mechanisms of socialist planning, which makes the final product dependent on the growth of inputs that the primary sectors are unable to deliver. Čihák (1997, 13) rightly calls this book a "lightening example" of research in macroeconomics in socialist Czechoslovakia.

23. Ján Ferianc (1927–1996) was an economist and politician, member of the Slovak National Council and the Federal Parliament. He served as a minister responsible for planning in the Slovak government in the 1970s. He graduated from the *VŠE*

Bratislava where he chaired the Department of Planning between 1952 and 1964. In the period of 1964–1968, Ferianc worked as a director of the Institute of Regional Planning in Bratislava. In 1958, he published *Národohospodárske plánovanie* (Planning of the National Economy) in two volumes.

24. In 1949, at the *Vysoká škola hospodárskych vied* (*VŠHV*, High school of economic sciences) in Bratislava, the predecessor of the *VŠE*, faculty who were not considered loyal was forced to leave the school. "From the eight professors of the School two remained, from forty-five assistant professors only fourteen" (Ekonomická univerzita 2011, 20).

25. In 1949/1950, the new regime founded the *Vysoká škola politických a hospodářských věd* (*VŠPHV*, High school of political and economic sciences). Furthermore, in 1948 *Vysoká škola obchodní* was first renamed *Vysoká škola věd hospodářských* (High school of economic sciences), then in 1951 it became *Fakulta hospodářských věd* (College of economic sciences) of the Czech Technical University. The institution came under attack because of the alleged influence by Rudolf Slánsky, a high-ranking communist leader executed in 1952. It was closed in 1953.

26. Benedikt Korda (Benő Kornreich, 1914–2010) studied at the Faculty of Natural Sciences of Charles University. He fled to Hungary in 1942 where he was drafted as forced laborer. After the war, he joined the communist party, worked at the Ministry of Energy, and graduated in statistics and insurance sciences at the *VŠSN*. Korda became professor in 1961, his main work *Matematické metódy v ekonomii* (Mathematical methods in economics) was published in 1967. In 1968, he left for Canada where he became a professor at the University of Alberta (see Závodský, 2013a).

27. Ján Svetoň (Ján Schweinert) was one of the leading Slovak statisticians specializing in demography. Between 1952 and 1966, he was head of Department of Statistics at the *VŠE*, and also president of the Slovak Statistical Office. Milan Kovačka worked as a statistical expert for the United Nations, Economic Commission for Africa. He published *Štatistické metódy* (Statistical Methods) in 1962. Anton Klas published *Ekonometrické modelovanie* (Econometric Modeling) in 1978. Anton Kotzig received a degree in mathematical statistics. From 1952 to 1958, he served as rector of the *VŠE*. From 1959 to 1964, he was the first director of the Mathematical Institute of the Slovak Academy of Sciences. Kotzig founded the Slovak school of the theory of graphs. In 1969, he visited Canada and stayed in Montreal till the end of his life.

28. See Laščiak et al. (1985, 1983), Sojka (1970), Sojka et al (1981), Unčovský (1985), and Unčovský et al. (1991). Fecanin, Laščiak, and Sojka participated in a one-year post-graduate study at Leningrad State University.

29. Later, other important mathematical economists, statisticians, and operations research specialists such as Michal Chobot, Michal Hatrák, Eduard Hozlár, Jaroslav Husár, Vladimír Mlynarovič, Ján Šimkovič, and Jozef Sojka joined the department.

30. In 1989, there were 35 instructors (five professors, five docents, and 25 assistant professors) at the Department of Statistics of the *VŠE*. Sixty percent of them were party members (Závodský 2013a, 527).

31. At the beginning of the normalization period, the *VŠE* Bratislava started dismissing politically unreliable faculty and staff. The university party organization,

consisting of about half of the teachers, was dissolved. From 260 party members 98 lost membership, and 19 were expelled from the party. Some of those who lost membership were forced to leave the school (Ekonomická univerzita 2011, 32).

32. Bedřich (Friedrich) Levčík became director of the Vienna Institute for International Economic Comparisons where Peter Havlík and Zdenek Lukáš were also active. Jiří Skolka and Jan Stankovský joined the Austrian Institute for Economic Research. Jiří Sláma worked at the Osteuropa-Institut in Munich, and Jiří Kosta was professor at Frankfurt University. Jan Mládek served as director of the International Monetary Fund. University of Reading hosted Luděk Rychetník, while Jaroslav Krejčí stayed at the University of Lancaster, and Pavel Pelikán at the University of Stockholm. Many Czechoslovak émigrés worked in the United States: Josef Brada joined Arizona State University and Oldřich Kýn joined Boston University, Zdeněk Drábek worked for the World Bank, Jan Švejnar taught at Columbia, and Jaroslav Vaněk at Cornell. Jan Vaňous established *PlanEcon*. Radovan Selucký and Jan Adam were active in Canada. Karel Kouba (2010, 30) mentions that after 1968, Fritz Machlup offered support to those economists who would leave Czechoslovakia for the United States. Also, some Slovak economists left the country, among others, Mikuláš Luptáčik, who became professor at the Vienna University of Economics and Business, and Anton Kotzig who became professor at University of Montreal.

33. The Soviet Union offered the Comecon countries a price mechanism that delayed the transmission of oil shocks to their economies. When the global price of oil stabilized, the terms of trade of these countries were still deteriorating *vis-à-vis* the Soviet Union. In addition, Czechoslovak exports were losing their positions on the world market (Levčík 1986, 86).

34. The grip of communist orthodoxy on the economic discourse is well described by the fact that, in the time of *perestroika*, Valtr Komárek (1985, 19) still needed to quote *Grundrisse* of Marx to support the view that production should not be understood only as a technical balance problem but as a social and economic issue.

35. The main outlet was *Politická ekonomie* (Political Economy) established in 1952 and issued by the Institute of Economics, Czechoslovak Academy of Sciences. *Ekonomicko-matematický obzor* (Economic and Mathematical Review) was founded in 1965 and published also by the Institute of Economics. *Finance a úvěr* (Finance and Credit) was established in 1951 and published until 1996 by the Ministry of Finance and later by Charles University. In Slovakia the leading journal was *Ekonomický časopis* (Economic Journal), founded in 1953 and issued by the Slovak Academy of Sciences.

36. Chapter 2 of the volume discusses material balances; in Chapter 3 Goldmann analyzes macroeconomy as a dynamic process; in Chapter 4 Janáček presents the theory of consumption; in Chapter 5 Kupka examines the dynamic theory of investment; in Chapter 6 Dyba writes about balance of payment adjustment; and in Chapter 7 Klacek describes the theory of production. In the second part of the book these authors present issues of adaptation, equilibrium, and growth. We agree with Čihák (1997, 21) that Goldmann belongs to the most important Czech economists of the socialist period due to his insistence on maintaining high professional standards.

37. "Toms' methodology was based on the connection of Marx's qualitative analysis with a quantitative analysis; to put it otherwise, a dialectic-materialistic approach with an econometric approach. [. . .] Toms was able to free himself from the need to see the laws of political economy of socialism everywhere. With one exception—the economy of time, i.e., the theory of efficiency—in Marxist terminology, the maximum rationality of expending societal labor in conditions of common ownership. Marx spoke of the economy of time as the first law of socialist society, and although this thesis had entirely disappeared from the work of Marxism-Leninism, it became Toms' life theme" (Doležalová 2018, 155).

38. Mlčoch (2000, 11) writes "In a private market economy, individuals can define property rights and freely buy and sell them—because they are defined in written codified law. In Real Socialism, there existed few formal rights. Instead, there were entitlements which individuals could enjoy only thanks to their status and under the protection of political and economic power structure. Generally, these entitlements were less easily divisible and transferable, even though trading of these entitlements did indeed occur using a form of barter."

39. František Turnovec graduated from Leningrad State University in mathematical economics in 1964. Between 1970 and 1989, he worked as a programmer for *Výskumné výpočtové centrum* (Research Computer Center) in Bratislava. He began his doctoral studies in 1967 but received his degree only in 1990 at *VŠE* Bratislava since he was not allowed to continue his studies during normalization. In 1998 he became professor at Charles University in Prague. In the second half of the 1990s Turnovec was director of the CERGE Institute in Prague.

BIBLIOGRAPHY

Allen, Roy George Douglas. 1971. *Matematická ekonomie*. Praha: Academia.

———. 1975. *Makroekonomická teorie*. Praha: Svoboda.

Arrow, Kenneth. 1971. *Společenský výběr a individuální hodnoty*. Praha: Svoboda.

Barnett, Vincent. 2008. "Economics in Soviet Union." In *New Palgrave Dictionary of Economics*, edited by Steven N. Durlauf and Lawrence E. Blume. London: Macmillan. https://doi.org/10.1007/978-1-349-58802-2_1576, accessed August 27, 2021.

Barvík, Jaromír, and Antonín Chyba. 1973. *Politická ekonomie*. Praha: SPN.

Benáček, Vladimír. 2010. "Zdroje identity a české tradice teoretické ekonomie." In Mlčoch 2010, 45–56.

Bernasek, Miloslav. 1970. "Czechoslovak Planning 1945–48." *Soviet Studies* 22 (1): 94–109.

Bouška, Jiří, Jiří Skolka, and Zdeněk Tlustý. 1965. *Meziodvětvová analýza*. Praha: SNTL.

Bouška, Jiří et al. 1976. *Systém ekonomicko-matematických modelů pro střednědobé plánování*. Praha: Ekonomicko-matematická laboratoř při Ekonomickém ústavu ČSAV.

Brus, Włodzimierz. 1964. *Modely socialistického hospodářství*. Praha: NPL.

Chytil, Zdeněk, and Milan Sojka. 2003. "České ekonomické myšlení v letech 1948–1969." *Politická ekonomie* 51 (4): 565–90.

Čihák, Martin. 1997. "Josef Goldmann: legenda české poválečné makroekonomie." *Politická ekonomie* 45 (1): 3–24.

Dantzig, George. 1966. Lineárne programovanie a jeho rozvoj. Bratislava: Slovenské vydavateľstvo technickej literatúry.

Dědek, Oldřich. 1989. "Teorie všeobecné ekonomické rovnováhy a optimálního plánování." *Politická ekonomie* 37 (11): 1281–94.

Doležalová, Antonie. 2018. *A History of Czech Economic Thought*. London—New York: Routledge.

Domar, Evsey David. 1957. *Essays in the Theory of Economic Growth*. New York: Oxford University Press. Translated into Slovak as *Teória ekonomického rastu a rovnováhy* (1966. Bratislava: Slovenská Akadémia Vied).

Dvořák, Jiří, and Tomáš Ježek. 1973. "Some Problems of Strain in the Manpower Balances." *Eastern European Economics* 11 (4): 60–85.

Dyba, Karel, and Václav Kupka. 1983. *Vnější nárazy a odezva hospodářské politiky*. Praha: Ekonomický ústav Československé akademie věd.

———. 1984. "Přizpusobení československé ekonomiky vnějším nárazům." *Politická ekonomie* 32 (1): 43–56.

Ekonomická univerzita. 2011. *Pamätnica Ekonomickej univerzity v Bratislave, 1940–2010*. Bratislava: EKONÓM.

———. 2012. *Spomienky a príbehy z dejín Ekonomickej university v Bratislave*. Bratislava: Sprint.

Ferianc, Jan. 1958. *Národohospodárske plánovanie I., II.* Bratislava: VŠE.

Folta, Jaroslav, and Pavel Šišma. n. d. "Emil Schoenbaum." https://web.math.muni.cz/biografie/emil_schoenbaum.html, accessed August 26, 2021

Frejka, Ludvík. 1951. *O kapitalismu a socialismu*. Praha: Svoboda.

George, Pierre. 1947. "Planning for Socialism in Czechoslovakia." *Science & Society* 11 (4): 327–39.

Goldmann, Josef. 1947. *Czechoslovakia, Test Case of Nationalization: A Survey of Post-War Industrial Development and the Two-Year Plan*. Prague: Orbis.

———. 1949. *Plánování, hospodářský zákon socialism*. Praha: Orbis.

———. 1973. *Od nestability ke stabilitě ekonomického růstu v ČSSR*. Praha: EÚ ČSAV.

———. 1975. *Makroekonomická analýza a prognóza*. Praha: Academia.

———. 1985. *Strategie ekonomického růstu*. Praha: Academia.

Goldmann, Josef et al. 1973. *Makroekonomická analýza za léta 1970–1972*. Praha: EÚ ČSAV.

———. 1978. *Úvod do makroekonomické analýzy*. Praha: Svoboda.

Goldmann, Josef, and Karel Kouba. 1969. *Hospodářský růst v ČSSR*. Praha: Academia.

———. 1984. "Terms of Trade, Adjustment Processes and the Economic Mechanisms (A Quantitative Approach)." *Acta Oeconomica* 32 (1–2): 137–60.

Hába, Zdeněk et al. 1978. *Politická ekonomie, socialistický výrobní způsob*. Praha: SPN.

————. 1983. *Politická ekonomie*. Praha: Svoboda.

Habr, Jaroslav. 1959. *Lineární programování*. Praha: SNTL.

Habr, Jaroslav. 1966. "A Contribution to the Theory of Sliding Plans." In *Problems of Economic Dynamics and Planning. Essays in Honour of Michał Kalecki*, 157–68. Oxford: Pergamon Press.

————. 1981. "Počátky formalizovaného myšlení v ekonomii u nás." In *Ekonomické modelování: Sborník referátu*, edited by ČSVTS—ŠBČS, Vol 1 Praha, 55–70.

Habr, Jaroslav, and Bedřich Korda. 1960. *Rozbor meziodvětvových vztahů*. Praha: SNTL.

Havel, Jiří, Jan Klacek, Jirí Kosta, and Zdislav Šulc. 1998. "Economics and System Change in Czechoslovakia, 1948–1992." In Wagener 1998, 213–63.

Hejl, Lubomír, Oldřich Kýn, and Bohuslav Sekerka. 1967. "Price Calculations." *Czechoslovak Economic Papers* 8: 6–81.

Hrnčíř, Miroslav, Karel Dyba, Vladimír Nachtigal, and Zdeněk Orlíček. 1978. *Vliv vnějších ekonomických vztahů na národní důchod*. Praha: Economic Institute of the Czechoslovak Academy of Sciences.

Horváth, Július. 2002. "The State of Economics in Slovakia." In Kaase, Sparschuh, and Wenninger 2002, 168–86.

Horváth, Julius, and Tomáš Krištofóry. 2017. "Early Reception of Austrian Economic Thought in Central Europe." Paper presented at the European Society for History of Economic Thought in Antwerp, May 18–20, 2017.

Horváth, Julius, and Vítězslav Sommer. 2018. "From Nationalization to Privatization: Understanding the Concept of Ownership in Czechoslovakia." In *Populating No Man's Land? Economic Concepts of Ownership under Communism*, edited by János Mátyás Kovács, 87–112. Lanham: Lexington Books.

Hudík, Marek. 2007. "František Čuhel (1862–1914)." *New Perspectives on Political Economy* 3 (1): 3–14.

Janáček, Kamil, Jan Klacek, and Růžena Vintrová. 1983. "Naléhavost obratu k intenzifikaci reprodukčního procesu v ČSSR v osmdesátých letech." *Politická ekonomie* 31 (12): 1311–14.

Janáček, Kamil et al. 1990. *Československá ekonomika na prahu devadesátých let*. Praha: EÚ ČSAV.

Ježek, Tomáš, and Václav Klaus. 1987. "Rozpory a dilemata Jánose Kornaie." *Finance a úvěr* 37 (2): 134–39.

Johansen, Leif. 1966. "Soviet Mathematical Economics." *Economic Journal* 76 (303): 593–601.

Kaase, Max, Vera Sparschuh, and Agnieszka Wenninger, eds. 2002. *Three Social Science Disciplines in Central and Eastern Europe: Handbook on Economics, Political Science and Sociology (1989–2001)*. Berlin: Gesis, Collegium Budapest.

Kalecki, Michał. 1965. *Náčrt teorie růstu socialistické ekonomiky*. Praha: NPL.

Kantorovich, Leonid, and Alexander Gorstko. 1976. *Optimálne rozhodnutia v ekonomike*. Bratislava: Nakladatelstvo Pravda.

Kantorovich, Leonid, Murat Albegov, and Vladimir Bezrukov. 1987. "Toward the Wider Use of Optimizing Methods in the National Economy." *Problems of*

Economics 29 (10): 5– 20. Originally published in Russian in 1986 (*Kommunist* 9: 44–54).

Kaufman A., and R. Cruon. 1969. *Dynamické programovanie*. Bratislava: Alfa.

Klacek, Jan, and Alena Nešporová. 1980. "Ekonomický růst v ČSSR—aplikace produkční funkce CES." *Politická ekonomie* 28 (6): 603–16.

Klacek, Jan et al. 1991. "Ekonomická reforma v ČSFR." *Politická ekonomie* 39 (9–10): 721–42.

Klas, Anton. 1978. *Ekonometrické modelovanie*. Bratislava: Alfa.

Klaus, Václav. 1979. "Metodologické problémy makroekonomického modelování." *Politická ekonomie* 27 (7): 697–706.

———. 1984. "Dr. Goldmann, ekonomická strategie a makroanalýza." In *Ekonomické modelováni*, ČSVTS–ŠBČS, Praha 1: 1–32.

———. 1988. "Příčiny zahraničně ekonomického problému." *Politická ekonomie* 36 (12): 1283–88.

Klaus, Václav, Kamil Janáček, and Václav Kupka. 1969. *Úvod do zkoumání inflace v československé ekonomice*. Praha: EU ČSAV.

Klusoň, Václav. 1982. *Adaptace v systémech plánování*. Praha: Institut řízení.

Komárek, Valtr. 1985. *Struktura československé ekonomiky*. Praha: Academia.

Komárek, Valtr et al. 1990. *Prognóza a program*. Praha: Academia.

Komenda, Bohumil et al. 1963. "Návrh tezí o zdokonalení soustavy plánovitého řízení národního hospodářství." Working Paper. Prague: Ekonomický ústav ČSAV.

Komenda, Bohumil. 1964. *Ekonomická funkce velkoobchodních cen*. Praha: Academia.

Komenda, Bohumil, and Čestmír Kožušník. 1964. "Některé základní otázky zdoko-nalení soustavy řízení socialistického národního hospodářství." *Politická ekono-mie, 12* (3): 219–72.

Korda, Benedikt. 1960. *Ekonomická statistika*. Praha: SNTL.

Korda, Benedikt et al. 1967. *Matematické metódy v ekonomii*. Praha: SNTL.

Kosta, Jiří. 1991. "O pracích českých a slovenských ekonomů v exilu." *Politická ekonomie* 39 (9–10): 825–37.

Kouba, Karel. 1966. "The Plan and Economic Growth." *Czechoslovak Economic Papers* 6: 7–21.

———. 1968b. *Plán a trh*. Praha: EÚ ČSAV.

Kouba, Karel, ed. 1965. *Politická ekonomie socialismu*. Praha: NPL.

———. 1968a. *Úvahy o socialistické ekonomice*. Praha: Svoboda.

———. 2010. "Teorie pravidel." In Mlčoch 2010, 29–36.

Kovačka, Milan. 1962. *Štatistické metódy*. Bratislava: Alfa.

Kowalik, Tadeusz. 1987. "Central Planning." In *The New Palgrave Dictionary of Economics,* edited by John Eatwell, Murray Milgate, and Peter Newman. London: Palgrave Macmillan.

Kožušník, Čestmír. 1964. *Problémy teorie hodnoty a ceny za socialismu*. Praha: Nakladatelství ČSAV.

Krejčí Jaroslav. 1977. "The Czechoslovak Economy during the Years of Systemic Transformation: 1945–1949." *Yearbook of East European Economics* 7: 297–344.

Kýn, Oldřich, and Pavel Pelikán. 1965. *Kybernetika v ekonomii*. Praha: NPL.

Kýn, Oldřich, Bohuslav Sekerka, and Lubomír Hejl. 1969. "A Model for the Planning of Prices." In *Socialism, Capitalism and Growth: Essays Presented to Maurice Dobb*, edited by C. H. Feinstein, 101–124. Cambridge: Cambridge University Press.

Lange, Oscar. 1965. *Teorie reprodukce a akumulace*. Praha: Svoboda.

Laski, Kazimierz. 1967. *Náčrt teorie socialistické reprodukce*. Praha: Svoboda.

Laščiak, Adam et al. 1985. *Dynamické*. Bratislava – Prague: Alfa, SNTL.

———. 1983. *Optimálne Programovanie*. Praha: Alfa.

Levčík, Bedřich. 1967. *Wage Policy and Wage Planning in Czechoslovakia*. Geneva: ILO.

Levčík, Friedrich. 1986. "The Czechoslovak Economy in the 1980s." In *East European Economies: Slow Growth in the 1980's. Vol. 3, Country Studies on Eastern Europe and Yugoslavia. Selected Papers submitted to the Joint Economic Committee of the Congress of the United States*, 85–108. Washington: U.S. Government Printing Office.

Levčík, Bedřich, and Jiří Kosta. 1968. "Koho reprezentuje socialistický podnik?" *Politická ekonomie* 16 (3): 239–47.

Markuš, Jozef. 1986. *Záujem o plánovanie a záujmy v plánovaní*. Bratislava: Pravda.

Matematický ústav Slovenskej akadémie vied (SAV). n. d. "Akademik Jur Hronec. Matematik." http://www.mat.savba.sk/MATEMATICI/matematici.php?cislo=82, accessed August 7, 2021.

Mises, Ludwig von. 2000. "The Equations of Mathematical Economics and the Problem of Economic Calculation in a Socialist State." *Quarterly Journal of Austrian Economics* 3 (1): 27–32.

———. 2013. *Notes and Recollections: With the Historical Setting of the Austrian School of Economics*. Indianapolis: Liberty Fund.

Mlčoch, Lubomír. 1967. "Alternativní chování podniku v decentralizovaném modelu socialism." *Politická ekonomie* 15 (11): 979–88.

———. 1990. *Chování československé podnikové sféry*. Praha: EÚ ČSAV.

———. 1992. "A Synthesis of Descriptive Analyses of a Traditional Model." *Prague Economic Papers* 4 (1): 311–32.

———. 2000. "Restructuring of Property Rights: An Institutional View." In *Economic and Social Changes in Czech Society after 1989: An Alternative View*, edited by Milan Sojka, Pavel Machonin, and Lubomir Mlčoch, 7–47. Budapest: Open Society Foundation.

Mlčoch, Lubomír. ed. 2010. *Soudobá ekonomie očima tří generací*. Praha: Karolinum.

Nachtigal, Vladimír. 1973. *Časové řady makroekonomických agregátu ČSSR za šedesátá léta a jejich metodologické problémy*. Praha: EÚ ČSAV.

Nemchinov, Vasilii et al. 1964. *Sovětští ekonomové k používaní matematiky v ekonomii*. Praha: Nakladatelství politické literatury.

Novák, Ilja, Benedikt Korda, and Jaromír Walter. 1956. *Statistické metódy*. Praha: Vysoká škola ekonomická.

Novák, Ilja, and Benedikt Korda. 1959. *Obecné metody statistiky*. Praha: Vysoká škola ekonomická.

Planometrie a optimální fungování socialistické ekonomiky. 1974. Sborník sovětských autorů. Praha: Svoboda.

Pontrjagin, L.S, V.G. Boltjanskij, R.V. Gramkrelidze, and J.F. Miščenko. 1964. *Matematická teorie optimálních procesů.* Praha: SNTL.

Problems of Economic Dynamics and Planning. *Essays in Honour of Michał Kalecki.* 1966. Oxford: Pergamon Press.

Robinsonová, Joan. 1975. *Jak porozumět ekonomické analýze.* Praha: Svoboda.

Rozsypal, Kurt. 1981. *Úvod do teorie a praxe národohospodářského plánování.* Praha: SNTL.

Rumler, Miroslav. 1965. *Keynes a soudobý kapitalismus.* Praha: NPL.

Rychetník, Luděk, and Oldřich Kýn. 1968. "Optimal Central Planning in a Competitive Solution." *Czechoslovak Economic Papers* 10: 29–44.

Rychetník, Luděk. 1968. *Úvod do matematické ekonomie.* Praha: Vysoká škola ekonomická.

Sojka, Jozef. 1970. *Ekonomická dynamika a rovnováha.* Bratislava: Epocha.

Sojka, Jozef et al. 1981. *Modelovanie národohospodárskych procesov.* Bratislava: Alfa.

Spulber, Nicolas. 1956. "Economic Thinking and Its Application and Methodology in Eastern Europe outside of Soviet Russia." *The American Economic Review* 46 (2): 367–79.

Státní plánovací komise. 1965. "Pokyny č. 55/1965 Sb." Ekonomické a právné informácie (EPI). https://www.epi.sk/zzcr/1965-55, accessed August 7, 2021.

Studihrad, Lukáš. 2018. "Vývoj výuky ekonomických oborů na ČVUT jako odraz sociálně-ekonomických změn." Master's Thesis, České vysoké učení technické v Praze, Masarykův ústav vyšších studií. Prague.

Tlustý, Zdeněk, and Vladimír Strnad. 1968. *Makroekonomické produkční funkce, technicko-organizační pokrok a substituce mezi výrobními faktory v ekonomice ČSSR.* Praha: VÚNP.

Toms, Miroslav. 1968. "Investice, inovace a Cobb-Douglasova produkční funkce." *Politická ekonomie* 16 (3): 260–75.

———. 1969. "Aplikace produkčních funkcí, ekonomícká teorie a hospodárská politika v Československu." *Politická ekonomie* 17: 131–44, 253–68, 322–36.

———. 1976. "Towards a Marxian Model of Capital Accumulation, Unemployment and Distribution." *Czechoslovak Economic Papers* 16, 3–70.

———. 1981. *Měření efektů v socialistické ekonomice.* Praha: Svoboda.

———. 1988. *Proces intenzifikace: teorie a měření.* Praha: Academia.

Toms, Miroslav, and Mojmír Hájek. 1965. *Dva modely ekonomického růstu.* Praha: EÚ ČSAV.

———. 1967. "Produkční funkce a hospodářský růst Československa v letech 1950–1964." *Politická ekonomie* 14 (1): 15–28.

Toms, Miroslav, and Michal Mejstřík. 1986. *Nerovnováha, kvalita výrobku a ceny plánované vybilancovanosti.* Praha: EÚ ČSAV.

Tříska, Dušan, and Václav Klaus. 1988. "Ekonomické centrum, přestavba a rovnováha." *Politická ekonomie* 36 (8): 817–30.

Turnovec, Frantisek. 2002. *Economics—Czech Republic*. In Kaase, Sparschuh, and Wenninger 2002, 50–64.

Unčovský, Ladislav.1985. *Operačná analýza v riadení podnikov*. Bratislava: Alfa.

Unčovský, Ladislav et al. 1991. *Modely sietovej analýzy*. Bratislava: Alfa.

Vencovský, František. 1997. *Dějiny českého ekonomického myšlení do roku 1948*. Brno: Nadace Universitas Masarykiana.

Wagener, Hans Jürgen. 1998a. "Between Conformity and Reform: Economics under State Socialism and Its Transformation." In Wagener 1998b, 1–32.

Wagener, Hans Jürgen, ed. 1998b. *Economic Thought in Communist and Post-Communist Europe*, Routledge.

Walter, Jaromír. 1981. "Počátky ekonomického modelováni v oblasti aplikované matematiky v letech 1930–1950." ČSVTS—ŠBČS, *Ekonomické modelování*, Sborník referátu, no. 1. Praha.

Walter, Jaromír, and Josef Lauber. 1975. *Simulační modely ekonomických procesů*. Praha: Alfa, SNTL.

Závodský, Prokop. 2013a. "60 let statistiky na Vysoké škole ekonomické v Praze." *Politická ekonomie* 61 (4): 515–35.

———. 2013b. "60th Anniversary of Statistics at the University of Economics in Prague." *Statistika* 93 (4): 87–96.

Zimmermann, Karel. 1999. "Celebrating Eighty Years of Professor Nožička." *Mathematica Bohemica*: 125 (1): 103–107.

Chapter 4

Theory and Political Economy of Central Planning in East Germany

Hans-Jürgen Wagener,
Udo Ludwig, and Knut Richter

This chapter focuses on central planning in East Germany.[1] Being—next to state and collective ownership—one of the two cornerstones supporting a socialist economic system as seen by East German Marxist-Leninist ideology, central planning as such never was questioned by the economics profession. The market as an alternative coordination mechanism hardly got any attention. What could be discussed theoretically and experimented with in practice were the scope, methods, and instruments of central planning.

Comprehensive surveys of the state of the art of East German economics of planning are scarce. In the German Democratic Republic (GDR), two textbooks are worth mentioning, one from 1957 (Rudolph and Friedrich 1957) and one from 1975 (Kinze, Knop, and Seifert 1975). In the West, socialist central planning attracted much attention, starting in Vienna with the Socialist Calculation Debate and ending with discussions of optimal planning models (see, for instance, Turner and Collis 1977). While, apart from the Soviets, Czechoslovak, Hungarian, and Polish economists are quoted widely, East German contributions never show up in this literature. This is not only due to the fact that they did not publish in English. After the collapse of the socialist economic system, we have the brilliant overview of Kornai (1992). His 45-page bibliography contains only one East German author: Bertolt Brecht.

Whether this neglect is fair is not the primary research objective of this chapter. Rather we will try to identify the main features of East German planning discourse and put them in their historical and political context. The chapter is divided in seven parts. To begin, there is a prolific tradition of debate on planning in the pre-communist period. Then, as said, the political economy of socialism considers central planning as one of its supporting pillars. In the 1960s, a cybernetic and mathematical revolution swept through from the Soviet Union. East German economic policy, however, was unimpressed and stuck to traditional approaches that are presented in section four. Over the course of time, they were complemented by forecasting and econometrics. The necessary statistical basis was provided by national accounting and input-output analysis. The chapter concludes with a brief summary.

PRE-COMMUNIST APPROACHES TO PLANNING

Karl Marx (in *Capital* I and III) and Friedrich Engels (in *Anti-Dühring*) have a simple vision of socialist economy. What Robinson Crusoe or the patron of the self-sufficient family farm did individually, socialist society will do collectively: to allocate its productive resources, above all labor time, directly to alternative uses taking account of the needs and wants of society. All the paraphernalia of capitalist society like markets, commodities, value, money, exploitation, and fetishism can be dismissed. It was the challenge for communists, socialists, and social democrats to show that this vision is practically feasible. Starting with Heinrich Gossen in 1854, renowned economists like Eugen Böhm-Bawerk, Friedrich Wieser, and Gustav Cassel were convinced of the contrary, paying special attention to the question of calculating optimal allocation plans or to the role of money and prices in a complex economic system (Chaloupek 2007).

Such doubts hardly could be removed by Karl Kautsky's (1902) rather naïve description of what should be done on the morrow of the revolution. It was the First World War which opened a new round of discussion, first by putting the economic war efforts under central control and secondly by awakening the expectation of imminent socialization after the war. Central planning not only had been proven possible in the eyes of many economists of the time but also promised a more rational governance of the economy than the blind play of market forces (Rathenau 1918; Neurath 1919). There was a lively discussion among socialists about the implementation of a socialist system, and also the liberal reaction did not take long to come. The extreme positions may be seen in Otto Neurath and Ludwig Mises whose ultra-liberal stance gave rise to neo-Austrian theory. In parallel with Mises ([1920] 1935), Max Weber ([1921] 2014, 71–81) compared calculation in kind and in money in *Wirtschaft und Gesellschaft*. What, in Weber's eyes, is crucial for economic rationality are effective prices. As to Neurath's ideal of the war economy, he remarks that it is predominantly a bankruptcy economy (*Bankerotteurswirtschaft*) (75). Its paramount objective reduces its governing principles to purely short-term technical considerations which can be performed in kind while long-term economic considerations, that is, the competition of aims and not of means for a single aim, remain rather primitive. The fault lines of the debate were the following:

- *Social technology and the new man or human nature and spontaneous development.* For Neurath (1925), as well as for Lenin, governance of the economic system was a problem of rational social technology. Liberals like Mises and later Friedrich Hayek thought in the tradition of Carl Menger in terms of a complex, spontaneously emerging order which largely precluded deliberate constructivist intervention.

- *Partial or full socialization which in terms of the post-1989 discussion can be interpreted as gradualism vs. shock therapy.* Kautsky (1922) was a fervent advocate of the former which had already earned him Lenin's scorn and the label "the renegade Kautsky." Neurath defended full socialization, by which he meant immediate transition to a centrally planned system but not necessarily comprehensive nationalization, which put him under pressure to show the workability of the new system.

- *Collectivism or syndicalism (or guild socialism).* For Marxists, but also for Mises, a socialist system was characterized by social ownership of the means of production and by central planning or collectivism. Karl Polanyi ([1922] 2005) ventured the idea of what he called "functional socialism." His corporatist construction received some critical reactions but then fell into oblivion as a participant of the socialization and calculation debate. Rathenau's approach was somewhat similar in terms of organization, although not socialist as it maintained private property, submitting it to a central planning authority.

- *Thus, the controversy was focused on the market and/or the plan.* Famously, Mises held that central planning is unable to generate prices mirroring supply and demand and, hence, to allocate productive resources rationally. This theorem already had been disproved by Vilfredo Pareto ([1906] 1966, 364) and Enrico Barone ([1908] 1935) who were little or unknown in postwar Vienna. If not theoretically impossible, Mises's argument may be interpreted as claiming practical impossibility.

- *A single measurement unit or multiple incommensurate units.* Liberals defended traditional accounting in monetary units. Marxists wanted a system free of value and money yet thought the necessary cost accounting should be done in labor values while the use value of goods can remain incommensurate. Neurath (1925) thought a one-dimensional monetary index is inadequate to represent the many dimensions of well-being and, therefore, profits are unsuitable optimization criterion. He went back to Robinson, stating that he needs no money and has only an ordinal preference scale with which to allocate his resources. The collective will need a preference scale, too. In case of conflicting individual preferences, the collective has to cut the knot and make a decision. This is quite a remarkable early contribution to social choice theory and to the theory of well-being (Lessmann 2007).

- *The question of the measurement unit leads to the dichotomy of money economy and in-kind economy* (*Naturalwirtschaft* as Neurath called it). If money valuation (or any other single unit valuation) is unacceptable, in-kind calculation becomes necessary. Naturally, this raised Mises's stern opposition, and Neurath did not succeed in definitely proving his case. He adduces convincing examples where monetary calculation obviously fails but is unable to show the reverse: that in-kind calculation generally is possible (Uebel 2007). At the time, Jakob Marschak (1924), who later aptly analyzed centralization and decentralization in economic organizations, was convinced that the problem could be solved. With linear programming of optimal plans it disappeared, in fact, since quantities and prices are two sides of the same coin.

- *Centralization and decentralization of information.* Neurath recognized the importance of statistics for central planning and implicitly was convinced that the necessary information could be obtained. Mises, and above all Hayek (1935), disagreed, not only because of the size of the task but also because a lot of relevant information is local and even tacit.

- *Consumer sovereignty, free consumption choice, and rationing.* Central planning and production organization in a huge single factory, as Neurath, and also Lenin proposed, is hardly conducive to consumer sovereignty, in which Neurath did not truly believe for the capitalist system. This was a point of critique of Kautsky (1922; see also Chaloupek 2007) who even ventured to demand freedom for producers but who also remained vague, since this looked hardly in agreement with socialist central planning. A huge single cooperative had earlier been Kautsky's (1892) vision for socialist production in a market economy with private ownership of the means of production (cf. his comments on the Erfurt Program of the Social Democratic Party of Germany). At the same time, everybody participates decentrally in the computation of value "in a double way: on the one hand, as a consumer and on the other, as a producer" (Mises [1920] 1935, 107). This is not how a capitalist system is functioning, Polanyi ([1922] 2005; [1925] 1979) objected. He asserted that such harmony of interests was possible only in his functional socialism in which individuals were simultaneously corporate members of producer and consumer organizations, thus having a democratic say in central planning.

The second, less theoretical experience with economic planning, the Nazi war economy, was studied critically in East Germany (Eichholtz [1969–1996] 2003) without due attention to planning methods and their economic, political, and social implications. This was provided in a thorough analysis by the head of the Freiburg School of German neoliberalism, Walter Eucken (1948), leading to a genuine theory of the centrally administered economy as he called it. Contrary to most economists, like Enrico Barone, Oskar Lange, and, later, Jan Tinbergen, he stated an essential difference between the centrally planned economy and the competitive market economy. In his view, they cannot be analyzed by the same theory but need self-contained approaches. The basic economic problem, scarcity, differs and most economic concepts assume a different meaning. Mixing the coordination mechanisms is impossible: "To believe in the possibility of grafting prices on to the mechanism of control in a centrally administered economy is to believe in a squaring of the circle" (Eucken 1948, 190). This dichotomous view of economic systems corresponds with Marxist-Leninist political economy. Of course, neoliberals have an absolute preference for market coordination, while Marxist-Leninists favor central planning.

Two developments of the 1930s are to be mentioned which might have improved planning practice. As Neurath had stressed, statistics are crucial for the success of the exercise, which was corroborated by the German experience: "This primary importance of statistics is a characteristic of the centrally administered economy" (Eucken 1948, 82). So statistics showed a remarkable progress in the interwar period in Germany (Tooze 2001). It may be assumed that this development was not lost on the GDR: two eminent East German scholars, Fritz Behrens and Felix Burkhardt, were statisticians trained in the 1930s. Secondly, in the 1930s, macroeconomics was developing, partly under the influence of Keynes (see, e.g., Grünig 1933; Föhl [1937] 1955). It introduced national accounting and opened an entire new field for state influence and planning. Parallel developments in the Soviet Union (see, e.g., Goskomstat [1926] 1993; Feldman [1929] 1969) should not be overlooked.

The early discourse on socialism and economic calculation could have been the starting point for economic theorizing in a socialist society. As a matter of fact, GDR political economy eagerly avoided any ties with non-Soviet-based debates. The leading East German textbook on the history

of political economy at least briefly mentions the bourgeois economic calculation debate triggered by Mises, not by Neurath, which, however "took place
independent of and unconnected with the Soviet discussion" (Meissner 1978,
437). The name of Lange remains unmentioned. Accordingly, the history of
political economy of socialism happened in the Soviet Union and nowhere
else. Taking notice of the Socialist Calculation Debate undoubtedly might
have benefited economic thinking on planning. A high-level East German
planning official remarked *post festum:*

> a bizarre problem which so far has found little attention in the literature on really
> existing socialism: Since there is no real comprehensive market with supply
> and demand in a centrally administered economy, value categories could not
> develop on an objective basis. How should their objective content be determined
> under such conditions? When calculating prices, for instance, one was reduced
> to taking the development on the capitalist world market as starting point.
> (Wenzel 1998, 43)

Mises could not have formulated it more succinctly.

CENTRAL PLANNING AS CORE ELEMENT OF
THE POLITICAL ECONOMY OF SOCIALISM

In the early postwar years, East and West applied state economic planning to
cope with the gigantic task of rebuilding a destroyed Germany and its economic fundament. This was not a question of principle but could be seen as
transitory political necessity. When it became clear that East Germany would
stay under Soviet influence and eventually become a socialist satellite state,
there was little choice as to the concrete implementation of the economic and
political system. "There is only one socialist planned economy as it is realized up to now only in the Soviet Union," wrote Willi Stoph (1948, 1139),
one of the highest-ranking GDR officials, in 1948. This sentence could serve
as a motto for the East German planned economy over the whole period
of its existence. Soviet planning practice, however, was not yet backed by
an elaborate political economy of socialism and planning theory. The East
German debate of the second half of the 1940s grappled with the problem
of economic planning under capitalism and socialism, the Marxists trying
to establish "real" planning possible only in a socialist system. Other views,
suggested even by a renowned Soviet economist like Evgeni Varga, were
attacked fiercely (Becker and Dierking 1989, 148–78; Krause 1998, 44–59).

  Most academic economists left the country by the end of the 1940s.
Soviet advisors and returning émigrés from the Soviet Union imparted their

knowledge about Soviet practice. The first Marxist economist appointed as a chair of Berlin University was Jürgen Kuczynski, who had just returned from the United States and who certainly was not a specialist in planning theory. When textbooks on the political economy of socialism became available, the GDR adopted the famous Stalinist text (Akademie [1954] 1955). During the reform period an East German textbook was commissioned but could not be published before 1969 when the reform was already over. Its use was discontinued in 1971, and it was replaced again by a Soviet textbook (*Lehrbuch Politische Ökonomie* [1970] 1972).

Marxist-Leninist political economy cannot be understood as economics proper. It is rather a social-historical science establishing the economic order of different historical modes of production and their laws of motion. As such, it provides the general framework of a socialist planned economy whose concrete working must be treated in a specialized theory of planning. Up to the writing of the first textbook (Akademie [1954] 1955) and Stalin's (1952) accompanying remarks, it was generally thought that the dictatorship of the proletariat was the basic law of motion of socialism and that economic laws are created deliberately by the proletariat, i.e., the party (Kohlmey 1967; Wittenburg 1979, 36). This conviction prevailed also in East Germany: "The plan is the basic economic law of socialism," Fritz Behrens wrote in 1949 (quoted in Becker and Dierking 1989, 321).

Stalin (1952) criticized this view as voluntarist and described economic laws of socialism as objective laws independent of human will. In contrast to capitalism, the economic laws of which operate behind the backs of individuals, the socialist planner has to apply these laws like an engineer applying the laws of mechanics. As formulated by Stalin and the textbooks, however, these laws appear as norms in need of specification to become operational. Marx ([1857] 1993, 173) had framed the often quoted first economic law: "Economy of time, to this all economy ultimately reduces itself. . . . Thus, economy of time, along with the planned distribution of labor time among the various branches of production, remains the first economic law on the basis of communal production." In the third volume of *Capital* he specified: "It is only where production is under the actual, predetermining control of society that the latter establishes a relation between the volume of social labor time applied in producing definite articles, and the volume of the social want to be satisfied by these articles" (Marx [1894] 1959, 138). Neoclassical microeconomics would appear to follow a similar allocation rule, if social want is interpreted as aggregate of individual demand. This need not be the case under socialism.

Stalin (1952, 45–46) highlighted two laws: the basic economic law of socialism and the law of the planned proportionate development of the national economy. Postulating the efficient use of resources by conscious planning, the second extends Marx's economy of time. The first substitutes profit maximization as an optimization rule requiring: "the securing of the maximum satisfaction of the constantly rising material and cultural requirements of the whole of society through the continuous expansion and perfection of socialist production on the basis of higher techniques." The school of mathematical economics also placed optimality and efficiency at the center of economic "laws" of socialism. The basic economic law defines in general terms the optimization rule of planning, planned proportional development, and the efficiency of economic activity. The law of value as a third component is the basis for material stimulation of production (Dadajan 1973, 18–27).

The conundrum of the law of value haunted socialist political economy and economic policy for years. We need not go into the details about the debate and may content ourselves with the statement that it boils down to a welfare equilibrium rule: "Generally speaking, the operation of the law of value leads to a division of social labor between its various applications, in which the relation of its effects to (socially indispensable) outlays of labor is the same for all of these applications" (Brus and Łaski 1964, 47).

The Soviet mathematical economist Viktor Novozhilov made clear that optimal planning neither contradicts nor restricts the operation of the law of value, as many political economists had assumed: "Full application of the law of value as objectively necessary . . . law presupposes the optimal organization of the socialist economy securing not only that optimal plans are formulated, but also that they are implemented. This fact corresponds to the duality theorem of linear optimization. It proves that optimal prices are the other side of the optimal plan" (Novoshilow [1967] 1970, 271).

Any economic planning has three criteria to fulfill: consistency, feasibility, and optimality. Specification of the basic economic law of socialism is by no means trivial, since it requires an optimal relation between consumption and investment or the choice of an optimal time horizon. In practice, such decisions were taken on political considerations more or less *ad hoc* by the party leadership. For the actual planning process the law of balanced, proportional development was the principal challenge. It should guarantee consistency and feasibility not only on paper but also in reality. Obviously, the list of proportions which have to be observed is endless not only on the micro-level of goods and services but also on the macro-level of monetary and financial aggregates. It is the crucial contention of Marxist-Leninists that central planners can do better in these fields than the spontaneous working of the market.

One rather controversial economic law of socialism maintains the faster growth of department I (production of means of production) compared to department II (production of means of consumption). As a general economic law it does not make much sense. As a policy guideline for industrialization in the Soviet post-revolutionary era this was quite logical.

While the theoretical argument for faster growth of department I originating from Lenin went unquestioned in the political economy of socialism, the policy argument for unbalanced growth, which could be derived from it and which was propounded by Evgeni Preobrazhensky ([1926] 1965), was heavily criticized still in the 1970s as a Trotskyite fiction (Schirokorad [1972] 1975). In the Soviet industrialization debate (Erlich 1960), Preobrazhensky had contrasted the law of value, that is, equal exchange, and the law of primitive socialist accumulation, that is, unequal exchange, with only the latter guaranteeing rapid development. In short, the peasantry had to pay one way or the other for industrialization. Preobrazhensky did not realize "that the problem had to be solved without hurting the interests of the broad masses of the working peasants on the basis of fortifying the alliance between the working class and the peasantry, since only such an alliance guarantees the stability of the dictatorship of the proletariat" (Schirokorad [1972] 1975, 164). This criticism, based on Bukharin's position in the debate (Bukharin, however, remained unmentioned because his name still fell under *damnatio memoriae*), must be seen in the context of the policy switch of 1971 in the Soviet Union and immediately afterwards in the GDR. When forced industrialization which Stalin had borrowed from Preobrazhensky was substituted for a more consumer-oriented approach corresponding to Bukharin's ideas.

In the postwar era, not only did the ever-shrinking peasantry pay for financing investment but also the worker and consumer in general. Increased work intensity and belt tightening were meant to create the material-technical basis for socialism. This was not received with universal enthusiasm and led to workers' protests and even uprisings (e.g., in the GDR in 1953). Temporary "new courses" had to calm the situation. But it was only in 1971 that the Soviet Union and in its wake the new Honecker leadership changed the general party line from creating the material-technical basis for socialism to "unity of economic and social policy." Similar developments could be seen in Gierek's Poland and in Hungarian "goulash communism." They did not lead, however, to balanced growth and equilibrium prices according to the law of value but to severe cuts in productive investment and an ever-increasing gap between fixed consumer prices and cost of production which had to be bridged by ever-increasing subsidies from the state budget.

A REVOLUTION THAT WASN'T

The Second World War initiated a far-reaching scientific revolution which deeply influenced the discipline of economics. Highly complex military-technical projects like automatic anti-aircraft systems, nuclear bombs, or cosmonautics could only be implemented with the help of new (overlapping) theoretical instruments firmly grounded in mathematics, to name just a few: linear programming, operations research, activity analysis, information theory, algorithm theory, control theory, search theory, computer science, theory of automata, artificial intelligence, game theory, and input-output analysis. These new instruments which branched into new scientific disciplines were concentrated and lavishly financed, as could be expected, in the two leading military powers—the United States and the Soviet Union. Anecdotal proof is the 1973 Nobel Prize for the Russian-born American economist Wassily Leontief and the joint 1975 Nobel Prize for Leonid Kantorovich and Tjalling Koopmans. The development of micro-electronics and informatics, which is still ongoing, is part of the story. The GDR failed to take part in this development in time and later paid a high price for catching-up.

The scientific revolution of the mid-twentieth century was oriented mainly toward organization, communication, and control of technical-economic processes. It has prompted two efforts to formulate an interdisciplinary meta-theory. For soon it became apparent that such theories were also applicable to many real-world phenomena outside the technical and economic sphere. Those two efforts complemented one another: cybernetics inaugurated by the mathematician Norbert Wiener and general systems theory proposed by the biologist Ludwig von Bertalanffy. They defined mechanical and economic as well as organic processes as systems to be organized and controlled according to similar principles which could be modeled mathematically. The central element of all these systems is information. "A core cybernetic insight was that any goal-directed system could be described alike, man or machine. Automation and intelligence were intersubstitutable" (Leeds 2016, 651). This is not the place to present a survey. Suffice it to say that the ideas of automatic control via feedback mechanisms and of self-organization were of particular interest for elites eager to plan and control social and economic processes. They must have been fascinated by the prospects of a rational scientific solution to their planning problems.

While the military-technical relevance of the new disciplines was immediately clear in the Soviet Union, the recognition of their socioeconomic importance, in particular of cybernetic and systems theories, took some time. There are good reasons for that. Mathematicians and mathematical economists are a different breed of people, with different scientific attitudes than Marxist-Leninist political economists, let alone party functionaries. A transition from the latter to the former would imply a veritable change of academic elites to which there must have been some resistance. The idea of automatic control and self-organization smelled of an attack on the political power of the party. To get their ideas accepted and implemented, the cyborg intelligentsia had to navigate carefully in the shallows of Marxist-Leninist ideology, even if their approaches did not really differ.

The first Soviet, and in its wake East German, reaction to cybernetics was dismissive: a bourgeois pseudo-science. But very soon the mathematicians made clear its potential. When Vasilii Nemchinov organized a high-level conference in Moscow in 1960 on mathematical methods in economics with the most brilliant mathematicians present, the proceedings of which were published in seven volumes, it was obvious to everybody that the event and its intentions had full political backing (Leeds 2016).

In East Germany nothing could happen without Soviet ideology and practice. It does not mean that cybernetics and the development of mathematical economics in East Germany was on par with Soviet developments. Far from that, for the conditions were totally different. There were neither huge military-technical projects triggering new scientific disciplines nor dozens of brilliant mathematicians pushing such new developments nor a generation of elder mathematical economists and their younger students. So it is little wonder that the history of cybernetics in the GDR is a totally different story told by Jérôme Segal (2001) and the volume of Frank Dittmann and Rudolf Seising (2007).

Cybernetics in the GDR was first of all a philosophical topic. This was due to the central role played by Georg Klaus.[2] He was fascinated by cybernetics, systems theory, and game theory early on: "The new science of cybernetics with all its social, scientific, and ideological ramifications is next to the scientific and technical handling of nuclear energy and starting cosmonautics the most important scientific event of our time. . . . Concerning its revolutionary effect, it can be seen in parallel to the discoveries of Copernicus, Darwin, and Marx" (Klaus 1961, 5).

As a philosopher, Klaus, of course, did not develop specified models and applications. But he invested great efforts in propagating the new disciplines and defending them against orthodox critics of whom there were quite a few. Knowing perfectly well and having experienced in practice the sensitive spots of orthodoxy, he was particularly eager to show that there are no contradictions between Marxism-Leninism and cybernetics and systems theory. What he attacked were scientifically unfounded ideological propositions in social sciences which led to irrational policies. To control social systems effectively one needs sound concepts and theories of economics and sociology. Only with new insights in the functioning of such systems can we construct better control schemes on the basis of cybernetics (Liebscher 2005). Like Nikita Khrushchev in the Soviet Union, Walter Ulbricht laid great hopes in such new insights and developments and said so at party gatherings. During the 1960s, cybernetics and systems theory enjoyed political backing from the highest level. Yet in the end, Klaus's efforts seem to have been in vain. Dialectical materialism felt threatened by cybernetics, as did official political economists and the orthodox party top leadership of the 1970s. They succeeded in fending off a cybernetic revolution.

Nevertheless, the short reform period of the 1960s saw an enhanced interest in exact theorizing. In the early 1960s young East German students were sent to the USSR to acquaint themselves with the new knowledge and skills. Economy and society breathed fresh air and, after endless ideological debates, business economists, mathematicians, and engineers expected to be able to make substantial contributions to economic science and efficiency. New institutes, working groups, and university chairs mushroomed everywhere.

One of the outstanding events, inaugurated in Berlin in 1964, was an international conference on mathematics and cybernetics in economics (*Mathematik und Kybernetik* 1965). It took place nine times till 1989 over varying intervals and brought together hundreds of specialists from all over the country as well as the Soviet Union, Eastern Europe, and Western countries. The venues outside of Berlin are indicative of the important role of provincial universities in developing mathematical methods and quantitative approaches in general: Dresden, Freiberg, Halle, Leipzig, Magdeburg, Merseburg, and Rostock.

Expectations had been great and rightly so. The first conference was attended, among others, by Vasilii Nemchinov and János Kornai and showed the great potential of mathematical planning techniques. But cybernetics also could be interpreted differently, and Gunther Kohlmey (1965),[3] himself neither a mathematician nor a cybernetician, used the opening of the conference to highlight the idea of a more or less self-regulating system steered by only a few control parameters fixed by the central planner. This implied a fully monetized economy, self-reliable firms, profit as the only performance indicator, and the market: "Without it the system is obviously not functioning" (7). Apparently, he interpreted the ideas of the 1963 reform (*Neues Ökonomisches System, NÖS*) as a blueprint of "socialist market economy" (which it was not), and cybernetics as its scientific foundation. Up to now, he wrote, socialism has been built "without the modern technical and scientific requisites of planning" (9)—a historical instance of the contradiction between productive forces and production relations. Approvingly, Kohlmey quotes "good old Bentham," having said that it is the task of science alone to show what people should do and how they should behave rationally. The challenge of the primacy of politics certainly was not appreciated in party circles.

Once more in 1968, Kohlmey (1968) combined the cybernetic approach with his favorite reform idea of a monetary socialist market economy. He interpreted a socialist planned economy as a dynamic, complex, goal-oriented system of governance and control consisting of interlocking hierarchical partial systems from the center to the firms. Such had been the description of the planned system by Nemchinov (1965, 23): "Social production can only be directed consciously on the basis of a completely defined system of macro-economic and micro-economic models." Nemchinov favored centralized planning and was interested in the behavior of the system. Kohlmey, in fact, favored markets and parametric planning and was more interested in the behavior of people.

In the planning mechanism, he claimed, governance should dominate over control: "A planned economy is a monetary economy. It is steered by monetary categories as reference values of the planning center and target values of the firm" (Kohlmey 1968, 119). Thus, he combined central and decentral elements in the planning process. Only then "the unity of planned economy and democracy becomes effective" (120). He distanced his view from the optimal planning approach of Johannes Rudolph (1962b; 1965). Evidently, the cybernetic paradigm could support quite different views of the economic system. The concept of planning the economic activity by rules and regulating mechanisms earned Kohlmey, again, the charge of revisionism and attack on democratic centralism, that is, on the power of the political leadership (Caldwell 2003, 173–80).

Mathematics did not revolutionize theoretical thinking in East German economics or the planning process. It was instrumentally oriented to concrete practical applications mostly in the field of business economics. This has been underlined by a book by Leonid Kantorovich and his colleagues at Halle University (Kantorovič 1985), where an operations research laboratory bearing his name designed respective programs. Werner Lassmann (1985) gave an overview of East German developments in this field.

Marxist-Leninist Organization science (MLO) was inaugurated in 1967 which was meant to incorporate systems theoretic and cybernetic thinking. In 1969 the Academy for MLO opened, only to be closed shortly thereafter. In 1968 a department of "Economic Cybernetics and Operations Research" was set up at Humboldt University, which by 1970 was renamed "Theory and Organization of Science" and reoriented accordingly (Fuchs-Kittowski 2007, 326). This signaled the end of the reform period and the end of cybernetic dreams. But it does not mean that cybernetics disappeared completely from the scene. Students of economics were taught a basic course of some 30 hours on "Cybernetics for Economists" (Schultze 2007). Still in 1990 a new textbook (Känel, Lauenroth, and Müller 1990) appeared, replacing an older one from 1971 (Känel 1971).

Back in 1967, a new textbook *Politische Ökonomie des Sozialismus und ihre Anwendung in der DDR* (Political economy of socialism and its application in the GDR) had been called for by the party. The team of authors was headed by Politburo member Günter Mittag. The draft had been discussed with First Secretary Walter Ulbricht, who contributed an extended preface, and with several of his Politburo colleagues (*Politische Ökonomie* 1969, 20). What could be more authoritative? The print run was said to have been almost one million (Nick 2011, 26)—for a population of some 17 million. The book was meant to represent the thinking of the economic reform initiated in 1963. When it came off the press in 1969, the reform was practically dead and Ulbricht's era almost at an end. With him the book disappeared from the shelves only two years after publication: "It also was forbidden to quote the book; it simply did not exist" (Krömke in Pirker 1995, 42).

It must have dawned on insiders that a change of ideological attitude was under way. Under socialist conditions this always meant a change of policy, in the actual case from Ulbricht to Honecker. The change expressed itself in a subtle linguistic switch: "the developed societal system of socialism" (*das entwickelte gesellschaftliche System des Sozialismus*), Ulbricht's political target of the 1960s, was substituted for "the developed socialist society" (*die entwickelte sozialistische Gesellschaft*) as the new catchword with no allusion to systems theory (Dittmann 2007, 33). Party chief ideologue Kurt Hager made clear the importance of the turn in an article in 1971 (quoted in Liebscher 2005, 169): "As important as cybernetics and systems theory are and shall remain, we naturally cannot allow that they assume the place of dialectical and historical materialism, political economy of socialism, scientific communism or socialist management science, that they get all-dominant and that the language of a special science becomes the political language of the party. The party thus would stop to be a Marxist-Leninist party."

The fate of cybernetics and systems theory in East Germany moved together with the changing political significance of reform thinking. Of course, mathematical methods always had been used in economics, in particular in statistics, financial and actuarial economics, and in simple calculations of production planning, which presuppose a systemic demarcation. Even after the discontinuation of the mathematical revolution in central planning, the development of mathematical methods, economic informatics, and operations research had a productive afterlife in the Soviet Union and the GDR: industrial ministries did set up the needed information systems within their own domain. "This resulted, quite naturally, in a transformation of the tool itself—from a vehicle of reform into a pillar of the status quo" (Gerovitch 2008, 347). The cybernetic revolution failed in the context of reform, but contributed to the better working of the traditional system.

To summarize, expectations undoubtedly had been too high or too myopic in both East and West. In Western Europe systems analysis and cybernetics did not really leave the academic sphere, with few exceptions like the 1972 and 1974 reports of the Club of Rome on limits to growth. In the East ideological reservations were preponderant, as shown. But it was a sequence of serious difficulties with the implementation of automated planning systems for the economy as a whole that led politics to abandon such projects in the early 1970s. Honecker declared at the eighth party congress in 1971: "By now it has finally been proven that cybernetics and systems research are pseudo sciences" (quoted in Segal 2001, 64). Such had been the official attitude some twenty years earlier.

THE ECONOMICS OF CENTRAL PLANNING

Central planning follows from centralized state ownership of the means of production and the dictatorship of the proletariat or the leading role of the Communist Party, in East Germany the *Sozialistische Einheitspartei Deutschlands* (Socialist Unity Party of Germany). Under socialism the economy is not a self-referential social system but obeys the principle of unity of polity and economy subject to the primacy of politics and democratic centralism (Kinze, Knop, and Seifert 1975, 29–37). This leads to a strict hierarchical system of decision-making and administration.

Within this systemic framework, planning becomes a technical task. As such it is treated in the two dominant textbooks published in 1957 (Rudolph and Friedrich 1957) and in 1975 (Kinze, Knop, and Seifert 1975). The latter was preceded by a shorter text (*Volkswirtschaftsplanung* 1974), the first edition of which had appeared in 1971, the year of the leadership and policy switch from Ulbricht to Honecker. This is fully reflected only in the final version of the textbook. Allusions to reform ideas such as decentralization, parametric planning, or market elements are avoided. What is presented is strict, hierarchical central planning using a system of balances with a rather brief mention of optimal planning.

It is remarkable that both books were written by the same team of authors from the High School for Economics (*Hochschule für Ökonomie*), even if in the latter case the team was somewhat larger. A similar team was also responsible for the definitive textbook on the socialist economy of the GDR (Kinze, Knop, and Seifert 1989). It testifies even more to the orthodox turn in economic thinking during the Honecker period. In the very year of the collapse of the system, there is no mention of reform needs or reform attempts, since there were not any. The socialist economy is represented as a complex administrative system. The list of literature at the end contains 88 scientific references, of which 20 pertain to Marx, Engels, and Lenin, as well as 108 references to legal documents and official pronouncements.

Material balances coordinating input and output of producing firms are the orthodox instrument of directive central planning. In fact, they make up only a tiny part of the total central plan which controls not only the productive sphere but all other sectors of economic, social, and cultural life, including science, and which, next to material input and output, uses a wide range of key indicators, ratios, coefficients, and norms to stimulate and control social development.

Balances are instruments to identify and control the material, financial, and personal proportions of production, circulation, and distribution of resources. As such, they are meant to guarantee the realization of the socialist economic law of planned proportional development. According to the traditional approach, single-item balances are drawn that confront the generation and utilization of material, equipment, and consumption goods (*Material-, Ausrüstungs-und Konsumgüterbilanzen, MAK-Bilanzen*). They can be addressed to individual production units and thus be controlled. They have a quantitative material, financial, territorial, and time dimension.

Given the huge amount of individual goods in any modern economy, material balances cover only the most important products at the central level. In the mid-1970s, the State Plan Commission was responsible for about 300 key items. The ministries added some 500 central balances. Together they covered more than 60 percent of manufacturing, albeit mostly in a highly aggregated form. This did not change much over time (Kinze, Knop, and Seifert 1975, 163; Rudolph and Friedrich 1957, 157). A so-called balance pyramid disaggregated the coverage to the levels of regions, combines (*Kombinate*), and firms, so that several thousand products were included in the balancing process in the end.

The most interesting theoretical question remains whether the method of material balances passes the test of consistency, feasibility, and optimality of planning. It is remarkable that the textbooks do not approach this question. It was treated by Western scholars in the 1950s (Hensel 1954; Montias 1959) who were optimistic about consistency and feasibility, while optimality was hardly conceivable in the case of purely in-kind balances. Marginal cost calculation hinges upon prices, the rational calculation of which had already been seriously questioned during the Socialist Calculation Debate and later by Eucken (1948) on the basis of the Nazi experience.

Compared with the 1957 textbook by Rudolph and Friedrich, the mathematical revolution of the 1960s clearly left its mark. The traditional system of single-item balances was complemented by so-called balance models, i.e., models of interconnectedness (*Verflechtungsbilanzen*), input-output and national accounting models, which guarantee consistency and allow for dynamics and tentative optimization. The shorter text (*Volkswirtschaftsplanung* 1974) gives much more room to these models than the final textbook, which may be due to still latent reform hopes, for input-output models imply a different form of planning than the traditional system of balances. "Application of the balance of interconnectedness as active instrument of planning presupposes an unambiguous definition of its function and its status in the process of planning. Presently, this is not perfectly clear" (130). For his directives addressed to firms, the planner needs a traditional system of single product balances which should be consistent with the interindustry balance. In addition, information problems are mentioned: data necessary for the first and second quadrant of an input-output table are hard to obtain, information on the third (value-added) quadrant is unavailable. It would have required a realistic price system (Kinze, Knop, and Seifert 1975, 184).

There is a marked difference between the preparatory volume (*Volkswirtschaftsplanung* 1974) and the final text (Kinze, Knop, and Seifert 1975) regarding the treatment of the optimization problem, which evidently was not mentioned in the pre-1960 textbook (Rudolph and Friedrich 1957). While the 1975 textbook devotes seven very general pages to this topic, the preparatory volume has a chapter of 85 pages focused on it. It is mainly based on the well-known contributions of Soviet scholars, many of whom had been translated into German, and on János Kornai's (1967; 1968) monograph and article in *Wirtschaftswissenschaft*. The Polish parallel to the preparatory volume's take on optimal planning (Porwit 1970) finds only a brief mention in the final textbook.

While a market economy has no explicit objective function—its welfare maximizing property being only a theoretical inference from competition and individual utility or profit maximization—the planned economy must formulate its overall objectives and, at least notionally, an optimization criterion. Collectivism follows its own rules. Methodological individualism, utility, and market behavior did not show up in the socialist textbooks of political economy. The final demand vector in input-output models was politically given. Highly interesting Soviet attempts—mainly at the Novosibirsk institute—to base the objective function of dynamic input-output models upon the analysis of consumption and utility had been translated into German (Waltuch 1972). This strand of research was taken up by the East German Academy Institute of Economics (Anders and Schwarz 1974) where Kohlmey (1966) already had advocated the explicit formulation of objective functions for optimal socialist planning. The Institute developed its own approach to estimating an objective function (Anders, Schwarz, and Klein 1976). It resulted in a utility function based on consumption, which was used in optimizing the relationship between consumption and investment. The model was tested using data from private household budgets and plausible assumptions on the time discount rate. These efforts did not go beyond the experimental stage.

The basic economic law of socialism defines the general objective with two shortcomings. It has, first, to be specified "in detailed, ideally quantitatively determined, practically manageable and controllable partial aims, which are aligned on the addressees" (*Volkswirtschaftsplanung* 1974, 257).

As with individual utility maximization, the collective planner has to form a preference ordering among these possibly conflicting partial aims. It is difficult, if not impossible (262), to aggregate them quantitatively in a comprehensive objective function for maximization as Neurath already had remarked. Second, the law does not operate automatically behind the backs of individuals. Despite its alleged objective character, it needs a political economy of specification and implementation which, in theory, results from democratic centralism and, in practice, is the privilege of party elites.

As to the optimization criterion, numerous variants are conceivable. Within optimization models the duality principle allows, in general, for two formulations: maximal output or minimal cost. Output maximization, either maximization of national income or maximization of consumption, plays a prominent role in general models (Kinze, Knop, and Seifert 1975, 205). Intuitively more accessible is minimizing the utilization of a scarce resource, in particular, labor, which is in accordance with Marx's first economic law. Different projects or methods easily can be compared with respect to their labor-saving properties. Since labor is not homogeneous, some difficult problems loom in the background (Granberg 1972, 55–58).

There are few theoretical difficulties as long as such production models of interconnectedness are formulated in material units and are subject to resource utilization criteria. Once profit maximization is postulated as "specific optimality criterion of socialist firms" (*Volkswirtschaftsplanung* 1974, 306), which by the mid-1970s must be regarded as a remnant of the reform discussion of the 1960s, the central plan and the interests of the firm may come into conflict. This problem is approached by strictly tying the firms to constraints, in particular, production assignments guaranteeing a resource distribution which allows to implement the general optimum (263). Clearly, the leeway for firm decisions is restricted, but with an appropriate stimulation system the firms may still be interested in profits and keep in line with the central plan.

Dovetailing the interests of the firm and the economy as a whole presupposes a rational price system—or the observation of the law of value—which turned out to be the central stumbling block of the socialist economy. This was theoretical conjecture since the early stages of the Socialist Calculation Debate. Rational prices also are needed to integrate material production models into the macro system of monetary balances by which the planner implements his economic policy and safeguards an overall equilibrium.

The step from economic reform thinking in the preparatory volume to orthodox (or political) argument in the final version of the textbook on planning becomes most visible in the discussion of prices. The price expresses the scarcity of a product. Across an economy, there should be only one price per product without any subsidies, so it is said. Important functions are to stimulate the most effective use of resources and to ensure the accord of personal and collective interests. The price is based on marginal cost (which is called differential expenditures [*Differentialaufwendungen*] to avoid the "bourgeois" term *Grenzkosten*) (*Volkswirtschaftsplanung* 1974, 306–10). Nothing of this theoretical background and terminology is to be found in the final textbook (Kinze, Knop, and Seifert 1975, 313–21) or in the textbook on the socialist economy (Kinze, Knop, and Seifert 1989, 232–46). They stress that price planning has to be kept firmly in the hands of the state and that prices in principle should be constant, in particular, consumer prices, which makes ever-growing subsidies unavoidable.

If prices are centrally planned, the planner needs an appropriate formula. An optimal price should stimulate the realization of the optimal plan and, at least in the context of reform economics, enable the firm to self-finance its outlays. This includes, intentionally, the self-finance of investment. There has been a fierce debate about the appropriate price formula. The central issue was the distribution of total surplus value or net profit: should it be distributed with a fixed rate in relation to labor cost, total cost, or capital cost? The first variant is orthodox given the labor theory of value. The second variant resembles cost-plus pricing in capitalism and had been used for the reform of industry prices in East Germany in the 1960s. The third variant, the so-called fund-related price (*fondsbezogener Preis*), corresponds to Marx's production price and finally is recommended for price planning (Nick 1968; Kinze, Knop, and Seifert 1975, 321). None of these variants stimulates the realization of an efficient plan as Dadaian (1973, 239–54) showed and which, according to him, can only be achieved by the shadow prices of this plan. In the eyes of the central planner, however, these have a major disadvantage: they are not constant but change with each change in data and plan. Of course, such changes happen continuously in reality. The history of East German price policy was a permanent struggle between changing internal and external conditions, between conflicting policy objectives, and between academic theory and political requirements. The resulting price system remained dysfunctional (Maier 1996).

FORECASTING AND ECONOMETRICS

Traditional Stalinist planning worked under the assumption that the party elites knew the future and were able to bring it about in a rational way. The contributions of Heinz-Dieter Haustein (1969; 1970) can be read as critique of traditional planning—what he did not make explicit. But he stressed the unity of forecast and plan with the forecast about feasible possibilities and constraints as a necessary basis for strategic decision-making. Western influences cannot be neglected in this context. Postwar planning experiments and especially macro-economic policy and planning required scientific forecasts of technical, social, and economic developments just in the same way as this was the case under socialism. When huge macro-economic models were constructed in the 1960s, forecasting became a hot issue (see, e.g., Gerfin 1964; Rothschild 1969).

Forecasting did not remain an academic exercise but was institutionalized in order to obtain information for long-term planning. In 1966 the State Plan Commission of the GDR established a forecasting department, and 17 permanent forecasting groups were set up in 1968 to project the development of different fields in science and technology as well as the economy and social relations. One motive was to derive strategies to catch up in relation to West Germany. The forecasting surge lost momentum after 1971, that is, the political change to Honecker and his departure from economic reform (Steinitz and Walter 2014, 91).

Mathematics-and statistics-based planning approaches with different time horizons were used already before the forecasting euphoria. In the beginning, trend and regression functions of single variables were extrapolated. Early in the 1970s, the State Plan Commission experimented with a one-sector econometric model (DÖM-1) describing the circular flow of goods in a closed state socialist economy. The main dependent variable, annual national income, was derived from gross production determined by capital stock (called *Grundfonds* to avoid capitalist concepts). The model consisted of seven regression equations and four defining equations and was brought up to draft plan variants (Bilow et al. 1974, 60).

From the mid-1970s onward, more complex models were designed. The State Plan Commission's DÖM-2 was a multisectoral model including foreign trade. It produced "a balanced equilibrium between production, capital formation, and consumption" (Bilow, Grahl, and Walter 1981, 64). Sectoral production was mapped by the dominant input-output relationships. The required capital and capital formation were estimated by the sectoral capital-output ratio, the required labor input by output and labor productivity. The model consisted of 115 regression equations and 117 defining equations. In line with the ruling doctrine of production, it covered only the circular flow of goods in the material sphere of production.

At the same time, the Institute of Economics at the Academy of Sciences constructed an econometric model complementing the circular flow of goods in an open economy by components of the circular flow of incomes relevant for consumption. It consisted of a core and several submodels covering in detail the production and use of goods as well as productive resources, labor, and capital (Wölfling, Biebler, and Schiele 1977). It is an equilibrium model with 146 regression equations and 61 defining equations. Equilibrium is reached when "macro-economic labor productivity can be realized at the level necessary to balance the resources of labor with its demand in the national economy" (18). The model has been tested by predicting national income produced for the first year after the estimation period.

Both the restricted technical possibilities for linking econometric submodels and extending the time horizon of planning and forecasting encouraged the research team of the Institute to proceed to system dynamics models (Wölfling 1981). Econometric models assume a certain structural stability of the economic system, that is, relatively invariant relationships between the main indicators of the national economy. This property determines their suitability for short-and medium-term predictions. Over longer periods of time, however, planning processes and projections have to cope with structural changes like far-reaching technical discontinuities, environmental repercussions, and institutional interventions.

This is the starting point for system dynamics models mapping the economy by a stock-and-flow methodology including feedback loops and nonlinearities that allow for simulating alternative sequences of action. The Institute of Economics initiated such models in the 1980s (Wölfling 1981), but they were verified only partially (Biebler 1981). A comprehensive system dynamics model was devised only at the end of the GDR for the transition from central planning to a market economy and was used to simulate different development scenarios for East Germany (Fleissner and Ludwig 1992).

Scholars of Humboldt University Berlin used a so-called econometric-demometric model for teaching purposes in the mid-1970s (Förster, Oertel, and Eckstein 1981). It describes the macro-economic circular flow of goods together with the reproduction of population. They are linked by supply and demand of labor. Output is determined by employment and capital stock. Production and expenditure of national income are calculated for an open economy. The circular flow of goods is supplemented by components of the income flow. Thus private consumption is modeled as function of net monetary receipts and saving deposits of the population. The model consisted of 22 stochastic regression equations and 10 defining equations.

In the 1980s, the Central Administration for Statistics experimented with an econometric model for the current calculation of annual national income. It was tested by comparing results and projections produced by conventional methods (Höschel 1986). This multisectoral model covers only the circular flow of goods using official input-output tables. Gross output is determined by capital stock and the input of intermediaries. National income produced is derived from final output. Disposable national income is modeled on planned capital formation and consumption. Simultaneously, gross investment determines the capital stock on the production side. The balance between production and expenditure of national income can be achieved by adjusting the control parameters. The model is a linear equilibrium model and consists of 150 stochastic regression and defining equations and 250 variables in total.

Forecasting is one way to approach the future. The other is innovation. As a matter of fact, the concept of innovation was alien to the GDR for most of the time. The leading economic encyclopedia (*Ökonomisches Lexikon* 1978–80) does not contain such an entry. Instead, the more abstract notion of scientific-technical revolution—toned down to scientific-technical progress by the 1970s—is described as an objective fact, to which one must adapt.

Haustein became familiar with the field of innovation research in the 1970s and wrote a couple of papers while fellow at the International Institute of Applied Systems Analysis at Laxenburg, Austria, from 1979 to 1983. He co-authored a book with Dimitar Ivanov and Hans-Heinrich Kinze (1988) introducing the concept of innovation. It shows the intense attention politics, in particular Politburo member Günter Mittag, who was responsible for the economy, paid to scientific-technical progress and international competitiveness. But the plans, decrees, normatives, and procedures that should support research and development and innovation were extremely bureaucratic and most likely inconducive to its generation. What is needed, claimed Haustein and his co-authors, are "a high flexibility of resource allocation and risk-seeking decisions" (63), hardly characteristic of centrally planned systems. "In the GDR basic innovations are managed by government orders" (171). The central planner selects one variant which he deems promising from the set of possible alternatives. The longer the planning horizon, the less certain are feasibility and optimality. Ex post, other variants may have been preferable.

THE STATISTICAL BASIS: NATIONAL ACCOUNTING AND INPUT-OUTPUT ANALYSIS

The development and application of quantitative methods led to new information and data systems for national accounting and input-output calculations, expanding thus the knowledge about structural interdependencies between production and final demand. The impulses were given by planning practice. But introducing mathematics to economic governance increased expectations about the possibilities of centrally organizing the economy as a whole. As shown, a revolution triggered by mathematics resulted in developing new planning instruments and new statistical information systems. This revolution happened, however, above all in research and teaching. Due to the dominance of traditional planning methods, the transfer to planning practice became sluggish. In addition, walling off planning and statistical institutions impeded the necessary flow of information between the developers and the users of the new instruments.

A certain theoretical restraint cannot be overlooked where the new methods interfere with political-economic propositions. Eventual contradictions between the relations that the indicators and equations of national accounting and input-output analysis are representing and the traditional theory (or ideology) are addressed rarely, let alone properly dealt with. The majority of mathematical economists did not explicitly hint at or express such contradictions. Using their technical jargon, mathematicians and statisticians somehow inhibited the transfer of knowledge from academe to economic thinking and planning practice.

National accounting, including input-output analysis, provides the raw data for macroeconomic growth, structure, and business cycle analysis. Due to different theoretical and political causes, there is no uniform system of such accounts. Two fundamentally different systems of national accounts have been approved by the United Nations: the System of National Accounts (SNA) mainly used in market economies and the Material Product System (MPS) of socialist planned economies which is based on the exclusive productivity of labor engaged in material production and which faded from use after the collapse of the Soviet system.

The MPS figured under the denomination "economic balance" (*Volkswirtschaftsbilanz*), and its roots went back to the formative years of the Soviet Union (Goskomstat Rossii [1926] 1993). The pioneering works followed Marx's theory of the reproduction of capital. Reproduction is Marx's concept of the circular flow describing the flow of goods and income in the context of maintenance and development of the main factors of production and their socioeconomic characteristics (or production relations). In order to keep up the continuity of the circular flow, certain proportions have to be observed in the production process resulting in the famous law of the balanced, proportionate development of the national economy. Such proportions (equilibria) between the production and utilization of goods in kind and the corresponding money incomes can be formulated for both a stationary and a growing economy (simple and extended reproduction). This was seen to be independent of the economic and social system (Akademie [1954] 1955, 611).

In 1956, the first Statistical Yearbook of the GDR (*Staatliche Zentralverwaltung* 1956, 90 *et seq.*) published an economic balance, i.e., a national account, for the years 1950–1955 which still was fragmentary in scope and detail, but was in line with Soviet-type accounting practice. At the time, the Central Administration for Statistics was headed by Fritz Behrens who had published on measuring economic aggregates already in the 1930s and 1940s (Behrens 1938; 1941) and in 1950 on national income in relation with Marx's theory of reproduction (Behrens 1950). In the context of a notorious debate on revisionism Behrens was removed from his position and his chair at Leipzig University in 1957 (Krause 1998, 121 *et seq.*; Caldwell 2003, 45–56).

A major change in the system of national accounting was caused by the economic reform of the 1960s. The firms were to be guided by self-financing and, at least on a trial basis, by the market, thus putting national income in the focus of economic policy and public awareness. The chief success indicator was to move from gross production to profit, an element of net production, with far-reaching consequences for the verification of economic activity. The change made necessary a readjustment of producer prices, the rise of which was not to be transmitted to consumer prices for political reasons. By implication the problem of subsidies was aggravated during the second half of the 1960s, and especially in the 1970s.

The general public received only scarce information about total production and national income on a few pages of the statistical yearbooks. An internal *Statistical Yearbook of the Social Product and National Income* (Statistisches Amt der DDR 1990) contained extended calculations and data on more than 100 pages. Only a small group of specialists had access to it, and from 1966 to 1989 it was classified as confidential.

Traditional production planning did not start from targets for aggregates but from individual products, among them several hundred so-called key products. Their production and distribution were registered and planned in material balances which were also calculated for some capital and consumer goods. The planning authorities had hoped for more precision and consistency by introducing input-output balances. They were expected to provide for exact and proportional planning of the total economy. In the second half of the 1950s, the Central Administration for Statistics undertook first experiments with input-output balances relying on Soviet (Kindelberger 1970, 621) and Hungarian experiences (Rudolph 1962a, 4). Under the leadership of Johannes Rudolph from the High School for Economics, a team of scholars from this institution, the State Planning Commission, and the Central Administration for Statistics presented in 1963 a balance for the year 1959 (Jäger, Karbstein, and Rudich 1963; Rudolph 1965).

The effort coincided with Walter Ulbricht's announcement of economic reform on the sixth party congress of the SED (*Sozialistische Einheitspartei Deutschlands*—Socialist Unity Party of Germany) which aimed at improving central planning with new instruments. For input-output scholars the political environment became more favorable, while proponents of central planning felt prompted to exaggerated propaganda. Economic historian Jürgen Kuczynski and political economist Helmut Koziolek wrote half a page in the party daily *Neues Deutschland*: "The input-output balance is the general staff map in our fight for a rapid and correctly proportional building of socialism"

(Kuczynski and Koziolek 1962, 4). Only a few years earlier, Koziolek (1959, 29) had called the mathematical model behind the inter-industry balances "nonsense" because it lacked a clear reference to orthodox political economy. He had dismissed as misjudgment Oskar Lange's view that saw an extension of Marx's theory of reproduction in the model.

Since 1968, symmetric tables were constructed which contained in their rows and columns the interrelationships of the producers and users of homogeneous product groups. The homogenized data allowed for the calculation of the matrix of coefficients of total material consumption, the so-called Leontief inverse. Under certain theoretical assumptions it shows the necessary structure of gross production if a certain final output of goods for consumption, investment, and export is aspired.

As a rule, an input-output table describes interrelations of homogenized product groups without any reference to institutional structure. Plans, however, are addressed to ministries on the higher level and to firms on the lower level. Product groups and institutional units had to be brought together. This happened in interconnected planning balances (*Planverflechtungsbilanzen*) which also allowed for controlling the relations of material and financial planning on an aggregate level (Graichen 1980; Kinze, Knop, and Seifert 1989, 558). The linking of output, final product, and extended reproduction of capital over the years is the object of dynamic input-output balances. The Institute for Economic Research of the Central Planning Commission occupied itself with building such models (Freimüller, Hertrampf, and Packeiser 1972). But these never reached practical applicability and were later discontinued (Kinze, Müncheberg, and Sange 1981, 217–18).

Input-output balances for the whole economy, even with more than 100 items, show too high a degree of aggregation for central planning of individual products down the pyramid of all economic organizations. In addition, they do not reflect the relations within the branches and combines. Optimization systems on the basis of such balances may be a useful analytical tool, but for the daily planning routine they are too complex and abstract. It is different with partial models of interconnectedness (*Teilverflechtungsbilanzen*). They analyze technically determined interrelations within firms, single branches, or production complexes in physical terms and can markedly improve the planning task on that level (Autorenkollektiv 1965). This is also the field of operations research which found a wide practical application in the socialist economy.

Moreover, a hybrid input-output balance was developed to bridge the gap between the national input-output balances in monetary terms and the partial balances in physical terms (*Natural-Wert-Verflechtungsbilanz*). It linked the information about the physical availability of about 600 products and their utilization, compiled in the balances of materials, equipment and consumer goods (*MAK-Bilanzen*), with the value of the total market output by organizational units. This type of balance had been created in the Institute for Economic Research of the Central Planning Commission. It was used, however, more for structural analyses of value chains than for planning activities (Kinze, Müncheberg, and Sange 1981, 219).

The input-output approaches mentioned so far belonged to the group of quantity models. However, efforts were made also to develop input-output price models (Kinze, Knop, and Seifert 1975, 212–13). They were of specific interest for the planning authorities in the time of the 1963–1969 NÖS reforms when price reforms took place. They allowed for evaluating, for instance, different types of price setting in individual stages of production and their cumulative repercussions on the total price level (Weisheimer 1969).

Constructing the correct proportions between quantities of gross output in order to generate a high net product became more and more difficult because of the increasing complexity of the economy. The planner was in need of new approaches. This led to the "discovery" of the final product which, of course, was well known to the builders of mathematical input-output models, but which political economists considered a deviation from Marxist orthodoxy. Some recognized, however, that the final product introduced a new perception of the production process (Altmann and Reichenberg 1979, 62–63). The final result of production actually includes not only consumer goods and means of production for extended reproduction but also means of production destined for replacement. Consequently, East German national accounting defined a new indicator "national income plus depreciation" which came quite close to the Western concept of gross domestic product (GDP) if we disregard the material–non-material dichotomy. The data were not published, and only the last issue of the internal yearbook of the social product contained a time series for 1970–1989 (Statistisches Amt der DDR 1990, 178–79). The turn to calculating a comprehensive final product, i.e., a GDP, was barred by the dogma of physical materiality of the production result.

In the 1970s, scholars recognized the importance of education and science, public health, and culture for economic productivity and urged for enlarging the boundaries of productive labor beyond the materiality of the product (Meyer 1984, 267 *et seq.*). In theoretical debates it was underlined that certain proportions between material and non-material production have to be observed (Koziolek 1979, 192). In the context of national accounting, however, the so-called "non-productive" branches of the economy remained consumers who never got upgraded to producers. Nevertheless, GDR statisticians calculated the performance of both sectors of the economy according to the same principles and constructed a new indicator for the economy as a whole—the total economic performance or GDP (Ludwig 1988, 22 *et seq.*; Hein 1988, 171 *et seq.*).

CONCLUSION

Central planning was one of the most conspicuous experiments in the political economy of the twentieth century. To a large extent, it started in pre-and post-First World War Vienna where the vision of Marx and Engels was worked out theoretically and immediately criticized heavily. It could not have passed unnoticed by Lev Trotsky and Nikolai Bukharin who spent some of the prewar years in this town. In the post-Second World War decennia, half the world was dominated by the idea. It ended in 1989 when the Iron Curtain and the Berlin Wall were pulled down. "The great illusion of communist ruling elites was to believe that the communist leviathan that they controlled could collect sufficient information, process it, and come up with adequately complex plans on that basis to politically prescribe—from the outside and from above—the optimal selective performance of social subsystems" (Merkel, Brückner, and Wagener 2019, 25). This illusion was exacerbated by the conviction of cyberneticians, above all in the late 1950s and 1960s, that the task could be performed elegantly by mathematical models of optimal planning. In the GDR, this conviction was not shared by most planners and political elite. As a device to improve central planning, optimal planning did not find enthusiastic support from reformers and, vice versa, optimal planners were little interested in market reforms. But both were explicit about their rejection of the orthodox approach to planning. When the cybernetic hype waned and optimal planning of the whole economy had become practically infeasible in the 1970s, the orthodox planning methods, however, gained renewed attention (Kinze, Knop, and Seifert 1989).

Of course, this was a big mistake for two reasons. First, the state of the East German economy had deteriorated gravely during the second half of the 1970s, and the 1980s testified to the inadequacy of the orthodox planning methods. In place of aborting the economic reforms of the 1960s, these reforms should have been implemented and further expanded. The reforms had (hesitantly) aimed at devolution of central planning, independence of firms, market relations, and profit orientation. Second, quantitative economics was a major intellectual revolution in socialist economics. Whatever were the merits of the political economy of socialism, it did not aspire to contribute to economic theorizing and the corresponding empirical research, as Lange already had made clear in 1935. Here, mathematical economics was a decisive step forward. It focused, like neoclassics, mainly on allocation and growth, but without a microeconomic and behavioral foundation.

The quantitative turn provided a sound basis for economic analysis and also a rapprochement to Western theory. (Such rapprochement was not necessary for a neoclassical Marxist like Oskar Lange.) To turn a back on mathematical economics and on reform economics at the same time was a sure move towards stagnation, ossification, and ultimate collapse. But the idea of central planning kept its allure among East German economists. Still in December 1989, the "young Turks" of Humboldt University Berlin (Brie and Land 1989, 1088–89) did not think further than to substitute the "subordination of economic subjects to the central administration" by the "linkage of all economic subjects to society, meaning democratic and public organizations influencing and controlling strategies in firms, combines, and municipalities."

NOTES

1. This work was supported by the Bundesministerium für Bildung und Forschung [01UJ1806DY].

2. Klaus (1912–74) started to study mathematics and philosophy in 1931 and was after three semesters imprisoned as an active communist for five years. He could resume his studies and academic career only in 1947. Already in 1950 he became professor for dialectical and historical materialism at the University of Jena, then moved to Humboldt University Berlin and finally to the Institute for Philosophy at the Academy of Sciences. His main fields of research were formal logic and theory and history of science and philosophy.

3. Gunther Kohlmey (1913–99) was arguably one of the best East German economists. He studied economics in Freiburg and Berlin in the early 1930s and, as a soldier, switched sides during the war in the Soviet Union. In 1953 he became founder and chief editor of the leading economic periodical *Wirtschaftswissenschaft*, in 1954 founding director of the Institute for Economics at the Academy of Sciences, and he held a chair at Humboldt University Berlin. After criticizing the orthodox bureaucratic system of governing the economy, as did Fritz Behrens and Arne Benary at the same time, he was attacked as revisionist in 1957 and lost all his positions to remain as researcher with the Institute of Economics (Krause 1998, 121–36). Nevertheless, his expertise was used in different functions later.

BIBLIOGRAPHY

Aganbegjan, Abel G., and Konstantin K. Waltuch, eds. 1972. *Gesellschaftlicher Wohlstand und Volkswirtschaftsplanung*. Translated from Russian. Berlin: Die Wirtschaft.

Akademie der Wissenschaften der UdSSR Institut für Ökonomie, ed. (1954) 1955. *Politische Ökonomie: Lehrbuch.* Translated from Russian. Berlin: Dietz.

Altmann, Eva, and Rudolf Reichenberg. 1979. *Die erweiterte sozialistische Reproduktion: Lehrhefte Politische Ökonomie des Sozialismus.* Berlin: Dietz.

Anders, Hans-Dieter, and Kunibert Schwarz. 1974. "Probleme der Modellierung einer sozialistischen Nutzensfunktion." In *Zum Bewertungsproblem im Sozialismus*, edited by Hans-Dieter Anders, Hans Schilar, and Kunibert Schwarz. 15–86. Vol. 12 of *Forschungsberichte des Zentralinstituts für Wirtschaftswissenschaften der Akademie der Wissenschaften der DDR.* Berlin: Akademie-Verlag.

Anders, Hans-Dieter, Kunibert Schwarz, and Thomas Klein. 1976. "Theorie und Praxis der Entwicklung einer sozialistischen Nutzensfunktion." Unpublished manuscript, Zentralinstitut für Wirtschaftswissenschaften der Akademie der Wissenschaften der DDR, Berlin.

Autorenkollektiv. 1965. *Teilverflechtungsbilanzen.* Berlin: Die Wirtschaft.

Autorenkollektiv. 1981. *Planungs-und Prognosemodelle: Erfahrungen, Probleme, Entwicklungstendenzen.* Berlin: Akademie-Verlag.

Barone, Enrico. (1908) 1935. "The Ministry of Production in the Collectivist State." In *Collectivist Economic Planning: Critical Studies on the Possibilities of Socialism*, edited by F.A. von Hayek, 245–90. London: Routledge.

Becker, Susanne, and Heiko Dierking. 1989. *Die Herausbildung der Wirtschaftswissenschaften in der Frühphase der DDR.* Köln: Verlag Wissenschaft und Politik.

Behrens, Friedrich. 1938. "Die Produktivität und ihre Messung." *Jahrbücher für Nationalökonomie und Statistik* 148: 416–29.

———. 1941. "Zusammenhang zwischen betriebswirtschaftlicher und volkswirtschaftlicher Statistik." *Allgemeines Statistisches Archiv* 30: 246–63.

Behrens, Fritz. 1950. "Bemerkungen zur Theorie des Volkseinkommens und der Akkumulation." *Finanzarchiv* N.F. 12: 49–60.

Biebler, Edith. 1981. "Bestimmung der Produktionsnachfrage im systemdynamischen Modell auf der Grundlage der Bedürfnisentwicklung." In Autorenkollektiv 1981, 185–98.

Bilow, Wolfram, Bernd Grahl, and Dieter Walter. 1981. "Das ökonometrische Modell DÖM-2: Ein Modell für die Analyse und Prognose der Volkswirtschaft der DDR." In Autorenkollektiv 1981, 56–63.

Bilow, Wolfram et al. 1974. "Erfahrungen und Probleme bei der Nutzung mathematisch-statistischer Methoden für die mittel-und langfristige Planung." *Wirtschaftswissenschaft* 22 (1): 58–75.

Brie, Michael, and Rainer Land. 1989. "Aspekte der Krise: Wege der Lösung." *Einheit* 44: 1084–89.

Brus, Włodzimierz, and Kazimierz Łaski. 1964. "The Law of Value and the Problem of Allocation in Socialism." In *On Political Economy and Econometrics: Essays in Honour of Oskar Lange*, 45–59. Warszawa: PWN—Polish Scientific Publishers.

Caldwell, Peter C. 2003. *Dictatorship, State Planning, and Social Theory in the German Democratic Republic.* Cambridge: Cambridge University Press.

Chaloupek, Günther. 2007. "Otto Neurath's Concepts of Socialization and Economic Calculation and his Socialist Critics." In *Otto Neurath's Economics in Context*, edited by Elisabeth Nemeth, Stefan W. Schmitz, and Thomas Uebel, 61–76. Vol. 13 of *Vienna Circle Institute Yearbook*. Vienna: Springer.

Dadajan, Vladislav S. 1973. *Ökonomische Gesetze des Sozialismus und optimale Entscheidungen.* Translated from Russian. Berlin: Akademie Verlag.

Dittmann, Frank, and Rudolf Seising, eds. 2007. *Kybernetik steckt den Osten an: Aufstieg und Schwierigkeiten einer interdisziplinären Wissenschaft in der DDR.* Berlin: trafo Verlag.

Eichholtz, Dietrich. (1969–96) 2003. *Geschichte der deutschen Kriegswirtschaft, 1939–1945.* 5 vols. Reprint. München: K.G. Saur.

Erlich, Alexander. 1960. *The Soviet Industrialization Debate, 1924–1928.* Cambridge, MA.: Harvard University Press.

Eucken, Walter. 1948. "On the Theory of the Centrally Administered Economy: An Analysis of the German experiment." *Economica* 15: 79–100, 173–93.

Feldman, Grigory A. (1929) 1969. *Zur Wachstumstheorie des Nationaleinkommens.* Translated from Russian. Berlin: Akademie Verlag.

Fleissner, Peter, and Udo Ludwig. 1992. *Ostdeutsche Wirtschaft im Umbruch: Computersimulation mit einem systemdynamischen Modell.* Braunschweig: Vieweg.

Föhl, Carl. (1937) 1955. *Geldschöpfung und Wirtschaftskreislauf.* 2nd Edition. Berlin: Duncker & Humblot.

Förster, Erhard, Gabriele Oertel, and Peter Eckstein. 1981. "Ein ökonometrisch-demometrisches Lehrmodell." In Autorenkollektiv 1981, 103–10.

Freimüller, Helmut, Irmtraut Hertrampf, and Manfred Packeiser. 1972. "Probleme bei der Bestimmung von Varianten der Entwicklung materieller Strukturen der Volkswirtschaft mit Hilfe dynamischer Verflechtungsbilanzen." *Wirtschaftswissenschaft*: 20: 696–721.

Fuchs-Kittowski, Klaus. 2007. Zur Herausbildung von Sichtweisen der Informatik in der DDR unter Einfluss der Kybernetik I. und II. Ordnung. In Dittmann and Seising 2007, 323–380.

Gerfin, Harald. 1964. *Langfristige Wirtschaftsprognose.* Tübingen: Mohr (Siebeck).

Gerovitch, Slava. 2008. "InterNyet: Why the Soviet Union did not Build a Nationwide Computer Network." *History and Technology* 24: 335–50.

Goskomstat Rossii. (1926) 1993. *Balans narodnogo khoziaistva Soiuza SSR, 1924–1926*, edited by P. I. Popov. Reprint, Moscow.

Graichen, Dieter. 1980. *Sozialistische Betriebswirtschaft: Lehrbuch.* Berlin: Die Wirtschaft.

Granberg, Aleksander G. 1972. "Die Zielfunktion des gesellschaftlichen Wohlstands und die Optimalitätskriterien in angewandten Modellen der Volkswirtschaft." In Aganbegjan and Waltuch 1972, 11–58.

Grünig, Ferdinand. 1933. *Der Wirtschaftskreislauf.* München: C. H. Beck.

Haustein, Heinz-Dieter. 1969. *Wirtschaftsprognose: Grundlagen—Elemente—Modelle.* Berlin: Die Wirtschaft.

————. 1970. *Prognoseverfahren in der sozialistischen Wirtschaft.* Berlin: Die Wirtschaft.

Haustein, Heinz-Dieter, Dimitar Ivanov, and Hans-Heinrich Kinze. 1988. *Innovationen in der sozialistischen Volkswirtschaft.* Berlin: Die Wirtschaft.

Hein, Ralf. 1988. "Zu einigen aktuellen Fragen der volkswirtschaftlichen Gesamtrechnung in der Staatlichen Zentralverwaltung für Statistik der DDR." In Zentralinstitut für Wirtschaftswissenschaften der Akademie der Wissenschaften der DDR. *Volkswirtschaftliche Gesamtrechnung der DDR: Karl-Marx-Symposium 1987;* Studien, Forschungsberichte, Kolloquien, Heft 3,171–81. Berlin.

Hensel, K. Paul. 1954. *Einführung in die Theorie der Zentralverwaltungswirtschaft.* Stuttgart: Gustav Fischer.

Hesse, Jan-Otmar. 2010. *Wirtschaft als Wissenschaft: Die Volkswirtschaftslehre in der frühen Bundesrepublik.* Frankfurt a.M.: Campus.

Höschel, Hans Peter. 1986. "Ein ökonometrisches Modell für Analysen und Vorausberechnungen des Nationaleinkommens der DDR." *Österreichische Zeitschrift für Statistik und Informatik* 16 (4): 213–39.

Jäger, Manfred, Werner Karbstein, and Georg Rudich. 1963. "Zu einigen Ergebnissen der Verflechtungsbilanz des Gesamtprodukts der DDR." *Wirtschaftswissenschaft* 11: 1374–99.

Kantorovič, Leonid V. et al. 1985. *Ökonomie und Optimierung.* Edited by Werner Lassmann and Hans Schilar. Berlin: Akademie Verlag.

Känel, Siegfried von. 1971. *Einführung in die Kybernetik für Ökonomen.* Berlin: Die Wirtschaft.

Känel, Siegfried von, Hans G. Lauenroth, and Johann A. Müller. 1990. *Kybernetik: Eine Einführung für Ökonomen.* Berlin: Die Wirtschaft.

Kautsky, Karl. (1892) 1965. *Das Erfurter Programm in seinem grundsätzlichen Teil erläutert.* Berlin: Dietz. https://www.marxists.org/deutsch/archiv/kautsky/1892/erfurter/index.htm, accessed May 04, 2021.

————. 1902. *Am Tage nach der sozialen Revolution.* Vol. 2 of *Die Soziale Revolution.* Berlin: Vorwärts. www.marxists.org/deutsch/archiv/kautsky/1902/sozrevolution/index.htm, accessed May 04, 2021.

————. 1922. *Die proletarische Revolution und ihr Programm.* Stuttgart: Dietz.

Kindelberger, Albert. 1970. "25 Jahre staatliche Statistik—eine Chronik: Zweiter Teil 1955 bis 1962." *Statistische Praxis* 11: 621–62.

Kinze, Hans-Heinrich, Klaus Müncheberg, and Heinz Sange, eds. 1981. *Langfristige Planung.* Berlin: Die Wirtschaft.

Kinze, Hans-Heinrich, Hans Knop, and Eberhard Seifert, eds. 1975. *Volkswirtschaftsplanung.* Berlin: Die Wirtschaft.

————, eds. 1989. *Sozialistische Volkswirtschaft.* Berlin: Die Wirtschaft.

Klaus, Georg. 1961. *Kybernetik in philosophischer Sicht.* Berlin: Dietz.

Kohlmey, Gunther. 1965. "Eröffnung." In *Mathematik und Kybernetik in der Ökonomie.* Internationale Tagung, 4–10. Berlin: Akademie-Verlag.

————. 1966. *Zielfunktionen des sozialistischen Wirtschaftens.* Vol. 4 of *Sitzungsberichte der Deutschen Akademie der Wissenschaften zu Berlin.* Berlin: Akademie-Verlag.

————. 1967. "Zur Entstehung der Theorie von der sozialistischen Wirtschaft." In *Oktoberrevolution und Wissenschaft*, 27–53. Berlin: Akademie-Verlag.

————. 1968. "Planen als Regeln und Steuern." *Probleme der politischen Ökonomie: Jahrbuch des Instituts für Wirtschaftswissenschaften* 11: 89 *et seq.*

Kornai, János. 1967. *Mathematische Methoden bei der Planung der ökonomischen Struktur*. Berlin: Die Wirtschaft.

————. 1968. "Theoretische Probleme bei Modellsystemen." *Wirtschaftswissenschaft*, 4.

————. 1992. *The Socialist System: The Political Economy of Communism*. Oxford: Clarendon.

Kosing, Alfred. 2005. "Habent sua fata libelli: Über das merkwürdige Schicksal des Buches Marxistische Philosophie." In *Denkversuche: DDR-Philosophie in den 60er Jahren*, edited by Hans-Christoph Rauh and Peter Ruben, 77c113. Berlin: Chr. Links.

Koziolek, Helmut. 1959. "Zur Behandlung des Nationaleinkommenskreislaufs bei Marx und die 'Synthese,' die Oskar Lange zwischen Marx und Leontief herstellte!" *Wissenschaftliche Zeitschrift der Hochschule für Ökonomie* 4 (1): 25–36.

————. 1979. *Reproduktion und Nationaleinkommen: Probleme und Zusammenhänge*. Berlin: Die Wirtschaft.

Krause, Günter. 1998. *Wirtschaftstheorie in der DDR*. Marburg: Metropolis.

Krömke, Claus. "Innovationen—nur gegen den Plan. Gespräch mit Claus Krömke." In Pirker et al. 1995, 33–66.

Kuczynski, Jürgen, and Helmut Koziolek. 1962. "Verflechtungsbilanz – Generalstabskarte der Wirtschaft." *Neues Deutschland*, November 17, 1962.

Lange, Oskar, 1935. "Marxian Economics and Modern Economic Theory." *Review of Economic Studies* 2: 189–201.

Lassmann, Werner. 1985. "Die Entwicklung und Anwendung von Optimierungsmethoden in der DDR." In Kantorovič et al. 1985, 97–193.

Lehrbuch Politische Ökonomie. Sozialismus. (1970) 1972. Edited under the leadership of Nikolai A. Tsagolov. Translated from Russian. Berlin: Verlag Die Wirtschaft.

Lessmann, Ortrud. 2007. "A Similar Line of Thought in Neurath and Sen: Interpersonal Comparability." In *Otto Neurath's Economics in Context*, edited by Elisabeth Nemeth, Stefan W. Schmitz, Thomas Uebel, 115–30. Vol. 13 of *Vienna Circle Institute Yearbook*. Vienna: Springer.

Liebscher, Heinz. 2005. "Systemtheorie und Kybernetik in der philosophischen Sicht von Georg Klaus." In *Denkversuche: DDR-Philosophie in den 60er Jahren*, edited by Hans-Christoph Rauh and Peter Ruben, 157–75. Berlin: Chr. Links.

Ludwig, Udo. 1988. Die volkswirtschaftliche Gesamtrechnung—ein Instrument zur statistischen Darstellung, Analyse und Prognose der intensiv erweiterten Reproduktion in der DDR. In: Zentralinstitut für Wirtschaftswissenschaften der Akademie der Wissenschaften der DDR, *Volkswirtschaftliche Gesamtrechnung der DDR*. Studien, Forschungsberichte, Kolloquien, Heft 3, 1–48. Berlin.

Maier, Wilfried. 1996. "Zur Preispolitik der DDR." In *Ansichten zur Geschichte der DDR. Vol. 4*, edited by Ludwig Elm, Dietmar Keller, and Reinhard Mocek, 243–98. Eggersdorf: Matthias Kirchner.

Marschak, Jakob. 1924. "Wirtschaftsrechnung und Gemeinwirtschaft. Zu Mises' These von der Unmöglichkeit sozialistischer Gemeinwirtschaft." *Archiv für Sozialwissenschaft und Sozialpolitik* 51: 501–20.

Marx, Karl. (1857) 1993. *Grundrisse: Foundations of the Critique of Political Economy*. London: Penguin.

Marx, Karl. (1867)1909. *Capital. A Critique of Political Economy. Vol I. The Process of Capitalist Production.* Chicago: Charles H. Kerr. oll.libertyfund.org/titles/marx-capital-a-critique-of-political-economy-volume-i-the-process-of-capitalist-production. Accessed 05–11–2021.

———. (1894) 1959. *Capital: A Critique of Political Economy. Vol. III, The Process of Capitalist Production as a Whole.* Moscow: Progress Publishers. www.marxists.org/archive/marx/works/download/pdf/Capital-Volume-III.pdf, accessed November 5, 2021.

Mathematik und Kybernetik in der Ökonomie: Internationale Tagung—Berlin, Oktober 1964; Konferenzprotokoll. 1965. Berlin: Akademie-Verlag.

Meissner, Herbert, ed. 1978. *Geschichte der politischen Ökonomie: Grundriss.* Berlin: Dietz.

Merkel, Wolfgang, Julian Brückner, and Hans-Jürgen Wagener. 2019. "System." In *The Handbook of Political, Social, and Economic Transformation,* edited by Wolfgang Merkel, Raj Kollmorgen, and Hans-Jürgen Wagener, 16–29. Oxford: Oxford University Press.

Meyer, Christian. 1984. *Die volkswirtschaftliche Gesamtrechnung der DDR: Methodik, Inkonsistenzen, Ideologie.* München: V. Florentz.

Mises, Ludwig von. (1920) 1935. "Economic Calculation in the Socialist Commonwealth." In *Collectivist Economic Planning: Critical Studies on the Possibilities of Socialism,* edited by F.A. von Hayek, 87–130. London: Routledge.

Montias, John M. 1959. "Planning with Material Balances in Soviet-Type Economies." *American Economic Review* 49: 963–85.

Nemchinov, Vasilii S. 1965. "Die Modellierung ökonomischer Prozesse." In *Mathematik und Kybernetik in der Ökonomie* 1965, 22–30.

Neurath, Otto. 1919. *Durch die Kriegswirtschaft zur Naturalwirtschaft.* München: Callwey. Extracts in Neurath and Nemeth 1994.

———. 1925. *Wirtschaftsplan und Naturalrechnung: Von der sozialistischen Lebensordnung und vom kommenden Menschen.* Berlin: Laub. Extracts in: Otto Neurath. 1979. *Wissenschaftliche Weltauffassung, Sozialismus und Logischer Empirismus.* Rainer Hegselmann ed. Frankfurt a.M.: Suhrkamp.

Neurath, Paul, and Elisabeth Nemeth, eds. 1994. *Otto Neurath oder Die Einheit von Wissenschaft und Gesellschaft.* Wien: Böhlau.

Nick, Harry. 1968. *Warum fondsbezogener Preistyp?* Berlin: Dietz.

———. 2011. *Ökonomendebatten in der DDR.* Schkeuditz: GNN Verlag.

Nowoshilow, W. W. (1967) 1970. *Die Messung von Aufwand und Ergebnis: Probleme der Messung von Aufwand und Ergebnis in der optimalen Planung.* Translated from Russian. Berlin: Die Wirtschaft.

Ökonomisches Lexikon. 3 vols. 3rd Edition. 1978–80. Berlin: Die Wirtschaft.

Pareto, Vilfredo. (1906) 1966. *Manuel d'économie politique.* Genf: Droz.

Pirker, Theo et al. 1995. *Der Plan als Befehl und Fiktion: Wirtschaftsführung in der DDR*. Opladen: Westdeutscher Verlag.

Polanyi, Karl. (1922) 2005. Sozialistische Rechnungslegung. In *Chronik der großen Transformation: Artikel und Aufsätze (1920–1947)*. Vol. 3, edited by Michele Cangiani, Kari Polanyi-Levitt, and Claus Thomasberger, 71–113. Marburg: Metropolis.

———. (1925) 1979. "Die funktionelle Theorie der Gesellschaft und das Problem der sozialistischen Rechnungslegung." In *Ökonomie und Gesellschaft,* 81–90. Frankfurt a.M.: Suhrkamp.

Politische Ökonomie des Sozialismus und ihre Anwendung in der DDR. 1969. Berlin: Dietz.

Porwit, Krzysztof. 1970. *Die Optimierung des Volkswirtschaftsplanes.* Translated from Polish. Berlin: Die Wirtschaft.

Preobrazhensky, Evgeni. (1926) 1965. *The New Economics.* Oxford: Clarendon Press.

Rathenau, Walther. 1918. *Die neue Wirtschaft.* Berlin: S. Fischer.

Rothschild, Kurt W. 1969. *Wirtschaftsprognose: Methoden und Probleme.* Berlin: Springer.

Rudolph, Johannes. 1962a. "Planen auf neue Art: Durch Verflechtungsbilanzen zur besseren proportionalen Entwicklung." *Neues Deutschland*, October 27, 1962.

———. 1962b. *Die Optimierung des volkswirtschaftlichen Produktionsplanes mit Hilfe der Volkswirtschaftsbilanz.* Berlin: Die Wirtschaft.

———. 1965. "Die Optimierung von Volkswirtschaftsplänen." In: *Mathematik und Kybernetik* 1964, 125–54.

Rudolph, Johannes, and Gerd Friedrich, eds. 1957. *Grundriss der Volkswirtschaftsplanung.* Berlin: Die Wirtschaft.

Schirokorad, Leonid D. (1972) 1975. "Das Problem des Regulators in der Wirtschaft der Übergangsperiode und im Sozialismus in der sowjetischen ökonomischen Literatur der zwanziger Jahre." In *Beiträge zur politischen Ökonomie des Sozialismus*, 156–70. Berlin: Dietz.

Schultze, Hartmut. 2007. "Kybernetik und die Ausbildung der Ökonomen in der DDR." In: Dittmann and Seising 2007, 433–44.

Segal, Jérome. 2001. Kybernetik in der DDR. Begegnung mit der marxistischen Ideologie. *Dresdener Beiträge zur Geschichte der Technikwissenschaften* 27: 47–75.

Stalin, Joseph W. 1952. *Economic Problems of Socialism in the U.S.S.R.* Moscow: Foreign Languages Publishing House.

Staatliche Zentralverwaltung für Statistik. 1956. *Statistisches Jahrbuch der DDR 1955.* Erster Jahrgang. Berlin: Deutscher Zentralverlag.

Statistisches Amt der DDR. 1990. *Statistisches Jahrbuch des gesellschaftlichen Gesamtprodukts und des Nationaleinkommens 1989.* Berlin.

Steinitz, Klaus, and Dieter Walter. 2014. *Plan—Markt—Demokratie: Prognose und langfristige Planung in der DDR—Schlussfolgerungen für morgen.* Hamburg: VSA Verlag.

Stoph, Willi. 1948. "Probleme der Wirtschaftsplanung." *Einheit* 3: 1138–48.

Tooze, Adam J. 2001. *Statistics and the German State, 1900–1945: The Making of Modern Economic Knowledge.* Cambridge: Cambridge University Press.

Turner, R. Kerry, and Clive Collis. 1977. *The Economics of Planning.* London: Macmillan.

Uebel, Thomas E. 2007. "Otto Neurath as an Austrian Economist: Behind the Scenes of the Early Socialist Calculation Debate." In: *Otto Neurath's Economics in Context,* edited by Elisabeth Nemeth, Stefan W. Schmitz, and Thomas Uebel, 37–59. Vol. 13 of *Vienna Circle Institute Yearbook.* Vienna: Springer.

Volkswirtschaftsplanung: Ausgewählte Studientexte. 1974. 3rd Edition. Berlin: Die Wirtschaft.

Waltuch, Konstantin K. 1972. *Entwicklungsproportionen und Befriedigung der Bedürfnisse.* Translated from Russian. Berlin: Die Wirtschaft.

Weber, Max. (1921) 2014. *Wirtschaft und Gesellschaft: Soziologie.* Tübingen: Mohr (Siebeck).

Weisheimer, Martin. 1969. "Volkswirtschaftliche Preismodelle im Großeinsatz." *Die Wirtschaft* 44.

Wenzel, Siegfried. 1998. *Plan und Wirklichkeit: Zur DDR-Ökonomie.* St. Katharinen: Scripta Mercaturae.

Wittenburg, Gertraud. 1979. "Zur Herausbildung und Entwicklung der politischen Ökonomie des Sozialismus." In *60 Jahre politische Ökonomie des Sozialismus,* edited by Autorenkollektiv, 9–52. Berlin: Akademie Verlag.

Wölfling, Manfred. 1981. "Eine systemdynamische Modellkonzeption für die langfristige Planung." In Autorenkollektiv 1981, 143–84.

Wölfling, Manfred, Edith Biebler, and Karin Schiele. 1977. "Ein ökonometrisches Modell der Volkswirtschaft der DDR." *Forschungsberichte des Zentralinstituts für Wirtschaftswissenschaften der Akademie der Wissenschaften der DDR,* Nr. 21. Berlin: Akademie-Verlag.

Chapter 5

Mathematical Economics Outside the Neoclassical Paradigm?

Evolution of Planning Concepts in Hungary under Communism

Gergely Kőhegyi and János Mátyás Kovács

This chapter seeks to unravel the puzzle of the sluggish Westernization[1] of economic thought during the communist period. Why did neoclassical economics that Hungarian economists of Marxist persuasion started sampling at the end of the 1950s strike roots only after 1989? Hungary gave the world theorists such as János Harsányi, Miklós Káldor, and János Neumann, and was famous for having one of the least closed and repressed economic research communities and launching one of the most radical market reforms in the Eastern Bloc. In our country the first models describing the planned economy by means of mathematical (partly neoclassical) instruments already were built at the turn of the 1950s and 1960s, and many of those instruments were taught in regular courses at Karl Marx University of Economics in Budapest from the early 1960s. Simultaneously, a growing number of Hungarian researchers followed in the footsteps of promising young scholars such as András Bródy and János Kornai, who rapidly became renowned in the international arena of modern economics. Borrowing the label accepted in the West (Kőhegyi 2010), they named themselves mathematical economists (in contrast to the official designation of "political economists"), and established special departments not only at research institutes and universities but also in major government agencies such as the Central Statistical Office and the Planning Office.[2] Both a symbolic breakthrough and institution building were

145

greatly facilitated by similar achievements of mathematical economists in the Soviet Union.

After carefully gauging the political mood, Hungarian scholars with an interest in quantitative economic research published their own journal *Szigma,*[3] and engaged in a busy multilogue with their peers in both the West and the East. Transnational communication resulted in long research stays, guest professorships, joint research projects and publications, not to speak of prominent positions in international academic organizations like the Econometric Society and the International Input-Output Association.[4] Why did this segment of the research community remain a minority in Hungary for about 30 years; a minority that—no matter how strong it was in scholarly terms—proved unable (or did not want?) to orchestrate a belated but genuine "neoclassical revolution?" How could mathematical economics thrive so long while resisting the temptation to join the neoclassical mainstream in the West?

We contend that the answer to these questions is to be found not only in a competing enticement by market reforms that kept the majority of Hungarian economists within the realm of verbal ("old") institutionalism, but also in the hope of comprehending the operation of the planned economy by means of input-output (I-O) analysis and improving economic performance through optimal planning based on linear programming. Obviously, any explanation relying on that hope, though necessary, cannot be sufficient since it dwindled as years passed. The historian also must clarify why the research program of optimal planning worked as a trap, easy to enter but difficult to exit even when more than enough evidence had been gathered about the failures of the program.

As so often in communist history, it would be easy to blame (self-)censorship for ensnaring economists in the trap for decades, at the very least gluing them in place unable to reach out in a neoclassical direction, thereby delaying Westernization. Ostensibly, the rapid success[5] of neoclassical thought in the Hungarian economic research community after 1989 makes such an explanation more than plausible (cf. Kovács 2002, 2012). It might seem that a number of gifted economists already had joined the "revolutionary movement" in a clandestine manner under communism and could not wait to "come out." Undoubtedly, there were some dedicated neoclassical-minded theorists among younger researchers during the late 1980s, some of whom had an opportunity to familiarize themselves with then-mainstream economic thought at Western universities and return home with that knowledge.[6] They served as catalysts of a neoclassical awakening after 1989, while the majority of members of the older generations of mathematical economists who had put all their faith in optimal planning did not jump on the bandwagon of neoclassical triumph.

Were they scared for good by the censors in the 1950s and 1960s? One could hardly accept this assumption knowing that optimal planners experienced a weakening of political control in Hungary long before the collapse of communism; some even enjoyed special privileges as advisors to or employees of the party-state. True, one must not disregard the recurrent intimidation of mathematical economists and their partial exclusion from official political economy. Nonetheless, after a while, mathematical reasoning in economic sciences ceased to be forbidden fruit, with all the excitement of its consumption. In terms of the Kádárist trinity of cultural policy[7] pursued from the early 1960s, mathematical economics was not prohibited but tolerated and then openly supported by the authorities. To put it bluntly, Hungarian mathematical economists had a relatively easy time for decades in the trap of optimal planning. They were convinced that they had found not only a political and existential but also a scientific *modus vivendi* by tacitly abandoning Marxist-Leninist textbook political economy without joining the neoclassical mainstream. They trusted the authenticity and success of their own research program and considered it at least as valuable by scholarly standards as any similar program initiated in the West. Returning to the basic research question of this chapter, we would like to check the assumption that, following a brief phase of devotion, the majority of Hungarian mathematical economists *did not want* to turn into veritable neoclassical thinkers, and quite sincerely so, driven—as time passed—by scientific preferences rather than political fears.

The first mathematical economists in Hungary were ready to make concessions without scruples by camouflaging (a) the divergence of their models that invoked an ideally technocratic vision of communism from the real world of bureaucracy in a Soviet-type planned economy, and (b) the similarities between their theories and the neoclassical ones. As usual, self-censorship resulted in self-cheating once these scholars fell in love with their concepts of optimal planning and made a virtue from necessity. They convinced themselves that a neoclassical turn would not only backfire politically but also would be scientifically superfluous and even harmful. As if the grapes were sour, they resisted the intellectual appeal of neoclassical thought by picking and choosing some of its instruments but ignoring its underlying philosophy and methodology. Instead of recognizing neoclassical economics as a Grand Theory, they considered it as a collection of technical recipes, from which one chooses the principle of optimization without whispering a word of praise about price theory. Moreover, even a frontal attack like Kornai's *Antiequilibrium* (1971) did not lead to irrevocable excommunication from the economic profession in the West. You safely could claim that the basic concepts of neoclassical economics (a) are unrealistic and reflect an ultra-liberal worldview replacing one extreme (state collectivism) with another (free-market individualism); (b) do not offer Eastern European economists an opportunity to comprehend their own economies better than their homemade theories do; and (c) deter the economists from searching for a "healthy" convergence in terms of both economic systems and theories describing them. *Nota bene*, from the 1970s, neoclassical thought, particularly, the traditional interpretation of its central category, general equilibrium, began to struggle with issues of self-confidence[8] (Lucas 1976; Kydland and Prescott 1982), opening up new (among others, neo-Marxist) vistas of criticism even among mathematical economists in the West.

At any rate, can mathematical economics prosper outside (or on the edge) of the neoclassical paradigm? Considering the example of Hungary and a majority of communist countries, yes, it definitely can. At least, it could in the past, for a long time, up to a certain point, resulting in theoretical discoveries and a whole range of experimental applications in the field of optimal planning. However, while the analytical results were promising, the normative project of "plan improvement"[9] failed following a series of trials and errors. Moreover, this project trapped many of its advocates even after the fiasco. Was it the West, where the idea of general equilibrium slowly lost its popularity, that finally opened their eyes? We rather assume that Hungarian mathematical planners eventually grew disappointed with the idea of optimization, more precisely, the idea of optimization *in a Soviet-type planned economy*, which failed exactly because it was tested in vivo in that particular economic system.

In order to assess the above conjectures, we will first sketch out the ways, in which mathematics enriched planning concepts in Hungary. Then the institutional preconditions of evolution of those concepts will be discussed. Here, we will focus on the Institute of Economics, a renowned research center attached to the Hungarian Academy of Sciences, in which two leading mathematical economists of Eastern Europe, András Bródy and János Kornai, worked in close proximity for many decades.[10] They took different approaches to the theory of planning in the "triumphant" period of optimization of central plans but eventually agreed on staying outside the realm of neoclassical economics in many essential respects. The conclusion will sum up the reasons why Hungarian mathematical economists lost their trust in rationalizing planning and examine what other research programs they chose instead.

Our study had to cope with the lack of secondary literature published by historians of economic thought in Hungary and beyond.[11] We did our best to fill this gap by participant observation, numerous old and new interviews with our colleagues, memoirs, and archival sources. The reader is warned about possible biases since one of the authors (Kovács) was affiliated with the Institute of Economics for more than 30 years.[12]

Traditions, Institutions, Experts

After planting the seeds for mathematical research into central planning during the 1960s, economic sciences in Hungary seemed prepared to reap the
first harvest by the 1970s. However, the first harvest also proved to be the
last. [13] The idea of rationality to be found somewhere outside the spheres of
textbook political economy and reform economics (market socialism) began
to fade away slowly but steadily.

The 1960s were still an unmistakable success story although the previous
10 to 15 years had been anything but promising. Even if anti-Jewish legisla-
tion before the Second World War, the war itself, and—following a few years
of relatively peaceful academic activity—the total Sovietization of social sciences had not nearly eradicated economic theory (and mathematical research)
in Hungary through murder, emigration, imprisonment, occupational ban,
and marginalization, the contingent of economists with mathematical skills
would have been very small. Like other countries in Eastern Europe, two
main strands of tradition dominated economic sciences in Hungary before
the war: the German Historical School and—to a lesser extent—the Austrian
School of Economics. Simply put, the former was open to the idea of major
state intervention, and even state ownership; the latter considered the introduction of central plans and collective property as large steps along the
"road to serfdom." This ideological difference notwithstanding, both schools
normally excluded formal models from economic analysis. The only areas
where quantitative reasoning found acceptance were in the systematization
of empirical data and rudimentary economic dynamics. Between the two
wars, the followers of the German Historical School in Hungary celebrated
the idea of planning and advocated a *dirigiste* economic regime, a "bounded"
or "managed" economy, as they called their ideal of corporative state capitalism. They formulated the planning procedures in verbal (let alone, elementary
mathematical) terms, and proposed that the institutional framework of the
central plan be patterned after the war economy as they knew it from the First
World War. [14]

One does not know, of course, what would have happened to research into
mathematical economics and its application to central planning in Hungary
if scholars like János Neumann or Miklós Káldor had not left the country
before the war. [15] Would they have survived and been permitted to work in the
academia, particularly, in the field of planning doctrines? To take the example of game theory, could Neumann have launched his research program,
teaching at a Budapest university from 1945 onward? Could Harsányi have
developed the theory further during the 1960s if he had not left the country
in 1948? [16] Similarly, would it have made a difference if the local forerunners
of econometric research such as István Varga and Mátyás Matolcsy had not

been silenced and imprisoned, respectively, after the communist takeover?[17] To put counter-factual questions aside, what is well-known is the sad fact that Varga was the only one from an older generation of eminent scholars who made a comeback in economic research during Hungary's communist era. Varga became influential for a short period around 1956, and at that time he focused on market reforms instead of experimenting with mathematical planning.[18] Those few who kept the fire of mathematical economics warm from before 1945, such as the econometricians Ede Theiss[19] and Kálmán Kádas, were marginalized.

Communist (or social-democratic) economists, well-versed in neoclassical thought like Oskar Lange in Poland, lacking, the supply of mathematical methods in economic analysis emerged from other sources: a few Western textbooks and Soviet works, cooperation with local mathematicians (like Alfréd Rényi in the case of Bródy and Tamás Lipták in that of Kornai), and engineering education (Péter Erdős and Ferenc Jánossy). Many of the freshly-baked planning experts (such as Augusztinovics, Kornai, András Nagy and Márton Tardos) were self-made mathematicians.

Despite the unfortunate prerequisites to a solid development of mathematical economics, the seeds of the discipline slowly came to fruition. Research and education managed to profit from an ironic combination of two unrelated political factors in the second half of the 1950s: (a) the growing legitimacy of applying mathematical methods in economic research in the Soviet Union and (b) the impasse of reformist thought in Hungary due to the crushing of the 1956 revolution by the same Soviet Union. Let us now consider the domestic institutional and cultural preconditions of the turn toward the mathematics of planning.

Starting with scholarly publications, a growing number of foreign-language books and periodicals on mathematical economics became available in the libraries of the main institutes of economic research and Karl Marx University of Economics in Budapest from the late 1950s. The same applied to translated works. Edited collections of articles and book excerpts published in the West or popular guides to the new discipline such as Szakolczai (1963, 1967), Andorka, Martos, and Szakolczai (1967), Hoch (1968), and Andorka (1970) made the breakthrough. Translations of volumes written or edited by Soviet economists and mathematicians (e.g., Nemchinov 1962, 1966; Khachaturov 1966; Pontriagin et al. 1968; Petrakov 1970; Novozhilov 1971) were also helpful.[20] The books of leading Western authors followed suit. For instance, Jan Tinbergen's *Econometrics* came out in Hungarian in 1957, William Baumol's *Economic Theory and Operations Analysis* in 1968, Edmond Malinvaud's *Méthodes statistiques de l'économétrie* in 1974, and a truncated version of Paul Samuelson's *Economics* in 1976.[21] Meanwhile, also important works by Oskar Lange (1965, 1966, 1967a, 1967b), Michał

Kalecki (1980, 1982),[22] and Wassily Leontief (1977, 1984) were published in translation. From the 1970s on, an avalanche of collections of papers written by other contemporary great theorists/Nobel laureates (such as Ragnar Frisch 1974, John Hicks 1978, Kenneth Arrow 1979, James Tobin 1984, Lawrence Klein 1986, Milton Friedman 1986, Gérard Debreu 1987, Miklós Káldor 1989) was launched by the *Közgazdasági és Jogi Könyvkiadó* (Economics and Law Publishing House). In some way, many prominent Hungarian mathematical economists and their disciples took part in translation and editing.

Numerous foreign authors spent some time in Budapest or met their Hungarian colleagues abroad.[23] Strong academic bonds emerged from these encounters (e.g., between Bródy and Leontief or Kornai and Arrow), not to speak of publications in excellent journals and publishing houses as well as prestigious collective volumes. Bródy's 1966 article in the *Quarterly Journal of Economics*, and Kornai's recurrent contributions to *Econometrica* (Kornai and Lipták 1962, 1965; Kornai and Martos 1973) set the bar very high.[24] The former published his books at North Holland and SAGE, the latter at North Holland and Oxford University Press.[25] Early on, they were invited to take part in edited volumes such as Bronfenbrenner (1969) in the case of Bródy; Malinvaud, and Bacharach (1967b) and Nove and Nuti (1972b) in the case of Kornai; and Bornstein (1975) in the case of Augusztinovics. The width of the stream of all these publications demonstrates not only the growing influence of Western (and, to a certain extent, Eastern[26]) scholarship on Hungarian economists but also the growing legitimacy of mathematical economics in the eyes of the authorities.

As will be shown, the domestic publications of Hungarian I-O scholars and optimal planners also started mushrooming in the 1960s and 1970s. The first English-language book on input-output analysis (Lukács et al. 1962)[27] was preceded or followed by a whole series of Hungarian-language works published, besides Bródy and Kornai, by Rudolf Andorka, Mária Augusztinovics, Péter Bod, Gusztáv Báger, Sándor Ganczer, Zoltán Kenessey, György Kondor, Béla Martos, Antal Máriás, András Nagy, Ferencné Nyitrai, Albert Rácz, András Simon, György Simon, András Simonovits, György Szakolczai, Márton Tardos, and others.[28] Later, when the trust in optimization diminished, scientific production did not decline but changed its face. The researchers diversified the models by including nonlinear and dynamic analysis or engaged in long-term planning. Both research strategies resulted in important English-language volumes (e.g., Martos 1975; Augusztinovics 1984). As regards scientific papers, in the beginning, the main periodical of the economic research community *Közgazdasági Szemle* (Economic Review) was reluctant to publish articles with a complex mathematical apparatus, but this attitude softened during the 1960s. With the publication of the journals *Szigma* and *Acta Oeconomica,*[29] mathematical economics slowly became a standard discipline in Hungary by the 1970s. For example, Bródy's and Kornai's papers of mathematical relevance on intersectoral relations and optimal planning began to appear in *Közgazdasági Szemle* in the late 1950s; from then on, just about every important work by the two authors was published in both Hungarian and English.[30]

However, one genre of academic writing was forbidden to most leading research economists: the university textbook. With the exception of Bródy's (1962a, 1962b) textbooks on linear and stochastic programming and a brief chapter written by Kornai (1969) on mathematical methods of planning for a textbook published by Karl Marx University, the articles and books of eminent scholars in the field featured at most in the reading lists of certain courses (or among the informal recommendations by some teachers). Up until 1989, just two of the scholars listed previously was offered a regular professorial job at the University of Economics. In the best case, the others were allowed to hold a few lectures and smaller seminars (Bródy 1994, 328; Kornai 2007, 209–11).

Leaving the terrain of scientific publications and jumping back to the time of the communist takeover, planning theories (both verbal and mathematical) were developed in Hungary by and large under the aegis of four institutions: Karl Marx University of Economics, the National Planning Office, the Central Statistical Office, and the Institute of Economics at the Hungarian Academy of Sciences.[31]

Karl Marx University: Teaching Mathematics, Ignoring Economics

Initially, Karl Marx University of Economics (*Marx Károly Közgazdasági Egyetem*) in Budapest was the only institution of higher learning that trained economists in Hungary.[32] Over time, the textbooks of political economy incorporated thoughts about market reforms, shortages, investment cycles, and so on, but even the textbooks published during the 1980s failed to discuss mathematical concepts of planning or other quantitative models in detail.[33] Although from 1961 courses were held and textbooks written on calculus, linear algebra, probability and statistics as well as operations research, the university relegated the theory of planning to the Department of Planning the People's Economy. This unit was small and had low prestige; initially, it completely ignored modern economics and, by and large, its textbook was a summary of what was taught by the Department of Political Economy about real socialism. It hardly included any information on the functioning of real-life planning regimes.[34]

Until 1960, the role of mathematics at the university was restricted to a simple repetition of high-school level basics (Forgó and Komlósi 2015). Even György Péter, an actuarial analyst who became president of the Central

Statistical Office, asserted in the 1950s that the four basic algebraic operations would be more than enough for an economist to know (Augusztinovics 2008, 1164). He served as head of the Statistics Department of the university from 1950. In contrast, Béla Krekó, a disciple of András Prékopa—"father" of operations research and probability theory in Hungary[35]—and assistant professor at the Mathematics Department, was committed to introduce the paradigm of optimization in the education of economists. He had futile discussions with the rectorate at the end of the 1950s. When he wanted to include game theory in the curriculum, one of its leading officials responded in an indignant style by saying, "Comrades, we have to preserve the university as a serious institution" (Forgó and Komlósi 2015, 3). Finally, Krekó was permitted to try out linear programming as an elective course with 20 to 30 students in 1959.

In 1961, he was allowed to invite the best 15 to 20 students in mathematics to take part in a new special program called *tervmatematika* (mathematics of planning). In this five-year program 60 percent of the courses were related to mathematics (calculus, linear algebra, cybernetics, mathematical programming, statistics, game theory, electrotechnics, and physics).[36] The program soon became popular, nurturing generations of mathematical economists. It launched a "deterministic" and a "stochastic" track. Although the program was also supervised by the Department of Planning, the planning courses were taught with hardly any mathematics. The term "neoclassical economics" popped up (if at all), followed by plain faultfinding comments, in lectures on the history of economic thought. The first textbook providing a general introduction into mathematical economics (including input-output analysis and a few neoclassical models) was not published until as late as 1989 (Zalai 1989).

Despite all efforts to the contrary, the quantitative methods courses remained theoretical because the university did not cooperate on a regular basis with either the Planning Office and the Statistical Office or the economic ministries. The courses were related neither to central planning nor to other important issues of macroeconomic research. Examples for optimization were rather taken from company life and referred to challenges such as which factors of production to purchase or how large an inventory to hold (Halpern 2020; Kőrösi 2020). The only textbook-like volume on models of long-term planning, written mostly by researchers at the Planning Office and translated into English and Russian (Augusztinovics 1979), was not taught at the university.

National Planning Office: Improving the Plan—Feeling Futile

The main institution responsible for the conceptualization and implementation of central plans was the National Planning Office (*Országos Tervhivatal*) founded in 1947. One of its main tasks was to coordinate the planning activities of the various ministries before they started negotiating with firms in the respective branches and to aggregate the outcomes of negotiations thereafter. Central planning was dominated by a traditional (verbal) political economy approach with a minimum of mathematical modeling during the entire communist period despite the fact that many attempts were made, inside and outside the Office, to apply advanced scientific tools that outshone the so-called "material balance method" borrowed from the Soviet Union, which did not require any more skill than elementary mathematics.

"The Central Planning Office was an <oasis> in Hungarian public administration. . . . A very flexible institution, in which it was important from the very outset that employees must have something in their head," remembered Augusztinovics (2012) long after its demise in 1990. She attributed this flexibility to the fact that—although the Office was a Soviet-style establishment—it was brand-new in the 1940s, free from the legacy of Austro-Hungarian bureaucracy (Augusztinovics 2008, 1165). From 1966 onward, the "mathematics of planning" program of Karl Marx University provided the Planning Office with good-quality experts. Collaborative projects with the Institute of Economics (*Közgazdaságtudományi Intézet*), which were launched during the early 1960s, also contributed to the growth of mathematical knowledge in the Office. Its Computing Center was founded in 1968.[37]

As regards planning as a scientific discipline, the Institute of Planned Economy (*Tervgazdasági Intézet*) that had been established between 1963 and 1966 under the aegis of the Planning Office set up a department of mathematical modeling. Here, Augusztinovics was employed as a leading researcher from 1964 to 1968. Before and after, she worked on financial balances and macro-modeling in general in various leading positions at the Office. Zsuzsa Bekker, who focused on growth models, joined the Institute a little later. The majority of researchers there produced verbal studies of central planning.[38] Among them was a brilliant thinker, Ferenc Jánossy, who invented iconoclastic theories of calculating national income and modeling economic development by using old-school statistical apparatus (Jánossy 1963, 1966). He was one of few scholars who—despite mastering higher-level mathematics—refrained from using it to improve planning and did not call himself a mathematical economist.[39]

In spite of all attempts at quantification, mathematical models played a major role only in medium-term, two-level (later, multi-level) planning, an initiative of Kornai in the 1960s (see below), and later in long-term planning, Augusztinovics's favorite field of study. Both were eventually futile undertakings but enjoyed an esteemed reputation among researchers due to the involvement of the two respected scholars, the parallel research programs in the West, and the relative freedom of scientific imagination. An open-minded scholarly approach to long-run economic processes remained exceptional in an organization whose everyday operation was based on a predominantly verbal (bookkeeping-style) planning of material balances for annual and five-year plans. In the beginning, the composition of such balances, including the final synthetic "chessboard balance" (intersectoral balance, $\acute{A}KM$ in Hungarian) describing the relationships among the main branches/sectors of the national economy, did not require advanced mathematical knowledge. However, the chessboard contained all the information necessary for embarking upon input-output analysis. Yet, despite the fact that, from the early 1960s, the chessboards were used as I-O tables and researchers in the Planning Office performed complex mathematical operations with them, the planning apparatus was bogged down in old Soviet habits of inter-and intra-departmental bargaining[40] when setting up the macro-plans and breaking them down, via various industry-level agencies (ministries, directorates, trusts, associations, and so on), to the level of individual firms. In this intricate—multi-level and multilateral—bargaining game mathematics played a subordinate role; quantitative procedures of some complexity were mostly referred to if they seemed useful for any of the actors in the game. The following is a telling story from the life of the Office:

> By the end of 1958, the *ex ante* national income . . . displayed a deficit of 13 billion Hungarian forints, an enormous amount at that time, some 10 percent of the national income . . . . (The expected price increase of material inputs was generally overestimated and the price index of outputs generally underestimated by Ministries and large firms.) The President of the Planning Office offered a prize: a bottle of French champagne for each recovered billion. Deficit-hunting went on in the Planning Office for several weeks without success.

> As a final resort, the management reluctantly consented to the compilation and repricing of a rather large interindustry table, something that was unknown and alien to traditional planning practices. "The chessboard game" began. Cell by cell, representatives of emitting and absorbing sectors had to meet personally and negotiate. . . . Within one week, all 13 billions were found. . . . We drank the 13 bottles of champagne and many more. (Augusztinovics 1995, 272)

Yet, instead of the computing center, plans were fabricated in the shady rooms of the Office, in which clerks rather than technocrats were making deals to finalize the planning indicators.[41] In order to achieve a meaningful selection of material balances, they had to solve numerous problems of measurement, commensurability, prioritization, and so on—problems all permeated by the conflicting interests of winners and losers, be they branch ministries, regional bodies, or ordinary firms. Moreover, these conflicts were mediated by a complicated network of party and state organizations including

non-economic institutions like the army. The outcome of bargaining processes overrode any results of optimal planning models during the crafting
stage of the central planning instructions that were turned into law. Provided
they had not overridden them, the same would have happened in the phase
of implementing the instructions, leading to an endless chain of retroactive
revisions of the planning figures (and amendments to the law). True, after a
while, the I-O models could be used to validate the changes made at the negotiating tables, either before the plan was approved or thereafter, much more
rapidly than earlier. Originally, the clerks were running from room to room in
the Planning Office with pencil and eraser in their hands in order to replace
a figure in the material balance of a particular product after their boss had
taken a phone call from an influential party politician or state bureaucrat.[42]
Augusztinovics lamented in retrospect: the mathematical models "remained a
façade all the time, they were in the best case thought-provoking but did not
ever become instruments of real decision-making. The real decisions emerged
from bargaining" (Augusztinovics 2000, 12–13).

Under such circumstances, one could not effectively test the applicability of
the input-output and optimal planning models,[43] even if the Statistical Office
delivered more accurate data as the years went by (see below) and the planners' toolbox expanded in step to include advanced mathematical methods.
Whether or not these models could have proven solid instruments of planning
at all was never determined. Mathematical economists did not have a choice
other than refining them in the hope of being perhaps listened to by the planning officials in the foreseeable future (cf. Ganczer 1973; Simon 1970, 1973;
Szepesi and Székely 1974). Since five-year planning continued until 1989,
the models did not cease to emerge in the Planning Office during the 1980s,
even after many mathematical economists had lost their faith in optimal planning. Quantification was, in the best case, suitable for underpinning a superficial check on the realism of plans produced by verbal techniques. While
in this respect their authors exerted some disciplining influence, they were
virtually powerless in affecting normative decisions.[44] Mathematical planners
in the Office encountered serious difficulties, for example, in identifying the
objective function, according to which the models should have been optimized. Beyond lamenting the lack of "clean" data and arbitrary changes in the
plans due to petty bargaining, this could have been the point where optimal
planners clashed with their principals the most vigorously.[45]

However, instead of insisting on new priorities in economic policy (hor-
ribile dictu, radically increasing living standards and slowing down economic
growth, or cutting military spending and trade with the Soviet Union), they
normally accepted most of the objectives defined by the ruling elite. Because
of firm political taboos, mathematical economists did not think of resisting the will of the nomenklatura publicly. They put up with pointing out

inconsistencies in the balances, smuggling a few new priorities into the plans, juggling with multiple draft plans, or playing mathematical tricks, mentioned by Augusztinovics above, which could modify the outcome of plan bargaining.[46] To the luck of optimal planners, by the mid-1980s, the top leaders of the Office and their advisors hardly could be distinguished from those of the Finance Ministry,[47] a stronghold of reform-minded economic policy and a think tank of late-communist transformation. In retrospect, the Planning Office seems to have been ready to engage in indicative planning, in which mathematical economists could have found ample space for themselves to experiment with Tinbergenian solutions. However, communism collapsed and the Office was closed, leaving behind a large gap in macro-coordination.

Central Statistical Office: From Chessboard to Econometrics

Hungary's tradition of statistical work on government level and higher education programs was informed by the German Historical School that laid the foundations for statistical research. The Central Statistical Office (*Központi Statisztikai Hivatal*) established in 1867 served as its strong institutional basis even after the communist takeover. Nevertheless, the Office was reorganized by a team led by György Péter, who worked as its president from 1948 to 1968.[48] In his view, a main task of the institution was to supply the Central Planning Office with reliable economic information. In the beginning, he had despised statistics as a discipline of calculating percentages (Köves 2005, 879) but later grew familiar with input-output analysis. While dutifully Sovietizing the statistical regime of the country, Péter developed a comprehensive observation system to measure the performance of state-owned firms. The first—experimental—version of the intersectoral balance was completed by the Office in 1957. In collaboration with the Planning Office, they accomplished a proper decomposition of the productive sectors in 1957 to create the first input-output table for Hungary by 1959 (Kenessey 1959).

In 1963, a special department was established within the Statistical Office to develop the economic applications of mathematical-statistical methods. Two years later, an econometric laboratory and a larger information processing laboratory (later, *Infelor*) was also set up.[49] While *Infelor* slowly became a quasi-independent company (Lampl 1971), the Econometric Laboratory remained within the Statistical Office. The members of the Laboratory (such as László Halabuk, Katalin Hulyák, László Hunyadi, Zoltán Kenessey, Judit Neményi, János Paizs, and György Szakolczai), were well-trained researchers in mathematics and statistics who started teaching one another modern econometric methods. They were driven by the urge to understand time series as well as linear and nonlinear regression analysis and other contemporary econometric techniques.[50] The early econometricians of the Office had to overcome the resistance of traditional German-style descriptive statistics reinforced by its Soviet version. In the 1950s and 1960s, official political economy rejected any stochastic approach to central planning, assuming "objective" certainty instead of probability in portraying economic processes. Unsurprisingly, the most educated—more importantly, neoclassical-minded—expert of econometrics in Hungary, Ede Theiss, had only an advisory affiliation with the Statistical Office.[51] Nonetheless, he was instrumental in launching the first experimental econometric macro-model of the Hungarian economy, M-1 (Theiss 1965; Halabuk, Kenessey, and Theiss 1965). The multidirectional causalities among the sectors had been captured with the help of a simultaneous system of stochastic equations. This method was in vogue in the West at the time, and the project including the estimations, forecasts, and simulations was successful enough. The next model, M-2, exerted influence on models in other communist countries; M-3 was a joint Czechoslovak-Hungarian initiative; and the authors of M-4 made an attempt at integrating econometrics and input-output analysis by incorporating an interrelated, deterministic, and stochastic input-output block in the model and representing the effects of non-material production closer to the SNA technique[52] than earlier (Halabuk 1971, 1976; Hulyák 1972; Hunyadi 2012). In 1982, some members of the Laboratory moved to the Institute of Economics. Here, they did not initiate collaborative projects with those researchers of the Institute who had already begun to run econometric programs themselves (Halpern 2020).

While economic theorists always complained that the Statistical Office delivered neither sufficient nor accurate information, the level of precision of the data increased remarkably in the communist era. Obviously, political biases, ranging from military secrets to artificial prices, continued to deform statistical information, and the lowest-level economic actors were astute enough to start plan bargaining already during the data provision phase. The planning bureaucrats would have magnified these errors and falsifications to their extreme if I-O analysts, optimal planners, and econometricians had not succeeded in confining distortion through their models time and again.

Institute of Economics: Making Mathematics Legitimate in Political Economy

The fourth institution that made a lasting contribution to developing planning concepts and methods in Hungary was the Institute of Economics at the Hungarian Academy of Sciences. In terms of original discoveries that might match similar results in mathematical economics in the West and the East, it proved the most productive in input-output analysis and optimal planning. Scientific innovation stood in strong correlation with the privileges the Institute's researchers enjoyed in accessing literature, choosing projects, fostering international relations, and publishing.

In the wake of Imre Nagy's "New Course," the Institute was established in 1954 with the aim of "laying the scientific foundations of economic policy." It published *Közgazdasági Szemle*, the main scientific monthly of the discipline to the present day in Hungary.[53] Founding director István Friss was appointed by the conservative faction of the Central Committee to counterbalance Nagy's reform program. However, a majority of affiliated researchers identified themselves with that program since they had been selected by Friss according to their scholarly talent rather than political loyalty.[54]

Even those among them who had some prior knowledge of mathematics refrained from applying quantitative research techniques at the very beginning.[55] They put faith in the possibility of restarting market reforms after the 1956 revolution, at least until the so-called Varga Commission that had suggested a further liberalization of planning was disbanded by the government in 1957. It was only during the later years of the first—militant—phase of Kádárist "consolidation" that several members of the younger generation, many of whom burned their fingers in 1956, felt persuaded to withdraw to a safer space within academia and use mathematics as a jargon of dissent.[56]

Amidst the post-revolutionary hangover, a number of frustrated market reformers were looking for a refuge where they could tide over hard times and from where they could emerge well-equipped with sound techniques of economic measurement, analysis, and prediction. They felt uneducated and inaccurate, and decided to overcome forced parochialism. Eagerly catching up with then-mainstream theories in the West, they wanted neither to fully renounce their Marxist convictions nor to exclude the possibility of rejoining reform programs at a future point. They hoped that—provided they could reassure their main adversaries about the political innocence of mathematical methods—the scientific language might protect them for the simple reason that it was impenetrable to the censors.[57] They did not anticipate, however, that such a discursive refuge could turn into a trap in the long run.

This strategy of self-camouflage did not prove entirely successful. Although Bródy's proud Marxist/collectivist stance as well as Kornai's sharp attack on general equilibrium theory may have demonstrated a fair degree of ideological obedience, suspicion toward mathematical economics burst out repeatedly. It was fueled by some leading scholars of the Institute, including deputy director Tamás Nagy, an influential reform economist and dedicated Marxist, even as late as the end of the 1970s.[58] Nevertheless, in the shadow of the Institute's persistent commitment to market reforms, mathematical-economic research programs continued to remain a tolerated (or provisionally supported) albeit secondary feature of the place. Prior to the introduction of the New Economic Mechanism (NEM) in 1968, the Institute of Economics served as a major pool of ideas on market reform and—under the directorship of the father of NEM, Rezső Nyers, from 1974 onward—became an academic stronghold levelling criticism at the counter-reform measures taken by the party-state after 1972/73. Mathematical knowledge did not count for much in this rearguard battle.

At the turn of the 1960s and 1970s, Bródy and Kornai were permitted to organize small research groups that attracted gifted young economists and mathematicians to the Institute. As mentioned, neither of them nor their close associates were allowed to teach regularly at Karl Marx University. Thus, they were not urged to build up a systematic body of knowledge in mathematical economics (Simonovits 2019). Yet, they affected many students of the university's "mathematics of planning" program through their works and numerous formal and informal discussions held at the Institute and even at the university.[59] The bulk of research into mathematical methods of planning in Hungary revolved around the Institute in concentric circles. For example, from the early 1960s onward, the Institute worked together with the Central Statistical Office and the computing center of the Planning Office (and later with its research institute) with hardly any friction. To an extent, cooperation was based on personal relationships[60] without aggressive political control. Astonishingly, the breakthrough of mathematical economics during the 1960s proved irreversible. In 1964, István Friss solemnly stressed that "if one could dispute the application of mathematics in economic science for a long time, there is no room for such doubts after the [positive] experiences during the past years" (Augusztinovics 1964, 65).[61] Apparently, this declaration was not just caused by internal lobbying by mathematical economists in the Institute but also by the influence of their Soviet colleagues, which resulted in mutual research visits and the publication of Nemchinov's path-breaking edited volume in Hungarian in 1962.[62] The process of legitimization seemed to end with an invitation, sent to Kornai who—accused of revisionism—had been fired in 1958, to rejoin the Institute in 1967. (The decision was made by Friss in both cases.)

As the previous sections suggest, there was a fairly cohesive group of dozens of scholars cultivating mathematical techniques of economic research in the partner institutions of the Institute of Economics.[63] Within the latter, two generations combined forces before 1989.[64] This was a small and stable research community, with two international stars surrounded by their associates who were barely threatened by external professional competition and enjoyed considerable freedom of thought within their research groups. However, ultimately they had to adjust to the mix of family atmosphere and quasi-feudal hierarchy prevailing in the Institute.[65]

During the 1960s and early 1970s, the majority of older researchers in mathematical economics focused on the theory of central planning in some sense. Professional solidarity among them was relatively strong for many reasons, ranging from the scientific vernacular they spoke to being occasional victims of harassment. The same applies to Bródy and Kornai who—irrespective of a growing divergence between their research programs and political attitudes—did not air their dirty linen in public.[66] The early research projects of the Institute in mathematical economics focused on input-output models (Ausch, Bródy) and optimal planning/programming (Kornai and Martos, András Nagy). Kondor and Simon studied both fields. According to Virág (1973), Simonovits (1996), and Csató (2019), the principal research fields covered by both generations in the Institute at the turn of the 1960s and 1970s were as follows: closed and open, static and dynamic input-output models, and the Neumann model (Bródy, Halpern), "searchlight programming" (Simon) as a decomposition procedure, nonlinear programming (Martos), equilibrium theory (Kornai), team theory (Simonovits) "vegetative" (non-price) control (Kornai, Martos, Simonovits, and Virág), queueing theory (Simonovits), planners' behavior (Lackó), decision theory (Tényi), growth models (Virág, Horváth, and Rimler), planning labor market and vocational training (Bondár, Horváth, and Tényi), consumption theory (Hoch, Ilona Kovács, Ördög, and Radnóti), and macroeconomic modeling (Kondor, Simon, and Gábor).

Interestingly, the most powerful academic initiative to rationalize medium-term central planning based on the idea of two-level planning came from outside the Institute of Economics in the course of the 1960s. Its pillars rested on a nearly decade-long cooperation of multiple state agencies and research institutes and embraced dozens of researchers under the guidance of Kornai, then formally still an outcast (Kornai 1965).

Ironically, mathematical economics became largely uncontested within the Institute only *after* Kornai's (1965) and Bródy's (1970) seminal works on optimal planning and input-output analysis, respectively, had been completed and the attraction of these research programs started petering out. At first sight, this cries for a political explanation, for it might seem as if mathematical methods were tolerated or even promoted once a growing number of researchers had abandoned applying them as means for intervening in the "high politics" of central planning. Accordingly, from that time on, they were free to build quantitative models of shortages, the labor market, shadow economy, and economic fluctuations, or even to indulge in the intricacies of economic control, just to name a few successful research projects, provided they did not challenge the institutional and ideological core of the five-year plans. Moreover, the model builders were permitted to use any mathematical techniques they thought opportune. Yet, in terms of methodology, some of the new models were more rigorously neoclassical than those of optimal planning, and the results of many of them were more explosive politically (see Postscript).

Undoubtedly, these models grew less normative and more descriptive and analytical in nature. However, with normativity their "meliorist" attitudes (cf. perfecting the planned economy) faded away and slowly were replaced by a cool-headed, impartial approach colored by a kind of "inverse normativity" pointing toward capitalism. Quite a few economists at the Institute were equipped to transition to neoclassical scholarly culture by the mid-1980s, at least as far as their mathematical expertise was concerned, and this had little to do with self-restraint in matters of high-ranking party and state affairs. Just the opposite happened: by then official political economy and its guardians in the higher echelons of the party-state became too weak to resist the proliferation of critical economic thought underpinned by an ever deeper mathematical knowledge. Nevertheless, this deepening never would have taken place without the groundbreaking contribution of the first cohort of input-output specialists and linear programmers.

At the same time, the members of the older generation—while pulling their disciples into mathematical economics as well as nurturing and safeguarding them—did not push them out from the "refuge," prompting them to convert to neoclassical economics. What is more, during the 1970s, they continued to refine I-O analysis and planning models, in harmony with close colleagues outside the Institute (e.g., Augusztinovics 1979).[67] True, their attention switched from five-year plans to planning economic processes in the long run (see below). It was only Márton Tardos (who joined the Institute in 1980) and András Nagy (who rejoined it in 1973) among the older scholars who acquainted some of the younger researchers with standard neoclassical thought—ironically, through its critique offered by new institutional economics.

This schematic story of the evolution of quantitative methods in economic research cultivated in the Institute of Economics would not stand the test of reality if, next to the textbook political economists and the mathematical economists, a third group of actors, the reform economists, were ignored. For example, the weakening of the party-state's resilience to criticism mentioned above was due, to a large extent, to the radicalization of reformist thought. Moderate or radical, the market reformers were similar to the textbook political economists (a rare species among the members of the Institute by the way[68]) in doing predominantly verbal research while reminding the observer of the mathematical economists when rejecting the sub-scientific discourse of the official textbooks. The reformers raised serious doubts upon state planning and contributed to its ideological disenchantment, which was received by many mathematical economists with mixed feelings. The latter also disapproved of the bureaucratization of planning and plan bargaining, namely, the distortion of scientific planning procedures by lobbies within the *nomenklatura*. However, they were afraid that the devaluation of central planning would eventually result in an overvaluation of the market and a decline in the quality of macro-management. Despite such disagreements, both groups shared the ideal of independent thinking, disliked parochialism,[69] cherished the memory of the 1956 revolution, and so on, that is, common attitudes sustaining solid bonds between their members. Furthermore, over the years, it was increasingly difficult to find a mathematical economist in the Institute who did not agree with the reformers on a considerable degree of marketization or even join verbal institutional research programs on that issue. To be sure, it was much easier for them to do so than for reform economists trying to learn how to build formal models.[70]

TWO PIONEERS IN ONE HOUSE: COMMON START, PEACEFUL RIVALRY, BIFURCATION

In terms of methodology András Bródy (1924–2010) and János Kornai (1928–2021) had chosen different points of departure for doing economic research on the planned economy. In the mid-1950s, the former opted for quantitative modeling while the latter chose verbal, quasi-sociological research. Later they took parallel roads leading to then-mainstream economics in the West. If space allowed we could write pages on the similarity of their social roots as well as political and cultural motivations—rich families, *Bildungsbürgertum*, cosmopolitan attitudes, Holocaust survival, joining the communist party and fascination with Marxism, the trauma of 1956, respect for scientific knowledge, a spirit of rebellion, and so forth—that would explain why the two young, self-educated intellectuals turned to Western economic theories. As mentioned, they helped (but also competed with) each other on their unfinished trip to neoclassical theory until they drifted apart. The causes of bifurcation of their research programs also would require a space dedicated to major differences in scholarly styles, attraction to other social/natural sciences, mathematical skills, demand for their works in scientific markets, political attitudes, and so on.

Bródy had introduced Kornai to input-output analysis whereas Kornai became more erudite in optimal planning than his friend and colleague. As Kornai (2018, 6) remembered, "in terms of methodology, Bródy (and many more Marxists, for example, Mária Augusztinovics) and I, who was not a Marxist but a fan of neoclassical theory in this phase of my life, were allies. ... We wanted to use mathematical methods, which forged a sort of alliance between us, I would say, complicity in the sense of understanding each other." Kornai imported Western-type research techniques, broke with Robinson

Crusoe-like routines of scientific organization and set up research teams whose members were assigned special tasks including literature reviews, case studies, model building, and testing, with particular attention to publication. While he benefited from a set of managerial skills, in addition to an ability to reinterpret and systematize ideas, Bródy was a lonely rider and a daring dreamer. "A majority of researchers in the Institute profited from or simply worked on projects developed from his flashes of inspiration" (Molnár 2019). Kornai carefully nourished many of his discoveries in comparison to Bródy who was not keen to flesh out his original insights in detail.[71] The role of the *enfant terrible* was always closer to his heart than that of the well-disciplined, widely respected researcher. Their younger colleagues had a chance to choose from these two scholarly attitudes or combine them freely.

The two charismatic scholars held sway over the research programs of the Institute of Economics in mathematical economics for a long period. In the beginning, Bródy's preoccupation with I-O models and Kornai's concentration on optimization complemented each other. Ironically, in working together on various projects, Bródy the Marxist grew less skeptical about neoclassical virtues than Kornai who had initially underpinned his studies of mathematical planning with neoclassical principles. Later, Bródy moved to the study of dynamic processes with a special interest in economic cycles and their mathematical complexities whereas Kornai, following a desperate struggle with general equilibrium theory, immersed himself in the scrutiny of disequilibrium with a renewed curiosity in institutional analysis. Meanwhile, problems of economic control, particularly whether it can lead to balanced growth, intrigued both of them immensely. The concept of equilibrium did not lose its appeal to them entirely even if they revisited it with growing suspicion. Bródy's (1994, 317) following words underline why their programs nonetheless diverged:

> Equilibrium is a very nice concept, without it one cannot do disequilibrium economics either. However, one also cannot create a theory that would guarantee, either via the market or the plan, that the equilibrium materializes. Moreover, and this applies to Kornai's works after *Anti-equilibrium*, my objection was that he wants to control the economy to adjust to an equilibrium that is again determined from outside.

András Bródy: From the End-of-Month Rush to the Kondratiev Cycles

Bródy's first inspiration to study economics came from Marxian political economy as he wanted to find an adequate mathematical structure for the reproduction schemes in *Capital*.[72] In the mid-1950s, he and his co-author Alfréd Rényi were unfamiliar with both Leontief's and Neumann's writings (Bródy 1994, 298). In examining centrally-managed price adjustment, they contended that prices with a given rate of profit are generated in an iterative process of circular adjustment where current prices emerge from the distortion of the unit cost in the previous period. Bródy and Rényi (1956) specified the conditions of convergence of this process. Later Bródy recognized that they accidentally had rediscovered the infinite series solution of the Leontief model—remarkably on the dual side.

In his early works Bródy also investigated the fluctuation of production in state-owned firms. Analyzing statistics of energy consumption by elementary tools of mathematics, he discovered that labor intensity sharply increased at the end of each month (*hóvégi hajrá*) (Bródy 1956). According to the key finding of this article, the cyclical characteristics of the production process were due to the periodic accounting of the fulfillment of planning targets, which was required by the branch ministries.

He also showed interest in the intersectoral foundations and computational methods of economic planning. Bródy's publications (1957, 1958, 1960a) were expository papers on input-output analysis, in which he demonstrated that the margin of error in the results of the I-O models is smaller than in the original data. Besides the ability of those models to display circular flows and cumulative effects in the economy as a whole, this was his main argument for their application, claiming that they provide robust conclusions concerning production structures, prices, and growth rates.[73] In addition to theoretical research, he participated in the computation of the first Hungarian SAM in the Central Statistical Office. At that time, Bródy (1960b, 954–55) protected his own model-building activity from excommunication by describing mathematical economics as "vulgar political economy," and accusing econometricians in the West (and the Hungarian Kálmán Kádas) of relying on the notion of "bourgeois rationality." He claimed that models cannot be borrowed from the West unless "one eradicates the last germs of bourgeois economics from them" and was embarrassed to read that Leontief's work had been said to be of "negative social value" in the United States because it helped manage a "totalitarian state." In retrospect, he portrayed his anti-Western attitudes as a blend of faith and opportunism (Bródy 1994, 348).

In 1961, Bródy defended his doctoral dissertation that summed up his knowledge of input-output analysis at the time, and this was his first attempt to clarify the Marxian background of I-O schemes. He proved the unicity of production prices and the rate of profit (Bródy 1962c). Later, he said that he recognized that this evidence was only a special case of Neumann's proof of the existence of general equilibrium (Bródy 1994, 314) although Neumann dealt with existence instead of unicity. In 1964, he continued working on the application of input-output models in Leontief's research group at Harvard where he cooperated with Anne Carter. In 1969, Bródy published a book with the title *Érték és újratermelés* (Value and Reproduction) that grew to be popular off the mainstream in the West. He regarded it as his *magnum opus* and had it translated into English under the title *Proportion, Prices and Planning: A Mathematical Restatement of the Labor Theory of Value* (Bródy 1970). The book departed from a closed, static, and deterministic model that drew from Lange, Leontief, and Neumann, and reinterpreted the turnpike theorem of equilibrium growth.[74] According to the author, the model reflected the duality of the Marxian concepts of use value and exchange value, could be directly applied to data, was computable, and was suitable for building consistent economic plans. Nevertheless, in his view, consistency was not tantamount to optimality:

> The model does not take decisions according to a given criterion of optimality, it does not automatize planning. It only makes for us possible to assess and compare relatively fast and simply some of the important consequences of decisions reflecting different economic policy considerations. (Bródy 1969, 12)[75]

> I did not believe in the Good Plan, but definitely trusted that the plan and the economy can be improved through model calculations. (Bródy 1994, 316)

Without attacking the theorists of optimal planning (including Kornai) head-on, Bródy cast doubts on the theory of optimal processes by pointing to (a) the vast number of constraints and control variables to be included in the I-O model if dynamized, which lead to difficulties in obtaining precise data and finding correct mathematical formulations, and (b) the possibility of sacrificing longer-term equilibrium for shorter-term optimization. More importantly, he alluded to the fact that the optimal planner is, in fact, not familiar with two things "only": the system to be controlled and the objectives, according to which it ought to be controlled.[76] However, rather than challenging directly the right of the party-state to determine the economic policy priorities (objective functions) of the central plan in Hungary (Bródy 1970, 147–53), he nailed down his own priorities, including a radical slowdown of economic growth, development of human capital, and avoiding overinvestment in fixed assets—suggestions identical to those of his friend Ferenc Jánossy.[77] Both of them thought that the market reformers of 1968 attributed too much importance to institutional change instead of calling for a balanced economic policy.[78] "If one wants to maximize something very much, what is one of the troubles with the planned economy, one will succeed in the beginning but fail in the end, even in fields where maximization was sought the most" (Bródy 1994, 325).

While continuing to refine his I-O models for decades (e.g., Bródy and Carter 1970a, 1970b; Bródy 1978, 1981, 1995, 2004a),[79] the problems of economic growth and development began to dominate Bródy's mind. A formative experience in studying economic dynamics was his encounter with Evsey Domar at MIT and Richard Stone in Cambridge in the mid-1960s. Upon return to Budapest, he aimed to clarify both the statics and the dynamics of economic systems, the latter with and without technological change (Bródy 1994, 315). This research endeavor gave an impetus for writing three books, including *Proportion, Prices and Planning*. Back in 1965, he had invented a simple model for economic growth. Departing from a closed dynamic Leontief model, he pointed out that the crucial factor restricting growth is human capital, in the Marxian sense of "production of workers" (Bródy 1966, 137). In Bródy's life the 1970s were devoted to resolute attempts to comprehend economic cycles. In 1980, he published a book entitled *Ciklus és szabályozás* (Cycles and Control) with the purpose of building a mathematical model of markets and cycles as suggested by classical authors such as Smith, Ricardo, Walras, and—obviously—Marx. He intended to derive the dynamic process of price formation from their texts (Bródy 1980, 44) and came to the conclusion that prices do not converge toward equilibrium but show a cyclical variation around it, which is analogous to the motion of a pendulum or a planet. In his model, product prices and quantities regulate each other (he calls this cross-control).[80]

Bródy (1980, 139) asserted that, according to the standard Marxist view of economic cycles, they were caused by the capitalist market even though cycles had existed before capitalism (see, e.g., the parable of seven years of great plenty and seven years of famine) and emerged also thereafter, in the planned economies. He searched for short and long cycles not only in economic and demographic time series like Kondratiev (Bródy 1997a, 1997b, 1999a, 1999b) but also in biological ones such as the pig cycle (Bródy 1994, 340). Bródy was interested in Goodwin's predator-prey model as well (Bródy and Farkas 1987). The theory of cycles served as a foundation for his explanation of economic crises in the world and errors in Hungarian economic policy. He wrote many articles in newspapers about this topic to a wider audience and published a popular book *Lassuló idő* (*Slowdown*) in 1985, which anticipated a global stagnation and many other economic maladies.[81]

As suggested above, Bródy (1994, 318) did not cease to believe in the labor theory of value but lost his faith in planning early on.[82] Instead of central planning, he envisioned a kind of economic self-regulation similar to that of physical and biological systems (cf. Kornai's concept of "vegetative control"). Thus, he was not really affected by the arguments of any of the conflicting parties in the Socialist Calculation Debate.[83] Indeed, he tried to integrate, to use his terminology, the "deterministic-causal" models of labor theory of value with the "teleological-optimizing" models of marginalism in the same mathematical framework and argued that these models bring identical results if the same data are fed into them (Bródy 1970, 50, 165). Seen as a follower of Wassily Leontief and Oskar Lange, heir of János Neumann, a mathematical interpreter of Karl Marx's theories, an adherent to Piero Sraffa and the Ricardian legacy, and one of the rediscoverers, with Michio Morishima, of the turnpike theorem, Bródy has been labeled a radical (heterodox) political economist of the 1968 generation until today, a neo-Marxist thinker who did not shy away from a critical dialogue with the neoclassical paradigm (Simonovits and Steenge 1997).[84] As Leontief put it politely,

> András Bródy's scientific contributions are marked by a creative, to some extent, dialectical combination of Eastern and Western streams of economic thought. On the one hand, it is rooted in the honorable tradition of classical economics interpreted by Karl Marx but carried forward by a sophisticated use of the analytical tools forged by modern neoclassical, mathematical economics. (Leontief 1997, VII)[85]

János Kornai: From Overcentralization to Shortage

Besides the impossibility of running reform-oriented empirical research projects in Hungary after 1956, Kornai's motivation to use mathematical methods stemmed from a real-world problem of central planning discussed in *Overcentralization*,[86] namely, the disincentives of firms to fulfill the plan. Following his dismissal from the Institute in 1958, he continued to examine the planning process in industry and began to tackle the issue of incentives by means of optimization.[87] He started sympathizing with neoclassical ideas of the time,[88] and in order to catch up with the state of the art, he relied on the support of the mathematical genius Tamás Lipták.[89] Their incentive-compatible optimization model generated complicated nonlinear programming problems whose solvability was not trivial. Although Lipták was arrested in 1957, Kornai managed to publish their research results (Kornai and Lipták 1959) with the support of the Ministry of Light Industry. When Lipták was released from prison, they summarized their findings in an English-language paper and submitted it to *Econometrica* for publication (Kornai and Lipták 1962). Its co-editor Edmond Malinvaud[90] proposed to accept the paper in an unchanged form. While the programming model dealt with the delicate issue of profit distribution, its authors exercised significant self-restraint. According to them, it is the state that performs the tasks of optimization on both upper and lower levels; the model does not tell whether the sum or the ratio of profit is to be maximized (if at all); it indicates the impact of choosing between these options on price policy but refrains from suggesting any solution.

Parallel to theoretical research, Kornai initiated an applied project of linear programming in industrial planning. First, he organized a large group of experts to model choices among different technologies in the cotton industry. They investigated the effects of major exogenous variables such as interest and exchange rates as well as export and import prices on the outcomes of the model. The project resulted in a competition within the group between linear programmers and input-output analysts. The latter, led by Bródy and later by Augusztinovics, already had collected experience in this field, but Kornai (2007, 140–42) insisted on assuming the endogeneity of technological change and the flexibility of the volume and structure of output, that is, properties excluded by I-O models with fixed technological coefficients and predetermined final consumption.

He extended this approach to the whole economy by decomposing the principal planning problem into linear programming subproblems and introducing an authentic algorithm to find and connect their optimal solutions. Yet, the habitual practice of the Planning Office was fundamentally different. True, the Office also planned macro-indices and decomposed them first into sectoral/branch indices, then into firm-level ones. However, as mentioned earlier, many (sometimes most) of these figures did not emerge from mathematical models but from a foggy web of pressure group interests and were modified in several rounds of multilateral bargaining, both horizontally and vertically. In reallocating resources, the Planning Office did not follow fixed rules of the game and mixed the principles of economic and political rationality.

A mathematical model for iterations like these, called by Kornai "two-level planning," again was built by Lipták.[91] He portrayed the bargaining segment of the linear programming problem in a game-theoretical framework as a polyhedral game. This was a surprisingly innovative idea because the game paradigm was hardly ever used by mathematical economists in the West in the early 1960s. The paper was first published in Hungarian in 1962, then in *Econometrica* in 1965. It became one of Kornai's most influential (and perhaps "most neoclassical") works. A reason for the success was the similarity of this two-level model with Lange's dual scheme of market socialism as reformulated by Malinvaud (1967).[92] Although the Kornai and Lipták paper did not refer to the debate between Hayek and Lange, not even to Lange's contributions to that debate, it also revolved around the question whether or not the central planner has perfect information. As is well known, the omniscience of the planning authority remained an axiom even in post-Stalinist official political economy for a long time. The authors touched on this taboo by postulating a so-called "overall central information problem" to be solved by the programmer. Another insult to the ruling ideology was the description of the planning process as a game (albeit, not a bargaining game), in which the center and the sectors have different strategies (i.e., different interests) that have to be coordinated. To reduce political risk, the paper reassured the reader that two-level planning only mirrored the actual dialogue between the center and the sectors: "the method proposed here is an attempt to *aid* this process of planning and counter-planning by means of *objective* criteria" (Kornai and Lipták 1965, 143, our emphasis). The authors stressed that the results of the two-level procedures could be useful in checking the consistency of the plan but abstained from interfering with the economic policy of the state through specifying the objective function of the model. In retrospect, Kornai (2007, 145–46, 181–83) claimed that they had managed to build an abstract (though unfeasible) model of perfect planning.

In 1963, Kornai got a job at the Computing Center of the Hungarian Academy of Sciences where the first mainframe computer had been installed in the country. There he launched the implementation of their planning concept. In order to avoid confrontation, Kornai did not question the legitimacy of the original targets of the five-year plan for 1966–1970 that he had promised to improve. Instead, he treated them as constraints of the model and experimented with various objective functions such as increasing the balance of current account in convertible currency or the value of private consumption (Kornai 2007, 148–49). Although he was unfamiliar with Arrow's impossibility theorem at the time, he instinctively resisted accepting a one-and-only welfare function defined by the communist ruling elite. He was firm in promising to not design an optimal plan and only to propose a better plan than that offered by verbal planners.

Yet, the original two-level algorithm in such a large model[93] was too complicated and had to be radically simplified. Thus, the results became much less precise and less true-to-life, while the computation process proved too slow to support the planners. Communication between the center and the sectors (not to speak of the firms) was clumsy and unpunctual, and the center proved intolerant to run enough iterations, which jeopardized the model's operation. Moreover, the input data were unreliable, intentionally distorted by the bargaining partners while the objectives and even the constraints were seldom defined by the policymakers clearly, often contradicted one another, and changed, following a chain of improvisations during the planning process. As a rule, the verbal planners were reluctant to reveal the sources of information they used in crafting the plans (e.g., when estimating the model coefficients), and—like their bosses—took the mathematical results seriously only if those supported their preconceptions. As a consequence, despite its scientific elegance, the Kornai and Lipták model could not be set up, computed, and implemented in planning unless one made a series of humiliating scholarly, political, or mundane technical concessions (Kornai 2007, 145–46, 155–56).

In other words, the "Faustian bargain" did not really work. The optimal planners offered the state their expertise in rationalizing planning (cf. the algorithm of "plan improvement") without making the communist rule questionable (they even helped prolong its existence), but the state did not provide in exchange proper data, sufficient computing infrastructure, or unambiguous economic policy goals and constraints, which were all necessary to run the planning model. Kornai's memoir testifies that in the early 2000s he still had a bad conscience because he had collaborated with the Kádár regime during its "consolidation" after 1956, for which he had excused himself earlier in the hope of increasing the welfare of Hungarians a little through optimizing the planning procedures. With the wisdom of hindsight, he did not find any other major advantage of this failed undertaking than its contribution to augmenting the mathematical knowledge of economists and releasing some of them from the ideological cage of textbook political economy (Kornai 2007, 147–57).

This is how Kornai remembered the reasons why the enthusiasm of his research team ebbed following five years of hard work to improve the central plan during the 1960s. His narrative borders on the Mises and Hayek impossibility thesis. However, some years after he had quit the terrain of optimal planning, he put his frustrations more diplomatically. Had he really managed to quit the project of ameliorating the planning system? Kornai related his model experiment in a book entitled *Mathematical Planning of Structural Decisions* (*A gazdasági szerkezet matematikai tervezése*) in 1965, published it in English in 1967. A slightly revised second edition came out in Hungarian in 1973 and in English in 1975. While outlining the difficulties of mathematical planning at length, none of these works alluded to the fact of impossibility. Instead, Kornai repeatedly comforted the reader, occasionally in a hopeful tone, about the need of central planning and its optimization *against all odds*. Although one "threw stones into the coffee mill," to use his phrase, that is, processed crude and unreliable data by sophisticated quantitative models, these models displayed the logical structure of planning decisions as well as revealed the inconsistencies of traditional plans and made these plans sounder. In sum, mathematical planning has a "pedagogical function": "it schools in rationality," it offers a "modest extension of rationality" (Kornai 1975, 426, 428, 523–25).

Even in the 1973 edition of the book he praised the procedure of plan improvement, the extension of two-level to multi-level planning, and a future construction of a pyramid of planning models and computing centers with the Planning Office on the top. In his view, the implementation of this vision—that "may rightly seem to be a utopia at a stage like the present"—basically will depend on the pace of development of computing capacity and expertise. Of course, planning does not have to be all-encompassing: it has to focus on "fundamental" economic processes (like capital investment) while the less fundamental ones can be left to the market (Kornai 1975, 377, 380). Incidentally, the years from 1972 to 1973 were the start of what was called "recentralization" or "counter-reform" in Hungary when the New Economic Mechanism suffered a serious backlash. In order to dull the edge of an anti-market interpretation of his reasoning, Kornai (381–84, 524) distanced himself from any kind of "computopia"[94] and claimed that his model does simulate market processes since the center actually distributes resources like an auctioneer. Nevertheless, he failed to explain why then a Lange or Malinvaud planning regime that imitates auction to a larger extent would be less realistic than his two-level planning scheme that was at least as dependent on ideal assumptions on the economic behavior of the main actors of the game.[95]

Meanwhile, Kornai's *Anti-equilibrium* came out in 1971, which passionately called at least two basic principles of optimal planning (equilibrium approach and optimization) into question. Two years after, the reader was surprised to see, as an explanation for the glaring contrast, Friedrich Dürrenmatt's cynical *bon mot* in the introduction to the second edition of the volume on planning: "He who never contradicts himself will never be read again" (Kornai 1975, XIII). Why criticize the very core of the neoclassical research program and republish shortly thereafter a volume on optimal planning, not to mention a few other articles on similar subjects (e.g., "plan sounding," see below) and participation in discussions on long-term planning in Hungary during the 1970s?[96] Undoubtedly, it was easier to satisfy the censors by contending that the Western mainstream was fatally flawed than by admitting that the rationalization of central planning proved to be an illusion. At the same time, if one goes beyond this simplistic political/moral explanation, it seems also likely that Kornai hesitated to decide which path of Westernization to take until he became absorbed in preparations for his subsequent book, *Economics of Shortage* (*Hiány*), that came out in 1980. Arriving at a crossroads, he could have insisted on the path he had chosen at the end of the 1950s, which led to neoclassical economics *and* made him an illustrious member of the international research community of planning theorists.[97] However, he also may have hoped that, by abandoning neoclassical theory (or correcting its allegedly fundamental mistakes), he would not have to give up his work on planning but could perhaps opt for modeling its indicative rather than directive (decentralized rather than centralized) varieties in the framework of a new—universal—systems theory suggested by *Anti-equilibrium*. This also would be a basically Western product but contain a larger-than-ever Eastern contribution. Simply put, he yearned to have his cake and eat it, too.

Kornai embarked on the second path without knowing the refusal he would provoke by challenging neoclassical economics so fiercely. The fact that he jumped from recognizing the failure of optimal planning into a blanket disapproval of general equilibrium theory and—more broadly—neoclassical economics was difficult for the representatives of the latter to digest. They believed, not without foundation, that Kornai threw the baby out with the bath water. Initially, *Anti-equilibrium* was received with deafening silence— except for soft applause from some "old-institutionalist" experts in the West and textbook political economists in the communist countries, both feeling justified in their contempt for the mainstream.[98] From a bird's-eye view, the decision to turn against neoclassicism while retaining the instruments of mathematical economics was a bold venture, even if Kornai could not know at the time that in some years Leonid Kantorovich would receive the Nobel Prize for his findings in a field very close to Kornai's research on optimal planning. Kornai was unaware of his "objective" boldness probably due to an optical illusion. Neither Tjalling Koopmans, who shared the prize with Kantorovich, nor Kenneth Arrow had dissuaded him from challenging general equilibrium theory when he visited them in the United States at the end of the 1960s. Reading the manuscript of *Anti-equilibrium*, these two eminent protagonists of the theory even helped strengthen the arguments of their Hungarian colleague,[99] but this could not prevent a third eminent protagonist Frank Hahn (1973) from publishing a devastating review of the book under the frightening title "The Winter of Our Discontent." It revealed Kornai's methodological naïveté reflected in his failure to make a distinction between the internal consistency of an abstract theory and its realism/applicability. Who said that we wanted to develop an empirically accurate "real science" that you require from us, asked an embarrassed Hahn.[100] Kornai was also reprimanded for (a) rejecting a workable and coherent scientific paradigm from the platform of a "vague and misdirected" research program, (b) using "his most vehement language to criticize what he has not properly understood," and (c) introducing dozens of new terms from his still non-existent theory, most of which were "empty boxes" (325–29).

Although the review was patronizing, it only mirrored Kornai's militant discourse and quasi-neophytic zeal against orthodoxy. To use Lakatosian language, besides a constructive criticism of the assumptions within the "protective belt" of the neoclassical research program, Kornai also called into question major axioms of its "hard core." His targets of criticism ranged from the principle of rationality based on optimization (this is what he considered the "original sin" of neoclassical theorists) and the maximization of profits and consumer utility, through using a normative concept of equilibrium, idealizing perfect competition, as well as disregarding increasing returns, non-price signals, and changing preferences, to the static and institution-free nature of the theory and its inattention to uncertainty. He accused the general equilibrium (GE) school of focusing on nothing else but these facets of economic systems, and hence, analyzing just one set of key economic features of the real world. In his opinion, its members actually dealt with partial rather than general equilibrium. Thus, they moved backward from the position of Léon Walras and have "become a brake on the development of economic thought" including "most of the work which is attributed to the <neo-classical school>. . . . The GE school makes the description of economic systems entirely too dull; it over-schematizes and impoverishes it" (Kornai 1971, 27–8, 30).

Part of the criticism could have been reasonable if neoclassical economists had not wanted to offer a complex but coherent *ideal* scheme instead of an empirically relevant "comparative systems theory" envisaged by Kornai. Similarly, his anti-equilibrium drive originating, to a large extent, in the dismal fate of optimal planning in communist countries certainly would have encouraged his potential allies to think twice about the pros and cons of the neoclassical paradigm if he had been able to substantiate that the project of plan improvement derailed exactly because of its optimization philosophy and not because of the fact that this philosophy was tested in planned economies. Moreover, *Anti-equilibrium* was permeated by strong doubts about market coordination and weaker ones about planning, which did not increase its popularity, even in non-libertarian circles of economic thought.

Later, Kornai saw, with a peculiar mix of regret and self-justification, his attack on neoclassical economics as rather unfortunate. He admitted to have made

> serious errors in the theoretical starting points of my [his] critique, within the philosophy of science. . . . Modelers can be accused of many mistakes, but not of abstracting from reality. . . . The market economy that actually operates under capitalism is far from the Walrasian ideal, but the ideal makes a useful gauge of how far reality lies from it. . . . I should have attacked not the purity of the theory (the abstract, unreal nature of its assumptions), but the wrong use of it in mainstream economics. The real addressee of the critique should have been mainstream teaching practices and research programs. (Laki 2006, 28–30; Kornai 2007, 183–85; 2018, 7–9)[101]

Following this confession, Kornai repeated some of the main points of the "indictment," submitted in his *Anti-equilibrium* more than 30 years before, concerning the notions of rationality, optimization, equilibrium, and so on. He called *Anti-equilibrium* a "semi-failure" and was proud to "grope in the right direction," adding that he might have employed a less offensive language, delayed the attack until his counter-theory matured, and trusted in the ability of the mainstream to progress (Kornai 2007, 185–90, 192–95). At the same time, he ignored an alternative road leading out of the impasse into which he had led his research program. Yet, given his never-ending interest in institutions, he might have joined the emerging stream of new institutional economics during the 1970s, combining neoclassical methodology with realism, that is, orthodoxy with his favorite heterodoxy.[102] Surely, as Kornai had hoped, he managed to contribute to a spread of mathematical culture among economists behind the Iron Curtain. Nevertheless, prior to 1989, he was probably just as successful in persuading them *not* to fall on their knees before the neoclassical school.[103]

All in all, Kornai did not accept Hahn's criticism[104] but took it as an act of exclusion, almost excommunication, decided not to burn his fingers again, and withdrew to his own safe territory, the study of planned economies. He wanted to prove that he had not been wrong when dismissing general equilibrium theory and embarked upon a kind of disequilibrium analysis, using some neoclassical instruments but also inventing a series of verbal means to study a new field, the economics of shortage. He assumed that this research program would offer him, as he said later, a "one foot in, and one foot out of the mainstream" position (Kornai 2007, 195) that was sufficiently Western in terms of methodological rigor but did not sacrifice the imagined realism of his own *Sonderweg* proclaimed in *Anti-equilibrium*.

Meanwhile, Kornai stopped bashing the neoclassical paradigm openly but did not forget his bitterness regarding the concept of equilibrium.[105] His research program became less universalistic: it did not aim at founding an overarching systems theory any longer. Following the excursion to occupy a place on the peak of economic sciences in the world, he tried to carve out a large niche for himself a little lower and slowly returned to his former role played as an "area studies" scholar. Here, he put up with examining disequilibrium in planned economies but never ceased to call himself a mathematical economist who combined formal models with verbal research of institutions that he had abandoned in the late 1950s.

Interestingly enough, this turn was preceded, like in the case of Bródy, by (a) further work on planning models (Kornai et al. 1971; Kornai, Dániel, and Rimler 1972; Martos and Kornai 1973; Kornai 1973), (b) a short digression to alternative approaches to economic development (Kornai 1972a), a polemic verbal study in favor of balanced growth,[106] and (c) a reexamination of the concept of economic control (Kornai and Martos 1973; Martos and Kornai 1981; Kornai and Simonovits 1977. Although the latter initiative might have evolved into a general theory again, Kornai dropped his anchor at studying "non-price control" (including "vegetative control"). These were favorite notions already in *Anti-equilibrium*, which have much more to do with planned than market economies and led him directly to studying the economics of shortage. This agenda reinforced his position as an esteemed expert of the economics of really-existing socialism but further alienated him from the research community of neoclassical economists while not bringing him into the fold of their heterodox critics.[107]

After a while, this kind of expertise concerned economic control rather than planning, and the normative attitude of plan improvement was replaced by the research objective of describing and explaining how planned economies are regulated with a special emphasis on non-price signals.[108] Simultaneously, the principle of optimization vanished from Kornai's research agenda, and with *Shortage* the share of mathematical reasoning also diminished in his work. He did not miss an opportunity to package the principal notions of his theory in mathematical formulae but failed to construct a synthetic model of shortage with their help.[109] Although in terms of verbal research, his book contained a great number of original approaches to concepts such as soft budget constraint, vegetative control, resource-constrained system, shortage versus slack, friction, queuing, and forced substitution among others, it applied formal models to illustrate rather than to profoundly analyze the planned economy as well as to measure its functioning. Thus, it could not catch up with the level of mathematical erudition of the disequilibrium school emerging at the time.[110] This is how Kornai remembered his debate, for instance, with Richard Portes and associates: they "had one huge advantage over me in these debates. They gleaned data from the statistics available to them. They were then able to make mathematical-statistical calculations, which undoubtedly impressed everyone. I could do little else than appeal to intuition or common sense; I could not oppose the quantified Portes models with likewise quantified Kornai models" (Portes and Winter 1980; Kornai, 2007, 249). He admitted that he realized too late that, despite the fact that the *Economics of Shortage* that he regarded as his *magnum opus* had a deeper insight than its rivals in the imbalances of communist economies, it would be outcompeted in the scholarly market. Indeed, the book's illustrative models construed to comprehend cause-and-effect relationships lacked the necessary explanatory force and econometric sophistication; furthermore, they were not tested on a critical mass of data.[111] His efforts to fill this gap eventually stumbled upon the collapse of communism: the time series data needed to substantiate his own interpretation of shortage could not be gathered any longer.[112]

An even greater disappointment for Kornai derived from his inability to identify a comprehensive and skillful mathematical portrayal of what he considered the main discovery of the book, the "soft budget constraint syndrome."[113] Such models were developed later by a number of scholars,[114] most famously by Mathias Dewatripont and Eric Maskin (1995). They employed game theory to capture the strategic interaction between firms and supporting organizations that bail them out. In their model interpreting the syndrome as a dynamic commitment problem, the actors maximize utility (payoff) and arrive at bargaining equilibria—the latter two concepts had been used by

Kornai back in the 1960s. Moreover, the primary reason for the soft constraint, paternalism as presented in *Shortage*, became a secondary issue that in the authors' view was neither a necessary nor a sufficient condition for comprehending the syndrome (Kornai, Maskin, and Roland 2003, 1111). In other words, the notion of paternalism was, in fact, abandoned, and thus the validity of the theory could be extended beyond the borders of the planned economy, fulfilling an old desire of Kornai.[115]

At the same time, it remained unclear whether paternalism could have been formalized and measured at all (cf. Kornai and Matits 1987a, 1987b), and whether—if one nevertheless sticks to murky explanations—this was really the best way to grasp the deeper political/ideological causes of the softness of budget constraints, or Kornai ought to have named directly at least a few powerful institutional factors such as state ownership, one-party rule, and Soviet occupation. In his memoir, he justified this choice with the need of self-censorship (Kornai 2007, 242–44, 253–55). Again, without passing any moral judgement on his decision, it had a heavy price in terms of scientific quality. If Kornai had not degraded his relationship with neoclassical economics dramatically, he might have gained inspiration from its new-institutional extensions and refined the notion of paternalism with the help of property rights, rent seeking, or principal-agent models, thereby not only showing political courage but also playing a pioneering role in universal economic research again, like he did at the time of inventing two-level planning. While many of his colleagues in the West[116] borrowed from new institutional economics among other subdisciplines in order to "consolidate" his concept of softness, he contented himself by saying "I did not use the term <institution> in every second paragraph as it recently has become fashionable to do, but I think I understood what a system means, and what the difference is between socialism and capitalism" (Kornai 2000, 654). If he had not thrown the concept of optimization overboard several decades before but assumed *some kind* of rationality in the behavior of the party-state, that is, if he had accepted that it can even maximize utility in a strictly economic sense of the word, then he might have arrived at the conclusion of his neoclassical-minded colleagues much earlier. They claimed that a bail-out of a state-owned enterprise can be in the best interest of the communist authorities not only because of purely political, ideological, reputational, and other considerations (which are also seldom immune to some economic motivation) but also of ordinary calculations of costs and benefits (Dewatripont and Maskin 1995).

During the 1980s, Kornai had almost everything at his disposal to crown his scientific career: the discovery of the importance of soft budget constraint, first-hand knowledge of the intricacies of the planned economy (and, as he says, "intuition and common sense"), mathematical skills, *Sitzfleisch*, embeddedness in Western academic culture,[117] and so on. At that time, one might think that nothing could prevent him from receiving the Nobel Prize virtually any time. Allegedly, he has been nominated quite a few times among the frontrunners since then. We suspect that Kornai's bad luck with the prize was rooted in his decision to launch a frontal attack against neoclassical economics, which, following a brief period of self-Westernization in the 1960s, led him back to the realm of area studies and left him without a reliable methodology. Capitalizing on the results of his authentic research programs accomplished in the "communist laboratory," he could have returned even more successfully than he did to the world of universal economic sciences via less self-censorship (if he had trusted more in the decay of the Kádár regime) and through borrowing from new institutional economics (if he had not continued to reject its neoclassical foundations). In both cases he chose a language the leading epistemic community of economists in the world did not want to speak. It seems that *sic* non *itur ad astra . . .* [118]

OUT OF THE TRAP? TENTATIVE CONCLUSIONS

To return to our working hypotheses, in the previous sections we witnessed how difficult it was for the adherents of optimal planning to leave this research program behind and release themselves from the trap that prevented them from becoming "regular" neoclassical theorists prior to 1989. In fact, they could not help facing[119] a long chain of serious shortcomings. They were shocked to realize that—despite improving the mathematical quality of their models and raising the capacity of computers to run them—their optimization efforts repeatedly stumbled upon the institutional/informational regime of the planned economy.

The optimal planners may have expected that, with the advent of the New Economic Mechanism in 1968, the termination of annual plans, and a shift from mandatory instructions to "indirect regulators," the "controlled market" would enhance transparency and accuracy by disciplining the actors through competition while some political taboos might disperse. Instead, they saw an even more chaotic system of planning arise, in which plan bargaining was replaced or complemented by "regulatory bargaining," to use the contemporary phrase. Apparently, capturing such a complexity of bargaining games by means of numerous small models of optimization instead of constructing a single Big Optimal Plan did not prove an attractive (or viable) scientific venture for mathematical economists in Hungary.[120] Yet, here again, an exchange of ideas with new institutional economists in the West probably could have been beneficial for both sides and paved the way for the Hungarian experts to reconcile themselves with neoclassical ideas without having to fear from ignoring real-world problems.

Unfortunately, the empirically grounded insights in the imperfections of optimization were not condensed in elegant scholarly theses. Instead, they sank into the tacit knowledge of mathematical economists. The research community of optimal planning in Hungary did not rethink the Socialist Calculation Debate in the light of the dismal experience of mathematizing central plans and challenge the axiom of rational economic calculation under communism.[121] Many of its members continued to refine the methodology of planning and moderate the worst outcomes of the bargaining games. They relaxed the initial—often prohibitively strict—assumptions, eliminated some of the simplifications of their models requiring homogeneity, linearity, closedness, determinism, staticness, and so on, and fine-tuned the estimation of data. The remedies also included disaggregation and "monetization" of the models, incorporating human capital and foreign trade and decentralizing the planning procedures (Augusztinovics 1981; Réti et al. 1981; Augusztinovics 1984, 43–85; Augusztinovics and Bod 1985; Ámon and Ligeti 1987; Sivák 1987). At the same time, the mathematical economists did not suggest any substantial change to the planning regimes. They, including Bródy and Kornai, demanded neither an irrevocable transition from imperative to indicative planning nor at least the dismantling of the central planning of capital investments, a major obstacle to marketization under the NEM.[122]

Those experts who were not locked up in the treadmill of the daily fabrication of plans turned to long-term planning,[123] which was much less exposed to the interplay of lobby interests than five-year plans. True, it was with diminishing hope that they were waiting for the arrival of an enlightened technocratic elite, to which they could have handed over a Great Plan of modernizing the Hungarian economy during the 1970s and 1980s. While planning became a less popular scientific undertaking, input-output models were prepared even in the 1990s (e.g., Halpern and Molnár 1997), and the perfection of I-O theory was not terminated for good. Besides Bródy, one of his followers, Ernő Zalai (1997, 2014), kept on publishing in this field during the 2000s. As to Augusztinovics, she closed the story of the research program by saying that "the heyday of Input-Output as a simple, transparent, deterministic, static linear model is . . . certainly over." She added though that its "subject matter has not been lost, . . . it has merely been transformed, incorporated into more complex structures. The subject matter . . . is the dual and circular nature of the economy in general" (Augusztinovics 1995, 275).

What about the two pioneers? Did the bifurcation of their research programs result in differences in their assessment of neoclassical theory? As suggested above, Bródy chose another way out of the trap. He lost faith in educating the communist decision-makers through planning models early on, and did not trust in market reforms either since he had second thoughts about both the efficiency of market coordination and the altruism of communist bureaucracy that was supposed to manage marketization—something that probably would jeopardize its own integrity.[124] Therefore, he elevated his research program to a higher level of abstraction and made efforts to identify organic links between the Marxian theory of labor value and input-output analysis (later even claiming that neoclassical theory is a special case of them)—not quite the best *rite de passage* to become a neoclassical economist. Remaining in the realm of mathematical economics, Bródy strived to prove that *all* economic systems suffer from cycles, any convergence toward market equilibrium is actually a cyclical oscillation around that, and economic dynamics can best be explained through a combination of classical (including Marxian) theory of labor value and marginalism—a contention again that did not really match standard neoclassical principles. As for his self-image, Bródy (1994, 325) liked to characterize himself as an heir of the classical tradition.

Kornai's was perhaps a more complicated case. It was neither an attraction to Marxism nor a high-level mathematical understanding of economic dynamics that prevented him from subscribing to the neoclassical paradigm. Unlike Bródy, he was not animated by abstract concepts of economic development ranging from the Neumann model to chaos theory, and distanced himself from both Marx (tacitly, quietly) and the neoclassical school (openly, loudly). Rather than finding the institutional architecture of the communist economy responsible for the failure of optimal planning, he blamed—with a dose of self-criticism—the "neoclassical illusions" blinding mathematical economists like himself. In passing, he alluded to the Socialist Calculation Debate and—while Bródy did not defy the legacy of Lange—Kornai disliked the Lange tradition as an unfortunate mix of Marxist and neoclassical thought and dropped skeptical remarks on Lange's "naiveté" in postulating a fruitful cooperation between the state plan and the regulated market. Here, he made no distinction between Hayek's classical liberalism and the neoclassical view of the market: both of them were rejected as *laissez faire* doctrines. After having left optimal planning behind, he continued to define himself as a mathematical economist but insisted on many of his former doubts about neoclassical thought. [125] Being "one foot out," however, prevented him from building new mathematical models as powerful as earlier.

Arguably, the failure of optimal planning did not prompt the two pioneers to critically examine the deep layers of the institutional world of the planned economy, no matter how knowledgeable they were about not only the economic sociology but also the social anthropology and psychology of central planning's main actors.[126] Refraining from thorough institutional studies could be justified by (self-)censorship and—until the mid-1960s—by the hopelessness of far-reaching economic reforms. Nevertheless, with the New Economic Mechanism appearing on the political agenda, ideological cautiousness did not require persistent skepticism toward the efficiency of market control, particularly not a frontal attack on neoclassical theory. As presumed in the first pages of our chapter, such attitudes and actions can hardly be explained if the historian solely focuses on political fears and ignores scientific preferences.[127]

It is our hope that the story we have told about the evolution of planning concepts in Hungary shed light on a whole series of sources of those preferences: Marxist indoctrination, misinterpretation of neoclassical theory as a bundle of abstract (unrealistic) ultra-liberal ideas, seeking a *modus vivendi* between communist and capitalist fundamentalisms, pride felt for authenticity and equality with the West in terms of scholarly discoveries, inertia of a large and initially promising research program, self-deception promoted by Western peers, and so on. Let us leave aside the questions of how justified and coherent these motives were and which author was inspired by which of them the most. Rudimentary answers to them were scattered in the notes attached to this chapter. Be as it may, it was the same motives (fixations?) that helped the former adherents of optimal planning avoid entering other dead-end streets, favored much too long in a number of communist countries, such as the decentralization of planning (e.g., on the basis of workers' self-management or on that of mega-enterprises) or, on the contrary, the organization of vast—centralized and automated—planning systems spirited by a sort of "computopia."

The I-O analysts and the optimal planners in Hungary had to accept the inevitable: what they once thought would become a hegemonic discourse and planning technique remained a negligible, auxiliary tool in the hands of the top *apparatchiki* of the party-state. Over time, hegemony was attained by another group of economists, the market reformers, by far the largest segment of the research community in Hungary. Witnesses to the failure of rationalizing the plan, they were comforted in their conviction that the agenda of marketization of the planned economy had no real alternative: depending on the boldness of their project, they claimed that central planning must be tamed or dismantled—but not optimized. The failure of optimal planners strengthened the pre-existing suspicion of many institutional reformers toward mathematical analysis as such, which in turn blocked their road leading to neoclassical economics.[128]

POSTSCRIPT ON ECONOMETRICS

The examples of Bródy and Kornai as well as their disciples demonstrate another comparative advantage *vis-à-vis* their colleagues in many communist countries. During the 1970s and 1980s, a growing number of mathematical economists in Hungary turned their backs on the normative strategy of improving central plans.[129] Although this turn was unspectacular, the program of producing a sound analysis of the planned economy (not just planning as such) with the help of mathematical instruments eventually replaced the intention of enlightening the *nomenklatura* and supporting the communist regime through "science-based" plans. While it was not always clear where optimal planning ended and where econometrics started,[130] many of the younger experts refused to construct overarching planning models and shape countrywide economic policies any longer. They indulged in econometric research and—after experiencing the imperfections of their own simultaneous macro-models—contented themselves with smaller-scale research projects that were to comprehend the real world of certain segments of the planned economy. The econometricians' scholarly choices stemmed neither from a deep sociological/political critique of planning under communist rule nor from a devotion to neoclassical principles. Nevertheless, they *nolens volens* kept a larger door open for Westernizing their research programs than I-O experts and optimal planners earlier (Kőrösi 1996).

Their role was controversial in other respects as well. In the field of quantitative economic research in general, empirical analysis was neglected for a long time. In retrospect, this may be surprising because in Hungary empirical studies served as a bridge connecting pre-and post-communist economic sciences. Subdisciplines such as labor and educational economics, health economics, financial economics, and empirical industrial organization, which applied econometric methods extensively, progressed more rapidly during the past decades. The roots of neglect stretch back to the early period of communism.

Back in the 1950s and early 1960s, empirical works containing statistical arguments were sporadic in Hungarian economic research. As mentioned, the foundation of the Econometric Laboratory at the Central Statistical Office brought some fresh wind into quantitative studies although its econometric investigations were not concatenated with models of mathematical economics in a way suggested, for instance, by the Cowles Commission's slogan of "theory and measurement."[131] Mathematical economists mostly avoided confronting their models with empirical data; therefore, the stage of verification was absent in their research agendas. This cannot be explained simply by the lack or bad quality of empirical information. Data served as a source of inspiration to generate a model (cf. Bródy's theory of cycles and Kornai's concept of overcentralization) or to support economic policy arguments (cf. the Laboratory's model series) rather than to precisely corroborate or falsify scientific hypotheses.[132]

During the 1970s, the situation changed slightly. The I-O models started including stochastic blocks (e.g., Hulyák 1972). The parameter estimations of production functions and the regression analyses of macro data began to infiltrate, quite unsystematically, the theoretical arguments instead of only helping solve practical problems and fill the input-output tables and SAM matrices. The authors were mostly self-made econometricians who chose their topics and methods often accidentally.[133] In the late 1970s and the 1980s, macro-econometric models still used the already outdated method of simultaneous equations (Kőrösi 1996, 359). The critique of simultaneous macro-econometric models (Lucas 1976; Sims 1980) did not affect this attitude for a while.[134]

A turn to more professional econometric research came only in the second half of the 1980s and in the 1990s. Younger researchers left I-O analysis and optimal planning for fields that were less macro-oriented and required robust evidence-based reasoning. To use the example of the Institute of Economics again, Halpern and Molnár started studying household statistics and corporate data that led them to so diverse research projects as the analysis of subjective welfare and industrial organization. Labor economists such as István Gábor, Károly Fazekas, János Köllő, and Gábor Kertesi explored employment and educational data and drew conclusions also with regard to gender and race economics.[135] A detailed case study made in the textile industry introduced some of them to both empirically and theoretically grounded procedures of neoclassical research.

The recognition of the problematic aspects of old-fashioned macro-econometric analysis discouraged some of the experts and micro-data methods became more popular. However, during the 1980s, there was no institution of higher education in Hungary to teach economists applied econometrics. Econometrics at the universities was regarded as part of the "high theory" of mathematical statistics. Symptomatically, the first generation of new-school econometricians like Gábor Kőrösi and László Mátyás learnt cutting-edge methods while teaching abroad (in Australia) in the 1990s, and returned to Hungary to cooperate with economists whose interest in micro-data analysis was greater than their knowledge of econometric methodology.

However, prior to 1989, this process of catching up with the West was not yet accompanied by a large-scale takeover of neoclassical principles and by a profound reconsideration of former assumptions and axioms of mathematical modeling, although a few young scholars (e.g., Imre Csekő, Júlia Király, János Vincze) decided to build their scientific careers on cultivating mainstream micro-and macroeconomics and finance.[136] A good example for the inertia of economic thinking was the way in which the computable general equilibrium (CGE) approach was received in macro-level modeling (Zalai 1983). Due to the flexibility of this approach, it could be used in input-output tables and SAM matrices without subscribing to the underlying philosophy of general equilibrium theory.[137] Similarly, the real business cycle (RBC) model proved too neoclassical to be adopted by Hungarian economists before 1989.

In sum, Hungarian econometricians built new pillars to support the bridge that input-output analysts and optimal planners had begun to erect in the late 1950s but only a few of them proved able to reach neoclassical economics situated on the opposite side of the abyss separating them. No matter how robust and sophisticated the new quantitative models became in comparison to those formulated by optimal planners, econometrics in communist Hungary (a) did not excel with significant original discoveries, and (b) failed to evolve into a compact discipline in close cooperation with micro-and macroeconomic theories. Unlike their peers beyond the Iron Curtain, Hungarian econometricians indulged in applied rather than basic research, the applications were scattered over a random variety of topics and were not underpinned by a tightly woven net of neoclassical concepts. In a sense, they moved ahead too quickly in the 1980s: they had to wait for the breakthrough of the other two core disciplines of neoclassical thought, micro-and macroeconomics, to progress further.

NOTES

1. This term will be used in our chapter in descriptive sense except when a scholar under scrutiny attaches a normative meaning to it.

2. The department of mathematical economics of the Hungarian Economic Association, the only professional organization of economists in the communist era, was established in 1962.

3. It was first issued by the Hungarian Economic Association in 1968. Béla Martos served as its editor-in-chief until 1990.

4. Bródy was one of the founders of the Association and Kornai was elected president of the Society in 1976.

5. While one can have second thoughts about the quality of the neoclassical breakthrough, its quantitative indicators, ranging from journal articles through university curricula to East-West research projects, show a sweeping victory of mainstream economics imported primarily from the West (see Kaase and Sparschuh 2002).

6. For example, László Csontos, Gábor Kertesi, Péter Pete, Balázs Váradi and others played a crucial role in setting up new neoclassical-style departments of economics at Budapest universities in the 1990s. Of course, these experts also felt happy about the fall of censorship, despite the fact that they were already lucky to not face a cruel "thought police" in the 1980s.

7. This was the infamous "3T" principle (in Hungarian: *tiltás, tűrés, támogatás*) distinguishing between prohibition, toleration, and support.

8. In fact, general equilibrium theory received quite a few punches that seemed devastating, but it managed to survive and prosper, resulting in a series of new models of computable and dynamic-stochastic general equilibrium (Kovács 2009).

9. "Improving," "developing," or "perfecting" the plan were terms used above all by the official rhetoric. The pejorative alternative was *tervkovácsolás* (hammering the plan) originating in the German word *Planschmied*.

10. As the reader will see, there is also a third hero in the story, Mária Augusztinovics, who would deserve a separate study. She was involved at each and every stage of research made by the two "pioneers" who probably would not have been able to reach the Parnassus of Hungarian economic thought without her help. A typical fate of an extremely talented female scholar, she was stuck willy-nilly on a lower level of scientific abstraction for a long time, striving to build optimal planning models in the Planning Office, even as late as the early 1980s. She could step out of the shadows of the two men only thereafter, when she switched to modeling life-cycles and pension systems. For a while, Augusztinovics was married to Bródy and was closer to him than to Kornai in terms of loyalty to Marxism.

11. For example, Szamuely and Csaba (1998), thus far, the most detailed overview published on the history of Hungarian economic thinking in the communist period, devoted less than a page to mathematical economists. The literature is dominated by works, in which the main representatives of the discipline and their associates share their memories with the reader or offer a snapshot of a certain stage of evolution in their scholarly field. Typically, these are brief texts, including published interviews and obituaries. Important (and refreshing) exceptions are Bródy's long biographical interview from 1994 and Kornai's voluminous memoir from 2007 (2005). A 1996 conference on "legacy, emulation, invention" in economics, in which numerous scholars, old and young, who conducted research in mathematical economics in any phase of their lives, made presentations also proved a very informative source, see Csekő (1996), Csontos (1996), Kőrösi (1996), Nagy (1996), Pete (1996), Simonovits (1996), Vincze (1996). Although normally Péteri (1993, 1997, 2002, 2017, 2019) do not focus on the nexus between mathematical economics and planning theory per se, they give valuable insights, based on careful archival research, in the political and sociological environment of their development. For the state of the art in writing the history of planning concepts in communist countries in general, see the Introduction and Conclusion of this volume.

The citations in this chapter were translated by us if no English-language translation was published.

12. For more on his personal attitudes to mathematical economics as experienced in the Institute, see Kovács (2016).

13. In preparing this section, we received useful research assistance from our students Dániel Baglyos, Barnabás Benyák, Zalán Cseresznyés, András Hetényi, Balázs Mayer, Tamás Sáfár, and Dániel Tordai.

14. Admittedly, that pattern fell short of the organization of central planning in the Soviet Union in both width and depth. However, the leading economists of the time such as Károly Balás, Frigyes Fellner, Farkas Heller, Mátyás Matolcsy, Ákos Navratil, Tivadar Surányi-Unger, and István Varga (even those who preferred Austrian economics) did not regard planning as a derogatory term. For those among them who flirted with the national socialists or later with the communists this was a natural ideological gesture. However, cautious liberals like Heller or liberal socialists like Károly Polányi did not reject some kind of state planning categorically, not to mention Károly Mannheim with his eulogy of planning in general.

15. Actually, Káldor had visited Hungary for some months at the turn of 1946/47 in order to advise the social-democrats but did not return there for about two decades. Then he paid only short family visits and gave lectures.

16. Béla Balassa, who emigrated in 1956, wrote his first book in the United States exactly on the planning system of Hungary. Would he have become "another Kornai" if he had decided to stay?

17. They were leading researchers in the *Magyar Gazdaságkutató Intézet* (Hungarian Institute for Economic Research) founded by Varga in 1927. On combining German-style institutional research with econometrics, see Varga (1947) and Theiss (1947).

18. For a brief period during and following the 1956 revolution, Varga replaced Friss as director of the Institute of Economics.

19. On his contribution to mathematical economics in Hungary, see note 51.

20. At the time, many Hungarian economists understood Russian. They could read not only the works of Leonid Kantorovich or Viktor Novozhilov in their original but also, for example, the Russian translation of Leontief (1953, 1958) on the U.S. economy. Kantorovich's (1965) seminal book on the best use of economic resources has never been translated into Hungarian (cf. Simon and Kondor 1962, 1963). In the 1960s and 1970s, the similarity between the 1968 economic reform in Hungary and the NEP aroused interest among Hungarian scholars about the ideas of Soviet mathematical economists such as Grigorii Feldman, Nikolai Kondratiev, and others.

21. The uncensored version of the book was released only in 1988.

22. The translation of Zbigniew Pawłowski's *Ekonometria* in 1970 also demonstrates the remarkable influence Polish scholars exerted on their Hungarian colleagues. The same applies to the translation of the 1977 book by the Czech theorist Josef Goldmann on macroeconomic analysis.

23. Kornai cherished the memory of his debut in Western high theory when in 1963, he met Maurice Allais, Sukhamoy Chakrawarty, Frank Hahn, Leo Hurwicz, Tjalling Koopmans, Lionel MacKenzie, Edmond Malinvaud, Roy Radner, and Richard Stone at a conference in Cambridge (Kornai 1996, 268).

24. Since then, just a few Hungarian economists have succeeded in publishing in these journals (see Medvegyev 1984; Simonovits 1975, 1978).

25. Martos (1975, 1990) were also published by North Holland that agreed on a joint publication project with the Budapest publishing house *Akadémiai Kiadó*.

26. This was the only phase of communist history in which Hungarian scholars maintained strong links to leading Soviet and other Eastern European mathematical economists and insisted on publishing in Russian as well.

27. For the first English-language review of the evolution of the new research program in Hungary, see Horvath (1963).

28. Although these experts contributed to each other's edited volumes, joint articles were rare among them. For example, Augusztinovics, Bródy, and Kornai did not publish scholarly papers together despite the fact that they were good friends for a long time. For collective volumes, see, for example, Bod et al. (1962), Lukács et al. (1962), and Juhász and Morva (1982).

29. This English-language journal was edited in collaboration with the Institute of Economics from 1966 onward.

30. Nevertheless, in the beginning, they also had to publish in marginal bulletins run by industrial organizations or in "official *samizdat*" like the working papers of limited circulation, which were produced by various research institutes.

31. For a fifth institution, see note 63.

32. It was founded as Hungarian University of Economics in 1948 to offer a full-time degree program in economics. The Sovietization of the university during the late 1940s was crowned by renaming it Karl Marx University of Economic Sciences in 1953. In fact, until the late 1980s, it taught political economy instead of economics despite a surge of programs in mathematical economics.

33. See, for example, Hámori (1986). On the eve of the collapse of communism, low-quality experimental textbooks on micro-and macroeconomics were written by members of the Department of Political Economy (Váradi 2007).

34. In 1972, students of planning theory (both verbal and mathematical) organized a strike against the course syllabus offered by the Department, and demanded to change the list of mandatory readings by replacing the official textbook with works of András Bródy, Ferenc Jánossy, János Kornai, Włodzimierz Brus, Jan Tinbergen, and selected authors from the Soviet 1920s and the Socialist Calculation Debate. The new textbook (Stark 1981) made a few insecure steps in this direction. On the development of research on mathematical economics at the Department, see Móczár (1980).

35. Prékopa was a student of Alfréd Rényi (mentor to and friend of András Bródy, see below) who taught operations research to mathematicians from 1958. His main research area was stochastic programming. The research groups and departments in operations research headed by him at two Budapest universities and the Academy of Sciences became strongholds of education and background studies of optimal planning (Prékopa 2018).

36. The curriculum was reorganized many times. Besides Béla Krekó and Jenő Szép who held mostly the calculus, linear algebra and operations research courses, Margit Ziermann, a student and co-author of Prékopa taught stochastic processes, and György Meszéna mathematical statistics. Later Géza Denkinger and István Dancs also entered the Department and taught core mathematics courses, Ferenc Forgó joined Szép in teaching game theory and János Paizs econometrics. In order to strengthen the ties to economic applications, Krekó published textbooks for each and every course, which were linked by pivoting techniques that allowed the solution of economic problems through computer programming (see, e.g., Krekó 1972).

37. In the early 1970s, it owned the highest-performance computer in Hungary (*ICL-4/70*). The first staff of about 40 operators were trained in London. The research affiliates included Bródy and Kornai. The main task of the Center was to prepare sectoral and central plans with the help of input-output analysis and later linear programming. The Kornai-Lipták model of two-level planning (see below) was also run here.

38. Nonetheless, the Institute and the Office raised a large group of quantitative experts including Gusztáv Báger, Zsuzsa Dániel, Éva Ehrlich, Sándor Ganczer, László Hunyadi, Tamás Morva, János Réti, Béla Székely, and György Szepesi. See also note 46.

39. "There are fans of <verbal> and <mathematical> approach among economists. I do not belong to either of them. Moreover, I consider the contrasting of the two methods a wrong alternative. If you please I am the enemy of verbal method if it is based on . . . empty abstractions. However, I am equally an enemy of . . . mathematization for its own sake" (Jánossy 1969).

40. The structure of departments within the Office matched that of the sectors and branches of the economy.

41. Augusztinovics remembers: the mathematical models "did not become influential, decisive instruments in planning . . . . Our first results were not to the liking of supreme economic policy leaders because one could not squeeze out of the models a larger than 3 percent growth on average . . . or force them to support that billions and billions would be poured into agriculture. Then, we had to be silent for a while. Of course, sooner or later one learns how to constrain everything in a model in a way that we get what we wanted to . . . " (Augusztinovics 2000, 45; see also Medvegyev 2015). For the advantages of I-O models in planning, see Augusztinovics (1995).

42. "In the practice of planning, future coefficients . . . are usually derived from various sources of information, experience and speculation. These are amalgamated, by intuition, conscious weighing, simple or more complex arithmetic, and pondering, into the most probable guess. This domain of planning must draw on technical expertise and knowledge, general economic know-how and political common sense" (Bródy 1970, 120). Augusztinovics (1984, 45) put it more bluntly: "The decision process is hierarchical and decentralized, even if it looks fully centralized. . . . The processes of elaboration and acceptance are intermingled: this dual process is called plan coordination. . . . The battle of figures, arguments, and interests takes place on the same battlefield."

43. For the remarkably small number of ministry-level models in the early 1970s, see Farkas (1973).

44. Ganczer (1973) reports this failure using the example of the Fourth Five-Year Plan (1971–1975). A large group of experts in the Planning Office was commissioned to elaborate a mathematical model for the plan too late, in March 1969. They wanted to go for sure and decided to work out a linear programming model that was much simpler than Kornai's inoperational two-level planning scheme (see below). While making the calculations, the plan was approved by the government in December 1970, based on data that were largely different from the ones the researchers applied to set up their model. The real plan and the model became incomparable; therefore, the former could not be checked by the latter, even retrospectively.

45. It is symptomatic that Augusztinovics (1995, 273) could not imagine that the suggestion made about popular voting on societal preferences by Ragnar Frisch in the early 1970s could ever become viable.

46. With time, a group of younger able experts crystallized around Augusztinovics, including, e.g., Tivadar Faur, Katalin Haraszti, Júlia Király, János Réti, Béla Székely, and György Szepesi, who were ideologically less committed to central planning and put forward economic policy goals compatible with the radical programs of market reform. Small wonder that they were disliked by officials coordinating the five-year

plans, a large majority of the Office's employees, whose work was managed by another department.

47. István Hetényi, a student of Farkas Heller at the pre-communist University of Economics, later professor of public finance, is probably the best example for continuity. He had supervised long-term planning in the Planning Office until 1980 when he left for the Finance Ministry to lead, as minister, the preparations for the last reforms of the planned economy. Hetényi was not the only reform-minded leader of the Planning Office in the communist era. He worked together with communist technocrats such as Miklós Ajtai, József Drecin, István Huszár, Ottó Gadó, Miklós Pulai, and Péter Vályi.

48. Péter frequently attended economic debates on market reforms in the 1950s and 1960s, criticizing overindustralization, emphasizing the role of profit incentives and marketization in general. He became one of the first reform economists in Hungary although he and the chief economist of the Office, Júlia Zala, seldom took part in open political battles. Following György Péter's mysterious death in 1969, his deputy István Huszár was appointed the new president of the Office. He had initiated in 1968 that János Paizs, a self-made econometrician, starts teaching econometrics at Karl Marx University (Hulyák 2014, 72).

49. The former was headed by László Halabuk and György Szakolczai, the latter by Ferenc Rabár.

50. They made parameter estimations of CES production functions for specific industries and input-output calculations for the Planning Office. The Laboratory also built forecasting models and took part in the calculation of price indexes (Szakolczai 1972; Halabuk 1971; Havass 2011).

51. Theiss advanced his knowledge of neoclassical economics at leading U.S. universities (Chicago, Columbia, and Stanford), worked with Ragnar Frisch and Henry Schultz, and published in *Econometrica* and the *Journal of Political Economy*. Instead of emigrating after 1945 or 1956, he exposed himself to humiliation, being deprived of organizing a Hungarian school of econometrics. From 1948, Theiss served as head of the Statistics Department at the University of Economics. In 1950, he was accused of "mathematical formalism" and dismissed. He was permitted to teach again (but only law students) in 1959. Instead of becoming a celebrated path-breaker of Western economics in Hungary, Theiss died as an isolated scholar. As so often in Eastern Europe, the subsequent generations had to reinvent what he had already known (Kádas 1980; Huszár 2008; Hunyadi 2012).

52. The M-4 model fitted into the pattern of Klein's LINK project that connected the trade accounts of several countries by uniform specifications to better understand trade flows.

53. The journal that had had various predecessors from 1874 on was founded in 1895. Between 1949 and 1954, it was called the *Hungarian-Soviet Economic Review* (Magyar-Szovjet Közgazdasági Szemle).

54. On Friss's professional and political ambiguities, see Péteri (1997, 2002, 2019). Among the recruited scholars Erdős and T. Nagy were prominent reform econo-mists of the time while their younger colleagues (e.g., Bródy, Kornai, A. Nagy, and

the maverick Tibor Liska) joined them in their struggle with the textbook political economists.

55. Bródy was a conspicuous exception (see below).

56. It did not help them that a number of the first mathematical economists in the communist era, such as Andorka, Szakolczai, Theiss and Varga, were stigmatized as "agents" of the previous regime.

57. "We did have to pour Marxist holy water on mathematical economics in order to be allowed to deal with it. When physicists realized that, by frankly admitting what they thought, they—like Giordano Bruno—committed themselves to the flames, invented mathematical physics that the clergy did not understand" (Bródy 1994, 294). "Mathematical language was incomprehensible to commissars, party officials, and all who kept watch on institutes, publishers, and journals. Having seen a few equations in a manuscript, they put it down with a shiver" (Kornai 2007, 152). Erdős chose a different strategy of survival. After 1956, instead of relying on his profound mathematical knowledge, he left the reform battles for research on capitalist economies and became a critic of Keynes.

58. He used to make condescending remarks about mathematical economists, which prompted Kornai (1981) to publish a bizarre article, full of self-critical comments on mistakes these economists made, in defense of the discipline. This is how Nagy invited Bródy to join his research group in the 1960s: "Andriska, come over to us, you are a smart researcher, but the precondition of your transfer is that you will not deal with mathematics because I do not understand it" (Bródy 1994, 300–301).

59. Meanwhile, Tamás Nagy taught political economy at the university, without any special reference to mathematical economics.

60. Not only Bródy and Augusztinovics were married. Kornai and Zsuzsa Dániel who also worked on mathematical planning were husband and wife as well. Bródy and Jánossy (who was the stepson of the Marxist philosopher György Lukács) were good friends and most of them maintained friendly relations with Martos, A. Nagy, and Tardos. The latter was son-in-law of Péter. As years passed, many of their younger colleagues joined this network.

61. In 1964–1965, a number of important Hungarian works in mathematical economics were published: for example, Bródy 1964, Kornai 1965, Simon and Kondor 1965, Theiss 1965.

62. The volume included a chapter written by Kantorovich on optimal planning.

63. A smaller research unit, the Institute of Market Research (*Konjunktúra-és Piackutató Intézet*) where, among others, János Gács, Kamilla Lányi, András Nagy, Gábor Oblath, Péter Pete, András Simon, and Márton Tardos worked for a long time also needs to be mentioned in this regard. In the 1960s, they were building optimal models for planning foreign trade and rationalizing the New Economic Mechanism, and later engaged in econometric research in various fields of macroeconomics. With time, Gács, Nagy, Pete, and Tardos moved to the Institute of Economics.

64. The older one included, besides Bródy and Kornai, Sándor Ausch, Anna Gelei, Róbert Hoch, György Kondor, Béla Martos, Éva Radnóti, and György Simon while the younger one consisted of Péter Bodó, Éva Bondár, Judit Barta, Győző Gábor, László Halpern, József Horváth, Zsuzsa Kapitány, Gábor Kertesi, Ilona Kovács,

János Köllő, Gábor Kőrösi, Mária Lackó, György Molnár, Miklós Ördög, Judit Rimler, András Simonovits, Judit Szabó, Tamás Tarján, György Tényi, and Ildikó Virág. Many of them focused on I-O analysis and/or optimal planning (and all of them applied some sort of formal models) at a certain point in their careers. While frequently leaving the country for conferences, longer research stays, or teaching, with the exception of Bodó and Kondor, none of them emigrated.

65. Normally, the younger researchers came from Karl Marx University or the Faculty of Mathematics of Loránd Eötvös University, and were recruited by the heads of the research groups who protected them from political intervention "from above" both inside and outside the Institute. With the gradual decline of political control, the young generation of researchers became dependent mainly on their group leaders, basically the same persons for decades. Fluctuation between the groups was weak, and loyalty overrode voice and exit.

66. Of course, their tongues were much sharper among themselves. For instance, Bródy (1994, 316) liked to call Kornai "the last advocate of Stalinist planning" and made fun of the alleged imperfections of his mathematical skills while Kornai ridiculed Bródy's Marxist nostalgia and superficial reading of literature. Otherwise, they respected each other and wrote cordial reviews about each other's books with only a few exceptions (cf. Kornai and Simonovits 1981), organized conferences together, and assisted each other abroad.

67. She left the Planning Office for the Institute in 1984.

68. In the Institute even the dedicated Marxists (such as Bródy, Erdős, Friss, Hoch and T. Nagy) distanced themselves from textbook political economists. The latter were called *polgazdos* ("polecon" may be the translation) with some contempt.

69. To be sure, all research on mathematical planning presented in this chapter was dwarfed by a great diversity of verbal approaches of mixed quality, thriving outside the Institute, to the problematic of planning. These approaches, which unfortunately we cannot cover here, equally embraced (1) the confirmation of traditional (Stalinist) principles of central planning and a large variety of (2) diluting or (3) denying them. To give examples, Kálmán Szabó (1960) represented the first, Ákos Balassa (1979) the second, and Tibor Liska (1988) the third approach. Sometimes, even those experts stuck to traditional principles (e.g., directive planning) who otherwise worked on optimization (cf. Morva 1965, 1966). As for research programs unfolding within the Institute, there were excellent verbal studies providing historical comparisons of planning regimes and policies in the Eastern Bloc from a reformist perspective and offering the mathematical economists original variables to model. See, for instance, Bauer (1981) and Soós (1986) on investment cycles.

70. The interest of younger mathematical economists in market reforms was facilitated by the fact that, in contrast to how their older colleagues felt in the early 1960s, they already were not enchanted by the idea of improving planning (see below).

71. György Molnár (2019) recalls that, as a young mathematician, he tried to correct one of Bródy's proofs. "It was full of mistakes and I was convinced and eager to show that his theorem was false. After having fixed the proof, I realized that the theorem was true. Bródy saw the truth somehow through the algebraic structure

of the input-output model but was not interested in puttering around the technical details at all."

72. His attraction to Marx cannot be explained if one disregards his intimate relationship with many members of the Budapest School of the "renaissance of Marxism," including his brother Ferenc, a philosopher as well as Lukács and his family (Bródy 1994, 292–96).

73. That is why Bródy was so skeptical about isolated calculations of investment efficiency, which were fashionable at the time and which actually contributed to the breakthrough of mathematization in official economic thought. He was not enticed by the econometric studies of the 1960s either since he deemed their results less robust than those of the I-O models (Bródy 1960b, 954; 1994, 313).

74. Bródy (1969, 43) was convinced that in terms of both the mathematical formulation of Marx's theory of reproduction and its combination with the turnpike theorem, he preceded Michio Morishima's discoveries.

75. These sentences were omitted from the English translation of the book.

76. Ironically, despite such reservations about optimal planning, he—unlike Kornai—did not give up the principle of optimization at the end of the 1960s (see below).

77. See, for example, Jánossy (1969). As Bródy (1994, 330) put it, "it almost did not matter to me . . . if Ferkó [Jánossy] published what I said or if I published what he said."

78. "One was permitted to chat about *how* things should be done but the *what is to be done* question, that is, the issue of economic policy, cannot be tackled while the mistakes were made there" (Bródy 1994, 322).

79. Between 1989 and 2004, Bródy served as editor-in-chief of *Economic Systems Research*, the journal of the International Input-Output Association.

80. Bródy was not satisfied with this book and decided not to publish it in English. It received a rather unfavorable review from his close colleagues (Kornai and Simonovits 1981) who missed non-price control, regulatory lags and the softness of budget constraint in Bródy's dynamic model, which they regarded as innovative but unrealistic and sloppy in many ways. Ironically, in the same year, Bródy (1981) published a paper on non-price control in a volume edited by Kornai and Martos. See also Bródy and Farkas (1987), Bródy (1997b).

81. Later Bródy (1994, 307–8) modified his concept of dynamics in the spirit of chaos theory, claiming that often there are neither stable equilibria nor stable cycles in the economy. Accordingly, the change in economic variables is completely irregular, but it stays near the equilibrium (Bródy 2004b).

82. "They believe that they have centralized [the economy], yet, they only created a totally impenetrable layer between the leaders and the ground level" (Bródy 1994, 307).

83. There is no trace in Bródy's writings of any serious reading of the main contributions to the debate.

84. In this capacity he was invited to write an entry on "Prices and Quantities" in the 1987 edition of *The New Palgrave Dictionary of Economics* (Bródy 1990).

85. Close to the end of his life, Bródy (1994, 311) was sad to have accused Leontief of plagiarism in Bródy (1964), the first book he wrote on I-O analysis.

86. This was his doctoral dissertation based on surveys and interviews with employees of state-owned firms on planning in the textile industry, which Kornai managed to publish in Hungarian right after the 1956 revolution and two years later in English. Although the book was regarded in the West as a work of economic sociology rather than economics, it was recognized as the first credible description of how the planned economy works.

87. For more on this, see Kőhegyi 2019. (This paper was supported by NKFIH No. 125374.)

88. At the end of the 1950s, Kornai decided to become a ("normal") Western economist, quit political life, and abandon Marxism but stay in Hungary as a dissenter rather than a dissident without rejoining the communist party. He began to learn higher mathematics and English and read neoclassical authors like Arrow, Hicks, Samuelson, and Solow (Kornai 2007, 123–24, 133).

89. He was a colleague of Alfréd Rényi. It was Bródy who made Lipták acquainted with Kornai. In 1965, Lipták who suffered from a serious mental disorder emigrated to the U.K. and ceased to assist Kornai. His place was filled by mathematical economists such as Béla Martos, Ágnes Matits, András Simonovits, and Jörgen Weibull. In his memoir, Kornai (2007, 157–58) explained why he—unlike a majority of contemporary economic theorists in the West—was exposed to support in quantitative analysis during his whole career. See also Lipták's obituary written by him (Kornai 1998).

90. Kornai's name became known in the West after Oxford University Press published *Overcentralization* in 1959 following the advice of John Hicks (Kornai 2007, 109, 139).

91. They assumed that the central planner allocates input and output quantity requirements among the sectors while lacking much of the information needed for such a decision. In order to fill in the information gaps, the sectoral planners solve their own optimization problems with some programming technique and send feedback to the central planner in the form of shadow prices received from the solution of the dual side of the programming tasks. The feedback signals serve to balance the initial quantity allocations by price adjustment according to the logic of market clearing. The reallocation of quantities is followed by a new round of sectoral optimization procedures and feedbacks. The iteration continues until the optimal plan is reached on both macro and sectoral levels. (The model ignored firm-level planning operations.)

92. However, in the Lange-Malinvaud model the center communicates with firms and top-down information is mediated by prices, in contrast to the Kornai-Lipták model where the center communicates with sectors and the dialogue is mediated by quantities. The bottom-up information coming from the firms is conveyed in the Lange-Malinvaud model by quantities to make the size of excess demand or supply transparent while in the Kornai and Lipták model such feedback is sent by (shadow) prices. As Kornai (2007, 145) remembers, they were not aware of Malinvaud's (1967) solution when inventing two-level planning.

93. Originally, the mathematical task of planning for the 1966–70 and 1971–75 periods included nearly 500 product groups, 52 sectors, 2,000 equations, 4,500

variables, and 2,000 constraints (Kornai 1975, 432–48). According to András Prékopa (2018), the refined and effective decomposition techniques published by George Dantzig and Philip Wolfe in 1960 as well as by Jacques Benders in 1962 were not known in Hungary in the early 1960s. In his 1965 [1967]/1973 [1975] book, however, Kornai (1975, 346, 381) discussed the Dantzig-Wolfe algorithm in great detail. By that time, he was also familiar with a version of the Lange-Malinvaud model using that algorithm. Nonetheless, he decided to apply the so-called "plan improvement" algorithm invented by Lipták (which Kornai named a "naïve variant" of the Dantzig-Wolfe technique) to adjust to the lack of computing capacity in the country. They did not expect this technique to reach an optimal solution but only to approach it somehow. In this way, they sacrificed important properties of the Dantzig-Wolfe algorithm such as convergence, finiteness, and monotonicity.

94. Although the program of optimization did not lack utopian elements, no serious mathematical economist in Hungary came up with a radical cybernetic vision of central planning. Such a vision was rarely proposed even by old-school planning officials (cf. Sík 1966). True, initially, Kornai did not deny that creating large computer networks hosting so-called model pyramids might make sense. Hungarian economists remained immune to an alternative utopia, too. It was cherished in the close vicinity of Hungarian optimal planners by Tibor Liska whose program of "entrepreneurial socialism" envisaged the replacement of central planning by a loose collection of competing business plans proposed from below by small private enterprises.

95. In his later works Kornai liked to call Lange's "competitive solution" naïve (see Conclusion).

96. At that time, with young members of his research team, Kornai made attempts, with no particular success, at building a vast macro-simulation model of the Hungarian economy to test alternative paths of growth. The model did not exclude optimization *ab ovo* (Kornai 2007, 232).

97. On the pride Kornai felt over the rapid fulfillment of this promise from among those he made to himself after 1956, see Kornai (2007, 154, 159–62). In his eyes, Westernization included cooptation in international academic networks of scholars like Frisch, Malinvaud, Stone, and Tinbergen who showed interest in macro-planning. In the beginning, such a cooptation did not conflict with recognition coming from equilibrium theorists.

98. Here is a remark by Mária Augusztinovics expressing the irony of the situation. Following the publication of *Anti-Equilibrium*, her boss in the Planning Office chided her as follows: "Why do you always jitter about the national income deficit? Kornai has already said that equilibrium is not necessary" (Augusztinovics in Laki 2006, 30).

99. The book "will make a fine obelisk on the burial mound of the general equilibrium theory," commented Arrow on the draft (Kornai 2007, 178). Let us not guess here whether Koopmans and Arrow (or Jacob Marschak and Roy Radner with whom Kornai also discussed his draft) were simply polite and did not want to frustrate a gifted scholar who, owing to his provenance, lacked the education and methodological sophistication they had, or were inclined to self-criticism and even self-irony. The optical illusion was rather a sort of cultural misunderstanding: probably, Kornai understood both the interest in his iconoclastic research program and the

compassion felt for his difficult career as an acceptance of his heavyweight criticism. He might have been misled also by the staunch opposition by Cambridge economists (particularly, that of Miklós Káldor) to general equilibrium theory. Kornai repeated and also anticipated some of Káldor's arguments, therefore, Hahn's malicious review actually may have targeted Káldor while Kornai was the scapegoat. On the relationship between Káldor and Kornai, and the similarities of their research programs, see Mihályi (2017).

100. Bródy also disliked Kornai's doubts about scientific abstraction but did not air his grievances publicly. This is how he remembered later: I could not share "his opinion that there is no fruit but apple, moreover, there is no apple but only a certain kind of apple, and in fact, . . . only this apple here at the bottom of the basket. This meticulousness leads nowhere" (Bródy 1994, 326). See also Pete (1996).

101. Instead of "mainstream economics," he wrote "neoclassical school" in the Hungarian original (Kornai 2005, 195).

102. Browsing through the bibliographies of his major works published before 1989, one finds a few authors such as Jacob Marschak, Roy Radner, and Herbert Simon who might have lured him in this direction. However, most of those experts who later became recognized as the *crème de la crème* of new institutionalism such as James Buchanan, Ronald Coase, and Douglass North were missing in the references. On unexploited opportunities in this regard, see Grosfeld (1992). Kornai also could have returned to Hungarian sources from the 1940s to couple mathematics and institutional analysis (see note 17).

103. He did not dissuade his students and younger colleagues from studying neoclassical authors. On the contrary, he told them to learn to know what they eventually had better not accept (cf. next note). See the discussion between Kornai and J. M. Kovács on these controversial aspects of *Anti-equilibrium* (Laki 2006, 14–17, 28–30). On Kornai's ambiguous impact on the Eastern European reception of mainstream theories in the West, see Vincze (1996), Klaus (1997), and Laki (2006). See also Gács and Köllő (1998), Maskin and Simonovits (2000), Bihari et al. (2018), and Simonovits (2018).

104. Introducing a Hungarian-language volume of Arrow's selected works in 1979, he wrote this: "I still consider the criticism expounded in my book *Anti-equilibrium* legitimate. . . . An economist who is not profoundly familiar with general equilibrium theory cannot be an educated expert mastering the profession seriously. . . . What is needed is not to reject [this theory] arrogantly but to surpass it in a well-prepared, critical and constructive manner" (Kornai 1979, 9–10).

105. In *Shortage* he even admitted that, instead of rejecting the notion of equilibrium as such, he should have only criticized the Walrasian concept of equilibrium (Kornai 1980, 143–47).

106. Here, he claimed that "truly harmonic growth is promoted by clever planning," and in itself the market does not produce harmony but can correct the plan (Kornai 1972a, 141).

107. Cf. Simonovits (2003) on what he calls "the Hungarian school of control theory." He lists Bródy (1973) among its important works. See also Martos (1990).

108. Kornai's cautiousness was reflected by the fact that he resisted the temptation to switch to a description of the planned economy as an overwhelmingly in-kind regime.

109. *Shortage* only contains two partial models built by Simonovits and Weibull on forced substitution as well as on queuing and friction, respectively, in its annex.

110. Nonetheless, in *Shortage* he confronted its members such as Robert Barro, Robert Clower, Herschel Grosmann, David Howard, and Richard Portes with reasonable verbal arguments on aggregate excess demand, household savings, and labor supply in a planned economy (Kornai, 1980, 476–80).

111. For other important counter-arguments, see Davis and Charemza (1989), Gomułka (1985), and Soós (1985).

112. Yet, during the 1980s promising attempts were made to study cases and build models to refine and/or test the principal hypotheses of *Shortage*. See, for example, Kapitány, Kornai, and Szabó (1984), Kornai and Matits (1987a, 1987b), Szabó (1988), Goldfeld and Quandt (1988), and Lackó (1989).

113. This concept motivated by consumer theory in microeconomics was to represent the situation in which a state-owned firm can count on a bail-out by the central planner if the firm's revenues do not cover its costs. Kornai (1986a; 2007, 265–67) regretted that, in 1984, his article on the soft budget constraint had been rejected by *American Economic Review* because of the excessively verbal style of his research project.

114. They include Erik Berglöf, Yingli Qian, Richard Quandt, Gerard Roland, Mark Schaffer, Jörgen Weibull, and Chenggang Xu.

115. For more on this, see Szabó (2015).

116. On the protracted reception of new institutional economics in Eastern Europe, see Kovács (2012).

117. Since the 1960s, he taught and researched at various Western universities from Stanford to Stockholm, and became a professor at Harvard in 1984 but never cut his relations with Hungary, claiming that his research material lay on the Eastern side of the Iron Curtain and admitting that there he always had a chance to rely on excellent mathematicians. An ahistorical question: would he have been more successful in modeling the soft budget constraint if Lipták had still been around?

118. Approaching 1989, Kornai gradually left the terrain of mathematical economics and devoted his time to the study of late communist reforms and the completion of his 1992 book on the *Socialist System*, a synthesis of decades-long research on the planned economy. For more on this, see the next volume of our series.

119. Facing the difficulties was not tantamount to admitting and explaining the failure. Just like Bródy and Kornai, the other former champions of optimal planning in Hungary also have not given a detailed historical account to this date about how and why their project ceased to exist.

120. Tardos (1968) tried to build a formal model for the regulation system of NEM, which was based on the Dorfman-Samuelson-Solow model of linear programming but did not test it by means of detailed calculations. Among those who started working on optimal planning at the turn of the 1950s and 1960s, just a very few (such as András Nagy and Tardos) anchored themselves in reform economics so firmly that,

from the 1970s onward, they stopped building quantitative models. This also meant that their interest in new institutional economics did not result in authentic formal models describing the planned economy undergoing market reforms.

121. Kornai (1986b, 1725–28) accepted some of Hayek's views indirectly, through passing judgement on Lange. It was only in 1991 that, criticizing state-led privatization, Kornai (1992a) referred to the Hayekian stance against "constructivism" approvingly the first time. In his book *The Socialist System* he admitted that "Hayek was right on every point in the debate [on socialist calculation]" (Kornai 1992b, 476).

122. For example, as shown earlier, Kornai (1967a [1975]) was still optimistic about centrally planned investments, and a total abolition of directive planning did not feature even in his writings on market reform during the second half of the 1980s (e.g., Kornai 1986b). Here, he rejected the attraction of "Galbraithian socialists" to large-scale state intervention but avoided to suggest the termination of five-year plans or at least of the gigantic central development programs. In his opinion, "ex-ante coordination" (whatever it may have meant) should have remained an important task of the central planner (1710, 1730–32).

123. For example, Augusztinovics played a leading role in modeling long-term plans for 1970–85, 1975–90, and 1980–2000. These were the least risky types of central plans: they were regarded as futurological visions rather than regular plans that had to be endorsed by the Politburo and fulfilled by the economic actors at all levels of the hierarchy.

124. Bródy's (1978, 180) opinion about state planning in both the East and the West was more than skeptical: planning "can be hardly left to the usual sort of politicians who will promise whatever is popular . . . and have a time horizon much shorter than the horizon considered in an economy-wide plan. . . . A plan is actually conserving the very power structure that gave rise to it."

125. Augusztinovics (2000, 17) was even more mistrustful: "the neoclassical theory does not want to understand but to cover up the reality of the capitalist economic system."

126. As young scholars in the 1950s and 1960s, Bródy and Kornai did empirical research in numerous firms (engineering and textiles, respectively) and gathered ample insider experience also about how the Planning Office and various branch ministries worked.

127. The trauma of the post-1956 retributions had a long afterlife. Kornai was not fully rehabilitated by his return to the Institute of Economics in 1967; the secret police did not stop harassing him from time to time. The last time Bródy had to undergo a disciplinary procedure in the communist party was in 1988. Yet, their fears stemmed increasingly from concerns about losing their jobs and privileges such as relative freedom of thought and travel as well as proximity to top decision-makers in the reformist camp while their worries about violent repression dwindled. Nevertheless, forced emigration (like in the case of some members of the Budapest School in the 1970s) remained a credible threat.

128. For more on this, see Kovács (2012, 2016).

129. For example, Gács and Lackó (1973) was a promising attempt to examine the behavior of central planners (instead of helping them improve planning) but their early initiative was hardly followed by their colleagues.

130. Kornai, for example, abandoned optimal planning, in which he had relied on econometric analyses, continued to apply econometric research in his later works, was active in the Econometric Society, but—as mentioned—insisted on the broadest possible designation and preferred to call himself a mathematical economist. This is how he remembered mathematical economics in Hungary during the 1960s: "we <two-levelers> formed one faction, but other groups emerged as well, such as the <input-outputters,> the econometricians, and the operations researchers. They often overlapped" (Kornai 2007, 153).

131. In the beginning, it was only Ede Theiss who worked in the spirit of this slogan in Hungary. He died at the end of the 1970s.

132. Kornai later became an exception in this regard when his disciples helped him verify the empirical relevance of his concepts.

133. For instance, at the Institute of Economics Mária Lackó investigated investment cycles, Miklós Ördög worked on the estimation of consumption functions, and György Simon on that of sectoral production functions. The example of László Hunyadi is revealing. As a self-taught econometrician, he had worked on planning models until—completing a large project on the impacts of change in energy prices on the Hungarian economy—he realized that the Planning Office ignored such econometric analyses, and in the mid-1980s he decided to move to Karl Marx University to teach instead of struggling for recognition within the economic administration (Hunyadi 2014).

134. Yet, the first article in Hungary on the "Lucas critique" was published by Kamilla Lányi as early as 1977.

135. Interestingly enough, a main motivation of this group came from sociologists (such as László Füstös and Róbert Manchin) who already applied first-generation statistical software (e.g., Socprog) in their empirical surveys, launched by István Kemény, on poverty and ethnicity (Köllő 2021).

136. The attraction of neoclassical concepts for certain econometricians survived Kornai's attack on general equilibrium theory. For example, when Ziermann (1977) reported on the annual meeting of the Econometric Society she presented not only the new results in times series analysis (to which she also contributed in the field of dynamic factor analysis) and multivariate regression but also in research on Pareto efficiency and decentralized allocation mechanisms.

137. Interestingly, the inertia was not overcome by some of promising international ventures (such as the LINK project, in which András Simon represented Hungary and the IIASA (International Institute for Applied Systems Analysis) where Ernő Zalai spent years in the first half of the 1980s) since these research communities were more pluralistic and did not exclusively favor the idea of general equilibrium.

BIBLIOGRAPHY

Ámon, Zsolt, and István Ligeti. 1987. "A tervezés kvantitatív módszereinek fejlesztése." *Tervgazdasági Fórum* 3 (3): 101–10.

Andorka, Rudolf, Béla Martos, and György Szakolczai, eds. 1967. *Dinamikus népgazdasági modellek.* Budapest: Közgazdasági és Jogi Könyvkiadó.

Andorka, Rudolf. 1970. *Mikromodellek.* Budapest: Közgazdasági és Jogi Könyvkiadó.

Arrow, Kenneth. 1979. *Egyensúly és döntés.* Budapest: Közgazdasági és Jogi Könyvkiadó.

Augusztinovics, Mária. 1964. "Ankét a matematikai módszerek gazdasági alkalmazásáról." *Az MTA Társadalmi-Történeti Tudományok Osztályának Közleményei* 14 (1–2): 65–68.

―――. 1975. "Integration of Mathematical and Traditional Methods of Planning." In *Economic Planning, East and West,* edited by Morris Bornstein, 127–48. Cambridge: Ballinger.

―――, ed. 1979. *Népgazdasági modellek a távlati tervezésben.* Budapest: Közgazdasági és Jogi Könyvkiadó. 1984. *Long-Term Models at Work.* Budapest: Akadémiai Kiadó.

―――. 1981. "Népgazdasági modellszámítások a VI. ötéves terv kidolgozásához." *Szigma* 14 (4): 229–38.

―――. 1995. "What Input-Output Is About." *Structural Change and Economic Dynamics* 6 (3): 271–77 (1996. "Miről szól az input-output modell?" *Közgazdasági Szemle* 43 (4): 313–20).

―――. 2000. "Pénz és terv—modellek és emberek." Interview by Krisztina Megyeri. In *Racionalitás és méltányosság,* edited by Júlia Király, András Simonovits, and János Száz, 7–20. Budapest: Közgazdasági Szemle Alapítvány.

―――. 2008. "Beszélgetés Augusztinovics Máriával." Interview by Miklós Lakatos. *Statisztikai Szemle* 86 (12): 1163–70.

―――. 2012. Interview with Mária Augusztinovics by András Pinkász, May 30, 2012. Manuscript.

Augusztinovics, Mária, and Péter Bod. 1985. "Practical Linear Programming in Macroeconomic Planning: The Case of Hungary." *European Journal of Operational Research* 22 (2): 204–15.

Balassa, Ákos. 1979. *A magyar népgazdaság tervezésének alapjai.* Budapest: Közgazdasági és Jogi Könyvkiadó.

Bauer, Tamás. 1981. *Tervgazdaság, beruházás, ciklusok.* Budapest: Közgazdasági és Jogi Könyvkiadó.

Baumol, William. 1968. *Közgazdaságtan és operációanalízis.* Budapest: Közgazdasági és Jogi Könyvkiadó.

Bihari, Péter, Lajos Bokros, Júlia Király, and András Vértes. 2018. "A Kornai-hatás." *Köz-Gazdaság* 13 (1): 29–44.

Bod, Péter et al., ed. 1962. *Az ágazati kapcsolati mérlegek összeállításának és felhasználásának kérdései.* Budapest: Akadémiai Kiadó.

Bornstein, Morris, ed. 1975. *Economic Planning, East and West.* Cambridge: Ballinger.

200   Gergely Kőhegyi and János Mátyás Kovács

Bródy, András. 1956. "A hóvégi hajrá és gazdasági mechanizmusunk." *Közgazdasági Szemle* 3 (7–8): 870–73.

———. 1957. "Input-output: Módszer a nemzetgazdasági folyamatok elemzésére." *Közgazdasági Szemle* 4 (2): 145–65.

———. 1958. "Az ágazati kapcsolatok mérlegének elméletéhez." *Közgazdasági Szemle*, 5 (8–9): 823–36.

———. 1960a. "Az ágazati kapcsolatok mérlege és a közvetett beruházások." *Közgazdasági Szemle* 7 (5): 561–80.

———. 1960b. "A közgazdasági <modellek> kérdéséhez." *Közgazdasági Szemle* 7 (8–9): 954–63.

———. 1962a. *Matematikai programozás: 1. Lineáris programozás.* Budapest: Tankönyvkiadó.

———. 1962b. *Matematikai programozás: 2. Sztochasztikus programozás.* Budapest: Tankönyvkiadó.

———. 1962c. "The Unicity of the Prices of Production and of the Average Rate of Profit." In *Input-Output Tables: Their Compilation and Use,* edited by Ottó Lukács et al., 243–49. Budapest: Akadémiai Kiadó.

———. 1964. *Az ágazati kapcsolatok modellje: A felhasznált absztrakciók, azok korlátai és a számítások pontossága.* Budapest: Akadémiai Kiadó.

———. 1966. "A Simplified Growth Model." *The Quarterly Journal of Economics* 80 (1): 137–46.

———. 1969. "The Rate of Economic Growth in Hungary, 1924–1965." In *Is the Business Cycle Obsolete?*, edited by Martin Bronfenbrenner, 312–27. New York: Wiley.

———. 1970. *Proportions, Prices, and Planning: A Mathematical Restatement of the Labor Theory of Value.* Budapest–Amsterdam: North-Holland. Originally published as 1969. *Érték és újratermelés: Kísérlet a marxi értékelmélet és újratermelési elmélet matematikai modelljének megfogalmazására.* Budapest: Közgazdasági és Jogi Könyvkiadó.

———. 1973. "Szabályozási modellekről." *Szigma* 6 (2): 93–103.

———. 1978. "Planning and Planning: Some Comments on Professor Wassily Leontief's Proposals." *Acta Oeconomica* 20 (1–2): 179–81.

———. 1980. *Ciklus és szabályozás: Kísérlet a klasszikus piac-és cikluselmélet matematikai modelljének megfogalmazására.* Budapest: Közgazdasági és Jogi Könyvkiadó.

———. 1981. "Készletről és nyereségről vezérelt zárt gazdaság." In *Szabályozás árjelzések nélkül,* edited by János Kornai and Béla Martos, 135–46. Budapest: Akadémiai Kiadó.

———. 1985. *Slowdown: Global Economic Maladies.* Beverly Hills: SAGE Publications.

———. 1990. "Prices and Quantities." In *The New Palgrave: Problems of the Planned Economy*, edited by John Eatwell, Murray Milgate, and Peter Newman, 218–26. London: Macmillan.

———. 1994. "Beszélgetés Bródy Andrással." Interview by János Mátyás Kovács. In *Miért hagytuk hogy így legyen? Tanulmányok Bródy Andrásnak,* edited by

Aladár Madarász and Judit Szabó, 271–348. Budapest: Közgazdasági és Jogi Könyvkiadó.

———. 1995. "Truncation and Spectrum of the Dynamic Inverse." *Economic Systems Research* 7 (3): 235–47.

———. 1997a. "A kétszáz éves ciklus és az Egyesült Államok I: A növekedési ráták alakulása." *Közgazdasági Szemle* 44 (2): 113–23.

———. 1997b. "A piac és az egyensúly: A neumanni és a kvázi-hamiltoni rendszer." *Közgazdasági Szemle* 44 (9): 738–55.

———. 1999a. "A kétszáz éves ciklus és az Egyesült Államok II: A kamatráták alakulása." *Közgazdasági Szemle* 46 (1): 35–44.

———. 1999b. "Rövid vagy hosszú ciklus? Új előrejelzés az ezredfordulóra." *Közgazdasági Szemle* 46 (7–8): 701–8.

———. 2004a. "Leontief zárt dinamikus modellje: Megoldások és értelmezések." *Közgazdasági Szemle* 51 (10): 924–35.

———. 2004b. *Near Equilibrium.* Budapest: Aula Könyvkiadó.

Bródy, András, and Alfréd Rényi. 1956. "Az árrendezés problémája." *Az MTA Matematikai Kutatóintézetének Közleményei* 1 (3): 325–35.

Bródy, András, and Anne Carter, eds. 1970a. *Contributions to Input-Output Analysis.* Amsterdam: North Holland.

———. 1970b. *Applications of Input-Output Analysis.* Amsterdam: North Holland.

Bródy, András, and Miklós Farkas. 1987. "Forms of Economic Motion." *Acta Oeconomica* 38 (3–4): 361–70.

Bronfenbrenner, Martin, ed. 1969. *Is the Business Cycle Obsolete?* New York: Wiley.

Csató, Katalin. 2019. "Az akadémiai közgazdasági gondolkodás formálódása a politika bordásfalán." IEHAS Discussion Papers No. 18, Hungarian Academy of Sciences, Institute of Economics, Budapest.

Csekő, Imre. 1996. "Választás és mechanizmus: Felületes ismerkedés az implementáció-elmélettel." *Közgazdasági Szemle* 43 (5): 420–30.

Csontos, László. 1996. "Túl jón és rosszon: a racionális döntések elméletének recepciója Magyarországon." *Közgazdasági Szemle* 43 (4): 326–31.

Davis, Christopher, and Wojciech Charemza, eds. 1989. *Models of Disequilibrium and Shortage in Centrally Planned Economies.* London: Chapman and Hall.

Debreu, Gerard. 1987. *Közgazdaságtan axiomatikus módszerrel.* Budapest: Közgazdasági és Jogi Könyvkiadó.

Dewatripont, Mathias, and Eric Maskin. 1995. "Credit and Efficiency in Centralized and Decentralized Economies." *Review of Economic Studies* 62 (4): 541–56.

Farkas, Katalin. 1973. "Ágazati terv-modell kísérletek (IV. ötéves terv)." *Szigma* 6 (1): 86–92.

Forgó, Ferenc, and Sándor Komlósi. 2015. "Krekó Béla szerepe a magyar közgazdászképzés modernizálásában." *Szigma* 46 (3–4): 137–58.

Friedman, Milton. 1986. *Infláció, munkanélküliség, monetarizmus.* Budapest: Közgazdasági és Jogi Könyvkiadó.

Frisch, Ragnar. 1974. *Dinamikus és kvantitatív közgazdaságtan.* Budapest: Közgazdasági és Jogi Könyvkiadó.

Gács, János, and János Köllő, eds. 1998. *A túlzott központosítástól az átmenet stratégiájáig: Tanulmányok Kornai Jánosnak*. Budapest: Közgazdasági és Jogi Könyvkiadó.

Gács, János, and Mária Lackó. 1973. "A Study of Planning Behavior on the National-Economic Level." *Economics of Planning* 13 (1–2): 91–119.

Ganczer, Sándor. 1973. *Népgazdasági tervezés és programozás*. Budapest: Közgazdasági és Jogi Könyvkiadó.

Goldfeld, Stephen, and Richard Quandt. 1988. "Budget Constraints, Bailouts, and the Firm under Central Planning." *Journal of Comparative Economics* 12 (4): 502–20.

Goldmann, Josef. 1977. *Makroökonómiai elemzés és előrejelzés*. Budapest: Közgazdasági és Jogi Könyvkiadó.

Gomułka, Stanisław. 1985. "Kornai's Soft Budget Constraint and the Shortage Phenomenon: A Criticism and Restatement." *Economics of Planning*, 19 (1): 1–11.

Grosfeld, Irena. 1992. "Reform Economics and Western Economic Theory: Unexploited Opportunities." In *Reform and Transformation on the Threshold of Change*, edited by János Mátyás Kovács and Márton Tardos, 62–79. London: Routledge.

Hahn, Frank. 1973. "The Winter of Our Discontent." *Economica* 40 (159): 322–30.

Halabuk, László. 1971. "The Activities of the Econometric Laboratory of the Central Statistical Office." *Acta Oeconomica* 6 (4): 381–85.

———. 1976. "Econometric Models and Methods: Research and Applications in Hungary." *Acta Oeconomica* 16 (1): 81–102.

Halabuk, László, Zoltán Kenessey, and Ede Theiss. 1965. "An Econometric Model of Hungary." *Economics of Planning* 5 (3): 30–43.

Halpern, László. 2020. Interview with László Halpern by Gergely Kőhegyi, January 7, 2020. Manuscript.

Halpern, László, and György Molnár. 1997. "Equilibrium and Disequilibrium in a Disaggregated Classical Model." In Simonovits and Steenge 1997, 149–60.

Hámori, Balázs, ed. 1986. *Politikai gazdaságtan 3*. Budapest: Közgazdasági és Jogi Könyvkiadó.

Havass, Miklós, ed. 2011. *A SZÁMALK és elődei*. Budapest: Számalk Kiadó.

Hicks, John. 1978. *Érték és tőke: A keynesi gazdaságtan válsága*. Budapest: Közgazdasági és Jogi Könyvkiadó.

Hoch, Róbert, ed. 1968. *Piac és vállalati árpolitika*. Budapest: Közgazdasági és Jogi Könyvkiadó.

Horváth, Róbert. 1963. "The Development and Present Status of Input-Output Methods in Hungary." *Economics of Planning* 3 (3): 209–20.

Hulyák, Katalin. 1972. "Plan of an Econometric Model Based on Input-Output Tables." *Acta Oeconomica* 8 (4): 433–43.

———. 2014. "Ötven éve alakult meg a Központi Statisztikai Hivatalban az Ökonometriai Laboratórium." *Statisztikai Szemle* 92 (1): 71–72.

Hunyadi, László. 2012. "Gondolatok Theiss Ede <A makroökonómiai modellek statisztikai problémái> című cikkével kapcsolatban." *Statisztikai Szemle* 90 (11–12): 1130–42.

————. 2014. "Beszélgetés Hunyadi Lászlóval." Interview by Gábor Rappai. *Statisztikai Szemle* 92 (6): 594–600.

Huszár, István. 2008. "Beszélgetés Huszár Istvánnal." Interview by Miklós Lakatos. *Statisztikai Szemle* 86 (3): 293–99.

Jánossy, Ferenc. 1963. *A gazdasági fejlettség mérhetősége és új mérési módszere.* Budapest: Közgazdasági és Jogi Könyvkiadó.

————. 1966. *A gazdasági fejlődés trendvonala és a helyreállítási periódusok.* Budapest: Közgazdasági és Jogi Könyvkiadó. 1971. *The End of the Economic Miracle.* White Plains, New York: International Arts and Sciences Press.

————. 1969. "Beszélgetés Jánossy Ferenccel." Interview by Varga Domonkos. *Valóság* 12 (5): 49–56.

Juhász, András, and Tamás Morva, eds. 1982. *A jövő tervezése—A tervezés jövője.* Budapest: OT Tervgazdasági Intézet.

Kaase, Max, and Vera Sparschuh, eds. 2002. *Three Social Science Disciplines in Central and Eastern Europe (1989–2001).* Bonn: GESIS/Social Science Information Centre (IZ).

Kádas, Kálmán. 1980. "Emlékezés Theiss Ede professzorra." *Statisztikai Szemle* 58 (10): 1022–27.

Káldor, Miklós. 1989. *Gazdaságelmélet—gazdaságpolitika.* Budapest: Közgazdasági és Jogi Könyvkiadó.

Kalecki, Michał. 1980. *A tőkés gazdaság működéséről.* Budapest: Közgazdasági és Jogi Könyvkiadó.

————. 1982. *A szocialista gazdaság működéséről.* Budapest: Közgazdasági és Jogi Könyvkiadó.

Kantorovich, Leonid. 1965. *The Best Use of Economic Resources.* Oxford: Pergamon Press. Originally published as 1959. *Ekonomicheskii raschet nailuchshego ispolzovaniia resursov.* Moskva: Akademiia Nauk SSSR.

Kapitány, Zsuzsa, János Kornai, and Judit Szabó. 1984. "Reproduction of Shortage on the Hungarian Car Market." *Soviet Studies* 36 (2): 236–56.

Kenessey, Zoltán. 1959. "A magyar népgazdaság ágazati kapcsolatainak mérlege." *Statisztikai Szemle* 37 (12): 1174–90.

Khachaturov, Tigran. 1966. *A beruházások gazdasági hatékonysága.* Budapest: Közgazdasági és Jogi Könyvkiadó.

Klaus, Václav. 1997. "Review of János Kornai's The Socialist System." In *Renaissance: The Rebirth of Liberty in the Heart of Europe*, 163–70. Washington DC: Cato Institute.

Klein, Lawrence. 1986. *Mérés és prognózis a gazdaságban.* Budapest: Közgazdasági és Jogi Könyvkiadó.

Kornai, János. 1959. *Overcentralization in Economic Administration: A Critical Analysis Based on Experience in Hungarian Light Industry.* Oxford: Oxford University Press. Originally published as 1957. *A gazdasági vezetés túlzott központosítása.* Budapest Közgazdasági és Jogi Könyvkiadó.

————. 1967a. *Mathematical Planning of Structural Decisions.* Amsterdam: North-Holland. Originally published as 1965. *A gazdasági szerkezet matematikai tervezése.* Budapest: Közgazdasági és Jogi Könyvkiadó.

————. 1967b. "Mathematical Programming of Long-Term Plans in Hungary." In *Activity Analysis in the Theory of Growth and Planning*, edited by Edmond Malinvaud and M. O. L. Bacharach, 211–31. London: Macmillan.

————. 1969. "A tervezés matematikai modelljeinek osztályozása." In *Népgazdasági tervezés és irányítás*, edited by Géza Kovács, 43–54. Budapest: Közgazdasági és Jogi Könyvkiadó.

————. 1971. *Anti-equilibrium*. Amsterdam: North Holland. Originally published as 1971. *Anti-equilibrium*. Budapest: Közgazdasági és Jogi Könyvkiadó.

————. 1972a. *Rush versus Harmonic Growth: Meditation on the Theory and on the Policies of Economic Growth*. Amsterdam: North-Holland.

————. 1972b. "Mathematical Programming as a Tool of Socialist Economic Planning." In *Socialist Economics: Selected Readings*, edited by Alec Nove and Mario Nuti, 475–88. Harmondsworth: Penguin Books.

————. 1973. "Some Intersectoral and Intertemporal Choice Problems: Hungarian Experience in Long-Term Planning." In *Economic Structure and Development*, edited by H. C. Bos, H. Linnemann, and P. de Wolff, 201–14. Amsterdam: North-Holland.

————. 1975. *Mathematical Planning of Structural Decisions*. Amsterdam: North-Holland. Second edition. Originally published as 1973. *A gazdasági szerkezet matematikai tervezése*. Második kiadás. Budapest: Közgazdasági és Jogi Könyvkiadó.

————. 1979. "Bevezetés." In *Egyensúly és döntés*, by Kenneth Arrow, 7–17. Budapest: Közgazdasági és Jogi Könyvkiadó.

————. 1980. *Economics of Shortage*. Amsterdam: North-Holland. Originally published as 1980. *Hiány*. Budapest: Közgazdasági és Jogi Könyvkiadó.

————. 1981. "On the Difficulties and Deficiencies of Mathematical Economic Research in Hungary." *Acta Oeconomica* 26 (1–2): 175–98.

————. 1986a. "The Soft Budget Constraint." *Kyklos* 39 (1): 3–30.

————. 1986b. "The Hungarian Reform Process: Visions, Hopes, and Reality." *Journal of Economic Literature* 24 (1): 1687–747.

————. 1992a. "The Principles of Privatization in Eastern Europe." *De Economist* 140 (2): 153–76.

————. 1992b. *The Socialist System: The Political Economy of Communism*. Oxford: Oxford University Press.

————. 1996. "Nagy András 70 éves." *Közgazdasági Szemle* 43 (3): 266–69.

————. 1998. "In Memoriam: Tamás Lipták." *Acta Oeconomica* 49 (3–4): 461–63.

————. 2000. "Tíz évvel a Röpirat angol nyelvű megjelenése után: A szerző önértékelése." *Közgazdasági Szemle* 47 (9): 647–61.

————. 2007. *By Force of Thought: Irregular Memoirs of an Intellectual Journey*. Cambridge MA: The MIT Press. Originally published as 2005. *A gondolat erejével: Rendhagyó önéletrajz*. Budapest: Osiris Kiadó.

————. 2018. "A Közgazdaságtudományi Intézet 1990 előtti történetéről." Lecture 2, edited version of the lecture given at the Institute of Economics, Budapest, April 12, 2018. https://www.mtakti.hu/wp-content/uploads/2018/10/Kornai2018-KTI-1990-elotti-torteneterol2.pdf.

Kornai, János, Zsuzsa Dániel, and Judit Rimler. 1972. "Macrofunctions Computed on the Basis of Plan Models." *Acta Oeconomica* 8 (4): 375–406.

Kornai, János, Zsuzsa Dániel, Anna Jónás, and Béla Martos. 1971. "Plan Sounding." *Economics of Planning* 11 (1–2): 31–58.

Kornai, János, and Tamás Lipták. 1959. A nyereségérdekeltség matematikai vizsgálata. Mimeo, Budapest: Közgazdasági és Jogi Könyvkiadó.

———. 1962. "A Mathematical Investigation of Some Economic Effects of Profit Sharing in Socialist Firms." *Econometrica* 30 (1): 140–61.

———. 1965. "Two-Level Planning." *Econometrica* 33 (1): 141–69.

Kornai, János, and Béla Martos. 1973. "Autonomous Control of the Economic System." *Econometrica* 41 (3): 509–28.

Kornai, János, Eric Maskin, and Gérard Roland. 2003. "Understanding the Soft Budget Constraint." *Journal of Economic Literature* 41 (4): 1095–136.

Kornai, János, and Ágnes Matits. 1987a. "The Softness of Budgetary Constraints: An Analysis of Enterprise Data." *Eastern European Economics* 25 (4): 1–33.

———. 1987b. *A vállalatok nyereségének bürokratikus újraelosztása.* Budapest: Közgazdasági és Jogi Könyvkiadó.

Kornai, János, and András Simonovits. 1977. "Decentralized Control Problems in Neumann Economies." *Journal of Economic Theory* 14 (1): 44–67.

———. 1981. "Bródy András <Ciklus és szabályozás>." *Közgazdasági Szemle* 28 (1): 115–20.

Kovács, János Mátyás. 2002. "Business as (Un)usual: Notes on the Westernization of Economic Sciences in Eastern Europe." In Kaase and Sparschuh 2002, 26–33.

———. 2009. *"Ex Occidente Flux*: Vita a makroökonómia hasznáról és a közgazdaságtan felelősségéről." *Közgazdasági Szemle* 56 (10): 881–912.

———. 2012. "Beyond Basic Instinct? On the Reception of New Institutional Economics in Eastern Europe." In *Capitalism from Outside? Economic Cultures in Eastern Europe after 1989*, edited by János Mátyás Kovács and Violetta Zentai, 281–310. Budapest: CEU Press.

———. 2016. "Minden, amit tudni akartam a matematikai közgazdaságtanról, de nem mertem megkérdezni." 2000 Irodalmi és Társadalmi Havi Lap. http://ketezer.hu/2016/11/minden-amit-tudni-akartam-matematikai-kozgazdasagtanrol-de-nem-mertem-megkerdezni/.

Kőhegyi, Gergely. 2010. "A királynő és a herceg: A közgazdaságtan matematizálódása a 20. század első felében." *Fordulat* 9 (1): 89–125.

———. 2019. "An Attempt to Ground Central Planning on a Scientific Basis: János Kornai and the Mathematical Theory of Planning." *Múltunk*, special issue: 210–27.

Köllő, János. 2021. Interview with János Köllő by Gergely Kőhegyi, January 15, 2021. Manuscript.

Kőrösi, Gábor. 1996. "Az átalakulás ökonometriája avagy az ökonometria átalakulása." *Közgazdasági Szemle* 43 (4): 356–62.

———. 2020. Interview with Gábor Kőrösi by Gergely Kőhegyi, January 13, March 12, 2020. Manuscript.

Köves, Pál. 2005. "Beszélgetés Köves Pállal." Interview by H. L. *Statisztikai Szemle* 83 (9): 878–84.

Krekó, Béla. 1972. *Optimumszámítás*. Budapest: Közgazdasági és Jogi Könyvkiadó.

Kydland, Finn, and Edward Prescott. 1982. "Time to Build and Aggregate Fluctuations." *Econometrica* 50 (6): 1345–70.

Lackó, Mária. 1989. "Sectoral Shortage Models." In *Models of Disequilibrium and Shortage in Centrally Planned Economies*, edited by Christopher Davis and Wojciech Charemza, 263–82. London: Chapman and Hall.

Laki, Mihály, ed. 2006. *Egy délután Kornaival*. Budapest: MTA Közgazdaságtudományi Intézet.

Lampl, Tamás. 1971. "Az Infelor Rendszertechnikai Vállalat gazdaságmatematikai munkái." Szigma 4 (3): 243–47.

Lange, Oskar. 1965. *Politikai gazdaságtan I*. Budapest: Közgazdasági és Jogi Könyvkiadó.

———. 1966. *Optimális döntések*. Budapest: Közgazdasági és Jogi Könyvkiadó.

———. 1967a. *Bevezetés a közgazdasági kibernetikába*. Budapest: Közgazdasági és Jogi Könyvkiadó.

———. 1967b. *Politikai gazdaságtan II*. Budapest: Közgazdasági és Jogi Könyvkiadó.

Lányi, Kamilla. 1977. "Egy előrejelzési paradoxon." *Szigma* 10 (1–2): 49–59.

Leontief, Wassily. 1953. *Studies in the Structure of the American Economy*. Oxford: Oxford University Press. Russian translation: 1958. Issledovaniia struktury ameri-kanskoi ekonomiki. Moskva: Gosstatizdat.

———. 1977. *Terv és gazdaság*. Budapest: Közgazdasági és Jogi Könyvkiadó.

———. 1984. *Gazdaságelmélet, tények és gazdaságpolitika*. Budapest: Statisztikai Kiadó.

———. 1997. "Foreword." In Simonovits and Steenge 1997, VII.

Liska, Tibor. 1988. *Ökonosztát*. Budapest: Közgazdasági és Jogi Könyvkiadó.

Lucas, Robert. 1976. "Econometric Policy Evaluation: A Critique." *Carnegie-Rochester Conference Series on Public Policy* 1 (1): 19–46.

Lukács, Ottó et al., eds. 1962. *Input-Output Tables, Their Compilation and Use*. Budapest: Akadémiai Kiadó.

Malinvaud, Edmond. 1967. "Decentralized Procedures for Planning." In *Activity Analysis in the Theory of Growth and Planning*, edited by Edmond Malinvaud and M. O. L. Bacharach, 170–208. London: Macmillan.

Malinvaud, Edmond and M. O. L. Bacharach. 1967. *Activity Analysis in the Theory of Growth and Planning*. London: Macmillan.

———. 1974. *Az ökonometria statisztikai módszerei*. Budapest: Közgazdasági és Jogi Könyvkiadó.

Martos, Béla. 1975. *Nonlinear Programming: Theory and Methods*. Amsterdam: North Holland.

———. 1990. *Economic Control Structures: A Non-Walrasian Approach*. Amsterdam: North-Holland.

Martos, Béla, and János Kornai. 1973. "Tervszondázás: a modellek szerkezete." *Szigma* 6 (1): 33–61.

———, eds. 1981. *Non-Price Control*. Amsterdam: North-Holland.

Maskin, Eric, and András Simonovits, eds. 2000. *Planning, Shortage and Transformation: Essays in Honor of János Kornai*. Cambridge MA: MIT Press.

Medvegyev, Péter. 1984. "A General Existence Theorem for von Neumann Economic Growth Models." *Econometrica* 52 (4): 963–74.

———. 2015. "Augusztinovics Mária és a 20. századi magyar közgazdaságtan." *Közgazdasági Szemle* 62 (6): 700–703.

Mihályi, Péter. 2017. "Kaldor and Kornai on Economics Without Equilibrium: Two Life Courses." *Acta Oeconomica* 67 (S1):47–66.

Móczár, József. 1980. "A Marx Károly Közgazdaságtudományi Egyetem Népgazdasági Tervezési Intézetének tudományos munkássága." *Szigma* 13 (3): 233–37.

Molnár, György. 2019. Interview with György Molnár by Gergely Kőhegyi,December 4, 2019. Manuscript.

Morva, Tamás. 1965. "Tervgazdálkodás, tervezési és irányítási módszerek." *Közgazdasági Szemle* 12 (4): 397–413.

———. 1966. "Tervszerűség és piaci mechanizmus a szocializmusban." *Közgazdasági Szemle* 13 (3): 273–85.

Nagy, András. 1996. "A *déjà vu*-től a *what's new*-ig." *Közgazdasági Szemle* 43 (4): 335–42.

Nemchinov, Vasilii. 1962. *A matematika alkalmazása a közgazdasági kutatásokban.* Budapest: Közgazdasági és Jogi Könyvkiadó.

———. 1966. *A népgazdasági tervezés és irányítás problémái.* Budapest: Kossuth Kiadó.

Nove, Alec, and Mario Nuti, eds. 1972. *Socialist Planning: Selected Readings.* Harmondsworth: Penguin Books.

Novozhilov, Viktor. 1971. *A ráfordítások és eredmények mérése.* Budapest: Közgazdasági és Jogi Könyvkiadó.

Pawłowski, Zbigniew. 1970. *Ökonometria.* Budapest: Közgazdasági és Jogi Könyvkiadó.

Pete, Péter. 1996. "Mi az általános az általános egyensúlyelméletben?." *Közgazdasági Szemle* 43 (5): 437–42.

Péteri, György. 1993. "The Politics of Statistical Information and Economic Research in Communist Hungary, 1949–56." *Contemporary European History* 2 (2): 149–67.

———. 1997. "New Course Economics: The Field of Economic Research in Hungary after Stalin, 1953–1956." *Contemporary European History* 6 (3): 295–327.

———. 2002. "Purge and Patronage: Kádár's Counterrevolution and the Field of Economic Research in Hungary, 1957–1958." *Contemporary European History* 11 (1): 125–52.

———. 2017. "External Politics—Internal Rivalries: Social Science Scholarship and Political Change in Communist Hungary." *East Central Europe* 44 (2–3): 309–39.

———. 2019. "By Force of Power: On the Relationship between Social Science Knowledge and Political Power in Economics in Communist Hungary." *History of Political Economy* 51 (6): 30–51.

Petrakov, Nikolai. 1970. *A szocialista gazdálkodási módszerek vitatott problémái.* Budapest: Közgazdasági és Jogi Könyvkiadó.

Pontriagin, Lev et al. 1968. *Optimális folyamatok elmélete.* Budapest: Közgazdasági és Jogi Könyvkiadó.

Portes, Richard, and David Winter. 1980. "Disequilibrium Estimates for Consumption Goods Markets in Centrally Planned Economies." *Review of Economic Studies* 47 (1): 137–59.

Prékopa, András. 2018. "Operációkutatás és alkalmazott matematika a SZTAKI-ban." *Alkalmazott Matematikai Lapok* 35: 5–11.

Réti, János, György Boda, Tivadar Faur, and Judit Simon. 1981. "A KV (központi volumen modell)." *Szigma* 14 (4): 239–68.

Samuelson, Paul. 1976. *Közgazdaságtan*. Budapest: Közgazdasági és Jogi Könyvkiadó.

Sík, György. 1966. "A tervezés tudományos színvonalának és a gazdaságirányítás reformjának kapcsolata." Közgazdasági Szemle 13 (4): 405–16.

Simon, György. 1970. *Gazdaságirányítás és népgazdasági optimum*. Budapest: Közgazdasági és Jogi Könyvkiadó.

———. 1973. "A reflektorprogramozás elvei és algoritmusa." *Szigma* (2–3): 115–26.

Simon, György, and György Kondor. 1962. "Kantorovics, L. V.: Az erőforrások legjobb felhasználásának gazdasági számítása." *Közgazdasági Szemle* 9 (1): 121–27.

———. 1963. "A gazdasági optimumszámítások problémái Kantorovics és Novozsilov műveiben." *Az MTA Közgazdaságtudományi Intézet tájékoztató közleményei* 2

———. 1965. *Gazdasági hatékonyság és árnyékárak*. Budapest: Közgazdasági és Jogi Könyvkiadó.

Simonovits, András. 1975. "A Note on the Underestimation and Overestimation of the Leontief Inverse." *Econometrica* 43 (3): 493–98.

———. 1978. "A Note on <Marx in the Light of Modern Economic Theory> by Morishima." *Econometrica* 46 (5): 1239–41.

———. 1996. "A magyar matematikai közgazdaságtan múltja, jelene és jövője." *Közgazdasági Szemle* 43 (4): 350–55.

———. 2003. "A magyar szabályozáselméleti iskola." *Közgazdasági Szemle* 50 (5): 465–70.

———. 2018. "Mit tanultam Kornai Jánostól?." *Köz-Gazdaság* 13 (1): 67–73.

———. 2019. Interview with András Simonovits by Gergely Kőhegyi, December 12, 2019. Manuscript.

Simonovits, András, and Albert Steenge, eds. 1997. *Prices, Growth and Cycles: Essays in Honor of András Bródy*. London: Macmillan Press; New York: St. Martin's Press.

Sims, Christopher. 1980. "Macroeconomics and Reality." *Econometrica* 48 (1): 1–48.

Sivák, József. 1987. "Illúzióvesztés vagy lépésváltás a modellezésben?." *Tervgazdasági Fórum* 3 (2): 58–62.

Soós, K. Attila. 1985. "A hiányjelenségek magyarázatához: keresletmennyiség és strukturális rugalmatlanság." *Közgazdasági Szemle* 32 (1): 86–98.

———. 1986. *Terv, kampány, pénz*. Budapest: Kossuth Kiadó—Közgazdasági és Jogi Könyvkiadó.

Stark, Antal, ed. 1981. *Tervgazdálkodás*. Budapest: Közgazdasági és Jogi Könyvkiadó.

Szabó, Judit. 1988. "Preliminary and Incremental Softness of the Budget Constraint: A Comment on the Gomulka-Kornai Debate." *Economics of Planning* 22 (3): 109–16.

———. 2015. "Szemben a mainstream közgazdaságtannal." *Buksz* 27 (1): 3–10.

Szabó, Kálmán. 1960. *A szocialista tervszerűség elméleti kérdései.* Budapest: Kossuth Kiadó.

Szakolczai, György, ed. 1963. *A gazdasági fejlődés feltételei.* Budapest Közgazdasági és Jogi Könyvkiadó.

———. 1967. *A gazdasági növekedés feltételei.* Budapest Közgazdasági és Jogi Könyvkiadó.

———. 1972. "Activities of the INFELOR Systems Engineering Institute." *Acta Oeconomica,* 8 (4): 445–54.

Szamuely, László, and László Csaba. 1998. *Rendszerváltozás a közgazdaságtanban közgazdaságtan a rendszerváltozásban.* Budapest: Közgazdasági Szemle Alapítvány.

Szepesi, György, and Béla Székely. 1974. "Optimal Path of Economic Growth in a Controlled Economic System." *Jahrbuch der Wirtschaft Osteuropas* 5: 221–241

Tardos, Márton. 1968. "Az új gazdasági rendszer szabályozó rendszerének modellje." *Közgazdasági Szemle* 15 (10): 1185–95.

Theiss, Ede. 1947. "Dinamikai közgazdaságtudomány és társadalmi folyamat." *Közgazdasági Szemle* 70 (3–4): 129–55.

———. 1965. "A makroökonómiai modellek statisztikai problémái." *Statisztikai Szemle* 43 (4): 399–411.

Tinbergen, Jan. 1957. *Ökonometria.* Budapest: Közgazdasági és Jogi Könyvkiadó.

Tobin, James. 1984. *Pénz és gazdasági növekedés.* Budapest: Közgazdasági és Jogi Könyvkiadó.

Váradi, Balázs. 2007. "Karl Marx Learns Microeconomics." Manuscript.

Varga, István. 1947. "A gazdasági élet fejlődése és a közgazdaságtan." *Közgazdasági Szemle* 70 (5–12): 257–74.

Vincze, János. 1996. "Van-e magyar út az elméleti közgazdaságtanban?." *Közgazdasági Szemle* 43 (4): 331–35.

Virág, Ildikó. 1973. "Az MTA Közgazdaságtudományi Intézetében folyó matematikai közgazdasági kutatásokról." *Szigma* 6 (1): 83–86.

Zalai, Ernő. 1983. "Egyensúly és optimum: A makrogazdasági modellezés két irányzatának összevetése." *Közgazdasági Szemle* 30 (2): 157–75.

———. 1989. *Bevezetés a matematikai közgazdaságtanba.* Budapest: Közgazdasági és Jogi Könyvkiadó.

———. 1997. "Production Prices and Proportions Revisited." In Simonovits and Steenge 1997, 280–301.

———. 2014. "Neumann versus Leontief: Két modell—két gazdaságkép." *Közgazdasági Szemle* 61 (11): 1245–78.

Ziermann, Margit. 1977. "ESEM 76." *Szigma* 10 (1–2): 106–8.

CENTRAL PLANNING IN POLAND, 1945–1989

The first postwar economic plan in the People's Republic of Poland was introduced by the Act on Economic Reconstruction in July of 1947. The plan for the years 1947–1949, prepared by the newly established Central Planning Office led by the respected economist Czesław Bobrowski (Kaliński 2012), aimed at rebuilding the country from the ruins of the Second World War. Therefore, most investments were allocated to a quick revitalization of prewar industrial capacities as well as to the reconstruction of the destroyed city of Warsaw. This led to long-lasting consequences because the opportunity to modernize machinery was overlooked, which resulted in relative technological backwardness and limited productivity growth (Bobrowski 1985). Although the primary goals of the plan—reigniting industrial production, eliminating large-scale unemployment, and increasing the share of manufacturing in the economy—were achieved, the problem of a deeper reconstruction of the Polish economy in the spirit of the communist ideal of state-led industrialization was left to the subsequent plans introduced in the 1950s and 1960s.

The first five-year plan covering the 1950–1955 period was developed by a group led by Minister of Economy Hilary Minc, who was a strong critic of Bobrowski's approach to planning. In January 1948 when the so-called "CUP debate"[1] started, planners were accused by Minc and his ministry of cherishing outdated, "bourgeois" economic views. The direct reason for the attack was the method used to calculate national income, which had been developed by Michał Kalecki and Ludwik Landau before the war, and included the private sector in trade and services. After Minc's memorandum published in the monthly of the communist party *Nowe Drogi* (Minc 1954), Czesław Bobrowski resigned and the Central Planning Office was replaced by the State Commission for Economic Planning led de facto by Minc. The Commission closely followed the Soviet example prioritizing investments in heavy industry, including the production of coal, steel, cement, industrial chemicals, ships, plastics, and machinery. It was declared that through the execution of the five-year plan the government wanted to lay the foundations of socialism in the country. Therefore, as in the Soviet case, the plan included the collectivization of individual farming (which eventually did not happen) and the nationalization of the remaining private firms in industry and trade (which was implemented successfully). This led to a substantial growth in heavy industry, which was, however, detrimental to other sectors of the economy: light industry, agriculture, and services. Despite large-scale migration from overpopulated rural areas to the cities, the standard of living did not rise that much as most of the investments were completed in industries that did not produce consumer goods. Shortages of basic necessities were not eliminated and the planners struggled with setting the prices at market clearing level until the end of the 1950s (Bobrowski 1984).

In spite of these problems, the next three five-year plans for 1956–1960, 1961–1966, and 1966–1970 largely continued the general direction taken in the previous decade. Relatively more resources were channeled to light industries but the absolute advantage of heavy industries was maintained (Jezierski and Leszczyńska 2010). Central planners continued to favor energy-intensive investments developing large capacities in fuel industry and power generation, including further development of coal mining (Kaliński 2012). This extensive model of economic growth resulted in substantial disparity between the needs of consumers and the profile of production. The commitment of the planners to heavy industry was strong, so in the third five-year plan they once again made large investments in the production of raw materials (Jezierski and Leszczyńska 2010). At the same time, the need to absorb the inflow of the Baby Boomer generation to the labor market led to the expansion of employment in already existing firms, hampering productivity growth. Once again, the growth of agriculture was slow and the shortages in the supply of food— especially meat—increased. Attempts to solve this problem by increasing prices resulted in massive social discontent and a change in the leadership of the Polish United Workers' Party in December 1970.

The new economic policy was presented as a "strategy of accelerated economic and social development" that aimed at combining fast economic growth with simultaneous improvement of welfare. The five-year plans of the so-called Gierek decade (1971–1975 and 1976–1980) predicted that the annual growth rate should exceed 4 percent—a figure that never materialized (Kaliński 1995). The optimism of the planners was based, among other things, on the assumption that the international loans financing planned investments will be re-paid through increased exports. International competitiveness was expected to rise thanks to the purchase of Western licenses. Substantial funds were directed to manufacturing, infrastructure, the energy sector, and mining. Due to large-scale malinvestment and the import of consumer goods, fast economic growth proved short-lived, ending with a crisis that stretched over the entire 1980s until the very idea of economic planning was abandoned. The efforts of consecutive governments of this period were focused much less on ambitious investments than on basic economic and political reforms that were eventually decided at the Round Table Talks with the democratic opposition, which ended the communist era in Poland in 1989.

CENTRAL PLANNING IN ECONOMIC
THEORY AND PRACTICE, 1940s–1960s

The Theory of the Optimal Plan

Quantitative research of the centrally planned economy in Poland between 1945 and 1969 was dominated by the economic program of Oskar Lange who, alongside with Michał Kalecki, was undoubtedly the most prominent Polish economist of the time. His international fame was established during his discussion with Friedrich von Hayek and Ludwig von Mises in the 1930s and 1940s on the hypothetical advantages of central planning over the market mechanism. In this discussion Lange suggested to replace the allocation function of the market (providing market prices) with manmade parameters generated by a controlled optimization procedure (providing shadow prices). In order to achieve this, he proposed the so-called programming method, which aimed at addressing the practical needs of the centrally planned economy. Details of this method were explained in the annex of Lange's *Political Economy* published in 1961 and further developed in his *Optimal Decisions: Programming Rules* (Lange 1964) as well as in his *Introduction to Economic Cybernetics* (Lange 1965). In these works Lange diverged from his prewar theory of market socialism and presented the utopia of an omniscient central authority that efficiently designs and implements very detailed plans for the entire economic system. It is debatable what caused this shift but some historians attribute it mostly to Lange's return to Poland during the peak of the Stalinist era and his flexible adaptation to its circumstances. Michał Kalecki, who arrived from the West several years later, displayed a more resilient intellectual integrity if one compares his publications before and after the war (Czarny 2016).

Oskar Lange heavily influenced an entire generation of Polish economists through his postwar works, including his popular textbook *Introduction to Econometrics* from 1958. Not surprisingly, most of quantitative economic research performed by Polish economists in the 1960s was based on the optimization techniques advocated by Lange. A typical model of this kind consisted of two basic elements: a goal function and constraints (Czerwiński et al. 1982). The goal function was meant to represent the value of private and public consumption, or the level of investment that enabled the growth of the economy, whereas the model constraints reflected the structural balances of the country's production capacity, the possible changes in the structure of consumption demand or foreign trade balances. The models were typically derived from Leontief's input-output procedure and took into account the expected supply of production factors.

These models, developed by Krzysztof Porwit (1966) and Paweł Sulmicki (1973), among others, were supposed to construct the "optimal plan" and determine the optimal solutions in the sense of the adopted criterion function. Porwit, who worked in the research department of the Economic Planning Committee of the Council of Ministers (*Komitet Planowania Gospodarczego przy Radzie Ministrów, EPC*) that in 1958 replaced the State Commission for Economic Planning, studied the applicability of computable models for regional planning but later became interested in economic reforms and abandoned quantitative research (Porwit 1998). At the same time, Jerzy Mycielski developed several more complex models of multi-level planning, in which he introduced novel theoretical approaches to model solving. A number of interesting theoretical results were attained, although they were rarely used by planners in the construction of real-life economic plans (Porwit 1969). The same applies to a related category of models developed for international trade. The value of these models prepared by Krzysztof Rey (in 1962), Aleksander Legatowicz (in 1964), and Jerzy Mycielski and Witold Piaszczyński (in 1969) was conceptual, and despite reasonable numerical results, they were not used in the practice of central planning (Mycielski and Piaszczyński 1966; Maciejewski 1968). Somewhat secondary to the above-mentioned approach were the models built to obtain shadow prices. These models adhered to the original concept of Lange dating back to the 1930s who proposed to replace various parameters normally generated by the interplay of demand and supply on the free market with shadow prices gained from mathematical models. Foreign trade models also were developed by Mycielski, Rey, and Piaszczyński (Mycielski and Rey 1961; Piaszczyński 1969;), who often worked in cooperation with Witold Trzeciakowski, a leading economist specialized in foreign trade research (Piaszczyński and Trzeciakowski 1963; Mycielski, Rey, and Trzeciakowski 1963). The best example of his approach is the model solved with the help of the Dantzig-Wolfe decomposition method (Trzeciakowski 1962a; 1962b; Bożyk and Trzeciakowski 1969), from which a group of shadow prices corresponding to the optimum solution were derived to determine the foreign exchange rates of the Polish zloty.

A completely separate path to studying central planning was proposed by Aleksy Wakar. Together with the group of younger economists (including Janusz G. Zieliński, Janusz Beksiak, and Urszula Libura) forming the so-called Wakar school (Beksiak 2006), he had begun to construct a theory in the early 1960s, which became known as the theory of direct account. They tried to understand the socialist economic system by means of general equilibrium methods, asserting that the socialist economy is divided into two decision-making processes: (1) planning and (2) management (Wakar et al. 1965). Therefore, one should distinguish between the construction of the plan and its implementation. The former is centralized while the latter can be centralized, decentralized, or mixed, depending on the nature of the associated instruments: commands, parameters, or both. Wakar contended that it is possible to steer a centrally planned economy indirectly through proper incentives for the managers of state-owned enterprises. This approach diverged strongly from Lange's who saw the central plan as an autonomous decision of the planner and devoted no attention to the problems of limited information and lack of motivation of managers and/or workers.

Formal Models and the Central Planner in the Golden Era of Economic Planning, 1950s–1960s

To what extent were optimization models used by planners in constructing real-life economic plans? In many of his works Oskar Lange stipulated that mathematical models would find their full application only in the planned economy, especially when computers will be powerful enough to solve sufficiently complex numerical problems. However, despite the fact that in the late 1960s computer technology was developed enough to allow for such simulations, it happened only in a few cases that the numerical solutions of the input-output models were applied as complementary tools for the construction of economic plans by the *EPC*. The reasons for the relative insignificance of this type of economic modeling for planning practice are the following:

- Attempts at treating the economy as a single large enterprise, in which the general manager controls even the most trifle details, led to the construction of huge, very disaggregated, and complicated formal structures. Large optimization models with tens of thousands of constraints and variables required a huge amount of information. Such data were practically unavailable for technical reasons. Moreover, planning models need not only historical but also prospective data, the attainment of which always required strong assumptions and uncertain estimates.
- A serious practical problem was posed by the definition of the economy's objective function. The universally adopted objective of macro-models, the maximization of total consumption, was far removed from the actual goals of the communist party.
- A variety of available models were not transformed into one—widely accepted—optimization tool for the entire planned economy for a long time. It was only in the 1970s that attempts were made at constructing such models in Hungary by János Kornai (1971; 1980) and in Poland by Zbigniew Pawłowski (1971) and Władysław Welfe (1973; 1976) but these belonged to a different family of macroeconomic tools.
- Mathematical modeling postulated by Lange did not fit in with the political bargaining process inherent in the planned economy. In the

real world the leaders of the party-state had powerful vested interests in individual regions or industrial branches (mining, military industry, steel production, and so forth), which were in conflict with any "optimal" plan proposed by a purely technocratic procedure. Despite the official rhetoric, they not only did not trust the "scientific method" of economic planning but also had no political reason to change their mind in this respect.

All this does not mean that the *EPC* did not try to incorporate formal tools into its work. In fact, attempts were made to build a large "integrated IT system" with a view of facilitating information flows within the huge enterprise meant to represent the national economy. Vast resources were channeled into studies of such systems as well as into their practical implementation; however, the results did not live up to the expectations.

ECONOMETRIC ASSESSMENT OF THE ECONOMY, 1960s–1980s

Classical Econometric Models of the 1960s–1970s

Until the second half of the 1950s, econometric models—in their narrow sense—were not taught in the courses of economics at Polish universities. This state of affairs was largely due to the dominant political doctrine. Econometric models perceive economic phenomena as stable, long-run relationships between different actors. At the same time, they assume that in the short run the economy may be perturbed from equilibrium by some stochastic disturbance. Official theoreticians questioned both of these assumptions. They claimed that in the centrally planned economy the relationships among individuals are of a basically deterministic nature, but the central planner, almost arbitrarily, may change them through conscious decision. Other doctrinal problems also explain the general rejection of econometrics as a viable tool for economists. Among them, Marxist political economy denied marginal analysis and—as a consequence—discarded the production function as a relationship between factors and product; a relationship implying that outputs reflect the marginal productivities of inputs.

With the end of Stalinism the orthodox interpretation of Marxism started to disappear from Polish universities, opening the door for a new generation of researchers. In the late 1950s, after the return of Michał Kalecki from abroad, a number of studies were carried out under his leadership, which used models of economic growth as tools for the analysis of the development of mixed—planned and market—economies (Kalecki 1982). Under his guidance, the first and only long-term economic development plan based on scientific methodology was prepared. Relying on his earlier models, Kalecki assumed that national income is the function of investments, the incremental capital output ratio, depreciation, and upgrading. The results of these works on planning economic development, however, were aggregated and—as such—their potential applications were limited. Thus, they were largely ignored by the State Commitee for Economic Planning. At the same time, Kalecki remained interested in broader questions of economic policy and his research did not focus solely on central planning (Kalecki 1964).

Nevertheless, the early 1960s brought the revival of Polish econometrics. The first estimate of the production function for postwar Poland was provided by Józef Pajestka (1961) in his doctoral thesis written under the guidance of Czesław Bobrowski. Soon afterwards, other researchers followed suit, including teams working at the Institute of Statistical and Economic Research of the Central Statistical Office, the Foreign Trade Research Institute, and the *EPC*. They all delivered their own estimates of various types (CES, VES, and others) of production functions. This research was supplemented by classical demand analyses of Zbigniew Pawłowski (1961) as well as the short-term time series forecasts of the annual economic plans carried out by the Central Statistical Office and the *EPC*. The work by a team at the Academy of Economics in Katowice led by Zbigniew Pawłowski culminated in the construction of the first—highly aggregated—econometric model of the national economy. The first version (Barczak et al. 1962) was followed by a more disaggregated one (Barczak et al. 1968). This model was second after the publication of the Hungarian econometric model (Kornai 1967), which put a planned economy under scrutiny. Of special interest is the research on multidimensional statistical analysis. Such studies were prepared mainly by Zbigniew Hellwig's research team at the Wrocław Academy of Economics (Hellwig 1977). Their methods thereafter were applied to other socialist economies in various empirical studies.

In this context it is worth to mention the attempts to estimate capacity utilization in Poland during the 1970s. One of the axioms of the planned economy was the assumption of full utilization of productive capacities. Yet, the reality of the Polish economy was very different. In the late 1970s, numerous studies made at the Gdańsk University and the Łódź University, as well as at the Institute of Statistical and Economic Research of the Central Statistical Office in Warsaw, revealed that production capacities were utilized only up to 60 to 70 percent, reflecting the pre-crisis state of the second half of the 1970s. This conclusion contributed to a growing criticism of the internal logic of the planned economy, which started spreading, especially among a new generation of Polish economists, including future reformers such as Waldemar Kuczyński and Leszek Balcerowicz.

Models of the National Economy in the 1970s–1980s

Although the first econometric model of Polish economy was published in the 1960s, the real boom for this kind of research started in the 1970s when large scale multi-equation models were developed in several research centers including the *EPC*. In 1972, it built its first aggregated annual model called KP-1.[2] In the following year, this model was expanded and named KP-2 by Wojciech Maciejewski and Józef Zajchowski (1974), and two years later the first quarterly model—KP-3k—was constructed (Maciejewski 1976). In spite of the fact that those models were constructed at the *EPC*, and therefore their authors were familiar with the expectations of the Council of Ministers, the results were used only partly in practice. The models served mostly academic purposes and impacted the planners only indirectly.

The same applies to the works of another, dynamic research group set up in 1971 at the University of Łódź. It was directed by Władysław Welfe and played a leading role in the community of scholars doing econometric studies of the Polish economy from the early 1970s onwards. Their models were used systematically for formulating medium-term forecasts or analyzing the implications of various scenarios of economic development. The results were regularly published, and both the academia and the decision-makers were persuaded of the potential usefulness of these studies for the practice of planning. A whole family of macro-models was created by this group (Welfe 1973; 1976; Klein 1982, Tomaszewicz 1983). In their subsequent versions, more and more disaggregated modeling techniques were tested. Initially, these were typical demand-and-supply models. Then the demand and supply sides were separated, which allowed for an indirect examination of the degree of equilibrium in the Polish economy. Furthermore, extensive research was made on modeling the pricing mechanism in the centrally planned economy and its financial sector.

A somewhat separate area of activity of the Łódź Center was the organization of annual international conferences on econometric modeling. Those conferences were attended by almost all econometricians from the communist countries who were involved in this type of research. For the majority of them this was the only opportunity to meet and listen to world celebrities such as Lawrence Klein, Herman Wold, Anton Barten, and Shirley Almon. These contacts and the very existence of econometric models for Poland made it possible for Welfe's group to join research into the models of global economy. One of the best-known projects in this area was the so-called LINK project, initiated in the United States in 1968 and headed by Klein. The main objective of this project was to construct a model of world trade, which offers possibilities to simulate economic policies of individual countries and—by linking these models—to study international trade and changes in world market prices. A model of trade within the Council for Mutual Economic Assistance (CMEA, Comecon) was proposed already at one of the first LINK conferences in Vienna in 1970. In the following years, models of trade between CMEA states were constructed at Łódź University. At the 1975 Toronto conference a leading Soviet econometrician, Stanislav Menshikov, presented a modified version of the Polish KP-1 model as a typical model for communist countries. From the mid-1970s on, Władysław Welfe was participating regularly in LINK activities, and the models prepared by his team (the so-called W family) were included in the integrated LINK model.

The new trends of econometric modeling in Poland were related primarily to the work of Wojciech Charemza from the University of Gdańsk. By the end of the 1970s, he initiated studies on models of the Polish economy under the conditions of disequilibrium. Therefore, similarly to János Kornai in Hungary, he rejected the assumption that a planned economy should be in permanent equilibrium. His approach was, however, different from Kornai's, who noted that disequilibrium prevailing in the centrally planned economy is substantially different from the classical notion of disequilibrium. Kornai found that in a centrally planned economy there is a constant excess of demand over supply and formulated a number of features of such a state of disequilibrium. He named this state of disequilibrium "shortage" and the socialist economy an "economy of shortage." Shortage was modeled as a concealed variable, that is, a variable that is not directly observable but felt.

Charemza (1981) dismissed the axiom of equilibrium in the planned economy but did not agree with Kornai's concept of shortage. Relying on the classical disequilibrium model, he applied the concepts proposed by Takatoshi Ito (1980) and developed further by Richard Portes and Richard Quandt (1989). Together with Mieczysław Gronicki, he was also the first in Poland to use the theory of rational expectations for the construction of the individual equations of the macroeconomic model in a disequilibrium setting (Charemza and Gronicki 1985). This late assessment of the socialist economy of Poland in the 1980s could not have—by definition—any impact on the practice of planning (which was already in crisis). Nonetheless, they contributed to the rapidly rising criticism of the inefficiency of the communist system, and reinforced the conviction by state officials and academics of the urgent need of substantial economic reforms. A follow-up to the debate about the notion of disequilibrium in the planned economy was a conference organized at the University of Birmingham, at which Kornai's views clashed with those of the advocates of the classical approach. The proceedings of the conference resulted in a book containing the opinions of both sides (Davis and Charemza 1989).

CONCLUSION

Any attempt at evaluating the evolution of quantitative economics in Poland during the communist era and its relation to central planning has to include two aspects: domestic and international.

Seen from a domestic perspective and compared to most Eastern Bloc countries, the achievements of the economic research community in Poland are significant because these countries (apart from the Soviet Union and Hungary) rarely contributed to the quantitative assessment of the planned economy. As early as the 1950s, optimization techniques were applied to find answers to the meaningful economic questions related to the research program initiated by the discussion between Oskar Lange, Friedrich von Hayek, and Ludwig von Mises in the 1930s. Moreover, using similar techniques, works by Witold Trzeciakowski, Jerzy Mycielski, Zygmunt Czerwiński, Krzysztof Porwit, and Paweł Sulmicki contributed to the theory of centrally planned economy in various fields but were not employed in the practice of central planning that mimicked simple Soviet patterns from the 1930s. The approach of central planners to econometric research changed after the thaw of 1956 when new vistas were opened for a young generation of econometricians and a family of practical models.

An original theory of planning and management under communism was proposed by Aleksy Wakar's team of the Warsaw School of Planning and Statistics. They distinguished between the planners and two categories of implementers: the "heads of socialist businesses" (managers) and the staff responsible for "executive work." From today's perspective, this can be seen as a form of principal-agent theory, adjusted to the reality of centrally planned economies. A particularly valuable and unorthodox contribution of the Wakar team was the strong attention they devoted to the motivations of workers and to the problem of the contradiction between these and the goals of the plan.

In the 1960s and 1970s, a wide spectrum of models were developed by Zygmunt Pawłowski, Władysław Welfe, Wojciech Maciejewski, and Józef Zajchowski. Some of these models were tested by the *EPC*; however, they remained marginal in terms of practical decision-making. Nevertheless, they increased the understanding of the malfunctioning of the communist system throughout the Polish economic community. This recognition was strengthened by the theoretical considerations of Wojciech Charemza about the nature of disequlibrium in centrally planned economies.

Seen from an international angle, the outcome of these inquiries, just like the majority of economic studies carried out in the Eastern Bloc was known only to a small number of people and rarely crossed the border between East and West. To put it metaphorically, it might be said that the accomplishments of Polish economics in the communist era matched the autarchic nature of the economic system of the country. The works of Oskar Lange on political economy and cybernetics, the contributions by Władysław Welfe to the LINK project, or by Wojciech Charemza to the development of non-classical econometric models were the only exceptions. Most of the other works, although of good quality, were following in the footsteps of international econometric research, supplementing it with necessary modifications reflecting the specifics of centrally planned economies.

At the same time, many Polish economists involved with central planning at some stages of their career lent their experience to developing countries. Michał Kalecki was Deputy Director at the Department of Economic Affairs of the United Nations between 1946 and 1955 when he was forced to resign (due to the McCarthyist mood of the era). He returned to the Warsaw School of Planning and Statistics where he established the Department of Economic Problems in Developing Countries and served as an advisor to many African and Asian countries experimenting with socialism at the time. Another Polish ex-planner (from the team of Czesław Bobrowski) who assisted the governments of developing nations was Jan Drewnowski. For many years, he worked as a director of the United Nations Institute for Social Development. Włodzimierz Brus, a staunch hardliner of the Stalinist era, was a special case. In the 1960s, he gradually changed his opinion and became an important critic of central planning, particularly following his forced emigration to the West in 1968. Brus proposed mixing the plan with the market in the framework of a far-reaching decentralization of decision-making and management (in accordance with the theory of the Wakar school). His views caught the attention of Chinese reformers, and—together with the Czech economist Ota Šik and, above all, the Hungarian János Kornai—he is considered today a main source of inspiration for the economic transformation in China under Deng Xiaoping (Góralczyk 2018).

NOTES

1. CUP stands for *Centralny Urząd Planowania* (Central Planning Office).

2. KP stands for *Komisja Planowania* (Planning Commision) as the model was designed within the EPC and was intended to be used for the assessment of the five year plan for 1971–1975.

BIBLIOGRAPHY

Barczak, Andrzej, Barbara Ciepielewska, Tadeusz Jakubczyk, and Zbigniew Pawłowski. 1964. "Próba budowy prostych ekonometrycznych równań wzrostu na przykładzie gospodarki Polski." *Ekonomista* 3: 545–64.

———. 1968. *Model ekonometryczny gospodarki Polski Ludowej.* Warszawa: PWN.

Barteczko, Krzysztof, Andrzej Bocian, and Tomasz Sapociński. 1984. *Makroproporcje wzrostu w latach 1986–1995.* Warszawa: IGN.

Beksiak, Janusz. 2006. "Aleksy Wakar—nauczyciel." *Gospodarka Narodowa* 205 (1–2): 109–114.

Bobrowski, Czesław. 1984. "Refleksje nad czterdziestoleciem PRL." *Nowe Drogi* 7: 26–32.

———. 1985. *Wspomnienia ze stulecia.* Lublin: Wydawnictwo Lubelskie.

Bocian, Andrzej, and Józef Zajchowski. 1972. "Makroekonomiczne modele analiz strukturalnych." *Ekonomista* 6: 123–57.

Bożyk, Paweł, and Witold Trzeciakowski, eds. 1969. *Efektywność handlu zagranicznego.* Warszawa: PWE.

Charemza, Wojciech. 1981. *Ekonometryczne modele nierównowagi: Problemy specyfikacji i estymacji.* Gdańsk: Uniwersytet Gdański.

Charemza, Wojciech, and Mirosław Gronicki. 1985. *Ekonometryczna analiza nierównowagi gospodarki Polski.* Warszawa: PWN.

Chojnicki, Zbyszko. 1966. *Zastosowanie modeli grawitacji i potencjału w badaniach przestrzenno–ekonomicznych.* Vol. 14 of *KPZK Studia.* Warszawa: PWN.

Czarny, Bogusław. 2016. *Szkice o ekonomii w Polsce 1949–1989.* Warszawa: SGH.

Czerwiński, Zbigniew. 1973. *Podstawy matematycznych modeli wzrostu gospodarczego.* Warszawa: PWE.

———. 1982. *Matematyczne modelowanie procesów ekonomicznych.* Warszawa: PWN.

Czerwiński, Zbigniew, Bogusław Guzik, Witold Jurek, Emil Panek, Henryk Runka, and Wacław Śledziński. 1982. *Modelowanie i planowanie wzrostu gospodarki narodowej* Warszawa: PWN.

Davis, Christopher, and Wojciech Charemza. 1989. *Models of Disequilibrium and Shortage in Centrally Planned Economies.* London: Chapman and Hall.

Domański, Ryszard. 1972. *Kształtowanie otwartych regionów ekonomicznych.* Warszawa: PWE.

Fisz, Marek. 1967. *Rachunek prawdopodobieństwa i statystyka matematyczna.* Warszawa: PWE.

Gajda, Jan. 1988. *Wielorównaniowe modele ekonometryczne: Estymacja—symulacja—sterowanie.* Warszawa: PWN.

Góralczyk, Bogdan. 2018. *Wielki renesans—chińska transformacja i jej konsekwencje.* Warszawa: Dialog.

Hellwig, Zdzisław. 1977. "Wielowymiarowa analiza porównawcza i jej zastosowanie w badaniach wielocechowych obiektów gospodarczych." In *Ekonometryczne modele rynku.* Vol. 1, edited by Władysław Welfe. Warszawa: PWE, 112–46.

Ito, Takatoshi. 1980. "Disequilibrium Growth Theory." *Journal of Economic Theory* 23 (3): 380–409.

Jezierski, Andrzej, and Cecylia Leszczyńska. 2010. *Historia gospodarcza Polski.* Warszawa: Key Text.

Kalecki, Michał. 1964. *Z zagadnień gospodarczo-społecznych Polski Ludowej.* Warszawa: PWN.

———. 1982. *Socjalizm: Funkcjonowanie i wieloletnie planowanie.* Vol. 3 of *Dzieła.* Warszawa: PWE.

———. 1984. *Socjalizm: Wzrost gospodarczy i efektywność inwestycji.* Vol. 4 of *Dzieła.* Warszawa: PWE.

Kaliński, Janusz. 1995. *Gospodarka Polski w latch 1944–1989: przemiany strukturalne.* Warszawa: PWE.

———. 2012. *Gospodarka w PRL.* Warszawa: IPN.

Klein, Lawrence. 1982. *Wykłady z ekonometrii.* Warszawa: PWE.

Kornai, Janos. 1967. "Mathematical Programming of Long-Term Plans in Hungary." In *Activity Analysis in the Theory of Growth and Planning*, edited by E. Malinvaud and M. Bacharach, 211–31. London: Macmillan.

———. 1971. *Anti-Equilibrium: On Economic Systems Theory and the Tasks of Research.* Amsterdam: North Holland Publishing.

———.1980). *Economics of Shortage.* Amsterdam: North Holland Publishing.

Lange, Oskar. 1958. *Wstęp do ekonometrii.* 1st Edition. Warszawa: PWN.

———. 1961. *Ekonomia polityczna. Vol. 1, Zagadnienia ogólne.* 2nd Edition. Warszawa: PWN.

———. 1964. *Optymalne decyzje—zasady programowania.* Warszawa: PWN.

———. 1965. *Wstęp do cybernetyki ekonomicznej.* Warszawa: PWN.

———. 1976. *Ekonometria.* Vol. 5 of *Dzieła.* Warszawa: PWE.

———. 1977. *Teoria programowania.* Vol. 6 of *Dzieła,.* Warszawa: PWE.

Maciejewski, Wojciech. Ed. 1968. *Zastosowanie metod matematycznych do analizy ekonomicznej*, Warszawa: Zakład Badań Koniunktur i Cen Handlu Zagranicznego.

———. 1976. *Zastosowanie ekonometrycznych modeli gospodarki narodowej.* Warszawa: PWE.

———. 1980. *Ekonometria stosowana: Analiza porównawcza.* Warszawa: PWE.

Maciejewski, Wojciech, and Witold Piaszczyński. 1968. *Ekonometryczne modele gospodarki narodowej.* Warszawa: PWE.

———. 1970. *Model prognozy handlu grupy krajów na przykładzie RWPG.* Warszawa: Komitet Przestrzennego Zagospodarowania Kraju (KPZK) PAN.

Maciejewski, Wojciech, and Józef Zajchowski. 1974. *Econometric Model of the Polish Economy KP-2.* Warszawa: KPZK PAN.

Minc, Hilary. 1954. *Głowne zadania gospodarcze dwóch ostatnich lat (1954–1955) Planu Sześcioletniego.* Warszawa: Książka i Wiedza

Mycielski, Jerzy, and Witold Piaszczyński. 1966. *A Mathematical Model of International Economic Co-operation.* Warszawa: KPZK PAN.

Mycielski, Jerzy, and Krzysztof Rey. 1961. *Analityczne kryteria efektywności wybranych grup towarowych.* Vol. 2 of *KPZK Studia.* Warszawa: PAN.

Mycielski, Jerzy, Krzysztof Rey, and Witold Trzeciakowski. 1963. "Optima całościowe a optima cząstkowe w planie handlu zagranicznego." *Przegląd Statystyczny* 10: 50–72.

Pajestka, Józef. 1961. *Zatrudnienie i inwestycje a wzrost gospodarczy.* Warszawa: SGPiS.

Pawłowski, Zbigniew. 1961. *Ekonometryczne metody badania popytu konsumpcyjnego.* Warszawa: PWN.

———. 1969. *Ekonometria.* Warszawa: PWE.

———. 1971. *Modele ekonometryczne równań opisowych.* Warszawa: PWN.

Piaszczyński, Witold. 1969. "Teoretyczne podstawy cen kalkulacyjnych (model cen dualnych)." In Bożyk and Trzeciakowski 1969: 112–143.

———. 1970. "Rachunek ekonomicznych efektów integracji krajów RWPG w zakresie wymiany." In *Integracja ekonomiczna krajów socjalistycznych*, edited by Paweł Bożyk, 72–93. Warszawa: KiW.

———. 1974. *Matematyczne modele teorii handlu międzynarodowego.* Warszawa: PWE.

Piaszczyński, Witold, and Witold Trzeciakowski. 1963. "Efficiency Prices and Economic Calculation in Foreign Trade." *Papers of the Regional Science Association* 10: 193–206.

Pluta, Wiesław. 1986. *Wielowymiarowa analiza porównawcza w modelowaniu ekonometrycznym.* Warszawa: PWN.

Portes, Richard, and Richard E. Quandt. 1989. "Macroeconomic Disequilibrium in Centrally Planned Economies: Comment." *Journal of Comparative Economics* 13 (4): 576–79.

Porwit, Krzysztof. 1966. "Regional Models and Economic Planning." *Papers of the Regional Science Association* 16: 43–61.

———. 1968. *Zagadnienia rachunku ekonomicznego w planie centralnym.* Warszawa: PWE.

———. 1969. *Metody planowania długookresowego.* Vol. 28 of *KPZK Studia.* Warszawa: PAN.

———. 1998. "Looking Back at Economic Science in Poland, 1945–96: The Challenge of system changes." In *Economic Thought in Communist and Post-Communist Europe*, edited by Hans-Jürgen Wagener. London/New York: Routledge, 80–157.

Sulmicki, Paweł. 1973. *Planowanie i zarządzanie gospodarcze.* Warszawa: PWE.

Sadowski, Wiesław. 1976. *Teoria podejmowania decyzji.* 6th Edition. Warszawa: PWE.

———. 1981. *Prognozy i decyzje.* Warszawa: PWE.

Tomaszewicz, Łukasz. 1983. *Zintegrowane modele gospodarki narodowej.* Warszawa: PWE.

Trzeciakowski, Witold. 1962a. *Problemy kompleksowego systemu efektywności bieżącej handlu zagranicznego.* Vol. 2 of *KPZK Studia.* Warszawa: PAN.

———. 1962b. "Model optymalizacji bieżącej handlu zagranicznego i jego zastosowanie." *Przegląd Statystyczny* 9 (1): 32–55.

———. 1978. *Indirect Management in a Centrally Planned Economy: System Constructions in Foreign Trade.* Warszawa: PWN.

Wakar, Aleksy. 1963. *Morfologia bodźców ekonomicznych.* Warszawa: PWN.

Wakar, Aleksy. 1965. *Zarys teorii gospodarki socjalistycznej.* Warszawa: PWN.

Welfe, Władysław. 1973. *A Medium-Term Econometric Model of the Polish Economy.* Vol. 8 of *Prace IEiS UL,* Łódź: Uniwersytet Łódzki. Łódź.

Welfe, Władysław. 1976. "The Unbalanced Econometric Macromodels Exemplified by the Model W1." In *Computing Equilibria—How and Why,* edited by Jerzy Los and Maria Los, 244–76, Amsterdam: North–Holland.

Chapter 7

The Failure of Communist Planning

A Perspective from Romania

Valentin Cojanu and Grigore Ioan Piroşcă

By 1990, Romania should have been known as a "multilaterally developed socialist state" according to the goal set by the secretary general of the Romanian Communist Party (PCR)[1] Nicolae Ceauşescu, at the tenth congress of the party in 1969 (Pasca 2015, 49). In line with the planning objectives of the mid-1970s, during the subsequent one and a half decades Romania would take off and "become an industrialized economy . . . on a level with many other countries considered to be developed" (Tsantis and Pepper 1979, 385). These goals hardly would have seemed unusual given the regime's determination to organize the economy along rational or "planned" lines, if they had not been formulated at a time when the economy began to run out of steam. Romania was experiencing a "dramatic decrease in efficiency of capital accumulation" from 32.1 percent between 1971 and 1975 to 17.4 percent in the period of 1986–1989 (Iancu and Pavelescu 2018), with "losses and subsidies" representing 9.6 percent of domestic income in 1979 (Axenciuc and Georgescu 2017, 114).

The discrepancy between political ambitions and economic reality was perhaps the most visible among the failures of communist planning in Romania. There are different perspectives, from which we can examine the concept of planning, for example, ideological, quantitative, and historical, to provide an answer to the seemingly simple question: why was economic reality so misinterpreted by the planners? Economists often refer to the absence of markets to explain the reason for the malfunction of central commands. This argument apparently shortcuts the debate without shedding light on specific circumstances that ultimately led to the failure of planning in Romania. On purely theoretical grounds, as one Romanian expert—a leading character in the subsequent narrative—reflects after a lifetime of work devoted to the intricacies of planning, the conflict between "free market" and "perfect planning" proves intractable rather than amenable to clear solutions. Both canons make similar assumptions—for example, about "shadow prices"—to reach formal solutions in terms of optimal programming, and both dispense sooner or later with the illusory presumption of "complete information" to allow for an increasing number of derogations from their disciplinary tenets (Emilian Dobrescu, personal communication to authors, March 31, 2019).

It would seem then more to the point to search for answers beyond the strict boundaries of economics. An encompassing framework perhaps would follow János Kornai's view eliciting the *political economy* of communism, that is, a study that overlaps the fields of "political science, sociology, social psychology, political and moral philosophy, and history" (Kornai 1992, 12). Given the scope of this volume, such an ample inquiry will not be pursued here, although it will inspire our approach. We aim at narrowing down the grand scheme to a version giving preference to the institutional foundations—writ large—of planning at the expense of its doctrinaire underpinning. Such an inquiry emphasizes issues, ranging from human to structural factors related to planning tasks and implementation (Ericson 2018) to "the abuse of power" (Carson and Coyne 2019) that concurred in derailing planning from its role as a coordination mechanism determining the allocation of scarce resources.

Mechanisms, people, events, and ideas evolving around planning, communism's most precious dogma, will be evoked in this chapter to understand why Romania, among its peers alone, failed so absolutely in achieving its development goals. Communist dogma was planted in diverse climates of social thought as they were nurtured in countries not as kindred as the slogan celebrating the brotherhood of communist nations implied. Our chapter sketches out two main characteristics of the Romanian communist regime, which combined to form a toxic approach to economic science and, eventually, to the practice of planning itself.

First, we cover the political commandment of disregarding independent thinking, past or present, which explains an unfortunate start from scratch and subsequent one-dimensional development of economic thought in postwar Romania. The overriding cultural norm of the regime was to severe links to any intellectual legacy and to obstruct any liberal manifestations of thought in radical forms. Several examples from the first years of communism (1948–1950) demonstrate how radical these forms were intended to be: imprisonment followed by the untimely death of great scholars, among them the renowned author of the theory of protectionism, Mihail Manoilescu, or the German-educated economist (and communist), Lucrețiu Pătrășcanu; neglect of original contributions by interwar Romania's outstanding economists such as Virgil Madgearu's first sketch of a five-year plan (*plan économique de longue durée*) submitted to the Supreme Economic Council in 1938 (Păun 2018); or the virulent attack against "bourgeois social science," which culminated in dismantling research areas associated with it: economic history, sociology, and demography (Zaman, Vasile, and Georgescu 2013, 7). Thus, when planning became an issue of political concern in the 1950s, the economists' profession already had been disfigured by political atrocities, its members having nothing at stake but to start from scratch, entering virgin territory.

Second, the disregard of authentic scholarly efforts, including works on planning as we will document below, paired up naturally with other conditions explaining the misconstruction of economic reality. Secrecy and amateurism in handling economic matters were conducive to a debilitating political control doomed to disrupt an emerging economy of some potential. The scale of the culture of concealment is relevant not only in putting the doctrine of planning in perspective but also in highlighting the research limits we had to confront in reaching our conclusions. The Romanian system of political control had "no precise counterpart in other communist regimes" and "arguably eclipsed even the Soviet archetype" (Bachman 1991, 135). The veiled approach to economic matters was shaped by censorship, amateurism, and mystification, indefatigable vices of communist planning in Romania. We conclude our chapter with reflections on the legacy of planning for the evolution of economic thought in post-communist Romania.

STARTING FROM SCRATCH I. THE EARLY PHASE OF THE PLANNING DOCTRINE

In Romania, almost singularly among other Eastern European countries, works of quantitative economics did not count among the intellectual heritage of would-be economists of the communist regime. To be sure, students of the Academy of Higher Commercial and Industrial Studies in Bucharest (now known as Bucharest University of Economic Studies, ASE), pioneering economic research and education in Romania from 1913 onward, could choose from among disciplines such as financial mathematics and insurance techniques during the interwar period. And even if the Academy's first rector—Anton Davidoglu, a renowned mathematician, who had defended his dissertation in the presence of such luminaries as Henri Poincaré—established several departments on mathematical topics, these did not coalesce in a Romanian school of applied mathematical economics (Herțeliu and Smeureanu 2017, 156–58). In fact, "until the 1960s, economic disciplines and mathematics were taught . . . without any connection between the two" (Iancu 2015, 57).

The main thrust of neoclassical economics emerging in Europe and the United States at the end of the nineteenth century was downplayed. To cast social and economic facts into mathematical formulae, a 1933 textbook on the *Principles of Political Economy* published in Bucharest instructed, "would imply adopting a metaphysics even more dangerous than that of <homo oeconomicus>" (Basilescu 1933, 73). Intellectual queries were, however, in no scarce supply. "Non–interventionism" had been adopted as an economic ideology at the start of the nineteenth century (Păun 2018), but it was the opposite creed which prevailed constantly in public and scholarly debates, although under various guises—protectionism and industrial policy, peasantism and dirigisme, corporatism and plannism, and Marxism. The legacy of the latter streams of interventionism proved so influential that even the communists, when starting to assert their nationalistic turn in the 1960s, "have identified themselves increasingly with the aspirations of the progressive intellectuals of the *ancien régime* who advocated industrialization under state guidance" (Ceauşescu 1966, quoted in Montias 1967, 231). All the promising manifestations of intellectual fervor during the interwar period came to an abrupt end in 1948 when the Soviet-inspired strategy for growth, "essentially a rather crude version of the Trotskyist Preobrazhensky's theory" (Dyker 1985, 3), was introduced in Romania by Moscow advisors (Iancu 2018) as an "obligation of respecting and faithfully copying in Romania of the Soviet economic model" (Zaman, Vasile, and Georgescu 2013, 13).

Adopting Soviet Economics

The policy for communist economic development or Marxian political economy, as it was commonly known in academic circles, postulated that industrialization represents the economic recipe for meeting the challenge of "catching up and overtaking" (Stalin) the advanced countries. In terms of economic policy, it must be based on larger investments in the production of means of production than in that of consumer goods (Kornai 1992, 172; Iancu and Pavelescu 2018).

Published from February 1948, *Probleme economice* (Economic Problems) was a journal instrumental in creating an intellectual platform for the new doctrine. Featuring editorials such as "Let us learn from the experience of the Soviet Union!" or "Helping the planner," the "special relationship" with the USSR—not a matter of choice, of course (Sovalov 1948)—was advocated on the premise of Soviet superiority. The latter was demonstrated by the success in overcoming the Great Depression of the 1930s and winning the Second World War as multiple contributions to *Probleme economice* emphasized at length in 1949. The credentials of Soviet economics were tested thus, and five-year plans were to be implemented in Romania, together with the other people's democracies, as ultimate tools of future economic growth. In 1949, Zeigler published "The State Plan of the People's Republic of Romania," a political declaration which presaged the dominance of Stalin's contributions and other papers of Soviet inspiration about socialist planning and the theory of value in a socialist economy until the mid-1960s. The objectification of work, as it was reflected in the *Stakhanovite* model,[2] which any worker should strive to embrace (Dumitru 1954), became the economic lesson of probably the greatest practical relevance in the early 1950s.

After Stalin's death in 1953, attempts at instilling economic science with domestic contributions paced themselves gradually. A new editorial section, "The life of entrepreneurial organizations" started appearing in *Probleme economice* at a time when the section "Let us learn from the experience of the Soviet Union!" was published only four times in 1954 until it was discontinued for good in 1955. At the same time, the range of economists' research interests expanded constantly with discussions on hitherto ideologically less desirable topics such as utility (Dan and Murgescu 1954), light industry (Avachian and Bernstein 1954), foreign economic systems (Schatteles 1956, classical economists (Mesaros 1955), productivity and national income (Alexiu and Rozen 1964; Catulescu 1964), and even about micro-and macroeconomics (Anghel 1964). References to the role of input-output analysis in planning also became part of the economic literature (e.g., Răvar and Hlevca 1961 cited in Murgescu Costin 1970; Schatteles 1967).

Command Planning

In 1948, the State Commission for Planning (SCP; *Comitetul de Stat al Planificării, CSP*) was established,[3] and it remained the highest-level decision-making body of command planning throughout the communist period. In the beginning, it could count only on scant expertise. Even in 1965, from a staff of 918, of which 625 were planners, at least two thirds had no professional background (Pașca 2015, 28). Their work was entirely dependent on political dictates and could not benefit from background reports. Discrepancies between plans and their results were "blatant" (Emilian Dobrescu, interview by the authors, March 17, 2016). It was not surprising that Leontief's input-output techniques were introduced to SCP planners with the help of "lowly high-school algebra with a little bit of matrix calculus as [a] supplement" (Schatteles 2007, 24–25).

Amid serious shortages during the 1950s, planning acquired a renewed interest as a formula to increase industrial output of consumer goods to meet people's needs. By the early 1960s, economics could refresh itself with a novel design: a discipline of studying the plan and planning as "a matter of political concern" (Paşca 2015, 131). The prioritization of the proportions of national income between consumption and accumulation was enshrined in the planning doctrine as a "political issue" (ASE 1970, 7).[4] In the first years of industrialization, the command imperative seemed almost benign, given the pressing task of advancing the country out of poverty. The mechanics of growth offered few alternatives to "the simple arithmetic of increasing the number of employees and the investment fund"[5] (Axenciuc and Georgescu 2017, 116; Iancu and Pavelescu 2018).

Drafted on plain sheets, the first *balances* (material, semi-product, and product balances), divided between production and consumption, exports and imports, as well as inventory fluctuations, were prepared for the first two one-year plans in 1949 and 1950. The planning period of five years was introduced in 1951–1955, followed by a six-year plan drawn up for 1960–1965, and a ten-year plan in the field of electricity for the period 1951–1960, which was considered an integral part of the 1951–1955 and 1956–1960 five-year plans (Iancu and Pavelescu 2018). The planning targets were disaggregated to lower institutional levels and became planning directives. However, in turning the planning targets into directives, the targets could be transformed through a procedure known as the "balance method" of planning: "a process of inching forward at repeated negotiations between the leading planners of the producers and the users" (Kornai 1992, 112).

With the five-year plan of 1966–1970, the planning environment grew in complexity due to at least two factors. The planning work expanded to include more hierarchical structures of economic control and implementation, and expertise became less of a scarce factor once the first generation of mathematical economists began contributing to the planning efforts toward the end of the 1960s. The work of estimating planning indicators began to rely on educated advice based on fairly reliable primary information and more rigorous forecast methods (Emilian Dobrescu, interview by the authors, March 17, 2016). Almost at the same time, rational planning thus had become both a strategic political preoccupation and a professional career option.

The elaboration and implementation work of the five-year plans developed along several layers of decision and control (Tsantis and Pepper 1979, 35ff.):

- The party formulated the strategy of development and the corresponding planning objectives at its congress preceding the elaboration of the plan.
- The enterprises made forecasts about the indicators of growth and output capacity, demand for current inputs, investment, and working capital. This information then circulated between the Ministry of Technical Material Supply and Fixed Assets Administration and the local authorities.

- At the sectoral level the plan took shape by aggregating, under guidance from the party, information from all enterprises.
- The ministries centralized information coming from branches/sectors and made efforts to match it with the requirements of the national strategy for development. Ministries could also decide, together with local authorities, to increase planning targets at the enterprise level.
- District and other local authorities developed plans for national and local use of resources. Although the specialization and location of future plants were local authorities' duty, ministerial representatives in every district's People's Council made sure that regional plans complied with higher-level plans.
- The SCP was responsible for collecting and coordinating all plans made by the ministries, as well as for ensuring macroeconomic consistency of material and synthetic balances. Finally, the draft of the national five-year plan was submitted to the Council of Ministers, then passed to the Political Executive Committee of the Romanian Communist Party.

The new context of planning in the late 1960s was radically different from earlier ones, not only because it contributed to the improvement of planning but also because, in a way reflecting the party's perverted beliefs, it made possible to distance the centralized world of planning even more from real economic needs and trends. Originally, the initiative to introduce a larger planning horizon covering the period 1967–1975 served to instill a more mature approach to planning. Drawing the main lines of development of the national economy between 1976 and 1980 was a request of a newly established body, clumsily entitled the "Central Commission for the Guidance and Coordination of the Entire Activity of Elaborating and Substantiating the Proposals for the 1971–1975 Five-Year Plan."

This framework lay in fact at the origin of a mechanism that made a simulacrum out of the general consultations on planning tasks between branches/sectors, ministries, regional authorities, and enterprises. It was virtually a conduit to obscure the accountability for decisions and place it instead, in case of failure, on anyone else, generally a political opponent (see Paşca 2015, 34ff.). The ever-more hierarchical state and party structures ensured decisions would be made in a small circle or even strictly by the general secretary of the party himself. Centralization only intensified after the overlapping of the party and the state decreed by Ceauşescu in 1967. An exemplar of the perverted mechanism emerged from the decision to establish the Supreme Council of Economic and Social Development in 1973, a new 300-member body, with both party and state affiliations, "to debate and approve state economic plans." Chaired by Ceauşescu, the Council's role relegated the constitutionally granted authority of the State Committee for Planning and the

Grand National Assembly in the planning process to "increasingly ceremonial" activities (Bachman 1991, 141).

Pale Rays of Light

The new scholarly openings, feeble and unidirectional as they were, augured well for an emerging class of economists. As one scholar recalls, between 1965 and 1973, "pale rays of light began to cross the ideological fog that covered the field of study of all social sciences" (Schatteles 2007, 23). This prospect may have been indicated by the still free and largely accessible collections of foreign flagship academic journals[6], access to international funds for the exchange of scholars, or translations of Western classics (e.g., Adam Smith, David Ricardo, and John M. Keynes), while Russian texts usually were read in the original. Scholars were free to choose from authors of both Marxist and "capitalist" credentials, although the latter were mostly within the realm of ideology-free, that is, quantitative, economics. (John K. Galbraith and Raymond Aron featured among the notable exceptions.) Classical works of mathematical economists from communist countries were readily available in Romanian (e.g., Kantorovich 1959; Leontief 1966; Lange 1965; Kalecki 1968; Kornai 1971), but prominent Western authors (e.g., Ramsey 1928; Allen 1956; Tinbergen 1960; 1964; Phelps 1961; Arrow 1962; Koopmans 1963; Maddison 1964) also were cited regularly.

The small window of opportunity made personal encounters in both the East and the West an important feature of the scientific life of Romanian scholars. Wassily Leontief and Nicholas Georgescu-Roegen were among the guests of the Institute of Economic Research (*Institutul de Cercetări Economice, ICE*) in Bucharest at the end of the 1960s (Zaman and Georgescu 2013 21–22). Regular Romanian-Soviet economic symposia were accompanied by a Romanian-French series organized jointly by the ICE with the Paris Institute for Applied Economics chaired by François Perroux. Other examples, such as the increased availability of research stays (in the United States, France, or the United Kingdom), or participation at international conferences (Zaman and Georgescu 2013, 2–7), testify to a growing institutionalization of scholarly contacts. Much of this process was explained by the new party line of rapprochement with Western countries for both economic and political reasons. (The turn was reflected by the negotiations on regional planning within Comecon, a topic we will tackle below.)

As the regime took firmer roots, the inherent difficulties of any novel endeavor were given a new dimension. Life beyond the political imperative of planning was a tough challenge: independent researchers fled the country early on, some remained and stubbornly held up the bar of honest analysis, whereas promising aspirants were uneasy about choosing between vocation and bureaucracy. All of them had to confront, sooner or later, bleak prospects in their profession.

STARTING FROM SCRATCH II. A NEW VENUE OF RESEARCH—MATHEMATICAL ECONOMICS

The doctrine of planning attracted talented researchers towards a new venue of research, mathematical economics, often for the sole reason that it helped them cope with or rather evade ideological limits (Iancu 2015; Schatteles 2015). Career advancement loomed full of promise. The "enhanced scientific nature" of the plan—as the SCP stressed in its 1967 official documents "under direct guidance" of the secretary general—would be only possible thanks to "professionals, technocrats, and scholars" of an estimated number of 40,000 (Pașca 2015, 130–31), applying "mathematical methods, cybernetics, and modern computing techniques" (Mănescu 1974). Consequently, during the 1960s, electronic computers became "politically respectable, step by step replacing the lathe as a symbol of socialist industrialization" (Schatteles 2007, 23).

Operationalization of Planning

The internal efforts of embracing the economics of planning were coordinated, if not expedited, under Soviet leadership, both political and professional. In 1964, the Comecon's Standing Commission for Statistics advised on staff exchanges and the elaboration of methodological principles for the Balance of Intersectoral Relationships (*Balanța legăturilor dintre ramuri, BLR*; in Russian: *Balans Mezhotraslevykh Sviazei*), a common phrase in the Soviet world for input-output analysis (Tövissi and Țigănescu 1969, 12, 14), and issued a report in November 1967. A conference held by the Romanian Communist Party in the same year led to the establishment of a working group within the State Committee of Planning to develop the necessary analytical tools,[7] and also to prepare the required staff of "economist engineers and mathematicians" (Murgescu 1970). The training efforts proved effective: the first BLR containing 74 industrial sectors was completed in 1972, and a second one for 27 sectors around 1974 (Tsantis and Pepper 1979, 44).

The advancement of quantitative expertise for planning was a direct result of party decisions. Major investments were channeled toward establishing regional computing centers already in the mid-1960s (Pașca 2015, 120). Romania became visible in international rankings of the production of home-grown mainframe computers (Herțeliu and Smeureanu 2017, 55, 91). Another example was the initiative Ceaușescu took to meet and send to the

United States a group of experts to acquire the know-how for constructing the BLR (Emilian Dobrescu, interview by the authors, March 17, 2016).

However, ideology and science never parted at any point along this road. Technical expertise increasingly became subdued to party directives. Presenting achievements as self-serving distortions of reality was recognized, at both the micro and macro level, as "another side of the communist economic system: its propensity to overstate, . . . to work around the plan" and to engage "in ingenious simulations and frauds" (Harrison 2012, 8). The parallel reality was created first by severe censorship to block information that could have jeopardized the political authority of the regime. Never knowing for sure what form the threat by the regime could take, the line of "ideological vigilance" (Schatteles 2007, 13) reigned supreme among formally appointed censors, for example, at the General Directorate of the Press or the Bureau of Secret Documents (BDS), or merely among subservient people at publishers or among scholars themselves. What was ideologically "correct" mostly was passed around by word of mouth, as one leading economist recalls (Aurel Iancu, interview by the authors, January 26, 2018).

The flow of economic data was among the first victims of censorship. In the mid-1960s, under serious shortages of consumers goods, a prominent American economist on a research visit in Romania found that key economic indicators[8] were no longer published. He collected nevertheless the "rate of accumulation out of national income" eventually from "a Polish source, reprinted in a Slovak daily paper" (Montias 1967, x). Between 1950 and 1979, absolute figures and comparable prices for a key indicator—domestic income—"were considered as trade secrets and strictly classified" (Axenciuc and Georgescu 2017, 115), as was an array of key sources[9] circulating "in a limited number of copies, 20–30 each, among the leaders of the party and the state" (Axenciuc and Georgescu 2017, 132).

The result was an economic picture that eventually deprived planning of practical validation. Distortions resulted from doctrinarian assumptions,[10] ideological goals to preserve "power and privilege for the party elite" (Bachman 1991, 135), and "official exaggerations" (Axenciuc and Georgescu 2017). Estimating the gaps between plan and economic reality would be a valuable field of counterfactual analysis.[11] Iancu (2018) suggests some landmarks to start with:

- The refusal to adjust the plan to the new realities in world markets during the 1970s and 1980s, such as rising oil prices, metallurgical and financial crises, inflation and increasing interest rates, and so on.
- The start of new, inefficient investment projects in the presence of a large number of delayed investments that never materialized.

- An obsession with the reduction of consumption norms in all economic branches at the expense of product quality.
- Early repayment of external debts irrespective of planning norms and warnings of large-scale economic and social imbalances (to be discussed in more detail later).

Upgrading the quantitative content of predictions remained an objective that did not meet the expectations even of the party officials in charge of planning. Manea Mănescu, who coordinated the elaboration of the 1971–1975 plan within the Central Committee (Paşca 2015, 130), revisited "the requirements of the science of managing socialist society" and concluded that scientific management "is still lagging behind the needs of planning" (Mănescu 1974, 8). External observers also remarked about the insufficient use of mathematical models, especially when contrasted with the practice (and experience) of other Eastern European economies (Tsantis and Pepper 1979, 44, 420). The lack of expertise may have been a natural effect of the belated progress of quantitative economics in Romania. As we will explain below, an equally important reason was the constant neglect, if not outright persecution, of educated opinion in economic matters.

Comecon—Planning the Socialist Camp

Comecon (Council for Mutual Economic Assistance, CMEA) was founded as a regional body of Eastern European countries[12] in Moscow in 1949, and was described as a replica to the Common Market in the main economic publications of the time (*Probleme economice* 1: 61–63). Up to 1955, it mostly provided a framework for bilateral commercial agreements between the member states. However, frictions in regional planning arose soon when, in 1956, the Council advanced a plan for establishing a pattern of specialization corresponding to the material balances of the countries. Eventually, the controversy about specialization proved an important factor in consolidating the political command over economic affairs in Romania.

In contrast to the European Economic Community, the communist bloc exhibited an extreme heterogeneity in economic development. The Soviet Union stood alone with its vast natural resources and political hegemony. The level of economic development of East Germany and Czechoslovakia outdistanced the least developed ones, Albania, Bulgaria, and Romania, while between the two groups, Hungary and Poland aspired to catch up with the advanced countries. Under these circumstances, the GDR and Czechoslovakia refused to shift the production of advanced technology goods to poor countries. In their view, specialization had to respond to differences in labor productivity, and therefore the less developed members were to import machinery in order to catch up with the rest (Kaigl 1959, quoted in Montias 1967, 196).

An additional issue originated in the way prices were stipulated in the contracts between Comecon members. In the inflationary environment after the Korean War, the Council decided to change price setting from prewar to current world market prices (Montias 1967, 191). The decision put poor countries' exports at a disadvantage due to their lower level of productivity. To overcome technological and productivity gaps, Romanian economists like Horowitz (1958), reminiscent of Manoilescu's theory of protectionism, argued that specialization within CMEA should be based not only on relative labor costs but also on the social costs of production. These can be higher due, for example, to foreign exchange shortages (Horowitz 1958, quoted in Montias 1967, 194).

Horowitz's point was of utmost relevance. Foreign loans were in great need and the primary source was the Soviet Union. By then, Gheorghe Gheorghiu-Dej, general secretary of the party since 1947, already had begun to assert an independent course for Romania's foreign policy. Between 1958 and 1959, borrowing from Western sources, including from the United States, was already in place (Montias 1967, 200). The foreign exchange thus accumulated helped balance external accounts (Montias 1967, 172) and finance purchases of technology for Romania's expanding industrial sector as well as pay for cultural exchange with the West (Bachman 1991, 54–55).

Between 1962 and 1964, several Russian economists elaborated on and promoted the concept of an "interstate economic complex or network" as a "new, superior and stable type of international socialist division of labor" (Murgescu 1964). At the Fourth Congress of the Geography Society of the Soviet Union held in Moscow in May 1964, the introductory lecture was entitled "Actual Issues of Economic Geography of the World Social System," in which Piotr Alampiev (1964) discussed the "world single social economy regulated under a single plan" with a separate management and planning identity. Alampiev went even further to claim the removal of national borders.

A different tack on cross-border issues, perceived in Romanian political circles as an attack on national sovereignty, came from Evgeny Valev, who published in 1964 an article on "Issues of Economic Development in the Danubian Districts of Romania, Bulgaria, and the USSR." He suggested the creation of a Lower Danubian Complex (Valev 1964) that would have included 48 percent of the Romanian population in an area equal to 42 percent of the country's territory (see map in Annex) and would have turned Romania into a specialized supplier of natural resources (Murgescu 1964).

Valev planned a precise specialization for the large metallurgical combinates in Galaţi, Hunedoara, and Reşiţa in Romania, Kremikovtsi in Bulgaria and the Dnieper region. Romanian officials, however, were reluctant to adapt domestic production to foreign demand. On this principle, Romania avoided integration with *Intermetall*, a Comecon association of steel producers dominated by companies from Czechoslovakia, East Germany, Hungary, and Poland.

Ultimately, Czechoslovakia and Germany were the only Comecon countries supporting the Soviet Union when, in 1963, it resuscitated a plan to reorganize Comecon according to the principle of national specialization. At a Comecon meeting in February 1963, Romania asserted its independent position "by stating publicly that it would not modify its industrialization program for regional integration" (Bachman 1991, 55). The regional planning of specialization was attacked vigorously by Romanian economists (see Murgescu 1964).

Nicolae Ceaușescu continued Gheorghiu–Dej's campaign of asserting Romanian nationalism. At first, the nationalist turn played well on the international arena. Romania entered the General Agreement on Tariffs and Trade in 1971 as its third communist member and also joined the International Monetary Fund and the World Bank soon thereafter. The share of non-Comecon countries became dominant in Romania's foreign trade in the 1970s and remained the same until today. In the meantime, however, what initially was perceived as openness and political courage among the Soviet satellites morphed into "primitive economic nationalism . . . exacerbated to absurd autarchic forms" in the late 1970s (Emilian Dobrescu, personal communication to authors, June 17, 2017). It was the start of a progressive decoupling of planning from the real balances of the economy or, as the process has been recalled lately, "de facto quasi-generalized voluntarism" (Ibid.) in matters of economic decisions. Actual planning began to resemble economics or any scholarly endeavor less and less.

PLANNING AND ECONOMICS

One of the proudest aspects of economic planning was its mathematical background. This belief, seemingly shared within the whole socialist camp (Katsenelinboigen 1986), virtually bonded economics and planning and strengthened confidence in the underlying rationale of a socialist economic system. The Nobel Prize awarded to Kantorovich in 1975 served as a living proof that "methods have ceased to be the privilege of non-Marxist political economy" (Postolache 1981, 75). However, ideological vigilance ultimately made room for doctrinaire ambivalence. The use of quantitative techniques may have been an expression not only of expertise necessary to make planning work but also of "apologetic purposes . . . to mask the character of the capitalist regime" (Nicolae-Văleanu 1975, 108).

Ideology eventually prevailed over reason in orienting economic policy, but not before allowing the budding practice of quantitative economics to develop into a full-fledged academic pursuit. Techniques such as linear programming, analytical statistics, and product optimization that emerged in the early phases were replaced gradually by research and university programs in the fields of econometrics and cybernetics that gained momentum in the 1970s.

In the 1960s, scholarship radiated from a three-pronged institutional core comprising (a) centers of economic analysis within the planning bureaucracy, namely, the Committee of State Planning, the General Directorate of Statistics, the Ministry of Finance, and the Institute of Planning; (b) the Institute of Mathematics (of the Romanian Academy of Sciences), until it was closed down in 1970; and (c) the departments of mathematics and statistics at the University of Bucharest, the Polytechnic University of Bucharest, Babeş-Bolyai University in Cluj, and Alexandru Ioan Cuza University in Iaşi.

Economics was taught only in Bucharest at ASE (Bucharest University of Economic Studies) until the late 1960s, or in the case of the doctoral program, until the early 1980s. In the last decade of the communist regime, ASE still churned out between 61 and 71 percent of economics graduates in Romania (Korka 2015, 41). The 1972 graduates of the Faculty of Economic Calculus and Cybernetics set up within ASE in 1965 were taught disciplines such as "probability theory and statistical mathematics," "computation systems," "programming," "economic cybernetics," and "operations research" by faculty coming from mathematics and polytechnic schools (Herţeliu and Smeureanu 2017, 65). These professors were the first to show the way to educate mathematical economists in Romania.

In 1966, the journal *Economic Computation and Economic Cybernetics Studies and Research* (ECECSR)[13] was published; it was dedicated to research areas such as analog computation, computer programming, mathematical and cybernetic modeling, operations research, and planometrics. It played a pivotal role in cementing a community of researchers with a quantitative background in economics. ECECSR enlisted support from mathematicians of interwar repute, such as Octav Onicescu, Grigore Moisil, and Gheorghe Mihoc, and attracted contributions from an increasing cohort of Romanian mathematical economists. By that time, the ASE had become a prominent member of a growing body of institutions—e.g., institutes of economic research of the Romanian Academy of Sciences, regional centers of computation belonging to the Central Institute of Informatics, or sectoral centers of economic analysis like the Institute of Research and Technological Design or the Institute of Construction—which began to contribute, with their own quantitative expertise, to the planners' work (Emilian Dobrescu, interview by the authors, March 17, 2016).

These were premises that would have promised a sound economic policy resting on solid theoretical pillars under any normal circumstances. However, the party undermined and, toward the end of the 1980s, de facto annihilated independent expert knowledge. Few choices were left for economists in search of the meaning of their science apart from those related to command planning.

Party Economics

A key driver of ambitious planning efforts was the belief borrowed from the Soviet Union that citizens were able to work hard, comply with the rigors of modern production, and disregard the shortcomings of everyday life, relying solely on their own socialist consciousness and national pride (Opriş 2019, 137). This conviction wavered and then hardened not long after party leaders had been confronted by the reality of massive proportions of defective exports of high-end industrial goods (79; Iancu and Pavelescu 2018). The motivation of the workforce seemed to be not in line with party ambitions, a verdict that only hardened after a visit Ceauşescu made to China and North Korea in 1971. In a high-ranking party assembly, he shared his favorable impressions with the audience: "There is a general mobilization of the people, from children to the elderly, everybody is mobilized, to learn, to work, no one rests. . . . To sum up, they possess good organization, discipline, and a healthy spirit" (quoted in Paşca 2015, 124). In the aftermath of the famous Asia experience, "the Party is always right" became a dictum that paralyzed virtually any independent, which is to say, apolitical initiative. Amateurism on the part of the political elite intruded on economists' discourse, including that of the planners.

More disturbingly, the secretary general, a shoemaker by profession, found a calling in uttering "teachings," "writings," or "opinions," which were to guide the political economy in the years to come. In 1971, putting faith in massive domestic investments to replace foreign technology in iron and steel production, he suggested to fire at once all experts from the ministries who advised against domestic production on grounds of cost efficiency and to replace them with "a few skilled people, workers, and technicians" (quoted in Opriş 2019, 271–72). Or, here is how he justified in 1985 his point on forced mobility of workers:

> If you do not have sugar beet, you do like this: you close the factory for two weeks, you build a stock of sugar beet, then you begin to work again when you have enough sugar beet to make the factory work at full capacity. . . . Do I have to teach you how to manage a factory? . . . If you have beet for only one month, then you work for one month, you do not keep the factory open for

three months. You close it and send people to some other place. (quoted in Opriş 2019, 135)[14]

The archives reveal today that the full extent of the malfunction of the planning process was well known among party leaders. A report from 1974 informed about:

> the poor correlation between financial norms and the tasks of the plan, . . . increasing inventories of inputs due to non-fulfilment of production targets, . . . the exceeding of the projected production costs, . . . the poor management and planning of investments, . . . and the usual breakdown of financial discipline and auditing. (Opriş 2019, 133–34)

A series of shocks of the 1970s—the start of the global oil crisis in 1973, the devastating Vrancea earthquake of 1977, and the rapid accumulation of external debt that rose to 27 percent of GDP in 1980 (Pelinescu, Cazan, and Iordan 2018)—could not but amplify the inherent weakness of the economic system.

The authoritarian tendency, toward which top-level economic planners still did not hesitate to express their criticism in the mid-1960s (Montias 1967, 2), became the unfortunate trademark of the country's economic management. "Deregulatory" measures were put in place between 1978 and 1980, whereby the "written directives" of the Party's Central Committee, drafted on Ceauşescu's direct order, overpowered laws and any other rules of legal effect (Emilian Dobrescu, interview by the authors, March 17, 2016). Starting in the 1970s, the personal influence of Nicolae Ceauşescu, accompanied by his wife, Elena, on economic policymaking and implementation transformed the country's command economy into a dual-command economy, in which centralized control and personal dictate would fight for supremacy. Their impact on society and economy was so deep and unusual as to prolong communist vices long beyond the time when the Iron Curtain fell.[15] With the benefit of hindsight, the erstwhile superlatives bestowed on "the Romanian model" cannot but express the fact that it was "the most highly centralized power structure in Eastern Europe" (Bachman 1991, xxi).

Beyond Command Planning: Building an Economic Culture of Sorts

Dissent or at least signs of apolitical economic thought were rare but not absent. A genuine culture of economic science emerged from disparate origins as diverse as the unaccomplished projects of émigrés, scattered groups of free thinking individuals, and even insiders in the planners' camp.

Until his emigration in 1972, Tiberiu Schatteles provided one of the most elaborate reflections on planning and the nature of economics in socialism.[16] His criticism came from several directions—philosophy, game theory, mathematical economics, statistics—which, taken together, frame a stylized portrait of what an independent researcher could have looked like in Romania: passionate about economics' various ramifications converging inevitably to discover the limits of planning under communism. Schatteles agrees with Ludwig Mises on the miscalculation problem in socialism[17] but offers a different explanation. In his view, the problem of rational calculation in socialism originates in the practice of planning, and not necessarily in the idea of planning. The context of strategic games illustrates "the possibility of unfathomable predictions in the process of planning work in socialism" (244). Mathematical economics serves to highlight "inconsistencies in the routine of planning thought" (279) and ultimately has the power to overwhelm the doctrinaire elements. For example, in inter-sectoral analysis "if we define the general development model, any discussion of the proportion between consumption and investment will be emptied of any significance, given the input-output relationships of the economy" (293).

Although original, insightful, and quite extensive, the work of Schatteles could not be circulated or appraised after he had left the country. When asked to name some "original economic papers" published in Romania between 1946 and 1989, Nicholas Spulber, a Romanian-born American professor and émigré of 1948, could not find a single example. He justified the harsh verdict by alluding to Romanian economists' disposition "to work on Stalinist models" (Aligică 2004, 77, 85). However, while the critical reaction by economists to official economic policy was muted at the time, exceptions did occur, and they were notable. Most probably, these attempts lacked the intellectual force to make breakthroughs, but, being as far from Soviet inspiration as possible, they harbingered a different path of economic research.

Emilian Dobrescu's work is one example. He is acknowledged as "the author of the first Romanian econometric models" (*Emilian Dobrescu at 75 Years* 2008) and as the Romanian economist with the longest uninterrupted series of publications since 1958. Dobrescu was president of the State Committee of Planning when, in 1981, he warned party officials at the highest level of command[18] about "the phenomena of abusive 'manipulation' of some value indicators" and pointed out that "economic policy is to consider the quantitative options of economic processes"[19] (Iancu and Pavelescu 2018, 10). In 1982, he cautioned again, this time in handwritten comments, against the "obsessive ambition" of "forcing quantitative rates . . . with consequences on living standards." (Dobrescu 2015)[20]

Given the whole magnitude of disastrous mismanagement, Dobrescu's reaction was remarkable not only because it credited an entire branch of dedicated practitioners[21] but also because it earmarked a turning point in the practice of economists. With all his intellectual and professional authority, he drew the attention of his fellow economists to the imposture that had creeped into their profession and to the less quantifiable, mostly social aspects of economic analyses.

By the mid-1980s, economic thinking was being driven gradually toward a mélange of "plan and market" economics. Pilat and Dăianu (1984) published a representative paper on this new approach. Against the backdrop of the declining share of industrial exports by Comecon countries to international markets, the authors made ample references to "the qualitative aspects of growth" largely neglected in the process of planning. They entered unchartered territory by advocating for an increased role for the market. As they put it, "the market, with all its shortcomings, remains an efficient mechanism," and the market and the plan should not "become incompatible."

Similar contributions were also the result of more or less organized gatherings of independent thinkers. By default, Bucharest was the center of these events, but places of intellectual fervor developed outside the capital as well. One example is a group at the Alexandru I. Cuza University in Iași. A local team of professors—Mihai Todosia, Ion Pohoață, Ion Ignat, Spiridon Pralea, Gheorghe Lutac and, for a while, Valeriu Coste (Ion Pohoață, personal communication to authors, September 15, 2019)—organized regular sessions, literally around a pile of books. Their enthusiasm largely was motivated by the efforts of Professor Todosia, rector and prominent party member, who exploited his personal liaisons with high-ranking officials in Bucharest to acquire new books from abroad. Those books were then photocopied clandestinely and assigned for debates based on "written comments."[22] Other sources of much longed-for literature consisted, for example, of the secret collection of the library of the Stefan Gheorghiu Party University in Bucharest, to which Professor Todosia had access, as well as of several other outlets such as the libraries of the French and the US embassies and the French Lectorate in Iasi.

CONCLUSION: REFLECTIONS ON THE LEGACY OF PLANNING THOUGHT IN ROMANIA

We set out this inquiry to understand why Romania's experience with communism led to a delusional approach to central economic management. As cautioned by Tolstoy's famous opening paragraph in *Anna Karenina* ("Happy families are all alike; every unhappy family is unhappy in its own way"), we attempted in this chapter to pass over the common experience of the communist countries with *dirigisme* and identified instead a specific Romanian way of coping with the economic miscalculation problem. We have seen planning emerge as a novel preoccupation of Romanian economists in the 1960s—virtually their only contribution to the development of economic thought since the interwar period. We conclude by emphasizing two of the lasting effects of that contribution, namely, on the practice of planning and on the history of economic ideas.

The practice of planning started under good auspices. Romania succeeded in producing expertise in terms of a critical mass of mathematical economists by the mid-1970s and a tangible rise in economic growth. For a country struggling to escape poverty in the 1950s, the economic effect was visible almost instantly due to the fact that "Stalinist classical socialism is repressive and inefficient, but it constitutes a coherent system" (Kornai 1992, xxv). Romania attained the 1938 level of economic development by 1950, its historically highest share in the world market (0.5 percent) in the 1970s, and became a middle-income country by the 1980s.

There were achievements that paralleled those of "the major regions under communism" (Harrison 2012), but at the time of the transition to productivity-driven growth, the limits of the political regime became evident. Planning significantly diverted from its course when its rational priorities changed hands from planners to an absolute party (and Ceaușescu's personal) command system. Starting from the Five-Year Plan of 1976–1980, the efficiency of capital accumulation dropped considerably below the average level recorded during 1951–1975 (Iancu and Pavelescu 2018). The annual average growth rate of aggregate output was in negative domain (–0.1 percent) during 1981–1988, whereas all other European socialist economies experienced positive growth in the range from 0.8 percent (Poland) to 2 percent (Soviet Union) (Kornai 1992, 200).

By the end of the 1980s, Romania became a country that lost both its growth potential and the ability of establishing economic priorities. The debates about the reform in the first post-communist years introduced many novel concepts such as free markets and property rights, which were translated almost overnight into the letter (though not the spirit) of policymaking. The goals of economic development were suspended by an almost visceral denial of planning. Since 1990, what one may generously call economic priorities have been configured through lobby interests, trade and integration arrangements with the European Union, or triggered by foreign investors.

At the same time, the work of economists evolved under more favorable circumstances. Surely, there were irrecoverable losses of their intellectual legacy; the prewar diversity of schools of thought have not returned until now. Marxism does not feed economic discourse any longer. Paradoxically, Romanian economic thought witnesses its revival in the new era thanks to the very skills honed for a long time by the planners. One of the milestones of this revival was the effort of Emilian Dobrescu to continue macroeconomic modeling. He pioneered the "mentor-disciple" pattern almost singularly in Romanian economics. Dobrescu's endeavor, highly supported by his new role as the author of the "Macro Model of the Romanian Market Economy" produced over seventeen years between 1996 and 2012, was facilitated by the founding of the Macroeconomic Modelling Seminar at the National Institute for Economic Research of the Romanian Academy in June 1990. The seminar still exists, demonstrating the legacy of planning expertise; since 2008, it has been called the Macroeconomic Modelling Center.

Quantitative knowledge took root in an ever-larger cohort of researchers as well as disciplinary domains. Economic science in Romania today identifies almost exclusively with a formal approach, according to which reasoning flows from method to premise and not the other way around. Divergent currents of thought still find their place, as, for example, a chain of centers devoted to Austrian economics shows, but they are still unable to create a rich intellectual climate of diversity and dialogue. Here communism left indelible scars. Investigating the concept of planning can be an illuminating exercise in finding the origins of harm and also in finding planning's beneficial influence on the growth of economic thought.

ANNEX

Figure 7.1: Valev Plan: The Lower–Danube Complex of Agricultural Specialization
Source: Adapted by authors from Valev (1964), 52, 54.

NOTES

1. PCR stands for *Partidul Comunist Român* (Romanian Communist Party).

2. In 1951, the communist party amended the law by introducing the concept of Stakhanovite labor for the most diligent workers exceeding the plan set by central authorities in their state-owned enterprise.

3. It was renamed State Committee for Planning in 1952 (Pelinescu, Cazan, and Iordan 2018).

4. "The distribution of national income between consumption and accumulation is of particular importance because increasing the accumulation fund to the detriment of the consumption fund means delaying the increase in the standard of living of the population, while increasing the consumption fund at the expense of accumulation fund means delaying the economic development of the country. Determining these proportions is a political issue" (ASE 1970, 7). See also the role of planning as underlined in the academic curriculum: "The main feature of management and organizational mechanism of economic activity in socialism is socialist planning" (Apostol et al. 1982, 87).

5. The accumulation fund is part of national income used in the form of investment and change in stocks in both the so-called productive and nonproductive sectors (Tsantis and Pepper 1979, xviii).

6. They included *Kyklos*, *Weltwirtschaftliches Archiv*, *The Quarterly Journal of Economics*, *Review of Economics and Statistics, Philosophy of Science*, *Journal of Political Economy*, and *Annals of Mathematics*.

7. Two research institutes at the SCP were in charge of operationalizing the planning tasks: the Institute of Planning and Prognosis focused on overall planning methodology and long-term forecasting techniques, and the Computer and Cybernetics Center for Planning dealt with the computations related to the plans and the sectoral models (Tsantis and Pepper 1979, 44).

8. These indicators included national income, the wage bill, the components of net investment, imports and exports in domestic prices and in constant foreign trade prices, agricultural procurements, retail and wholesale price indices, costs and profits in industry (Montias 1967, ix).

9. The sources included the studies of the Ministry of Finance, the Balance Sheet of Economic and Financial Results (1970–1988), the Centralized Financial Plan (1980–1984), Reports of General Account for the Ending of the Financial Year (1978–1983), the State Budget (1980–1986), and the Analysis of Domestic Income (1950–1959).

10. For example, non-material services (in comparable prices) were excluded from the value of national income, as well as fixed capital consumption from official statistics until 1990 (Axenciuc and Georgescu 2017, 122).

11. A World Bank study from 1985 points to estimations of material production with ±5–6 percent error margin, and of GDP with an even wider margin, "possibly of ±10–12 percent" (cited in Axenciuc and Georgescu 2017, 116). GDP values were published by the National Institute of Statistics starting in 1980 (115).

12. It embraced Albania, Bulgaria, Czechoslovakia, East Germany, Hungary, Poland, Romania, and the Soviet Union.

13. *Studii şi cercetări de calcul economic şi cibernetică economică.* The journal has been published continuously since 1966. It was edited in the Faculty of Economic Calculus and Cybernetics set up within ASE in 1965. The faculty had three sections—mechanization and automation of economic calculus, economic statistics, and economic cybernetics. From 1978 to 1990, it became known as the Faculty of Economic Planning and Cybernetics (*Facultatea de Cibernetică, Statistică şi Informatică Economică: n.d. Istoric*).

14. The fear of losing their established home and lifestyle suddenly by being moved to other plants in the country made people accept any social injustice that may have arisen from such hasty judgments. In the summer of 1989, when the *Oltcit* car factory ran out of liquidity with dire consequences for wage payment, no one complained. The factory was willing to pay 2,249 workers out of 3,675 only 54.6 percent of the monthly wage (see Vasile 2013, quoted in Opriş 2019, 139).

15. The far-reaching changes in popular values in Romania, changes wrought by a highly centralized government that concentrated power in the hands of a very small political elite, are discussed cogently in Bachman (1991, 106ff.). For a splendid reflection on moral imperatives under communism, see Kornai (1992, 57ff.).

16. Unless otherwise specified, the citations come from Schatteles (2007). This book gathers some of his most important contributions between 1967 and 1972.

17. "[It] is not a very solid argument . . . that the socialist state, being in possession of <complete information> on the economic process, is in any case able to make the calculations necessary for the efficient functioning of the economy" (Schatteles 2007, 279).

18. He spoke at the Joint Plenary of the Central Committee of the Communist Party and the Supreme Council of Economic and Social Development on November 25–26, 1981.

19. He criticized the inclusion of the positive balance of trade and the reserves in the material balances (together amounting to 9 percent of the national income planned for 1983) in the fund of consumption. This inflated the share of the consumption fund from 61.5 to 70.5 (Iancu and Pavelescu 2018).

20. The commentary comes from his July 16, 1982 personal statement to the Central Committee and was published in Ionete (1993).

21. It goes beyond the scope of this chapter to credit all the merits of these experts throughout the period. See Cojanu (2017) for a preliminary analysis preceding this research project. See Ionete (1993), Pilat (2006), and Ban (2011) for reference works on communist Romania's economic thinkers.

22. An *ad hoc* list of authors included Mark Blaug, Eugen Böhm-Bawerk, Fernand Braudel, Henri Denis, Emilian Dobrescu, John Galbraith, Friedrich Hayek, Eli Heckscher, Emile James, Stanley Jevons, John Keynes, Thomas Kuhn, Carl Menger, Ludwig Mises, Andre Piettre, Karl Popper, Karl Pribram, Joan Robinson, Wilhelm Röpke, Joseph Schumpeter, Werner Sombart, Immanuel Wallerstein, Leon Walras, and Max Weber. Mathematical economics was also represented by Evsey Domar, Nikolai Fedorenko, Nicholas Kaldor, Michał Kalecki, Leonid Kantorovich, János Kornai, Edmond Malinvaud, Vasilii Nemchinov, Viktor Novozhilov, and Piero Sraffa.

BIBLIOGRAPHY

Academia de Studii Economice (ASE). 1970. *Conducerea planificată a economiei naționale*. București: Editura Didactică și Pedagogică.

Alampiev, Piotr. 1964. *Materialy k IV Siezdu Geograficheskogo Obshchestva SSSR Simpozium "V."* *Geografiia sotsialisticheskikh stran*. Leningrad: AN SSSR..

Alexiu, P., and A. Rozen. 1964. "Eficacitatea economica a activității productive și cresterea venitului național." *Probleme economice* 1: 18–31

Aligică, Paul Dragos. 2004. *Tranziții economice: Convorbiri cu Nicolas Spulber*. București: Humanitas.

Allen, Roy G. D. 1956. *Mathematical Economics*. New York: St. Martin's Press.

Anghel I. 1964. "Continutul teoriilor microeconomice si macroeconomice." *Probleme economice* 1: 58–71.

Apostol, Gheorghe P., Gheorghe Cretoiu, Costin Murgescu, and Florea Burtan. 1982. *Economie politică*, București: Editura didactică și pedagogică.

Arrow, Kenneth J. 1962. "The Economic Implication of Learning by Doing." *The Review of Economic Studies* 29 (3): 155–73.

ASE Facultatea de Cibernetica, Statistica si Informatica. n.d. "Istoric." http://www.csie.ase.ro/istoric, accessed July 7, 2021.

Avachian, A., and O. Bernstein. 1954. "Industria ușoară și bunurile de larg consum bazat pe economii reale dedicate investițiilor." *Probleme economice* 3: 23–36.

Axenciuc, Victor, and George Georgescu. 2017. *Romania's Gross Domestic Product and National Income 1862–2010*. Bucharest: Editura Academiei Române.

Bachman, Roland D., ed. 1991. *Romania: A Country Study*. Washington DC: Federal Research Division, Library of Congress.

Ban, Cornel. 2011. "Neoliberalism in Translation: Economic Ideas and Reforms in Spain and Romania." PhD Dissertation, Department of Government and Politics, University of Maryland College Park. http://drum.lib.umd.edu/bitstream/1903/11456/1/Ban_umd_0117E_11923.pdf, accessed July 7, 2021.

Basilescu, A. N. 1933. *Principii de economie politică*. Vol. 1. București: A. T. Doicescu.

Carson, Byron, and Christopher J. Coyne. 2019. "Knowledge and Power: Hayek's Dual Problems with Planning." GMU Working Paper in Economics No. 19–12. https://papers.ssrn.com/sol3/papers.cfm?abstract_id=3301967##, accessed August 11, 2021.

Catulescu A. 1964. "Productivitatea muncii în industria usoară." *Probleme economice* 1: 45–57.

Ceaușescu, Nicolae. 1966. *Partidul Comunist Român—Continuator al luptei revoluționare și democratice a poporului român, a tradițiilor mișcării muncitorești și socialiste din România.* București: Agerpres.

Cojanu, Valentin. 2017. "The Rise of Mathematical Economics in Communist Romania." *History of Economic Ideas* XXV (3): 41–65.

Dan, Em., and C. Murgescu. 1954. "Aspecte ale cresterii productiei marfa in agricultura RPR." *Probleme economice* 2: 37–49.

Dobrescu, Emilian. 2015. "Adnotări la problema acumulării în România anilor '70–'80." Manuscript, February 20, 2015.

Dumitru V. 1954. "For Growing Output of Metallic Merchandises in Heavy Industries." *Economic Issues* 1:44.

Dyker, David A. 1985. *The Future of the Soviet Economic Planning System.* London—Sydney: Croom Helm.

Economic Computation and Economic Cybernetics Studies and Research. http://www.ecocyb.ase.ro, accessed August 11, 2021.

"Emilian Dobrescu at 75 Years." 2008. *Romanian Journal of Economic Forecasting* 9 (1): 5–16.

Ericson, Richard E. 2018. "The Growth and Marcescence of SOFE: System for Optimal Functioning of the (Socialist) Economy." Paper presented at the AEA Conference, January 2018. https://www.aeaweb.org/conference/2018/preliminary, accessed July 7, 2021.

Harrison, Mark. 2012. "Communism and economic modernization." Draft of 11 June. https://warwick.ac.uk/fac/soc/economics/staff/mharrison/public/communism_modernization.pdf, accessed October 7, 2021.

Herţeliu, Claudiu, and Ion Smeureanu. eds. 2017. *Facultatea de cibernetică, statistică şi informatică economică la semicentenar,* Bucureşti: Editura ASE.

Horowitz, M. 1958. "Despre unele particularităţi şi limite ale acţiunii legii valorii în comerţul exterior socialist." *Probleme economice* 4: 10–20.

Iancu, Aurel. 2015. "Pionierat în abordarea şi dezvoltarea economiei analitice în România." *Academica* XXV (2): 56–59.

———. 2018. "Observaţii şi propuneri la lucrarea privind 'Activitatea de planificare economică." Manuscript.

Iancu, Aurel, and Florin Marius Pavelescu. 2018. *Creştere economică, acumulare şi dezechilibre în România: perioadei comuniste.* Bucureşti: Institutul Naţional de Cercetări Economice.

Ionete, Constantin. 1993. *Criza de sistem a economiei de comandă şi etapa sa explozivă.* Bucuresti: Editura Expert.

Kaigl, V. 1959. "Zakonomernosti razvitiia ekonomicheskikh otnoshenii mezhdu stranami mirovoi sotsialisticheskoi sistemy." *Voprosy filosofii* 3:37–39.

Kalecki, Michał. 1968. *Zarys teorii wzrostu gospodarki socjalistycznej.* Warsaw: Panstwowe Wydawnictwo Naukowe.

Kantorovich, Leonid V. 1959. Ekonomicheskii raschet nailuchshego ispolzovaniia resursov [Economic Calculation of the Best Use of Resources]. Moskva: Akademiia nauk SSSR.

Katsenelinboigen, Aron J. 1986. "Mathematical Economics in the Soviet Union: A Reflection on the 25th Anniversary of L. V. Kantorovich's Book, *The Best Use of Economic Resources.*" *Acta Slavica Iaponica* 4: 88–103.

Koopmans, Tjalling C. 1963. "On the Concept of Optimal Economic Growth." Cowles Foundation Discussion Papers 163, Cowles Foundation for Research in Economics, Yale University.

Korka, Mihai. 2015. "Contrast Between Pre-Reform and Post-Reform Curricula at the Faculty of Trade at the Bucharest University of Economic Studies." In *Between*

Bukharin and Balcerowicz. A Comparative History of Economic Thought under Communism. Position Paper Romania, edited by Bogdan Murgescu and Dragos Aligica. Manuscript, 35–61.

Kornai, János. 1971. *Anti-equilibrium*. Budapest: Közgazdasági és Jogi Könyvkiadó.

———. 1992 (2007). *The Socialist System: The Political Economy of Communism*. Oxford: Clarendon Press.

Lange, Oskar. 1965. *Wstep do cybernetyki ekonomicznej*. Warsaw: Panstwowe Wydawnictwo Naukowe.

Leontief, Wassily. 1966. *Input-Output Economics*. New York: Oxford University Press.

Maddison, Angus. 1964. *Economic Growth in the West—Comparative Experience in Europe and North America*. New York: Twentieth Century Fund.

Madgearu, Virgil. 1938. *Orientations générales destinées à service à l'élaboration d'économique de longue durée*. Bucharest.

Mănescu, Manea. 1974. "The Institutionalization of Planning in Romania (1948–1973)." *Revue Roumaine des Sciences Sociales. Série de Sociologie* 18: 3–9.

Mesaros, E. 1955. "Teorii neo malthusiene despre populație." *Probleme economice* 10: 111–29.

Moldovan, Roman.1964. "Perfecționarea continuă a planificării—factor important pentru înfăptuirea politicii economice." *Probleme economice* 8:40.

Montias, John Michael. 1967. *Economic Development in Communist Rumania*. Cambridge: The MIT Press.

Murgescu, Costin. 1964. "Concepții potrivnice principiilor de bază ale relațiilor economice dintre tările socialiste—Despre 'complexul economic interstatal,' în general și despre concretizarea lui 'dunăreană' în special." *Probleme ale Relațiilor dintre țările socialiste, Biblioteca Viața Economică* 2: 3–30. http://www.cnsas.ro/documente/istoria_comunism/documente_programatice/1964%20Relatiile%20economice%20dintre%20tarile%20socialiste.pdf, accessed July 7, 2021.

———. 1970. "Cuvînt înainte." In *Analiza input–output. Teoria interdependentei ramurilor economice (Input–Output Economics)*, by Wassily Leontief, 9–28. București: Editura Științifică.

Nicolae-Văleanu, Ivanciu. 1975. *Gândirea economică burgheză și lumea contemporană*. București: Editura Politică.

Opriș, Petre. 2019. *Aspecte ale economiei românești în timpul războiului rece (1946–1991)*. București: Editura Trei.

Pașca, Vlad. 2015. "Cincinalul 1971–1975 în România socialistă: Mecanismul decizional între tentații tehnocratice și primatul politicului." Teza de doctorat, Universitatea București.

Păun, Nicolae. 2018. "Doctrine economice. Liberalism—intervenționism în modernitatea românească." Manuscript.

Pelinescu, Elena, Leonard Cazan, and Marioara Iordan. 2018. "Planificarea și prognoza economică." In *Economia României după Marea Unire. Vol. 2, Economia sectorială*, edited by Aurel Iancu, George Georgescu, Victor Axenciuc, and Constantin Ciutacu. București: Editura Academiei Române.

Phelps, Edmund S. 1961. "The Golden Rule of Capital Accumulation." *American Economic Review* 51 (4): 638–43.

Pilat, Vasile. 2006. *Funcţionarea economiei naţionale*. Bucureşti: Rosetti Educational.

Pilat, Vasile, and Daniel Dăianu. 1984. "Current Development Problems of European Socialist Economies." *Revista Română de Studii Internaţionale* (May–June): 227–40. Retrieved from Foreign Broadcast Information Service, East Europe Report—Economic and Industrial Affairs, 24 of August 1984, JPRS–EEI–84–096.

Postolache, Tudorel. 1981. *Restructurări în economia politică*. Bucureşti: Editura Politică.

Ramsey, Frank P. 1928. "A Mathematical Theory of Saving." *Economic Journal* 38 (152): 543–59.

Răvar, Ion, and Maria Hlevca. 1961. "Probleme metodologice ale balanţei legăturilor dintre ramuri a producţiei şi repartiţiei produsului social." *Revista de statistică* 6.

Schatteles, Tiberiu. 1956. "Unele probleme ale comerţului exterior şi diviziunii internaţionale a muncii în lumea capitalistă." *Probleme Economice* 10: 78–92.

———. 1967. "Agregarea ramurilor la elaborarea balanţei legăturilor dintre ramuri." *Revista de Statistica* 16: 21–28

———. 2007. *Economie, epistemologie si previziune*. Bucureşti: Tritonic.

———. 2015. "Studiul economiei—sinteza unei aventuri." *Academica* XXV (2): 48–55.

Sovalov, A. 1948. "The Capitalist Economy Crisis." *Probleme economice* 4: 90–93.

Tinbergen, Jan. 1960. "Optimum Saving and Utility Maximization over Time." *Econometrica* XXVIII (April): 481–89.

———. 1964. *Central Planning*. New Haven: Yale University Press.

Totu, Ioan V. 1984. "The Contribution of Economics to Romania's Economic Development During the Past Decade." Research Report 24: Economy, Society and Culture in Contemporary Romania, Anthropology Department Research Reports series, University of Massachusetts—Amherst. http://scholarworks.umass.edu/anthro_res_rpt24/24, accessed July 7, 2021.

Tövissi, Ludovic, and Eugen Ţigănescu. 1969. *Balanţa legăturilor dintre ramuri*. Bucuresti: Editura Ştiinţifică.

Tsantis, Andreas C., and Roy Pepper. 1979. *Romania—Industrialization of an Agrarian Economy Under Socialist Planning*. A World Bank Country Study. Washington, DC: The World Bank. http://documents.worldbank.org/curated/en/308951468762951181/Romania–Industrialization–of–an–agrarian–economy–under–socialist–planning, accessed July 7, 2021.

Valev, Evgeny. 1964. "Probleme dezvoltării economice a raioanelor dunărene din Romînia, Bulgaria şi U.R.S.S." *Probleme ale Relaţiilor dintre ţările social-iste, Biblioteca Viaţa Economică* 2: 47–59. http://www.cnsas.ro/documente/istoria_comunism/documente_programatice/1964%20Relatiile%20economice%20dintre%20tarile%20socialiste.pdf, accessed July 7, 2021.

Vasile, Valentin. 2013. "Sub imperiul ispitei. Autoturismul, românii şi Securitatea în anii 70–80." *Caietele CNSAS* VI (1–2): 259–80. https://www.academia.edu/36130042/Caiete_CNSAS_nr_11_12_2013_pdf, accessed July 7, 2021.

Zaman, Gheorghe, Valentina Vasile, and George Georgescu, eds. 2013. *Institutul de Economie Națională: 60 de ani de cercetare științifică 1953–2013*. București: RCR Editorial.
Zeigler S. 1949. "Planul de stat al Republicii Populare a României." *Probleme economice* 1: 36–47.

Chapter 8

Communism = Soviet Power + Planning

Planning and Mathematical Economics in the Soviet Union

Andrei Belykh

In one of his notes Lenin formulated an idea which later became a widely known slogan: "communism = soviet power + electrification." It is much less known that the plan of electrification (*GOELRO*) was the only possible economic plan for Russia's development from Lenin's viewpoint. It was this fact that prompted the title of this chapter. Undoubtedly, the history of planning in the USSR can explain the country's economic history during the Soviet period. The development of planning was influenced by attempts to use mathematical methods that were expected to improve the quality of planning, to convert it into a truly scientific paradigm, and thus to achieve visible economic effects.

Various aspects of the history of planning in the USSR and its relationship with mathematical economics have been studied in a number of works such as Zauberman (1960; 1975), Smolinski (1971), Ellman (1973), Sutela (1984; 1991), Belykh (2007), Boldyrev and Kirtchik (2013), Leeds (2016), and Feygin (2017). This chapter will concentrate on the evolution of planning concepts in the USSR. Moreover, it will analyze the impact of mathematical ideas on the theory and practice of planning. In the course of its development, the Soviet economy and planning lived through several stages characterized not only by different levels of centralization but also by different uses of in-kind (natural, physical) and monetary indicators. In a simplified form, four historical models of planning and management can be presented:

Model 1: Centralized system with natural indicators
Model 2: Centralized system with monetary indicators
Model 3: Mixed system with natural indicators
Model 4: Mixed system with monetary indicators

A centralized system implies that the economy is understood as a unified factory with a single center of planning. In this system planning and management are exercised either primarily by means of natural indicators (Model 1) or by means of monetary indicators (Model 2). In a mixed system, centralized planning is combined with the operation of enterprises enjoying different degrees of independence. Model 3 depicts centralized planning and enterprise management on the basis of natural indicators. According to Model 4, centralized planning uses monetary indicators while the enterprises have different degrees of independence. These models do not exclude the existence of state enterprises operating on the market together with private companies (like in the period of the new Economic Policy [NEP]) or more or less independent state enterprises (like in the late Soviet period).

By examining the history of Soviet planning and its interaction with economic theory, we will come to the conclusion that mathematical economics played an important role in the improvement of the planning system but failed to solve basic problems of the socialist economy no matter what model it happened to experiment with.

PREHISTORY—PLANNING CONCEPTS BEFORE 1917

In Russia the idea of planning originated at the beginning of the twentieth century. It was actively propagated by the journal *Industry and Trade (Promyshlennost i Torgovlia)* published by the All-Russian Council of Conventions of Industries and Trades. In the editorial article of the first issue of 1909 it was clearly stated:

> We badly need a working plan for our financial and economic policy. . . . Otherwise, we shall not be able to find any way out of the economic impasse. . . . To transform Russia from an ignorant, hungry and stagnant country into an educated, well-fed and vigorous one, we need to take just one small step: to unite separate departmental programs into a single unified plan for the economic and financial development of Russia. (*Minuvshii god* 1909, 3, quoted in Mau 2017, 81)

The First World War became an additional impulse for state planning. In 1915, four special committees were formed to deal with problems of defense, transport, fuel, and food, respectively. These committees headed by government ministers included representatives from the State Duma as well as from local governments and municipal councils. Among the members were scholars like Vladimir Groman who later became known as an outstanding statistician and economist. The committees were established with the purpose of supporting industrial enterprises, with military enterprises as the first priority. This period also witnessed the beginning of price regulation. In February 1915, local authorities were granted the right to prohibit the export of agricultural products from their regions (*gubernii*). Moreover, they were allowed to establish an upper limit on grain prices and to requisition food at reduced prices.

The demand for planning and state regulation came from industrialists, state officials, and economic experts. The famous economist Mikhail Bogolepov started working on the development of the theory of planning. According to him, "an economic plan should include concise but extremely necessary information. Balanced development means the choice of what is most necessary at a given moment" (Bogolepov 1916, 46). The official note of the Ministry of Finance from January 1916 stated: "Departmental policy must be changed for governmental policy based on a single plan, obligatory for all departments. The future of Russia strictly demands to create due regularity of state economic transformations" (quoted in Mau 2017, 122).

In comparison with the rest of the world, Russian economic thought in the nineteenth century was relatively backward. In 1890, when Alfred Marshall's *Principles of Economics* was published, an article appeared in Russia, which attempted to take a "neo-classical approach," that is, to combine classical value theory with marginal utility and marginal productivity theories. It was written by Mikhail Tugan-Baranovsky (1890), which, while it did not display originality, marked the beginning of a closer cooperation with Western economics. Similar approaches were adopted by Vladimir Dmitriev (1974) and Evgenii Slutsky (1927), whose works became known worldwide much later.

Thus, the foundations were laid for further developments in the field of mathematical economics. Mathematical methods gained general acceptance, and some experience was acquired in the mathematical modeling of economic phenomena. The development of management and planning systems required reliable statistical data on the economy. The beginning of the twentieth century in Russia brought a significant progress in statistics. At that time, Russian statisticians Vladimir Groman and Pavel Popov, who later made a great contribution to constructing the planning system, started their scientific investigations.

MAKING AN ECONOMIC SYSTEM WORK, 1917–1929

During the Civil War, the main economic tasks faced by the Bolsheviks included the organization of the provisioning of the army and the food supply of the civil population. Under War Communism, large, middle-sized, and many small enterprises were nationalized. Food supply was based on requisitioning. Core objectives were neither industrial development nor the organization of the planning system but survival and the distribution of resources. In November 1918, this led to the establishment of the Committee of Utilization for 19 basic products. In 1919, their number grew to 44, and in 1920, to 55. (Kritsman 1921a, 16). In fact, War Communist economic management corresponded to Model 1.

It was only logical that in such a situation various concepts of a money-free economy emerged. They were analyzed by Leonid Iurovskii (1928, 98–129). The main difficulty was to determine a unit for comparing economic goods. One of the solutions proposed was the labor unit, so-called *tred* (*trudovaia edinitsa*). This idea was strongly supported by Stanislav Strumilin. Aleksandr Chayanov put forward an alternative concept, that of money-free calculation. In his work *The Concept of Efficiency of the Socialist Economy* he made an attempt to demonstrate that accounting based on natural indicators is sufficient. It was in this work, as far as we know, that the notion "political economy of socialist society" was introduced (Chayanov 1921, 27).

Chayanov suggested that these natural indicators be compared by means of a numerical scale. He wrote that in a socialist society only "such an input of labor and capital" is considered to be expedient "which, compared with another use of the same amount of labor and capital, will offer a bigger output of product" (Chayanov 1921, 18). According to him, the center should manage the national economy by means of a system of norms that substitute the market and its prices. He hoped that such indicators would make it possible to calculate a general success index for each economic unit, which can be used in the process of management. In our classification scheme such an arrangement corresponds to Model 3. Iurovskii (1928, 107) noted that Chayanov's concept conforms with the principles formulated by Otto Neurath, although they drew similar conclusions independently. Actually, Chayanov had anticipated ideas of economic management, which in the 1960s and 1970s were advocated by some Soviet mathematical economists.

During the 1920s, mathematical methods made rapid progress in Soviet economics for a variety of reasons. Difficult economic conditions demanded rapid solutions to economic problems, especially in the organization of planning and finance. Under the New Economic Policy, many non-communist economists worked for the government. Some of them were quite competent in mathematics. As for the Marxists, their application of mathematical methods in planning was legitimized by Marx's schemes of reproduction. Equilibrium theory as developed by Aleksandr Bogdanov was considered compatible with Marxism at the time and provided the basis for the use of mathematical models in economics, which hitherto had been applied only in natural sciences (Belykh, 1990). Bogdanov's ideas influenced the prominent Bolshevik Nikolai Bukharin, who was the first to suggest a mathematical formalization of Marx's schemes of "expanded reproduction." As Leon Smolinski noted:

> the rise of mathematical economics during the NEP period can be interpreted as a response to the challenge posed by the emergence of the Soviet economy during the years of War Communism. When their Western colleagues were still largely preoccupied with the finer points of marginal utility theory, . . . Soviet mathematical economists were opening up new frontiers in economic research. (Smolinski 1971, 140)

These new frontiers included the planning of national economy, the theory of inflation, and the problems of economic growth. The most attention was given to problems of planning: first to economic balances and later to the problems of economic growth.

Discussions on the methodology of planning began in 1920. It was understandable that War Communism, with its administrative allocation of resources and high inflation, led to planning techniques that used physical indicators. As a result, a major contribution to economic science was made. In January 1921, Bogdanov delivered a presentation at a conference on "scientific organization of labor and production," in which he advocated an authentic system of planning. It relied on the idea of chain links between branches/sectors of the economy. The existence of such links, including feedback links, determined certain proportions in the economy. Any possible increase in the output of a particular good would be dependent upon the input factor in scarcest supply. Bogdanov named this rule "the law of the minimum" (Bogdanov 1921a).

The starting point of Bogdanov's planning methodology was a calculation of the ultimate needs of the population. To cater for these needs, consumer goods had to be produced, which entailed the utilization of producer goods. In turn, the production of producer goods entailed the production of other producer goods. The elaboration of the plan was conceived as an iterative process. Bogdanov did not use the terms "technological" or "input-output" coefficients, but he did make it clear that for the output of any given product, inputs of other products have to be imputed. This was an important contribution to what later became known as input-output analysis.

Adopting the same approach, Lev Kritsman published several articles on the methodology of planning in *Ekonomicheskaia Zhizn* (Economic Life), which were later published in book form (Kritsman 1921b). Kritsman developed Bogdanov's iterative process further, adapting it to the real economy and dividing goods into three groups: those produced in the state sector, those purchased in the private sector, and those purchased abroad. He defined the task of planning as "to determine the size of branches of the economy in such a way that they will be able to develop without disturbance, producing the maximum possible while utilizing existing resources" (44). Kritsman already used the term "input coefficients" *(koeffitsienty raskhodovaniia)* and emphasized that the reliability of planning depends on the reliability of these coefficients. In 1922, he proposed to use a kind of chessboard table in planning (Kritsman 1922, 24–25).

Analyzing the impact of Kritsman and Bogdanov on Soviet planning, Thomas Remington did not connect explicitly their approach to the development of input-output analysis. Nevertheless, he realized that the iterative process proposed by Bogdanov and Kritsman was "the <missing link> between the hazy visions of a national economic table of Quesnay or Marx and the innovative efforts by Vladimir Groman, Vladimir Bazarov and other *Gosplan* leaders in the 1920s to devise a <balance> method of planning" (Remington 1982, 591).[1]

Another important contribution to the development of planning theory was made by Stanislav Strumilin. In January 1921, he put forward a solution to the optimization problem. The utility function (a kind of social welfare function) was to be maximized. The quantities of labor devoted to the production of different goods were variables, and the single constraint was the total labor fund for the year. From a formal point of view, this approach did not differ greatly from Western models of consumer behavior and from the model built by Tugan-Baranovsky (1890). However, Strumilin (1921) tried to elaborate on the notion of objective social utility and to apply the concept of optimization to planning the national economy. Later, Strumilin became a prominent Soviet economist and academician. However, loyal to traditional Marxist political economy, he never reprinted this article. In the 1960s, he was rather critical of mathematical economists such as Leonid Kantorovich and Viktor Novozhilov.

Both Bogdanov and Strumilin were influenced greatly by the economic system of War Communism. Thus, prices were practically irrelevant in their schemes, and they conceived of the plan as being elaborated by a central authority and implemented by all economic units. From the very beginning, mathematical models were linked to administrative planning in their mind. Strumilin thought that his approach was irrelevant under the New Economic

Policy, but it would become instrumental when the state could directly determine all prices.

Although Lenin was acquainted with the debate on a unified (single) economic plan, he was very critical about it. In his opinion, the articles by Kritsman and other economists like Vladimir Miliutin and Iurii Larin contain empty rhetoric, a kind of theoretical reasoning that has nothing in common with reality. The only viable plan was *GOELRO*, prepared by a team of more than 180 experts who had been working on it for 10 months. This plan was calculated to last for 10 years. Lenin drew a comparison between Karl Ballod's book *State of the Future*[2] and *GOELRO* by saying that Ballod's plan remained a one man show and "was up in the air" while in Soviet Russia *GOELRO* would be fulfilled (Lenin 1970, 342–43).

It was not before War Communism failed that planning was subjected to theoretical analysis in the works of Bogdanov, Kritsman, and Strumilin. Nevertheless, these scholars continued to presume that the socialist economy should be a centrally governed organization. As a contrast, it became absolutely clear for some scholars in the early 1920s that such a model cannot be efficient. Famously, the first work substantiating the impossibility of "economic calculation in a socialist commonwealth" was a paper by Ludwig Mises (1920). In Russia a similar thesis was formulated by Boris Brutskus. In August 1920, he set forth his views in a talk to an academic audience. In 1922, he published his ideas in a series of articles in the journal *Ekonomist*. Brutskus thought that rational economic calculation is based on a universal principle of decision-making that requires commensuration of different kinds of inputs and the output. According to Brutskus, the use of natural accounting—the method advocated by Chayanov and Bukharin for this purpose—was inappropriate.

It might seem that a socialist economy gives a clear chance to organize production not "from below," by means of value accounting, but "from above," using a rational plan. However, such an approach requires production to be focused on needs. Thereby, it is necessary to be able to commensurate various needs of different individuals, which is impossible without market prices. In Brutskus's (1935, 44) words, "the weakest point of the socialist economic system lies in the efforts made by the socialist state to gather all the functions of distribution into the hands of its bureaucracy." In this connection "an economic system which possesses no mechanism for co-ordinating production with the needs of society cannot be maintained. Socialism overcomes the <anarchy of capitalist production> by substituting it for a condition of super anarchy; and in comparison with this <super anarchy> capitalism presents a picture of the utmost harmony" (49). Bureaucratization results in the lack of entrepreneurial spirit, in authoritarian distribution of commodities, in limitation of peoples' freedom, and in reducing economic efficiency. After Brutskus had published his papers, he was condemned to exile in autumn 1922.[3]

With the introduction of the New Economic Policy in 1921, requisition was replaced by tax in kind, and private trade was allowed. Alongside the remaining state property of the main companies, private entrepreneurs appeared in industry, too. In the language of our chapter that meant the emergence of Model 4. The NEP brought quick results in terms of economic recovery. Further economic development became one of the central issues of planning. The first planning body to emerge was the Commission for Electrification founded in February 1920. The *GOELRO* plan was ready by the end of the same year and approved at the Eighth Congress of Soviets held in December. In February 1921, the General Planning Commission (*Gosplan*) was established with the purpose "to work out a unified state economic plan on the basis of the electrification plan . . . and to exercise general control over its implementation" (*Polozhenie* 1944). *Gosplan* was headed by Gleb Krzhizhanovskii, the former chief of the *GOELRO* Commission.

A new journal *Planovoe Khoziaistvo* (Planned Economy) was launched in 1924. During the 1920s, it was open to a free exchange of views and published many important articles on mathematical economics. A top priority of the journal was working out the methodology of planning, which would enable experts to draw up real plans and to implement them. Krzhizhanovskii developed the idea of a system of plans: a one-year plan, a five-year plan, and a general (ten-to fifteen-year) plan.

The first economist to discuss the methodology of perspective planning in detail was Bazarov. He suggested a genetic approach based on the extrapolation of existing trends and a teleological approach relying on target tasks formulated by the central planning body (Bazarov 1924). The genetic approach was contingent on the use of a complex mathematical apparatus, constructing curves that describe the dynamics of economic indicators and extrapolating them. Moreover, this approach also implied that the economy is in equilibrium state. In fact, these two approaches determined two basic lines of economic policy, namely, central planning focused on achieving predetermined target tasks and flexible planning that takes into account the actual trends of the economy. According to the common view of the time, the body responsible for teleological approach was *Gosplan*, whereas the genetic approach was represented by the People's Commissariat of Finance (*Narkomfin*), Iurovskii being one of its leading figures. True, initially, *Gosplan* (with Groman and Bazarov still working there) adhered mostly to the genetic approach.

An outstanding role in shaping the policy of *Narkomfin* was assigned to the Conjuncture Institute (*Koniunkturnyi Institut*) founded within *Narkomfin* and headed by Kondratiev. His ideas on planning were developed in his fundamental paper "Plan and Forecast." This paper warned against drawing up detailed perspective plans with a great number of figures or plans that were not based on economic analysis. He wrote: "We are not strongly against the quantitative expression of perspectives in perspective plans" (Kondratiev 1989, 127). However, Kondratiev was absolutely sure that "the core of perspective plans is not in detailed numerical calculations but in determining and substantiating the most important probable and preferable trends in the development of national economy" (132). Kondratiev's attitude towards numerical calculations in perspective plans can be described best by the title of a famous article by Lenin: "Better Fewer, But Better."

An active advocate of the genetic approach in *Gosplan* was Groman, who put forward the idea of dynamic coefficients. A passionate supporter of equilibrium state in the economy, Groman thought that this state could be described by means of a system of statistical coefficients over time. In his opinion, the postwar recovery of the national economy resulted in a return to prewar ratios expressing equilibrium conditions (Groman 1925, no. 1, 98). Among the best-known coefficients were the shares of agriculture and industry in gross production. Prewar figures amounted to 37 and 63 percent, respectively. This ratio was suggested to be used as a reference point of planning in a document that was to become a prototype of central plans, the so-called "Control Figures of the National Economy for 1925–1926" (*Kontrolnye Tsifry*). The methodological part of the work on these figures was done by Bazarov, Groman, and Strumilin.

An alternative to market equilibrium was a system of real prices that caused severe imbalances in the Soviet economy. This problem was analyzed in Novozhilov's (1926) article "Deficit of Goods." As far as we know, this was the first paper in which he applied mathematical calculations to support his conclusions. His main idea was the following: if goods are not sold at their cost value, then "the more production expands, the stronger goods' famine (*tovarnyi golod*) is" (Novozhilov 1972, 58). To illustrate it, Novozhilov built a simple model, in which one consumer good is produced from one raw material. As a practical measure against shortage, he advised raising prices to restore market equilibrium.

Since the socialist economy was considered to be organized efficiently as well as centrally planned, it was natural that ideas on optimal planning emerged. An important contribution to the theory of optimization was made by the prominent economist Bazarov. In his view, there were three basic requirements for any optimal economic plan:

> First, the progress of national economy from its present state to the target indicated in the General Plan must be smooth. . . . Second, the economy must be conceived of as a harmonious, organic whole, a system of mobile equilibrium,

which is as stable as possible. . . . The third precondition of optimality is that the path chosen as leading to the goal projected in the General Plan should be the shortest possible. (Bazarov 1926, 10)

The idea that one of the criteria for optimization should be the minimum time necessary for reaching the final goal was quite reasonable. However, during the 1920s neither Bazarov nor any other Russian economist was able to develop a formal optimization model for such an approach. There were at least two reasons for this. First, mathematical tools to describe the optimal functioning of the economy were not yet available. Second, the task of defining a target that the economy should reach in ten to fifteen years was too complicated.

Better practical results were achieved in the construction of economic balances. As mentioned, the reproduction schemes of Marx served as the starting point for the inventors of the Control Figures of the Central Statistical Board, Pavel Popov, Lev Litoshenko, and others. In 1926, the Board published the Balance of the National Economy of the USSR (Popov 1926). The first versions of this balance came out in 1925, and this work was positively reviewed by Wassily Leontief who had just graduated from Leningrad State University. Leontief wrote:

What is essentially new in this balance when it is compared with the usual economic investigations such as the American and English censuses, is the attempt to embrace in figures not only the output but also the distribution of the national product, so as to obtain in this way a comprehensive picture of the whole process of reproduction in the form of a kind of *Tableau Économique*. (Leontief 1925, 254)

This balance contained the "chessboard" tables for the first time.

A further step was taken by Moisei Barengolts, who in 1928 created a chessboard table for twelve branches of the economy of the USSR. Barengolts also discussed the idea of technological coefficients and argued that, in the absence of technological and price changes, these coefficients could be considered as stable. In his opinion, such coefficients would help explain the links between the various branches of economy (Barengolts 1928, 329). The history of input-output analysis in Russia has been analyzed by several authors (Treml 1967; Clark 1984; Belykh 1989; 2007). It is still unknown to what extent Leontief was familiar with the Russian works mentioned above and whether or not they influenced the formation of his own theory.[4]

Calculations of balances per se could not lay the foundations for annual plans. These were called Control Figures to express the intention to control economic processes rather than planning them. An alternative to the genetic approach was the teleological one. According to the latter, it is necessary to set target tasks, describe possible scenarios of economic development, and also to formulate the rule of choosing the best scenario that should be centrally announced to include the target tasks. The teleological approach played an important role when preparing the First Five-Year Plan. Strumilin took an active part in this work. In his view, the main task of the plan was "the redistribution of existing productive forces of society, which would enable it to expand reproduction at a maximum rate possible, optimally and without any crisis, with the aim of maximum satisfaction of current needs of working people and the quickest progress on the way of reconstructing society" (Strumilin 1927, 17).

At this time, the drawing-up of perspective plans was already well underway. In April 1926, a five-year plan commission had been set up in *Gosplan,* but it did not have a monopoly to formulate such plans. These were prepared by the Supreme Soviet of the National Economy (*VSNKh*), people's commissariats, and various republican and local planning bodies. In his report to the Fifteenth Party Congress in 1928, Krzhizhanovskii informed the participants that 50 drafts of five-year plans had been made by that time. Debates about different variants of *Gosplan*'s and *VSNKh*'s plans continued from 1927 to 1929. Meanwhile, the target tasks of the plan were permanently raised. It was only in March 1929 that the First Five-Year Plan for 1928–1932 was approved by the Presidium of *Gosplan*. It was adopted in two versions, initial and optimal, by the Fifth Congress of Soviets in May. The plan covered the period 1928–1933, which meant that, in fact, it was endorsed much later than its official starting date.

The establishment of the planning system in the USSR and the introduction of five-year plans raised questions about long-term planning and the rates of economic growth. In 1928, Grigorii Feldman put forward his own model of economic growth—another pioneering contribution to mathematical economics. His model was used for calculating the general plan of the national economy for a period of fifteen years. Feldman was convinced that "it is impossible to imagine that a phenomenon as complicated as the national economy could be planned by a simple method" and that "perfect planning can be implemented only on the basis of mathematical theory" (Feldman 1928, no. 12, 177–78). He modified the Marxian theory of reproduction and divided the economy into two parts: one, in which "simple reproduction" took place, and another which provided the means for "expanded reproduction." Evsey Domar, who was the first in the West to draw attention to Feldman, interpreted this binary distinction along Marxian lines as a reference, on the one hand, to the production of the means of production and, on the other, to the production of consumer goods.[5]

Feldman's model was used by the Commission for the Preparation of the General Plan, which was headed by Nikolai Kovalevskii (1928; 1930). At the discussions of the plan the majority of participants were not against using mathematical models in planning and made useful critical remarks and suggestions. It seemed that the Commission could continue its work to develop the plan. However, that was not to be.

During the 1920s, mathematical economics was a fast-developing branch of Soviet economic thought. Its impact on concepts of planning was fairly significant. This healthy development was interrupted abruptly (Erlich 1960). Difficulties with grain procurement in 1928 served as the economic justification for radical changes in economic policy and the revival of War Communist methods. The political defeat of the so-called "right deviation" headed by Bukharin had important consequences for Soviet economic science. In his speech to a conference of Agrarian Marxists in 1929, Stalin denounced equilibrium theory as anti-Marxist. He called for "the development of reproduction theory and the balance of the national economy" because "what the Central Statistical Board published in 1926 as a balance sheet of the national economy is not a balance sheet, but a juggling with numbers. Nor is the manner, in which Bazarov and Groman treat the problem of the balance sheet of the national economy suitable" (Stalin 1929). Soon afterwards, both Groman and Bazarov, together with Chayanov, Kondratiev, Litoshenko, Iurovskii, and many other gifted economists were arrested under the false pretext of being members of counter-revolutionary organizations—the *Prompartiia* (Party of Industrialists), the Menshevik Bureau, or the *Trudovaia Krestianskaia Partiia* (Working Peasants Party).[6]

At the show trials of these organizations many of the defendants, including those who worked for *Gosplan*, were accused of wrecking and sabotage, attempts to intercept the process of industrialization, and support of foreign intervention. In 1930, many *Gosplan* employees were arrested. In fact, 1930 marked the turning point in the evolution of economics in the Soviet Union because the most prominent scholars were repressed. The number of economic journals was reduced drastically, the volume of scientific publications decreased, and their quality deteriorated. As Gregory Grossman (1953, 316) rightly put it, "economic literature disappeared with the economists themselves."[7] As early as 1928, the Conjuncture Institute was separated from *Narkomfin* and attached to *TsSU* (Central Statistical Board). The prominent scholar, former head of *TsSU* Pavel Popov was appointed the head of the institute. Having lost its previous status, the institute could not attain a high level of scientific research. In 1930, *TsSU*, a relatively independent agency, was transformed into the Department for Accounting of *Gosplan*,[8] and the Conjuncture Institute was closed.

STALIN'S ADMINISTRATIVE SYSTEM, 1930–1953

In the early 1930s, the basic economic law of socialism was deemed to be the dictatorship of proletariat. Prices were considered a political rather than an economic matter. Theories of the optimal size of industrial and agriculture enterprises were despised as "bourgeois." The intensive search for "wreckers and saboteurs" greatly damaged the planning organizations. The application of mathematical methods in economics was condemned as "formalism," and later as "idealism." Finally, these methods were called "anti-Marxist." As early as 1931, Kuibyshev (1937, 78), who was head of *Gosplan* from 1930 to 1934, discovered a "statistical-arithmetical deviation" in planning.

Under these new conditions, the leaders of the party-state felt no need for economic discussions or even for correct economic statistics. While mathematical economists had advocated balanced growth and tried to identify the real limitations of the economy, politicians were inclined to use revolutionary methods in planning, too.[9] As a consequence, from 1931 until Stalin's death in 1953, the use of mathematics was practically banned in Soviet economic thought, alleging that it was non-Marxist (at best). In 1933, two important publications—part of Marx's (1933) "Mathematical Manuscripts" and the recollections of Paul Lafargue (1933) on Marx—appeared that may have influenced some economists and politicians. Lafargue quoted Marx: "science becomes mature only after it has reached the point where it can make use of mathematics" (8). However, these books had little impact.

After a number of "bourgeois" economists who frequently used mathematical methods had been purged in 1929–1930 (Jasny 1972), in the mid-1930s, it was the turn of the Marxists. Strumilin was criticized severely and lost his important position in *Gosplan*. Feldman was arrested in 1937 and freed only in 1953. In 1936, the trial of "Trotsky's center" was held, which sentenced former People's Commissar of Finance Grigorii Sokolnikov to imprisonment for ten years. He was murdered in prison. In 1938, Bukharin was put on trial and killed. In 1937–1938 Chayanov, Kondratiev, and Iurovskii were condemned again and executed.

In fact, mathematical analysis of the economy was banned. Still, economists continued working in this field, and, for example, Kondratiev managed to carry out his investigations even from prison. He planned to write a serious book devoted to the dynamic of economic development. He built a model of differential equations for 10 variables and noted that the results obtained were "wonderful." In his opinion, constructing and solving the equations was "a real discovery that makes it possible to construct a new important sector of theoretical economics" (Kondratiev 1993, 632). He tested his formulas on real data of the economies of Great Britain and the United States. This test allowed him to draw the conclusion that, provided some variables are known, his model can forecast changes in other variables. Unfortunately, Kondratiev could not complete his book, and the larger part of the manuscript was lost.

After the *TsSU* balances were criticized fiercely by Stalin, the compilation of consolidated balance sheets of the national economy was stopped. Yet, it was practically impossible to develop balances in planning without using the notion of equilibrium even if it was associated with "the people's enemy" Bogdanov and Bukharin. In the 1930s, the only related—detailed and published—documents were the following: "Materials on the Balance of National Economy for 1928, 1929 and 1930," "Materials on the Balance of National Economy for 1935" and the similar collections for 1937 and 1938 were concise and classified. This made it easy for the government to declare great successes in fulfilling the plans. The First Five-Year Plan was to last from October 1, 1928 to October 1, 1933.[10] In January 1933, the Central Committee announced that it was implemented by the end of 1932. Later researchers demonstrated that it was not the case (Jasny, 1972).

The Second Five-Year Plan was drawn up for the period 1933–1937. Again, it was adopted with nearly a year's delay at the beginning of 1934. It was marked by some mitigation of economic policy and more realistic planning. *Gosplan*'s experts tried to work out more balanced plans. This tendency was reinforced when Nikolai Voznesenskii started working at *Gosplan*. After his predecessors Valerii Mezhlauk and Gennadii Smirnov had been arrested, Voznesenskii was appointed head of the institution in January 1938. He introduced several important innovations: procedures for checking plan fulfilment, organizing a network of local agents of the central plan, planning labor recruitment for industry, using material and equipment balances, making attempts at long-term planning, and so on (Harrison 2002, 21–23). Furthermore, in February 1938, a financial department was set up in *Gosplan* following the instruction of Voznesenskii.

Paradoxically, it was during this period that the foundations of what became known as the theory of optimal planning were laid. In 1938–1939, starting with the study of the so-called "Plywood Trust problem," Leonid Kantorovich, then a young mathematician at Leningrad University, discovered linear programming. While this problem seemed to pertain to the field of microeconomics, its economic implications made programming extremely important for general macroeconomics and planning. Kantorovich formulated the problem as follows: let there be eight different peeling machines and five different types of wood to be peeled. How could one determine the use of machines that would maximize wood production in specific fixed proportions? Kantorovich discovered that this problem is only one example of a whole bundle of mathematical problems, namely, that of arriving at an optimum of a linear function with linear constraints. For such a problem the optimal solution is on the boundary of the possibility set. Therefore, the classical approach of Lagrangian multipliers was not applicable. Kantorovich invented his own method. Each constraint has a corresponding variable that he called a "resolving multiplier."

He published these results in 1939 (Kantorovich 1939). In addition to the Plywood Trust problem, he analyzed a large number of other economic problems and provided analytical and geometrical proofs for the resolving multipliers method. The geometrical proof showed that resolving multipliers determine a hyperplane separating two convex sets determined by the conditions of the optimization problem. Kantorovich (1940) proved that, for the problem of minimizing a convex objective function with a compact feasibility set, the criterion for the optimal solution is the existence of a linear function passing through the optimal solution and having the same value as the objective function. In modern terms, this linear function determines the optimal plan of the dual problem.

Already at that time Kantorovich understood that an optimal plan is inseparable from prices. "It is somewhat ironic that at practically the same time that the great debate over the feasibility of socialism was taking place between Oskar Lange and Friedrich Hayek in England, a Russian unknown to them had proved the mathematical existence of planned socialist prices" (Gardner 1990, 644). We may add that, obviously, in the 1930s and 1940s, Kantorovich as well as other Soviet economists were not aware of the Socialist Calculation Debate (Hayek 1935; Lange and Taylor 1938).

In 1941, Kantorovich was drafted as a major and sent to Iaroslavl, where he was involved with military research at the navy school. In 1942, he completed the first version of his book on the efficient use of economic resources. Kantorovich sent its synopsis to *Gosplan* but the reply was negative. Then, he prepared a concise version of the book and forwarded it to Voznesenskii in person.[11] In this work he proved that his estimations were more accurate value indices than those produced by *Gosplan* and suggested that they should be used as prices. These materials were passed over to the head of *TsSU*, Vladimir Starovskii, whose review again turned out to be negative.

Kantorovich delivered lectures on this work in a number of institutions but did not find sufficient support. During a discussion in 1943, a professor of statistics, Boris Iastremskii, commented as follows: "Kantorovich suggests the optimum, and who else suggests the optimum? The fascist Pareto, Mussolini's favorite" (Kantorovich 2002, 60). In his memoirs, Kantorovich writes that, in view of such attitudes, he tried to avoid using the term "economic" to describe a problem and referred instead to a problem of the "organization of production." Also, he could not openly discuss the implications of resolving multipliers (55). Working on optimal planning became dangerous, and he abandoned economic research. After the war, Kantorovich was engaged in mathematical work for the Soviet nuclear program, which in 1949, brought him the Stalin Prize and enabled him to return to economics and publish some of his earlier works.

Kantorovich's ideas influenced Novozhilov, who wrote an important article in 1943 (published in 1946) in which he outlined a new procedure for planning. The elaboration of the plan was regarded as a solution to an optimization problem, in which the total sum of labor inputs is to be minimized, with constraints on the quantity of available capital goods to be allocated to different investment projects. In his procedure, the so-called norms of "inversely related expenditures of labor" (*zatraty obratnoi sviazi*) played a crucial role. Using what was in fact Kantorovich's method of resolving multipliers, Novozhilov (1946) showed that the optimal solution to his problem is attained if, for each final product, an investment project is adopted, which has the lowest sum of actual labor costs and amount of other inputs multiplied by their norms of inversely related expenditures. Gregory Grossman (1953, 330) has pointed out that "these norms are, of course, actually the interest rate on capital and the scarcity rents of physical resources" and that Novozhilov's concept was close to the idea of opportunity costs.

Novozhilov's problem of plan determination was actually a mixed-integer linear problem but this was not presented explicitly. Thus, his recourse to the method of linear programming and his use of shadow prices were, strictly speaking, not correct. Also, and this is more important, his new approach to planning logically leads to the reevaluation of the whole economic mechanism. Opportunity costs must be included in prices, cost accounting must be introduced as their basis, and planning procedures must be changed. Moreover, the labor theory of value has to be reappraised.

Grossman thought that Novozhilov's solution was similar to the general equilibrium systems of Léon Walras and Enrico Barone, which Novozhilov himself denied. It would be interesting to know whether their works were familiar to him. Being an educated economist who had graduated from Kiev University before 1917, Novozhilov might well know of the work of Walras (most probably, he had not read Barone). It seems, however, that his theory was much more affected by the practice of Soviet planning, with its iterative procedures of attaining balances of physical products, and distribution of limited resources. Novozhilov's theory was not accepted at that time. He was heavily criticized and fired from Leningrad Polytechnic Institute.

Another important event of this period was the appeal of Vasilii Nemchinov in 1946 for the creation of Soviet econometrics that he interpreted as a theory of mathematical calculations in planning (Nemchinov 1967, 182). At that time, this was rejected as a "bourgeois" idea, a Western invention. Nemchinov, who was president of the Academy of Agricultural Sciences, was fired in 1948 after having attempted to protect genetics from the onslaught of Trofim Lysenko. Nemchinov was accused of "idealism," the evidence for which, allegedly, was his adherence to the formalist, "bourgeois" methodology of using mathematics in biology and economics (*O teoreticheskoi rabote* 1948, 79, 80–82). Mathematical economists were criticized ferociously, and their careers were ruined. Nonetheless, they were fortunate if they were not arrested or killed.

In 1949 many party and state leaders were repressed in Leningrad. By this time Voznesenskii had already been a member of the Politburo. In 1947 he published his book *War Economy of the USSR in the Years of the Patriotic War* (Voznesenskii 1979), which was awarded the Stalin Prize of first degree in 1948. However, in 1949, he was regarded as a member of the "Leningrad group," and a criminal case had been fabricated against *Gosplan*. Its officials were accused of setting too low plans for industrial development and losing classified documents. As a result, in March 1949 Voznesenskii was removed from *Gosplan* and withdrawn from the Politburo. In October 1949, he was arrested and, a year after, executed. During the purges in *Gosplan*, more than 10 percent of the 1,400 employees were dismissed or transferred to another job (Gorlitskii and Khlevniuk 2011, 301).

It was at this time that information leaked out about the United States having produced its first computer. This accelerated attempts to build a computer, attempts that had already been made in the Soviet Union before the war. In 1951, a team under the leadership of Sergei Lebedev constructed a computer—the first one in the USSR and continental Europe. In 1952, computers M-1 and M-2, designed by the team of Isaak Bruk, started working (Pospelov and Fet 1998, 10). Although computers originally were used for military purposes, they paved the way for a broader application of mathematical methods to economic calculations.

ATTEMPTS TO REFORM THE SYSTEM, 1954–1985

It was only after the death of Stalin that real changes began in economic research. In 1954, the first Soviet textbook of political economy was published, which, among other things, recognized the law of value under socialism. Cybernetics, which had been denounced as "bourgeois" science, was rehabilitated (Gerovitch 2002). Of considerable importance was the fact that research in the field of cybernetics, computers, and programming was carried out mostly by the army. All books on these issues published in the late 1950s were written by military scientists (Pospelov and Fet 1998, 10). One of the main organizers of research in the field of cybernetics, Aksel Berg, was deputy minister of defense.[12] In 1954, Kantorovich (1954) wrote a paper with a telling title "The Importance of Modern Computers for Human Culture," but it had to wait for publication for 50 years.

When, after the Twentieth Congress, partial de-Stalinization continued, economic theorists got some fresh air. The first experiments with the calculation of input-output tables already had begun in 1957, and Kantorovich (1957) was able to publish his optimization model for macro-planning. In 1958, Anatolii Kitov (1958, 23–24) advocated the extensive use of computers in planning and proposed the organization of an all-union system of computing centers processing economic information and performing all necessary calculations.

De-Stalinization also meant that it became permissible to translate and publish books by Western scholars. This played an important role in the development of mathematical economics in the USSR. In the late 1950s, several famous works came out in the Russian language such as *Cybernetics* by Norbert Wiener (1958), *Studies in the Structure of the American Economy* by Wassily Leontief et al (1958), and *An Introduction to Cybernetics* by W. Ross Ashby (1959). Another evidence of changes was Leontief's visit to the USSR in 1959. He delivered a lecture to the students of the Institute of World Economy and International Relations of the Soviet Academy of Sciences and also met with scholars and experts from *Gosplan* and *TsSU*.[13]

In 1957, the Laboratory of Mathematical Methods in Economics (*Laboratoriia ekonomiko-matematicheskikh metodov*) was organized and headed by Nemchinov at the Soviet Academy of Sciences. This laboratory became the center of input-output studies, and in 1958–1959 it prepared several regional input-output balances. As a result, the Central Statistical Board launched the preparation of an input-output balance of the national economy. Kantorovich and Novozhilov played a major part in this revival of Soviet mathematical economics.

The years 1959–1960 were of crucial importance. In 1959, Kantorovich was allowed to publish his book *Economic Calculation of the Best Use of Resources* (Kantorovich 1959)[14] that was based on his 1942 manuscript. Nemchinov (1959) also edited the first collective volume of the series *The Use of Mathematics in Economic Research*. In this volume Kantorovich's work of 1939 was republished, and Novozhilov's (1959) major article "Measurement of Costs and Results in a Socialist Economy" (*Izmerenie zatrat i rezultatov v sotsialisticheskom khoziaistve*)[15] was included. In April 1960, an all-union conference on "The Application of Mathematical Methods in Economics" was organized by Nemchinov. The materials of the conference were published in six volumes. This conference laid the organizational foundations and completed the official recognition of this new branch of Soviet economic science.

The conclusion of Alfred Zauberman in his study on the books of Kantorovich (1959) and Nemchinov (1959) is quite typical of the time: "The extent to which mathematical tools and techniques may add to efficiency in Soviet economic planning and control can and will be only empirically established. . . . The two books discussed have especially affected the tone of economic thought and put it at an important theoretical and doctrinal crossroads. Where will it go from here?" (Zauberman 1960, 12). It was clear that the new approach of mathematical economists was capable not only of improving a number of planning techniques on micro and macro levels but was a challenge to ideological and political standards. In his review of Kantorovich's book, Robert Campbell (1960, 731) stated that "the book is a testimony to the proposition that the problem of economic theory is to show how to maximize output from scarce resources, and this portion of its message alone will mean a revolution in Soviet economic thinking."

The situation was changing indeed. In October 1959, a computing center was established within *Gosplan*. The order was signed by Aleksei Kosygin, then deputy head of *Gosplan*. In the beginning, the center (in 1963, it was renamed Main Computing Center of *Gosplan*) employed 60 persons. *Gosplan* started preparing balances of the national economy, using input-output models. In 1962, at its Twenty-second Congress, the party adopted a new program that envisaged communism to be built in 20 years. This period would witness the development of "cybernetics, computers, which should be used in planning and management" (XXII Congress 1962, 280).

However, at the beginning of the 1960s, the level of mathematical culture of economists was rather low. On the initiative of Kantorovich, a so-called "sixth year" of studies was organized at the Department of Economics of Leningrad State University (Dmitriev 2006). After five years of education, the best 25 students continued their studies for an extra year. Then, this number was increased by 13 (i.e., 11 students from Russia and two from Czechoslovakia[16]). For these students, several lecture courses were held by Kantorovich. Among the students of this year were Aleksandr Anchishkin and Stanislav Shatalin, who later became members of the Academy of Sciences. Education in mathematical economics was also introduced at Lomonosov University in Moscow.

In May 1963, the Central Committee and the Council of Ministers issued a resolution "On Improving the Management of Computers and Automated Systems Employed in the National Economy." This included several decisions aimed at accelerating the production of computers and enhancing their use. It stated that the application of computers in planning was limited by the absence of "sufficiently developed mathematical methods." The Central Economics and Mathematics Institute (*Tsentralnyi Ekonomiko-Matematicheskii Institut, TsEMI*) of the Soviet Academy of Sciences was founded in accordance with the resolution. In 1965, *TsEMI* began publishing a new journal *Ekonomika i matematicheskie metody* (Economics and Mathematical Methods[17]). In 1965, Kantorovich, Nemchinov, and Novozhilov were awarded the Lenin Prize— "for developing linear programming and economic models." This was the most prestigious award available to a scientist in the USSR, and it signaled the official approval of mathematical economics by the Soviet authorities. In 1975, Kantorovich received the Nobel Prize in economics.[18] However, there still remained a substantial distance between the formal recognition and actual implementation of mathematical methods in the economy as a whole and in planning in particular.

There were a variety of reasons—scientific, technical, administrative, and political—for the rather complicated relations between planners and mathematical economists. These reasons were studied primarily in the Western literature (Hardt et al. 1967; Ellman 1973). From a theoretical point of view, linear models, balances, and input-output analysis faced practically no opposition. Nemchinov's analysis of the work of Dmitriev cunningly had ascribed Russian origins to these techniques. Marx's writings on reproduction also conferred legitimacy. Finally, Leontief himself was not particularly critical of the Soviet system. For these reasons, the work of *Gosplan* on input-output tables made good progress.

Optimization was a different matter. Optimal planners tried to introduce new categories into economics and propose new planning techniques. Of great importance was Kantorovich's "objectively determined valuations" (*ODV*s) and Novozhilov's "differential costs." These indices were to be obtained from the calculation of the optimal variant of the plan. They were connected with each scarce resource and basically coincided with the optimal solution of the dual problem. According to Kantorovich and Novozhilov, these indices should play a major role in the process of price determination and planning. In the West their approach was interpreted as a "search for a new theory of value," and with good reason (Campbell 1961, 403). This was indeed an attempt to reformulate the labor theory of value in modern terms.

Kantorovich and Novozhilov were accused by conservative critics of a departure from Marxism and an adherence to the concepts of Western economics. This criticism had occurred already in the 1940s. Kantorovich and Novozhilov argued that their concepts were quite compatible with Marxism and that they were developing the labor theory of value. They also tried to distance themselves from the Western mainstream. There is no doubt that such a position was the only possible way of defense at the time. However, it is difficult to judge in retrospect whether the two scholars were absolutely sincere.

The main features of optimal planning were summarized by Kantorovich as follows:

> it will consist in the simultaneous drawing up of the outlines of a plan and of economic indicators (*ODVs*): it will be calculated for implementation at various levels; it will proceed by consecutive stages, by gradual implementation and by coordination of short-term with long-term planning; it will furnish planning solutions of a flexible rather than a final character. These should be adjusted in the process of plan fulfillment and supported by economic accounting and a system of incentives. (Kantorovich 1965, 146–47)

The idea of the indivisibility of plan and prices was advocated frequently by Kantorovich. Of course, these prices were to differ from the existing system of prices. They should include payments for scarce resources and, in fact, should reflect market factors—demand and supply—in some way.

Such an approach was strongly opposed by conservative political economists who exerted influence on *Gosplan*. Articles expressing a skeptical attitude toward optimal planning frequently appeared in *Planovoe Khoziaistvo*. Further to the fact that optimal models were deemed to be non-Marxist and similar to Western market models, they were also criticized for being incompatible with the real economy and with the practical issues of pricing and planning. Yet, the models Kantorovich proposed were of a technical-economic nature and did not exhibit market relations. Unsurprisingly, after his discussion of the mechanism of planning and the process of gradually increasing the accuracy of *ODVs*, Kantorovich insisted that—while his approach was "outwardly reminiscent of the process of competition in the capitalist world"—in reality "one differs radically from the other." Under his scheme "the problem, instead of the actual competition on the market, is one of competition among plans and methods in the process of planning calculations" (Kantorovich 1965, 150). Thus, there is no real market and no real prices, but only evaluations, used in the process of formulating the plan. Apparently, at that time, Kantorovich was unacquainted with the Socialist Calculation Debate. Nevertheless, unintentionally, his work elaborated on Lange's arguments against Mises and Hayek. Later, Kantorovich explicitly expressed his belief that the *ODV* concept undermined their thesis regarding the inefficiency of the socialist economy (Gaetano 1984, 79).

Novozhilov took a similar approach. The market did not feature in his concept of planning either. In the models of both Kantorovich and Novozhilov there was a single objective function and no market. Thus, prices were needed for the implementation rather than the preparation of the plan. At the same time, the idea that the optimal plan could not be separated from a rational price system was crucial. Both scholars argued for indirect centralization, and appealed for the use of economic regulation of prices and for cost accounting. At the same time, their models targeting the determination of the optimal plan portrayed a fully centralized system.

Thus, in fact, their models described an economic system corresponding to Model 2 suggested above, that is, a centralized economy with value indicators. However, in the authors' view, their ideas were to promote more those economies whose governance was centralized and had relatively independent enterprises using the prices of the optimal plan. According to our classification, this would correspond to Model 4, namely, a mixed economy with value parameters (prices).

This inconsistency gave rise to opposing interpretations with serious implications. The criticism by Kantorovich and Novozhilov of the existing economic mechanism could be used as an argument in favor of a kind of economic reform that would provide more decentralization, a greater role of the market in the allocation of resources, and rational prices. However, an alternative interpretation envisaged development in quite the opposite direction, whereby the construction of the optimal plan would be concentrated in a single center and based on the processing of huge amounts of information relating to all economic units. The basic task of these units would then boil down to a straightforward implementation of the optimal plan as defined by the center.

Kantorovich and Novozhilov themselves were more inclined to interpret their models along reformist lines. In this regard, Nemchinov's late works are quite important since they deal with the problems of economic reform. His core idea was the transition from directive to flexible planning. The latter should be based on state orders to enterprises, whose implementation should be stimulated economically rather than ordered administratively. Nemchinov, who died in 1964, considered the use of mathematical methods an indispensable part of any planning process. An important proposition of mathematical economists at that time was the introduction of payment for the use of natural resources and means of production.

By and large, Soviet economists could be classified in the following way:

Group 1: traditional (verbal) economists with conservative views
Group 2: mathematical economists with conservative views
Group 3: traditional (verbal) economists with reformist views
Group 4: mathematical economists with reformist views

Traditional economists were (official) political economists adhering to Marxist concepts as formulated in the USSR. But there were also progressive-thinking scholars among them who acknowledged the necessity of market reforms. Undoubtedly, Kantorovich, Nemchinov, and Novozhilov, as well as the larger part of mathematical economists, belonged to Group 4. Meanwhile, some traditional theorists (e.g., the reputable economist Yakov Kronrod) sharply criticized mathematical approaches but supported the idea of reforming the Soviet economy. They formed Group 3.

After Aleksei Kosygin became prime minister in 1964, a group of economists prepared an economic reform project in one year. According to Nikolai Baibakov (2012, 123), the head of *Gosplan* from 1965 to 1985, Kosygin considered mathematical methods and computers important tools to improve planning. With the so-called "Kosygin reform" of 1965, enterprises became the main economic units; the number of centrally planned indicators that applied to them was reduced from thirty-four to nine; and they could set up an incentive fund of their own. However, no real transformation of the administrative system was proposed. Although the concept of reform incorporated some of the ideas of Kantorovich, Novozhilov, and Nemchinov, it was not based on any developed mathematical model of the new economic system or the planning process. In a way, the situation resembled the mid-1920s: the economy was not influenced directly by plans calculated with the help of mathematical models. Instead, the planning system adopted certain procedures elaborated by economists adept in quantitative analysis.

The need for reform was dictated by the declining rates of growth of the Soviet economy. The main idea was to increase its efficiency. From this point of view, the period 1966–1970 has been regarded by economic historians very positively, although some of them demonstrated that the rates of economic growth continued to decline (Khanin 1991, 146). In the mid-1960s, it was expected by some experts that the use of mathematical methods and computers in planning would double the rate of economic growth (Glushkov, Dorodnitsyn, and Fedorenko 1964; Novozhilov 1972, 264). In fact, there was no breakthrough in the use of mathematical models in the planning process. Nevertheless, input-output studies flourished, numerous optimal models were created, and dynamic models were developed.

In the second half of the 1960s, the evolution of mathematical economics resulted in the concept of *SOFE* (System for Optimal Functioning of the Economy) that was invented by the scholars of *TsEMI* headed by Nikolai Fedorenko (1968; 1999). In this concept the economy was viewed as a hierarchical system, with an inherent objective function. Planning was seen as a task of optimization of the objective function under the constraints of scarce resources. Owing to the complexity of the economy, a completely centralized planning regime was thought to be impossible. The guidance of the local units was to be based on prices calculated as *ODV*s. From this general approach, several major proposals for the reform of the planning system were derived. Planning was conceived of as an iterative process, integrating plans with different time horizons. An all-union system of collecting, processing, and transmitting information was regarded as the technical basis of planning. At the top level, decisions were to be made in aggregate terms; at the lower levels disaggregation would take place for all scarce resources; *ODV*s (or shadow prices) were to be imputed; and economic accounting (*khozraschet*) was to be widely used.

After the invasion of Czechoslovakia in 1968, the idea of market reform became politically inexpedient. When the deputy head of *Gosplan* Aleksandr Bachurin suggested in 1969 that large enterprises should be allowed to manage their exports themselves, the minister of foreign trade, Nikolai Patolichev called him the "Soviet Ota Šik" and the proposal was firmly rejected (Bachurin 2000, 115). In the USSR there was a gradual shift back to a higher level of centralization in planning and regulation. Although the use of mathematical methods in planning continued to be recognized as useful, the practice of planning remained basically unaffected in the 1960s. Even input-output models were not wholly integrated in the planning procedures, owing to various informational, organizational, and institutional difficulties (Hardt et al. 1967).

At the Twenty-fourth Congress of *CPSU* in 1971, a program was adopted for the development of automated systems of management on a large scale. The task of creating an All-Union State System of Automated Management (*OGAS, Obshchegosudarstvennaia avtomatizirovannaia sistema*) was announced. One of the central parts of this system was to be the Automated System of Planning Calculations (*ASPR, Avtomatizirovannaia sistema pla-novykh raschetov*) (Cave 1980; Conyngham 1982). A main "ideologist" of *OGAS* was Viktor Glushkov, who thought that computers could calculate and help implement economic plans without the market. This position was received very favorably by many *Gosplan* officials. Glushkov and his colleagues viewed the Soviet economy as Model 2, that is, a centralized system with prices playing a technical rather than a real economic role. Although they used a quite progressive (modernist) rhetoric, they belonged to the economists of Group 2 because they argued in favor of a completely controllable administrative system relying on an all-encompassing computer network.

However, notwithstanding the approval by the party, *OGAS* was not established. Its protagonists explained its failure by the potentially high costs involved. Glushkov considered the complexity and expenditure of the *OGAS* program comparable with the Soviet nuclear and space projects. But the main reason was different. The leaders of the party-state did not think that such a system would really be necessary for the country's economic development (Revich and Malinovskii 2014, 181–86). *OGAS* could have been effective only if it had been coupled with changes to the whole economic mechanism.

There were other crucial points. Automatization of the traditional planning process does not make it more efficient. One wrong decision made within one hour is not better than the same decision made in a week. Most importantly, the hierarchical nature of the planned economy often was underestimated by the adherents of automatization. In the real world, the different economic institutions within the hierarchy had their own self-interest, so, for example, enterprises would never disclose complete information about their activities to the ministries.

During the 1970s, Soviet economic performance deteriorated further, which was reflected in a decline in the rates of growth of basic economic indicators. The authorities tried to solve the problem by increasing centralization and by modest changes in the system of management. The proposals of mathematical economists for the improvement of the economic mechanism became less and less radical. They attempted to develop a system of models for planning, in which elements of decentralization, flexible planning, concentration on long-term planning, and consideration of the stochastic nature of the economy were taken into account. This provided important mathematical tools for the description of the economy.

The systems of planning models proposed by *TsEMI* scholars were studied by Pekka Sutela (1984). He cited a number of typical *Gosplan* criticisms of *TsEMI*, in which *SOFE* was characterized as:

> an attempt to introduce a special concept of <optimal planning> in order to supplant the supposedly nonscientific, empirical planning, to unite the vulgar theory of utility with the labor theory of value, to borrow notions from bourgeois theories (marginal utility theory, the notion of market socialism and the theory of factors of production, the idea of automatic regulation of the socialist economy by <prices of the optimal plan>). (Bor and Logvinov 1975, 135)

Such criticism clearly had parallels with the controversy between proponents of administrative planning and the reformists during the 1970s and with the debates of the 1920s. Sutela followed the above quotation with the just comment: "Ironically enough, in the same issue [of *Planovoie Khoziaistvo*] there was a review by the journal's chief editor of Michael Ellman's book of 1973. Ellman was judged to be anti-Marxist and anti-Soviet for exaggerating the disagreements among Soviet economists" (Sutela 1984, 146).[19]

The System for Optimal Functioning of the Economy became the most famous concept of application of mathematical methods to planning and management of the Soviet economy. It still attracts researchers' attention (Ericson 2019). Nevertheless, even in the Central Economics and Mathematics Institute, *SOFE* was rather an umbrella for diverse research programs covering sometimes unrelated areas. Moreover, mathematical applications were carried out in other research institutes, too. In particular, the Institute of Economics and Industrial Engineering of the Siberian branch of the Soviet

Academy of Sciences contributed greatly to research in mathematical economics. This institute, headed for a long time by Abel Aganbegian, published the progressive journal *EKO*. The Economic Research Institute of *Gosplan* also conducted serious work on developing planning models and other practical applications, in particular, intersectoral balances.

In the sphere of education a certain degree of coexistence was achieved between mathematical economists and political economists. A good example were the courses at the Department of Mathematical Economics of the Faculty of Economics of Leningrad State University. Here, students were taught courses on political economy of capitalism and socialism, but there were no courses on macro-and microeconomics. However, the course "Models of the national economy"[20] was held not only for students of this department but also for those of the Department of Political Economy. Moscow State University implemented a similar combination. There, from 1970 to 1983, the head of the chair of mathematical methods in economic analysis was Shatalin.

The Economic Faculty of Moscow State University established its Mathematical Economics School in 1967. Here, students taught secondary school pupils mathematics and economics. In 1978, a similar school was established at Leningrad State University by a group of young economists, including the author of this chapter. Nevertheless, in the most popular textbook of political economy for students of economics, the description of mathematical methods in planning took less than one and a half pages out of 543 (Rumiantsev 1978, 161–63). Part of the textbook, which was devoted to price formation, presented the primal and dual problems of linear programming. Here, it was stressed that prices and dual prices have "principally different economic meaning" (308). The model of intersectoral balance was described only in one textbook for economists edited by Nikolai Tsagolov (1970, 500–502), head of the Department of Political Economy of the Economic Faculty of Moscow State University from 1957 to 1985. The books of Western scholars continued to be translated. The list of books recommended for mathematical economists included Hukukane Nikaido's *Convex Structures and Economic Theory* (1972),[21] and Michael Intriligator's *Mathematical Optimization and Economic Theory* (1975).

Parallel to theoretical discussions, the integration of mathematical methods in the practice of planning continued, though at a snail's pace. In 1977, the first stage of the Automated System of Planning Calculations *(ASPR)* was introduced, and the second stage followed suit in 1985. The results were far from satisfactory. In *ASPR* about 5,000 different tasks (*zadachi*) were accomplished, but most of them consisted of processing primary information. The system was developed for making routine work easier (*dlia oblegcheniia*) rather than for the improvement of management (*ne dlia uluchsheniia*) (Kantorovich, Albegov, and Bezrukov 1986, 50).

For the efficient use of mathematical methods, information was crucial. Existing statistical data were inadequate; it was necessary to collect new, reliable data. However, all statistical data were collected at enterprise level and then transferred via economic branches and their management structures to central bodies. Optimal plans were supposed to use resources in the "best way," therefore they were "taut" plans. Enterprises and ministries were interested only in plans that permitted them to have hidden resources—so as to be able to fulfill the plan easily. Kantorovich correctly stated that since optimal plans were taut plans, those enterprises and branches of economy, which adopted such plans, found themselves in a worse situation than traditionally operating units. Therefore, in the second stage of *ASPR* the number of tasks was reduced because the ministries stopped providing the necessary data (Kantorovich, Albegov, and Bezrukov 1986, 49).

During the 1970s, apart from introducing the Automated System of Planning Calculations, numerous other attempts were made to improve planning. It was acknowledged that the center cannot solve a variety of economic problems, especially those connected with technological progress, during one five-year period. In 1971–1972, under the leadership of Aleksandr Anchishkin, Stanislav Shatalin, and Iurii Iaremenko, the Economic Research Institute of *Gosplan* made the first attempt to work out the concept of economic development for the period between 1976 and 1990. In July 1979, the Central Committee of the party and the Council of Ministers adopted a joint proclamation "On the Improvement of Planning and Economic Measures to Increase Industrial Efficiency and Quality." This envisaged the preparation of a complex program of technological development for 20 years. It was suggested that the program be prolonged every five years and the necessary corrections be done. Such programs were compiled for the periods 1981–2000, 1986–2005 and 1991–2010.

Meanwhile, even simple optimization problems very rarely were solved in planning. The growing difficulties encountered in economic practice made the theory of optimal functioning of the economy less and less realistic. The impact of mathematical methods on planning remained marginal. This state of affairs triggered a growing criticism of mathematical economics in both Soviet and Western literature during the 1980s. Sutela (1984, 203), for example, judged *SOFE* to be a failure. This attitude coincided with that of Soviet leaders. After the death of Brezhnev in 1982, Iurii Andropov became the general secretary of the party and Konstantin Chernenko was responsible in the Politburo for ideological issues. In June 1983, Chernenko gave a speech in which he openly criticized *TsEMI*:

> Much was expected of the Institute of Sociological Studies and of the Central Economics and Mathematics Institute. . . . However, we have yet to be provided

with comprehensive, concrete investigations of social phenomena and pressing economic problems. The party organizations of these scientific institutes
should pay more attention to issues concerning the planning and management
of research. (Chernenko 1984, 575)

Obviously, economists were unable to give real solutions to the "pressing economic problems" of the Soviet Union in official publications. In this
regard, *TsEMI* was no more to blame than other economic research institutions. The real reason why the party criticized the institute was political:
TsEMI offered a rather liberal atmosphere for research, many economists
were in favor of market reforms, and a number of Jewish scholars in the
institute emigrated to Western countries. As a result of the attack, *TsEMI* was
divided into two institutes. In 1986, part of it was established as the Institute
of Economic Forecasting of the Soviet Academy of Sciences (*INP*). In 1990,
INP issued a new economic journal *Problemy Prognozirovaniia* (Problems
of Forecasting).

In our opinion, the criticism of *SOFE* was one-sided. It is true that it had
major shortcomings and contradictions, some of which were inherited from
the Kantorovich-Novozhilov paradigm. The application of the concept of
optimality to a society with different social groups that have different goals
and interests is questionable. Thus, the idea of prices as *ODV*s derived from
the optimal plan is unconvincing. Certainly, proposals for a rapid construction
of a comprehensive computer network were too optimistic. At the same time,
a successful application of mathematical methods in planning, or, indeed, of
any scientific method of management, is impossible in a command economy.
Mathematical economists should not be the first to be blamed for the stagnation of the economy and of Soviet economics.

PERESTROIKA **AND TRANSITION**
TO THE MARKET, 1985–1992

Serious political and economic changes in the Soviet Union began with
Mikhail Gorbachev's *perestroika* in 1985. At first, the economic objectives
were rather modest: improvement and acceleration. Nevertheless, changes in
the planning system were remarkable soon. In 1986, the Twelfth Five-Year
Plan adopted by the Twenty-Seventh Party Congress had a less directive
character than its predecessors. This was transparent even from its title
"Main Directions of Economic and Social Development of the USSR for the
Period 1986–1990 and Prospects for the Year 2000." In preparing the plan,
input-output models as well as forecasting methods were used.

This congress also approved the revised version of the 1961 party program. One of the targets set by the revised program was "to dramatically move forward in the automatization of production, including the transition to automatic plants and enterprises, and to systems of automated management and design. Electrification, chemicalization, robotization, computerization and biotechnologies will be implemented on a much larger scale" (*Materialy* 1986, 141–42). In the revised text the need for optimal solutions was frequently articulated.[22]

The deterioration of the performance of Soviet economy by the late 1970s and the 1980s made the need for radical economic reform evident. In 1987, the concept of such a reform was adopted by the Central Committee. The reform envisaged enterprise autonomy, the replacement of directive planning by a system of state procurement combined with a flexible investment and financial policy, the creation of a strong cooperative sector, price reform, a comprehensive use of rigorous economic accounting (including payments for all resources), joint ventures with Western companies, and progress towards the convertibility of the ruble.

In a speech given in June 1987, Gorbachev announced a "radical reconstruction" (*korennaia perestroika*) of the Soviet economy and quoted an article of Nemchinov published in the party journal *Kommunist* in 1964:

> The primitive understanding of relationships between large and small economic systems can only build an ossified and mechanical system, in which all control parameters are given ahead of time, and the entire system is structured top-down at each moment and each point. Such a . . . system will slow social and technical progress, and, under the pressure of the real forces of economic life, will sooner or later break. (Gorbachev 1987, 42)

The economic concept of radical reconstruction incorporated many ideas proposed by mathematical economists. From 1982 to 1985, ten volumes of the series *Voprosy optimalnogo planirovaniia i upravleniia sotsialisticheskoi ekonomiki* (Problems of Optimal Planning and Management of the Socialist Economy) were published. These works summarized the ideas developed in the *SOFE* framework. A review article published in *Kommunist* stressed that "several basic ideas of *SOFE* . . . correspond to modern views on the restructuring of economic science and the system of management of the economy" (Valenta et al. 1987, 121).[23] However, by 1987, this estimation was in conformity with official state policy. At that time, *SOFE* did not prove radical enough and was, consequently, unrealistic.

Meanwhile, *TsEMI* remained the most liberal academic research institute in Moscow. It was there that the meetings of the Club *Perestroika* were held. This club was organized by Leningrad economists and run by Vilen Perlamutrov, head of one of *TsEMI*'s laboratories. Meetings were held on a regular basis from March 1987 onward. The club united representatives of various democratic movements who discussed the problems of reforms. Strangely, researchers from *TsEMI* did not take an active part in these meetings.

Under *perestroika*, the ideas of mathematical economists on the improvement of planning were no longer of prime importance. Nevertheless, some mathematical economists did draft major reform projects. For example, Shatalin was one of the leaders of the group preparing the first program of market reforms named "500 Days."[24] However, reformers of the *perestroika* period were much more interested in the lessons of *NEP* and in contemporary reforms taking place in Eastern Europe.

With the dissolution of the USSR and the introduction of market economy, *Gosplan* ceased to exist in 1991. Its journal *Planned Economy* was renamed *Economist*.[25] Since Soviet-type central planning no longer exists, we can say that "the saga of mathematical economics in planning" came to an end. In a sense, the situation was the opposite of the end of the 1920s. In 1939, Slutsky wrote in his autobiography: "When capitalist society collapsed and the outlines of a planned socialist economy emerged, the basis for the problems that I was interested in as a mathematical economist disappeared" (quoted in Chetverikov 1959, 259).[26]

What is the status of mathematical economics today? Branches of mathematical economics such as input-output analysis and optimal planning have found new tasks. Input-output studies can no longer be viewed as a means of obtaining economic indicators that can then be assigned to enterprises as directive plans. Such studies now serve long-term planning of the basic proportions of the economy, the forecasting of the structure of the economy, and the analysis of current business cycles.[27] Similarly, optimization can no longer be seen as a tool for the elaboration of a detailed and comprehensive economic plan. Even so, procedures for the selection of the best variant of development should be an important part of economic policy.

The illusions of the period of "mathematical revolution" have been abandoned. However, the transition to a market economy has created new possibilities for the application of mathematical methods. Statistical publications have become more comprehensive and, hopefully, more accurate. This enhances the availability of economic data needed for mathematical models especially in forecasting. In fact, market forces, however chaotic they might seem in the short run, are more predictable than voluntary decisions made by communist leaders.

In higher education, political economy is no longer the discipline studied by economists. Today, the key textbooks used are on economics: macroeconomics, and microeconomics. In the early 1990s, these were translations of Western works; by now good Russian textbooks exist side by side their Western peers.

CONCLUSION

To sum up, we have seen that Soviet mathematical economics enjoyed a period of great creativity during the 1920s. In the Stalinist years, despite restrictions, there were further important theoretical achievements. In the post-Stalin period, mathematical economics gained acceptance in Soviet economic thought, substantially influencing general economic culture and improving economic analysis. During the Soviet era, mathematical economists experienced difficulties in making a practical contribution to Soviet planning. However, since the 1990s, their discipline has assumed a role in Russia, which does not differ greatly from that in other countries.

NOTES

1. Remington believed that "it was Kritsman who first put forward the principles of iterative balancing and material budgets as a method for the construction of a general economic plan" (1982, 599). However, Kritsman first published an article on this issue in *Ekonomicheskaia Zhizn* on February 20, 1921, and Remington referred to a later presentation of Bogdanov (1921b), made on April 4, 1921. But, in fact, this presentation was a short version of his paper delivered to the January conference mentioned above. Although Kritsman's name does not figure on the list of participants of this conference, a comparison of the texts in terms of general approach and terminology strongly suggests that Kritsman was acquainted with Bogdanov's ideas. Thus, the precedence appears to belong to Bogdanov.

2. The second edition of Karl Ballod's book, published in 1919, was translated into Russian and published in 1920.

3. He was forced to emigrate together with other Russian intellectuals (Glavatskii 2002). Chayanov, Kondratiev, and Iurovskii were also on the list of the secret police but—due to the support of governmental officials—they could remain in Russia.

4. In 1989, I sent him my paper (Belykh 1989). In his letter of December 6, 1989, he wrote back: "Thanks for sending me your interesting paper on the origin of input-output analysis. Some of what you say in it is new to me."

5. Domar (1957) considered Feldman's model to be similar to Western models of economic growth developed later. This error was reflected in the translation of Feldman's work into English. An accurate and detailed analysis of Feldman's research program was offered by Jones (1975).

6. Bogdanov had died in 1928. Undoubtedly, if he had been alive he also would have been persecuted.

7. It is worth remembering Joseph Brodsky's observation in his Nobel lecture (Brodsky 1987): "In a real tragedy, it is not the hero who perishes; it is the chorus."

8. In 1931, it was "upgraded" and became the Accounting Board of *Gosplan*. In 1941 the old name—Central Statistical Board—was returned. In 1948 the Board was separated from *Gosplan* and subordinated directly to the Council of Ministers of the USSR.

9. For example, in 1930, in several issues of the party newspaper *Leningradskaia Pravda* (February 5–9) the first page carried a section entitled "There are no bad or good plants and factories, there are bad and good managers," ignoring the objective constraints of economic development.

10. In the 1920s, the so-called "economic year" starting on October 1, did not coincide with the calendar year.

11. Kantorovich also wrote letters to Stalin and Molotov (they are available in his archives). However, it is not known whether these letters actually were sent to the addressees.

12. He was arrested in 1937 but managed to leave prison and was restored in his military rank, which was next to impossible at that time (Pospelov and Fet 1998, 551).

13. Leontief also visited the USSR in 1979 and then several times during *perestroika*. He initiated the foundation of a research center named the "Leontief Center."

14. For the English translation, see Kantorovich (1965).

15. The article was expanded to become his main book (Novozhilov 1967).

16. Juraj Fecanin and Adam Laščiak were among the first foreign students of mathematical economics in the Soviet Union.

17. The Russian word *ekonomika* means both "economics" and "economy."

18. Kantorovich is still the only person in Russia who was given such an important award. He received the Nobel Prize together with Tjalling Koopmans.

19. Sutela referred to Glagolev (1975, 132–33).

20. When the author of this chapter sat an exam for this course, he was asked two questions: one on the input-output model and another on the Arrow–Debreu theorem of the existence of equilibrium.

21. This book contained the only proof of the Kakutani fixed-point theorem available at that time in Russian.

22. The vocabulary of the program included the following terms: optimal structure of the economy, optimal ratio of consumption and investment, optimal relations between private and public interests, optimal decisions in management, and so on.

23. Valenta was a corresponding member of the Czechoslovak Academy of Sciences.

24. Another member of this group was Leonid Grigoriev, organizer of the mathematical economics school at Moscow State University.

25. Ironically, this was the name of Brutskus' journal in 1922. The title of *Kommunist* also changed: now it is named *Svobodnaia Mysl* (Free Thought).

26. Slutsky worked at the Conjuncture Institute of Kondratiev and decided to specialize in pure mathematical research. This proved to be a fortunate decision since nearly all the staff members of the Institute were repressed.

27. For more information, see, for example, Ksenofontov et al. (2018).

BIBLIOGRAPHY

Ashby, Ross W. 1959. *Vvedenie v kibernetiku*. Moscow: Inostrannaia literatura.

Baibakov, Nikolai. 2012. "Iz zapisok zampreda." In *Kosygin: Vyzov premiera*, edited by Nikolai Baibakov, Viktor Grishin, and Vadim Kirpichenko, 119–34. Moscow: Algoritm.

Bachurin, Aleksandr. 2000. "Reforma A.N. Kosygina i ee preodolenie komandno-administrativnoi sistemoi." In *Planovaia Sistema v retrospektive*, edited by Iurii Olsevich and Paul Gregory, 108–119. Moscow: MGU, TEIS.

Ballod, C. 1919. *Der Zukunftsstaat: Produktion und Konsum im Sozialstaat*. Stuttgart: J.H.W.Dietz Nachf.

Barengolts, Moisei. 1928. "Emkost promyshlennogo rynka v SSSR." *Planovoe Khoziaistvo* 7: 325–98.

Bazarov, Vladimir. 1924. *K metodologii perspektivnogo planirovaniia*. Moscow: Gosplan.

———. 1926. "O metodologii postroeniia perspektivnykh planov." *Planovoe Khoziaistvo* 7: 7–21.

Belykh, Andrei. 1989. "A Note on the Origins of Input-Output Analysis and the Contribution of the Early Soviet Economists: Chayanov, Bogdanov and Kritsman." *Soviet Studies* 41 (3): 426–29.

———. 1990. "Theory of Equilibrium and Economic Discussions of the 1920s." *Soviet Studies* 42 (3): 571–82.

———. 2007. *Istoriia rossiiskikh ekonomiko-matematicheskikh issledovanii: Pervye sto let*. Moscow: URSS.

Bogdanov, Aleksandr. 1921a. "Organizatsionnaia nauka i khoziaistvennaia planomer-nost.'" In *Trudy pervoi vserossiiskoi initsiativnoi konferentsii po nauchnoi organi-zatsii proizvodstva*. Vol. 1, edited by N. Gushchin, 8–12. Moscow.

———. 1921b. "Organizatsionnye printsipy edinogo khoziaistvennogo plana." Vestnik statistiki 4–5 –6: 40–45.

Bogolepov, Mikhail. 1916. *O putiakh budushchego: K voprosu ob ekonomicheskom plane*. Petrograd: Izdatelstvo Ministerstva Finansov.

Boldyrev, Ivan, and Olesia Kirtchik. 2013. "The Culture of Mathematical Economics in the Postwar Soviet Union." Working paper WP6/2013/05. Moscow: Publishing House of the Higher School of Economics.

Bor, Mikhail, and Stanislav Logvinov. 1975. "O knigakh <Kompleksnoie narodnok-hoziaistvennoie planirovanie> i <Problemy planirovaniia i prognozirovaniia>" Planovoe Khoziaistvo 9: 134–41.

Brodsky, Josef. 1987. "Nobel Lecture." https://www.nobelprize.org/prizes/ literature/1987/brodsky/lecture/, accessed November 8, 2020.

Brutskus, Boris. 1935. *Economic Planning in Soviet Russia*. London: George Routledge & Sons, Ltd.

Campbell, Robert W. 1960. Review of *Ekonomicheskii raschet nailuchshego ispol-zovaniia resursov*, by L.V. Kantorovich. *American Economic Review* 50 (4): 729–31.

————. 1961. "Marx, Kantorovich, and Novozhilov: *Stoimost'* Versus Reality." *Slavic Review* 20 (3): 402–418.

Cave, Martin. 1980. *Computers and Economic Planning: The Soviet Experience.* Cambridge: Cambridge University Press.

Chayanov, Aleksandr. 1921. "Poniatie vygodnosti sotsialisticheskogo khoziaistva (opyt postroeniia bezdenezhnogo ucheta sovetskikh khoziaistv)." In *Metody bezdenezhnogo ucheta khoziaistvennykh predpriiatii* 5–76. Moscow: Gosizdat.

Chernenko, Konstantin. 1984. *Izbrannye rechi i stati.* Moscow: Politzdat.

Chetverikov, Nikolai. 1959. "Zhizn i nauchnaia deiatelnost E.E., Slutskogo." *Uchenie zapiski po statistike* 5: 254–70.

Clark, David. 1984. "Planning and the Real Origins of Input-Output Analysis." *Journal of Contemporary Asia* 14 (4): 408–29.

Conyngham, William J. 1982. *The Modernization of Soviet Industrial Management.* Cambridge: Cambridge University Press.

Dmitriev, Anton. 2006. "Stanovlenie ekonomiko-matematicheskogo napravleniia na ekonomicheskom fakultete leningradskogo gosudarstvennogo universiteta. *Primenenie matematiki v ekonomike* 16: 194–205. Saint Petersburg: University Publishing House.

Dmitriev, Vladimir K. 1974. *Economic Essays on Value, Competition and Utility.* Edited by Domenico Nuti, Cambridge: Cambridge University Press.

Domar, Evsey. 1957. "A Soviet Model of Growth." In *Essays in the Theory of Economic Growth,* 223–61. New York – Oxford: Oxford University Press.

Ellman, Michael. 1973. *Planning Problems in the USSR.* Cambridge: Cambridge University Press.

Ericson, Richard E. 2019. "The Growth and Marcescence of the 'System for Optimal Functioning of the Economy' (SOFE)." *History of Political Economy* 51 (S1): 155–79.

Erlich, Alexander. 1960. *The Soviet Industrialization Debate 1924–1928.* Cambridge, Mass.: Harvard University Press.

Fedorenko, Nikolai. 1968. *O razrabotke sistemy optimalnogo funktsionirovaniia ekonomiki.* Moscow: Nauka.

————. 1999. *Vspominaia proshloe, zagliadivaiu v budushchee.* Moscow: Nauka.

Feldman, Grigorii. 1928. "K teorii tempov rosta narodnogo dokhoda." *Planovoe Khoziaistvo* 11: 146–70; 12: 151–78.

Feygin, Yakov. 2017. "Reforming the Cold War State: Economic Thought, Internationalization, and the Politics of Soviet Reform, 1955–1985." Doctoral Dissertation, University of Pennsylvania. https://repository.upenn.edu/edissertations/2277, accessed August 23, 2020.

Gaetano, Donato. 1984. *L'economia sovietica: Uno sguardo dall'interno.* Milano: Franco Angeli.

Gardner, Roy. 1990. "L.V. Kantorovich: The Price Implications of Optimal Planning." *Journal of Economic Literature* 28 (2): 638–48.

Gerovitch, Slava. 2002. *From Newspeak to Cyberspeak: A History of Soviet Cybernetics.* Cambridge: MIT Press

Glagolev, Vladimir. 1975. "Spekulativnii proisk d-ra Ellmana." *Planovoe Khoziaistvo* 9: 132–33.

Glavatskii, Mikhail. 2002. *"Filozofskii parokhod": god 1922. Istoricheskie etiudy.* Ekaterinburg: Izdatelstvo Uralskogo Universiteta.

Glushkov, Viktor, Anatolii Dorodnitsyn, and Nikolai Fedorenko. 1964. "O nekotorykh problemakh kibernetiki" *Izvestiia* September 9, 1964.

Gorbachev, Mikhail. 1987. "O zadachakh partii po korennoi perestroike upravleniia ekonomikoi." In *Materialy Plenuma Tsentralnogo Komiteta KPSS, 25–26 iiunia.* 6–70. Moscow: Politizdat.

Gorlitskii, Jorem, and Oleg Khlevniuk. 2011. *Kholodnyi mir: Stalin i zavershenie stalinskoi diktatury.* Moscow: ROSSPEN.

Groman, Vladimir. 1925. "O nekotorykh zakonomernostiakh, empiricheski obnaruzhivaemykh v nashem narodnom khoziaistve." *Planovoe Khoziaistvo* 1: 88–101; 2: 125–41.

Grossman, Gregory. 1953. "Scarce Capital and Soviet Doctrine." *Quarterly Journal of Economics* 67 (3): 311–43.

Hardt, John P., Marvin Hoffenberg, Norman Kaplan, and Herbert S. Levine, eds. 1967. *Mathematics and Computers in Soviet Economic Planning.* New Haven – London: Yale University Press.

Harrison, Mark. 2002. *Soviet Planning in Peace and War, 1938–1945.* Cambridge: Cambridge University Press.

Hayek, Friedrich, ed. 1935. *Collectivist Economic Planning.* London: George Routledge & Sons Ltd.

Intriligator, Michael. 1975. *Matematicheskie metody optimizatsii i ekonomicheskaia teoriia.* Moscow: Progress.

Iurovskii, Leonid. 1928. *Denezhnaia politika Sovietskoi vlasti (1917–1928).* Moscow: Finansovoie Izdatel'stvo.

Jasny, Naum. 1972. *Soviet Economists of the Twenties: Names to Be Remembered.* Cambridge: Cambridge University Press.

Jones, Hywel R. 1975. *An Introduction to Modern Theories of Economic Growth.* London: Thomas Nelson & Sons Ltd.

Kantorovich, Leonid. 1939. *Matematicheskie metody organizatsii i planirovaniia proizvodstva.* Leningrad: Leningrad State University.

———. 1940. "Ob odnom effektivnom metode resheniia nekotorykh klassov ekstremal'nykh problem." *Doklady AN SSSR* 28 (3): 212–15.

———. 1954. "O znachenii elektronno-vychislitelnykh mashin dlia chelovecheskoi kultury." In Kantorovich, Kutateladze, and Fet. 2004. 2: 21–26.

———. 1957. "O metodakh analiza nekotorykh ekstremalnykh planovo-proizvodstvennykh zadach." *Doklady AN SSSR* 115 (3): 414–44.

———. 1959. *Ekonomicheskii raschet nailuchshego ispolzovaniia resursov.* Moscow: AN SSSR. Translated: (Kantorovich 1965).

———. 1965. *The Best Use of Economic Resources.* Oxford: Pergamon Press.

———. 2002. "Moi put v nauke." In Kantorovich, Kutateladze, and Fet. 2002. 1: 22–75.

Kantorovich, Leonid, Murat Albegov, and Vladimir Bezrukov. 1986. "Shire ispolzo-vat optimizatsionnie metody v narodnom khoziaistve." *Kommunist* 9: 44–54.

Kantorovich, Vsevolod, Samson Kutateladze, and Iakov Fet, eds. 2002⁻2004. *Leonid Vitalievich Kantorovich: chelovek i uchenii.* 2 vols. Novosibirsk: SO RAN, Geo.

Khanin, Grigorii. 1991. *Dinamika ekonomicheskogo razvitiia SSSR.* Novosibirsk: Nauka, Siberian Department.

Kitov, Anatolii. 1958. *Elektronnye vychislitelnye mashiny.* Moscow: Znanie.

Kondratiev, Nikolai. 1989. "Plan i predvidenie. In *Problemy ekonomicheskoi dinamiki.* 91–134. Moscow: Ekonomika.

———. 1993. *Osoboie mnenie. Izbrannye proizvodeniia v 2-kh knigakh.* Vol 2. Moscow: Nauka.

Kovalevskii, Nikolai. 1928. "Metodologiia plana rekonstruktsii." *Planovoe Khoziaistvo* 4: 7–45.

———. 1930. "K postroeniiu generalnogo plana." *Planovoe Khoziaistvo* 3: 117–44.

Kritsman, Lev. 1921a. Edinyi khoziaistvennyi plan i Komissiia Ispol'zovaniia. Moscow: Gosizdat.

———. 1921b. *Ob edinom khoziaistvennom plane.* Moscow: Gosizdat.

———. 1922. *Novaia ekonomicheskaia politika i planovoie raspredelenie.* Moscow: Gosizdat.

Ksenofontov, Mikhail, Aleksandr Shirov, Dmitrii Polzikov, and Aleksei Iantovskii. 2018. "Otsenka multiplikativnykh effektov v rossiiskoi ekonomike na osnove tablits zatraty–vypusk." *Problemy prognozirovaniia* (2): 3–13.

Kuibyshev, Valerian. 1937. Stat'i i rechi. Moscow: Partizdat.

Lafargue, Paul. 1933. *Vospominaniia o Markse.* Moscow: Partizdat.

Lange, Oskar, and Fred Taylor. 1938. *On the Economic Theory of Socialism.* Minneapolis: University of Minnesota Press.

Leeds, Adam. 2016. "Spectral Liberalism. On the Subjects of Political Economy in Moscow." Doctoral Dissertation, University of Pennsylvania. Accessed August 23, 2020.

Lenin, Vladimir. 1970. "Ob edinom khoziaistvennom plane." In *Polnoie sobranie sochinenii v 55 t.* 42: 339–47. Moscow: Gospolitizdat.

Leontief, Wassily. 1925. "Balans narodnogo khoziaistva." *Planovoe Khoziaistvo* 12: 254–58.

Leontief, Wassily, Hollis Chenery, and Paul Clark. 1958. *Issledovanie struktury amerikanskoi ekonomii.* Moscow: Gosstatizdat.

Marx, Karl. 1933. "Matematicheskie rukopisi." *Pod Znamenem Marksizma* 1: 15–73.

Materialy. 1986. Materialy *XXVII sezda KPSS.* Moscow: Politizdat.

Mau, Vladimir. 2017. *Gosudarstvo i ekonomika: Opyt ekonomicheskikh reform.* Moscow: Delo.

Minuvshii God. 1909. "Minuvshyi god." *Promyshlennost i Torgovlia* 1: 1–3.

Mises, Ludwig E. 1920. Economic Calculation in the Socialist Commonwealth. Reprinted in Hayek 1935, 87–130.

Nemchinov, Vasilii, ed. 1959. *Primenenie matematiki v ekonomicheskikh issledovaniiakh v 3-kh t.* Vol. 1. Moscow: Sotsekgiz.

Nemchinov, Vasilii. 1964. "Sotsialisticheskoie khoziaistvovanie i planirovanie proizvodstva." *Kommunist* 5: 74–87.

———. 1967. *Izbrannye proizvedeniia v 6 t.* Vol. 1. Moscow: Nauka.

Nikaido, Hukukane. 1972. *Vypuklye struktury i matematicheskaia ekonomika.* Moscow: Mir.

Novozhilov, Viktor. 1926. "Nedostatok tovarov." *Vestnik finansov* 2: 75–96. Reprinted in Novozhilov 1972, 51–79.

———. 1946. "Metody nakhozhdeniia minimuma zatrat v sotsialisticheskom khoziaistve." *Trudy Leningradskogo Politekhnicheskogo Instituta.* 1: 322–37.

———. 1959. "Izmerenie zatrat i rezultatov v sotsialisticheskom khoziaistve. In Nemchinov 1959, 42–113.

———. 1967. *Problemy izmereniia zatrat i rezultatov pri optimalnom planirovanii.* Moscow: Ekonomika.

———. 1972. *Voprosy razvitiia sotsialisticheskoi ekonomiki.* Moscow: Nauka.

O teoreticheskoi rabote. 1948. "O teoreticheskoi rabote v oblasti statistiki." *Voprosy Ekonomiki* 5: 79–90.

Polozhenie. 1944. "Polozhenie o Gosudarstvennoi Obshcheplanovoi Komissii." February 22, 1921, 161–62. Moscow: Upravlenie delami Sovnarkoma SSSR.

Pospelov, Dmitrii, and Yakov Fet. eds. 1998. *Ocherki istorii informatiki v Rossii.* Novosibirsk: SO RAN.

Popov, Pavel, ed. 1926. "Balans narodnogo khoziaistva SSSR za 1923/24 god." *Trudy Tsentralnogo statisticheskogo upravleniia* 29 (1): 632.

Remington, Thomas F. 1982. "Varga and the Foundations of Soviet Planning." *Soviet Studies* 34 (4): 585–600.

Revich, Iurii, and Boris Malinovskii. eds. 2014. *Informatsionnye tekhnologii v SSSR: Sozdateli sovetskoi vychislitelnoi tekhniki.* Saint Petersburg: BKhV-Peterburg.

Rumiantsev, Aleksei. ed. 1978. *Politicheskaia ekonomiia. Uchebnik. T.2, Sotsialism—pervaia faza kommunisticheskogo sposoba proizvodstva.* Moscow: Izdatel'stvo Politicheskoi Literatury.

Slutsky, Evgenii. 1927. "O slozhenii sluchainykh velichin kak istochnike tsiklicheskikh protsessov. *Voprosy Koniunktury* 3 (1): 34–64. Translated into English: 1937. *Econometrica* 5: 105–46.

Smolinski, Leon. 1971. "The Origins of Soviet Mathematical Economics." *Jahrbuch der Wirtschaft Osteuropas* 2: 137–53.

Stalin, Iosif. 1929. "Concerning Questions of Agrarian Policy in the USSR." In *Collected Works. 12:* 147–178. Moscow: Foreign Languages Publishing House.

Strumilin, Stanislav. 1921. "Formula khoziaistvennogo plana." *Ekonomicheskaia Zhizn* January 22, 1921, 14: 1–2.

———. 1927. "K perspektivnoi piatiletke Gosplana na 1926/27–1930/31." *Planovoe Khoziaistvo* 3: 17–54.

Sutela, Pekka. 1984. *Socialism, Planning and Optimality.* Helsinki: Societas Scientiarum Fennica.

———. 1991. *Economic Thought and Economic Reform in the Soviet Union.* Cambridge: Cambridge University Press.

Treml, Vladimir G. 1967. "Input-Output Analysis and Soviet Planning." In Hardt et al. 1967, 68–146.

Tsagolov, Nikolai. ed. 1970. *Kurs politicheskoi ekonomii T. 2, Sotsialism.* Moscow: Ekonomika.

Tugan-Baranovsky, Mikhail. 1890. "Uchenie o predelnoi poleznosti khoziaistvennykh blag kak prichine tsennosti." *Iuridicheskii vestnik* 6 (2): 192–230.

Valenta, Vítězslav, Aleksandr Granberg, Raimundas Raiatskas, and Aleksei Rumiantsev. 1987. "Optimizatsionnyi podkhod k ekonomike: rezultaty i uroki." *Kommunist* 14: 120–24.

Voprosy. 1982–1985. *Voprosy optimalnogo planirovania i upravleniia sotsialisticheskoi ekonomikoi.* V 10 t. Moscow: Nauka.

Voznesenskii, Nikolai. 1979. *Izbrannie proizvedeniia.* Moscow: Politizdat.

Wiener, Norbert. 1958. *Kibernetika ili upravlenie i sviaz v zhivotnom i mashine.* Moscow: Sovetskoe radio.

XXII Congress. 1962. *XXII siezd KPSS: Stenograficheskii otchet.* Vol. 3 Moscow: Gospolitizdat.

XXIV Congress. 1971. *XXIV siezd KPSS: Stenograficheskii otchet.* Vol. 1 Moscow: Gospolitizdat.

Zauberman, Alfred. 1960. "New Winds in Soviet Planning." *Soviet Studies* 12 (1): 1–13.

———. 1975. *The Mathematical Revolution in Soviet Economics.* London: Oxford University Press.

Chapter 9

Mathematical Economics, Economic Modeling, and Planning in Yugoslavia

Jože Mencinger

Following a few words of introduction, the chapter starts with a general description of the development of the Yugoslav economy and economic theory in the communist era. Then, the state of economics in the country before 1945 will be described, focusing on the influence of Russian émigrés. The next section will describe the rebirth of economics under communism and the eminent role of Branko Horvat in developing mathematical research in economic sciences. It will be followed by a discussion of input-output analysis and econometric modeling in Yugoslavia. Finally, directive and indicative planning will be examined as well as the return of the idea of planning in the form of "social planning" during the 1970s. The Annex presents a statistical analysis of indicative planning and provides estimates of economic performance shaped by systemic changes.[1]

The chapter tries to stress the divergence in economic theories, mathematics in economics, and planning between Yugoslavia and other communist countries. An important difference was that theoretical discussions in my country lagged behind actual economic development. Obviously, this originated in other well-known differences stemming from self-liberation during the Second World War, the break with the Soviet Bloc in 1948, and the introduction of workers' self-management.

ECONOMIC SYSTEMS AND THEORIES:
INTRODUCTORY THOUGHTS

In studying the economic history of former Yugoslavia, four systems/periods can be distinguished: *administrative socialism* (1946–1952), *administrative market socialism* (1953–1962), *market socialism* (1963–1973), and *contractual socialism* (1974–1990).[2] This is a normative demarcation because four postwar constitutions (passed in 1946, 1953, 1963, and 1974) are used to spot the starting year of each period. Evidently, such a demarcation is open to criticism. First, it creates the perception of abrupt changes, which did not occur. Secondly, some far-reaching institutional adjustments preceded the constitutions, others were introduced after them. Thirdly, the gaps between the ideology represented by constitutions, their actual normative setting, and reality were always substantial. Fourthly, some of the economic policy changes affected economic development more than constitutional changes did. For example, this was the case with two major economic reforms in 1961 and in 1965. Although more significant changes in the economic system were introduced in 1961 than in 1965, it is the economic reform of 1965 that was considered by many Yugoslav and foreign economists the breaking point between the more successful period before 1965 and the less successful one thereafter (Horvat 1971; Sapir 1980). Indeed, the introduction of new market mechanisms in 1965 and restrictive economic policies that followed triggered a crisis with increased open unemployment, particularly in 1967.[3]

The periodization above can be observed in the use of mathematical instruments and economic models. In the second period, the use of mathematics was limited to input-output tables and simple growth models, which are appropriate tools for dealing with the supply side of the economy when growth is limited by scarce inputs (cf. János Kornai's shortage economy), while in the third period standard econometric models, appropriate for the exploration of the demand side, also appeared.

While in most Eastern European countries economic reforms were politically unwanted or communist leaders were skeptical about them, reforms in Yugoslavia mainly were inspired by top policy-makers. Until 1960, most of the discussions neither were put on paper nor published. Scholarly articles were published mostly without proper references. There was a general feeling of a complete break with the pre-communist past, and so there seemed nothing important to refer to. At the same time, professional literature was almost completely descriptive, which was partly due to the fact that many university departments of economics were established after the war and employed a faculty with no theoretical training. Furthermore, economists were busy with changing the institutions and not with the debates of why these changes happened or whether they were needed. Attention was mainly focused on what Yugoslav economists called the "economic system." Economic policy in a traditional sense—the use of a set of policy instruments in a given framework—hardly existed. Problems encountered generally were solved by changing the institutional framework. This was easier in Yugoslavia than in other communist countries because both the influence of the Soviet Union and the obedience of local leaders to Moscow were far less pronounced from the very beginning.

The assumption that the Yugoslav economic situation requires a special approach to economic theory was supported by exaggerated estimates of devastation to the country during the war. Allegedly, two-fifths of an extremely undeveloped manufacturing industry was destroyed, and 1.7 million people out of fifteen million were killed during the Second World War. This contributed to a complete break with prewar economic thinking and reduced the need to discuss theoretical issues.

In administrative socialism the answers to four basic economic questions (what? how? to whom? and when?) were, at least in principle, given by political leaders. They made the decisions on consumption, organization of production, income distribution, and savings/investments. The major goal at the time was to transform a backward, predominantly agricultural society into a socialist industrial society. Directive planning was believed to create a path to the final goal. Economic science from before the Second World War was considered obsolete and replaced by Stalin's law on proportional socialist development and citations from Marx's writings. However, the break between Yugoslavia and the Soviet Bloc in 1948 altered everything. A new system that would differ from the Soviet one was badly needed and quickly invented. When the First Five-Year Plan that started in 1947 was terminated abruptly in 1948, so also was belief in Stalin's law. In less than one year, the concept of administrative socialism included the objective of the free association of producers who do not need planners to tell them what to do (Kidrič 1949; 1950a,b).

The economy was affected heavily by the break. The five-year industrialization plan imbued with hopes for rapid growth had only been initiated when suddenly the contracts were broken and supplies of equipment and materials were interrupted. While trade with the countries of Eastern Europe in the period of 1946–1948 stabilized around 50 percent of overall exports and 42 percent of overall imports, by 1949, it was reduced to one-third and canceled entirely in 1950. Due to a total boycott, the country was cut off from the East completely and still separated from the West. Initially, Yugoslav leaders refused any benefits provided by Western countries, including the Marshall Plan. Indeed, the country felt isolated in a hostile world, which contributed to the idea of non-alignment later. The situation changed quickly due to U.S. assistance following its break with the Soviet Bloc.

Regardless of how useful the move from central planning was in the long run, Yugoslavia profited from some components of the First Five-Year Plan that focused on energy production (in accordance with Lenin's belief in electrification as a prerequisite to communism) and heavy industry. While faith faded that development of the sector producing investment goods should outstrip the production of consumer goods, investments stubbornly were directed at infrastructure. This led to rapid growth in the 1950s when central planning and rationing already were abolished. This was the most successful period of Yugoslav economic history under communism. In this period, economic success and the experiment of self-management fascinated Western economic theorists, some of whom became admirers of the "Yugoslav economic miracle."[4]

The ideological grip on economic science softened in the early 1950s, which resulted in a gradual rediscovery of forgotten economic theories needed to explain the behavior of consumers and producers. Aleksander Bajt's PhD dissertation, *Marxov zakon vrednosti* (Marx's Law of Value), defended in 1953, was a pathbreaking attempt to combine contemporary Western economics and Marxism. The dissertation was followed by an eruption of economic analyses, books, and published dissertations such as Maksimović (1958), Dabčević-Kučar (1957), Lavrač (1956), and Černe (1960). Ideological boundaries disappeared. Samuelson's famous textbook of elementary economics was translated into Yugoslav languages and used at economics departments. A rapid expansion of university courses in economics reflected the constant change in the economy. Economic publications began to flourish and authors started writing books rather than articles. However, publishing abroad remained a rare habit. The only real limit to economic research was the actual ability of a researcher to understand and apply mathematical and statistical procedures.

There is one thing which helped quantitative analysis in Yugoslavia from the very outset. Contrary to centrally planned economies where company-level data were not available to the general public, the Social Accounting Service in Yugoslavia was permanently publishing them in so-called "green books" that enabled researchers to prepare econometric studies based on cross-section, time series, and panel data.

Before the Second World War and also thereafter, economics was a subject taught at law schools rather than schools of economics and often provided practical knowledge instead of focusing on theoretical issues. While schools of economics already existed in Zagreb and Belgrade between the two wars, such a school was established in Ljubljana only after the Second World War as a faculty of law and economics. The tradition of teaching modern economics within law schools persisted; they were much less engaged in teaching Marxism.

Discussion among Yugoslav economists was facilitated by influential weeklies and monthlies. *Gospodarska Gibanja* (GG—Economic Movements), a monthly of the Economic Institute of the Law School (EIPF), known as the "Bajt Institute," in Ljubljana focused on Yugoslav economic policy and introduced new methodological tools, particularly in econometrics. Its first issue was published in June 1971. Throughout its almost 50-year history, GG presented the economic situation in Yugoslavia (and after the end of Yugoslavia, in Slovenia) from a critical perspective. The golden age of the periodical were the 1980s when it was also published in Serbo-Croatian as *Privredna kretanja Jugoslavije* (PKJ—Economic Movements of Yugoslavia). Aleksander Bajt and other members of his institute (Velimir Bole, France Križanič, Jože Mencinger, Franjo Štiblar) were arguing that the economic system and the economic policy determine the behavior of economic units; therefore, the latter cannot be blamed for results that differed from the goals of the center.

Ekonomska politika, a Belgrade weekly was established by Boris Kidrič and Kiro Gligorov in 1952 to promote socialist market economy as an alternative to Soviet-style centrally planned economy. The weekly became very influential; most of the large Yugoslav firms were among its subscribers and supporters. Particularly in the 1970s, *Ekonomska politika* published articles of reform-oriented economists, journalists, managers, and politicians such as Dragiša Bošković, Kiro Gligorov, Vladimir Gligorov, Ljubomir Madžar, Ante Marković, Jože Mencinger, Stjepan Mesić, Milutin Mitrović, Marko Nikezić, Latinka Perović, Žarko Puhovski, Dragan Veselinov, and Veselin Vukotić, most of whom influenced Yugoslav economic and political thinking, to use official rhetoric, by "undermining" the hegemony of the communist party. In the 1980s, the weekly fought against the nationalism of Serbian Academy of Arts and Sciences and criticized economists who opposed the market economy and capitalism.

Although there were no barriers in expressing even radically pro-capitalist views since the 1960s, most Yugoslav economic theorists and social scientists were adjusting their opinions to what was considered appropriate ideologically at any given moment. For example, in 1974 when a new Constitution was passed and "contractual socialism" and social planning were introduced, these scholars published a record number of books and articles supporting the new institutional setup.

In the 1950s and 1960s, one already could observe fundamental changes in and new approaches to economic methodology. In the period of administrative market socialism, the rationing of goods gradually was replaced by the market mechanism, and this created the need to explain the behavior of consumers when they maximize utility under the constraint of prices and incomes. Mathematics provided the necessary analytical tools. The situation was similar on the supply side where instructions by planners were replaced by the decisions of company managers on how to combine inputs to produce output. True, in this period, the control of wage determination and savings/investment decisions were retained by the state. The dichotomy in decision-making can be well observed in teaching economics, for example, in the textbook *Politična ekonomija* (Political Economy) published by Aleksander Bajt in 1958, which was a unique combination of Alfred Marshall's economics with Marxism. In the first part (microeconomics) Marshall's tools derived from the principles of utility maximization were used in presenting demand and supply. The second part (macroeconomics), however, insisted on Marx's explanation of relative wages and income distribution between labor and capital, and Marxian reproduction schemes were used to explain the functioning of the national economy. In fact, Yugoslav economists did not care very much for what Marx said or did not say. Marxism remained a kind of lip service paid by citing Marx and Engels. A shift from macro- to microeconomics was also evident. Macroeconomics became a marginal subject even at the three leading universities (Belgrade, Zagreb, and Ljubljana), and economics was replaced gradually by business studies while the schools retained the name "faculty of economics."[5]

In Yugoslavia there were no economists either before or after the war who—similar to Oskar Lange in Poland—would have believed that a centrally planned economy could compete and overcome capitalist economies with the help of computers. Despite being an ardent socialist, Lange deplored the Marxian labor theory of value on grounds of neoclassical price theory. As mentioned, in Yugoslavia it was Bajt who tried to mix Marxist and neoclassical principles in economics, albeit not in the same fashion. Both Lange and Bajt advocated the use of market tools in economic planning. Lange proposed that the Central Planning Board set prices via a "trial and error" procedure, making adjustments once shortages and surpluses occur, rather than relying on free competition. Planners would pick arbitrarily a price for a product manufactured in state-owned firms and raise or reduce it, depending on whether it resulted in shortages or gluts. After this experiment was run a few times, additional mathematical methods would be employed to plan the economy. Raising prices would encourage firms to increase production, driven by their desire for larger profits, and in doing so eliminate shortages. Lowering prices would encourage firms to curtail production in order to prevent losses and eliminate surpluses. In Lange's opinion, such a simulation of the market would be capable of effectively managing supply and demand.

Proponents of this idea argued that such an economy combines advantages of a market economy with those of a planned economy.

As a contrast, Bajt did not look for a simulated system because, by and large, the Yugoslav economy was a workable market economy, even if price setting by the government was practiced widely under both administrative socialism and administrative market socialism. In the first period, agricultural goods were rationed and their prices kept low for two reasons: to "persuade" farmers to join the collective farms and to transfer revenues from agriculture to industry. This policy was not abolished until the mid-1960s when—in the course of the 1965 reform—agricultural prices were first frozen, then increased and freed. After 1965, the regulation of prices in Yugoslavia became similar to that in most capitalist countries, in which time and again, governments set prices in some sectors, particularly, in public services and in industries controlled by monopolies (e.g., energy and transportation). In general, price control in Yugoslavia ceased to be a device for manipulating the structure of the economy. Rather, it served the fight against inflation which became one of the major economic problems after 1965. Constant interference in price setting (freezing and thawing) was used in times of high inflation as well as in the hyperinflationary period before the breakup of the country.[6]

ECONOMICS IN YUGOSLAVIA BEFORE 1945

Economic science in Yugoslavia between the two wars was influenced heavily by scholars who emigrated from Russia after the October Revolution and occupied many teaching positions at three Yugoslav universities: in Belgrade, Zagreb, and Ljubljana. They brought along economics that flourished in the first decades of the twentieth century in the Russian empire. A number of them worked as professors in fields such as law, technology, and philosophy. Many of the younger Russian émigrés became students at the universities and/or members of different scholarly and political associations. (There were 1,400 Russian students at Yugoslav universities in the 1928/29 schoolyear.) The most known among "Russians" were Evgeni Spektorsky, Todor Taranovsky, Mikhail Chubinsky, Aleksei Shcherbakov, Evgeni Anichkov, Nikolai Bubnov, Alexander Soloviev, Vladimir Farmakovsky (see Brglez 2015). Alexander Bilimovich (1876–1963).[7] Economics taught by him closely followed the lines of economic analysis offered by John Bates Clark, Irving Fisher, Alfred Marshall, and Vilfredo Pareto, to mention only a few leading theorists of the time. Bilimovich contributed papers to economic journals such as *Econometrica, Weltwirtschaftliches Archiv, Journal des économistes, Revue d'économie politique*, and *Quarterly Journal of Economics*. Curricula at the Law School offered lectures on monetary theory, economic cycles, social policy, history of economic thought, price theory, and theory of planning. Bilimovich's colleagues included Ludvik Bohm, (economic policy, agrarian policy, geopolitics), Franc Eller (finance, budget, and taxation), Mirko Kovač (demography and statistics), Vladimir Murko (public finance), Albin Ogris (statistical analysis), Alojz Rant (public finance), Adolf Vogelnik (statistics), and Cyril Žebot (modern economic structures). Yugoslav economic journals of the interwar period also deserve mention, such as *Revue économique et financière de Belgrade*, *Privredni Pregled* (Economic Review), or *Arhiv za pravne i društvene nauke* (Archive of Legal and Social Sciences), the last two surviving until today. Economic science in Yugoslavia did not lag much behind contemporary economic knowledge in the region. The articles and textbooks published by Yugoslav scholars discussed concepts of rational decision-making, transaction costs, positive and normative economics, as well as static and dynamic equilibrium. At the same time, they had practically no links to socialist economic thought emerging in other Eastern European countries. On the contrary, the Russian émigré economists were hostile to the ideas of communist planning. For instance, in discussing the Great Depression, Bilimovich's textbook *Uvod v ekonomsko vedo* (Introduction to Economics), published in 1933, vehemently refused planning as a solution for the economic crisis and proposed what many years later became known as social market economy. Of importance for our topic is chapter five of the book on methodology in economic sciences. It starts with a discussion on deductive and inductive approaches in economics and the criteria of a proper methodology, which is followed by an assessment of the advantages and disadvantages of mathematical tools. According to Bilimovich, the use of mathematics enables the scholar to make precise statements that can be tested by statistical data or econometric models.

Two other Slovenian economists should be mentioned in this respect: Cyril Žebot (1914–1989) and Andrej Gosar (1887–1970). Žebot was professor at the Law School and editor of the daily *Jutro*; he emigrated to the United States in 1947 and is most known for his book *Slovenija včeraj, danes, jutri* (Slovenia Yesterday, Today, Tomorrow), in which he pleaded for an independent Slovenia decades before independence (Žebot 1967). Gosar, an influential Christian socialist economist and politician, was sent to a concentration camp by Germans and was ignored completely after the war. Allegedly, he was "forgotten" because the communist leader Edvard Kardelj (1910–1979) stole his ideas on self-management.

Before the Second World War, two main traditions dominated the analysis of economic problems in Yugoslavia: the German Historical School and

Austrian marginalism. While in the former, top-down government intervention and even *dirigisme* were inherent parts of economic policy, in the latter these were largely rejected. Regarding the role of mathematical reasoning, both schools refused it as misleading and normally excluded formal models from economic analysis. The efforts made by Bilimovich and his colleagues notwithstanding, the only area where quantitative reasoning found acceptance was the systematization of empirical data and rudimentary economic dynamics.

Even such a—mathematically rather poor—economics practically disappeared after the war, together with scholars who died, retired, were forced into retirement, or left the country in the wake of communist takeover. The economic profession of the time by and large was unaware of what economics is really about and what the basic concepts—such as scarcity, choice, allocation, and preferences—mean. For example, for Boris Kidrič (1949) who was a main architect of the Yugoslav economic system in both the first and the second periods, Stalin's law on proportional development was the essence of economic science, state property was the highest form of ownership, and planning was the fundamental tool of socialist economic management. However, in less than a year after this publication, the idea of free association of direct producers appeared on the political scene (1949; 1950a, b). Those having doubts like Milovan Đilas, who wrote the famous book *Nova klasa* (New Class), were persecuted, as were all those who did not side with Tito in his battle with Stalin. While economists and other social scientists continued quoting Marx, this habit became as irrelevant as Stalin's law.

REBIRTH OF ECONOMICS AND THE
ROLE OF BRANKO HORVAT

There is no doubt that the scholar who made the far largest contribution to the rebirth of economics in communist Yugoslavia was the controversial theorist Branko Horvat (1923–2001). He rediscovered economics in a still ideologically dominated, evidently uninspiring atmosphere. Specifically, he was also the first among Marxist economists in Yugoslavia who justified the use of mathematics in economic sciences and planning.

After moving from Zagreb to Belgrade, Horvat started delivering lectures that reopened vast landscapes of contemporary economics. The result of Horvat's transfer to Belgrade was, however, much more significant in another respect. In 1958, he was invited to the Federal Planning Agency to form and head the Department of Economic Research and Methodology of Planning which in 1963 became the Yugoslav Institute of Economic Research. A major step in promoting contemporary economic science was his creation of the Postgraduate School of Economics within the institute. Such celebrities as George Kuznets and John Johnston taught at the school. The institute was the first in the country among economic institutes to be equipped with a powerful electronic computer reflecting the technological level of the time. The journal *Economic Analysis*, which he established and remained the editor of, resembled, in both content and form, the best contemporary economic journals in the world. By publishing more than six hundred articles in professional journals, at least ten of which appeared in the most prestigious international journals such as *The Economic Journal*, *American Economic Review*, *The Journal of Economic Literature*, *Kyklos*, *The Journal of Comparative Economics*, and *The Journal of Development*, Horvat was by far the most prolific author in Yugoslavia. He also published some thirty books, of which quite a few were translated into some 18 languages.

It is also interesting how he shifted from one subject to another in parallel to the institutional development of the Yugoslav economy. The first field of Horvat's interest was planning, which led to a series of articles summarized in his book *Ekonomska teorija planske privrede* (Theory of Planned Economy) (Horvat 1961), which was at the time of publishing one of the very few volumes devoted to the real functioning of a planned economy. The next field was structural analysis culminating in his book on intersectoral economics and related models (1962a). Relevant in this context is also his book on economic models published in the same year (1962b). Horvat's analytical ability came to the most vivid expression in his book on the theory of production and technological progress (1970), which was on the very frontier of academic writings in the field. Abstract theory of mathematical structures leading to production functions, mathematical derivations of basic relations in the theory of production, decomposition of the rate of growth, and alternative concepts of the neutrality of technical progress are all ingredients of this fascinating book, which is concise and uses clean and rigorous definitions. Simultaneously, Horvat (1969) offered an analysis of business cycles in Yugoslavia, in which he demonstrated that—maybe only because of planning failures—the self-managed economy displays cyclical movements while pretending to be a planned economy.[8] Another field of Horvat's research work was the linkages between economic trends and economic policy interventions. He emphasized that economic policy cannot be efficient without an appropriate institutional framework, a regulative machinery that in Yugoslavia was referred to as the economic system. His monograph on postwar economic policy (Horvat 1971) induced one of the liveliest discussions among Yugoslav economists. According to Horvat, primary, genuine, and predetermined relations do not have to be sought at the lowest level of the economic system but can be identified at the highest systemic level. His authoritative institutional study *The Political Economy of Socialism* was known widely and cited (Horvat 1982). With this he wanted to lay the foundations of a genuinely structured socialist economy and society.

In his contributions to the theory of behavior of the self-managed firm, which was his lifelong research subject, Horvat (1972; 1975) radically rejected Benjamin Ward's[9] (1958) objective function of maximizing income per worker and gave a critical summary of the then available interpretations of the self-managed economy. Many analysts thought in the 1970s that self-management generates considerable differences between firms in income per worker and, consequently, unjustifiable differences in take-home pay. A decade earlier, Horvat (1962b) had offered a clear account of what differences are unavoidable, economically functional, and warranted in terms of the prevailing morality in Yugoslavia. These were times when self-management frequently was analyzed by foreign economists who—like Ward—discussed the consequences of the income-per-worker maximand leading to the backward bending supply curve that implies that a firm with such a curve is inefficient. Horvat disputed Ward's findings by claiming that one would get a similarly strange result by maximizing profit per unit of capital. In addition to these numerous and voluminous works, he published comprehensive studies in sectoral economics, notably on the oil industry, where he discussed the issue of economics of scale. National income accounting was also one of the areas of his professional pursuits.

Horvat was one of the few economists in Yugoslavia with a deep knowledge of and sincere inclination toward Marxism. Ironically, in the early stages of Yugoslav communism, he had been stigmatized as a non-Marxist and even anti-Marxist. In 1962, he published a book on economic models (Horvat 1962b) at a time when most economists did not even know what a model was and what was to be done with the incomprehensible mathematical formulae through which the models had been developed. It was therefore easier to proclaim him anti-Marxist. When most former "Marxists" became "monetarists" after the collapse of communism, Horvat as a Marxist resolutely denied the desirability of restoring capitalism. Indeed, while approving privatization, he supported the idea that the companies should be owned by workers.

INPUT-OUTPUT ANALYSIS AND
ECONOMETRIC MODELING

The Croatian economist Mijo Sekulić (1919–1996) can be considered the father of Yugoslav input-output (I-O) analysis. He also studied the application of I-O models in the preparation of central plans and published a voluminous book *Međusektorski modeli i strukturna analiza* (Intersectoral Models and Structural Analysis) in 1980. In this work Sekulić examined important theoretical and empirical problems related to formulating dynamic models and iterative solutions, defining multipliers, performing numerical calculations, applying the RAS method, and building regional models. The latter was a key issue because of the republican structure of Yugoslav economy. The first experimental input-output table for the Yugoslav economy was composed in 1957. In 1962, tables disaggregated to 8, 15, 37, and 76 sectors were published, and the Federal Statistical Office started producing larger and larger I-O tables regularly in two-year intervals. In the beginning, no distinction was made between domestic and imported products, but later imports were considered a specific input sector. Input-output analysis laid the foundation for CGE (computable general equilibrium) models used in the 1980s and influenced the methodology of the so-called S distance models, in which the differences in all economic and social variables or aggregates were expressed in time (Sicherl 1992).

As said before, the first up-to-date computer started working in Branko Horvat's institute in Belgrade where the first simple growth models of Harrod-Domar type were built. Their authors presumed that the development of national economy was determined by the supply and accumulation of capital. In Yugoslavia, the first model of this kind was created by Dančika Nikolić in 1963; in later years, a number of similar growth models were built by researchers of the Belgrade institute. Strangely enough, they did not enter the field of Klein-type modern econometric models for many years.

In the early 1970s, the first proper Klein-type econometric model appeared in a PhD thesis by the author of this chapter, "Quarterly Econometric Model of Yugoslav Economy," at the University of Pennsylvania (Mencinger 1975). It was based on Keynesian economics, with the demand side determining the evolution of the economy. The formal presentation of the model is the following:

$$AY_t + \sum B_j Y_{t-p} + \sum C_j X_{t-p} = e_t$$
$$t = 1 \ldots \ldots n.$$

A   k * k matrix of coefficients of endogenous variables;
B   k * k matrix of coefficients of lagged endogenous variables;
C   k * m matrix of coefficients of exogenous variables;
Y_t k * 1 vector of the values of current endogenous variables;
Y_{t-I} k * 1 vector of the values of exogenous variables;
e_t k * 1 vector of residuals;

m   number of exogenous variables;
k   number of equations or number of endogenous variables;
p   longest lag in the model;
n   number of observations.

The model tries to explain medium-term fluctuations and growth of the Yugoslav economy. It can be considered a Keynes-Klein type "demand-driven" econometric model with some room for equation specifications related to the nature of a developing socialist market economy. The central equation is the gross national product (GNP) definition by the components of final demand, which are explained on the aggregate level.

In analyzing consumption, the traditional approach is followed. Thus, the level of real consumption depends on real disposable income defined as the sum of personal incomes (wages) and social transfers. Investments in fixed assets were defined originally as exogenous to the model and only later became endogenous variables dependent on interest rates as exogenous variables. The foreign trade block consists of export and import equations. The assumption of infinite price elasticity for the supply of imports and demand for exports appears realistic for a small country. On the one hand, imports are explained by domestic demand and relative prices adjusted for exchange rates. On the other hand, exports are explained by foreign demand, expressed by imports of the Organization for Economic Cooperation and Development (OECD) countries. Real wages in the productive sector are explained by productivity; a dummy for the period after 1980, in which wages were to a great extent directly influenced by economic policy measures, is added to the wage equation. Wages in the public sector are determined by wages in the business sector.

Because output is determined by final demand in the short run, the production function determines the demand for productive factors. As far as labor is concerned, this means that the employment function (instead of the production function) implies proper causality direction, while the production function is used to present potential output. Unemployment is basically a long-run structural problem determined by the difference between long-run supply of labor contingent on demographic factors and the actual stage of development, and demand for labor is determined by actual output. The price block of the model bridges the real and nominal sectors. The method of price determination follows the pattern often used in macro-econometric models of medium size: a behavioral equation for overall price changes is estimated and GNP deflator is determined by identity. The central variable in the price sector is the index of producers' prices. Its specification is based on the variable mark-up principle. Three cost factors appear in the price equations: unit labor costs, import prices, and costs produced by governments on all levels in the form of taxes and contributions. Price deflators of final demand categories are derived from changes in producers' prices.

The first model, using quarterly data for the 1961–1974 period, consisted of 51 equations with 17 exogenous variables. The coefficients were estimated by ordinary least squares (OLS) method; the Gauss-Seidel method was used for the solution of the model; stochastic simulations were done; and static and dynamic multipliers were calculated. All these were made possible by the computer and, particularly, by statistical software from the University of Pennsylvania. In the following years, the model was expanded to 91 equations, which were estimated for the 1965–1979 period by Bole and Mencinger (1980). The methods were improved with two stage least squares (TSLS) and limited information maximum likelihood (LIML) techniques, a modified Gauss-Seidel solution method, stochastic simulation, and spectral analysis.

To some extent, the frontiers in econometrics shifted from Belgrade to Ljubljana where two institutes, the Economic Institute of the Law School (EIPF) and the Institute for Economic Research (IER), were competing. EIPF specialized in quarterly and monthly models and short-term predictions while IER specialized in yearly models and medium-term predictions. The main goal of the EIPF models was economic policy analysis. The results were presented annually in November at the conferences of the Yugoslav Economic Association and could be applied by federal authorities in formulating economic policies for the next year. Whether they were actually applied is hard to tell. It is more likely that the authorities rather used models built in Belgrade.

Of course, econometric models had appeared in Yugoslavia earlier. Thus, Cobb-Douglas production functions were estimated on cross-section data already in the 1960s using Briggs logarithmic tables and calculators as well as data from the Yugoslav textile industry. The amount of work that nowadays can be done in seconds required many hundreds of hours. Once appropriate software became available, the spread of econometric models accelerated greatly, also reaching other research fields: inflation (Bajt 1967; Mencinger 1971), fiscal sector (Kranjec 1976), balance of payment (World Bank 1979), and so forth.[10] EIPF introduced a number of methodological innovations. The best known was the improvement by Velimir Bole (1975) of the seasonal adjustment procedure X-11 in the so-called "impulse trend," which increased the stability of the procedure. In order to make short-term predictions, monthly econometric models were built (*Mesečni napovedni model konjunkture I, II, III*). Furthermore, EIPF published occasional papers dealing with relevant economic issues such as consumption, unemployment, inflation, exchange rate, effective tax rates, and so forth.

PLANNING

Directive Planning

The Yugoslav planning regime attracted much less attention in professional circles than other features of the Yugoslav economic system. There are many reasons for that. The First Five-Year Plan could hardly be called a plan. It was an ambitious proclamation of desired goals that had very little to do with real planning and even less with reality. Yugoslavia was a federation and industrial enterprises belonged to three groups: enterprises of federal importance (e.g., power generation and heavy industry), republican importance (most other industries), and local importance (small-scale industry and trade, and practically all other businesses, with the exception of some barbers and shoemakers). This excluded any unified regulation. The plan consisted of orders to increase industrial investments triggering rapid growth in heavy industry and reallocating labor and capital from agriculture to manufacturing.

Due to the complicated regional structure and the low level of development, all major theoretical and actual problems of centrally planned economies came to the fore immediately. Authorities at different levels were incapable of predicting future trends, and there was a lack of incentives at each level of the hierarchy as income was guaranteed. Companies cheated the planning authorities by underestimating their own capacities and slightly overfulfilling the planning targets as this brought them rewards. A large overfulfillment would have been risky because the planning authorities might have enhanced the requirements for the next period. It was said that plan implementation relied on orders given by telephone. At any rate, in 1949, Yugoslavia formally ceased to be a centrally planned economy.

Indicative Planning

After some years without planning, in 1957, it returned as a kind of indicative planning in the form of five-year plans and yearly plans called resolutions that were passed by the federal and republican parliaments. According to the logic of indicative planning, for example, in France at the time, economic units did not need to know that they were "planned"; they were only supposed to properly react to economic policy incentives while planners had to be able to implement the plans by economic policy measures influencing the behavior of the "planned" economic units. If the planners do not use these measures, they become forecasters. This was the case in Yugoslavia in the period 1957–1985.[11]

Did Yugoslav planners learn? This question is relevant also for other "planned" economies which pretended that they planned the economic processes. If they had really planned them, the economies would have collapsed soon; cheating by planners at all levels of the hierarchy was a strong pillar of required flexibility. Did over- or under-fulfillment of the previous plan affect the figures of the current plan? Did over-fulfillment increase optimism and under-fulfillment increase cautiousness? This may have resulted in oscillations of differences between the plans and reality—a consequence of the "ratchet principle" observed in the centrally planned economies (Keren et al. 1983). While a small number of observations does not allow proper econometric analysis, the existence of similar oscillations in Yugoslav macro-planning was confirmed (Mencinger 1986).

Social Planning and General Equilibrium

The disappointment with the results of market reforms (not only with their economic but also social and, particularly, political results) during the third period of system change was decisive for the revival of confidence in planning. However, one had to invent a planning system consistent with the idea of "contractual socialism" that had been introduced in the early 1970s as a response to the fact that the market economy endangered the political monopoly of the communist party. The basic characteristics of the new planning regime called "social planning" were the following:

1. All economic and regional entities plan. Planning is non-hierarchical, or it is done "from below." It consists of a micro-and a macroeconomic part; the former means planning by companies, the latter the planning by regional authorities at different levels.
2. Exchange of information on predetermined planning indicators is obligatory for all; coordination is required in priority activities.
3. Income is the major item being planned.
4. Plans are codified by self-management agreements that are instruments of microeconomic coordination and by social contracts that are instruments of macroeconomic coordination. The consent of every institution concerned is required for codification.
5. Planning is a medium-term undertaking every five years. The planning process is, however, continuous for all participants. It includes yearly estimates of plan fulfillment and yearly adjustments.

While the fulfillment of plans in directive and indicative planning is based on exogenous enforcement and on the assumption of rational behavior of economic units, social planning rests on endogenous enforcement. It should be a result of participation by all economic units in the planning process and of coordination among them. Before analyzing the theoretical and actual limits of social planning, one should consider the differences between planning and prediction or the collection of wishes. We can talk of planning only if the planner has well-defined and quantifiable goals, tools for achieving the goals, and is able to ensure their fulfillment. None of these features existed in the case of social planning. Indeed, even the households' decisions on how they will spend family income in the current month can be called planning because the households are able to ensure the fulfilment of their plans, which the "planners" in social planning were unable to do.

Although social planning exhibits some of the characteristics of both directive and indicative planning, it is significantly different from them as well as from planning systems in other countries. In some respect it came close to French planning in the 1950s, which was also based on exchange of information and communication between the most important economic decision-makers.

Social planning was part of system changes introduced in the Yugoslav economy in the early 1970s, during the fourth (i.e., the last) period. In a way, it belonged to a set of other strange ideas emerging at that time. The major reason for the change was the fear that the communist party-state was threatened by "technocrats" (company managers) who gained power, particularly, in successful firms and were reluctant to obey politicians. Indeed, they were turning into a kind of well-paid nobility of decision-makers who could easily manipulate workers and local political leaders. The general phrase invented for the curtailment of their power was "the need for deepening self-management."

As in the past, the new idea was accepted smoothly by "economic science." Critical writings were overlooked. Yet, social planning was based on the participation of all economic subjects concerned, which meant that there were more than 65,000 planners. Planning was obligatory at different levels of the government (federation, republics, local communities), and in companies (basic organizations of associated labor, different associations), which would have had to coordinate their plans. Let us suppose that there was only one external factor of uncertainty with three possible values (good, medium, bad). The system would have required about 50,000 alternative plans. With two factors the number of plans would have grown to 14 million while four factors would have increased the number of plans to three billion. Before reaching that number, the whole adult population of Yugoslavia should have been engaged in preparing a single five-year plan.

If we ignore differences in terminology the system of social planning is theoretically similar to the neo-classical concept of general equilibrium on future markets (Ardalan 1980). The basic problem of the latter is how to determine proper market signals in advance. Failure causes a loss of part of gross domestic product, thus inefficiency. This can be prevented by exchanging information among economic units and concluding obligatory ex ante contracts on supply and demand. In this way, market uncertainty caused by ignorance of intentions and actions of other economic units can be reduced to a large degree. However, avoidance of losses, even theoretically, is possible only if there is competition on the product market and on the markets of production factors, if every unit participates in the process of information and coordination, if no new actors appear on the market, and if market uncertainty is the only form of uncertainty.

The basic similarity between general equilibrium on the future markets and social planning is that both are contingent on an increasing amount of information about the future and on the reduction of market uncertainty. They should enable a flexible adaptation of production capacities. Like negotiations on the way to general equilibrium end with binding agreements, the negotiations in the framework of social planning also end with self-management agreements and social contracts. Social planning thus would limit the role of government that does not even appear in the concept of general equilibrium.

The spiritual father of social planning was Edvard Kardelj, who stood behind most of the Yugoslav reforms, good or bad. The idea of social planning was one of the utopias that had nothing to do with planning. In reality, planning became a kind of ceremony, and it was considered as such also by most participants.[12]

ANNEX

Statistical Analysis of Indicative Planning and Changes in the Economic System

How well did indicative planning work in Yugoslavia? Did plans have any impact on actual economic development? The answer to the second question is no. Did plans contain targets or forecasts? Did planners possess proper tools for the implementation of their plans? Was the construction of plans and their adoption by the parliament a mere ritual? Let us pretend that indicative planning worked in Yugoslavia, and the government was actively seeking to control the development of the economy and disposed of the means to make such control effective. This was not the case. The discrepancies between planned and actual growth rates between 1957 and 1976 cannot be interpreted as planning errors but rather as forecasting errors.

The analysis of the relationship between planning targets and plan fulfill-ments consists of three parts. The first part considers the midterm or five-year plans. The second part deals with the short-term or annual plans, and with the relationship between midterm and annual plans. In the third part, the behavior of planners as forecasters is analyzed. The inquiry into the midterm plans is based on six macroeconomic growth targets of six midterm plans in the 1957–1985 period, and the study of annual plans in the 1968–1985 period covers three macroeconomic growth targets. The number of planning targets for the analysis of planners' behavior is reduced to two only: growth figures of net material product and industrial production.

Table 9.1 presents the quality of "planning" for six planned items in six midterm plans by mean absolute error defined as $MAE = 1/n^* \sum /P_i\text{-}A_i/$ where P denotes planned growth rates and A actual growth rates over time and across aggregates.

Planners were more precise in easier-to-plan aggregates such as industrial production (Q) and employment (L), less precise in planning agricultural production (A), and net material product (NMP) and were the least precise in planning foreign trade flows, imports (M) and exports (E). They gener-ally overestimated growth (except in the 1957–1961 plan). The differences between the planned and actual growth rates increased considerably after 1976. This challenges the general belief that there was not much planning before 1976 and more planning after 1976, when faith was restored in plan-ning and the new system of social planning was introduced. However, one could argue that increased discrepancies between actual and planned figures were caused by the fact that the tasks of planners after 1976 became much harder because of changes in the world economy (oil crisis) reverberating in the indebted Yugoslav economy.

Table 9.1 Quality of Midterm Plans in Yugoslavia, 1957–1985

Source: author's compilations from Statistički Godišnjak Jugoslavije 1989 1990. NMP—net material product, Q—indus-trial production, A—agricultural production, L—employment, M—imports, E—exports; MAE—mean absolute error

	Over time					
Plan	1957–61	1961–65	1966–70	1971–75	1976–80	1981–85
MAE	2.18	3.85	3.85	2.34	4.46	4.23
	Across Aggregates					
Aggregate	NMO	Q	A	L	M	E
MAE	2.46	1.61	2.40	1.52	6.20	5.60

Annual plans should augment the implementation of midterm plans by adjusting to actual development within the planned period. One could therefore expect that annual plans were closer to reality than midterm plans. Nevertheless, yearly plans often lacked numerical figures, which were replaced by statements such as "more than," "fast," "faster than," "slower," and so forth. This reduces the number of planning targets to be analyzed to three (net material product, industrial production, and employment) and shortens the period under scrutiny to 1968–1985.

The characteristics of the yearly plans of NMP for the period 1968–1985 are summarized in Figure 9.1 while data on growth included in midterm plans and on actual growth extend to the period 1957–1985.

Figure 9.1 indicates that fluctuations of actual growth over growth envisaged in midterm plans were enormous, which in the period 1957–1967 was mainly due to fluctuations in agricultural production. Actual growth lagged behind growth planned in midterm plans by 3.7 percentage points. In the period 1968–1985 actual average growth lagged behind average yearly planned growth by 0.29 percentage points. Fluctuation of actual growth (coefficient of variation KV= 0.69) exceeded fluctuations in planned growth (KV=0.37) presented in Table 9.2.

Figure 9.2 indicates that in the 1970s there was no systematic lagging of actual growth behind planned growth, while in the 1980s actual growth systematically lagged behind planned growth.

How successful were changes in the economic system? Table 9.3 demonstrates cyclical development.

The data speak for themselves. They show the catastrophic results of agricultural policy in the 1940s, accompanied by a large fall of exports, partly caused by the break between Yugoslavia and the Soviet Union, and a high growth of industry. The next period (1952–1962), when ideological nonsenses dominating economic policy were abolished, became the most successful stage of economic development in Yugoslavia. Slowdown of growth, galloping inflation, and mass unemployment followed thereafter. Finally, general stagnation and hyperinflation in the last period indicated the end of the system and of the country.

Table 9.2 Statistics of Yugoslav Indicative Planning 1957–1967 and 1968–1985

Source: author's compilation from Table 9.1

	1957–1967			*1968–1985*		
	actual	midterm	difference	actual	planned	difference
Average	6.12	8.93	-3.71	4.52	4.81	-0.29
Standard error	5.4	1.58		3.1	1.8	
KV	0.9	0.17		0.69	0.37	

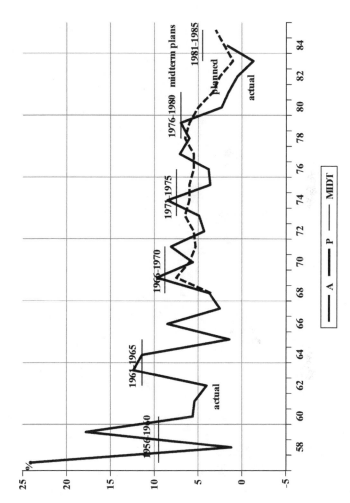

Figure 9.4: Indicative Planning in Yugoslavia 1957–1985 *Source:* author's compilation from Statistički Godišnjak Jugoslavije 1989–1990.

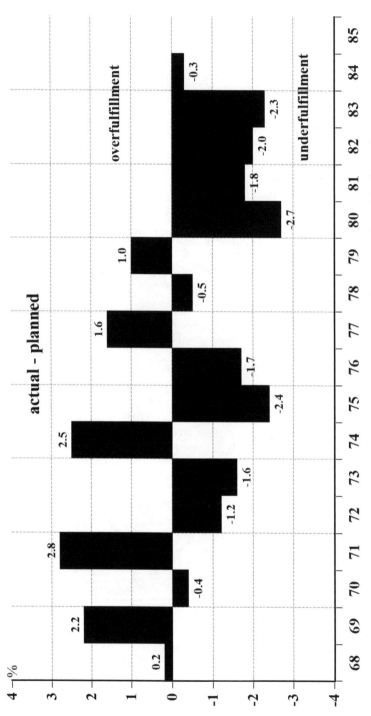

Figure 9.2: Errors of Planners in Annual Plans 1968–1985 *Source:* author's compilation from Statistički Godišnjak Jugoslavije 1989–1990.

Table 9.3 Systemic Changes and Development

Source: author's compilation from *Statistički Godišnjak Jugoslavije 1989* 1990.

Period	1946– 1951	1952– 1962	1963– 1973	1974– 1984	1980– 1984	1985– 1991
Rates of growth (in percent)						
GDP	2.3	8.3	6.5	3.9	2.6	-0.1
Industry	12.9	12.2	8.6	5.4	2.7	-0.1
Agriculture	-3.1	9.2	3.1	2.1	1.6	0.2
Employment	8.3	6.8	2.4	3.6	2.4	1.2
Export in USD	-3.1	12.0	14.0	13.3	10.1	9.4
Imports in USD	3.6	10.1	16.6	11.8	-2.0	0.3
Fixed investments		11.5	5.3	11.8	-2.0	-0.5
Private cons.		6.5	6.4	2.8	-0.5	2.1
Retail sale prices		8.6	13.0	28.3	40.2	105
Ratios						
Investment/GDP		41.9	38.9	35.2	30.2	20.3
Capital/output		2.28	2.23	2.64	2.82	
Labor/output		8.87	2.42	1.86	1.82	
Unemployment rate		5.01	7.58	18.3	14.2	16.5
Export/import rate		64.7	69.4	68.9	74.8	80.5

NOTES

1. This chapter may be biased as its author actively participated in shaping economic development in Yugoslavia and knew most of the decision-makers in person.

2. For more on this, see Mencinger (2018).

3. The crisis indirectly enhanced the openness of the country by resulting in the employment of more than one million Yugoslavs abroad (the peak was reached in 1972 before the oil crisis). This became a convenient solution: besides decreasing unemployment, it resulted in enormous amounts of remittances sent home by Yugoslav guest workers.

4. For example, Jaroslav Vanek published a renowned book *General Theory of Labor-Managed Market Economies* in 1970, in which he wanted to prove that such economies are the most efficient. The author of this chapter confronted Vanek's and Branko Horvat's theoretical claims with empirical data indicating that a labor-managed economy is more efficient indeed in keeping open unemployment low and transform it into socially more acceptable hidden unemployment, but less efficient in controlling inflation and ensuring higher rates of growth (Mencinger 1986).

5. Universities offered more and more MBA courses because these were very profitable ventures. Such courses were normally paid for by the participants or their companies.

6. In a related discussion during the 1960s, Yugoslav economists made attempts to define what was to be the proper price in a socialist market economy. There were two

different views. One group, including Bajt and Horvat, asserted that the proper price in a self-managed economy is the so-called production price that meets two requirements: it should be proportional to relative wages and equalize return on capital. The other group claimed that prices should be determined by relative wages only.

7. He studied law in Kiev and received his doctorate in economics, finance, and statistics in Saint Petersburg. Upon arrival in Yugoslavia he became professor of economics at the Ljubljana University Law School where he stayed for 25 years, teaching economics and statistics until 1943 when the Italian government closed the university.

8. Again, this was one of the truly rare works in the field; the only other covering the same area was the book co-authored by Nikola Čobeljić and Radmila Stojanović (1966).

9. Far the most productive, influential, and critical foreign scholar on the economic theory of Yugoslav self-management was Benjamin N. Ward, who taught at University of Berkeley for more than three decades. His main research fields were comparative economic systems and the methodology of economics. The former included research on mathematical techniques in Soviet planning, comparative economic development (Yugoslavia, Greece, Chile, and so forth), and economic planning in the West.

10. An overview of economic and econometric models was presented in Mencinger and Pfajfar (1986).

11. For a detailed analysis of midterm plans in Yugoslavia, see Annex.

12. Ironically, the decay of contractual socialism began with a planning decision, more exactly, with the so-called "planned borrowing abroad." In the Yugoslav national plan for the period 1976–1980, a loan of USD 11.5 billion and a repayment of the old debt of USD 5.2 billion were foreseen. Yugoslavia's gross debt abroad increased from USD 6.6 billion in 1975 to USD 21.1 billion in 1981, or 220 percent of GDP (Cemović 1985; Štiblar 1991).

BIBLIOGRAPHY

Ardalan, Cyrus. 1980. "Workers' Self-Management and Planning: The Yugoslav Case." *World Development* 8 (9): 623–38.

Bajt, Aleksander. 1953. *Marksov zakon vrednosti*. Ljubljana: Pravna Fakulteta.

———. 1958. *Politična ekonomija (kapitalizma)*. Ljubljana: Gospodarski Vestnik.

———. 1967. "Yugoslav Economic Reforms, Monetary and Production Mechanism." *Economics of Planning* 7 (3): 200–218.

Bilimovič, Aleksander. 1933. *Uvod v ekonomsko vedo*. Ljubljana: Jugoslovanska knjigarna. Bole, Velimir. 1975. *Izločanje sezone iz časovnih vrst*. Ljubljana: Ekonomski Inštitut Pravne Fakultete.

Bole, Velimir, and Jože Mencinger. 1980. *Ekonometrični model Jugoslovanskega gospodarstva*. Ljubljana: EIPF.

Brglez, Alja. 2015. "Ruski znanstveniki v Kraljevini Jugoslaviji." Monitor ISH 17 (1): 151–76.

Cemović, M. 1985. *Zašto, kako i koliko smo se zadužili: Kreditni odnosi Jugoslavije sa inostranstvom*. Beograd: Institut za unapredženje robnog prometa.

Černe, France. 1960. *Planiranje in tržni mehanizem v ekonomski teoriji socilizma.* Ljubljana: Cankarjeva založba.

Cobeljic, Nikola, and Radmila Stojanovic. 1966. *Teorija investicionih ciklusa socijalistickog razvoja.* Beograd: Institut za ekonomska istrazivanja.

Dabčević-Kučar, Savka. 1957. *J.M. Keynes: Teoretičar državnog kapitalizma.* Zagreb: Kultura.

Horvat, Branko. 1961. *Ekonomska teorija planske privrede.* Beograd: Kultura.

———. 1962a. *Međusektorska analiza*, Zagreb: Narodne novine.

———. 1962b. *Ekonomski modeli*, Zagreb: Ekonomski institut.

———. 1964. *Towards a Theory of Planned Economy.* Beograd: Yugoslav Institute of Economic Research.

———. *Privredni ciklusi u Jugoslaviji*, Beograd: Institut ekonomskih nauka, 1969. (Business Cycles in Yugoslavia, International Arts and Sciences Press, New York, 1971.)

———. *Privredni sistem i ekonomska politika Jugoslavije*, Beograd: Institut ekonomskih nauka, 1970.

———. 1971. "Yugoslav Economic Policy in the Post-War Period: Problems, Ideas, Institutional Developments." *American Economic Review Supplement* 61: 71–169.

———. *Ekonomska politika stabilizacije*, Zagreb: Naprijed, 1976.

———. 1972. "Critical Notes on the Theory of the Labor-Managed Firm and Some Macroeconomic Implications." *Economic Analysis* 6: 291–94.

———. 1975. *Self-Governing Socialism: A Reader.* New York: International Arts and Sciences Press.

———. 1982. *The Political Economy of Socialism.* New York: Sharpe.

Keren, Michael, Jeffrey Miller, and James Thornton. 1983. "The Ratchet. A Dynamic Managerial Incentive Model of the Soviet Enterprise." *Journal of Comparative Economics* 7 (4): 347–67.

Kidrič, Boris. 1949. "Kvalitet robno-novčanih odnosa u FNRJ." *Komunist* 1: 33–51.

———. 1950a. *Privredni problemi FNRJ.* Beograd: Kultura.

———. 1950b. "Teze o ekonomiji u prelaznom razdoblju u našoj zemlji." *Komunist* 6: 1–20.

Kranjec, Marko. 1976. "A Self-Managed Fiscal System and the Allocation Function of Fiscal Policy." *Journal of Public Economics* 5 (3–4): 325–36.

Lavrač, Ivan. 1956. *Maršallov zakon tražnje.* Ljubljana: RSS.

Maksimović, Ivan. 1958. *Teorija socializma u građanskoj ekonomskoj nauci.* Beograd: Nolit.

Mencinger, Jože. 1971. "Inflacija potraznje ili inflacija troskova?" *Ekonomska analiza* 1–2: 1–16.

———. 1975. *A Quarterly Macroeconometric Model of the Yugoslav Economy.* University of Pennsylvania, Philadelphia. PhD dissertation.

———. 1986. "The Yugoslav Economic Systems and Their Efficiency." *Economic Analysis* 20 (1): 31–43.

———. 2018. "Social Property and the Market: An Uneasy Symbiosis in Yugoslavia." In *Populating No Man's Land: Economic Concepts of Ownership under Communism*, edited by János Mátyás Kovács, 261–86. Lanham: Lexington Books.

Mencinger, Jože, and Lovro Pfajfar. 1986. "Makroekonomski modeli u Jugoslaviji." *Ekonomist* 39 (2): 156–70.

Sapir, André. 1980. "Economic Growth and Factor Substitution: What Happened to the Yugoslav Economic Miracle?" *Economic Journal* 90 (358): 294–313.

Sekulić, Mijo. 1980. *Međusektorski modeli i strukturna analiza.* Zagreb: Informator.

Sicherl, Pavle. 1992. "Integrating Comparisons Across Time and Space: Methodology and Applications to Disparities within Yugoslavia." *Journal of Public Policy* 12 (4): 377–403.

Statistički Godišnjak Jugoslavije 1989. 1990. Beograd: Savezni Zavod za Stat.

Štiblar, Franjo. 1991. "Zunanja zadolženost Jugoslavije in njenih federalnih enot." *Teorija in praksa* 28 (7): 745–58.

Vanek, Jaroslav. 1970. *The General Theory of Labor-Managed Market Economies.* Ithaca: Cornell University Press.

Ward, Benjamin .1958. "The Firm in Illyria: Market Syndicalism." *American Economic Review* 48 (4): 566–89.

World Bank. 1979. *Yugoslavia: Self-Management Socialism and Challenges of Development.* Baltimore: John Hopkins University Press.

Žebot, Ciril. 1967. *Slovenija, včeraj, danes in jutri.* Klagenfurt: Mohorjeva založba.

Conclusion

Rationality Found and Lost? In Search of a New Historical Narrative of Optimal Planning

János Mátyás Kovács

The history of economic thought under communism can be portrayed as a long chain of human disasters. Economic theorists could end up in jail or be executed for a policy idea, a scientific method, or just a phrase blacklisted by the censors. In brighter times, repression "only" led to forced emigration, employment and publication bans, travel restrictions, and harassment at the workplace, which also could result in illness or death. Mathematical economists suffered from such sanctions until the late 1950s, and even afterwards. From the 1960s, their *métier* became much freer, attaining, in the worst case, a status of a semi-official discipline. Thus, the specter of tragedy invoked in the Introduction may seem like an exaggeration—unless it referred to the first postwar generation of mathematical economists in the Eastern Bloc. They were crestfallen after experiencing one failure after another in advancing optimal planning, their signature research program, which they hoped, with Panglossian optimism, would establish the best of all possible worlds in universal economic science.

Interestingly enough, while some disenchantment does transpire from the reminiscences of the elite of optimizers, their personal accounts seldom contain much self-criticism such as: borrowing the theory of general equilibrium, I ignored its philosophical and methodological underpinnings; I underestimated the Mises-Hayek arguments on the impossibility of rational economic calculation in a collectivist system; I put too much trust in the improvability of the planning regimes; I was blinded by the highest-level acknowledgement coming from the West; I made too many concessions to the Central Planner and got stuck with the research program even after I had known that it was hopeless; I neglected cooperation with the market reformers and did not use my mathematical knowledge to work with them on a new theory of the planned economy, which could have relied on a critical analysis of its institutions including the party-state.

It can be heartbreaking for scholars to face the ruins of their lifetime achievement. But what explains that, until today, a majority of historical analysts have pulled their punches when writing the history of optimal planning? A systematic overview of the literature of the past sixty years should elucidate such a discretion and assist the reader in deciding whether our research group has managed to go beyond the state of the art. This will be a fairly unconventional review: instead of a dry summary of the main arguments, I will initiate conversation with my fellow historians.

CIRCLING AROUND THE SOCIALIST CALCULATION DEBATE (AND THE COMPUTER)

The positive biases of the first observers[1] originated in a long-awaited turn in communist economic thought, which liberated numerous groups of gifted researchers suffering under oppressive regimes. The usual orientalist prejudices were moderated by the respectable traditions of mathematical economics in Russia and the Soviet Union and the scientific discoveries made by scholars like Leonid Kantorovich, János Kornai, and Oskar Lange parallel to their counterparts in the West. In fact, early observers aired some concern about what might come after the stage of "hurray, optimal planning is here." Nevertheless, as indicated in the Introduction, they did not find fault with the lopsided (technique-oriented) takeover of the neoclassical paradigm, ignoring the Socialist Calculation Debate, or the statist leanings of the optimizers. They were also fairly uninterested in the ambiguous relationship between the "plan improvers" and the market reformers and insensitive to the principal moral dilemma of many Marxist (and a few non-Marxist) mathematical economists who cooperated with the communist government. These economists were tormented by the following: what if the leading communist officials agree to our advice and the planned economy turns into a *perpetuum mobile* supporting authoritarian rule with our help? In an era of "cyber-optimism" generating dreams about vast automated control systems, this did not seem an unfounded worry.[2]

In a sense, sympathy was understandable, and not only because of the Eastern European provenance or socialist commitment of many Western analysts.[3] Besides the hopes of convergence, the rise of the Soviet School of Mathematical Economics and its influence upon the Eastern European research communities raised hopes about progress in economic thinking in the Soviet empire, notwithstanding the publication of the notorious 1954 textbook of political economy (Ostrovitianov et al. 1954). Peter Wiles' (1964, 16) sarcastic remark about optimal planners who would like to replace perfect competition with "perfect computation" was a rare bird. The sympathizers argued the following way: Soviet-style pseudo-scholarship has an encouraging alternative at last; its followers use our professional economic discourse but they are not rootless in their own scientific environment.[4] In Alfred Zauberman's (1975, 9–11) words, they had left behind the "five fingers plus abacus" technique long before. An authentic scientific movement came into being (powered by the *shestidesiatniki*, the generation of the 1960s), but—despite all support rendered by the Kremlin and symbolized by Stalin and Lenin Prizes—its protagonists faced resistance by both academia and politics time and again. Even those among the benevolent observers who were less enthusiastic about mathematical planning thought that things could not get worse than they had been under verbal planning safeguarded by the official political economy, the "discoveries" of which did not exceed Stalin's "basic law of maximum satisfaction of society's needs." They trusted in a (never materializing) future, in which planning would have a proper theory at last and no *apparatchik* can say that two plus two is five because of Party demands. John Michael Montias (1967, 244) went as far as to predict the imminent end of separation between Eastern European and Western economics.

Justifying a "Revolution"—the Founding Narratives

Let me first bring the example of seminal works published by three leading analysts from the West: Alfred Zauberman, Michael Ellman, and Pekka Sutela who dominated the scene of historical analysis of Soviet planning concepts from the 1960s. All of them were extremely knowledgeable about the field and well-supplied by their Soviet colleagues with insider information. Although they did not follow closely the evolution of mathematical economics in other Eastern European countries, their books stand out from the sea of journal articles of the time.[5]

Zauberman who, in the 1950s, had pioneered an interpretation of the *oeuvre* of Soviet mathematical economists, introduced the romantic term "mathematical revolution" in 1975[6] to signal the birth of a new methodology in Soviet economic thought, with a special emphasis on the research program of optimal planning (which he earlier called "planometrics"). He put faith in the program's "organic development" (Zauberman 1975, 52) irrespective of the fact that in the first half of the 1970s it entered, as he said, its "post-elation" phase (41). The pinnacle of criticism in his case was a mild disagreement with Kantorovich who had hoped that the application of mathematical methods in central planning would result in a quick rise in the national product (45).[7] Instead of speaking of a failing project of social engineering or a utopia, Zauberman thought to witness just some unavoidable skepticism in the research community due to exaggerated expectations generated during the 1960s (52). Otherwise, he was convinced that the optimal models grew in sophistication, the computers became faster and faster, the ideological brakes got weaker, and the mathematical breakthrough was irreversible, also because Soviet economic science sought to become international (47). Official political economy was on its way to be pushed aside by the "relatively exact" discipline of mathematical economics (43–44). This would not make the labor theory of value disappear (19–20) since marginalism emerged in the USSR as a method of computation rather than a "subjectivist" philosophy of economic calculation. Apparently, the question of whether the application of the new algorithms could unleash (not just a mathematical but also) a neoclassical revolution at a certain point did not interest Zauberman.[8] He spoke of rationality in the context of a simplistic scheme of minimum costs versus maximum benefits (19), which would bring the concept down to earth from Marxist-Leninist political economy that considered rational economic behavior an innate property of the Central Planner (2–3).

Zauberman knew that (a) most of the optimal models were either mathematically correct or realistic; (b) in the Eastern Bloc not a single one- or five-year plan was built on optimal schemes (at most, the consistency of certain parts of some of them was checked by these). Nevertheless, he presumed that all was not lost that was delayed, hoping that even the political/ideological obstacles of the Brezhnev era would dwindle because the regime was doomed to boost productivity. Accordingly, the notorious lack of truthful economic information was not an unsurmountable *quality* problem originating in the very core of the planning system but a provisional difficulty owing to the still too large *quantity* of data demanded by the models and to the "inertia of the planning and controlling apparatus" (52) causing lags in providing the necessary data. Yet, healthy incentives and "closer and closer collaboration between the Soviet planner and the scientist" (53) should help. In sum, all economic actors involved with planning were portrayed as benevolent warriors of a common good, and "informational incongruities" (i.e., not severe systemic distortions) stemmed from organizational and cognitive bottlenecks rather than powerful vested interests at all levels of the planning hierarchy (41).[9]

The author did not cast serious doubts even on the most daring endeavor of mathematical economists in the Soviet Union, the establishment of a nationwide automated (self-adjusting) system of planning and control (35–36). According to him, the ultimate guarantee for success was the gradual shift in official economic theory thanks to co-opting the winning combination of input-output analysis and linear programming. Undoubtedly, these models brought along intricate problems related to aggregation, the lack of dynamic and stochastic approach, insistence on linearity and so on, but these were, in Zauberman's view, purely *technical* difficulties that certainly would be overcome by the evolution of mathematics and computer science. Sooner or later, the Central Planner would be unable to ignore what *logically* derived from the process of optimization, namely, concepts such as "equilibrium," "social utility," "shadow prices," and "duality" in general. These would support the marketization program of verbal reformers advocating the monetization and decentralization of the planned economy (19).[10] The "market or computer" choice was out of date (34–37). The models would produce a world of consistency and feasibility, forcing the economic actors to "declare their hands." Even if the supreme leaders continued to take the final decisions behind the scenes, they would have to choose from among mathematically viable alternatives (18). They would need to refrain from rule of thumb and *ad hoc* decisions as well as from an obsession to overfulfill the plans, which would upset the harmony of optimality.

During the 1970s, Michael Ellman took up the torch from Zauberman in a less optimistic mood, sharing Kornai's skepticism about the neoclassical underpinnings of optimal planning. As early as 1973, he reproached Soviet mathematical economists for going too far in trusting in general equilibrium and the healing force of the market as well as attributing too little importance to mobilizing social support for their optimal plans (Ellman 1973, 176–90).[11] For him, mathematization without a proper neoclassical turn was not an odd episode to be explained but a desirable combination: he demanded less Walras (129) and more Keynes and Marx (179, 182–83) in terms of economic theory to attain, in the end, Jan Tinbergen's ideal of indicative planning in both the East and the West.[12] In this respect, he went far beyond Zauberman. Ellman overlooked the concessions the mathematical planners made by accepting the privileges of the Central Planner in defining the economic policy priorities of the optimal models and reserving the right to diverge from the plans at any time. To him, most of the optimal planners seemed to be reform-minded experts, covert or overt adherents of *khozraschet* as if Evsei Liberman and Leonid Kantorovich had merged into one individual.

Ellman saw the imperfections of verbal planning clearly but—similar to Zauberman—did not take the Austrian-style reservations about the rationality of "collectivist economic planning" seriously.[13] In Ellman's eyes, economic rationality was not threatened by optimization models that lacked vital information and were built on severely biased data and absurd mathematical assumptions such as the linearity of programming procedures and fixed coefficients of the I-O models (31), but rather by the fact that the optimizers were actually inconsistent market reformers. Allegedly, they wanted the planners to apply capitalist categories like price, wage, interest, profit, and rent provided by their model calculations, as well as the resulting "objectively determined valuations"[14] of the resources, while other segments of the planned economy (above all the institutions including the incentives) would remain the same (57). Hence, a hybrid system would come into being, combining the disadvantages, as he wrote, of both the "administrative" and the "*khozraschet*" economies: waste, rigidity, and technological standstill with weak growth, slow structural change, and rising social inequality.

Discussing the social base of optimal planning, Ellman was appreciative of the state bureaucrats. He contended that optimization represented the vested interests of experts who wanted to crowd out the *apparatchiki* from the planning process despite the fact that this group administered "society as a whole and thus had to place the requirements of society as a whole above its own sectional interest" (136). Thus, optimal planning was depicted as an ideology rather than a scientific undertaking (139, 179) that included outmoded propositions anyway. Allegedly, it suffered from a "hypertrophy" of market orientation and rational organization of production, focusing on allocation and choice instead of growth and social cohesion (100, 178). "It was an attempt to replace one doctrine, political economy, which provides the ideological legitimation for rule by the bosses, by another doctrine, optimal planning, which legitimizes the rule of the white-collar intelligentsia" (141). In this sense, he also lamented the heavily mathematical discourse and the quixotism of the researchers who might have sought stronger social backing of their program, for instance, by lobbying not only for "the old bourgeois liberal program (civil liberties)" but also for workers' self-management (126, 175).

Insisting on an impartial interpretation, Ellman raised doubts about both the computer and the market, challenging the project of a nationwide automated control system while also blaming a few radicals (and disregarding the moderates, an overwhelming majority by the way) among the optimizers who, in his opinion, risked social polarization, inflation, and unemployment by introducing shadow prices, taxing capital investment, or demanding the closure of loss-making enterprises. These radicals (scholars like Igor Birman or Viktor Volkonskii), he claimed, did not even shy away from advocating a transition from directive to "consultative" planning, thereby irritating the "responsible officials" (127).[15] Yet, "if enterprises were simply instructed to maximize profits and given a free hand, the experience of capitalist firms suggests that they might well operate with considerable waste and inefficiency" (54). In the thick of such criticism, the reader can hardly find praise about the benign effects of the optimal planners' research program in enhancing the efficiency of investments in certain branches, improving production schedules and the location of industries, reducing shortages, stocks, and waste, as well as in enabling the Central Planner to temper taut plans and choose among plan variants (189–90).

Among the founding narrators Pekka Sutela (1984) was perhaps the most cognizant of the stagnation and decline of optimal planning in the Soviet Union during the 1970s. Prior to *perestroika* that depreciated mathematical economics and rehabilitated market reform, he nuanced Zauberman's concept of a "mathematical revolution" by emphasizing the continuity of verbal research programs. He challenged those analysts who squeezed the researchers into two camps: mathematical economists and textbook political economists. While Ellman spelled out the reformist inclinations of the former, Sutela stressed that the political economists also approached Western economics by accepting certain ideas of market reform. However, he disregarded a third camp, more influential in some other communist countries, the camp of verbal reformers who had left official political economy behind yet resisted the temptation of mathematics.

Did anything change that explained Sutela's detached attitude that lacked both Zauberman's admiration of and Ellman's suspicion about optimal planning? Yes, with time, it became clear that any refinement of the macro-level optimal planning models was insufficient to convince the Central Planner to implement them, trusting that their economic benefits would balance their political costs. The late Brezhnev regime was not ready to launch a marketization project similar to the Kosygin reform in the 1960s, which could have been combined with the optimization of planning on various levels of the economic hierarchy. Moreover, the institutional buildup of mathematical economics also slowed down during the years of *zastoi,* and the main strongholds and leading scholars of the discipline were arguing with each other persistently. Although Zauberman and Ellman did not cease to follow these developments during the 1970s and 1980s, they failed to revise their attitudes.[16] Thus, it was Sutela who realized that the program of optimal planning actually had withered away and only the fingernails of the dead continued to grow. "It is difficult not to judge [the program] as a failure," wrote Sutela (1984, 203) politely.

He was barely interested in the mathematical intricacies of SOFE (System of the Optimal Functioning of the Socialist Economy) that became the new official label for scientific planning in the Soviet Union by the 1970s. Rather, he wanted to examine the political economy of the program by focusing on the cultural background of its creation. As he put it, if earlier works "have . . . regarded SOFE as an alien body within Soviet economics, this study weighs the scales in the opposite direction. SOFE is regarded here . . . as part of Soviet Marxist thought (12)." In Sutela's—iconoclastic—opinion, the neoclassical principles of optimal planning fit well with official Soviet political economy (which he considered a pseudo-science), mainly because both had a strong normative thrust and propensity for social engineering (87).[17] In contrast to what was customary to assume at the time, he blamed the neoclassical paradigm for its inherent normative bias toward the plan.

Accordingly, the optimal planner and the textbook political economist equally claim to be able to define a Good Society, the economy of which is rationally organized, balanced, and maximizes some sort of social utility. The former devises, under the supervision of the rulers, the objective function of a programming model while the latter—like Stalin—the "basic economic law of socialism." Nevertheless, Sutela did not mind that within this framework of official political economy SOFE proved unable to develop its neoclassical features into a full-blown theory because—following Kornai—he was convinced that such a theory could not meet the triple requirement of being theoretically sound, realistic, and also acceptable for communist rulers. Apparently, while Ellman denigrated the optimal planners by presenting them as agents of some erratic marketization, Sutela tarnished their fame by presenting them as experts who were deep down textbook Marxists, if not diehard Stalinists (116).[18] He knew that both political economy and mathematical economics had multiple shades in Soviet scholarship. However, he did not bother to engage in a thought experiment about the opportunity for optimal planners to modify their research program to become genuinely neoclassical (aborting, for instance, the labor theory of value), less normative, and more instrumentalist and even perhaps more realistic.

Sutela carefully mapped the institutional environment of mathematical economists in the Soviet Union, focusing on the political context of their scholarly work. However, he did not explain why these scholars failed to elaborate a coherent—mathematically equipped—theory of the planned economy despite the fact that, as he noted, they had already started checking the applicability of game theory to such an endeavor. Why did they stop short of exploring the institutional conditions of the planning process if—as top advisors—they were daily winners or losers of conflicts among the various power centers of central planning and knew the interests, strategies, and routines of the economic actors firsthand? Why did they not venture to trace the institutional games of planning, ranging from petty bargaining over pieces of information serviced by the firms, through the ongoing improvisation of the planning bureaucracy and its arbitrary intervention into model building, all the way up to the *placet* given by the Politburo to the five-year plan (or to the changes in the mandatory planning targets two months later)? Why did the optimal planners shut their eyes to an orgy of irrationality that did not recede for decades? Were they scared, tired, or both, or did they trust in incremental improvements or—on the contrary—in a gradual delegitimization of central planning as such? Did they believe that their mathematical algorithms (stochastic methods, simulation and so forth) would be able to cure the millions of fake data fed into their models (126–27) or discipline the economic actors who were eminently interested in secrecy, cheating, and falsification? Did they expect the Central Planner to be happy about the curtailment of its own power and to disclose say, the statistics of military production to the model builders in the hope of receiving a less inconsistent five-year plan in exchange? Did the top rulers have reliable figures about top-secret matters at all? Why did a number of optimal planners begin to be attracted by radical market reforms during the 1980s (107) and work on econometric rather than programming models?[19]

Sutela let most of these questions pass, although he got very close to the answers in discussing the selection of planning goals by the optimal planners. He recognized that the choice of the objective function of the programming task was a crucial criterion for the intellectual historian in identifying the position of mathematical planners on the axis stretching between being an opportunistic advisor to the communist regime and its brave critic. Sutela reported that, even in the early 1980s, the majority of "Sofeists" agreed to the party's leading role in determining the common goals of society (98). Only some experts like Aron Katsenelinboigen and Nikolai Petrakov proposed that either the model itself should generate the objective function or citizens at large should do so through their market preferences and/or following some democratic procedure (cf. "compositional" versus "decompositional" goal formation [187–88]). The latter solutions would have been tantamount to a kind of liberal-democratic decision-making (like in the propagandistic ideal of Yugoslav self-management in the 1970s[20]). Sutela considered these options so unlikely to materialize in the USSR that he did not pay special attention to them.

As regards the future of SOFE, Sutela's interpretation was pessimistic but permissive. According to him, the research program "became an appendix of traditional planning methods, a compensation for the economic reform that had miscarried" (121). "It has really not shown what an optimal social-ist society might look like. It has certainly not provided for a strategy of transition to such a state, nor has it persuaded Soviet decision-makers of the need and possibility of such a transition. Furthermore, it has not provided us with an economic theory of really existing socialism" (203). All criticism notwithstanding, he did not deem the research program theoretically flawed *sui generis* but only infeasible in the context of the Soviet planned economy of the time. He alluded to a chance for continuation with these two cryptic sentences: "The basic alternative to the normative and abstract SOFE would certainly be a positive and critical social analysis but there is no evidence of circumstances having become any more favorable for such an orientation. SOFE may now be seen as a dead end, but finding a workable new course may prove difficult" (154).[21]

Austrian challenge

As we will see, some components of the founding narratives determined the way in which history-writing has approached optimal planning until today. Continuity was not broken, even by powerful interventions by members of the New (or Contemporary) Austrian School of Economics during the 1980s and 1990s. Yet, they did their best to reinstate the Mises-Hayek thesis into historical analysis, noticing that optimal planning revived the promise of rationality, which they thought had been disproved by the "old" Austrians for good in the Socialist Calculation Debate almost half a century before. This was a vital probe indeed because the School's propositions about the impossibility of both rational calculation and exact computation of the state of equilibrium were contested by cutting-edge models of optimal planning and the rapid development of computers. In addition, unlike in the 1930s when the Lange models were less mature in mathematical terms and enchanted only a few specialists such as Abba Lerner and Fred Taylor, the Soviet School of Mathematical Economics used highly complex algorithms and had a considerable entourage among scholars and state officials in the Eastern Bloc. The latter were willing to engage in large-scale experiments to optimize central control of their national economies. Finally, the heavy artillery deployed by Mises against the labor theory of value seemed to become expendable as many optimal planners slowly let go of this theory.

The arrival of new, technically well-equipped and politically influential discussion partners did not prompt Mises and Hayek or neo-Austrian scholars such as Don Lavoie and Peter Boettke either to prepare a comparative historical survey of the real-socialist planning concepts or to map the mathematical features and the political/sociological background of those concepts.[22] Instead, they revisited the key message of their own school,[23] the emphatic rejection of the possibility of rational calculation (planning). They tried their best to protect that message against the pro-Lange discourse of eminent Western economists such as Abram Bergson, Frank Knight, Joseph Schumpeter, and Benjamin Ward, a discourse that enhanced the legitimacy of Eastern European optimal planners a great deal (Lavoie 1981). The decline of optimization attempts did not surprise the neo-Austrians at all. This was what the Austrian School had always expected to happen. Thus, the members of its new generations did not feel the need to write the second act of the drama of optimal planning. How could we speak of a tragedy, they might ask themselves, if the hero's aspirations were fatefully flawed from the very outset? Why should we indulge in dissecting the new calculation procedures (be they "non-competitive" or "competitive") if Mises and Hayek had already proven the basic fallacies of any such procedure?

Similarly, the neo-Austrian experts were uninterested in the scope and quality of neoclassical elements in the optimal models since they did not hold the general equilibrium paradigm in high esteem.[24] They missed a dynamic/ evolutionary and institution-centered view of the economy, which focuses on property, incentives, entrepreneurship, and the like and finds disequilibrium where mainstream economists search for perfect equilibrium, nothing else (cf. Lavoie 1981; Kirzner 1988). As a final trump, they repeated the Hayekian question addressed to Lange in the 1930s: why bother with simulation if real thing exists? Why fabricate a (less efficient) socialist market if one can borrow one from a (more efficient) capitalist economy? Ironically, they extended their doubts to the market reformers who actually were quite close to them in terms of favoring institutional analysis, praising rivalry and entrepreneurship, and playing around with private ownership. With no scruples, these reformers were put under the heading of "social engineers" next to the optimal planners.[25]

Reinstating the Mises-Hayek arguments implied a rearrangement of its internal proportions. Like the labor theory of value, the issue of computation lost its former significance. Owing to the progress of electronic computers and the invention of decomposition methods, the thesis of the impossibility of *computing* the state of equilibrium was overshadowed by the impossibility of *calculating* it. The neo-Austrian theorists also bracketed the old—fairly scholastic—debate whether rational calculation was deemed by their predecessors impossible in theoretical or practical terms or both. Rather they reached for the reasoning of Mises and Hayek, claiming that all efforts of optimization stumble upon a lack of reliable data.[26] In a planned economy (a) the actors, be they planners or those whose economic behavior they plan, are interested in concealing and distorting information due to their respective shares in informal property rights in the world of formally social ownership (Lavoie 1985, 143–44, 173–78; Boettke 1995; Boettke and Anderson 1997); (b) even if—against their own incentives—they were willing to provide accurate statistics, they would be unable to do so because a large part of economic knowledge/information, for example, data on change in technology and consumers preferences, are by definition inarticulate, tacit, contextual, or simply unavailable to them (unlike in a capitalist economy where these data emerge and spread in the market process, i.e., in a competition between agents of private property) (Lavoie 1985, 103–104, 160–61, 171–72; 1986, 8–10); and (c) even if they possessed true-to-life information ex ante, these pieces of dispersed (local) knowledge could only be centralized with the help of market prices.[27] However, provided that the authors of the planning models want to avoid these crucial quandaries by simulating the market, they must tell how exactly the process of simulation is to be organized. How will the Walrasian *tâtonnement* function in the real world?

The Austrians had regarded Lange as just another Marxist utopian thinker already in the 1930s. Witnessing the rise of hopes for computer-based plano-metric control from the late 1950s, they could not but smile when they saw he had taken it much further in the meantime. Famously, Lange ([1964] 1967) claimed that the market works as an obsolete computer coordinating supply and demand in a cumbersome way.[28] In response, the neo-Austrian analysts refined Hayek's views on the essential "unrealism" resulting from the artifi-cial design of communication between the planning office and the companies, that is, of the trial-and-error process that was assumed to clear the market. They asked, for example, how central plans could adjust flexibly to changes in the economic environment if production started only after all iterations of matching supply and demand were completed and the plans were supposed to remain untouched until the new series of iterations were terminated. How can the optimal planners feed data into their models, when much of the data only emerge (have to be discovered) during the very implementation of those models? This paradox suggested that the truly impossible undertaking would not be the solution but rather would be the formulation of the simultane-ous equations of the programming tasks (Lavoie 1985, 91). As a final blow, referring to Leonid Hurwicz, they added that in dual systems, such as the one devised by Lange, it is the plan that would adjust (*ex post*) to the market and not conversely as expected by the optimal planners (95).

In the liberal *Zeitgeist* of 1989, discussions on optimizing the central plan became a research topic almost as untimely as the controversies about improving mercantilist regimes in the eighteenth century. When at the begin-ning of the new millennium, the tide turned and the communist past regained some academic interest, the historians already lived in another *Zeitgeist* that was often critical of liberal doctrines. However, those who disliked the Austrian arguments have proved unable to integrate and complete the found-ing narratives to explain why and how optimal planning actually failed. They tried to provide a richer history of the research program by amalgamating economic, political, social, and intellectual history-writing as well as apply-ing "thicker description" and "closer reading." Nevertheless, their works suffered either from anti-neoliberal resentment or—on the contrary—from forced impartiality.

A "Neoliberal Conspiracy"

The stubborn attempts at optimizing central planning started rehabilitating key notions of neoclassical economics such as rationality, scarcity, choice, marginal utility, equilibrium, that is, notions that almost had been eradicated at the end of the Soviet twenties. Following 1989, the process of reha-bilitation gained momentum. The upsurge of neoclassical economics under post-communism was an enormous accomplishment (regardless of whether one liked it or not) after decades of indoctrination against "subjectivist economic theories." A witch hunt seemed to end, which connected Nikolai Bukharin's ([1919] 1927) vitriolic assault on the "economic theory of the leisure class" with the last—maybe less arrogant—textbook of political economy published in any of the communist countries in the second half of the 1980s.

A peculiar novelty in the post-1989 literature on the evolution of optimal planning was the appearance of authors like Johanna Bockman (2007; 2011; 2012; Bockman and Eyal 2002; Bockman and Bernstein 2008) and Gil Eyal (2000; 2003) who did not consider the landslide victory of neoclassical thought in Eastern Europe during the 1990s a laudable development at all. They reinvented Ellman's arguments against the "hypertrophy of market orientation" under the influence of the writings of Philip Mirowski (2002; 2009; Mirowski and Plehwe 2009) on neoclassical economics (especially its links to cybernetics) and on what he described as the "neoliberal thought collective." They also borrowed heavily from the anti-neoliberal literature of the early 2000s produced by scholars such as David Harvey, John Kelly, Dieter Plehwe, and Monica Prasad. Fearing the advent of a "neoliberal hegemony," Bockman and her co-authors were captivated by two—alleged—traits of neoclassical theory: its socialist origins and evolution into neoliberalism. They challenged neoclassical economics *not* on Austrian grounds[29] but because they assumed that neo*classicism* cultivated by mathematical economists in the communist era had been a catalyst for the revival of the Mises-Hayek tradition often labelled by them nonchalantly as neo*liberalism.*

No matter how far they left behind the earlier narrators of the optimization story in terms of research methodology, these analysts did not tell the second part of the story. In their view, optimal planning was sentenced to death at the moment *Homo Oeconomicus* (in whatever disguise) appeared in the first models of the research program. Like Ellman, they lamented that—although general equilibrium theory also can be used to justify the rational allocation of resources by the state—it paved the way for the planned economies to the capitalist market as a result of cooperation (bordering on conspiracy) of academic, economic, and political elites, both Eastern and Western.[30] Allegedly, these wove strong transnational networks cross-cutting the Cold War divide. Consequently, state fundamentalism was replaced by market fundamentalism, instead of choosing a "third way" that—unlike market socialism—would be immune to capitalist temptation.[31] Moreover, the pre-1989 liberal awakening in Eastern Europe and China (however sluggish that had been) came to be regarded by these observers not only as a manifestation of neoliberal wrongdoing but also as one of its sources and testing grounds.

The authors of this strand mostly were uninterested in the twists and turns of the evolution of mathematical economics. They put the optimal planners in the same pigeon hole as the market reformers whom they also considered proto-neoliberal thinkers. According to Bockman (2011, 1), the neoclassical theorists in Eastern Europe were exploited if not cheated: "neoliberal capitalism was a parasitic growth on the very socialist alternatives it attacked." To increase confusion, she called these theorists socialists or leftists (whatever these words mean). Allegedly, they eagerly wanted to have their research program "translated" (Latour) into mainstream neoclassical economics in the West and, at the same time, to catch up with that mainstream, which was—somewhat paradoxically—co-produced by them in "Eastern Europe as a laboratory for economic knowledge" (Bockman and Eyal 2002). To put all this in the language of cultural anti-imperialism, they were depicted as self-made "Reagan robots" (Bockman 2011, VII) who, obsessed with the goal of self-colonization, did not realize that Western neoliberals used them as useful idiots to prove the popularity of their own teachings. This interpretation overlooked the expressly collectivist/statist attitudes of the mathematical planners (and the fact that they often obediently advised communist leaders). Alternatively, it was presumed that these advisors, just like supposedly all neoliberals, loved strong states led by authoritarian-minded "social planners" if those pursue free-market policies (218, 220).

These analysts were right to assert that seen from a global perspective "the majority of mainstream neoclassical economists have not advocated neoliberalism" (215). Furthermore, they also claimed correctly that Eastern European optimizers contributed to the development of the neoclassical paradigm in certain fields. Yet, it might have been sound to refer to the split egos of these theorists and portray them as *half-hearted* importers or (re) inventors of *selected* neoclassical ideas rather than full-blown Walrasian thinkers. Undoubtedly, through general equilibrium theory one could borrow the *language* of market competition and rational calculation. Nevertheless, according to the creed of the overwhelming majority of optimal planners, in the real world both competition and calculation could be organized by the communist state as well, and moreover, better than by the capitalist market.

Even with such limitations, the thesis of the neoclassical-neoliberal nexus seems to be a huge overstatement. To put it bluntly, should we suppose that those, who the day before yesterday had begged the communist Central Planner to apply shadow prices, asked the "neoliberal social planner" to privatize the pension system yesterday? It would be, I believe, a more plausible assumption that it was not the minority but only a miniscule faction of optimal planners who could not wait to see the coming of "neoliberal dictators" ready to follow their advice once the communist dictators fell. Similarly, is it not a hasty generalization to equate communist authoritarian rule with early post-communist liberalization even if it was directed from above?

Revisiting the Soviet Case

Approaching our contemporary period, one encounters a growing number of historians who seem somewhat dissatisfied with the militantly anti-neoliberal discourse of researchers like Bockman and Eyal (Leeds 2016a, 369) but agree with them on refuting the widespread truism that both neoclassical and neoliberal economic ideas were imported from the West.[32] Trying to prove the "homegrownness" of these ideas in the USSR, they also reveal political and sociological curiosity and explore plenty of archival and oral sources. As ex-post participant observers, they often portray the research strategies and institutions of the mathematical economists with anthropological precision. Nevertheless, they can be reproved for being "completely apolitical.... What is lost in this cultural-institutional sociology of science is the sound of the grinding wheels of institutional competition, political coalition building, and their associated economic outcomes" (Feygin 2017, 214). To be sure, the criticized members of the group adhere to the founding narrators not only in forming political opinions cautiously but also in an insightful and accurate reading of original texts.

The group includes younger scholars such as Ivan Boldyrev, Till Düppe, Yakov Feygin, Olessia Kirtchik, Adam Leeds, Benjamin Peters, and Eglė Rindzevičiūtė but also more senior scholars like Vincent Barnett, Richard Ericson, Slava Gerovitch, Wade Hands, and Joachim Zweynert. Many dozen cross-references as well as several joint publications and conferences show a remarkable intellectual cohesion among them. Working on the evolution of economic thought in Russia and the Soviet Union, many of these analysts focus on mathematical economics, with a special interest in cybernetics and, in turn, optimal planning. They borrow a great deal from Slava Gerovitch (2002), Philip Mirowski (2002), Roy Weintraub (2002), and Erickson et al. (2013) and attribute a great importance to the Cold War in modernizing economic thought in the Soviet Union.[33]

In their writings the optimal planners are not portrayed as steadfast Western-type neoclassical thinkers who in the second half of the 1980s finally gathered enough courage to show their true colors as neoliberals. Boldyrev and Kirtchik (2017, 6–8), for example, coin the term of "latent neoclassical" economists and Leeds (2016a, 51–58) writes about "spectral liberals" to show the ambiguities and intellectual constraints of the research program. Boldyrev and Kirtchik (2014, 436) argue that the Walrasian paradigm of general equilibrium could not be "<simply> extended to a different intellectual space . . . extension requires a work of interpretation and adaptation to a new context."

Hands (2016, 16–18) goes further by pointing to essential differences in economic philosophy and methodology[34] between Walras's original theory and its dominant interpretations in the Soviet Union: "on the Soviet side, the goal was to use Walrasian equilibrium to help model a centrally planned economy with a single representative agent . . . . On the Western side, the goal was to use individual optimization to help model the general equilibrium of a perfectly competitive economy . . . . Walrasian theorizing was primarily demand- and utility-focused, while Soviet mathematical economics was supply- and production-focused. . . . Western literature was not computationally oriented; it was more concerned with <how possibly> than <how actually.>"[35] In his view (6–7), the compatibility of Leontief and Neumann with Marx does not mean that Marx is also compatible with Walras.[36]

A detailed comparison with other countries of communism or with the work of verbal economists, be they official political economists or market reformers, is not among the top priorities of these analysts.[37] Rather, they carefully reconstruct the different types of mathematical economists by making distinction not only between input-output analysts and linear programmers or between builders of equilibrium and disequilibrium models but also between experts who favored all-encompassing automated systems of hierarchical state control and who advocated a certain degree of decentralization and/or marketization (e.g., Leeds, 2016a, 346–47). Symptomatically, only the fans of automatization are labeled by them as utopian thinkers. Regardless of the *sui generis* interventionist position of the optimal planners and their strong advisory links to (and partial cooptation by) the *nomenklatura*, they are merely depicted as "techno-scientists" (Rindzevičiūtė 2010, 289–91; Leeds 2016b, 636–39), "partisan technocrats" (Boldyrev and Düppe 2020, 264–73), or members of a "Technocratic International" (Feygin 2017, 260). According to Leeds (2016a, 58), their expert knowledge helped mill the Soviet regime from inside (from "the heart of the state") step by step. There is a consensus among these historians with regard to the amorphous epistemic culture and disciplinary identity of the mathematical economists, their proximity to natural and technical sciences as well as their controversial relationship with cybernetics as a strange umbrella concept and cover discourse (Rindzevičiūtė 2010; Leeds 2016a; Boldyrev and Kirtchik 2017, 2–6, 8–9). They were "stuck between the method and the discipline," writes Boldyrev and Kirtchik (2017, 8–9), suggesting that the application of mathematical techniques does not necessarily make someone a genuine mathematical economist in its Western sense, that is, a neoclassical theorist. However, the question of how this intermediary position between politics and science, and among various scientific disciplines, helped conserve the interventionist/collectivist attitudes of the optimal planners does not seem to provoke the observers' mind.

The flipside to the lack of anti-neoliberal fervor is a weak interest in the Austrian problematic. Apart from identifying some cybernetic fantasists among Soviet economists at the time, these authors do not claim that the optimal planners were cherishing utopian dreams about the rationalization of the planned economy. They barely deal with the fact that even those among the mathematical economists who were not blind to institutionalist approaches got stuck with a—rather neutral—concept of economic mechanism (Leeds 2016a, 173–82; Feygin 2017, 243) instead of leaving the program of regulating/planning the market for that of privatization. The fact that Soviet planning experts kept on propounding state-collectivist views is often overlooked[38] and makes it difficult for the reader to gauge the real depth of both the neoclassical and the liberal commitment of those experts. As a result, one might get the impression that the insistence of optimizers on bettering the central plan stemmed from a fear from retribution rather than from the "stickiness" of their collectivist attitudes.

A promising development has been that some of the authors mentioned above started bridging the gap in literature, which divided the proliferation of optimization attempts during the 1960s and their disappearance with the advent of *perestroika*. In other words, the second act of our drama has begun to be written. For instance, Ericson (2019) coins the term "marcescence" to cover the stagnation and decline of SOFE. The poetic expression (meaning leaves that wither without falling off) denotes the devastating effects of the ideological and political interference by the party-state on the research program but does not refer to the ultimate impossibility of properly designing and implementing rational central plans for the economy as a whole. It suggests that the green leaves were still fresh and healthy in spring. True, Ericson (173–74) talks about the "unrealizable dream" and "unresolvable issues" of optimal planning. Nonetheless, alluding to the informational chaos and incentive incompatibilities of the planned economy as well as to the indeterminate nature of the objective function of any society (unless it is ruled by a dictator), he only calls these "practical problems" that are "highly unlikely" to overcome. Like the founding narrators, most of the analysts in this group consider the difficulty with the objective function crucial. As Leeds (2016b, 355) puts it, "the objective function is nothing other than a name for the economic sovereign." Rindzevičiūtė (2010, 303–4) rather stresses the problems of formalization, the lack of powerful computers, and the slowness of gathering information: "it took two to three years to collect information for a branch optimizing model and about two years for a district model and about five years were needed to collect the information for a more complex model."

Although other members of the group offer thought-provoking studies of the work of leading Soviet mathematical economists like Emmanuil Braverman, Leonid Kantorovich,[39] and Viktor Polterovich, (cf. Boldyrev and

Kirtchik 2014; Kirtchik 2019; Boldyrev and Düppe 2020) as well as elaborate case studies of cybernetic research and its co-evolution with the economics of planning (Rindzevičiūtė 2010; Leeds 2016b), the Kosygin reform (Feygin 2017), or the anthropology of Moscow economists (Leeds 2016a), a number of main actors and scenes of the play are still absent, not to mention the simultaneous plays staged in other communist countries. Also, a comprehensive narrative of the consecutive phases, the external and internal drivers and the alternative ways of decline (marcescence) has not been offered yet.[40] Nevertheless, valuable fragments waiting for a synthesis already have been produced.

Reading the texts of these historical analysts, one sees repeated attempts made by Soviet mathematical economists, which result in repeated fiascoes (theoretical and/or practical), ranging from the dynamization and stochasticization of equilibrium models, through the introduction of game-theoretical schemes of planning, concepts of disequilibrium and non-price control, all the way down to experimenting with man-machine systems. Sometimes, the fiascoes led to a reversal of the history of economic thought: while earlier mathematicians moved to economics, a few decades later the mathematical economists sought refuge in mathematics, building increasingly abstract models. Alternatively, one could abandon the normative use of mathematics,[41] leave behind the domain of planning, and start applying formal models based on one's econometric knowledge acquired in solving optimization problems, in the analysis of the communist economy and the forecasting of its performance.[42] However, as Feygin (2017, 243) remarks, one also could limit one's mathematical ambitions and return to help the traditional planners or, on the contrary, leave mathematical economics for verbal institutionalism mixed with radical Austrian ideas during the agony of communism.[43] In any event, in this labyrinth of research programs aiming to show the Soviet economists the way out of the realm of recurring failures, many optimal planners could think that *perhaps* the next attempt at improving the central plan would be successful.

Insider View?

Earlier I spoke about two ways in which history-writing could respond to the Austrian challenge: resentment and disregard. Those who, in principle, could have combined the virtues of the challenge and both kinds of response (while avoiding their vices) and capitalized on exclusive local knowledge were the historians of economic thought living in the communist countries that experimented with optimal planning. However, such historians were rare, many of them lacked mathematical expertise and/or stayed under surveillance. Andrei Belykh's pioneering book (2007) published in 1989 on the history of mathematical economics in the Soviet Union (which stops the narration in 1965) raised expectations that similar volumes would come to light in other communist countries, too, right after the collapse of the regime. One of the main reasons for publishing our book is that following 1989, such works[44] did not emerge *en masse*. Their lack is barely compensated for by a special genre mentioned in the Introduction: personal reminiscences by leading mathematical economists, both emigré scholars and those who did not leave the region.

A RESEARCH PROGRAM WITH A SOFT CORE

By the end of this volume, the reader has become acquainted with nine country cases that reflect nine evolutionary paths of the same research program: optimal planning and, more broadly, mathematical economics. Do the national chapters offer sufficient evidence to substantiate our comments on the state of the art and, more importantly, to surpass it in key respects? I will condense the answer to this question in the next six points.

Scholarly Identity: A Neoclassical Program of Sorts?

In my view, a large majority of optimal planners were half-hearted and technique-oriented rather than "latent" neoclassical economists. When they did not shout from the rooftops that they were Walrasian thinkers, this was not only (or mainly) due to self-censorship or lack of self-confidence. Most of them candidly believed Marx and Walras to be combinable.[45] Even if we suppose that the optimizers read the relevant neoclassical authors attentively, they were much more interested in the mathematical language these authors spoke than in the *Weltanschauung* and methodology underpinning it. They accepted without second thoughts the Pareto-Barone "equivalence thesis," that is, an interpretation of the Walras model according to which, *in principle*, the "ministry of production" of a collectivist state may not achieve worse results in finding macro-equilibrium than the free market. This also explained why they became resistant to the Austrian criticism of Lange's position in the calculation debate.

General equilibrium theory (GET) was, for the optimal planners, an *operational device* of rational resource allocation by the state (maybe with a little help from the market) instead of a logically consistent, abstract scheme that is called "general" exactly because it was built on stylized hypotheses concerning the market (perfect competition, zero uncertainty, no institutions, and so on) in accordance with the principle of methodological individualism. The suspicion among the mathematical planners about the free-market foundations of neoclassical economics was so widespread that even scholars such as János Kornai, who by the 1970s managed to get rid of many of his state-collectivist fixations, were captivated by it. He reacted to his own failure to build a coherent theory of optimal planning by scapegoating the "unrealistic" premises and *laissez-faire* ideology of GET. This theory can be beautiful mathematically, he admitted, but it is naïve, self-centered, and unworldly, thereby mistaken and unable to serve as "real science," to cite Kornai's favorite term.[46] Such criticisms were not always grounded in scientific arguments; they also originated in the fear of being strait-jacketed by a new one-size-fits-all worldview just after ridding themselves of Stalinism and searching for a "third way."

The optimal planners were not mesmerized by the neoclassical paradigm, to say the least. Maybe at a certain point, some of them became ready to (secretly) say good-bye to key principles of Marxism, but even they mistook the principle of methodological individualism for individualism in the sense of egoism. It is difficult to explain why even the best-educated minds such as Branko Horvat, Leonid Kantorovich, János Kornai, and Oskar Lange were hesitant to jump over their own shadows even at times when political repression subsided and they achieved the privileged status of the "less vulnerable." Apparently, they were anxious about a situation in which subscribing to Paul Samuelson or Kenneth Arrow might end up in agreement with Milton Friedman and Friedrich Hayek.

The premises of GET were deliberately idealistic, but they became twice as idealistic once coupled with unrealistic hypotheses regarding the planned economy. On an abstract level, the optimal planners described planning as a system, in which all necessary pieces of information are available on time, their flow among the levels of institutional hierarchy is free, there are no vested interests in distorting information, no bargaining games, and so on, and the Central Planner is capable of revealing and concentrating inarticulate and dispersed knowledge. While many of these scholars criticized GET for assuming perfect competition in the market, they suggested, in an ideal case, a perfect lack of competition, friction, disturbance, etc., in central planning.

Further, the optimal planners could not really cope with a dual problem of direct translation. On the one hand, they used a stylized theory of market competition as a manual for operating a workable regime of central planning in the real world. On the other, they wanted to apply the model of a simple programming task (with a small number of static variables as well as with well-defined constraints and objective function) that was solvable in a factory workshop, to an extremely complex assignment of finding equilibrium in the national economy as a whole. To use Lakatosian language, the research program was shaky, incoherent, and fatally incomplete in both its hard core and protective belt. Its core should have been hard in terms of irrefutability while its changeable belt should have protected the irrefutable propositions contained by the core. This included the underlying hypothesis of "plannability" (*planiruemost, Planbarkeit*)[47] that went far beyond the prediction of future conditions of the economy. It pertained to (a) the theoretical and practical preparation as well as the implementation of central plans by the party-state, and (b) the postulate of their improvement via optimization. "Perfecting (developing, coordinating) the plan" and "making the plan more scientific" were phrases invented to describe that postulate.

However, the core lacked a fundamental theory (even if a stylized one) of the micro-and macroeconomic features of the economy presumed to be planned and the economic behavior of the party-state presumed to be able to plan. That theory should have explored, simultaneously with the economy's institutional, behavioral, and informational characteristics, some of its basic driving forces as well, especially those related to changes in technology and consumer preferences in not completely isolated economic systems of great complexity. It seems that either in order to comply with the need to make unavoidable simplifications in their models or to reflect the gray reality of everyday life in economies of shortage, the optimal planners' mind was dominated by the image of a Robinson Crusoe-type planned economy with brutally limited consumer choice, sluggish innovation, autarky, and the like. They knew, for example, that even small changes in human taste would put sand in the wheels of planning but were sure that the hindrances could be overcome with the help of advanced (dynamic, non-linear, and stochastic) models.

The hard core of the research program was not only incomplete but, ironically, rather soft in clarifying crucial issues of optimization such as the definition of the objective function or the "mechanism design" of the economy. For example, the former contained a number of burning questions about who determines (and measures) the needs of society (Fehér, Heller, and Márkus 1983). As regards the protective belt, it also displayed confusion caused by often retaining the doctrine of labor value while also calculating in marginal utility; defining rationality in a sloppy fashion as a technical term; and by mixing normative and descriptive/analytical approaches. The belt was also short of an elaborate concept of supply to replace or complement that of demand in GET. Price determination (e.g., accounting versus real prices) was also a vague issue. Moreover, the optimization procedures were reduced to "naked" mathematical algorithms of input-output analysis and programming, which served, for instance, to decompose the models and ensure their convergence to the optimal solution. These were not only naked but also often empty because, by definition, one could not expect to fill them with correct real-world information. In fact, seeing such a "gappy" research program without solid conceptual pillars, one did not even know what belonged to the core and what to the belt, and whether optimal planning had had a progressive phase at all before it began to degenerate (see below). Any clairvoyance was also disturbed by the fact that the protective belt continued to be packed with the heavy symbolism of communist planning hailing scientific foresight, the primacy of the state, and collectivist culture in general.

What do I mean by a sloppy, primarily technical definition of rationality? As mentioned in the Introduction, the optimal planners focused on instru-mental (goal) rationality rather than value rationality. The latter would have provoked the censors by asking disturbing questions, for example, about trade-offs between armament programs and social welfare. It would be unfair to reprimand the optimizers for conformism in retrospect. Yet, a hint at the non-moral origins of their instrumentalist attitudes seems opportune here. The logical chain linking the Cold War, vast military research projects, cybernet-ics, operations research, optimization, the computer, the algorithm, and eco-nomic planning in both the East and the West was so strong and convincing that moral reservations about the crimes of communism or "only" its forced irrationality could hardly compete with it. Similarly, the admiration felt for mathematics, engineering, systemic rules of behavior, and exact methods placed *rationality above reason* even though the latter can be more humane, flexible, and—according to John Rawls—has a palpable ethical component.[48]

With time, attempts were made at inserting realistic elements (e.g., bar-gaining) and their related mathematical techniques (e.g., game theory)[49] in the program as well as advancing unorthodox procedures like a democratic selection of the objective function. However, slowly and unnoticeably, the program imploded *in terms of economic theory* before it could fail in the real world. It could not really go wrong in practice because most optimal plans had broken down before they were tested *in vivo*. Unnoticeably, I say, because there circled a more spectacular enemy around the research program than its scientific imperfection. It emerged from the ruling elite, without the initial support of whom optimal planning could not have entered the his-tory of economic thought. But the same elite could cancel assistance if it suspected too much realism or iconoclasm in the optimal models or simply did not find them helpful. As a consequence, the optimizers had plenty of chances for shifting responsibility for the "marcescence" of the program to the Central Planner.

To be sure, this was not a cynical act; many of them sincerely believed in a trade-off between oppression and sound planning, hoping that democracy would cure the maladies of their theory in the future.[50] Regardless of recur-rent fiascoes, they kept on building optimal macro-models for years until the political market for these dried up during the second half of the 1980s. A critical introspection could have opened the eyes of the optimal planners to see that the research program was faulty from its very inception and in that sense its failure was coded into the program's core. Scientific central planning did not work (either on the drawing board or in the form of projects implemented by the planning office), even when it was backed or tolerated by strong groups within the *nomenklatura*.

Were the inbuilt damages of optimal planning reparable? To an extent, they surely were but with paradoxical consequences. When scholars began to improve the research program, for instance, by borrowing critical thoughts on the actual institutional setup (incentives, mechanisms, ownership forms, and so forth) of the planned economy from the market reformers, they found themselves in a vacuum because those thoughts implied that the communist economy was not reformable beyond a certain limit. Surpassing this limit would require privatization and democratization instead of regulated marketization under one-party rule. However, why would an economy of private owners need/acknowledge an overarching optimal plan that eradicates the free choice of economic actors in crucial respects? Hence, if the scientific planners did not intend to quit their research program they were interested in preserving the dominance of some sort of collective ownership. In other words, if they wanted to go on with their optimization experiments, they had better long not for capitalism but market socialism without communist dictatorship—another debatable vision by the way.

Pattern of Evolution I: Explaining Rise

Is it easier to portray the rise of an economic theory than its fall? The state of the art suggests this truism. If indulging the first act of our drama risks stealing the show from the second, one would not have to do more than identify the causes of decay to balance the story. However, the country studies by our research group convinced me that, by examining those causes, optimism about the first act may recede noticeably. It became clear that many of them had loomed large in the concept of optimal planning already in the very beginning. This encouraged me to reconsider not only the program's fall but also its rise.

Thus far, historians have not felt the urge to ask in what sense was optimal planning "better" than its predecessor. Rather than assessing the program's quality rigorously with standard tools of science studies, it was enough to cite two random sentences on planning from any of the official textbooks of political economy to attest to a vast improvement relative to them. Following a carnival of irrationality, even a pale hope for rational reasoning would shine. The intellectual strength of the new research program seemed self-evident also because its rise was extremely troublesome as far as political recognition was concerned, but the optimizers managed to overcome much of the resistance of the censors.[51] Unfortunately, defeating an intellectually weak rival can camouflage one's own deficiencies.

Be as it may, the rehabilitation of mathematics in economic research confirmed some basic methodological requirements of sound economic inquiry; consolidated key institutions of research, education, and advocacy (offering jobs to thousands of mathematical economists in the Soviet world); and promoted the inclusion of researchers in international networks. All these offered the historians motives for a story of a tiresome but triumphant breakthrough, first in the Soviet Union, then in the other communist countries, followed by repeated battles for survival and a final victory. The story would start on the day when Kantorovich first tried to sell the party ideologues the notion of shadow price as "objectively determined valuation" and would end with the award ceremony of his Nobel Prize.[52] Yet, the latter was not given to him for being one of the founding fathers of optimizing *mandatory central* planning in a *communist* economy but for much less and something different. He received the prize for his "contributions to the theory of optimum allocation of resources, [the demonstration of] how economic planning in his country could be improved, [and for showing] how the possibility of decentralizing decisions in a planned economy is dependent on the existence of a rational price system, including a uniform accounting interest rate to form a foundation for investment decision" (Nobel Prize 1975). Sharing the prize with Koopmans also suggested that it was not meant to justify optimal planning as a means of a potentially total macro-control of a non-private and non-market economy, a veritable Grand Design. Instead, it aimed to recognize the fact that the mathematical techniques simultaneously invented in the East and the West gave a chance for economists with *normative* attitudes to experiment with a large variety of "small designs" in the field of the optimum allocation of resources.

Hence, examining the research program from the perspective of "eternity," that is, of the evolution of universal economic thought, one is prompted to ask a few—somewhat ahistorical—questions of a spoilsport nature to test the "rise and fall" sequence. For example, after a while, optimal planners ceased to be contented with designing micro-and mezzo-projects (cf. Kantorovich and the Plywood Trust problem) but, thinking big, stretched their models far beyond the size of those built by Koopmans and most of his colleagues in the West.[53] Should we consider this change a sign of a rising theory? Initially, it seemed so that, with time, most deficiencies of verbal planning could be eliminated and optimization would result in perfect allocational efficiency on the macro level. However, the emerging nationwide models endangered the research program in both theory and practice and eventually contributed to its collapse. In all probability, less would have been more. Many of the serious shortcomings of optimal planning could have been avoided if its protagonists stuck to attempts at solving operations research-type problems in selected firms, industries, or regions rather than continuing the Kautskyan tradition of imagining the national economy as a large firm to be optimized.[54] Does it make sense calling a research program progressive, which—driven sometimes by megalomaniacal goals—maneuvered itself early on into various dead-end streets such as the utopia of automated macro-control? Moreover, most of its representatives did not try to escape or reach out, at least for a Tinbergenian solution, a less determined Grand Design, by switching to indicative (non-mandatory) and decentralized planning by the government. This would have bordered on prognostics and promised modest but more reliable optimization models by also paying attention to genuine (non-simulated) market processes in the private sector. In sum, given the global postwar supply of ideas on mathematical planning, it would have been possible to emulate alternative avenues of progress.[55]

Choosing ambitious, Soviet-style optimal planning implied high scholarly "opportunity costs" in another respect, too. Obviously, one could skim the edges of central planning and the related official political economy without much mathematical finesse, with the help of the verbal research programs of market reform. These programs, too, had a number of methodological flaws[56] but promised a quicker access to a future positive theory of the planned economy, a theory absent from the core of optimal planning. While most reform economists were also collaborating with the party-state, their empirical curiosity was much stronger and normative leanings slightly weaker than those of the optimizers. They disliked the rigid hierarchy of the economy ruled by a party-state and started toying with the idea of (limited) economic liberalization much earlier. It is also true, however, that the reformers used a less accurate, and even messy scientific discourse. What if the optimal planners had not embarked upon their road to nowhere but helped the verbal reformers formalize their analytical thoughts about the communist economy? What is still regarded as the rise of optimal planning was in certain respects a persistent waste of time that could have been spent on merging the two research programs.

As a result of such a synthesis, the national research communities probably could have approached a then brand-new research program in the West earlier. Like mathematical economics in the communist countries, New Institutional Economics, and particularly Public Choice, began to bloom from the turn of the 1950s and 1960s. Knowing the institutionalist tradition of Marxist economists, the mathematical talent of some, the reformist prehistory of several mathematical economists in the Eastern Bloc, and their local knowledge of massive government failures, they could have even overtaken some of their Western colleagues in developing the neo-institutionalist program.[57] If this volume revolved around market concepts (as our next volume will), I would hasten to ask whether the market reformers, stuck in their own cul-de-sacs, were not wasting time as well. Here, it suffices to say that, owing to the rivalry of the two groups, their research programs ran in parallel for more than thirty years without barely profiting from synergy.[58]

In principle, nothing prevented the optimal planners from asking what kind of utility the various actors of the planned economy try to maximize. They could have modeled why and how these actors bargain about the planning figures and distort data.[59] However, that would have required a critical rethinking of the "rules of the game" of central planning and a careful mapping of the actors' behavior (with a special emphasis on the *nomenklatura*). This map might have included principal-agent problems, asymmetric information, adverse selection, moral hazard issues, informality, bargaining, rent-seeking, shirking, subgoal pursuit, logrolling, pork barreling, and the like.[60] The mathematical economists were aware of many of these intricacies of the planned economy, but they lacked the scientific language to convert empirical knowledge into theory. If they had not been well-read in the rapidly growing literature in fields such as property rights, market and government failures, law and economics, and transaction costs (which in some countries would not have been their fault at all), they still could have used concepts like "ratchet effect," "hoarding," "Micawber principle," or "taut planning." After all, many of these concepts emerged in economic Sovietology and Comparative Economic Systems with their own or their reformer colleagues' assistance. However, rather than focusing on the institutional texture of the planned economy, they cast doubts on the heuristic value of the notion of *Homo Oeconomicus* by contending that in such an economy the main actors would follow irrational goals if the optimal plans did not discipline their behavior.

Today, the spread of optimal planning would appear as a less successful period in the history of communist economic ideas if we took into account the unexploited opportunities for progress. Should we blame isolation for the missed chances? I would not think so because some preconditions of exchange of ideas between East and West and East and East (see below), not to mention interaction between the various groups of the national research communities, were given from the very beginning, at least in certain countries. Also, the prospects for physical and intellectual encounters between scholars widened as the years passed by. Mutual misunderstandings aside, the optimal planners in the East and operations researchers (activity analysts) in the West spoke dialects of the same technical language. Despite the applause coming from the West and the enthusiasm of the pioneer-optimizers, the transnational multilogue also could have made them more cautious. Still, they showed a clear propensity for overstretching their research program.

Well, we returned to our basic puzzle mentioned in the Introduction: why did economic theorists in the communist countries so often become captives of what we call the "trap of collectivism?" To answer this question, one has to get rid of the widespread practice of deriving the imperfections of their concepts primarily from political repression. For brevity, let me name this the "thought police fallacy." Blaming censorship (or self-censorship) was a favorite element of the tale of woe told by mathematical economists. A brief description of the reasons for the fall of optimal planning next should explain why this may be a necessary but fairly weak account.

Pattern of Evolution II: Explaining Fall

Above, I paraphrased an old Soviet joke about Marxist philosophers who worked hard to answer a burning question of real socialism: is there life *before* death? Had optimal planning risen before it began to fall? Now, let us check the opposite: was there a fall after the rise? This is also a tricky question because in our case there was no *caesura* separating the two. The end was preprogrammed in the beginning, and the fall overlapped the rise; therefore, it is close to impossible to make a clear distinction between them. This is not to say that, taking the whole lifespan of optimal planning, there was no difference in the quality and growth of publications, stability of academic institutions, or in the enthusiasm of researchers between the start and the end. However, the gist of the research program is another matter.

So far, I have used the term "stagnation and decline" instead of fall to indicate the lack of a turning point (or points) or a peak (or a plateau) dividing rise and fall, and invoked the structure of Greek tragedies to reveal the absence of catharsis in the plot. Now, let me collect the main causes of the gradual decay, capitalizing on evidence provided by the national chapters.

Beyond Realism and Elegance

The Mises-Hayek-type reasons for the dysfunctions of rational planning came to the fore early on when researchers were confronted with the task of gathering information they wanted to feed into their models. Most of them did not know that the following questions had been asked many decades before:[61] should we measure products in physical units or in labor time in order to aggregate them? If prices are used for measurement, how reliable are they in a planned economy? Is the necessary information about quantities and prices available at all at the start of the planning process? What if they change thereafter? How can scattered information be synthetized? Are the economic actors interested in providing the optimal plan with truthful data and complying with the planning instructions in the phase of implementation? Do they know these data at all? All answers to such questions were ambiguous and insecure; in addition, they had to be translated into robust mathematical operations. Meanwhile, the models grew too large (even compared to the rapidly expanding capacity of computers) and clumsy, especially if the experts

wanted to loosen some of the simplifications such as homogeneity, closedness, linearity, staticness, and determinism, which led them far away from the
real world. Yet, a more realistic model did not prove necessarily more elegant
in mathematical terms and more workable in the planning practice.

However, witnessing the mushrooming of experimental models and the
attraction the research program made to gifted mathematical economists all
over the world, the optimizers reassured themselves that these difficulties
would be overcome through scholarly invention and reasonable theoretical
compromises. The models would become increasingly complex and realistic, the computers astronomically faster, and—consequently—the criticisms
pointing to unsurmountable institutional/informational problems with the
optimal plan outdated. In this optimistic mood the deepest wounds cut by the
Austrian critique were frivolously ignored (concerning, e.g., calculation in
labor time, reliance on artificial prices, or centralization of dispersed and tacit
knowledge) and never healed by mathematical sophistication.

Life in the Jungle

Initially, it seemed that the ideological resistance to optimization was broken
for good when the Central Planner agreed to the rehabilitation of mathematical methods. It took a long time until it became clear that political support
was utterly conditional. The optimal planners were not allowed to decide
on key components of their models such as the objective function and the
constraints; they were deprived of essential information about certain sectors of the economy; and the rulers also reserved the right to not reveal their
preferences precisely and alter or dump the complete optimal plan at their
will. Obviously, the luminaries of the Austrian School could not predict these
specifics of planning under one-party rule, like they could not know either
how fiercely the verbal planners would resist the inflow of mathematics in the
daily practice of the national planning offices ("drawing up I-O chessboard
tables may be fine but please do not mess around the planning goals and
instructions," they said). Mises and Hayek foresaw the detrimental effects
of collective ownership (especially in the form of centralized state property)
on incentives to calculate rationally, innovate, and behave as entrepreneurs
instead of bureaucrats. Nonetheless, it was impossible for them even to guess
the absurdity of the "ordinary business of life" in the jungle of institutions of
a planned economy (cf. Lewin 1973; Harrison 2005).

If they had had the slightest idea of the complicated web of vested interests
and bargaining strategies in the planning process then they probably would
not have spent much time discussing such elevated theoretical issues as the
controversial nature of labor value or the emergence of economic knowledge
in the market. Austrian critics of collectivism simply would have drawn the

conclusion that economic rationality would be suffocated by misinformation, secrecy, ignorance, informality, political intervention, non-economic preferences, and the like.

Virtually all data providers in the planned economy were cheating without any scruples, and the only hope for rational decision-making was, to quote the writer Péter Esterházy (2004, 5), that "it is deucedly difficult to tell a lie when you don't know the truth." However, it took the majority of scientific planners decades to recognize that these were deep structural defects and could not be fixed either by mathematical tools or administrative/managerial practices such as moral persuasion, disciplinary action, and stricter monitoring. Until then, the optimizers could presume that their mission was not entirely impossible and *perhaps* the next round of experiments would succeed. They also needed time to reckon with the sad fact that it did not help much when—rather reluctantly—they borrowed ideas from the reform economists and injected a modicum of decentralization or marketization in their planning projects to raise efficiency.

Inertia and Conviction

Paradoxically, such disappointments would likely have deepened if a genuine comprehensive central plan (not just its truncated or simulated version) had ever been prepared by the optimal planners and it had enjoyed lasting support from powerful lobbies within the ruling elite. Then they would not have been able to close their eyes to its ultimate bankruptcy. The optimizers could not be sure whether or not their plans would be dispensed with any moment and they would be thrown before the lions, that is, exposed to attacks by vigilant political economists, or angry bureaucrats from the Planning Office and the party center. The researchers were dragged back and forth by the political class, and the academic institutions were incited against each other and pulled into hopeless intra- and interdepartmental fights of the ruling elite. Ironically, the optimal planners slowly lost confidence in support coming from the party-state while still firmly believing in the central role played by the same party-state in their planning models. Blaming the *apparatchiki* for the failing plans delayed facing the theoretical shortcomings of their own research program. Eventually, they put up with polishing their models, fortune-telling, assessing risks, and issuing early warnings. Some of them moved to the field of long-term planning where one could breathe more freely; many others, however, continued to take part, though more reluctantly, in what was called in Hungary "plan coordination," revealing, in the form of simple quantitative terms and causal relationships, the constraints of the unchained fantasy of the supreme decision-makers.

At a certain point, the waves of frustration and fatigue of scholars reached some groups of the *nomenklatura*, who began to switch their patronage from the optimization of central planning to marketization and even privatization of the planned economy. Not quite independently from this, the existential anxiety of mathematical economists subsided in most countries. There remained only two—strongly related—reasons for them to continue building optimal models for the Central Planner even in "softliner" communist regimes: scholarly inertia and collectivist conviction.[62] The former explained the insistence of optimal planners on staying within the discipline of mathematical economics, often submerging in econometrics, growth theory, or research on production functions, economic regulation, business cycles, disequilibrium, and so on, that is, in fields related to optimal planning, but also in forecasting and even futurology.[63] The latter was evidenced by the fact that normally these experts did not join the camp of market reformers, in particular, not their radical wing. They had second thoughts about communist and (later) post-communist liberalization and made fun of turncoat political economists who covered the distance between "Marxism and monetarism" in a few seconds.[64] Similarly, very few of them became champions of New Institutional Economics, even after 1989.[65]

To return to the image of marcescence, from the 1970s, the leaves started drying but did not fall off the tree of the research program. What explained the belief that optimal plans failing in the past *perhaps* would become successful in the near future? I have alluded to a number of reasons thus far, including myopia, self-deception, opportunism, and so on, which are not directly related to fear from the thought police. Let me elaborate on them from the perspective of the "inertia/conviction" connection. Much of the communist messianism of mathematical economists turned into social-democratic pragmatism as years elapsed and their theories opened up to adopt market socialist (initially, *khozraschet* socialist) elements. However, they did not receive powerful messages from their key reference groups for decades, which would have persuaded them to take a step further and start thinking about an exit from the research program. The recurrent attacks by political economists, on whom they looked down (calling them, for example, parrots[66]), only reinforced their beliefs. As for the market reformers, their verbal discourse and liberal pretensions did not enchant the optimizers. Moreover, the reformers could not issue warnings about the dangers of state interventionism because their projects were also contingent on cooperation with the party-state and seemed to be equally unsuccessful as those of the scientific planners in practical terms. Finally, the Western peers of the optimizers did not cease to encourage them with prestigious prizes, joint publications, conference invitations, etc., suggesting that they were producing cutting-edge knowledge. However, this support weakened after Kantorovich's Nobel Prize. General equilibrium theory began to fade in the West, concepts of disequilibrium and rational expectations appearing as strong competitors.[67] The neoconservative turn in the second half of the 1970s (Milton Friedman was awarded the Nobel Prize just a year after Kantorovich and Koopmans) started eroding two other pillars of optimal planning, its inherent statism and hope for convergence between East and West.

An overwhelming majority of the optimizers' research community developed a professional identity that relied not only on international solidarity between input-output analysts and linear programmers but also on the feelings of superiority of mathematical economists vis á vis their colleagues doing verbal research.[68] This worked as a regular demarcation criterion for the disciplinary status of optimal planners. The initial investment in the "cultural capital" of their research program was large enough to not let it go easily. Besides accumulating exclusive scientific knowledge and developing institutional and political routines in order to increase that capital, the optimal planners combined these with ideological and even emotional ingredients. For years, many of them were convinced that by finding rationality in a post-Stalinist economy they fulfilled the old dream of the left, and the marriage of optimization and humanization in the framework of a scientific program with global outreach was just around the corner. If you seriously think that you hold the stone of the wise in your hand and are imbued with a historical mission, it will be very hard for you to admit that this stone is almost worthless, at least as far as your mission of perfecting the central plan is concerned. Even if you were ready to realize this after much hesitation and self-torture, you have already fallen in love with your own ideas in the meantime—a tempting opportunity to overstretch your program, in particular if you found a comfortable place in the trap of collectivism. The market reformers were often ridiculed for "reform mongering," a sort of lucrative business pursued at the border of science and politics. Well, "plan mongering" became a similar job for optimal planners once they managed to stabilize their institutions of research and education. Nevertheless, their relationship with the Central Planner was far from being balanced: what the optimizers profited from their advisory position was a considerable (but not irrevocable) protection that manifested itself in some freedom of thought, travel, publication and the like, higher incomes, and a chance for cooptation in the *nomenklatura*. The protector's only risk was that the protected could take a look at his cards.[69]

Thus, beating a dead horse, you could build up a life work (cemented by formal academic status), and hardly anything was more depressing for you as a scholar than to admit that maybe you would not bequeath but a few model specifications or simulation algorithms to posterity. Meanwhile, the main lesson of your professional life could have been a brief warning like this:

"Think twice before you engage in central planning again! Optimization will not help."

Plans without Tests

This was a schematic view of acknowledging/denying the decline of the research program by its adherents. The causes were listed in a chronological rather than a ranking order. In some respects, the story may remind the reader of the evolution of ownership concepts described in our previous volume (Kovács ed. 2018, 325–29). From among the similarities let me choose only one. Why did the "perhaps effect" work so long? How could the optimizers continue to craft plans between two fiascoes again and again? Beyond the numerous reasons depicted above, one must not ignore a principal problem of scientific logic, testability. Why would an unrelenting experimentation end if the boundaries between success and failure are vague? Because political interference was daily business, one always could think that planning failures were brought about by it rather than by deep-seated theoretical flaws of the optimal plans. How do we know that, at a certain point in time, an optimal plan is better or worse than the other if both contain not only different mathematical structures but also different data sets and different inbuilt political compromises? Furthermore, neither of the two will be implemented and we will not be able to gauge the difference between their predictive powers.

What remains is barely more than a comparison of the two planning projects according to their mathematical abilities and beauties. By crossing the country lines, decisions on quality become even more insecure because a planning project regarded by a national research community as a conspicuous failure could be relaunched in another country without any difficulty after some years. Errors do not exclude further trials and one can always blame, not without foundation, the hard constraints of making experiments: the poor technical conditions (lack of computing capacity and skilled planning officials, red tape, permanent time pressure due to chaotic organization, and so on), the company directors and the planning bureaucrats of various state agencies who fake data, or the top policymakers who change priorities overnight and ignore the final version of the "scientific" plan, preferring the traditional methods of verbal planning.

East-West and East-East Exchanges of Ideas

As the review of the relevant literature showed, three intertwined narratives dominate when it comes to the transnational diffusion of ideas of optimal planning: (a) the research program had strong Russian/Soviet roots; (b) in contrast to the usual West-East direction, important ideas (original discoveries) of the program traveled also from the USSR to the West[70]; (c) the new knowledge exerted a decisive influence on mathematical economists in other communist countries. These narratives originate in an extraordinary interest of the authors in the Soviet history of economic thought—a plausible bias. Undoubtedly, the re-legitimization of mathematical economics in the USSR created a pattern for researchers in the Eastern Bloc to follow. The institutional stabilization of the Soviet School of Mathematical Economics also offered the optimal planners in other communist countries an excellent opportunity to justify their struggle for recognition. Nonetheless, these served as a base of reference ("if new ideas are not blacklisted in Moscow then why should they be in Prague or Sofia?") rather than triggering off an actual emulation of theories invented in the center of the empire.

The Soviet experts tried to find allies in the satellite states but the local specialists were not emissaries sent by their superiors in Moscow. To read Kantorovich or Novozhilov was not a must and not the only option either. Polish optimal planners learned the basics of the research program first from Oskar Lange (Kantorovich studied him as well), while Hungarians followed scholars like Kenneth Arrow, Robert Dorfman, Paul Samuelson, and Robert Solow.[71] For instance, in his *Anti-equilibrium* Kornai (1971, 351–55) reprimanded Katsenelinboigen for assuming the existence of a welfare function for the whole society and Kantorovich for controlling the economy via shadow prices.

Self-education prevailed in all countries for many years, and reading was promoted by the translation of cutting-edge works of a great number of prominent mathematical economists. As the Bulgarian case shows, understanding Russian was helpful not only in borrowing ideas from Soviet scholars but also in reading Western authors whose works were translated into Russian language. To give other examples of mutual and indirect impacts, Vasilii Nemchinov learned linear programming from the English-language book of a young Hungarian mathematician Béla Krekó (Leeds 2016a, 259). The writings of the East-German Georg Klaus affected many Soviet cyberneticians and optimal planners (Rindzevičiūtė 2010, 302).[72] The optimizers took over input-output analysis from Leontief who was at least as American as Russian. To show the fragility of ethnic classification in an East-West context, one may consider the case of John Neumann whose growth model made an enormous influence on the optimal planners: can he be reasonably considered a Hungarian, therefore, Eastern scholar?

U.S. activity analysts and cyberneticians exchanged key ideas with their Soviet colleagues during the Cold War, contributing to the evolution of scientific planning as well.[73] Was Koopmans the first or was Kantorovich, or their discoveries were truly parallel?[74] What about priority issues in the cases of Lange and Malinvaud versus Kornai, Dantzig and Wolfe versus Kornai, or Volkonskii versus Kornai in various planning models?[75] Was the "West" affecting the "East" or vice versa? *À propos* Kornai, his self-criticism as an optimal planner was ground-breaking, affecting other Eastern European researchers such as Tibor Schatteles (a Hungarian in Romania), Aron Katsenelinboigen, and Viktor Polterovich. To be sure, even if these experts often did not speak each other's mother tongue, they met at various conferences,[76] visited each other on both sides of the Iron Curtain, read each other's works in translation, and published in each other's countries. Optimal planners from Eastern Europe studied at Soviet universities. Certainly, many of the new ideas were not homegrown but were not dictated by Moscow either. (True, a Soviet precedent was useful.[77]) Yet, not only Kornai but also even more cautious experts such as the Bulgarian Evgeni Mateev took the courage to diverge, for instance, from Kantorovich's theory openly.

The Soviet bias in the literature on the history of mathematical economics in the communist period was understandable but led to an optical illusion. It obscured the fact that long before the Soviet School of Mathematical Economics could begin to establish itself as a stronghold of optimal planning at the turn of the 1950s and 1960s, historic changes had taken place in economic research in the West (above all in the United States). The defeat of (old) institutionalism in the second *Methodenstreit* after the war and the victory of neoclassical synthesis, the surge in operations research/activity analysis, the triumphal march of general equilibrium theory and econometrics as well as the mathematization of economics in general were at least as decisive developments contributing to optimal planning in terms of High Theory as the simultaneous rise of computer science, systems theory, or economic cybernetics (Weintraub 2002; Backhouse and Salanti, eds. 2001). These were the times, say, between the seminal book *Linear Programming and Economic Analysis* published by Dorfman, Samuelson, and Solow in 1958 and Samuelson's (1970) self-ironical *bon mot* from 1970—"Before I won a Nobel, I felt my omniscience. Now I know it."—which reinforced the self-confidence of mathematical economists not only in the West but also in the East.

National Types?

Did this network of transnational impacts emanate from well-distinguishable national types (schools) of the research program? Was there, for example, a Polish (Lange), Hungarian (Kornai), or a Soviet (Kantorovich) school of optimal planning, which showed characteristic traits different enough to construct a fair typology? In writing the Conclusion of a volume like this, one is tempted to apply conventional distinctions between the country types of communist economies such as conservative and reformist, hardliner and softliner, state-collectivist and self-managed. In order to diverge a little from these—often fuzzy—adjectives, our previous volume introduced another division running between "conformists" and "explorers," that is, between countries in which economists complied with the concept of social owner-ship and countries in which many of them searched for innovative solu-tions in property relations, drifting gradually toward the idea of large-scale privatization. In fact, there were countries in which no major innovation in scientific planning took place, while in others (above all in Hungary, Poland, and the Soviet Union) the specialists excelled with several original discover-ies. Nonetheless, in contrast to the colorful world of ownership doctrines in which one country opted for centralized state property, another for managerial ownership, yet another for workers' self-management, following an irregular schedule, optimal planning was much more homogeneous in both space and time. With the obvious exception of Yugoslavia,[78] all countries from the GDR to China traveled along similar paths through the overlapping rise and fall of the research program.[79] These paths reflected a certain degree of ideological radicalization in the long run. Yet, a large majority of optimal planners were only able to scratch the armor of dominant state control since they remained loyal to the idea of some kind of an *imperative* central plan. Meanwhile, the ownership reformers (who belonged to the group of the most liberal-minded economists among the market reformers) challenged *nomenklatura* owner-ship by punching holes in that armor.

The optimizers varied in terms of timing their planning projects. Some of the countries (the Soviet Union, for sure) were early birds; some others, like China and Romania, were latecomers. In one country frustration with the program appeared at a relatively early stage (Hungary); in another the experts are still fabricating optimal planning models (China).[80] However, if we descend from the national level to that of the individual scholars we encounter a number of similar types in the different countries. These types vary not so much in the mathematical techniques they employ but in the ways in which they interpret plannability, a principal constituent of the hard core of the research program.

As for the techniques, optimal planners worked out numerous new algo-rithms as years passed by. Originally, the protective belt of the program included input-output analysis and linear programming. These were comple-mented with and refined by a large variety of mathematical instruments like game theory, non-linear, dynamic, and stochastic analysis, general equilibrium models, and so on. In this sense, the program was considered progressive with good reason.[81] In hindsight, one could create typologies comparing, for instance, those scholars in each country who experimented with non-linear programming with those who preferred to develop the theory through applying stochastic methods in order to protect the hard core.[82]

However, I am afraid that such a classification scheme would not help tackle our basic problem of whether or not optimal planning was doomed to decline because its "degeneration," to use again a term coined by Imre Lakatos, was much less related to the components of the protective belt than to those of the hard core. Owing to the refinement of mathematical methods, the belt did become more protective but not to such an extent that it could resist attacks against the core, which gained strength from the increasingly obvious lack of "plannability."[83]

In an attempt to identify real types, I suggest to examine the main varieties of reaction to the paradox annoying Oskar Lange already in the 1930s when he pondered the dangers of bureaucratization.[84] To rephrase his Leninist discourse, he wanted to know how the party-state could be strengthened and weakened at the same time by means of economic theory. Is there a way, in which the Central Planner concedes to not abusing the power it earns, profiting from the expert advice given by mathematical economists? How to ensure that the Central Planner observes the rules of the game (above all, complying with the requirement of free consumer and labor markets), does not derail the process of scientific planning, stretching from data collection to the endorsement of the plan, and accepts the optimal model's normative conclusions in the course of its implementation? In other words, how can the optimal planner convince the ruling elite about the advantages of having much less to do and, as a consequence, much less power to intervene? Will the Central Planner want to commit suicide?

To answer these questions, the optimal planners first had to get rid of Leninist illusions, according to which it was the working class and the party that would tame the Central Planner (if this would be necessary at all) and look for institutional obstacles to excessive state intervention. Like the verbal reformers, the mathematical planners started moving toward the market, sometimes echoing reformist suggestions for liberalization, but stopped at different points on their way. The ideal of a centralized regime of imperative planning did not vanish entirely from their scientific agenda. Some of them were even ready to make a U-turn and go back to "classical" Soviet planning in terms of centralization and mandatory targets, choosing its updated—automated—version. Otherwise, optimization projects with or without inbuilt elements of controlled marketization were mushrooming in many countries. These projects included key components of what analysts like to call the Soviet, Hungarian, or Polish schools but stretched beyond these in many respects.[85] They can be squeezed into four pigeonholes (ideal types):

Optimization within the Old Planning Regime

This is a prolongation of the traditional scheme of central planning, practically without any misgivings about its hierarchical nature. The first optimal plans of the post-Stalin era continued to consider the Central Planner both omniscient and omnipotent, an institution that—similar to other actors at lower levels of the planning hierarchy—has no vested interests whatsoever. It is supposed to be capable of collecting and processing correct information and sharing the job of preparing the optimal plans with mathematical economists (and computers). Its only imperfection is the exposure to the expert knowledge of scientific planners, but these must accept whatever the Central Planner wants to include in their models and quit the planning process in the phase of implementation. Selected results of the models become imperative planning tasks to be disaggregated by the center and fulfilled by intermediary organizations all the way down to enterprises.

Instead of suggesting to transform the command economy into an "advice economy," to play with words, this project retains military mobilization as the main organizational principle of planning and confines the efforts expected from the optimizers to raising the quality of commands. Hence, enterprises are not considered active "plan makers" but data providers and passive "plan takers." The entire procedure is allegedly transparent, the tasks are technical, that is, not "contaminated" by market-type decisions, and all actors serve a common cause without informational-institutional frictions. Kantorovich's original attempts at linear programming and the first models built by TSEMI researchers were among the real types of this endeavor.

Optimization in a Plan-and-Market Regime

This project admits that the Central Planner has limited powers in both acquiring correct information and implementing planning decisions. Nevertheless, it is still deemed to be unselfish and worth being assisted by "the science" in controlling some self-interested lower-level state institutions including enterprises. These need to be incentivized to reveal information and comply with the center's will. The optimal plan is presumed to deliver the proper incentives to channel the energy of informal bargaining into plan making. Here the principle of tit for tat is regretfully acknowledged. Once the optimal plan is completed, these institutions turn into passive plan takers. Similar to the previous project, the Central Planner is entitled to govern the entire planning process and dominate the optimal planners by disrespecting the rules of optimization any time. Still, it has to acknowledge the virtues of some decentralization and indirect control as well as to create a few quasi-market institutions like *khozraschet* in order to oil the planning machinery. Planning thus

becomes an interactive and iterative venture with multiple rounds of negotiation between the center and its inferiors, in which the last word belongs to the
former and nothing is enshrined in contract. At the end of the final round, the
Central Planner is assumed to become omniscient and omnipotent again. In
the phase of implementation no bargaining is permitted.

This ideal type derives from a great number of real types and their blends[86]
that differ in the degree of doubt about the "innocence" of the main actors.
Initially, for instance, in the Lange models, not only the higher echelons of
the economic hierarchy had been presumed to lack vested interests but also
the lower ones. As mentioned, red tape was considered a risk but the need for
negotiation was explained rather by the fact that the task of macro-planning
was too complex and the enterprises were better informed about their own
situation than the planners. Later, the suspicion toward all participants of
central planning grew and the optimal planners had to face the hard task of
designing models that reduce the flow of distorted data from below, arbitrary
interference from above, and both from between the two levels. The real
types embodied many dozen attempts at executing that task. They range from
one- to two- to multi-level planning models with or without games. They
also differ in the structure and size of information required from the actors
and of instructions or normatives resulting from the model calculations as
well as in the space left by parametric planning for the actors to maneuver.
In these models the iterations of the draft plans between the various levels of
hierarchy may start from below and from above; they may apply input-output
schemes of diverse depth and width and use or produce different kinds of
prices (including shadow prices), or no prices at all; the calculations may or
may not result in profits and rents as planning normatives—one might list the
differences *ad nauseam* without leaving the core of the research program.[87]

In the last analysis, it was the Central Planner who remained the plan
maker and decided on how much of its power might be sacrificed and how to
compensate for the loss. These projects did touch on some main taboos of the
planning concept canonized by official political economy, but they continued
to bestow so much power on the party-state that its intrusive character could
not compare to that of a detached Walrasian auctioneer. The latter was an
idol for many optimal planners—a mediator who processes data but does not
coerce and punish the real actors. As for the planning normatives, they were
not immune to being transformed by the authorities into mandatory instructions at will. Even in the best case they were artificial (accounting-style)
indicators generated by the planning model instead of produced by flesh
and blood agents of the market. To return to the military analogy, the "cap-
tains of industry" were obliged to inform their superiors about the combat
force of their units and allowed to complain about the quality of food or the

quantity of ammunition but were strictly prohibited to resist the commands of the general.

Democratizing the Planning Regime

Relative to the previous two ideal types, this one aims at depriving the center of the exclusive right of defining the *telos* of the planned economy when formulating the constraints and objective function of the programming model. If the citizens were allowed to vote, for example, on the desirable patterns of consumption, the rate of economic growth, or the share of military investments, then the party-state could have much less chance to abuse power.[88] Heretic thoughts like "consultative" rather than "directive" (Birman 1968) or "compositional" rather than "decompositional" (Petrakov in Sutela 1984, 187–88) planning were put forward only by a small minority of mathematical economists even in Yugoslavia where they could have made use of the self-management rhetoric of the ruling elite in certain periods of communist history.[89] Be as it may, a discussion whether a democratically defined social utility function exists at all (cf. the Arrow paradox) did not even begin among researchers.

Some of the optimal planners saw clearly that democratic participation in planning needs legal guarantees to defend the weaker party in the negotiations, be it an enterprise or the whole society. In order to prevent the Central Planner from ignoring or amending a popular vote or any of its promises made to enterprises, they advocated for the introduction of contractual relations (e.g., *khozdogovor*) among the various actors or, for example, of formalized procedures for bidding for resources. In this way, the contractual partners might establish transparent market relations. These initiatives, as so many others, remained on paper, possibly saving their authors from new frustrations.

Automatic Planning

This type of planning project steps out of the plan-and market paradigm to return, with a cybernetic twist, to the realm of the end-of-nineteenth-century collectivist visions of a world governed by benevolent manmade machines. The idea of total automation of central planning, an extremist version of what was called "computopia" in the 1960s, replaces the Central Planner with a centrally managed network of computers that have no interests, preferences, or biases whatsoever. Still, their omniscience and omnipotence are beyond question. Thus, any constraint on state planning would be superfluous and even harmful. Unlike most of the previous projects, some elements of this were tested in the Soviet Union during the 1970s and 1980s. Originally, the size of the project was thought to be comparable with the Soviet nuclear and space programs. In other countries (e.g., in the GDR and Bulgaria) the automatization program was aborted at an even earlier stage.[90]

Although at first sight, automatization seems to be a plainly hyper-centralist apotheosis of state-based planning, some of its followers wanted to exclude not only the market (and even money) from improving the plan but—boldly— also the Central Planner. The mathematical algorithm was supposed to be the plan maker while all institutions in the vanishing economic hierarchy were thought to become simple plan takers. It was hoped optimistically that the so-called "automated management and planning systems" (ASU, ASPR, OGAS) were decentralized and impersonal enough to resist the interventions of the party-state. Unsurprisingly, however, it turned out that these systems were designed to be "*centrally* decentralized," to use an oxymoron, and not neutral at all. They were exposed to those politicians who decided on power distribution encrypted in the software to be installed in the computers and on the data. They were also presumed to determine the constraints and objective functions of the optimal planning models. In these models the problem of rational calculation was overshadowed, in a cybernetic daze, by that of optimal control. The "Austrian suspicion" about institutional/informational frictions was ignored, which explained much of the failure of the entire project.[91]

At the same time, automatization of planning had its own enemies within the ruling elite. Suggesting in a dictatorship that the dictator should obey the instructions of an automatic machine was a hopeless initiative. How can the "leading role of the party" be defined in an optimal model, asked the official ideologues. What if the optimal solution determined by the machine does not match the "interests of the working class"? What if it harms industries, firms or regions that the party wants to favor? An optimal plan is by definition rigid: if it promises the best solution how could we bend it to attain our own goals went the argument. Hence, disappointment with automatic optimization was preprogrammed in the genes of large lobbies within the *nomenklatura*, first of all in those of potential losers. Therefore, if they disliked optimization then they disliked its automatic variants even more. The optimal planners recognized rather late that it was not by chance that—as ironic as it may have been—the official political economy of communism had not developed its own theory of planning in the course of so many decades. Today, it is already a commonplace conclusion that it did not need such a theory because a rigorous (mathematical) doctrine would have grossly limited the liberty of the ruling elite in taking macroeconomic decisions.

To avoid misunderstanding, neither the ideal nor the real types outlined above were arranged in a chronological order. Many of them appeared in the research program simultaneously, especially if all countries in our sample are considered. This is another reason for the claim made earlier that the rise and the fall of optimal planning overlapped and the final decline was preceded by a longer period of stagnation.

Status and Role within the Research Community: "Optecons," "Polecons," and "Refecons"

Sociology and politics, and more broadly put, the non-economic external drivers of change in economic sciences of the communist era, will be the subject of our fourth volume in the series. There we will discuss standard themes ranging from the institutions of research and education, through the socio-cultural features of the epistemic communities, to the political control over scholars. Here I will only gather from the chapters of the present volume a few elements missing or hiding in the literature, which pertain to conflict and cooperation between the optimal planners and either the political economists or the market reformers. To simplify my account, I will call them "optecons," "polecons," and "refecons."[92]

In the previous sections it has become clear that the community of optecons was layered in many ways. It included empiricist I-O analysts just like linear programmers with normative aspirations; those among them who focused on mathematical techniques and those who also advocated institutional changes like the refecons or opposed such changes like the intransigent polecons; and those who cherished close contacts with the ruling elite and those who were forced to emigrate. Obviously, intermediary types abounded. In any event, the best way to demarcate optimal planning from the other two economic subdisciplines was the language its representatives spoke, although there were also a few refecons who were well-versed in mathematics. Above, I used the word "rivalry" repeatedly to describe not only conflict but also cooperation between the three groups. As mentioned, the state of the art is rather uncertain about their interactions. For example, Ellman portrayed the optecons as refecons, even if inconsistent ones, whereas Sutela and Feygin regarded also part of the polecons (the *tovarniki* in the Soviet Union) as refecons, while Bockman believed that both the optecons and the refecons were proto-neoliberal thinkers. I am afraid that by remaining on this level of generalization, one cannot understand why the research program of optimal planning "degenerated," was often left alone by its potential ally, the theory of market reform, got locked in its own inertia, was trapped by collectivist traditions, and found an emergency exit to mainstream mathematical economics only during the last hours of communism.

Undoubtedly, optimal planning was a prime terrain for middle-of-the-road solutions. It offered an excellent chance for scholars to (a) distance themselves from the theory of central planning as glorified by official political economy *without* demanding sweeping market reforms; (b) work together with the reformers *without* becoming liberal thinkers; (c) borrow certain instruments of neoclassical economics *without* accepting its original philosophy; and (d) break with the parochialism and Byzantine atmosphere of the communist academia and join the international community of modern (data-based, formalized, computerized, and so forth) scientific research driven by competition *without* hurting the rules of censorship. To put it bluntly, they could open up to the West without having to turn their back on the East. This stunt was, of course, contingent on observing the taboos of the communist regime and collaborating with it as expert advisors or planning officials at various levels of the party-state. As an optecon you could be a fellow of a research institute today, a head of department in the Planning Office tomorrow, and a member of the Central Committee the day after tomorrow, or just the other way round. To cite Albert Hirschman, exit and voice were rare; instead, loyalty based on a mix of conviction, inertia, and survival instinct prevailed. The optimal planners rarely became dissidents; they were dwarfed by market reformers in this respect.

While the optecons had much in common with both of their rivals, they did not foster equidistant relations with them. The recurrent ideological attacks launched by the polecons scared the optecons,[93] whereas the competition with the refecons was more peaceful. For a mathematical planner to forge an alliance with the latter was almost a natural move, but with the former it was rather a tactical compromise. At a certain point, an optecon could not team up with a polecon who believed in the "dialectics" of economic laws including the freedom of the Central Planner to change them. Both the optecons and the refecons were dissatisfied with the performance of central planning and wanted to improve it through evolutionary change. Imbued with the optimism of social engineering, both promised Rationalization (writ large) in their scientific programs. However, the market reformers pledged to make the planned economy rational by changing the behavior of economic actors through new institutions rather than training them, like the mathematical economists proposed, how to conduct themselves "more scientifically" in the framework of the old ones. The optecons did their best to reveal the inexactitude and sterility of official political economy, but they also criticized the methodological sloppiness of market reformers.[94] Nonetheless, they more easily could agree together on the values of scientific quality, transparency, innovation, East-West exchange of ideas, and so on, more than any of them with the polecons. It happened time and again that reformers became optimal planners and *vice versa*, or these two egos coexisted in the soul of the same scholar for a while.[95]

Then why did cooperation between the optecons and the refecons not prove to be a long-term solution leading to the integration of their research programs? Was the hubris of the former the main reason for their isolation? Or did the majority of optecons count as excessively interventionist and, therefore, opportunist[96] in the eyes of the refecons? Or, on the contrary, were some optecons irritated by those refecons who—as young Stalinists—had denounced "bourgeois" (mathematical) economics in the early 1950s?[97] Or was it the optimal planners' preference for formal analysis to verbal-institutional study that alienated the reformers from them? Most likely, all these reasons contributed to the sharpening of the demarcation lines around the optecons' research program, which stiffened their professional status and roles. In addition, adhering to the principle of *divide et impera*, the ideological supervisors of economic sciences were always keen on inciting conflicts between the two groups, threatening both with excommunication for heresy. As a result, the marriage between neoclassical knowledge and institutional experience did not take place and in the declining phase of the optimization program the scientific planners had to console themselves with other research fields within mathematical economics.[98]

IS OPTIMAL PLANNING *PASSÉ*?

The readers may put down our volume in a rather sad mood. They have been presented a research program that, moving back and forth, ended up as a typical Eastern European project of innovation in technology or business life. Ingenious ideas, comparable to those in the West, struggled for recognition in a demotivating social environment. They seemed successful at the outset, were overblown with the fervor of neophytes and instrumentalized by politics, failed in practice but did not vanish. The program moved ahead producing ambitious models on this side of the Iron Curtain at a time when it already began to retreat on the other. The inventors tried their best to save the original ideas of the program by fine-tuning its technical components in order to make it work outside the laboratory. Meanwhile, optimal planning cracked under the burden of its own ambiguities and fallacies, and the fiasco could not be primarily attributed to censorship and other machinations of the thought police. Experimentation was stopped by an abrupt change in the real world, the collapse of communism, that made the optimization efforts as a whole questionable in retrospect. During the implementation of the program, many of its followers got too close to the ruling elite and narrowed the opportunities for alternative inventions. As one of my interview partners in Hungary put it, optimal planning, just like alchemy performed in royal courts centuries ago, will certainly be exhibited in the virtual museum of human thought, but we will not know if the stone of the wise produced by it accelerated or slowed down the progress of science.

This is the seamy side of our story. Admittedly, our comparative research program on the evolution of economic ideas under communism was (and is) a little schizophrenic. Besides reminding the reader of epic failures, we also would like to show the sunny side of that evolution without, of course, persuading anyone to repeat the communist adventure. The Introduction could not conceal that we launched this book project with rather gloomy working hypotheses. Today, we see the intricacies of planning concepts more clearly and have revised some of our assumptions concerning, among other things, the two stages of evolution, the meaning of rationality, and the typology of optimal planning accordingly. As a result, the overall appraisal of the research program has not got significantly brighter. However, it became clear that in scholarly terms optimal planning proved to be the most creative and influential research program in economic science of the communist era. Indisputably, it enriched universal economics in many crucial fields such as input-output modeling, linear programming, general equilibrium theory, welfare economics, mechanism design theory, control theory, and—indirectly— concepts of disequilibrium. Yet, it was probably the greatest merit of these scientific discoveries that they revived the Socialist Calculation Debate,[99] in most cases eclipsing the work of market reformers, not to speak of textbook political economists, in terms of scholarly quality. In the Eastern Bloc as a whole, the optimizers did much for the rehabilitation of mathematical culture (and, more broadly, of the ideal of exactitude, quantification, and formalization) in economic thought in general and for the takeover of key concepts of neoclassical economics in particular. For example, no matter if leading mathematical economists had contended tactfully or hoped sincerely that the Marxian labor theory of value would not suffer from the conceptual apparatus of optimization, it did suffer immensely. More than thirty years after the collapse of communism, hardly anyone among serious economic theorists tried to resuscitate this theory in the ex-communist countries.

In a wider context, taking back the notion of economic rationality and starting to "decollectivize" it inflicted vast damage on the once celebrated concept of central planning. Maybe, to nuance the title of this chapter, not all important aspects of rationality were found by the optimal planners but some of the aspects they found did not get lost again. The requirement of coupling the concept of rationality with individual (and later with institutional) choice as cornerstones of standard economic inquiry survived and was carved in stone in the course of the neoclassical upswing under post-communism. Last but not least, descending from High Theory to earthly matters, optimal planners were rightly proud of generating indispensable empirical knowledge and its rational assessment by means of input-output analysis. To sum up, these accomplishments helped the economists climb out from the hole in which they sank at the end of the Soviet twenties, but their dream about the reintegration of Eastern and Western economic thought, capitalizing on their own theoretical discoveries and local empirical knowledge did not come true. The most exciting and rewarding opportunity, namely, to attain rapprochement via New Institutional Economics remained largely unexploited in communist times.[100]

And so, our volume could not be finished with anything close to a happy ending, not even in the sense of what Jürgen Habermas called *nachholende Revolution* at a societal level. Arguably, catching up with standard neoclassical thought gained momentum *after* the communist system had collapsed. Prior to 1989, reintegration was severely inhibited by the fact that none of the leading theorists of optimal planning admitted the failure of their mission clearly, and such an admission (not an apology, of course) is still due.[101]

Their sending of a "Never again!" message might have moderated expectations today about reigniting the Socialist Calculation Debate and challenging the impossibility thesis with the magic bullets of our age, artificial intelligence, including machine learning,[102] which offer behavioral intent prediction, datafied knowledge production, algorithmic governance, and so forth. Like it or not, economists of a collectivist persuasion who are familiar with these novel disciplines and methods have begun to claim that real-time insights in production and exchange as well as in changes in technologies and consumer preferences are possible. Moreover, they add, there is also decent chance to collect and centralize near-perfect information by eliminating the distortion of data by fallible humans.[103]

Certainly, Big Data and AI oblige economists to rethink the century-long debate, and it is very likely that some of the Austrian arguments will need to be amended or abandoned. Owing to the fact that during the past two decades the very notion of data has expanded rapidly (including non-verbal information *en masse*), their quality has improved immensely, their collection and processing have become far more accurate and faster than ever before, and short-term market prediction can rely on real-time information managed by self-correcting models operating on online platforms (cf. "anticipatory shipping"). Today, any of the big tech companies uses more data (and more efficiently) than the national planning office of a large country in the communist epoch. Nevertheless, crucial elements of the Mises-Hayek position, notably, those related to tacit knowledge and distorted information, seem to remain valid even in an imagined non-hierarchical collectivist economy. Also, it is doubtful whether the AI models are capable of sustaining longer-term planning and can release themselves from the prison of the past and the present, say, in deciding on technology and consumer taste in the future. The old question of "How to craft plans based on knowledge we do not have?" still waits for an answer. Finally, are the extremely complex new models really computable, or—returning to the beginning of the calculation debate—will the would-be planners have to face an "impossibility (of computation) thesis" again?

In any event, rationality seems to be back again, allegedly taking the wind out of the Austrians' sails. "Why wouldn't we try to optimize the economy again?" ask some new-collectivist thinkers—but at this point without one-party dictatorship and imperative planning, yet with dominant collective ownership, workers' self-management, decentralized planning, and regulated markets?[104] Optimizers in the previous century experimented in the framework of vertical collectivism. *Perhaps* under the rule of horizontal collectivism and with the help of machine learning, the program of optimal planning will work. *Perhaps* . . . , and the trap of collectivism may close again.

The world has just begun to fear the use of artificial intelligence by dictatorial regimes. Thus far, these have focused on surveilling and brainwashing their citizens.[105] But what will happen if the Big Brother decides to switch to the control of the national economy as a whole, trusting in a conversion from "platform capitalism" to a sort of "platform collectivism?" Hopefully, and very likely, this will not work or at least will not work efficiently. Nevertheless, knowing the disastrous consequences of an earlier failed experiment with macroeconomic control starting with the First Five-Year Plan at the end of the 1920s, one does not look forward to witnessing another six-decade-long bankruptcy.

NOTES

1. In the pre-1989 period, these scholars were among the most credible analysts of the rise of mathematical economics in the English-speaking world: Edward Ames, Abram Bergson, Morris Bornstein, Robert Campbell, Martin Cave, Maurice Dobb, Robert Dorfman, David Dyker, Michael Ellman, Alexander Erlich, George Feiwel, Philip Hanson, John Hardt, Paul Hare, Richard Judy, Michael Kaser, Carl Landauer, Don Lavoie, Herbert Levine, Moshe Lewin, John Michael Montias, Egon Neuberger, Alec Nove, Mario Nuti, Jan Prybyla, Peter Rutland, Leon Smolinski, Nicolas Spulber, Pekka Sutela, Vladimir Treml, Benjamin Ward, Peter Wiles, Eugene Zaleski, and Alfred Zauberman.

2. Even Aron Katsenelinboigen (1980, 30) who emigrated from the USSR in 1973 and had a strong opinion about many of his Russian colleagues showed understanding, for example, for the leaders of the mathematical economics movement: ". . . one could view Nemchinov as a collaborator with the Stalinist regime. The refusal of a creative person to collaborate with a totalitarian regime is a moral act of selfless asceticism, difficult for most people. Activity, with its possibility for creation, is too important. Moreover, a young person once fallen into the rut of collaboration finds it difficult to leave. Such is the subjective side of the behavior of many scholars in totalitarian regimes. However, this activity has some positive aspects. Since the

regime is already formed, the presence of decent people with power can, in changing conditions, result in a renewed moral atmosphere and the creation of new directions in science."

The market reformers faced the same dilemma. Recently, János Kornai (2019) who, following the 1956 revolution, had already been confronted with this ethical predicament and opted for (half-hearted) collaboration, likened himself to Frankenstein for advising Chinese communist leaders to liberalize their economy in the 1980s and thereby contributing to the rise of a new authoritarian empire. See also note 80 and 105.

3. There were important reasons for the Western specialists to express cautious opinions about the research programs of their Eastern Bloc colleagues. They felt compassion for their peers exposed to repression; at the same time, they wanted to do field research—a forgivable motive for sure. For the story of how an American scholar's articles caused difficult moments in the life of Kantorovich, see the chapter on the Soviet Union in this volume, Campbell (1960; 1961) and Boldyrev and Düppe (2020, 271).

4. They can look back on the noble tradition of Russian mathematics from before the 1917 revolution and the world-famous economists of the 1920s like Aleksandr Chayanov, Grigorii Feldman, Vladimir Groman, and Nikolai Kondratiev who spoke the language of mathematics fluently. True, this fame had not been shining bright until historians like Alexander Erlich (1960) and Nicolas Spulber (1964) rediscovered these scholars in the early 1960s. Interestingly, Evgeny Slutsky and Boris Brutskus were not among them at the time. For many years, the Vladimir Dmitriev—Aleksandr Bogdanov—Pavel Popov—Wassily Leontief—Leonid Kantorovich lineage was more acceptable in the USSR, especially after Leontief was permitted to re-enter his fatherland. For Leontief's symbolic blessing to this history of ancestry, see Leontief (1960).

5. The reading list of the most important journal articles on the evolution of optimal planning would be incredibly long if one also took into account, beyond the authors listed in note 1, scholars publishing in French, German, and other languages.

6. In his foreword to Zauberman (1975, VII–VIII) Gregory Grossman also used this word but elegantly distanced himself from the author' enthusiasm. Prior to this book, Zauberman was a co-editor of a pathbreaking work on *Planometrics* in 1967. In 1976, he published a voluminous book on *Mathematical Theory in Soviet Planning*, which provided a rich background material to the book discussed here.

7. This is how Aron Katsenelinboigen (2009) remembered one of his conversations with Kantorovich: "He said that <if the government supports me all economists will think like me in five to seven years. And a new era will begin in the economy of our country>."

8. In an earlier article Zauberman (1969, 2) examined the "rapprochement between East and West in mathematical economic thought." He drew a very optimistic picture of mutual help in developing new mathematical techniques but remarked that it was not sure that the "reconciliation of historical materialism and econometric formalism" would be successful.

9. Similar to Oskar Lange in the Socialist Calculation Debate, Zauberman (1975, 52) was contented with a vague complaint about socialist bureaucracy, particularly, the "inertia of the planning and controlling apparatus."

10. Zauberman knew that, besides the prices, the dual side of the models could deliver the optimal size of capital investment, profit, and interest. However, he did not realize that while the rehabilitation of these categories helped the market reformers, it also stole the show from them because the optimal size was specified by the computer instead of emerging in the market process.

11. This book was a sequel to Ellman (1971).

12. Surprisingly, a few years later, he published a sharp-tongued article against Tinbergen's convergence theorem. See Ellman (1980).

13. Some years before, he settled the issue of economic rationality for himself with these words: "What Barone and Mises did not realize is that it is perfectly possible for an economy to function, and in many respects perform exceedingly well, even if the plans are inconsistent and micro irrationalities abound" (Ellman 1968, 27). Ten years later, he amended his position a little, though remained far from promulgating the Austrian "impossibility thesis": "the theory of decision making implicit in the Marxist-Leninist theory of planning is inadequate because it ignores the fundamental factors of partial ignorance, inadequate techniques for data processing, and complexity" (Ellman 1978, 249). "Subordinates may transmit inaccurate information, the process of transmitting information may destroy some of it, and the addressees of information may not receive it" (251). "In this respect the Marxist-Leninist theory of planning suffers from the same weaknesses as neo-classical price theory" (255). These remarks did not go much beyond Lange's or Zauberman's criticism of "bureaucratization."

14. Cf. the chapter on the Soviet Union in this volume.

15. The picture of self-centered marketeers did not differ much from the one painted by textbook political economists and hardliner politicians in the communist countries as well as by certain theorists on the New Left. See also Ellman (1968) published in the *Socialist Register*.

16. Meanwhile, both scholars lost interest in studying optimal planning: Zauberman published on the history of game theory in the Soviet Union and Comecon trade while Ellman focused on planning and market reforms in a comparative perspective. Ellman's 1979 volume on *Socialist Planning* (republished in 1989 and 2014) discussed mathematical methods less and less.

17. In 1966, the SOFE guru Nikolai Fedorenko put this less mildly when he spoke about "descriptive" versus "constructive" political economy to distinguish old-school textbooks from optimal model building. His outspoken older colleague Aleksandr Lur'e added: official political economy was not descriptive but destructive (Ellman 1973, 9).

18. He argued that not only the older generation of Leonid Kantorovich, Vasilii Nemchinov, and Viktor Novozhilov but also their younger colleagues such as Nikolai Fedorenko and Stanislav Shatalin were sincere devotees of central planning in some collectivist (not necessarily administrative-hierarchical) framework. Their

affirmative attitude could not be explained solely by self-censorship (Sutela 1984, 92–97, 198–99).

19. Sutela (1991, 40) already took a larger distance to the optimal planners and their illusions: the planning bureaucracy was "regarded as unselfish servants of the system with no power aspirations or interests of their own. All the <petty tutelage> was simply seen as a consequence of a badly designed hierarchical division of labor, not as a natural way of exercising ownership rights in a situation where the planners and ministries were responsible for the performance of <their> empires. Since the late sixties, however, the bureaucrats have often been accused of sabotaging the reform of 1965. During the seventies planners generally supported the mechanization of plan calculations but fiercely opposed any reform that would lessen their concrete power over resource allocation."

20. Cf. the chapter on Yugoslavia in this volume.

21. Some years later, Sutela (1991, 45) reassessed optimal planning in an even more pessimistic mood. He discovered Mises and Hayek but did not reject Lange and subscribe to the impossibility thesis. Witnessing how during *perestroika* the idea of market reform replaced that of improving the plan in the hearts and minds of a number of Soviet mathematical economists, he gave up any hope about a "workable new course." SOFE, wrote Sutela "really has no place for money as a liquid asset, credit, foreign trade or the conversion of military production. Questions of competition, ownership, the legal framework and entrepreneurship are all absent. This was the technocratic and romantic phase of Soviet economic reformism."

22. The same applies to David Prychitko (2002) who offered a powerful critique of the decentralized projects of communist planning (particularly in Yugoslavia), complementing the writings of his close colleagues on central planning. Peter Boettke's (2000a) pioneering series of volumes republishing most of the important contributions to the consecutive waves of the Socialist Calculation Debate contained only some of the relevant essays of Eastern European scholars. Lavoie (1986) was supported by a rich review of the literature but his Eastern European sources were dwarfed by references to Western star economists.

23. Both Mises in the various editions of *Human Action* ([1949] 1966, 694–711) and Hayek in *The Fatal Conceit* (1988, 85–88) confined themselves to a general summary of their thoughts on socialist calculation. Also, they retained their suspicion about formal analysis. As Mises ([1949] 1966, 698) says, "the mathematical economist, blinded by the prepossession that economics must be constructed according to the pattern of Newtonian mechanics and is open to treatment by mathematical methods, misconstrues entirely the subject matter of his investigations. He no longer deals with human action but with a soulless mechanism." Hayek (98) talks about macroeconomics that "seeks casual connections between hypothetically measurable entities" and "may sometimes . . . indicate some *vague* probabilities" as well as about mathematics, "which must always impress politicians" and "is really the nearest thing to the practice of magic." Although the new generations of Austrian economists made friends with mathematics, the reservations of their predecessors about mathematical methods poisoned the climate of the ongoing debate on rational calculation. Also,

they gave an advantage to the neoclassical experts who felt reinforced to regard the Austrian discourse as imprecise, ideological talk.

24. On differences between Austrian and neoclassical theory in interpreting the concept of rationality, see Lavoie (1986, 10–14). On the limitations of neoclassical analysis, see Lavoie (1985, 100–113) and Boettke (2000b, 8–22).

25. Apparently, they accepted Mises' ([1949] 1966, 703) paternalistic words in *Human Action*: the socialist reformers "want people to play market as children play war, railroad, or school. They do not comprehend how such childish play differs from the real thing it tries to imitate." Boettke (1990; 1993) examined the reform economists with more compassion but showed little interest in them in the long period between the NEP and *perestroika*.

26. Rothbard (1991, 72) warned the optimal planners about the danger of building "garbage in, garbage out" models.

27. As Lavoie (1986, 9) puts it, ". . . the essence of the <knowledge problem> argument is not simply that plant managers know things that the Central Planning Board does not or the communication of this knowledge from the former to the latter would . . . entail the cost of losing some data or accuracy. The problem is rather that the relevant knowledge is inarticulate. The producers know more than they can explicitly communicate to others. While the market marshals this dispersed knowledge without requiring its articulation all these market-socialist models necessarily require the full articulation of localized knowledge to the Central Planning Board during the <dialogue.>"

Boettke (1990, 36) enumerated the main difficulties of socialist calculation and planning as seen by the Austrian School: "(1) property rights and incentive problems, (2) problems of informational complexity, (3) epistemological (tacit knowledge) problems, (4) the totalitarian problem." The last point pertained to the underlying hypothesis, according to which central planning *logically* presupposes some kind of dictatorship. Boettke (2001, 41) summed up the Austrian message succinctly: ". . . socialism is *impossible* precisely because the institutional configuration of socialism precludes economic calculation by eliminating the emergence of the very *economic* knowledge that is required for these calculations to be made by economic actors."

28. Here, Lange ([1964] 1967, 158) proudly declared: "my answer to Hayek and Robbins would be: so what's the trouble? Let us put the simultaneous equations on an electronic computer and we shall obtain the solution in less than a second." See also Rothbard (1991).

29. On the contrary, they tended to demonize the Austrian School as a refuge for free-market fanatics (while borrowing some of their arguments about evolutionary institutional analysis).

30. "International and domestic political elites created a package of neoliberal ideas to take advantage of the changing political situation around 1989. These elites, as well as right-wing economists and activists, co-opted critical, transnational socialist discussions and presented them, along with a narrow version of neoclassical economics, as calls for private property, hierarchy, and markets within capitalism. In doing so, they distorted the neoclassical economic discussion of socialism and markets into

neoliberal ideology." ". . . Around 1989, these elites began to implement neoliberalism . . . " (Bockman 2011, 12, 217).

31. This expectation was supported by prominent economists such as Pranab Bardhan and John Roemer (1992) who, attributed the failure of market socialism to the lack of democracy (instead of the lack of market and private property) and trusted in some sort of rational macro-planning. See their sharp dispute with Andrei Shleifer and Robert Vishny (1994).

32. This is how, for instance, Feygin (2017, VIII) starts his dissertation: "I challenge the prevailing historiographical narrative that so-called Soviet <liberals> <learned from the West> and instead show that reform-minded economists became equal partners in trans-European intellectual communities."

33. Feygin (2017, 4) talks about "cold-war science" to refer to a critical impact of geopolitical drivers on mathematical economics in the USSR. Vincent Barnett (2009) and Joachim Zweynert (2006; 2018) examine the evolution of Soviet economic thought in a much longer perspective and are more sensitive to methodological nuances. See also Barnett and Zweynert (2008).

34. Citing Bert Hamminga, Hands (2016, 3) employs the term of a "set of elementary plausibility convictions."

35. Cf. Dorfman (1976).

36. See also Leeds (2016a, 274, 351). Boldyrev and Düppe (2020, 272) note that, surprisingly, Kantorovich was "never seriously interested in general equilibrium theory or game theory."

37. Feygin and Leeds are clear exceptions. However, perhaps due to the fuzzy designations used in the USSR at the time, they regard both the *tovarniki* who were part of the official political economy (but advocated the broadening of the "commodity-money relations") and the *khozraschet*-prone optimal planners as market reformers/socialists. Feygin's (2019) *tovarnik* hero is Yakov Kronrod who, to say the least, did not maintain a friendly relationship with the optimal planners.

38. Boldyrev and Kirtchik (2014) and Boldyrev and Düppe (2020) mention the socialist leanings of Polterovich and Kantorovich several times. Leeds (2016a, 295–96), too, speaks of Novozhilov's Marxist beliefs, but he is also unsure to what extent these experts were turncoats defending their "true" positions against the censors. It is only Feygin (2017, 9) who says explicitly that many Soviet mathematical economists were "dedicated Soviet patriots and Communists who were trying to deal with problems of the modern territorial state that thinkers west of the Iron Curtain were grappling with at the exact same time." As an exception within this group, Zweynert (2006, 189–92) stresses the devotion of Soviet economists, verbal or mathematical, to social engineering.

39. On Kantorovich, see also Bockman and Bernstein (2008).

40. Referring to Hayden White, Rindzevičiūtė (2010, 290) dislikes evolutionary schemes based on a simple "rise and fall" dichotomy. Leeds and Feygin are uninterested in the logic of the decline of optimal planning: Leeds (2016a, 343) applies the term "accomodation" for decline while Feygin (2017, 6, 156–262) sees the Brezhnev years not as a period of stagnation and decay but that of "conservative reform," in which "a gradual improvement of technical elements of Soviet planning practice"

took place. True, Feygin also talks about "the closing of the soviet economic mind" during these decades (242). Finally, Boldyrev and Düppe (2020, 278) refuse to think about the evolution of Kantorovich's work "in terms of success or failure."

41. Kantorovich, for example, quits the field of macro-optimization during the 1970s.

42. Leeds (2016a 289–90) maintains that with time, "input-output models changed from description and prescription to prediction. This was perhaps the greatest effect of input-output modeling." On the opportunities to switch to econometric research, see Feygin (2017, 81, 268–81).

43. Cf. Leeds' (2016a, 379–422) case study of the "Gaidar Boys" and the concept of the "administrative market." In his view "the optimal planners were normative theorists. They did not systematically study the institutions of the Soviet Union. They created an ideal mathematical structure, and then dreamed up institutions that might realize it. . . . In contrast, the young economists were empirical theorists. They began not from the math but from the institutions as they actually existed" (418).

44. Most of them were cited in the national chapters such as Caldwell (2003), Doležalová (2018), Kaase, Sparschuh, and Wenninger (2002), Krause (1998), Mau (2017), Mlčoch (2010), Szamuely and Csaba (1998), Wagener (1993; 1998); see also Mau (1990; 1995), Shukhov and Freidlin (1996), and Zhang et al. (2016). Many "insiders" published brief chapters in the Palgrave collection on the planned economy (Eatwell et al. ed, 1990). This volume represented the last (and surprisingly soft) word on planning by the international research community before the 1989 revolutions.

45. Cf. the section "Revisiting the Soviet Case" above, especially Hands (2016) and Boldyrev and Kirtchik (2017). For a long time, Western observers did not attribute as much attention to the conceptual differences between neoclassical and optimal planning models as to the linguistic tricks with which mathematical economists in the communist countries tried to camouflage the similarities by inventing special terms for optimality, utility, or the shadow price and prove that Marx, Engels, and Lenin were forefathers of mathematical modeling as a guarantee for scientific accuracy.

46. Here Kornai returns to the "German" position in the first *Methodenstreit*. For more details, see the chapter on Hungary in this volume.

47. The quasi-axiom of plannability ("intrinsic governability," to use Roumen Avramov's phrase) had had a long history before it became associated with imperative central planning at the turn of the nineteenth and twentieth century. The concept did not come out of the blue. Without recapitulating the evolution of planning doctrines prior to the October Revolution, one can safely claim that the birth of the idea of War Communism, that is, the first (failed) attempt at some kind of mandatory macroeconomic control under Soviet rule, was contingent on a whole series of synergetic effects. They included Marxism and its interpretation by German social democrats, the end-of-century utopias in Europe and beyond and their influence on Bolshevik thought, the idea of *Naturalwirtschaft*, the theory of the German war economy, as well as their common philosophical background of a collectivist variety of evolutionary optimism backed by a positivist approach to social sciences. Nevertheless, the spell of plannability could not have survived safely without the three alleged success stories of the interwar period: Stalinist and national-socialist planning and the New Deal.

The approval of planning to be performed by central government agencies could be articulated in cautious understatements like those of John Maynard Keynes in his 1926 essay on "The End of Laissez-Faire" but also in crude nazi or fascist slogans swarming in their party programs. It could be expressed in the Hegelian language of Marx detesting spontaneity and saluting the class consciousness of the proletariat, in technocratic terms applied by Otto Neurath or Walther Rathenau to praise in-kind regulations in a war economy, and also in the romantic style of utopian novels such as William Morris's *News from Nowhere* (1890) and Edward Bellamy's *Looking Backward* (1887). You could be a parliamentary democrat like the protagonists of the New Deal, a fan of *Räterepublik* like Neurath, or an economic advisor and politician serving a dictatorial regime like Hjalmar Schacht, Nikolai Voznesenskii, or later Oskar Lange.

Approaching our research field, the economist subscribing to the idea of plannability after 1945 could be of social-democratic and communist persuasion, a heir of "military Keynesianism," to use Michał Kalecki's phrase describing the economics of national socialism, like the Hungarian Béla Csikós-Nagy and Mátyás Matolcsy, a fan of Henry de Man's doctrine of *planisme*, maybe in Romania, a "bourgeois" economist like the Czech Karel Engliš combining Keynes' program with the teachings of the Austrian School of Economics in his theory of the "regulated economy," or a steadfast Marxist who like Lange applied neoclassical instruments to prove the rationality of a centrally administered economy. (The term "wartime capitalistic socialism" coined by the Bulgarian liberal Assen Christophoroff resignedly reflects such hybrid doctrines well.) Even the attitudes of many scholars in the interwar to private property were bad predictors for being an enthusiast of central planning. One finds among its devotees of German national socialism who, while resisting large-scale nationalization, endorsed strict governmental planning as well as various socialists and social-liberals ranging from the old Karl Kautsky to the young Karl Polányi who also disliked all-encompassing and hierarchical state ownership but favored some kind of—democratically designed—central planning. Moreover, a number of Russian agrarian (*neo-narodnik*) economists like Aleksandr Chayanov may be mentioned in this regard who insisted on the freedom of small-and medium-sized peasant property (private or communal) but also acknowledged central planning based on a certain degree of state coercion. (See also the chapter on the GDR in this volume.)

48. See Rawls (2005, 49) and the excellent books by Gerovitch (2002) and Erickson et al. (2013). The latter called my attention to Rawl's opinion.

49. One of the most exciting problems of the evolution of mathematical economics under communism is why game theory did not succeed to conquer the discipline in spite of the early discovery of its usefulness by eminent scholars like Viktor Volkonskii and Yurii Gavrilets in the Soviet Union, Tiberiu Schatteles in Romania, or Kornai and Lipták in Hungary even if they replaced the term "bargaining" with those of "dialogue" and "negotiation." Also, no mathematical incompatibility was to be expected since a linear programming task can be described in a game-theoretic form. In order to model the interplay of main economic actors in the planned economy, the optimizers should have defined the strategies of these actors, including that of the Central Planner—a risky venture for sure. For instance, they should have asked

"what the Soviet rulers maximized" just like Kontorovich and Wein (2009) did many years later. Below, we will see that approaching New Institutional Economics could have helped them raise such questions. In any event, it seemed much easier (and more elegant) to construct a single Big Optimal Plan than to find the optimum in thousands of smaller but important games and aggregate their outcome on the macro level. For Lubomir Mlčoch's concept of institutional games, see the chapter on Czechoslovakia.

50. For more on faith and opportunism/cynicism as well as on their covert and overt variants, see note 2 and 18. Koopmans described Kantorovich after their meeting in 1965 as a person of "self-imposed political cautiousness . . . beyond the call of duty and necessity" (Boldyrev and Düppe 2020, 274). Katsenelinboigen (1980, 43–44) recalls that "I did not succeed in understanding whether it was out of tactical considerations or from conviction that he wanted to reconcile shadow prices with labor value." The chapter on Hungary in this volume brings many examples of this dilemma by comparing the approaches of Bródy and Kornai to censorship. The following words of Schatteles (1970, 196) also demonstrate ambiguity between expressing loyalty to communist principles and accepting part of "capitalist criticism": Mises's "rationality postulate is essentially a capitalist one from which he tries to prove the impossibility of socialism. But the problem of computation in socialism is—and must be—beyond the question thus put. For the economist, the social system is a <fact of the world,> his task being the study of this fact and to compute the computable in the field of planning practice defined by this very <world>." Multiple examples for the durability of Marxist views of prominent mathematical planners such as Mária Augusztinovics, Aleksander Bajt, András Bródy, Emilian Dobrescu, Josef Goldmann, Branko Horvat, Evgeni Mateev, or Miroslav Toms can be found in the national chapters.

51. See note 45. Andrei Belykh quotes a critic of optimization from 1943: "Kantorovich suggests the optimum, and who else suggests the optimum? The fascist Pareto, Mussolini's favorite" (see the chapter on the Soviet Union). The censors and their allies among the official political economists had a hard time when they accused the mathematical economists of formalism, subjectivism, revisionism, anti-Marxist deviation, or being the Trojan horse of bourgeois economics but did not really understand the jargon these spoke. Accordingly, it was not the excellence of optimal planning theory that convinced them of relaxing the grip on the experts but its expected utility in running the economy and strategic importance in military affairs. At any rate, the process of recognition was very slow if one considers the fact that Kantorovich, Novozhilov, and Nemchinov had worked out the basic principles of optimal planning in 1939, 1943, and 1946, respectively (cf. the chapter on the Soviet Union).

52. Between the two, in 1965, Novozhilov, Kantorovich, and Nemchinov (posthumously) were awarded the Lenin Prize: of similar importance was the fact that step by step they succeeded in occupying strategic positions in economic research and education as well as within *Gosplan* and other key institutions of the party-state. An important milestone in the international recognition of optimal planning was Leontief's Nobel Prize in 1973.

53. The Walras model of general equilibrium pertains to the economy as a whole but does not contain an overarching objective function. At the same time,

the Dorfman-Samuelson-Solow model of linear programming does not aim at macro-optimization. Cf. Koopmans (1957) and Dorfman, Samuelson, and Solow ([1958] 1987).

54. While trying to craft big optimization models with moderate success, many optimal planners put up with smaller ones. Mathematical experts in China enjoyed the advantages of latecomers, skipped the overambitious phase of optimal planning, and have continued to work on smaller-scale projects until today. See the chapter on China in this volume. See also note 80.

55. I have no room in this chapter (nor enough knowledge) to discuss the troubled fate of indicative planning in market economies.

56. Cf. Kovács (1990; 1992).

57. For reasons why this East-West cultural encounter did not take place, see Aligică and Terpe (2012), Avramov (2012), Franičević (2012), Kochanowicz (2012), and Kovács (2012).

58. This came in handy for the textbook political economists (see below).

59. See note 49. The chapter on Hungary includes the example of verbal reform economists Tamás Bauer and Attila K. Soós, revealing the sad fact that their deep knowledge of planning regimes in many communist countries were hardly processed into mathematical models to increase its accuracy and testability.

60. János Kornai (1959; 1980) had started examining some of these phenomena in *Overcentralization* in the 1950s, that is, before he began to work on optimal planning, and returned to them in *Shortage* during the 1980s. See the chapter on Hungary.

61. In fact, some of these questions already had been asked by Boris Brutskus (1935) in Soviet Russia simultaneously with Mises in the early 1920s.

62. On conviction, see note 2, 18, and 50. Of course, institutional inertia also mattered, especially in the case of model builders who could not do armchair research on their own but were exposed to cooperation with fellow scientists and assistants, not to speak of the availability of computer centers. See also the term "plan mongering" below.

63. The scientific career of Józef Pajestka is a good example for how one gets from the estimation of production functions in Poland to sketching up megatrends of civilization.

64. See the chapter on Yugoslavia.

65. A remarkable exception is a group of Russian scholars, including Sergei Guriev, Konstantin Sonin, and Ekaterina Zhuravskaia. For more on their scientific and political attitudes, see Leeds (2016a, 431–40). A little earlier, the concept of the "administrative market" seemed to provide a promising opportunity for reform-minded and mathematically literate economists (like Piotr Aven, Anatolii Chubais, Vitalii Naishul, and Viacheslav Shironin, some of whom became members of the Gaidar team later) to join forces under the auspices of a similar research program (Leeds 2016a, 361–419).

66. See the chapter on Czechoslovakia.

67. A number of mathematical economists in our countries (e.g., Eduard Braverman, Viktor Polterovich, Wojciech Charemza) turned to disequilibrium analysis but with much less commitment against GET than János Kornai in his *Anti-equilibrium*.

Cf. Boldyrev and Kirtchik (2014), Kirtchik (2019), and the chapters on Hungary and Poland.

68. This feeling originated not only in the dramatically poor record of textbook political economy but also in the traditional prestige of mathematical sciences, especially in the Soviet Union. Leeds (2016a, 261) cites a founding member of the first economic-mathematical laboratory in Moscow Vladimir Kossov: "We felt like people defending ourselves with weapons against the savages. We could read, formulate the task, propose calculations. It gave us a sense of enormous moral superiority." Let me add that frequently pride was also due to a simplistic engineering view of planning: "I am right because my calculations were correct and my <machine> seems to work in the real world." (See note 17 on constructivism versus destructivism.)

Mathematical planners ridiculed the verbal specialists as bookkeepers preoccupied with their simplistic balances. Yet, the scorn often pertained neither to the bureaucratic attitudes of the "accountants" nor the roughness of their calculations but rather to the fact that this method of planning was considered to be heavily exposed to arbitrary political intervention, far more so than the complicated quantitative operations suggested by the optimizers.

69. For more on this "Faustian bargain," see the chapter on Hungary.

70. Optimal planning is probably one of those few fields in economic sciences, in which the *ex oriente lux* thesis is not without any foundation (see below). Eminent economic theorists (including Nobel Prize winners such as Arrow, Frisch, Hayek, Hurwicz, Koopmans, Leontief, Ostrom, Samuelson, Sen, Solow, Tinbergen, and Williamson) in the West have profited from outstanding scientific discoveries made in the communist world or—indirectly—from challenges stemming from not-so-outstanding scholarly products fabricated there, or—even more indirectly—from the reality of the planned economy.

71. Philip Hanson (2003, 97) remembers visiting a laboratory in TSEMI in 1964 where he saw "the excellent economist Viktor Volkonskii and a group of young women, all math graduates, armed with copies of Samuelson's *Foundations of Economic Analysis* and English-Russian dictionaries."

72. See the chapter on the GDR.

73. Cf. Gerovitch (2002, 264–88), Rindzevičiūtė (2010), Erickson et al. (2013, 1–21), Düppe (2016), Leeds (2016b), and Feygin (2017, 260–323).

74. Cf. Bockman and Bernstein (2008), Düppe (2016), Boldyrev and Düppe (2020).

75. See the Hungarian chapter.

76. For example, Schatteles (1970) was originally presented at a conference in Novosibirsk. Soviet mathematical economists took part in regular meetings in Warsaw, Prague, Budapest, and Berlin but visited Yugoslavia as well (Katsenelinboigen 2009). In these cities they could also meet top scholars from the West (Boldyrev and Düppe 2020, 267) but some of them, like Koopmans and Leontief, traveled to Moscow. In the framework of his LINK project, Lawrence Klein visited many countries of Eastern Europe and China. IIASA in Laxenburg, Austria was also a crucial place of East-West encounters. Łódź provided home for an annual workshop of econometricians. Even in Bucharest there were regular symposia with Soviet and French experts, respectively, in the brief period of opening at the turn of the 1960s and 1970s. Experts from the

planning offices met regularly under the aegis of the Comecon but also by crossing the Iron Curtain (cf. Guarné 2018). For more details, see the national chapters.

77. For Vasilii Nemchinov's role in establishing the Economico-Mathematical Laboratory in Prague and Sofia, see the chapters on Czechoslovakia and Bulgaria.

78. Here mathematical economists were much less enchanted by optimal planning and accepted the basics of neoclassical economics and standard econometrics (cf. the "Klein connection") earlier than in most communist countries. As mentioned, leading scholars like Aleksander Bajt and Branko Horvat did not give up their Marxist views entirely but supported not only macro-but also microeconomic analysis of planning once imperative central planning was replaced, first by indicative, then by so-called "social" planning. Simulating market socialism by means of optimal models was not popular among local experts since the Yugoslav economy had fragile but real markets. Another difference was that economic theorists working in and on the country discovered early on that these markets were exposed to heavy government intervention (a kind of informal planning) and tried to develop the existing neoclassical models of Yugoslav self-management with the help of new-institutional techniques. See the chapter on Yugoslavia.

79. The chapter on the GDR demonstrates that the rise could be interrupted (cf. "the revolution that wasn't"). Cybernetics became a philosophical discipline, input-output research did not develop into optimal planning, and in 1971 (!) cybernetics and systems theory was condemned by the supreme party leader as pseudo-sciences.

80. Understandably, in our comparison China is always the (instructive) outlier. The first chessboard table of its national economy was completed during the Cultural Revolution in 1974. When Chinese scholars could have started to work out optimal plans, the country embarked upon a long journey of reforms that made imperative macro-planning questionable step by step: first through deregulation, then through privatization. Indirect macro-control became the rule, which relied on standard (Western) macroeconomic models and was implemented by means of monetary and fiscal incentives rather than mandatory planning targets even in the state sector that was shrinking anyway. Large-scale administrative decentralization (e.g., fiscal federalism) also required indicative methods of planning instead of imperative ones.

Ironically, unlike other communist countries before, in China the establishment of "centrally planned commodity economy" and later of "socialist market economy," to use the official designations, did not result in an upsurge of optimal planning. On the macro level, optimization was rather used in forecasting and checking the consistency of the annual and five-year plans that have not ceased to exist until today (However, since 2006, the "ministry of ministries," the National Commission for Development and Reform, does not carry the term "planning" in its name.). Of course, targeted interventions by the party-state in economic life abound, but these are not arranged in formal mandatory instructions. Nevertheless, informal recentralization can turn into a formal one. What is today outside the plan can get inside it tomorrow, and optimal planners may face an increasing demand for their services. Currently, the Chinese Society of Optimization, Overall Planning and Economic Mathematics has about 17,000 members (Chow 2005; Chen, Guo, and Yang 2005; Lin, Liu, and Tao 2013; Zhang 2016).

81. Undoubtedly, progress was contingent on the cultural baggage of mathematical knowledge economists brought along from the pre-communist era. Here the Soviet scholars had no strong competitors. Moreover, as the national chapters show, the ascent of mathematical economics in Belgrade, Berlin, Prague, and Sofia also was promoted by Russian émigré scholars (e.g., Oskar Anderson and Aleksandr Bilimovich) between the two wars. Nonetheless, in searching for the sources of quantitative methods in economics under communism, the chapter authors found in these countries a whole series of indigenous economic theorists, both communists and non-communists, who studied mathematics prior to 1945.

82. One can observe an interesting difference among the countries in the attitudes of mathematical economists to econometrics. While in most countries it served the transition from optimal planning to standard neoclassical research during the agony of communism, in Poland and Yugoslavia it evolved parallelly to optimization or even replaced it.

83. According to the joke spreading all over Eastern Europe before 1989, if the central plans had been correctly implemented the communist system would have crumbled much earlier.

84. Lange (1936, 70) regarded this a decisive threat to the survival of his model of market socialism in a really-existing planned economy: "By demonstrating the economic consistency and workability of a socialist economy with free choice neither in consumption nor in occupation, but directed by a preference scale imposed by the bureaucrats in the Central Planning Board, we do not mean, of course, to recommend such a system. . . . Such a system would scarcely be tolerated by any civilized people."

85. The chapters of this volume help preserve the memory of eminent scholars of their time, input-output analysts and linear programmers, who have not been given enough light in the shadow of the Lange-Kantorovich-Kornai triumvirate. Here is a very short list of them: Mária Augusztinovics, András Bródy, Xikang Chen, Emilian Dobrescu, Josef Goldmann, Jaroslav Habr, Branko Horvat, Evgeni Mateev, Krzysztof Porwit, Tiberiu Schatteles, Mijo Sekulić, Ivan Stefanov, Miroslav Toms, Aleksy Wakar, and Zhang Shouyi. No matter what role some of them played in communist politics or scientific management at certain stages of their lives, their work is part of the (more and more) hidden treasures of economic thought in their countries. Obviously, Soviet scholars, ranging from Nemchinov and Novozhilov to Katsenelinboigen and Volkonskii, have received much more attention in the history of economic ideas.

86. With time, Kantorovich and the TSEMI experts approached this type (Nemchinov called it "flexible planning") whereas Kornai, Schatteles, and Wakar started from here. While Wakar's theory of "direct account" was based on the paradigm of general equilibrium, it also yielded insights into problems of incentive incompatibility in a planned economy, thereby anticipating neo-institutional conclusions. See the chapter on Poland and the Soviet Union.

87. In the cavalcade of planning models it was enough for the Central Planner to change somewhat the definition of "strategic industries/products" that need intensive state control, or insert new constraints or a modified objective function in the model,

and—as a consequence—the initially market-friendly versions of optimal plans returned to the traditional planning schemes.

88. Cf. Volkonskii (1967; 1973), Katsenelinboigen, Lakhman, and Ovsienko (1969), Petrakov (1971a, b), in which forbidden themes like the pluralism of interests and social goals as well as market feedbacks were discussed. Earlier, János Kornai also refused to calculate with a single objective function but did not demand to establish a democratic procedure for coordinating interests. See the Soviet and Hungarian chapters.

89. Josef Goldmann drew a similar conclusion with regard to popular discussion on planning goals. See the chapter on Czechoslovakia.

90. The attraction of automatization was so great that in the beginning even a pragmatic like Kornai could not resist it entirely (see the chapter on Hungary).

91. See the chapter on the Soviet Union. Cf. Gerovitch (2002, 279–88), Peters (2016, 107–90), Katsenelinboigen (1980, 147–56), Ericson (2019, 162–71), Leeds (2016b, 663–66), Feygin (2017, 255–58). The Soviet experiments with automated planning systems were not unique at the time: see Stafford Beer's *Cybersin* (Synco) project supported by Salvador Allende's government in Chile (Medina 2006; Morozov 2014).

92. Cf. Leijonhufvud's (1973) "econological" parody about the Math-econs, Micros, Macros, and Devlops. Compare with another typology of economists (mathematical versus verbal and reformist versus conservative) in the chapter on the Soviet Union.

93. The best documented stories have been told about the political humiliation of the Soviet optimal planners at TSEMI and other research institutes and university departments, particularly during the 1970s. For example, in the course of ideological cleansing following the occupation of Czechoslovakia in 1968, it was not only market socialism that featured among the accusations levelled against TSEMI but also the "too high" proportion of Jewish researchers in the institute (Birman 2001, 241–76; Katsenelinboigen 1980, 78–80; 2009; Leeds 2016a, 237, 340, 395; Sutela 1991, 83–94). In Prague the Institute of Economic Sciences at the Law Faculty of Charles University, which was regarded as a "nest of revisionists" was closed in the period of "normalization." Mathematical economists were not safe from recurrent attacks in more permissive communist regimes either. See the chapters on the Soviet Union and Hungary.

94. While mathematical economics and the theory of market reform did not merge, optimal planning did contribute to the development of the theory of marketization in some way. It prompted reformers to say goodbye to some of the fuzzy notions of the official discourse (e.g., commodity production, the interest of the people's economy, material incentives) and think in terms of well-defined economic actors who want to maximize some kind of utility but planning instructions and other state regulations force them to join the informal economy.

95. The refecons who normally came from the realm of official political economy and retained some loyalty to Marxism seldom returned there. On the contrary, owing to the successive radicalization of refecons, the road to teaching at universities was

blocked by the polecons for many of them until communism started imploding in the 1980s. A conversion between the optecons and the polecons was virtually impossible.

96. In private conversations the liberal-minded optimal planners used to combine the following self-justifications (which initially were similar to those of the market reformers): first, the regime will only change (if at all) in the long run; second, what we are doing can be seen as a gradual and peaceful destruction of the planned economy by injecting the poison of rationality in its body and eliminating the *raison d'être* of a large part of the planning apparatus; third, provided our suggestions are accepted by the rulers, the life of our fellow citizens will improve.

97. See the chapters on Czechoslovakia, Hungary, and Poland.

98. "Consoling" is meant here with a grain of salt. A key change, namely, the turn to econometric studies, presented in most chapters of this volume, could not really comfort those scholars who had been used to normative research with a direct impact on the economy, an academic position of high prestige embedded in the planning regime at its higher echelons, and a distinguished status in the international scientific community.

99. It is perplexing to see how many times the participants of the debate thought that it ended with their victory. Austrian theorists of different generations, Lange, even Koopmans belong to them. Koopmans (1951, 7), for example, praised George Dantzig, saying that his model "is an abstract allocation model that does not depend on the concept of a market" and as such it disproves Mises's impossibility thesis.

100. See note 57.

101. Among the eminent optimizers, it was Kornai who proved to be the most self-critical. For the limitations of his "repentance," see the chapter on Hungary.

102. I learned a lot in conversation with Péter Bodó about the role these disciplines can play in economic planning.

103. For anticipating some of these developments by Emmanuil Braverman, see Kirtchik (2019, 200). For a selection of the rapidly growing literature on whether AI can guarantee rational calculation under collectivism, see Cockshott and Cottrell (1989; 1993a,b), Laibman (2002), Jablonowski (2011), Morozov (2014; 2019), Phillips and Rozworski (2019), Feygin (2019), Van Den Hauwe (2019), Nieto and Mateo (2020), and Daum and Nuss (2021). On the possibility of bringing the labor theory of value back in economic calculation, see Cockhshott and Cottrell (1989). For a most recent critique of "cyber-communist" projects, see Wang, Espinosa, and Peña-Ramos (2021).

104. As mentioned, Bardhan and Roemer (1992; 1993) started groping in this direction right after the collapse of communism by resuscitating the doctrine of market socialism. Since then, the ideas of industrial democracy, cooperativism, participatory economics, and so on have continued to appear in different forms on the Left. (See, e.g., the project of "investment and consumer councils" in Nieto and Mateo (2020).) For earlier and later comments on concepts of decentralized socialism, including the murky experiment with "social planning" in Yugoslavia, see Prychitko (1988; 2002). Meanwhile, modern macroeconomics, with its varying families of models (ranging from "computable general equilibrium" through the "real business cycle"

to "dynamic stochastic general equilibrium"), does not seem to attract the would-be planners like the Walras model did almost a century ago.

105. The system of grading them by means of a "social credit" system in China is a case in point. For an ambitious program of a democratic architecture of a "plan-oriented market economy system" controlled by artificial intelligence, see Wang and Li (2017).

BIBLIOGRAPHY

Aligică, Paul Dragoș, and Horia Terpe. 2012. "Institutionalism, the Economic Institutions of Capitalism, and the Romanian Economic Epistemic Community." In *Capitalism from Outside? Economic Cultures in Eastern Europe after 1989*, edited by János Mátyás Kovács and Violetta Zentai, 263–80. Budapest: CEU Press.

Avramov, Roumen. 2012. "The Sinuous Path of New Institutional Economics in Bulgaria." In *Capitalism from Outside? Economic Cultures in Eastern Europe after 1989*, edited by János Mátyás Kovács and Violetta Zentai, 223–40. Budapest: CEU Press.

Backhouse, Roger, and Andrea Salanti, eds. 2001. *Macroeconomics and the Real World*. 2 vols. New York: Oxford University Press.

Bardhan, Pranab, and John Roemer. 1992. "Market Socialism: A Case for Rejuvenation." *Journal of Economic Perspectives* 6 (3): 101–16.

———, eds. 1993. *Market Socialism: The Current Debate*. New York: Oxford University Press.

Barnett, Vincent. 2009. *A History of Russian Economic Thought*. London: Routledge.

Barnett, Vincent, and Joachim Zweynert. eds. 2008. *Economics in Russia: Studies in Intellectual History.* London: Routledge.

Bellamy, Edward. 1887. *Looking Backward 2000–1887*. Cambridge: The Riverside Press.

Belykh, Andrei. (1989) 2007. *История российских экономико-математических исследований: Первые сто лет.* Moscow: URSS.

Birman, Igor. 1968. *Optimal'noe programmirovanie*. Moscow: Ekonomika.

———. 2001. *Ia—ekonomist (o sebe liubimom)*. Moscow: Vremia.

Bockman, Johanna. 2007. "The Origins of Neoliberalism between Soviet Socialism and Western Capitalism: A Galaxy without Borders." *Theory and Society* 36 (4): 343–71.

———. 2011. *Markets in the Name of Socialism; The Left-Wing Origins of Neoliberalism*. Stanford: Stanford University Press.

———. 2012. "The Long Road to 1989: Neoclassical Economics, Alternative Socialisms, and the Advent of Neoliberalism." *Radical History Review* 112 (Winter): 9–42.

Bockman, Johanna, and Gil Eyal. 2002. "Eastern Europe as a Laboratory for Economic Knowledge: The Transnational Roots of Neoliberalism." *American Journal of Sociology* 108 (2): 310–52.

Bockman, Johanna, and Michael Bernstein. 2008. "Scientific Community in a Divided World: Economists, Planning, and Research Priority During the Cold War." *Comparative Studies in Society and History* 50 (3): 581–613.

Boettke, Peter. 1990. *The Political Economy of Soviet Socialism: The Formative Years. 1918–1928.* Boston: Kluwer Academic Publishers.

———. 1993. *Why Perestroika Failed: The Politics and Economics of Socialist Transformation.* New York: Routledge.

———. 1995. "Credibility, Commitment and Soviet Economic Reform." In *Economic Transition in Eastern Europe and Russia: Realities of Reform*, edited by Edward Lazear, 247–75. Stanford: Hoover Institution Press.

———. ed. 2000a. *Socialism and the Market.* 9 vols. London: Routledge.

———. 2000b. "Towards a Theory of the History of Socialist Planning." In *Socialism and the Market.* Vol 1, edited by Peter Boettke, 1–39. London: Routledge.

———. 2001. *Calculation and Coordination.* London: Routledge.

Boettke, Peter, and Gary Anderson. 1997. "Soviet Venality: A Rent-Seeking Model of the Communist State." *Public Choice* 93 (1–2): 37–53.

Boldyrev, Ivan, and Till Düppe. 2020. "Programming the USSR: Leonid V. Kantorovich in Context." *The British Journal for the History of Science* 53 (2): 255–78.

Boldyrev, Ivan, and Olessia Kirtchik. 2014. "General Equilibrium Theory Behind the Iron Curtain: The Case of Victor Polterovich." *History of Political Economy* 46 (3): 435–61.

———. 2017. "The Cultures of Mathematical Economics in the Postwar Soviet Union: More Than a Method, Less Than a Discipline." *Studies in History and Philosophy of Science* 63 (June): 1–10.

Brutskus, Boris. 1935. *Economic Planning in Soviet Russia.* London: Routledge.

Bukharin, Nikolai. (1919) 1927. *Economic Theory of the Leisure Class.* Moscow: International Publishers.

Caldwell, Peter. 2003. *Dictatorship, State Planning, and Social Theory in the German Democratic Republic.* Cambridge: Cambridge University Press.

Campbell, Robert W. 1960. Review of *Ekonomicheskii raschet nailuchshego ispolzovaniia resursov*, by L.V. Kantorovich. *American Economic Review* 50 (4): 729–31.

———. 1961. "Marx, Kantorovich, and Novozhilov: *Stoimost'* Versus Reality." *Slavic Review* 20 (3): 402–18.

Chen Xikang, Ju-e Guo, and Cuihong Yang. 2005. "Chinese Economic Development and Input-Output Extension." https://www.iioa.org/conferences/15th/pdf/chenxikang.pdf. Accessed November 15, 2021.

Chow, Gregory. 2005. "The Role of Planning in China's Market Economy." *Journal of Chinese Economic and Business Studies* 3 (3): 193–203.

Cockshott, Paul, and Allin Cottrell. 1989. "Labour value and socialist economic calculation." *Economy and Society* 18 (1): 71–99.

———. 1993a. "Calculation, Complexity and Planning: The Socialist Calculation Debate Once Again." *Review of Political Economy* 5 (1): 73–112.

———. 1993b. *Towards a New Socialism.* Nottingham: Spokesman Books.

Daum, Timo, and Sabine Nuss. 2021. *Die unsichtbare Hand des Plans: Koordination und Kalkül im digitalen Kapitalismus*. Berlin: Dietz Verlag.

Doležalová, Antonie. 2018. *A History of Czech Economic Thought*. London: Routledge.

Dorfman, Robert. 1976. Preface to *Mathematical Models in Economics: Papers and Proceedings of a U.S.-U.S.S.R. Seminar*, edited by Sydney Shulman. New York: National Bureau of Economic Research.

Dorfman, Robert, Paul A. Samuelson, and Robert M. Solow. (1958) 1987. *Linear Programming and Economic Analysis*. New York: Dover Publications.

Düppe, Till. 2016. "Koopmans in the Soviet Union: A Travel Report of the Summer of 1965." *Journal of the History of Economic Thought* 38 (1): 81–104.

Eatwell, John, Murray Milgate, and Peter Newman. eds. (1987) 1990. *Problems of the Planned Economy. The New Palgrave*. New York: Norton.

Ellman, Michael. 1968. "Lessons of the Soviet Economic Reform." *Socialist Register* 5: 23–53.

———. 1971. *Soviet Planning Today: Proposals for an Optimally Functioning Economic System*. Cambridge: Cambridge University Press.

———. 1973. *Planning Problems in the USSR: The Contribution of Mathematical Economics to Their Solution, 1960–1971*. Cambridge: Cambridge University Press.

———. 1978. "The Fundamental Problem of Socialist Planning." *Oxford Economic Papers* 30 (2): 249–62.

———. 1979. *Socialist Planning*. Cambridge: Cambridge University Press.

———. 1980. "Against Convergence." *Cambridge Journal of Economics* 4 (3): 199–210.

Ericson, Richard. 2019. "The Growth and Marcescence of the 'System for Optimal Functioning of the Economy' (SOFE)." *History of Political Economy* 51 (S1): 155–79.

Erickson, Paul, Judy Klein, Lorraine Daston, Rebecca Lemov, Thomas Sturm, and Michael Gordin. 2013. *How Reason Almost Lost Its Mind*. Chicago: University of Chicago Press.

Erlich, Alexander. 1960. *The Soviet Industrialization Debate 1924–1928*. Cambridge: Harvard University Press.

Esterházy, Péter. 2004. *Celestial Harmonies*. New York: Ecco.

Eyal, Gil. 2000. "Anti-Politics and the Spirit of Capitalism: Dissidents, Monetarists, and the Czech Transition to Capitalism." *Theory and Society* 29 (1): 49–92.

———. 2003. *The Origins of Postcommunist Elites: From Prague Spring to the Breakup of Czechoslovakia*. Minneapolis: University of Minnesota Press.

Fehér, Ferenc, Ágnes Heller, and György Márkus. 1983. *Dictatorship over Needs: An Analysis of Soviet Societies*. Oxford: Basil Blackwell.

Feygin, Jakov. 2017. "Reforming the Cold War State: Economic Thought, Internationalization, and the Politics of Soviet Reform, 1955–1985." PhD. diss., University of Pennsylvania. Accessed November 15, 2021. https://repository.upenn.edu/edissertations/2277.

———. 2019. "The Honest Marxist: Yakov Kronrod and the Politics of Cold War Economics in the Post-Stalin USSR." *History of Political Economy* 51 (S1): 100–126.

———. 2019. "On the Limits of a New AI-inspired Gosplan System." *Financial Times*, April 19. Accessed November 15, 2021. https://www.ft.com/content/a91b4f53-8d98-3e4b-b270-b59d4ae9e22a.

Franičević, Vojmir. 2012. "Soft Institutionalism: The Reception of New Institutional Economics in Croatia." In *Capitalism from Outside? Economic Cultures in Eastern Europe after 1989*, edited by János Mátyás Kovács and Violetta Zentai, 241–62. Budapest: CEU Press.

Gerovitch, Slava. 2002. *From Newspeak to Cyberspeak: A History of Soviet Cybernetics*. Cambridge: The MIT Press.

Grossman, Gregory. 1975. Foreword to *The Mathematical Revolution in Soviet Economics*, by Alfred Zauberman. Oxford: Oxford University Press.

Guarné, Isabelle. 2018. "Mandatory Planning versus Indicative Planning? The Eastern Itineraries of French Planners (1960s-1970s)." In *Planning in Cold War Europe, Competition, Cooperation, Circulations (1950s–1970s)*, edited by Michel Christian, Sandrine Kott, and Ondřej Matějka, 71–96. Berlin - Boston: De Gruyter.

Hands, D. Wade. 2016. "Crossing in the Night of the Cold War: Alternative Visions and Related Tensions in Western and Soviet General Equilibrium Theory." *History of Economic Ideas* 24 (2): 51–74. https://www.researchgate.net/publication/313579329_Crossing_in_the_night_of_the_cold_war_Alternative_visions_and_related_tensions_in_Western_and_Soviet_general_equilibrium_theory.

Hanson, Philip. 2003. *The Rise and Fall of the Soviet Economy*. London: Pearson Education.

Hayek, Friedrich. 1988. *The Fatal Conceit: The Errors of Socialism*. London: Routledge.

Harrison, Mark. 2005. "The Fundamental Problem of Command: Plan and Compliance in a Partially Centralised Economy." *Comparative Economic Studies* 47 (2): 296–314.

Jablonowski, Mark. 2011. "Markets on a (Computer) Chip? New Perspectives on Economic Calculation." *Science & Society* 75:3, 400–418.

Kaase, Max, Vera Sparschuh, and Agnieszka Wenninger, eds. 2002. *Three Social Science Disciplines in Central and Eastern Europe (1989–2001)*. Bonn: GESIS/Social Science Information Centre (IZ), Collegium Budapest.

Katsenelinboigen, Aron, Lakhman Iosif, and Yurii Ovsienko. 1969. *Optimal'nost i tovarno-denezhniie otnosheniia*. Moscow: Nauka.

Katsenelinboigen, Aron J. 1978. "L. V. Kantorovich: The Political Dilemma in Scientific Creativity." *Journal of Post Keynesian Economics* 1 (2): 129–47.

———. 1980. *Soviet Economic Thought and Political Power in the USSR*. New York: Pergamon Press.

———. 2009. "Predisposition: Vospominaniia. O Vremeni, O Liudiakh, O Sebe." https://web.archive.org/web/20120331012012/http://predisposition.us/category/memoirs/, accessed October 30, 2021.

Keynes, John Maynard. 1926. *The End of Laissez-Faire*. London: Hogarth Press.

Kirtchik, Olessia 2019. "From Pattern Recognition to Economic Disequilibrium: Emmanuil Braverman's Theory of Control of the Soviet Economy." *History of Political Economy* 51 (S1): 180–203.

Kirzner, Israel. 1988. "The Economic Calculation Debate: Lessons for Austrians." *The Review of Austrian Economics* 2 (1): 1–18.

Kochanowicz, Jacek. 2012. "Have Polish Economists Noticed New Institutionalism?" In *Capitalism from Outside? Economic Cultures in Eastern Europe after 1989*, edited by János Mátyás Kovács and Violetta Zentai, 203–22. Budapest: CEU Press.

Kontorovich, Vladimir, and Alexander Wein. 2009. "What Did the Soviet Rulers Maximise?" *Europe-Asia Studies* 61(9): 1579–1601.

Koopmans, Tjalling. 1951. "Introduction to Activity Analysis of Production and Allocation: Proceedings of a Conference." In *Cowles Commission for Research in Economics Monograph 13*, edited by Tjalling Koopmans, 1–12. New York: John Wiley & Sons.

———. 1957. *Three Essays on the State of Economic Science*. New York: MacGraw Hill.

Kornai, János. 1959. *Overcentralization in Economic Administration*. Oxford: Oxford University Press.

———. 1980. *Economics of Shortage*. Amsterdam: North-Holland.

———. 2019. "Economists Share Blame for China's 'Monstrous' Turn: Western Intellectuals Must Now Seek to Contain Beijing." *Financial Times*, July 11, 2019.

Kovács, János Mátyás. 1990. "Reform Economics: The Classification Gap." *Daedalus* 119 (1): 215–48.

———. 1992. "Compassionate Doubts about Reform Economics (Science, Ideology, Politics)." In *Reform and Transformation; Eastern European Economics on the Threshold of Change*, edited by János Mátyás Kovács and Márton Tardos, 299–333. London: Routledge.

———. 2012. "Beyond Basic Instinct? On the Reception of New Institutional Economics in Eastern Europe." In *Capitalism from Outside? Economic Cultures in Eastern Europe after 1989*, edited by János Mátyás Kovács and Violetta Zentai, 281–310. Budapest: CEU Press.

———. 2018. "Expeditions to No Man's Land: Comparing Economic Concepts of Ownership under Communism. An evolutionary View." In *Populating No Man's Land: Economic Concepts of Ownership Under Communism,* edited by János Mátyás Kovács, 287–340. Lanham: Lexington Books.

Krause, Günter. 1998. *Wirtschaftstheorie in der DDR*. Marburg: Metropolis.

Laibman, David. 2002. "Democratic Coordination: Towards a Working Socialism for the New Century." *Science & Society* 66:1, 116–129.

Lange, Oskar. 1936. "On the Economic Theory of Socialism, Part One." *Review of Economic Studies* 4 (1): 53–71.

———. (1964) 1967. "The Computer and the Market." In *Capitalism, Socialism and Economic Growth*, edited by Charles Feinstein, 158–61. Cambridge: Cambridge University Press.

Lavoie, Don. 1981. "A Critique of the Standard Account of the Socialist Calculation Debate." *The Journal of Libertarian Studies* 5 (1): 40–87.

———. 1985. *Rivalry and Central Planning: The Socialist Calculation Debate Reconsidered.* Cambridge: Cambridge University Press.

———. 1986. "The Market as a Procedure for Discovery and Conveyance of Inarticulate Knowledge." *Comparative Economic Studies* 28 (1): 1–19.

Leeds, Adam. 2016a. "Spectral Liberalism: On the Subjects of Political Economy in Moscow." PhD diss., University of Pennsylvania, 2016. Accessed November 18, 2020. http://repository.upenn.edu/edissertations/1828.

———. 2016b. "Dreams in Cybernetic Fugue: Cold War Technoscience, the Intelligentsia, and the Birth of Soviet Mathematical Economics." *Historical Studies in the Natural Sciences* 46 (5): 633–68.

Leijonhufvud, Axel. 1973. "Life Among the Econ." *Western Economic Journal* 11 (3): 327–37.

Leontief, Wassily. 1960. "The Decline and Rise of Soviet Economic Science." *Foreign Affairs* 38 (2): 261–72.

Lewin, Moshe. 1973. "The Disappearance of Planning in the Plan." *Slavic Review* 32 (2): 271–87.

Lin, Justin Yifu, Mingxing Liu, and Ran Tao. 2013. "Deregulation, Decentralization, and China's Growth in Transition." In *Law and Economics with Chinese Characteristics: Institutions for Promoting Development in the Twenty-First Century*, edited by David Kennedy and Joseph E. Stiglitz, 467–90. Oxford: Oxford University Press.

Mau, Vladimir. 1990. *V poiskakh planomernosti: iz istorii razvitiia sovetskoi ekonomicheskoi mysli kontsa 30-ikh—nachala 60-ikh godov.* Moscow: Nauka.

———. 1995. "Perestroika: Theoretical and Political Problems of Economic Reforms in the USSR." *Europe-Asia Studies* 47 (3): 387–411.

———. 2017. *Gosudarstvo i ekonomika: Opyt ekonomicheskikh reform.* Moscow: Delo.

Medina, Eden. 2006. "Designing Freedom, Regulating a Nation: Socialist Cybernetics in Allende's Chile." *Journal of Latin American Studies* 38 (3): 571–606.

Mirowski, Philip. 2002. *Machine Dreams: Economics Becomes a Cyborg Science.* Cambridge: Cambridge University Press.

———. 2009. "Postface: Defining Neoliberalism." In Mirowsky and Plehwe 2009, 417–56.

Mirowski, Philip, and Dieter Plehwe, eds. 2009. *The Road from Mont Pèlerin: The Making of the Neoliberal Thought Collective.* Cambridge: Harvard University Press.

Mises, Ludwig. (1949) 1966. *Human Action.* New Haven: Yale University Press.

Mlčoch, Lubomír, ed. 2010. *Soudobá ekonomie očima tří generací.* Praha: Karolinum.

Montias, John Michael. 1967. "Soviet Optimizing Models for Multiperiod Planning." In *Mathematics and Computers in Soviet Economic Planning*, edited by John Hardt et al., New Haven: Yale University Press.

Morgan, Mary. 2012. *The World in the Model. How Economists Work and Think.* Cambridge: Cambridge University Press.

Morozov, Evgenii. 2014. "The Planning Machine." *The New Yorker*, October 13, 2014.

———. 2019. "Digital Socialism? The Calculation Debate in the Age of Big Data." *New Left Review* 116–17: 33–67.

Morris, William. 1908. *News from Nowhere*. London: Longmans, Green and Co. https://gutenberg.org/cache/epub/3261/pg3261-images.html, accessed November 15, 2021.

Nieto, Maxi, and Juan Mateo. 2020. "Dynamic Efficiency in a Planned Economy: Innovation and Entrepreneurship without Markets." *Science & Society* 84: 42–66.

Nobel Prize. 1975. "Press release." NobelPrize.org. Accessed November 15, 2021. https://www.nobelprize.org/prizes/economic-sciences/1975/press-release/.

Ostrovitianov, Konstantin et al. 1954. *Politicheskaia ekonomiia*. Moscow: Gospolitizdat.

Peters, Benjamin. 2016. *How Not to Network a Nation: The Uneasy History of the Soviet Internet*. Cambridge: MIT Press.

Petrakov, Nikolai. 1971a. *Khoziaistvennaia reforma: Plan i ekonomicheskaia Samostoiatel'nost*. Moscow: Mysl.

———. 1971b. *Nekotorye voprosy upravleniya sotsialisticheskoi ekonomiki*. Moscow. TsEMI.

Phillips, Leigh, and Michal Rozworski. 2019. *The People's Republic of Walmart: How the World's Biggest Corporations are Laying the Foundation for Socialism*. New York: Verso Books.

Prychitko, David. 1988. "Marxism and Decentralized Socialism." *Critical Review* 2 (4): 127–48.

———. 2002. *Markets, Planning, and Democracy: Essays after the Collapse of Communism*. Cheltenham: Edward Elgar.

Rawls, John. 2005. *Political Liberalism*. New York: Columbia University Press.

Rindzevičiūtė, Eglė. 2010. "Purification and Hybridisation of Soviet Cybernetics: The Politics of Scientific Governance in an Authoritarian Regime." *Archiv für Sozialgeschichte* 50: 289–309.

Rothbard, Murray. 1991. "The End of Socialism and the Calculation Debate Revisited." *The Review of Austrian Economics* 5 (2): 51–76.

Samuelson, Paul. 1970. "Is There Life after Nobel Coronation?" NobelPrize.org. Accessed November 15, 2021. https://www.nobelprize.org/prizes/economic-sciences/1970/samuelson/article/.

Schatteles, Tiberiu. 1970. "Macroeconomic Models, Economic Growth and the Reality of Planning Practice." *Revue Roumaine des Sciences Sociales*, Série des Sciences Économiques 14 (2): 195–208.

Shleifer, Andrei, and Robert Vishny. 1994. "The Politics of Market Socialism." *Journal of Economic Perspectives* 8 (2): 165–76.

Shukhov, Nikolai, and Mikhail Freidlin. 1996. *Matematicheskaia ekonomiia v Rossii (1885–1995)*. Moscow: Nauka.

Spulber, Nicolas. 1964. *Foundations of Soviet Strategy for Economic Growth*. Bloomington: Indiana University Press.

Conclusion

Sutela, Pekka. 1984. *Socialism, Planning, and Optimality: A Study in Soviet Economic Thought*. Helsinki: Finnish Society of Sciences and Letters.

———. 1991. *Economic Thought and Economic Reform in the Soviet Union*. Cambridge: Cambridge University Press.

Szamuely, László, and László Csaba. 1998. *Rendszerváltozás a közgazdaságtanban közgazdaságtan a rendszerváltozásban*. Budapest: Közgazdasági Szemle Alapítvány.

Van Den Hauwe, Ludwig. 2019. "Ludwig von Mises' Argument against the Possibility of Socialism: Early Concepts and Contemporary Relevance." In *The First Socialization Debate (1918) and Early Efforts Towards Socialization*, edited by Jürgen Backhaus, Günther Chaloupek, and Hans Frambach. Springer

Volkonskii, Viktor. 1967. *Model optimal'nogo planirovaniia i vzaimosviazi ekonomicheskikh pokazatelei* (A Model of Optimal Planning and the Interdependence of Economic Indicators). Moscow: Nauka.

———. 1973. *Printsipy optimal'nogo planirovaniia* (Principles of Optimal Planning). Moscow: Ekonomika.

Wagener, Hans-Jürgen, ed. 1993. *The Political Economy of Transformation*. Heidelberg: Physica-Verlag.

———, ed. 1998. *Economic Thought in Communist and Post-Communist Europe*. London: Routledge.

Wang, Binbin, and Xiaoyan Li. 2017. Big Data, Platform Economy and Market Competition. A Preliminary Construction of a Plan-Oriented Market Economy System in the Information Age. *World Review of Political Economy* 8 (2): 138–161.

Wang, William Hongsong, Victor Espinosa, and José Antonio Peña-Ramos. 2021. "Private Property Rights, Dynamic Efficiency and Economic Development: An Austrian Reply to Neo-Marxist Scholars Nieto and Mateo on Cyber-Communism and Market Process." *Economies* 9: 165. https://doi.org/10.3390/economies9040165 accessed November 15, 2021.

Weintraub, Roy. 2002. *How Economics Became a Mathematical Science*. Durham: Duke University Press.

Wiles, Peter. 1964. "Imperfect Competition and Decentralized Planning." *Economics of Planning* 4 (1): 16–28.

Zauberman, Alfred. 1967. *Aspects of Planometrics*. New Haven: Yale University Press.

———. 1969. "The Rapprochement Between East and West in Mathematical-Economic Thought." *The Manchester School of Economics and Social Studies* 37 (1): 1–21.

———. 1975. *The Mathematical Revolution in Soviet Economics*. Oxford: Oxford University Press.

———. 1976. *Mathematical Theory in Soviet Planning: Concepts, Methods, Techniques*. London: Oxford University Press.

Zhang, Shouyi, Tongsan Wang, and Xinquan Ge. eds. 2016. *Quantitative Economics in China. A Thirty-Year Review*. Singapore: World Scientific Publishing.

Zweynert, Joachim. 2006. "Economic Ideas and Institutional Change: Evidence from Soviet Economic Debates 1987-1991." *Europe-Asia Studies* 58 (2): 169–92.
——. 2018. *When Ideas Fail. Economic Thought, the Failure of Transition and the Rise of Institutional Instability in Post-Soviet Russia*. London: Routledge.

Index

abstract, abstraction, 20, 27, 32, 130, 133, 170, 173–74, 180–81, 185n10, 188n39, 195n100, 302, 327, 336–38, 378n99

activity analysis, 14n9, 115, 352

algorithm, 26, 34, 64, 118, 169, 170–71, 194n93, 322, 326, 328, 339–40, 349, 353, 358, 363

All-Union State System of Automated Management (*OGAS*), 278, 358

Anderson, Oskar, 21, 47n1, 57, 376n81

anti-liberal(ism), 45, 330–31, 333, 335

Antonov, Ventsislav, 29, 31–32, 37, 41–45, 49nn15–21, 50nn25–29

apparatchik, 88, 321, 324, 347

Arrow, Kenneth, 91, 151, 170, 173, 193n88, 194n99, 195n104, 286n20, 338, 351, 357, 374n70

artificial intelligence, 118, 363–64, 379

Augusztinovics, Mária, 150–51, 154, 156–57, 163, 169, 179, 185n10, 186n28, 188nn41–46, 190n60, 194n98, 197nn123–25, 372n50, 376n85

Austrian School of Economics, 8, 29, 84, 149, 328, 346, 368nn27–29, 371n47

Austrian suspicion, 10, 358

Automated System of Planning Calculations (*ASPR*), 278, 280–81, 358

Bajt, Aleksander, 296–99, 316n6, 372n50, 375n78

balance, 14n8, 25–26, 40, 56, 86, 97, 101n34, 123–24, 129, 131–34, 154, 157, 170, 214, 232, 239, 247n9, 259–60, 264, 266, 268, 270, 272–74, 306, 374n68;
chessboard balance (table), 155, 157, 260, 264, 346, 375n80;
of interconnectedness, 124, 133;
intersectoral (interindustry), 56, 69n2, 125, 133, 157, 235, 280;
material/financial (monetary), 23, 35, 85, 101n36, 123–24, 126, 132, 154–56, 232–33, 237, 248n19.
See also input-output analysis

Balassa, Béla, 91, 186n16

Balcerowicz, Leszek, 12, 218

Ballod, Karl, 261, 285n2

Barnett, Vincent, 333, 369n33

Barone, Enrico, 111, 113, 270, 337, 366n13

Bazarov, Vladimir, 260, 262–64, 266

Behrens, Fritz, 99n20, 113, 115, 131–32, 136n3

Beksiak, Janusz, 215
Benáček, Vladimír, 89, 91, 97n6
Benary, Arne, 136n3
Berg, Aksel, 271
Bergson, Abram, 328, 364n1
Bertalanffy, Ludwig, 118
Big Data, 60, 363
Bilimovich, Alexander, 299–
    301, 376n81
Birman, Igor, 7, 324
Bobrowski, Czesław, 99n20,
    212, 218, 222
Bochev, Stoyan, 21, 47n3
Bockman, Johanna, 9, 331–33, 359
Boettke, Peter, 8, 328, 367n22,
    368nn25–27
Bogdanov, Aleksandr, 32, 259–61, 268,
    285n1, 285n6, 365n4
Böhm-Bawerk, Eugen, 29, 84,
    110, 248n22
Boldyrev, Ivan, 10, 255, 333–34,
    369n36, 369nn38–39
Bolshevik, 20, 258–59, 370n47
Bortkiewicz, Ladislaus, 29
Brezhnev, Leonid, 10, 281, 322,
    325, 369n40
Bródy, András, 145, 148, 150–52,
    159, 160–61, 164–69, 175, 179,
    180–82, 184n4, 185nn10–11,
    186n28, 187nn34–35, 187n37,
    189n54, 190n55, 190n58, 190n60,
    190n64, 191n66, 191n68, 191n71,
    192nn73–74, 192n77, 192nn79–
    84, 193n85, 193n89, 195n100,
    195n107, 196n119, 197nn124–27,
    372n50, 376n85
Brus, Włodzimierz, 91, 99n20,
    187n34, 211, 222
Brutskus, Boris, 261–62, 286n25,
    365n4, 373n61
Bukharin, Nikolai, 13n6, 117, 135, 259,
    261, 266–68, 331
Bulgaria, 12n1, 19–53, 237–38, 247n12,
    351–52, 358, 371n47, 375n77

calculation, 8, 10, 14n8, 21, 28, 32,
    36–37, 44, 56, 64, 83, 97n2, 109,
    110–14, 122, 124, 129, 130, 132–33,
    166–67, 176–77, 179–80, 187n34,
    188n44, 189n50, 192n73, 196n120,
    197n121, 243–44, 248n17, 258–59,
    261, 263–64, 269–72, 274–75, 278,
    280–81, 304, 319–20, 322, 324,
    328–29, 332, 337, 346, 356, 358,
    362, 363, 366, 367nn19–23, 368n27,
    374n68, 378n103;
    See also rational calculation
capitalism, capitalist, 3–6, 9, 13–14, 21,
    30–32, 40, 42, 48n12, 69, 83, 85,
    110, 112–15, 127–28, 149, 162, 167,
    174, 177, 181, 190n57, 197n125,
    234, 239, 261, 275, 280, 284, 297–
    99, 303, 324, 329, 331–32, 341, 364,
    368n30, 371n47, 372n50
Ceauşescu, Nicolae, 227, 233, 235,
    239, 241–42
censorship (self-censorship, political
    control), ix, 146–47, 177–78, 180,
    184n6, 229, 236–37, 345, 360–61,
    367n18, 372n50
centralization/decentralization, 23, 26–
    27, 30, 45, 86, 112, 123, 168, 172,
    181–82, 211, 222, 233, 255, 275–76,
    278–79, 323, 334, 346–47, 354–55,
    373n60, 375n80
centrally planned economy, 113,
    214, 216–17, 219–20, 297–98,
    307, 334, 375;
    theory of, 221.
    See also planned economy,
        Central Planner
Charemza, Wojciech, 220–22, 373n67
Chayanov (Chaianov), Aleksandr, 258,
    261, 266, 267, 293n3, 365n4, 371n47
cheating, falsification, 147, 307–8,
    327, 332, 347
Chen, Xikang, 57, 61, 70n9, 376n85
China, 7, 10, 12n1–3, 55–80, 211, 222,
    241, 331, 353, 373n54, 374n76,
    375n80, 379n105

Christophoroff, Assen, 21–22, 371n47

Cold War, coldwarism, 3, 6, 10,
12n1, 15n15, 36, 331, 333, 340,
351, 369n33,

collectivism/collectivist, 2, 4, 10, 12n2,
20, 35, 111, 125, 147, 159, 319, 323,
332, 334–35, 337–38, 340, 344,
346, 348–49, 353, 357, 359, 363–64,
366n18, 370n47, 378n103;
horizontal, vertical, 2, 364;
trap of, 1, 344, 349, 359, 364

Comecon (Council for Mutual
Economic Assistance, CMEA), 41,
87, 101, 220, 234–35, 237–39, 244,
366n16, 375n76

commodity-money relations, 15,
369n37, 377n94.
See also socialist market economy

communism/communist, 1–6, 8–12,
13nn4–6, 14n7, 14n9, 15nn10–11,
15n13, 16n16, 19, 21–24, 28–30, 32–
33, 35, 37, 44–47, 48n7, 55, 81–85,
87–88, 90–93, 95–96, 98nn14–15,
99n21, 100nn25–26, 101n34, 109–
10, 117, 122, 135, 136n2, 145–48,
150, 152, 154, 157–58, 171, 173–74,
176, 177–82, 184, 184n2, 185n11,
185n14, 186n26, 187n33, 189n47,
190n56, 196n118, 211–13, 219–22,
227–31, 234, 236–37, 239–40, 242–
46, 248n15, 248n21, 255, 258–61,
266, 273, 284, 293–96, 300–1, 303,
319–20, 325–27, 330–34, 336–37,
340–44, 348, 351–52, 357–63, 365,
366n15, 367n22, 369n38, 370n45,
370n47, 371n49, 372n50, 373n59,
374n70, 375n78, 375n80, 376nn81–
83, 376n85, 377n93, 378n95,
378nn103–4;
party, 8, 22, 57, 88, 92–93, 99n21,
100n26, 123, 163, 193n88,
197n127, 212, 216, 227, 233,
235, 247nn1–2, 248n18, 297,
308–9, 347;

Politburo, 121–22, 130, 197,
271, 281, 326;
ruling elite (*see also nomenklatura*),
93, 135, 156, 170, 340, 347, 354,
357–59, 361.
See also party-state

Comparative Economic Systems,
7, 316, 344

computation, computable 25, 35, 37, 64,
88, 112, 165–66, 170, 183, 184n8,
215, 240, 247n7, 304, 322, 328–29,
334, 363–64, 372n50, 378n104;
perfect computation, 321

computer, computer science 27, 37–38,
81, 83, 86–87, 118, 170, 178,
187nn36–37, 194n94, 216, 235, 240,
271–73, 277–78, 282, 322–24, 328–
29, 302, 304, 306, 320, 323, 330,
335, 340, 345–46, 352, 355, 357–58,
366n10, 368n28

computing center, computerization,
57, 102, 154–55, 160, 170–71,
235, 247n7, 272–73, 283, 298,
360, 373n62

computopia, cyber-optimism, 7, 172,
181, 320, 357

conformists and explorers, 353

constructivism, constructivist
rationalism, 6, 111,
197n121, 374n68.
See also rationality

contract responsibility
system, 64, 70n16

Control Figures, 263–64

control theory, 66, 67, 68, 118,
195n107, 362;
vegetative (non-price) control,
161, 167, 175–76

convergence theorem, 3, 366n12

conviction (faith), 1, 4, 34, 36, 39,
115, 135, 146, 156, 159, 165, 167,
179, 181, 220, 230, 241, 296,
311, 321, 347–48, 360, 369n34,
372n50, 373n62

corporatism, corporatist, 111, 230

Cultural Revolution, 57, 63, 64, 375n80
cybernetic(s), cybernetician, 10, 14n9,
    25, 27, 55–56, 66–68, 81, 89, 110,
    118–23, 135, 153, 194n94, 214, 222,
    235, 240, 247n7, 248n13, 271–73,
    331, 333–36, 340, 351–52, 357–
    58, 375n79
cycle, cyclicity, 21, 24, 32, 42–43,
    47n1, 56, 62, 65, 131, 152, 164,
    167, 180, 182–83, 185, 191n69,
    192n81, 198n133, 284, 300, 302,
    348, 378n104
Czechoslovakia, 81–109, 158, 237, 239,
    247n12, 273, 278, 377n93

Dăianu, Daniel, 244
Dantzig, George, 15n10, 49n13, 91,
    194n93, 215, 351, 378n99
Debreu, Gérard, 151, 286n20
democratic centralism, 121, 123, 126
democratization, 327, 341, 357, 377n88
demonetization, 37, 44
Deng, Xiaoping, 55, 222
descriptive vs analytical vs normative
    approach, 22, 32–38, 41, 65, 130,
    133, 148, 156, 158, 162, 168, 173,
    176, 181, 235, 240, 269, 294,
    298, 300, 302, 326–27, 336, 339,
    342–43, 354, 356, 359, 366n17,
    370n43, 378n98
Dewatripont, Mathias, 176
dictator(ship), 3, 115, 117, 123,
    267, 332, 335, 341, 358, 364,
    368n27, 371n47
dirigisme, 22, 45, 149, 230, 244
disciplinary identity, 68, 228, 334, 349
discovery, 11, 32, 119, 134, 148, 158,
    164, 176–77, 181, 184, 192n74, 267,
    296, 320–21, 351, 353, 362–63,
    371n49, 374n70
dissenter, dissident, 193n88, 360
Dmitriev, Vladimir, 257, 274, 365
Dobrescu, Emilian, 243, 245, 246,
    248n22, 371n50, 376n85

Domar, Evsey, 48n9, 91, 167, 248n22,
    265, 285n5, 304
Dorfman, Robert, 196n120, 351, 352,
    364n1, 373n53
Düppe, Till, 10, 333, 369n36,
    369n38, 370n40

Eastern Europe, 7, 9–10, 12nn1–3, 32,
    42, 120, 147–49, 186n26, 189n51,
    195n103, 196n116, 229, 237,
    242, 284, 294–95, 300, 320–21,
    328, 331–32, 352, 361, 367n22,
    374n76, 376n83
East-West, 9, 11, 14, 184n5, 350, 351,
    360, 373n57, 374n76
econometric(s), econometrician, 21, 26–
    28, 32, 38–39, 47n1, 49n14, 55–58,
    61–63, 68, 81, 83, 89–91, 94–95,
    100n27, 102n37, 110, 127–29, 146,
    149–50, 157–58, 165, 176, 181–84,
    186n17, 187n36, 189n48, 189n51,
    190n63, 192n73, 198n130, 198n133,
    198n136, 211, 214, 217–22, 240,
    243, 270, 293–94, 296–97, 300, 303–
    6, 308, 316n10, 327, 336, 348, 352,
    365n8, 370n42, 374n76, 375n78,
    376n82, 378n98
economic growth, 19, 34, 38, 41–43, 45,
    56, 58–60, 62–63, 82, 90–91, 93–94,
    99n22, 122, 131, 156, 166–67,
    213, 217, 231, 245, 259, 265, 277,
    285n5, 311, 357;
economic knowledge, 9, 11, 300, 329,
    332, 346, 368n27;
        dispersed, 329, 338, 346, 368;
        local, 9, 33, 112, 329, 336, 343,
        363, 368n27;
        tacit (inarticulate), 112, 179, 329,
        338, 346, 363, 368
economic laws of socialism, 13, 115–17,
    124, 267, 301, 326
economic policy, 15, 20–21, 37, 42,
    45, 58, 95, 110, 116, 126, 128, 132,
    156–57, 159, 166–67, 170–71, 182,
    188n41, 188n46, 192n78, 213, 218,

230, 240–43, 256, 258, 262, 266, 268, 284, 294, 295, 297, 300–2, 305–7, 312, 323

economic reform, 24, 30, 36, 90, 122, 126, 128, 132, 135, 180, 186n20, 215, 220, 276–77, 283, 294, 327, 367n21.

See also market reform, reformer

economics:

bourgeois, 15n13, 25–26, 30, 38, 48n12, 49n19, 64, 92, 114, 119, 127, 165, 212, 229, 267, 270–71, 279, 324, 361, 371n47, 372n51;

mainstream, 4–5, 20–21, 25, 29, 30, 32, 38, 46, 61, 82, 88, 90, 94, 146–47, 159, 163, 166, 172–75, 183, 184n5, 195n101, 195n103, 274, 329, 332, 359.

See also neoclassical economics

Ellman, Michael, 7, 255, 279, 321, 323–26, 331, 359, 364n1, 366nn11–17

emigration, emigré, 91, 93, 149, 186n16, 189n51, 191n64, 193n89, 197n127, 222, 243, 282, 285n3, 299–300, 319, 359, 364n2

empirical, 21, 24, 29, 36, 38–40, 57, 60, 69n1, 90, 135, 149, 168, 173–74, 179, 182–83, 197n126, 198n132, 198n135, 218, 273, 279, 301, 304, 315n4, 343–44, 362–63, 370n43

Engels, Friedrich, 110, 123, 135, 298, 370n45

Engliš, Karel, 83–84, 98n14, 371

epistemic culture, 334

equilibrium/disequilibrium, 5, 14n9, 15n12, 32, 35, 37, 40, 42–44, 46, 65–67, 101n36, 116–17, 126, 128, 130, 161, 164, 166–67, 172–76, 180, 183, 192n81, 194nn97–99, 195nn105, 217, 219–20, 259, 262–63, 266, 268, 286n20, 300, 323, 328–30, 334, 336–38, 348–49, 351, 362, 373n67;

partial/general, 4, 22n9, 32, 35, 37–38, 42, 58, 65, 133, 148, 159, 164–65, 173–75, 183, 184n8,

194n99, 195n104, 198nn136–37, 215, 270, 304, 308, 310, 319, 323, 329, 331–34, 337, 348, 352–53, 362, 369n36, 372n53, 376n86, 378n104.

See also general equilibrium theory

equivalence thesis (Pareto-Barone), 337

Erdős, Péter, 150, 189n54, 190n57, 191n68

Ericson, Richard, 333, 335,

Eucken, Walter, 113, 124

evolutionary, 329, 337, 360, 368n29, 369n40, 370n47

exchange of ideas, 3, 95, 178, 262, 309, 344, 350, 351, 360

experimentation, 2, 20, 23, 36, 44, 47, 48n5, 49n20, 65–66, 93, 96, 98n11, 109, 125, 128–29, 132, 135, 148, 150, 157–58, 170–71, 187n33, 222, 256, 272, 296, 298, 304, 326, 328, 336, 341–42, 346–47, 350, 353, 361, 364, 377n91, 378n104

expert, 4, 6–10, 20–21, 85, 87, 92, 96, 100n27, 149–50, 154, 158, 169, 173, 175, 178–79, 182–83, 184n6, 186n28, 187n38, 188n42, 188n44, 188n46, 191n69, 195n102, 195n104, 211, 228, 236, 241, 248n21, 257, 261–62, 268, 272, 277, 323–24, 326–27, 329, 334–35, 345, 348, 351–55, 360, 368n23, 369n38, 372n51, 373n54, 374n76, 375n78, 376n86.

See also planning expert

Eyal, Gil, 9, 331, 333

Faustian bargain, 171, 374n69

fear, 5, 10, 24, 88, 147, 178, 181, 197n127, 248n14, 309, 331, 335, 338, 348, 364

Fecanin, Juraj, 93, 100n28, 286n16

Fedorenko, Nikolai, 248n22, 277, 366nn17–18

Feldman, Grigorii (Grigory), 32, 49n17, 186n20, 265–67, 285n5, 365n4,

Feygin, Yakov, 10, 333, 336, 359,
    369nn32–33, 369nn37–40
forecast(ing), prognostics, 25, 27–28,
    34, 41, 55, 57–58, 60, 68, 110, 127–
    30, 158, 189n50, 218–19, 232, 247,
    263, 268, 282, 284, 307, 310–11,
    336, 343, 348, 375
formalization, 14n8, 19, 177, 259, 335,
    357, 360, 362.
        See also models
Friedman, Milton, 36, 338, 349
Frisch, Ragnar, 47n1, 99n20, 188n45,
    189n51, 194n97, 374n70
Friss, István, 159–60, 186n18,
    189n54, 191n68

Galbraith, John, 234, 248n22
game theory, 27, 55, 59, 63, 65–66,
    71nn20–21, 118–19, 149, 153, 176,
    187n36, 243, 326, 340, 353, 366n16,
    369n36, 371n49
general equilibrium theory (GET),
    37, 58, 159, 164, 173, 175, 183,
    184n8, 194n99, 195n99, 195n104,
    198n136, 331–32, 337–39, 352, 362,
    369n36, 373n67;
        computable general equilibrium
        (CGE), 183, 304, 378n104
Georgescu-Roegen, Nicholas, 234
German Democratic Republic (GDR),
    109–44, 237, 239, 247n12, 351, 353,
    358, 375n79
German Historical School of
    Economics, 84, 98n9, 149, 157, 300
Gerovitch, Slava, 333, 371n48
Gheorghiu-Dej, Gheorghe, 238–39
Gierek, Edward, 117, 213
Gligorov, Vladimir, 297
Glushkov, Viktor, 278
GOELRO (State Commission
    for Electrification of Russia),
    255, 261–62
Goldmann, Josef, 85, 90, 94, 98n13,
    99n21, 101n36, 186n22, 372n50,
    376n85, 377n89

Gorbachev, Mikhail, 282–83
government failure, 343–44
Grand Design, 342–43
Groman, Vladimir, 257, 260, 262–63,
    266, 365n4
Grossman, Gregory, 266, 270, 365n6

Habermas, Jürgen, 363
Habr, Jaroslav, 82, 89–90, 99n18–
    19, 376n85
Hahn, Frank, 173, 175, 186n23, 195
Hands, Wade, 369n34, 370n45, 333–34
Harsányi, János (John), 145, 149
Haustein, Heinz-Dieter, 127, 130
Hayek, Friedrich, 6, 8–9, 37, 49n20,
    111–12, 169, 171, 180, 197n121,
    214, 221, 248n22, 269, 275, 319,
    328–31, 338, 345–46, 363, 367n21,
    367n23, 368n28, 374n70
History/evolution of economic ideas/
    thought, 8, 10–12, 15n15, 19–20,
    48n12, 153, 229, 245, 300, 319, 333,
    336, 340, 351, 362, 376n85
Homo Oeconomicus, 9, 230, 331, 344
Honecker, Erich, 117, 122–23, 128
Horvat, Branko, 49n13, 293, 301–4,
    315n4, 316n6, 338, 372n50,
    375n78, 376n85
Hungary, 8, 12n2, 29, 45, 90, 99n21,
    100n26, 145–211, 216, 220–21, 237,
    239, 247n12, 347, 353, 361, 371n49,
    372n50, 373n59
Hurwicz, Leonid, 186n23, 330, 374n70

ignorance, myopia, 20, 32–33, 36–37,
    39, 41, 44, 49nn17–18, 82, 152, 162,
    174, 181, 193n91, 198n133, 218,
    300, 310, 319, 323, 346–48, 350,
    358, 366n13
impossibility thesis, 10, 44, 328–29,
    335, 363–64, 366n13, 367n21;
        Arrow, 170, 357;
        Mises-Hayek, 8, 111, 171, 261,
        319, 328–29, 331, 345, 363,
        372n50, 378n99

incentive, 23, 37–38, 40–41, 70n16, 82, 93, 163, 189n48, 216, 275, 277, 307, 322, 324, 329, 335, 341, 346, 355, 368n27, 375n80, 376n86, 377n94
individualism, 2, 20, 147, 338; methodological, 125, 337–38
inertia, 10, 41, 181, 183, 198n137, 322, 347–48, 359–60, 366n9, 373n62
informal (grey, shadow) economy, 46, 161, 377n94
information/data, 4, 9, 13n6, 21, 26–28, 33, 35, 38–40, 43, 56–60, 62–63, 65–66, 82, 86, 90, 95–96, 97n3, 112, 118, 122, 125, 127–28, 130–35, 149, 152, 155–58, 165–66, 168–71, 176, 178–79, 182–83, 188n42, 188n44, 193nn91–92, 216–17, 232–33, 236, 257, 267, 271–72, 276, 278, 280–81, 284, 296, 300–1, 306, 308–10, 312, 315n4, 321–23, 326, 329–30, 335, 338–39, 345–47, 350, 354–56, 358, 360, 363, 366n13, 368n27;
complete/incomplete, 34, 216, 228, 248n17, 279, 306;
distorted (fake), 4, 35, 170, 327, 329, 338, 344, 347, 350, 356, 363;
perfect/imperfect, 34, 169, 363
input coefficients, 35, 37, 169, 259–60, 264
input-output (I-O) analysis (model, table), 4–5, 14, 23, 25–29, 32–33, 35–38, 40–41, 48n5, 55–61, 67, 70, 81, 86, 89, 110, 118, 124–25, 128–34, 146, 151, 153, 155–58, 161, 162, 163–67, 169, 179–84, 187n37, 188n41, 189n50, 191n64, 192n71, 192n73, 193n85, 198n130, 214, 216, 231, 235, 243, 259–60, 264, 272–74, 277–78, 282, 284, 285n4, 286n20, 293–94, 303–4, 323, 334, 339, 349, 351, 353, 356, 359, 362, 370n42, 375n79, 376n85;
duality of, 35, 116, 126, 166, 193n91, 269, 274, 280, 323, 366n10;

input-occupancy-output model, 61, 70n9
institutional(ism), 8, 22–23, 45–46, 49n15, 63, 69n2, 129, 133, 148–50, 157, 161–64, 166, 173, 175, 177–78, 180–81, 186n17, 195n102, 196n116, 197n120, 228, 232, 234, 240, 278, 294–95, 297, 302–3, 325–26, 329, 333, 335–36, 338–39, 341, 343–44, 346, 348–49, 351, 354, 359, 361–63, 368n27, 368n29, 372, 373n62, 375n78, 376n86;
institutional/informational friction, 355, 358.
See also New Institutional Economics
interest, self-interest, 8, 20, 28, 31, 113, 117, 126–27, 155, 169, 170, 179, 188n42, 197n120, 217, 245, 279, 281–82, 286n22, 322, 324, 326, 338, 346, 355–58, 366n10, 367n19, 377n88, 377n94
intervention(ism), 2, 12n3, 14n8, 20–21, 24, 45, 84, 111, 129, 149, 191n65, 197n122, 230, 266, 301–2, 326, 328, 334, 347–48, 354, 358, 361, 374n68, 375n78, 375n80.
See also dirigisme
irrationality, 13n4, 82, 119, 326, 340–41, 344, 366n13.
See also rationality
Iurovskii (Yurovsky), Leonid, 258, 262, 266–67, 285n3

Jánossy, Ferenc, 150, 154, 166, 187n34, 190n60, 192n77
Ježek, Tomáš, 95
Johansen, Leif, 90, 91

Káldor, Miklós (Nicholas), 145, 149, 151, 186n15, 195n99, 248n22
Kalecki, Michał, 40, 48n9, 90–91, 99n22, 151, 212, 214, 217–18, 222, 248n22, 371

Kantorovich, Leonid, 3, 5, 8, 37, 91,
    118, 121, 173, 186n20, 190n62,
    239, 248n22, 260, 268–77, 281–82,
    286n11, 286n18, 320, 322–23, 335,
    338, 342, 348–49, 351–52, 355,
    365nn3–4, 365n7, 366n18, 369n36,
    369n38, 370nn40–41, 372nn50–51,
    376nn85–86
Kardelj, Edvard, 300, 310
Katsenelinboigen, Aron, 7, 327,
    351–52, 364n2, 365n7, 372n50,
    376n85, 377n88,
Kautsky, Karl, 110–12, 342, 371n47
Keynes, John Maynard, 30, 43, 48n9,
    113, 190n57, 234, 248n22, 304–5,
    323, 371n47
khozraschet, 8, 278, 323–24, 348,
    355, 369n37
Khrushchev, Nikita, 119
Kidrič, Boris, 297, 301
Kirtchik, Olessia, 10, 333–34, 369n38
Klacek, Jan, 92, 94, 101n36
Klaus, Georg, 119, 136n2, 351
Klaus, Václav, 95
Klein, Lawrence, 57, 91, 99n20,
    189n52, 219, 304–5, 374n76, 375n78
Knight, Frank, 328
Kohlmey, Gunther, 120–21, 125, 136n3
Kondratiev (Kondratieff), Nikolai,
    49n17, 164, 167, 186n20, 262–63,
    266–68, 285n3, 286n26, 365n4
Koopmans, Tjalling, 3, 15n10, 40, 118,
    173, 186n23, 194n99, 234, 286n18,
    342, 349, 351, 372n50, 374n70,
    374n76, 378n99
Korda, Benedikt, 89, 92, 97n6,100n26
Kornai, János, 4, 7–8, 13n6, 32, 36, 42,
    49n18, 91, 109, 120, 125, 145, 147–
    48, 150–52, 154, 159–61, 163–64,
    166–82, 184n4, 185n10, 186n16,
    186n23, 186n28, 187n34, 187n37,
    188n44, 189n54, 190nn57–58,
    190n64, 191n66, 192n76, 192n80,
    193nn86–90, 193n92, 194nn93–99,
    195nn99–106, 196nn108–13,

196nn118–19, 197nn121–22,
    197nn126–27, 198n130, 198n132,
    198n136, 216, 220, 222, 228,
    248n22, 294, 320, 323, 326, 338,
    351–52, 365n2, 370n46, 371n49,
    372n50, 373n60, 373n67, 376nn85–
    86, 377n88, 377n90, 378n101
Kosta, Jiří, 90, 92, 101
Kosygin, Aleksei, 273, 277, 325, 336
Kouba, Karel, 90, 99n21, 101n32
Kovalevskii, Nikolai, 266
Koziolek, Helmut, 132–33
Kritsman, Lev, 260–61, 285n1
Kronrod, Yakov, 277, 369n37
Krzhizhanovskii, Gleb, 262, 265
Kuczynski, Jürgen, 115, 132, 218
Kýn, Oldřich, 89–90, 101n32

labor theory of value, 69n2, 127, 167,
    270, 274, 279, 298, 322, 326, 328–
    29, 362, 378n103
laissez faire, 180, 338, 371
Lakatos, Imre, 15n9, 173, 338, 354
Lange, Oskar, 8, 15, 25, 32, 36, 49n20,
    66, 90–91, 99n20, 113–14, 133,
    135–36, 150, 166, 168–69, 172, 180,
    193n92, 194nn93–94, 197n121, 211,
    214–16, 221–22, 269, 275, 298, 320,
    328–30, 337–38, 351–52, 354, 356,
    366n9, 366n13, 367n21, 368n28,
    371n47, 376nn84–85, 378n99
Larin, Iurii, 261
Laščiak, Adam, 93, 95, 100n28, 286n16
Lavoie, Don, 8, 328, 364n1,
    367n22, 368n27
law of value, 116–17, 126, 271, 296
Leeds, Adam, 10, 333–35, 369nn36–38,
    369n40, 370nn42–43, 374n68
Lenin Prize, 274, 321, 372n52
Lenin, Vladimir, 15n11, 57, 92, 111–12,
    117, 123, 255, 261, 263, 296, 370n45
Leontief (Leontiev), Wassily, 14, 35,
    37–38, 40, 48n9, 49n19, 118, 133,
    151, 165–68, 186n20, 193n85,
    214, 231, 234, 264, 272, 274,

286n13, 334, 351, 365, 372n52,
374n70, 374n76
Lerner, Abba, 328
liberal(ism), 2, 5, 20, 22, 45, 50n27,
98n8, 110–11, 159, 180, 185n14,
228, 282–83, 324, 327, 330–31, 333,
335, 343, 348, 353–54, 360, 365,
369n32, 371n47, 378n96;
neoliberal(ism), 9, 10, 30, 113, 330–
33, 335, 359, 368n30;
spectral liberalism, 333;
ultra-liberalism, 110, 147, 181
Liberman, Evsei, 323
linear programming, 14n9, 26–27, 35,
61, 64–65, 81, 87, 89, 96, 99n18,
112, 118, 146, 153, 161–62, 168–69,
187n37, 188n44, 196n120, 240,
268, 270, 274, 280, 323, 334, 349,
351–53, 355, 359, 362, 371n49,
373n53, 376n85;
constraints, 4, 15n12, 34, 36, 60,
67, 70n11, 82, 126–27, 166,
170–71, 176–77, 192n80, 194n93,
196n113, 196n117, 214, 216, 260,
268–70, 277, 286n9, 298, 338,
346, 347, 357–58, 376n87;
objective (goal) function, 4, 41, 82,
125–26, 156, 166, 170, 214, 216,
269, 275, 277, 303, 326–27, 335,
338–40, 346, 357–58, 372n53,
376n87, 377n88.
See also programming
LINK project, 189n52, 198n137, 219,
222, 374n76
Lipták, Tamás, 150, 168–70, 187n37,
193n89, 193n92, 194n93,
196n117, 371n49
Litoshenko, Lev, 264, 266
Lurie, Anatolii, 91

Madžar, Ljubomir, 297
Malinvaud, Edmond, 49n14, 150–51,
168–69, 172, 186n23, 193n92,
194n93, 194n97, 248n22, 351

management, manager, 13, 22–23, 26–
28, 33–34, 36, 38, 41, 49n20, 56, 64–
65, 68, 81, 86–87, 89, 95, 122, 155,
163–64, 181, 211, 215–16, 221–22,
237–38, 242, 244, 247n4, 255–58,
273, 278–83, 286n9, 286n22, 293,
296–98, 300–3, 308–10, 319n9, 324,
327, 347, 353, 357–58, 364, 368n27,
375n78, 376n85
Mannheim, Károly (Karl), 185n14
Manoilescu, Mihail, 228, 238
marcescence, 10, 335–36, 340, 348
marginal utility theory, marginalism,
44, 168, 180, 257, 259, 279, 301,
322, 330, 339
market:
administrative, 297, 299,
370n43, 373n65;
marketization, 15n11, 62, 163, 179–
81, 189n48, 323, 325–26, 334,
341, 347–48, 354, 377n94;
market reformer (*see also* reform
economist), 5, 8, 11, 13, 15n13,
83, 159, 162, 166, 181, 320, 323,
329, 332, 334, 341, 343, 348–49,
353, 359–60, 362, 365n2, 366n10,
369n37, 378n96;
market socialism, market socialist,
3, 9, 13n6, 15n11, 83, 149, 169,
214, 279, 297, 299, 331, 341, 348,
368n27, 369n31, 375n78, 376n84,
377n93, 378n104
Marschak, Jakob (Jacob), 112,
194n99, 195n102
Martos, Béla, 151, 161, 184n3, 186n25,
190n60, 190n64, 192n80, 193n89
Marx, Karl, 2, 3, 8, 13n5, 15n11, 31,
36, 57, 69n2, 70n10, 94, 101n34,
102n37, 110, 115–16, 119, 123,
126–27, 131, 133, 135, 164–68,
180, 192n74, 259, 260, 264–65, 274,
295–96, 298, 301, 323, 334, 337,
362, 370n45, 371n47
Marxism, 14n8, 20, 25–26, 29–31, 33,
35, 37, 40, 42, 55, 62, 69n2, 82, 88,

90, 92, 94, 102n37, 111, 114–15,
134, 136, 145, 148, 159, 163–64,
168, 180–81, 185n10, 190n57,
190n60, 191n66, 191n68, 192n72,
193n88, 217, 230, 234, 239, 245,
259–60, 266–67, 275–76, 279,
296–98, 301, 303, 320, 325–26,
330, 338, 343, 345, 348, 369n38,
370n47, 371n47, 372nn50–51,
375n78, 377n95;
    Marxism-Leninism, 2, 4, 11,
    15n13, 88, 102n37, 109, 113,
    115–16, 118–19, 121–22, 147,
    322, 366n13
Maskin, Eric, 176
Mateev, Evgeni, 25, 28–30, 33–35, 37,
    352, 372n50, 376n85
mathematical:
    culture, 5, 175, 273, 362;
    knowledge (skills), 149, 154–55,
        160, 162–63, 171, 177, 190n57,
        191n66, 320, 376n81;
    language (jargon), 11, 13n5, 86,
        131, 159, 161, 190n57, 324,
        337, 372n51;
    methods/techniques/tools, 3, 5, 7,
        15m13, 25–29, 31–32, 47, 48n10,
        82, 87–89, 91, 96, 100n26, 119–
        20, 122, 150, 152, 156, 159–61,
        163, 168, 235, 255, 257–59, 264,
        267, 271–74, 276–82, 284, 298,
        300, 316n9, 322, 334, 340, 342,
        346–47, 353–54, 359, 365n8,
        366n16, 367n23;
    revolution, 110, 122, 124,
        284, 321, 325
mathematical economics/economist:
    4–7, 10–12, 14n8, 15n13, 21, 24–26,
    31, 32, 49n14, 55–57, 61, 67, 82–83,
    88–91, 94–96, 99n17, 100n29, 116,
    118–19, 131, 135–36, 145–65, 168–
    69, 173, 175, 178–82, 185nn11,12,
    186nn20–26, 190nn56–58–59–61,
    191nn69,70, 193n89, 194n94,
    198n130, 229, 232, 234–35, 240,

243, 245, 248n22, 255–62, 265–67,
271–74, 276–77, 279–85, 319–28,
331–37, 342–57, 359–62, 364nn1–2,
367nn21–23, 369nn33–38, 370n45,
371n49, 372n51, 373n67, 374n76,
375n78, 376nn81–82, 377nn93–94;
    education (teaching) of, 5, 12,
        20, 22, 25–26, 49n13, 61, 84, 87,
        92–93, 95, 98n9, 129–30, 134,
        149–50, 152–53, 157, 174, 182–
        83, 178n36, 187nn32–35, 189n48,
        191n64, 194n99, 229, 241, 273,
        280, 284, 286nn16–24, 297–99,
        316n7, 332, 342, 349, 351, 359,
        372n52, 371n47, 377n95
mathematician, 15n13, 24, 27, 32, 82,
    118–20, 131, 150, 160, 187n35,
    191n71, 196n117, 229, 235, 240,
    268, 336, 351
mathematics, 14, 15n13, 24–26, 36,
    49n16, 49n18, 64–65, 68, 81–83, 88,
    90–91, 97nn6–7, 118, 120–21, 128,
    130, 136n2, 148, 152–55, 157–60,
    165, 187n36, 190n58, 193n88,
    195n102, 229–30, 240, 259, 267,
    271–72, 280, 293–94, 298, 300–1,
    323, 325, 336, 340, 346, 359, 364n5,
    367n23, 376n81;
    of planning, 15n13, 150,
        153–54, 160;
    rehabilitation of, 342, 346
mathematization, 11, 19, 29, 47, 83,
    188n39, 192n73, 323, 352
maximization, 41–42, 82, 116, 125–26,
    166, 173, 216, 298
mechanism design, 339, 362
Methodenstreit, 84, 352, 370
methodological, 10, 11, 15n9, 16n19,
    27, 40, 43, 49n15, 49n22, 125, 173,
    194n99, 235, 263, 297, 306, 319,
    337–38, 342–43, 360, 369n33;
    micro/macroeonomic(s), 3, 8, 13n7,
        26, 34, 37–38, 40, 43–45, 48n5,
        50n29, 55, 57–60, 62, 65, 67–68,
        69n4, 70n11, 70n13, 84, 94, 99n22,

101n36, 113, 115, 121, 128–29, 131,
135, 153, 161, 183–84, 186n22,
187n33, 190n63, 196n113, 216,
220, 231, 233, 245–46, 268, 280,
284, 298, 305, 308, 311, 339, 358,
364, 367n23, 370n47, 375n78,
375n80, 378n104
military/army, 6, 9–10, 81, 90, 117–19,
156, 158, 217, 257–58, 269, 271,
286n12, 327, 340, 355–57, 367n21,
371n47, 372n51
Minc, Hilary, 212
Mirowski, Philip, 331, 333
Mises, Ludwig, 8, 37, 49n20, 84,
97n3, 110–12, 114, 171, 214,
221, 243, 248n22, 261, 275, 319,
328–29, 331, 345–46, 363, 366n13,
367n21, 367n23, 368n25, 372n50,
373n61, 378n99
Mlčoch, Lubomír, 95, 102n38,
370n44, 372n50
mobilization, 36, 241, 355
model:
    closed, 166–67, 179, 345–46;
    decomposition of, 157, 161, 194n94,
    215, 327, 329, 357;
    deterministic, 39, 153, 158, 166–
    67, 179, 217;
    dynamic, 58, 61, 67, 69n2, 95,
    192n80, 277, 304;
    formal, 4, 14n8, 149, 163, 175–76,
    191, 196n120, 216, 301, 336;
    linear, 38, 179, 274;
    mathematical, 8, 16n19, 25, 27,
    48n12, 56, 58, 62, 88, 94, 133,
    135, 154, 156, 167, 169, 180,
    183, 188n41, 188n44, 215–16,
    327, 257, 259–60, 266, 277, 284,
    370n45, 373n59;
    Neumann, 161, 180;
    static, 37, 39, 64, 70n9, 161, 166–67,
    173, 179, 300, 306, 338, 345–46;
    stochastic, 14n9, 64–65, 129–30,
    152–53, 158, 182, 184n8,

187nn35–36, 217, 279, 306, 323,
326, 336, 339, 353, 378n104
modern, modernization, modernity,
2–3, 6, 20, 33, 63, 65–67, 84, 89,
94, 120, 124, 145, 152, 157, 168,
179, 212, 235, 241, 269, 272, 274,
278, 283, 297, 300, 304, 333, 360,
369n38, 378n104
Montias, John Michael, 35, 321, 364n1
Morishima, Michio, 49n14, 168, 192n74

Nagy, András, 150–51, 161–62, 189n54,
190nn60–63, 196n120
Nagy, Tamás, 159, 189n54,
190n59, 191n68
naïve, naiveté, 20, 110, 173, 180,
194n93, 194n95, 338
nationalism, nationalist, 11,
230, 239, 297
nationalization, 1–2, 20, 85,
111, 212, 371
Nemchinov, Vasilii (Vasily), 48n10, 82,
91, 99n20, 119–21, 160, 248n22,
270–74, 276–77, 283, 351, 364n2,
366n18, 371nn51–52, 375n77,
376nn85–86
neoclassical economics (school), 7–8,
11, 37–38, 145, 147–48, 153, 162,
172–78, 180–81, 184, 195n101,
189n51, 230, 330–33, 337, 360, 362,
368n30, 375;
    neoclassical revolution (turn),
    9, 19, 40–41, 46–47, 146–47,
    184n5, 322–23;
    latent neoclassical, 333.
See also mathematical economics
Neumann, János (John), 48n9, 145, 149,
161, 165–66, 168, 180, 334, 351
Neurath, Otto, 110–14, 126, 258, 371
New Economic Mechanism (*NEM*),
160, 172, 178–80, 190n63, 196n120
New Economic Policy (*NEP*), 13n6,
15, 186n20, 213, 256, 258–59, 262,
284, 368n25

New Economic System (*NÖS*),
120, 134, 277
New Institutional Economics, 162, 175,
177–78, 196n116, 197n120, 343,
348, 363, 372n49
Nobel Prize, 3, 8, 62, 118, 173, 178,
239, 274, 286n18, 342, 348–49,
372n52, 374n70
nomenklatura, 1, 6, 13, 46, 88, 95, 334,
341, 344, 348–49, 353, 358
normalization, 83, 89–91, 93, 95, 99n21,
100n31, 102n39, 377n93
Novozhilov, Viktor, 49n17, 91, 116,
186n20, 248n22, 260, 263, 270, 272,
274–77, 282, 351, 366n18, 369n38,
372nn51–52, 376n85

objectively determined valuation (*ODV*),
274–75, 277–78, 282, 324, 342
omnipotence, omniscience, 3,
169, 352, 357
operations research, 14n9, 56, 63, 81,
87, 89, 95–96, 100n29, 118, 121–22,
133, 152–53, 187nn35–36, 198n130,
240, 340, 342, 344, 352
opportunism (conformism), 42, 88, 159,
165, 283, 295, 327, 332, 340, 348,
353, 361, 372n50
optecon, 359–61, 378n95
optimal (mathematical, scientific) plan,
planner, 4, 6, 8–11, 14n9, 15n14,
27, 81, 112, 116, 127, 135, 147,
151 156–58, 166, 170–71, 178,
181–84, 193n91, 194n94, 214–17,
269, 274–76, 279–82, 321, 323–62,
367n19, 368n26, 369n37, 370n43,
372n49, 373n54, 375n80, 377n87,
93, 378n96;
moral dilemma of, 8, 320.
See also plan, planner
optimal (mathematical, scientific)
planning, 3–11, 14n8, 9, 15n9,
16n16, 19, 27–28, 32–37, 49n20,
56, 64, 81, 87, 89–91, 94, 109, 116,
120–21, 123, 125, 135, 146–48, 150,
152, 156, 161, 163–64, 166, 171–74,
181–83, 185n10, 187n35, 190n60,
62, 191n64, 69, 192n76, 196nn119–
120, 198n130, 263, 268–69, 275,
279, 283, 284, 319–25, 327–28,
330–33, 335–45, 343, 348–54,
358–64, 365n5, 366n16, 367n21,
369n40, 370n45, 372nn50–52,
373nn54–60, 374nn68–70, 375nn78–
80, 376n82, 377n94;
rise and fall of, 342, 345,
353, 369n40.
See also planning
optimization, 5, 8, 10, 14n8, 25–28, 56,
59, 63–65, 67, 70n11, 70nn15–18,
96n1, 112, 116, 124–26, 133, 147–
48, 151, 153, 164, 166, 168, 171–74,
176–79, 191n69, 192n76, 193n91,
194n94, 194n96, 214, 216, 221, 240,
260, 263–64, 269–70, 272, 274, 277,
280–81, 284, 323–25, 328–29, 331,
334–36, 339–43, 346, 348–50, 354–
55, 358, 361–62, 370n41, 372n51,
373nn53–54, 375n80, 376n82
orthodox/heterodox, 28–29, 38, 83, 90,
93–94, 98n15, 101n34, 119–20, 123,
126–27, 133–35, 136n3, 168, 173,
175–76, 217, 221, 340, 168
ownership (property), 1–3, 10–11,
13n6, 22, 33, 49n20, 56, 59, 69, 95,
102nn37–38, 109, 111–12, 123, 125,
129, 149, 177, 245, 262, 301, 322,
329, 341, 344, 346, 350, 353, 364,
367n19, 367n21, 368n27, 368n30,
369n31, 371n47

Pajestka, Józef, 218, 373n63
Pareto, Vilfredo, 48n9, 111, 198n136,
269, 299, 337, 372n51
parochial(ism), 33, 159, 163, 360
party-state, 1–2, 4, 6, 8, 13n4, 13n6,
47, 94, 147, 160, 162, 166, 177,
181, 217, 267, 278, 309, 320, 335,
339, 343, 347–48, 354, 356–58, 360,
372n52, 375n80

Pătrăşcanu, Lucreţiu, 228
Pawłowski, Zygmunt, 186n22,
   216, 218, 221
perestroika, 10, 28, 42, 282, 286n13,
   325, 335, 367n21, 368n25
perhaps effect, 350
Perlamutrov, Vilen, 283
Péter, György, 152, 157, 189n48
Petrakov, Nikolai, 327
plan:
   annual (one-year), 86–7, 96,
      175, 178, 218, 232, 262, 264,
      311–14, 375;
   five-year, 12n3, 20–22, 42–43, 58,
      62, 65, 70n19, 85–87, 99n21,
      155–56, 161–2, 170, 179,
      188nn44–46, 197n122, 212–13,
      229, 231–33, 245, 262, 265, 268,
      281–82, 295–96, 307, 309, 311,
      322, 326–27, 375n80;
   long-term (general, perspective),
      21, 86, 128, 151–54, 172, 179,
      189n47, 197n123, 257, 263–66,
      268, 275, 279, 284. *See also*
      planning horizon
   single (unified), 238, 256;
   taut, 281, 325, 344
plan bargaining, 48n6, 155–62, 169–70,
   176–79, 326, 338, 340, 344, 346,
   355–56, 371n49
plan coordination, 86, 188n42,
   275, 309, 347
plan fulfillment (over-and under-),
   197n123, 261, 275, 308–9, 355
plan improvement (perfection), 3–4, 8,
   10, 26, 93, 133, 135, 148, 154, 162,
   170–76, 184n9, 194n93, 198n129,
   228, 233, 255–56, 265, 277, 281,
   284, 321, 339, 349, 360, 369n40
plan makers/takers, 355–58
plan mongering, 349, 373n62
plan and market, 355, 357
planisme, 371n47
plannability, 3, 13n4, 339, 353–
   54, 370–71n47

planned economy, 4, 6, 8, 20–21, 42,
   55–56, 62, 68, 70n10, 85–86, 90,
   91–94, 99, 113–15, 120–21, 125,
   145–47, 154, 162–63, 166, 176–82,
   189n47, 193n86, 196n108–110
   –118, 197n120, 214, 216–21, 262,
   279, 284, 297–99, 302, 307, 320,
   323–29, 334–35, 338–48, 357, 360,
   370n44, 371n49, 374n70, 376nn84–
   86, 378n96;
   planned commodity economy, 57,
      62, 375n80;
   command economy, 242, 282, 355
planner:
   Central Planner, 3,4, 13n4, 15n12,
      120, 127, 130, 169, 193n91,
      196n113, 197n122, 216–17,
      320, 322–23, 325, 327, 332,
      338, 340, 346, 348–49, 354–60,
      371n49, 376n87
planning:
   administrative (state), 3, 57–8,
      69, 85, 98, 132, 162, 185n14,
      197n124, 240, 256, 260, 279, 357;
   automated, automatic, automatization
      of, 27, 123, 181, 357–58, 377n91;
   as a ceremony/ritual, 234, 310;
   as a cooperative game, 95;
   as a smoke screen, 95;
   centrally decentralized, 358;
   consultative, 233, 324, 357;
   counter-planning (both-direction
      plans, alternative plan), 48n6,
      86, 98n12;
   decentralized, 343, 364;
   directive, direct, 14, 86–7, 93,
      191n69, 197n122, 283–
      84, 295, 307;
   enterprise-level, 14;
   ex ante/ex post, 13n4;
   expert, 10, 87, 150, 246, 335;
   genetic/teleological approach to,
      168, 262–65;
   flexible, 262, 275–76, 279, 376n86;
   hierarchy, 322, 355;

imperative (command, mandatory),
2, 3, 13–4, 13n4, 48n6, 94,
178–79, 231, 241–42, 326,
342–43, 353–56, 364, 370n47,
375nn78–80;

imperfection (deficiency, failure)
of, 7–8, 173, 180–1, 188n44,
196n119, 227–28, 278, 281, 302,
319, 323, 325, 338, 340, 342,
350, 358, 363;

indicative, 3, 14n7, 36, 157, 172,
179, 293, 307–13, 323, 343,
373n55, 375nn78–80;

in-kind (natural, physical) vs
financial (monetary), 13n6, 21,
35–36, 85, 112, 124, 133, 255–56,
258, 261, 370n47, 371n47;

national types of, 11, 352–55;

parametric, 14n9, 121, 123, 356;

regime (system), 8, 37, 86, 171–72,
186n16, 256–58, 265, 277, 282,
307–8, 322, 355, 357, 378n98;

regional, 100n23, 215, 233–
34, 237, 239;

two-and multi-level planning, 98n12,
154, 161, 169–72, 177, 187n37,
188n44, 193n92, 215, 356;

verbal, 5, 321, 323, 342, 350;

planning bureaucrats (officials,
technocrats), 4, 36, 41, 46–7, 147,
155–56, 158, 188n46, 189n47,
194n94, 237, 240, 271, 278, 324,
326, 334, 347, 350, 360, 366n9,
367n19, 376n84

planning concept (canon, doctrine,
paradigm, theory), 2–3, 5, 7, 10–12,
14n7, 19, 21, 23, 26, 32–34, 46, 89,
114–15, 121, 145, 148–49, 152, 158,
170, 181, 185n11, 187n34, 221, 227,
229, 232, 235, 246, 255–57, 260,
275, 300, 321, 328, 336, 356, 358,
362, 366n13, 370n47, 372n51

planning instruction (directive, target,
task, figure), 85–86, 94, 156, 165,

228, 232–33, 247n7, 307, 311–12,
326, 344–45, 355, 375n80, 377n94

planning norms, normatives, 86, 115,
124, 130, 237, 242, 258, 270, 356

planning office (board, commission,
committee), 4, 11, 22, 28, 45,
57–58, 69n3, 85, 95, 98n10, 15,
132–34, 145, 152–57, 160, 169,
171, 185n10, 188n44, 189n47, 50,
191n67, 194n98, 197n126, 198n133,
212, 215, 222n1, 262, 298, 330,
341, 346–47, 360, 363, 375n76,
368n27, 376n84;

Gosplan (State Planning Committee),
4, 260–86, 372n52

planning period (horizon), 116, 129–30,
197n124, 233, 232

planning process (procedure), 4, 14n7,
23, 88, 94–95, 99n17, 116, 121,
149, 163, 168 170–71, 179, 234,
242, 270, 276–78, 308–9, 324, 326,
345–46, 355

planometrics, 14, 240, 321, 365n6

Plehwe, Dieter, 331

Plywood Trust problem, 268–69, 342

Poland, 12n3, 29, 90, 117, 150, 211–26,
237, 239, 245, 247n12, 298, 353,
373n63, 376n82, 376n86

Polanyi (Polányi), Karl (Károly), 111,
113, 185n14, 371n47

polecon, 359–60, 378n95, 191n68

political economy, 2, 4, 15n13, 20, 22,
24–26, 29–31, 42, 46, 48n8, 48n12,
57, 81, 88–89, 92, 97n4, 99n16,
101n35, 102n37, 109, 113–17,
121–22, 125–26, 133, 135, 152, 158,
164–65, 187n32, 190n59, 214, 217,
222, 230, 239, 241, 258, 260, 271,
280, 284, 298, 321–22, 324–26, 331,
341, 356, 358, 360, 366n17, 369n37,
374n68, 377n95;

descriptive/constructive/
destructive, 366n17;

official (textbook), 5–7, 15n13,
82, 91, 94, 147, 149, 158, 162,

169, 171, 321–22, 325–26, 343, 356, 358–60, 366n17, 369n37, 374n68, 377n95;
verbal, 14n8, 154
Polterovich, Viktor, 335, 352, 369n38, 373n67
Popov, Pavel, 257, 264, 266, 365n4
Portes, Richard, 176, 196n110, 220
Porwit, Krzysztof, 215, 221, 376n85
positivism, positivist, 4, 21, 30–31, 43, 370n47
preferences, 8, 35, 112, 126, 173, 188n45, 301, 327, 329, 339, 346–47, 357, 363, 376n84
Prékopa, András, 153, 187nn35–36, 194n93
Preobrazhenskii (Preobrazhensky), Evgenii (Yevgeni), 117, 230
price, 4, 21, 23, 35–37, 41, 44–45, 50nn27–28, 57–58, 60–62, 70n13, 70n16, 85–86, 91, 93, 97n2, 101n33, 110–14, 116–18, 124–27, 132, 134, 147, 155, 158, 161, 165–67, 169, 173, 175–77, 189n50, 192n80, 192n84, 193nn91–92, 198n133, 213–14, 220, 236, 238, 247n8, 247n10, 257–58, 260–61, 263–64, 267, 269–70, 274–80, 282–83, 298–300, 305–6, 315n6, 324, 329, 336, 339, 342, 345–46, 356, 366n10, 366n13;
shadow price, 61, 70n16, 127, 193nn91–92, 214–15, 228, 270, 278, 323–24, 332, 342, 351, 356, 370n45, 372n50
principal-agent theory, 177, 221, 334
privatization, 197n121, 303, 335, 341, 348, 353, 375n80
production function, 25–26, 32, 38, 49n21, 58, 90, 182, 189n50, 198n133, 217–18, 302, 305–6, 348, 373n63
profit, 36–37, 112, 116, 120, 125–27, 132, 135, 150, 165, 168, 173, 189n48, 247n8, 298, 303, 324, 356, 366n10

programming, 25, 34, 65, 95, 153, 161, 168, 187n36, 193n91, 214, 228, 240, 268, 271, 323, 326–27, 330, 338–39, 357;
dynamic, 27, 64–65, 67, 96n1;
non-linear, 64–65, 161, 168, 353;
stochastic, 152, 187n35.
See also linear programming
Public Choice, 36, 343

Qian, Yingli, 196n114
Quandt, Richard, 196n114, 220
quantitative, quantification, 14n8, 24, 29–31, 36, 47, 49n16, 55–60, 62, 65, 68–69, 85–86, 97n6, 102n37, 120, 124, 130, 135–36, 146, 149, 152–56, 159, 161–63, 171, 182, 184, 184n5, 187n38, 193n89, 197n120, 211, 214–15, 221, 227, 229, 234–35, 237, 239–40, 243, 246, 263, 277, 296, 301, 347, 362, 374n68, 376n81

ratchet effect, 308, 344
Rathenau, Walther, 111, 371n47
rational calculation, 124, 243, 328–29, 332, 358, 367n23, 378n103;
(im)possibility of, 10, 328
rationality, 4–6, 8, 15n12, 15n15, 36, 102n37, 110, 149, 165, 169, 171, 173–74, 177, 211, 220, 319, 322–23, 328, 330, 339–40, 347, 349, 362, 364, 366n13, 368n24, 371n47, 372n50, 378n96;
value/instrumental (goal) rationality, 6, 340.
See also irrationality
rationing, 36, 112, 296–97
Rawls, John, 340
real business cycle (RBC), 43, 183, 378n104
realism, realistic, 7, 9, 27, 45, 125, 156, 172–73, 175, 268, 281, 305, 322, 326, 340, 345–46
refecon, 359–61, 377n95

reform economics, reform economist, 10, 13n6, 127, 136, 149, 159, 162–63, 189n48, 189n54, 196n120, 211, 343, 347, 368n25, 373n59

reformer, 5, 8, 11, 13n6, 15n13, 20, 33, 44, 49n17, 83, 87, 135, 159, 162–63, 166, 181, 218, 222, 284, 320, 323, 325, 329, 332, 334, 341, 343–44, 348–49, 353–54, 359–62, 365n2, 366n10, 368n25, 369n37, 377n94, 378n96;

Remington, Thomas, 260, 285n1

Rényi, Alfréd, 150, 165, 187n35, 193n89

research institute, academy of sciences:
Center for Forecasting Science, Chinese Academy of Sciences, 58;
Central Economics and Mathematics Institute, Soviet Academy of Sciences, 273, 279, 281;
Central Institute of Informatics, Romania, 240;
China Aerospace Academy of Systems Science and Engineering, 69n4;
China Aerospace Economic Research Center, 69n4;
Chinese Academy of Social Sciences, 57–58;
Conjuncture Institute, Soviet Union, 262, 266, 286n26;
Czech Institute of Labor, 89;
Econometric Laboratory, Central Statistical Office, Hungary, 157, 182;
Economico-Mathematical Laboratory, Bulgarian Academy of Sciences, 26, 375n77;
Economic Research Institute of *Gosplan*, Soviet Union, 280–81;
Foreign Trade Research Institute, Poland, 218;
German Institute of Technology, Brno, 84;
German Institute of Technology, Prague, 84;
Hungarian Institute for Economic Research, 186n17;
Institute for Economic Research, Central Planning Commission, GDR, 133–34;
Institute for Economic Research, Ljubljana, 306;
Institute for Philosophy, Academy of Sciences, GDR, 136n2;
Institute of Computational Mathematics, Chinese Academy of Sciences, 64;
Institute of Economic Forecasting, Soviet Academy of Sciences, 282;
Institute of Economic Research, Bucharest, 234;
Institute of Economics, Academy of Sciences, GDR, 125, 128–29, 136n3;
Institute of Economics and Industrial Engineering, Siberian branch of the Soviet Academy of Sciences, 279;
Institute of Economics, Chinese Academy of Sciences, 56;
Institute of Economics, Czechoslovak Academy of Sciences, 82, 89, 94, 99n16, 99n21, 101n35;
Institute of Economics, Hungarian Academy of Sciences, 148, 152, 154, 158, 160–62, 164, 183, 186n18, 187n29, 190n63, 197n127, 198n133;
Institute of Economy, Bulgarian Academy of Sciences, 26;
Institute of Market Research, Budapest, 190n63;
Institute of Mathematics, Chinese Academy of Sciences, 56;
Institute of Mathematics, Romanian Academy of Sciences, 240;

Institute of Planned Economy, National Planning Office, Budapest, 154;

Institute of Planning, Romania, 240, 247n7;

Institute of Planning and Prognosis, Romania, 247n7;

Institute of Regional Planning, Bratislava, 100n23;

Institute of Research and Technological Design, Romania, 240;

Institute of Statistical and Economic Research, Central Statistical Office, Poland, 218;

Institute of World Economy and International Relations, Soviet Academy of Sciences, 272;

International Institute for Applied Systems Analysis, Laxenburg, 31, 198n137;

Karl Marx Higher Institute of Economy, Sofia, 23;

Laboratory of Economics and Mathematics, Czechoslovak Academy of Sciences, 82;

Laboratory of Mathematical Methods in Economics, Soviet Academy of Sciences, 272;

Mathematical Institute, Slovak Academy of Sciences, 100n27;

Moscow Institute of Economic Statistics, 92;

National Game Theory Research Institute, China, 66;

National Institute for Economic Research, Romanian Academy, 246;

National Institute of Statistics, Romania, 247n11;

Statistical Institute for Economic Research, Sofia University, 21;

Yugoslav Institute of Economic Research, Belgrade, 301

resolving multiplier, 269–70

revisionism, 121, 132, 160, 372n51. *See also* Marxism

revolution, 9, 15n13, 57, 63–64, 95, 110, 116–20, 122, 124, 130, 135, 146, 273, 284, 321–22, 325, 363, 370n44, 375nn79–80;
    Bolshevik (October), 20, 299, 365n4, 370n47;
    1956 (Hungary), 156, 159, 163, 186n18, 193n86, 365n2

Rindzevičiūtė, Eglė, 10, 333, 335, 369n40

Robbins, Lionel, 84, 368n28

Romania, 227–53, 352–53, 371n47, 371n49

Rozsypal, Kurt, 85, 87, 98n15

Russia, 81, 84, 255–92, 299, 320, 333, 373n61

Samuelson, Paul, 15n10, 48n9, 91, 150, 193n88, 196n120, 296, 338, 351–52, 373n53, 374nn70–71

Schatteles, Tiberiu (Tibor), 7, 243, 248n16, 352, 371n49, 372n50, 374n76, 376nn85–86

Schumpeter, Joseph, 248n22, 328

scientific research program, 2–6, 8–9, 11–12, 14n9, 15n10, 16nn18–19, 81, 88, 90, 146–49, 154, 159, 161, 163–64, 172–75, 178–82, 186n27, 191n69, 194n99, 221, 279, 285n5, 319–21, 324–27, 330–33, 335–53, 356, 358–59, 361–62, 365n3, 373n65;
    hard core, protective belt of, 173, 338–40, 353, 354;
    progressive/degenerating, 15n9, 339–40, 343, 353, 359

secret, secrecy, 28, 158, 229, 236, 244, 327, 338, 347

Shatalin, Stanislav, 91, 273, 280–81, 284, 366n18

shortage, 44, 49nn17–18, 88, 92, 95, 152, 161, 168, 172, 175–77, 211,

213, 220, 231, 236, 238, 263, 294,
298, 324, 339
Šik, Ota, 86, 90–91, 222, 278
Simonovits, András, 151, 161, 191n64,
193n89, 196n109
simulation, simulated, 9, 15n11, 28, 56,
58, 60, 62–63, 66, 129, 158, 172,
194n96, 216, 219, 236, 298–99, 306,
326, 329, 347, 349
Skinner, Quentin, 11
Slovakia, 84, 97n7, 101n35
Slovenia, 297, 300
Slutskii (Slutsky), Evgenii (Yevgeni),
84, 257, 284, 286n26, 365n4
Smolinski, Leon, 259, 364n1
social democracy, social-democrat(ic),
110, 112, 150, 186n15, 348,
370n47, 371n47
social engineer(ing), 3, 322, 326, 329,
360, 369n38
socialism, socialist, 3–4, 6, 8, 13nn4–5,
20–21, 25, 30–32, 35, 37, 40, 50n26,
55–57, 62, 64, 68–69, 83, 86–89,
91–95, 97n3, 98n11, 99n18, 99nn21–
22, 101n36, 102nn37–38, 109–17,
120–28, 131–33, 135, 152, 175,
177, 185n14, 194n94, 197nn121–22,
212, 215, 218, 220–22, 227, 231,
235, 237–39, 241, 243, 245, 247n4,
248n17, 256, 258, 261, 263, 267,
269, 271–72, 275, 279–80, 283–84,
295, 297–98, 300–1, 303, 305,
315n6, 320, 326–29, 331–32, 345,
366n9, 367n23, 368n25, 368n27,
368n30, 369nn37–38, 370n47,
372n50, 375n80, 378n104;
administrative market
socialism, 297, 299;
administrative socialism, 295, 299;
contractual socialism, 297,
308, 316n12;
guild socialism, 111.
See also market socialism
Socialist Calculation Debate, 21, 32,
36, 44, 109, 114, 124, 126, 167, 179,

180, 187n34, 269, 275, 320, 328,
362–63, 366, 367n22
socialist market economy, 55, 57,
62, 64, 68–69, 120, 297, 305,
315n6, 375n80.
See also market socialism
socialization, 70n10, 110–11
social market economy (*Soziale
Marktwirtschaft*), 300
social welfare function, 82, 260
SOFE (System of the Optimal
Functioning of the Socialist
Economy), 277, 279, 281–83, 325–
27, 335, 366n17, 367n21
soft budget constraint, 36, 176–77,
196n113, 196n117
Sonderweg, 175
Soviet School of Mathematical
Economics, 328, 351–52
Soviet Union, 8, 10, 31, 47, 56, 71n20,
82, 90, 93, 97n2, 98n8, 98n11,
101n33, 110, 113–14, 117–20, 122,
131, 136n3, 146, 150, 154, 156,
185n14, 211, 221, 230–31, 237–39,
241, 245, 247n12, 255–92, 295,
312, 320, 322, 325–26, 333–34, 337,
342, 353, 357, 359, 366n16, 370n43,
371n49, 374n68
Sovietization, 149, 187n32
Spulber, Nicholas, 243, 364n1, 365n4
Sraffa, Piero, 168, 248n22
Stalinism, Stalinization, 3, 13n6, 15n11,
23, 82, 115, 117, 127, 169, 191n66,
191n69, 214, 217, 222, 230–31, 243,
245, 266–68, 271, 285, 286n11, 295,
301, 321, 326, 338, 349, 355, 361,
364n2, 370n47;
de-Stalinization, 82, 272;
Stalin Prize, 270–71
Stalin, Joseph (Iosif), 15, 13n6, 115,
117, 231, 266–68, 271, 286n11, 295,
301, 321, 326
statism, statist, 8, 10, 320, 332, 349,
statistics, statistical, 14n8, 21, 25–26,
28–30, 33, 48n5, 57, 60–61, 71n21,

81, 83, 89–90, 92–93, 96, 97nn5–7, 98n10, 99n21, 100nn26–27, 100n29, 110, 112–13, 122, 128–32, 145, 152–54, 156–58, 160, 165, 176, 182–83, 187n36, 189n51, 198n135, 218, 221–22, 235, 240, 243, 247nn10–11, 248n13, 257, 263–64, 266–67, 269, 272, 281, 284, 286n7, 293, 296, 300, 304, 306, 310, 316n7, 327, 329;
Stefanov, Ivan, 26, 29, 376n85
stone of the wise, 349, 361
Stone, Richard, 99n20, 167, 186n23, 194n97
Strumilin, Stanislav, 258, 260–61, 263, 265, 267
Sun, Yefang, 56
Sutela, Pekka, 7, 279, 281, 321, 325–27, 359, 364n1, 367n19, 367n21
systems theory, 56, 89, 118–19, 122, 172, 174–75, 352, 375n79

Tableau Économique, 264
taboos, 42, 156, 169, 178, 356, 360
Tardos, Márton, 150–51, 162, 190n60, 190n63, 196n120
Taylor, Fred, 49n20, 328
technocrat, techno-scientist, 4, 10, 20, 26, 36, 41, 45–47, 147, 155, 179, 189n47, 217, 235, 309, 334, 367n21, 371n47
Theiss, Ede, 150, 158, 189n51, 190n56, 198n131
thought police, 15n13, 184n6, 345, 348, 361
Tinbergen, Jan, 47n1, 99n20, 113, 150, 157, 187n34, 194n97, 323, 343, 366n12, 374n70
Toms, Miroslav, 94, 102n37, 372n50, 376n85
tovarnik, 359, 369n37
trial and error, (*tâtonnement*), 24, 37, 298, 329–30
Trotsky, Leon (Lev Trotskii), 117, 135, 230, 267
Trzeciakowski, Witold, 215, 221

Tsagolov, Nikolai, 280
Tugan-Baranovskii (Baranovsky), Mikhail, 257, 260
Turnovec, František, 89, 96, 102n39
turnpike theorem, 32, 166, 168, 192n74

university:
    Academy for Marxist-Leninist Organization Science, GDR, 121;
    Academy of Agricultural Sciences, Soviet Union, 270;
    Academy of Economics, Katowice, 218;
    Academy of Mathematics and System Science, Chinese Academy of Sciences, 58;
    Alexandru Ioan Cuza University, Iaşi, 240;
    Babeş-Bolyai University, Cluj, 240;
    Bucharest University of Economic Studies, 240;
    Charles-Ferdinand University, Prague, 97n4;
    Charles University, Prague (Department of Informatics and Operations Research; Institute of Economic Sciences, Law Faculty), 89–90, 96n1, 97nn5–6, 100n26, 101n35, 102n39, 377n93;
    Comenius University, Bratislava (Institute of Statistics, Law School), 97n7;
    Czech Technical University, Prague, 97nn5–6, 100n25;
    Czech University, Prague, 83–84;
    Fudan University, Shanghai, 57;
    Gdańsk University, 218, 220;
    German University, Prague, 84, 97n6;
    Graduate School of the Institute of Economics, Prague, 94;
    Halle University, 121;
    High School for Economics, GDR, 123, 132;

High School of Business,
    Bratislava, 97n7;
High School of Economics, Prague,
    89, 92, 96n1, 98n15;
High School of Economic Sciences,
    (Institute of Economics;
    Department of Mathematical
    Economics, Institute of
    Socioeconomic Statistics),
    Bratislava, 92–3, 99n23, 100nn24
    –27–30–31, 102n39;
High School of Political
    and Economic Sciences,
    Prague, 100n25;
Higher School of Economics,
    Svishtov, 29;
Humboldt University Berlin
    (Department of Economic
    Cybernetics and Operations
    Research; Department of Theory
    and Organization of Science), 29,
    121, 129, 136;
Karl Marx Higher Institute of
    Economy, Sofia (Research
    Institute for Forecasting of the
    Socioeconomic Development of
    Bulgaria), 23, 25–26, 28, 30;
Karl Marx University of Economics,
    Budapest, 145, 150, 152,
    154, 160, 187n32, 189n48,
    191n65, 198n133;
Kiev University, 270;
Law School of Brno University, 92;
Law School of Comenius
    University, 97n7;
Law School of Ljubljana University,
    297, 300, 306, 316n7;
Leipzig University, 132;
Leningrad Polytechnic Institute, 270;
Leningrad State University, 100n28,
    102n39, 264, 273, 280;
Łódź University, 218, 220;
Loránd Eötvös University, 191n65;
Masaryk University, 97n5;

Moscow State University
    (Mathematical Economics School,
    Economic Faculty), 280, 286n24;
Polytechnic University,
    Bucharest, 240;
Postgraduate School of Economics,
    Yugoslav Institute of Economic
    Research, 301–2;
Renmin University, China,
    57, 60–61;
Sofia University (Law Department),
    21, 29, 49n16;
Stefan Gheorghiu Party University,
    Bucharest, 244;
Technical University, Prague, 83;
University of Bucharest (Department
    of Mathematics, Department of
    Statistics), 240;
University of Economics,
    Bratislava, 89;
University of Economics, Prague, 89;
University of Jena, 136n2;
University of Ljubljana (Economic
    Institute of the Law School),
    298–99, 306, 316n7;
Warsaw School of Planning and
    Statistics, 221–22;
Wrocław Academy of
    Economics, 218
utopia, utopian, 1, 4, 10, 34, 171,
    194n94, 214, 310, 322, 330, 334–35,
    343, 370n47, 371n47

Valev, Evgeny 234, 246
Vaněk, Jaroslav, 315n4, 101n32
Varga, István, 149–50, 159, 185n14,
    186nn17–18, 190n56
Volkonskii, Viktor, 324, 352, 371n49,
    374n71, 376n85
Vorobyov, Nikolai, 65, 71n20
Voznesenskii, Nikolai, 268–69,
    271, 371n47

Wakar, Aleksy, 211, 215–16, 221–22,
    376nn85–86,

Walras, Léon, 48n9, 167, 174, 248n22, 270, 323, 334, 337, 372n53, 379n104

Walrasian, 4, 8, 14n9, 35, 37, 174, 195n105, 329, 332–34, 337, 356

War Communism, 13n6, 48n7, 258–61, 370n47

war economy, 81, 110, 113, 149, 271, 370n47, 371n47

Ward, Benjamin, 303, 316n9, 328, 364n1

wartime capitalistic socialism, 21, 371n47

Weber, Max, 6, 110, 248n22

Weintraub, Roy, 6, 333

Welfe, Władysław, 216, 219–22

Westernization, 145–46, 172, 178, 182, 194n97

Wiener, Norbert, 118, 272

Wieser, Friedrich, 84, 98n9, 110

Wiles, Peter, 321, 364n1

Wolfe, Philip, 194n93, 215, 351

workers' self-management, 181, 293, 296, 300, 303, 308–10, 316n9, 324, 327, 353, 357, 364, 375n78

Wu, Jiapei, 56, 66

Xu, Chenggang, 196n114

Yue, Minyi, 63–64

Zauberman, Alfred, 7, 273, 321–23, 325, 364n1, 365n6, 365n8, 366nn9–10, 366n13, 366n16

Zhang, Shouyi, 376n85

Zweynert, Joachim, 333, 369n33, 369n38

About the Editor and Contributors

ABOUT THE EDITOR

János Mátyás Kovács worked as permanent fellow at the Institute for Human Sciences (IWM), Vienna between 1991 and 2018. From 2009 to 2019, he taught history of economic thought at the department of economics, Eötvös Loránd University, Budapest. Kovács joined RECET at the University of Vienna in 2019. His research interests include the intellectual history of Eastern Europe under communism and the political economy of new capitalism. Some of his recent publications include: "Brave New Hungary: Mapping the 'System of National Cooperation'" (2019, co-edited with Balázs Trencsényi); "Populating No Man's Land: Economic Concepts of Ownership under Communism" (2018); "Vom Zweifel zur Scham. Sieben falsche Vorhersagen über das postkommunistische Ungarn," *Transit* (2017/50).

ABOUT THE CONTRIBUTORS

Roumen Avramov is member of the Academic Advisory Council of the Centre for Advanced Studies Sofia (CAS). He has published on economic history, monetary economics, and the history of economic ideas under communism. His publications include "Communal Capitalism. Reflections on the Bulgarian Economic Past" (vol. 1–3, 2007); "Money and De/Stabilization in Bulgaria, 1948–1989" (2008); "'Salvation' and Abjection. Microeconomy of State Anti-Semitism in Bulgaria, 1940–1944" (2012); "The Economy of the 'Revival Process'" (2016) (on the Anti-Turkish Assimilation Campaign, 1984–1989). He edited the series "Bulgarian National Bank. Selected Documents, 1879–1990" (eight volumes, 1999–2009).

Andrei Belykh is the head of the Laboratory for Public History at the Russian Presidential Academy for National Economy and Public Administration. He received his PhD in economics from St. Petersburg State University of Economics where he lectured from 1982 to 1993. From 1993 to 2017 he worked in international and Russian banks. His research interests include history of economy and economic theory, history of finance, and history of mathematical economics. He is the editor of the Russian-language book series *Economic History in the Past and Present*, and *Ministers of Finance in Russia.*

Maciej Bukowski is assistant professor at the University of Warsaw, Faculty of Economic Sciences and president of WiseEuropa think-tank. His academic interests include economic history, political economy of economic and energy transformations, and public finance. His recent publications include "Urbanization and GDP per Capita: New Data and Results for the Polish Lands, 1790–1910" (2019); "Economic Transition in Silesia" (2020); and "Green Recovery: From Crisis to Sustainable Recovery" (2021). In the past he was member of the Group of Strategic Advisors to the Polish Prime Minister, member of the European Expert Group on Sustainable Finance and co-author of the European Taxonomy of Sustainable Finance.

Valentin Cojanu is professor of economics and international competition at Bucharest University of Economic Studies (ASE). His publications cover the thematic areas of trade and development: market integration, international specialization, competitiveness, and international competition. He has been head of the Doctoral School in Economics and International Business since 2013 and manages the Program of Microeconomics of Competitiveness offered by Harvard Business School in the school of Economics and International Business. In 2007, he founded the *Journal of Philosophical Economics*, covering areas of interest connected with the reorientation of economics towards landmark philosophical ideas about society and modern thinking.

Kaloyan Ganev is associate professor at the Sofia University St. Kliment Ohridski. His research interests are in macroeconomic modeling (growth and business cycles), applied econometrics, and economic history. He has published the book *Business Cycles: Theories and Models* (2015, in Bulgarian), and a number of scientific articles related to modeling economic developments in Bulgaria and in other EU countries. He has played a key role in the elaboration of several large-scale policy simulation and forecasting models used actively by the Bulgarian Council of Ministers, Ministry of Finance, and Ministry of Labour and Social Policy.

Julius Horváth is professor at the Central European University in Budapest/ Vienna. He is also a member of Academia Europea, a former dean of the business school, and former head of the department of economics at Central European University. His research focuses on the political economy of international money, history of economic thought, and post-communist economic transformation. He has published in a variety of peer-reviewed journals. He was a member of the State Accreditation Committee in both the Slovak and the Czech Republic and the Chair of the Slovak Economic Association. In 2020, he published the book *Introduction to the History of Economic Thought in Central Europe* at Palgrave.

Gergely Kőhegyi is assistant professor of economics, managing director of the Applied Economics BA program, and head of economics module in the Mathematical Economics and Finance program at the Corvinus University of Budapest. He is former head of the department of economics and director of ELTECON programs at the Eötvös Loránd University. His research focuses on the history and philosophy of economic ideas, especially on the mathematization of economics in the period of the marginalist revolution, in the first decades of the twentieth century, and during the communist era in Eastern Europe.

Xiuli Liu is professor at the Academy of Mathematics and Systems Science, Chinese Academy of Sciences, and director of the Laboratory of Economic Analysis and Forecasting Science. Her research fields are mainly focused on input-output analysis linked with econometric models; complex macroeconomic system modeling and forecasting of natural resources, environment and population, policy simulation, and decision support. She has published over ninety articles in peer-reviewed journals, three monographs, and co-edited twelve books. Her achievements were awarded with the National Science and Technology Progress Award in China, The First China Science & Technology Award for Young in Decision Science, and the Dayu Hydropower Technology Achievement Award First Prize.

Udo Ludwig is professor emeritus of economics at Leipzig University. He retired from the Halle Institute for Economic Research. He studied economic cybernetics at the University of Leningrad, USSR. Up to 1991, he held leading positions at the Institute of Economics, German Academy of Sciences in Berlin (GDR) and the Statistical Office of the GDR. His main interests are economic growth and business cycles and national accounting. He is the author of numerous publications on economic development in the new Lands of Germany. They include "Economic Convergence Across German Regions in Light of Empirical Findings," *Cambridge Journal of Economics* (2006), and "Explaining Persistent Unemployment in Eastern Germany," *Journal of Post Keynesian Economics* (2007) (co-author: John Hall).

Wojciech Maciejewski is professor emeritus at the University of Warsaw Faculty of Economic Sciences. His academic career focused on econometrics, economic forecasting, and applications of econometric models to the policy design. In the 1970s he was head of the Mathematical Models Department in the State Planning Commission where he developed models for the assessment of the national government's investment plans. His publications include "Econometric Models of Centralized Planning of the National Economy. The Current State of Art" (1973, revised 1983); "The Use of Simulation with Econometric Models in the Planning of the National Economy" (1977); "Socioeconomic Crises in Poland: A Model Approach," *Eastern European Economics* (1986); "Macroeconomic Forecasts in Transition—Polish Projections in the '90s," *East European Transition and EU Enlargement* (2001).

Jože Mencinger is professor emeritus of economics at the University of Ljubljana and member of the Economic Institute of the Law Faculty. He gained a PhD in economics from the University of Pennsylvania. He served as director of the Economic Institute between 1993 and 2001, and 2008 and 2013. From 1998 to 2005 he was rector of the University of Ljubljana. In 1990/1991 he joined the government of Slovenia as deputy prime minister and minister for economic affairs. His research interests include econometric analysis, the self-management system, economic policy, post-communist transformation, and privatization. His recent publications include "The Impact of FDI in CEE Countries and the Outlook for the Future of CEE and SEE" (2010); "Economic Convergence of New Member States: Opportunities and Risks" (2012); "From the Collapse of Socialism to the Crisis of Capitalism: Experiences of Central and Eastern European Countries" (2013); and "Social Property and the Market: An Uneasy Smbiosis in Yugoslavia" (2018).

Stefan Petranov is professor at Sofia University St. Kliment Ohridski, where he has also served as chair of the department of economics. He was a visiting professor at the University of Delaware (USA) and the University of Osnabrück (Germany). He was frequently invited to give lectures and short-term seminars in government institutions, international organizations, universities, and private companies such as the European Central Bank, the European Parliament, ING-Bulgaria and others. His research interests cover privatization, economics of transition, investments, corporate governance, shadow economy. He was winner of the national award "Economy in Light" for his research in the field of shadow economy. His articles have been published in international peer-reviewed journals and publishing houses. Among them are "Process of Privatization in Bulgaria" (1997), "The First Wave of Mass Privatization in Bulgaria and its Immediate Aftermath" (2000), "The Financial System in the Bulgarian Economy" (2001), and "Foreign Direct Investments to Bulgaria" (2003).

Grigore Ioan Piroşcă is dean of the faculty of theoretical and applied econmics and former head of the department of economic doctrines and communication at Bucharest University of Economic Studies. His main academic interests include the history of economic thought and economic epistemology, the labor market, and sustainable education policies. He coordinated scientific research projects within his university or in partnerships. His publications include, among others, "Economics Between Arguments: The Quest for a Positive Science" (2018); "Methodology and Perspectives of Value Judgments in Economics on Equilibrium" (2017); and "Austrian School Perspectives on Liberalism" (2012).

Minghui Qin is currently pursuing a doctorate degree in management science and engineering at the Academy of Mathematics and System Science, Chinese Academy of Sciences. She holds a master's degree (2019) in management science and engineering from the Academy of Mathematics and System Science, Chinese Academy of Sciences, and a bachelor's degree (2016) from the Xiamen University in mathematics. Her research interests are mainly in water environmental management, as well as forecasting of grain yields, national nutrition, health, and water demand.

Knut Richter is professor emeritus of industrial economics at European University Viadrina Frankfurt (Oder). He is currently professor of business economics at St. Petersburg State University. As a scientist with an East German background (TU Chemnitz) and a PhD in economic cyberenetics from the Leningrad University he is a critical analyst of the economies of the former Eastern Bloc. His publications include highly ranked English-, German-, and Russian-language papers and books on economic modeling and environmental processes and systems.

Hans-Jürgen Wagener is professor emeritus of economics at European University Viadrina Frankfurt (Oder) and Rijksuniversiteit Groningen, The Netherlands. His scientific interests center on economic systems, European integration, and history of economic thought. His publications comprise, among others, "Economic Thought in Communist and Post-Communist Europe" (1998); "Constitutions, Markets and Law. Recent Experiences in Transformation Economies" (2002, co-edited with Stefan Voigt); "The

Handbook of Political, Social, and Economic Transformation" (2018, co-edited with Wolfgang Merkel and Raj Kollmorgen); and, in German, "Socialist Economics in the Stress Field of Modernization: A Historical Comparison between East Germany and Poland" (2021, co-authored with Maciej Tymiński and Piotr Koryś).

Xin Xiang is currently a PhD candidate in management science and engineering at the Academy of Mathematics and Systems Science, Chinese Academy of Sciences. He holds a bachelor's degree (2018) from Soochow University in mathematics. His research interests are mainly in forecasting methods and input-output techniques.

Shan Zheng is a data analyst in Glodon Company Limited. She holds a master's degree in quantitative economics from the Academy of Mathematics and Systems Science, Chinese Academy of Sciences, and a bachelor's degree in mathematics and applied mathematics from Lanzhou University. Her main research interests are machine learning, econometric models, and the prediction of household consumption.